C

CONSTITUTIONAL GOVERNMENT AND DEMOCRACY

A BLAISDELL BOOK IN POLITICAL SCIENCE

CONSTITUTIONAL GOVERNMENT AND DEMOCRACY

Theory and Practice in Europe and America | **Fourth Edition**

CARL J. FRIEDRICH
Harvard University

BLAISDELL PUBLISHING COMPANY

A Division of Ginn and Company

WALTHAM, MASSACHUSETTS • TORONTO • LONDON

to Lenore

Preface to the Fourth Edition

It is now more than seventeen years since the last edition of *Constitutional Government* was made. In the meantime, momentous changes have taken place in the world which have greatly affected the theory and practice of constitutionalism. In America, a series of decisions by the Supreme Court have opened up deep issues and revived somewhat sleepy ideological concerns over the meaning and content of this oldest of "written" constitutions. Regimes which were new in 1949 have in the meantime achieved a measure of stability — in India, in Germany, in Japan, in Italy. In France, the familiar constitutional order of parliamentary democracy has been transformed into a presidential system. In Britain, Labour has become an ever-more effective agent of the collectivist age. The unification of Europe has raised constitutional issues of a new and perplexing kind. Finally, the so-called emergent nations have adopted, rejected, and adapted constitutionalism in a bewildering array of successive charters. Change has been the order of the day, from the limited alteration of a procedural rule in parliament to the revolutionary transformation of entire regimes.

But not only have the "facts" evolved rapidly and kaleidoscopically, but knowledge about these facts has also greatly increased. The expanding scope of empirical and more particularly quantitative studies in the advanced countries has been accompanied by ever-more numerous studies of particular regimes, and the swift rise of new groups of political scientists in country after country has added enormously to our knowledge and understanding, as well as our bewilderment.

Finally, but by no means unimportantly, theoretical discussion and argument has gained in perspective and depth. Without particular authors being named, it will be evident to anyone familiar with the field that numerous contributions to the theory of constitutional politics and democracy have been offered since 1950. This theorizing has in part been stimulated by the persistent claim of the totalitarians that theirs is a valid alternative *constitutional* order, or at any rate a more perfect democracy. The discussion of what constitutes a "genuine" or "real" or "true" democracy has shown considerable vigor in recent years, and there is no end in sight. The universal desire to secure popular assent to the rulers' right to rule — the key to legitimacy —

has produced new varieties of democracy and constitutionalism, qualified by adjectives such as "popular" which are more often signs of a particular ideological orientation than of new analytical insight. Still, they are all part of the ongoing debate within which the present work is cast and executed.

It is obvious that no one could hope to do full justice to all these trends, to evaluate fully and adequately all the authors and laborers in the field, without allowing the book to grow into a many-volumed enterprise. The task of keeping an overview, of providing a general analysis, cannot be shirked. It is as much part of science, scholarship, and learning as is the discovery of new facts, or the fashioning of new hypotheses. An effort has been made to do justice to as much of the new as is compatible with retaining or restating that which is old. To keep hold of the old truths is crucial in political theory and practice. The political scientist must seek the middle road between excessive traditionalism and heedless novelty seeking. In such an effort, he is bound not to satisfy everyone in all respects.

In speaking of the theoretical and analytical work of the past two decades, I cannot avoid making specific reference to my own work, not because I necessarily consider it more important than that of others, but because issues have therein been treated, positions developed, and hypotheses formulated which I can only allude to in the present work. It actually forms one of a trilogy of which the other two are *Totalitarian Dictatorship and Autocracy*, 1956 (with Z. Brzezinski), of which a new completely revised edition appeared in 1965, and *Man and His Government*, 1963. Besides these two systematic works, *The Philosophy of Law in Historical Perspective*, 1958, revised edition 1963, treats a basic issue of constitutionalism historically. Especially germane to *Constitutional Government and Democracy* are three other topical studies of mine, *Constitutional Reason of State*, 1957, *Transcendent Justice — The Religious Dimension of Constitutionalism*, 1964, and *The Impact of American Constitutionalism Abroad*, 1967. Other works are mentioned in the bibliography.

One of the most important sources for review providing guidance for such a revision as the present one is of course the critical evaluation by other students of the field. There have been many over the years, both in this country and abroad. Some of these have been general evaluations, others have concerned particular aspects or propositions. I have tried to allow for them, at the appropriate places in this new edition, and acknowledge wherever possible these ongoing labors. Sometimes, of course, one is puzzled, as in the case of Giovanni Sartori's fine discussion of constitutionalism and the ensuing argument with W. H. Morris-Jones in the APSR; for he speaks of his proposition as "preliminary," though it might more appropriately be called "terminal," for it sums up, in a magistral fashion, that we have been discussing. As he himself said at the end of his rejoinder to Morris-Jones, it may be well "to realize that Western constitutionalism as a whole is ever more faced with similar problems and with a common challenge." Writers like K. C. Wheare, Karl Loewenstein, Herbert Spiro, Hitchner and Harbold, Georges Burdeau, Hermens, B. de Jouvenel, and Dolf Sternberger have all significantly contributed to the ongoing discussion, as have Harry Eckstein and David Apter, who gathered some of these and others into their stimu-lating *Comparative Politics — A Reader,* 1963. In spite of methodological differences, the empirically based functional approach seeking to formulate theoretical propositions based upon ascertained and confirmed matter-of-fact has remained and probably will remain dominant, along with descriptively analytical studies of regimes in their particularity. For it is well to know how a political system works in its concrete reality.

Some of the revisions have been suggested by translations which have appeared; a Spanish one in 1946, a German one in 1954, a French one in 1958, an Italian one in 1965, and so forth. Others resulted from the effort not to allow the work to expand and therefore to replace older by newer material which seemed more central. Thus chapter I and the chapter on federalism have been completely recast, all others revised and frequently amplified by new sections. Chapter XXVI is newly added, but based upon my recent writings. Some of the omissions, and more especially sections and paragraphs dealing with aspects of totalitarian regimes and general theory, have been condensed or omitted, since they are treated in the above-mentioned works.

The bibliography and notes have also been extensively revised. Actually, all the notes have been rewritten and older items in the references have been replaced by more recent ones. This seemed justifiable to save space, especially since the former editions are readily available for reference, when needed. The same holds true for chapter XXI of the previous edition, con-taining a sketch of European party history.

I have tried to acknowledge my indebtedness to fellow scholars by appro-priate reference to their work — a tradition which is regrettably neglected by some scholars, even when they actually derive their very hypotheses from one's writings. But there are of course always others, especially younger ones and practitioners of the art of politics, whom one cannot thus thank for their help and information. Since the list would be a very long one, in light of the rich life of cooperation and teaching which I have been privileged to live these past seventeen years, I must hope that they will feel sufficiently rewarded by the goodness of their deed, should they ever stumble across these pages.

But there are several more immediate helpers whom I feel I must thank for their devoted labors. First of all, Valerie Greenberg, who helped in editing and typing an often almost illegible mass of marginal notes and inserts composed over many years, and finally produced a printable manuscript. But I have also been greatly assisted by Jane M. deLong, who out of her special knowledge and concern with France helped me recast those numerous sections and passages where the Fifth Republic has changed the ways of French politics. On the bibliography Suzanne Bodenheimer and Hans Friedrich Lorenz reviewed many professional journals for me in order to make the net more tight than one's ordinary professional attention to the ongoing work could be. Last but not least, the greatest friend of many years to whom the volume is once more dedicated will have to abide by the thanks which she will of course protest against.

> How heavy do I journey on the way,
> When what I seek, my weary travel's end,
> Doth teach that ease and that repose to say
> "Thus far the miles are measur'd from thy friend!"

Ashwood
New Boston, N. H.
April 5, 1967   C. J. FRIEDRICH

Preface to the Third Edition

The Fascists have been vanquished and the capacity of constitutional democracy has been once more demonstrated in striking fashion. Yet as this revised edition of *Constitutional Government and Democracy* goes to press the future seems as uncertain as it did nine years ago, before the United States entered the Second World War. The "unnecessary war," Winston Churchill has called it. But was it unnecessary? Churchill meant that adequate precautions would have given sufficient warning to Hitler, who was encouraged by a policy of appeasement and vacillation. But how were such precautions to be secured? The failure of the United States and Great Britain to adopt any satisfactory safeguards is no doubt a serious indictment of their constitutional systems, not to speak of the systems of France and other European countries. In some ways it is perhaps as serious an indictment as that of the Weimar Republic when it allowed itself to be overthrown by Hitler. Yet is it not asking too much of a free people that they should calmly envisage the prospect of war? It is not necessarily the chosen few of exceptional insight who will be prepared to travel so perilous a road?

There would be little need now for recalling these problems, already clearly defined in 1941, were it not for the fact of the conflict between "East and West," that sharp antagonism which has arisen between the United States, Great Britain, France, and their friends on one hand and the Soviet Union and her associates on the other. This conflict is once again a conflict of ideas concerning government, economics, and the good life, but more especially concerning constitutionalism. For while both parties to the global antithesis proclaim themselves champions of "democracy" — both making it amply clear that they do not mean what the others mean — it is only the Western powers who insist upon constitutionalism. More especially the basic rights of human beings are central to the Western position — their right to live without fear of arbitrary arrest and punishment, their right to express themselves freely in accordance with their convictions, and finally their right to work and to enjoy the fruits of their labor. But it is a position which is more easily stated in general terms than applied in concrete and actual politics. Not only are there limits beyond which no community can allow such rights and freedoms to go lest it invite anarchy, but the willingness to condone a lack of agreement on all fundamentals, except on these basic procedures of the democratic process itself, entails risks which may prove fatal in the face of a determined and totalitarian opponent.

In short, the assessment of constitutional democracy in all its ramified manifestations, theoretical and practical, has lost none of its urgency of ten years ago. Continued critical re-examination in the light of new facts and deeper insight, of broader experience and a sharpened sense of values, is indeed of the essence in the cooperative process upon which constitutional democracy depends for its success. In revising the earlier edition, an effort has been made to live up to this task of critical scholarship. While the basic approach remains, the varied experiences of the past ten years provide numerous occasions for revision of detail, as well as for some major additions. Two entirely new chapters have been added, one on problems of local government, the other on socialization and planning, and half a chapter has been added to the discussion of constitutional dictatorship to outline the hitherto neglected problems of military government. My experience in the intervening years, as well as a number of studies and inquiries, had convinced me that a consideration of constitutional democracy without attention to "grass-roots democracy" must remain incomplete. My work and studies in the field of propaganda and public opinion, and more especially of the control of radio broadcasting, as well as my experience in the teaching and practice of military government, all pointed toward this conclusion. On the other hand, no one who considers the shape of constitutional development in postwar Europe can help realizing that socialization and planning are becoming, for better or for worse, established features of constitutional democracy. And in spite of American protestations to the contrary, the United States herself is deeply involved in these trends. On the regional level, for instance, I had the pleasure of helping to shape the *Plan for Greater Boston* (1945), which was accorded first prize by a group hardly to be classified as radical. On the international level, the United States, by putting forward the Marshall Plan, urged and at times insisted upon the very planning which those Europeans who had talked loudest but had done least hesitated to put into effect. Even on the national level the efforts in Britain, France, and Sweden, to name only three, lacked the full democratic backing without which their success within the setting of constitutional democracy could not be considered even probable, as I had opportunity to learn at first hand when accompanying the Congressional Committee on Foreign Aid (Herter Committee) to Europe in 1947. But the importance of grass-roots democracy as well as the vicissitudes of careless planning (involved as it was in the Level of Industry Plan) was highlighted for me during my experience in Germany in 1946, 1947, and 1948. Ever since my experience during the war as Director of the Civil Affairs Training School at Harvard University, the problem of what place to assign to military government in the constitutional order had seemed to me of vital importance. This practical experience and an examination of the bitter controversies in both Britain and the United States surrounding the conduct of military government have led me to the conclusions now embodied in this volume.

Regretfully, it was decided to eliminate the chapter dealing with methodological problems. My hope is to offer a more comprehensive treatment of these matters in a separate volume about two years hence. In the meantime, the publishers have kindly agreed to reprint the chapter as a separate brochure, to be available to those who do not possess the first edition. A revision of this chapter to bring it up to date in terms of my views as shaped by experience with area studies and continued association with sociologists, anthropologists, and social psychologists — an association which I greatly value — would have meant expanding it to several times its present length. This seemed impracticable in view of the somewhat greater scope of the new edition as it is here being offered.

Besides the acknowledgements contained in the preface to the first edition of *Constitutional Government and Democracy* (reprinted below), I wish to thank especially my friend and colleague John M. Gaus, who kindly read both of the new chapters and offered valuable help, and to Theodore S. Baer and Lester Hawkins, who gave similar help. I also feel that I ought to record my genuine appreciation of the assistance of my colleagues in the School for Overseas Administration, especially Professors Merle Fainsod, Talcott Parsons, Clyde Kluckhohn, Charles Cherington, and Douglas Haring, and to my associates in the Greater Boston Contest, who included, besides Cherington and Parsons, Professors Seymour Harris, Walter Bogner, and Al Simpson, as well as Mr. George Walker. Finally, it would be unfair not to say a word of thanks to the men whose association I was privileged to share through "thick and thin," more especially General Lucius DuB. Clay, Messrs. Henry Parkman, J. A. Panuch, and Charles M. LaFollette, and Dr. Richard S. Scammon as well as Drs. Edward H. Litchfield, Hans Simons, and Kenneth Dayton; also Colonels John Raymond and J. L. Harbaugh, and Mr. Seymour Bolten. These men all labored hard in the vineyard of constitutional democracy in Germany, barren though the ground is, beset by uncomprehending critics at home and abroad among our Allies and erstwhile enemies.

I have had as well the devoted assistance throughout of Mrs. Dorothy

Smith and Mrs. Shirley Coyne, who rendered the kind of continued and cheerful aid without which such books as this one would hardly ever be written. I should also like to thank the library staffs at Harvard University and at Concord for continued friendly and unfailing courtesy.

Concord, Massachusetts
Armistice Day, 1949   C. J. FRIEDRICH

Preface to the Second Edition

This book is written for those who are puzzled about the future of constitutional government and democracy. It tries to show the present disturbances in proper perspective by setting them off against the ground swell of long-range secular trends. In these days of profound crisis when the international civil war has once more come out in the open, it is undoubtedly, an act of faith, for both the writer and the publisher, to bring out a new edition of *Constitutional Government*. Four years ago, when the first edition was published, there had been no Munich, the French Republic seemed firmly entrenched behind the Maginot line, and the smaller countries of Europe, Czechoslovakia, Denmark, Norway, Holland, and Belgium, if not Poland, were joined with Sweden, Finland, and Switzerland in carrying forward the constitutional tradition. And yet, in a deeper sense, the outlook for constitutionalism was more uncertain then. The British people were in an appeasing mood and America hid her face in the sand. There was little aggressive belief in the future of democracy and free institutions. Many people who were then indifferent, if not cynical, have since rediscovered the essential of constitutionalism: a vivid appreciation of the rights of free men. In the preface to the first edition, I wrote: "Within the lifetime of this generation, the present barbarities will be abandoned, and finer, more noble conceptions of life will reassert themselves. There are great latent reservoirs of faith in a higher morality which were overgrown with the slime of nineteenth-century decadence. I do not propose to know how the creative sensibilities will manifest themselves. I will confess to a faith in their potential strength." The English people have already given proof of this prediction.

The present edition is almost a new book. Not only have revisions been made on almost every page, but a new first chapter has been added to give historical perspective to the rise of constitutionalism, and the role of executive leadership has been brought out more fully in the light of recent events, English and Dominion material has been given greater emphasis as contrasted with French and German, and many other minor changes made. It may be asked by some why anything should be retained about the ill-fated German Republic or even France. The answer would seem to be that we can learn as much from our failures as from our successes. And since the purpose of this volume is definitely to do more than summarize descriptively what various governments are like, such failures are often needed to point up the central tenets concerning the work of constitutionalism. For constitutionalism is probably the greatest achievement of modern civilization, without which little or none of the rest is conceivable. Under it, for the first time in the history of man, has a measure of freedom and well-being been achieved for the common man. There is nothing complete or final about this achievement, but it is a great achievement just the same. To understand, even partially, the conditions for the success of this system is, it seems to me, the most important task of political science. What is here offered is no final answer. But it is the best the author could do. And it is considerably changed in at least one important respect from the first edition. At that time, it was assumed, following Balfour and others, that agreement on fundamentals was a necessary condition of constitutionalism. That tenet has now been abandoned. In fact, constitutionalism is about the only system of government which seems able to get along without such agreement on fundamentals. It is part of the organization of freedom that this should be so.

I have enjoyed so much help and stimulation from the discussion with friends throughout the years during which this book has reached its present scope that I am utterly incapable of setting a suitable memorial for each of them individually. Wherever I could, I have tried to emphasize in the bibliography such special debts. But some of the greatest benefits I have derived from men and women who have not written anything, and their share in shaping my thoughts must remain obscure.

It may be permissible to mention, however, those who have taken part in the arduous and trying task of reading the manuscript and the proof. In the first edition, Jane Barbour, William Yandell Elliott, Rupert Emerson, H. Schuyler Foster, William P. Maddox, George Pettee, David Riesman, Jr., Frederick M. Watkins, Harold Winkler, and the whimsical person to whom this volume is dedicated, have all lent a helping hand. Since then, so many more have come to my aid that it seems impossible to list them. I have particularly appreciated those friendly critics who have called my attention to flaws in the presentation and argument. It is hoped that they will find the new edition improved in the right direction. Besides these scholars, Emily Whitman, Helen Parsons, and Miriam Berry have rendered great assistance in preparing the new manuscript and bringing the bibliography up to date.

Beechwood Hill Farm
Brattleboro, Vermont
July 4, 1941

C. J. FRIEDRICH

Contents

VIII

IX

X

XI

XII

XIII

PART III
The Functioning Processes of Constitutional Government

XIV

XV

XX

XXI

PART IV
Tensions, Breakdowns, Adjustments

XXII

XXIII

PART 1

MODERN GOVERNMENT:

NATURE

AND DEVELOPMENT

The Development of Modern Constitutional
Government in Theory and Practice

I

Introduction · Modern political science and Aristotle · The ideology of
constitutionalism · Constitutionalism and Christianity · National unification
· Material factors of unification · Political factors of unification · The
Roman law as a formative force · The state · Sovereignty · The problem
of responsibility · Reason of state · Developmental administration: core
of the state · Constitutionalism · England's leadership in constitutionalism
· The spread of constitutionalism · The living constitution · Democratization of constitutionalism · Socialism and constitutionalism · Conclusion

Introduction · Democracy has been the battle cry of the twentieth
century. Everyone is for democracy as he understands it. In the United
States democracy means the existing scheme of things, or some idealized
version of it, or even what the men of Philadelphia intended the constitution
to be. In Britain, too, it means whatever one considers the government and
politics of the country to be, but also more particularly what the Labour party
aspires to and has been seeking to accomplish, when it has been in power.
In the Soviet Union and Communist China, such American and British views
are laughed at as reactionary. According to each, their particular brand of
Communism is "true" democracy, perfect democracy. Such a democracy presupposes a classless society and can only come after capitalism has been
destroyed by the dictatorship of the proletariat. Since the end of the Second
World War, and especially in the period of the Cold War, these clashes of
outlook have become acute.

Is all this conflict pure madness? Do words have no meaning, and is that
all propaganda? What is the ascertainable difference between constitutional
and "popular" democracies? One answer could be: in America and England
there is open competition for political power among many groups, whereas
in the Communist states it is concentrated in one group, the Communist
party, often headed by one man, but in any case by a very small set of men.
This concentration does not mean, of course, that there are not a good many

others who participate in the exercise of this power, but it does mean that their participation takes place at the discretion of the dictator or the dictatorial collective.[1]

Division of power is the basis of constitutional democracy. It is what is meant by constitutionalism. Constitutionalism may be monarchical or it may be republican, it may be aristocratic or democratic, and it has been all of these. When people in America speak of "democracy," they usually mean constitutional democracy. Of course, there are those who would define democracy simply as the rule of the majority, without any constitutional framework within which such majority decisions are to be made. Such absolute democracy is, however, rare in the history of political institutions, and is nowhere to be found in contemporary Europe or America.

Constitutionalism is an achievement of the modern world. It is a very recent achievement, and it has by no means become stabilized. Indeed, it is a complex system of providing for orderly change, and there is no reason for assuming that the need for change will come to an end in the immediate future. Both nationally and internationally, we are confronted with gigantic tasks. Changes are taking place which rival in magnitude any the world has seen. Technological advance multiplied human contacts and has revolutionized economic life and warfare. Constitutionalism has provided a setting for these changes in some cases, and it has failed to do so in others. Both the promoters and the opponents of change have been dissatisfied. They have declared constitutionalism bankrupt, and have proceeded to erect governments of an absolutist type. Their systems, marking a return to older methods of government, have brought many men to a fuller appreciation of the importance of constitutionalism. Much more than appeared to be challenged at first, is actually at stake. Science and art and religion, the whole realm of free creative effort, are in fact threatened. It is clear, at last, that there can be no more important study than the study of the conditions of the rise of constitutionalism in general and constitutional democracy in particular. The crisis has revealed the poignancy of Aristotle's claim that the study of politics, of the working of government, is the most important study of all. Without an understanding of politics, man's other works are in danger of being destroyed.

Modern political science and Aristotle · Aristotle's philosophy has probably exercised a deeper influence upon the Western mind than any other source except the teachings of Christianity. Nowhere has this influence been more all-pervading than in the field of politics. Monarchists and republicans, aristocrats and democrats, idealists and realists — all have drawn upon *the* philosopher for inspiration and authority. And yet, the realities of

Western development have made Aristotle's analysis more and more inadequate, until today a student of imagination, sent to consider contemporary politics in terms of Aristotelian theory, might well report that the Republic of Andorra would be the place of greatest interest.[2]

There are a number of reasons for this divergence of modern politics from Aristotle, but two stand out as of greatest importance. Philosophically, it is probably not too much to say that the concept of the *state* crystallized during the Renaissance. It was the mainstay of political theory in the age of absolutism, as developed by writers like Bodin and Hobbes. It received its final apotheosis in Hegel; Hegel and his followers have inspired both conservative and radical thinking throughout the West during the last hundred years. The state, modeled upon the Greek concept of the polis, was deified by them as the concrete embodiment of all value as represented by man's culture. The rise of key words in politics, of symbols, is usually associated with the rise of new forces in political society. The word *state* crystallized in the sixteenth and seventeenth centuries, because secular rulers who wanted to achieve absolute power needed a symbol that they could set against the church, something that would be awe-inspiring and clothed with an abstract corporate halo. Hobbes typically concludes the *Leviathan* with a violent denunciation of the church.

This deification of the state, of the government, was a gross misrepresentation of the Greek and Aristotelian concept of the polis. The Greek Olympus with its many gods had permitted each polis to share in the deity through a special local favorite, such as Athens' Athene. Governmental offices were closely related to priestly ones, and in many cases overlapped. Thus the polis was really a church as well as a "state," and the two were so closely intermingled that a man's religious as well as his political allegiance was bound up in such a polity. By associating the general ideas rooted in this reality with the mere government of monarchical administrators, the mythmakers of state and sovereignty not only distorted the Aristotelian political philosophy, but they saddled our culture with a heritage of which the totalitarian states of our time are the penultimate sequel. These totalitarian states have once again come to claim the whole man in the name of secular ideology; yet for the vast masses this claim is abstract and impersonal. In any case, little of what Aristotle has to say concerning the polis can be rightly said of modern *government*. The word *state* has been the vehicle for confusing the issue.

The approach of the great Greek philosophers to politics was basically static. They sought stability as a primary goal of politics. When they wrote of ideals like justice and happiness, they thought of them as eternal verities, as something unalterable and changeless. To be sure, Aristotle's *Politics* contains a theory of revolution and change in political orders, but his interest was motivated by the question: how can it be prevented? The idea that change and even revolution might be positive, creative forces of great value was alien to them. Hence they explained and to some extent justified slavery, because it seemed to have an essential function in the established order of things.

The modern, the Western way is to emphasize *becoming*, to see change as not only inevitable, but also as desirable, at least at times. Therefore the stress is upon the history of institutions and ways of behavior. The outlook is dynamic. It is preoccupied with processes and functions. For the modern political scientist moral judgments are specific; we do not care so much whether George III was a good man in vague abstract terms, but whether in pursuing the policy he did concerning the colonies he violated the standards of free government or not. Thus monarchy, the very word which for Aristotle essentially meant rule by one man when directed to good purposes, has for the modern mind become a historical term. Broadly speaking, it designates a peculiar kind of political ruler whose legitimacy is founded upon blood descent surrounded by a religious halo, and who, no matter how limited may be the extent of his governing functions, is thereby enabled to represent the people. The monarch is the symbol of the living growth of a unified culture pattern of which the political order is but an aspect. What made France a monarchy in the time of Richelieu was not the rule of one man — Richelieu — but the fact that there existed by divine grace a hereditary king from whom Richelieu derived his authority and legitimate powers. The modern scientific approach is interested in questions of historical fitness, in evolutionary patterns. From such historical considerations there results a very different attitude toward change. Change is looked upon as intrinsically necessary and unavoidable. The question is, therefore, how to turn such change to good account, how to adapt political life to the changing social context in order to secure the greatest satisfaction for the people.[3]

The ideology of constitutionalism · How then did modern constitutionalism develop? What is its background? The Christian tradition emphasizes ideas and ideals. Western man's interest in history and evolution has therefore often taken the road of exploring the rise of ideas and ideologies. Constitutionalism has been traced in its relation to liberalism, to rationalism, to individualism. Each one of these general philosophies has indeed contributed its fair share to the making of constitutionalism. But a different perspective results, depending upon which one of these ideologies is emphasized. Liberalism, the most recent of the three, is certainly at variance with socialism; hence if constitutionalism is linked with liberalism, it seems reasonable to conclude that it is about to pass away. Rationalism is the most general and is associated with many different forms of culture; if constitutionalism is the political outgrowth of rationalism, it acquires a more universal significance. But rationalism has been dominant in societies the constitutional order of which did not much resemble modern constitutionalism. Again, individualism crystallized in the period when modern constitutionalism began to take shape. To this individualism, constitutionalism owes the development of the doctrine of individual rights, which in some ways is the distinguishing feature of modern, in contrast to ancient and medieval, constitutionalism. Any sequence of ideas is difficult to trace, because the interrelations are so numerous. Political science, though vividly cognizant of the role of ideas, has turned often to the more material aspects of political institutions. The economic interpretation of history produced an economic interpretation of politics.

Inquiries into the economic setting of modern constitutionalism have led to the assertion that it is associated with capitalism and imperialism.[4] This is not merely a coincident in time, it is held; the more thoroughly constitutionalized countries are also those which have advanced farthest in the direction of either capitalism or imperialism or both. Great Britain would, of course, furnish the outstanding example. Behind both capitalism and imperialism, modern industrialism appears as the basic material setting. From such a standpoint capitalism and imperialism may be transitional phases of a technology which persists. In other words, industrialism and constitutionalism appear to be linked and may persist together even after the industrial economy has become socialized. It is an ongoing process with which we shall be much concerned in later chapters. In the Scandinavian countries, in Great Britain and Australia, in India and many other developing countries, this process is in full swing. Constitutionalism is itself a potent political ideology, along with those to which it is linked by history and development.

Wherever new nations emerge, wherever old nations renew themselves, in India and Italy, in Nigeria and France, new constitutions are the order of the day. Whenever a revolution, even a Communist one, is successfully consummated, a constitution is issued. Even beyond the sphere of the national community, regional unions and the world-wide United Nations seek to structure their alleged community in a constitution. And yet many of these constitutions are feeble and ineffectual, subject to rapid erosion and replacement by other ones. Constitutionalism, in spite of its world-wide appeal, lacks some of the firm self-confidence of former days. Why do constitutions encounter so many difficulties, engender so many tensions and troubles? In order to understand and answer this question, it is necessary to see constitutionalism as embedded in the belief system of Western Christianity and the political thought that expresses its implications for the secular order. The weakening of that belief system has also weakened the secular ideology of constitutionalism.

Constitutionalism and Christianity[5] · In asserting that modern constitutionalism is part of Christian culture, one follows a present belief that all cultural manifestations are to be seen as emanations of a consistent system of values, interests, and beliefs. This does not mean that a particular manifestation, such as constitutionalism, is strictly limited, of course. Such parochialism would be quite wrong. Many political phenomena, such as will be treated later in this book, occur in many contexts. How else would comparative government be possible? By pointing out the cultural and ideological context of constitutionalism and constitutional democracy, the range of its possible applicability is not restricted to its original context. Its extension may, however, present very special problems, as may indeed the weakening of the beliefs and values upon which its growth depended originally.

Probably the most distinctive religious root of modern constitutionalism is the Christian belief in the dignity and worth of each person, each human being, no matter how lowly. For if we ask what is the political function of a constitution, we find that the core objective is that of safeguarding each member of the political community as such a person. Each man is supposed to possess a sphere of genuine autonomy. The constitution is meant to protect the *self;* for the self is believed to be the (primary and ultimate) value. This preoccupation with the self, rooted in Christian beliefs, eventually gave rise to the notion of rights which were thought to be natural. Hence the function of a constitution may also be said to be the defining and maintaining of human rights. The constitution is to protect the individual member of the political community against interference in his personal sphere. Among these rights, that of each person's right to his own political conviction was and is paramount.

Medieval constitutionalism was far removed from this conception. And yet it laid the foundation for it. By developing the idea that man is entitled and indeed called upon to render resistance to a ruler who violates the Christian natural law, that is, who becomes a tyrant interfering with man's religious (Christian) duties, it took the first step in the direction of the recognition of a *universal* right to *any* religious conviction. For both Thomas Aquinas and John Fortescue, it was crucial that a government be subject to legal restraints; government was best when instituted by law. From here the road leads to English seventeenth-century constitutionalism, but before this development is traced, it is necessary to sketch the constitutionalism embodied in conciliarism.

Conciliarism is, in a sense, the application of medieval constitutionalism to the church itself. The ecclesiastical insistence upon the need for subjecting all authority to legal restraints was claimed to apply to the church. Effective participation of the lower ecclesiastical orders and even of the laity was demanded in the councils that were called upon to formulate the law. In this discussion, the constitutional aspect became increasingly explicit. From William of Ockham to Nicholas of Cusa, the idea of consent as a vital ingredient of law gained ground, and the question of how to organize the expression of such consent was faced. Church councils appeared in analogy to feudal representative assemblies, such as the English parliament, and their traditional participation in establishing the law was claimed to be applicable to the government of the church.

Even though the conciliar movement failed, there can be little doubt that it spread some of the key ideas of constitutionalism. Thus reinforced, constitutionalism might have triumphed throughout Europe in a broader secular form, had it not been thwarted by the countervailing arguments arising from religious dissension and civil war.

National unification · Constitutionalism, wherever it appears, is a refinement of ordinary government. In any society, there is practically always some sort of government, no matter how inadequate, but only a firmly established government is capable of being constitutionalized. In the evolution of the Western world, this meant that national unification had to precede constitutionalism. It is here that the great difference may be seen between Germany and Italy, as contrasted with England and France. Some small countries, like Sweden and Holland, offer interesting parallels. England became unified at an early date, when Italy was completely divided; hence constitutionalism could make substantial headway in England in the seventeenth century, but not in Italy. The only real exception is provided by Switzerland, and Switzerland, throughout the earlier period, was not so much a constitutional order as a league of small-town and rural cantons for the defense of the kind of local autonomy which national unification destroyed in the large territorial realms. It thus came to pass that a communal sentiment of political loyalty, based upon the common enterprise of joint defense against their feudal overlords, came into existence among the Swiss people which surpassed the national-cultural feelings of its German-, French-, and Italian-speaking components. This powerful, yet distinctive, group feeling had become so well rooted by the time nationalism triumphed throughout Europe that it could act as the basis of an effective constitutionalism in 1848. As far as the United States are concerned, historians are in disagreement as to whether a nation had come into being by 1776. National sentiment there certainly was, and the more ardent revolutionaries talked in terms of themselves as "Americans." But the very fact that it had to be asserted proves that for many others the predominant sentiment was local, and foreign observers were often greatly impressed with the divisive factors. The great Chateaubriand, looking at "states without community of religion and interests" which had been "peopled by different stocks," even at the beginning of the nineteenth century could still ask: "How many centuries will be needed to make these elements homogeneous?" De Tocqueville was frankly skeptical; he saw the federal government "grow daily weaker" and believed that it was "the Union which is in danger." He felt that the Union was "merely an accident" and therefore clearly not the creation of a nation.

National unification was carried out by medieval and early modern kings. Feudalism, though providing some national and even international unity, rested upon the autonomy of local lords, with towns acquiring a species of constitutionalism under royal or imperial charter. In a struggle raging for many centuries, certain kings succeeded in extending their centrally controlled rule. It is quite arbitrary to single out a particular ruler, such as Henry VIII of England or Louis XI of France, as the "founder." These long-drawn-out conflicts had many ups and downs. Their course is marked by decided upswings of royal power and of the services which the kings controlled, only to be followed by retrogressions accompanied by the inevitable dispersion of power. Nor was this process by any means a uniform one in the several countries. Thus in England, under the Norman and early Plantagenet kings, remarkable strides were made toward centralization, but the period of Magna Charta is marked by the ascendancy of the local lords. The consolidation which followed was almost entirely lost during the Wars of the Roses, which in turn paved the way for Tudor absolutism. In France the development was no less turbulent, yet it resembled the English case in that it steadily progressed toward greater consolidation of the nation. In Germany and Italy, on the other hand, the forces of disintegration gained the ascendancy. This is, at any rate, true for the nation as a whole; but within the more limited areas of city-states and principalities, centralizing forces were, in turn, victorious. The histories of Florence and Venice, no less than those of Bavaria and Brandenburg-Prussia, bear witness to this trend.

In all these countries, the late Middle Ages witnessed the rise of a medieval constitutionalism which rested upon the dualism of king or crown and estates (see below, pp. 128 ff.) The persistence of certain elements of this medieval constitutionalism in England had tended to obscure the fact that there, as elsewhere, modern constitutionalism is a distinctive development which was possible only after national unification had provided an effective central government. The disappearance of the universal church as an ever-present counterpoise to the national monarchies was probably also important. Practically a century was consumed in the process of stabilizing the Anglican (National) Church in England; only when that process was completed, and the king-pope James I set forth his claim to totalitarian authority, had the moment come for modern constitutionalism. Thus it can be seen that developments followed a different path in each country, and hence no single time schedule can be made out for the history of constitutionalism. But nowhere do we find modern constitutionalism until an effective central government has been brought into existence. This needs to be remembered when constitutionalism in developing countries is in question.

Material factors of unification · Various causes, military, economic, geographic, religious, and nationalist, have been offered to explain this progress of national unification. These several factors are conditions of unification, centralization, and bureaucracy. They may conveniently be divided into the material and the political. Both are important. Among the material factors, the economic one has received the greatest attention.[6] Writers on mercantilism have dealt extensively with the economic side of unification. In the early period the expansion of trade played a decisive role. It created a need for better police protection and security in transportation and communication. The story of these activities is a long and complicated one, but there is little disagreement concerning the fundamental facts as revealed in the mounting trade figures in Venice, Florence, Antwerp, London, Frankfurt, and many other centers of urban progress. The citizenry of London and Paris, as well as the imperial cities of Germany, were, on the whole, willing supporters of the princely overlord against local feudal barons, regarding him as the likeliest guarantor of the public peace. But in Italy, where the development of trade was perhaps most marked, the cities did not support such a central head; these cities, in fact, offered the most violent opposition to imperial as well as papal pretensions. Here traders preferred to rely upon the growing power of their own city. This led to incessant warfare between the cities, which eventually, in the age of Machiavelli, brought foreign intervention and subjugation. It was the success of Northern monarchs in integrating and pacifying their kingdoms which in part inspired Machiavelli's ardent concern with Italian unification.[7] In the Europe north of the Alps, by increasing the security of commercial intercourse, these political developments provided a fertile field for the expansion of trade activities.

During the later phase of the evolution of modern government, when differentiated bureaucracies were being established all over Europe, the industrial revolution with its growing number of manufacturing establishments is said to have "caused" the expansion of governmental services. There can be no doubt that the growth of these industries provided an important concomitant condition of governmental expansion; still, it is more nearly true that the governments caused the industries to grow. In fact, the term "mercantilism," generally used for characterizing this age, suggests just that type of governmental participation and stimulation in the economic realm.

Another factor making for unification was the military. The military cause or determinant is most clearly seen when we consider the development of various weapons and techniques of warfare during these centuries.[8] If we compare the military establishments of early modern times with those prevalent in the Middle Ages, we discover three important technical differences: (1) they are very much larger; (2) their main force consists of infantry; (3) they are equipped with firearms and guns. Besides these three technical differences, there are three important administrative contrasts: (1) the military establishments are permanent (standing armies); (2) they are mercenary, or at any rate regularly paid; (3) they possess a central command, entrusted to a professional officer corps. The story of how all these changes came about differs considerably for the various countries. Even more important, in England the military establishment was predominantly naval, while on the Continent the army occupied the center of attention. Army and navy exercised a similar effect upon the growth of central administration; but a navy proved less dangerous to constitutionalism than an army. In the first place, as irregular forces become standing mercenary armies, expensively equipped, they require ever-increasing sums for their sustenance and thereby oblige the prince to perfect his tax-gathering machinery. Officials must be hired and organized, not only to collect the taxes, but to break down local resistance and to give assistance to those groups in the community which promise larger tax returns through the development of industry and manufacture. Again, the large size of the armies presupposes the organization of offices for collecting the food for men and horses as well as for distributing it. Finally, the development of a professional officer corps suggests a similar hierarchy for the administrative services. Obviously, if one starts from the military development as a fact, he could undertake to explain the entire evolution of modern government from that viewpoint. Actually this military development itself is as much "caused" by the evolution and growth of modern government; for in the struggle with local lords, as well as in the conflicts which arose between the several kingdoms, we recognize the most powerful stimulants to this military progress. Modern infantry first appeared in Switzerland, where peasants on foot defeated the Austrian duke's cavalry; it appeared again in the Hundred Years War when the newly organized archers gave the victory to England, until Charles VII of France succeeded in establishing his regular infantry. In short, we find that military and governmental development stimulate each other as concomitant aspects of the same process.

Attempts have been made from time to time to explain the evolution of modern government largely in terms of geography.[9] The distinctive evolution of government in England has provided seemingly convincing proof of such arguments. England's island position obviously facilitated her subordination to one government and the accompanying centralization by making foreign assistance to the weaker party relatively difficult, if not impossible. On the other hand, England has always been an island. The difficulty under which any geographic explanation labors is the static character of all geographic conditions. Growth is change, and cannot be explained by what has always been. Consequently, we find that those who would make us believe that geography was the final cause always slip in an unexplained, but firmly asserted, "natural" tendency of the "state" to grow. This natural tendency toward growth once accepted, it is easier to make probable that the governments of England, France, and Switzerland, for example, grew the way they did, because mountains, rivers, plains, and other such "facts" conditioned the particular form of their growth. There is little in the geography of Burgundy, to pick an example at random, which would lead us to conclude affirmatively that it was to become part of France rather than of Germany. Nor can the general assertions about the relation of climate to national character, first expounded by Aristotle, be considered adequately tested scientific hypotheses. Of the three causes or conditions which we have considered so far, the geographic, though from the point of view of the natural scientist the most "natural," would appear to be the least likely to explain satisfactorily unification of the national governments.

Political factors of unification · The determinants or conditions which we have so far discussed have been of the material, non-political sort. But there are other determinants which condition men's behavior through their minds without reference to a material factor. The broadest and most inclusive interpretation of this type is that which sees modern governments essentially as attempts at a realization of the social teachings of the Christian churches.[10] In medieval political life all moral and legal restraints of governmental authorities were reinforced by ecclesiastical sanctions, including pressure upon individual rulers. The Reformation disrupted the unity of faith which lent to such ecclesiastical restraint its essential legitimacy. It greatly intensified the older doctrine of a right of resistance, and in turn reinforced the monarch's efforts to surround his office with the halo of a "divine right." The Protestant inclination to make the prince the head of the church as well as the state became important in that it gave the state a new kind of ecclesiastical sanction by allowing it to participate in the symbolism of a mystical body, a divinely ordained superentity. Naturally, the Catholic rulers of the Counter Reformation, more especially Philip II of Spain, strove to achieve a comparable status. The sanctification of such worldly offices in turn permitted the idea to spread that the office, and not the officeholder, was entitled to such profound veneration, and that the officeholder must display a corresponding regard for the duties and responsibilities of his office. The life stories of individual leaders, such as Cromwell and Coke, the Great Elector and Henry IV, Gustavus Adolphus and the princes of Orange, reveal the force of these ideas in shaping their own conduct as well as the standards which they set for their officials. Such religious ideas were therefore a concomitant condition of the evolution of modern government.[11]

Another important explanatory "cause" of modern governments is the nation, or the national spirit. This factor is closely linked to religion, for if nationalism is not a religion, as has been pretended, it certainly has been a secular substitute for religion since the French revolution. Both in England and France this nationalist explanation of a national unification has found many advocates, on account of the strength of the national tradition in these countries. Fundamentally, it is held under this theory that modern constitutional government (England) or modern centralized governmental machinery (France) is the work of a "national genius," a collective group spirit, as it were, which created the government as we know it. Letters and statements of politicians and officials abound with more or less unctuous references to their devotion to the national cause, and there can be no question that the development of a public, as compared to a royal, service was greatly aided by the emergence of national consciousness. The nation as the sum total of the cultural environment offered a welcome substitute for the person of the king. Cromwell and Richelieu are alike in their allegiance to their country, their nation. The French revolution immensely intensified these sentiments, and carried them into other lands where they had previously not been important. But it is easy to exaggerate the causative importance of this factor. Some modern states arose where there was no nation, nor any national spirit. Countries like Prussia and the Hapsburg domains rivaled England and France in the perfection of modern governmental machinery.[12]

The problems of the emergent nations, so called, has led to extended discussions of the process of "nation building." The close link between state and nation — they are often mistakenly identified with each other — causes the rulers of a state to strive to bring a nation into being, because without it the state is weakened. This was not always true for political order in the past; vast empires have existed without anything like a nation providing the infrastructure. But there is another facet of this link between nation and state: nations are not always built; they may grow and then seek to build a state. This has been the case of Germany, of Italy, even of India.

The case of India raises another question, for India is not very much like a Western nation, such as France. We have broadened our concept and have given it a more general connotation than it has traditionally had. Empirically speaking, in the light of present realities, such as the United *Nations,* a nation is any cohesive group possessing independence within the confines of the international order. A nation provides a constituency for a government effectively ruling it and receiving from it the acclamation which legitimizes its government in confronting the governments of other nations. In light of this transformation, nation building is now a matter of building group cohesion and loyalty for purposes of international representation and domestic planning. This may be done by an already existing state, or by others — for example the Zionist movement — and it may unify very divergent groups, tribal conglomerates, ancient principalities, former colonies, or even existing nation-states (as in Europe). European nation-states in their development may provide some paradigmatic comparisons; they surely do not exhaust the possibilities.[13]

The Roman law as a formative force · There is one political factor which deserves special emphasis, on account of its formative importance, and that is the Roman law.[14] For law is essentially the embodiment of the established forms of recurrent social behavior patterns. This is the reason why all political, economic, and sociological studies are impossible without an adequate analysis of the legal forms with which a particular activity or process has been clothed. The political scientist is interested in the system of law as a whole, the political function it serves, because of the formal elements it happens to contain. Roman law greatly aided unification and centralization, because royal judges everywhere (imitating the papal legates) tended to employ the Roman law during the later Middle Ages and early modern times. It was long believed that this was not so in England, but more recent investigations have shown that the impact of the Roman law is merely more obscure, because it lay farther back in time in England. Why should the royal judges have used the Roman law? Until the idea of man-made law, of legislation, was definitely established, the greatest obstacle to the king's or prince's efforts toward centralization and expansion of the royal jurisdiction was the multitude of local laws, embodied in eternal custom. As against this obstacle, the Roman law offered an ideal weapon. It was a more ancient and therefore seemed an almost divine system of law, this law of the Roman Empire as embodied in the Institutes, the Digests, and the

Code of Justinian. Emperor and pope alike sought in its provisions weapons against traditional local customs; the several national kings soon followed their example. French lawyers developed the famous doctrine that the French king is *imperator* (emperor) in his own kingdom. He can, therefore, draw upon the Roman law in which were presumably embodied the principles of a *common* law of the whole kingdom. With the help of this doctrine, the jurists, called *Legists*, slowly succeeded in breaking down the feudal organization.

It is perfectly obvious that in the process of interpretation and application the Roman law was twisted, and arbitrary selections from its tenets gave it a wholly different flavor from the one it had possessed when it regulated the social life of the Eastern Roman Empire. Yet, it so happened that the Roman law, being the law of a highly developed commercial community, contained many principles which were better adapted to the needs of the emerging commercial classes than the local customs of a cruder agricultural society. Its urbanity, you might say, strengthened its position and insured it the support of the rising townsfolk everywhere.

These notions were powerfully reinforced by the emphasis on law in the Old Testament. Ancient Judaism in fact played a decisive role in shaping the origins of Western concepts of law. For the One God reveals himself very differently from the Greek and Roman gods. Jahweh, was clearly distinguished from the gods of peoples surrounding ancient Israel by his preoccupation with the law. The Old Testament is full of acts of legislation, of stories about God's struggle to secure their observation and enforcement, of rewards and punishments. Christians derived a dual obligation from this heritage: on the one hand, the Ten Commandments; on the other hand, the warning against mere obedience to law, that is to say, against hypocrisy. It is not sufficiently realized how extraordinarly potent has been the influence of these religious notions upon Western legal thought, and through it upon behavior in law and politics. It joined with Roman law in shaping the development of both church and state.[15]

The essentially *political* significance of the impact of Roman law has at times been overlooked, because it came much earlier in England and France than in Germany. The dreamlike aspirations of the medieval German emperor had prevented "nationalization" of the Roman law. Therefore the true "reception" of the Roman law, as the process was baptized by German scholars, came only when ultimate political authority passed to the several territorial princes in the sixteenth and seventeenth centuries. Then suddenly these princes commenced to put the Roman law to the same use to which it had earlier been put by the kings of France, England, and Spain; for they no longer needed the local law for combating imperial pretensions. But here, as there, it served the purpose of consolidating and centralizing scattered feudal realms, facilitating commerce, and last, but not least, rendering abstract and impersonal the relation of official and prince, as well as that of prince and people, by the Roman doctrine of magistracy.

The state · The Roman law itself did not develop a state concept in the modern sense. However, the Roman *civitas* or *res publica* comes closer to the modern idea of the state than any Greek notions regarding the polis or city. Similarly, the Roman practices of government in the republican period more nearly resembled modern constitutionalism than anything else in the world of antiquity. Indeed, they have often been equated, but mistakenly. For the modern state concept — and that of the constitution associated with it, though by way of juxtaposition — was born of the Western church concept. The state as a concept was forged by political theorists as a tool of propaganda for absolute monarchy. Jean Bodin and those who followed him wished to give the king's government a corporate halo roughly equivalent to that of the church. The "state" was the "estate" of the king; in France, where the idea was first most sharply stated, the word *État* to this day covers both estate and state. In setting off the state against church and empire, Jean Bodin provided an effective rationalization for the centrifugal and particularistic forces which eventually led to the modern nation-state.[16]

A very large gloss has in the course of centuries covered the groundwork which Bodin first laid. Yet, fundamentally all definitions of sovereignty still revolve around Bodin's original ideas, including the modern notions of the state as a "sovereign juristic association" or "person." Every state, said Bodin, is the government of an association of families, and in order to be well ordered it requires a single sovereign, that is to say, a person or group of persons who possess supreme legislative power; a sovereign, therefore, can change any existing law.[17] It is clear that the state and the sovereign are here linked in such a way as to be in effect Siamese twins; these artificial twins became one when the state itself was proclaimed sovereign, first by Hugo Grotius and more commonly in the nineteenth century.

As an ideology for monarchical absolutism, the concepts of state and sovertignty were perfect. They provided the absolute rulers with an excuse for establishing unrestrained control over all lesser associations, including the church. Seventeenth-century writers, especially Thomas Hobbes and Baruch Spinoza, further radicalized the doctrine by founding it upon natural law, thus eliminating the possibility, still recognized by Bodin, that natural law might be pleaded as a ground for limiting state authority. Only in Britain, where the idea of modern constitutionalism was developed in antithesis of the "state" concept in the course of the revolutionary struggles of the seventeenth century, did the doctrine fail. When Sir Edward Coke snorted that sovereignty and the common law were not suitable bedfellows, he may have been echoing medieval ideas, but these medieval ideas of a government effectively restrained by law were soon converted into a more explicit constitutional structure in the *Instrument of Government* (see below, p. 135 f.). Only in the nineteenth century, through Jeremy Bentham and John Austin, did the notions of state and sovereign gain an entering wedge into English legal thought, but legal practitioners have remained troubled by the implications. It is all very well to claim that parliament or the majority of the people is "sovereign," but the moment one does so it becomes impossible to maintain the idea of a constitutional system, with its protection for the individual and the minority against arbitrary action of the majority in parliament or out. Absolutism in its various forms provides for a concentration of power, while constitutionalism provides for a divided exercise of power. This is the ancient idea of a mixed system of government, and hence arguments about democracy do not properly apply; by definition, a constitutional democracy is one which does not grant *all* power to the majority. This issue dramatically presented itself again in Europe after the Second World War, when in France, Italy, and Germany the Communists came to plead for unrestrained and absolute majority rule in the name of democracy.

The "state" concept when linked with that of sovereignty seeks to comprehend under one concept the antithetical systems of absolutism and constitutionalism. This is sometimes done by asserting that the state exercises a "monopoly of force." This emphasis on coercion does not fit the cooperative community. If persuasion, or, more broadly speaking, consent, is given the place which it in fact occupies from time to time in the management of political communities by providing a basis for power and authority, the antithesis between the sovereign state and the self-governing community becomes clear.[18]

A political community is governed in one of two ways. Either a constituent group (see below, ch. VIII) has organized a pattern providing for the expression of consent by a substantial body of *citizens* (the common man), or a conquering group has set up a system of controls providing for effective constraint of the *subjects*. The antithesis is an abstract and theoretical one and there are many communities which fall into intermediary patterns. But the basic difference is of great importance in assessing even these communities. It was to idealize a government based on constraint that the concepts of "state" and "sovereignty" were developed. Any close analysis reveals that the central bureaucracies, supported by growing military establishments, conquered the medieval constitutional systems from within, and established the monarch as the symbolical figurehead of a system in which they became the final arbiter of what should be done.

Sovereignty · A very important political corollary of the idea of state and sovereignty, however, was the depersonalizing of governmental relationships. To put this another way, against feudalism the trend toward legislative unification and centralization found its most challenging expression in the doctrine of sovereignty. It was the theoretical culmination of a long secular trend in France and elsewhere. Sovereignty rendered impersonal the relation of the king to his subjects. Under feudalism, all such relationships were patterned upon the personal fealty of lord and vassal. That is to say, the principle of the relation between the lord (*dominus*) and the vassal was personal "mutuality." Such personal relationship must needs be limited in extent, and was therefore ill-adapted to wide territorial realms. The hierarchy of the mutual relationships which feudal society had tried to evolve in the effort to bridge the gap had shown a dismal tendency toward disintegration and anarchy. This tendency had resulted from the growth of complex intermediary authorities which opposed the prince's rule. To escape from this confusion it was then asserted that no true government existed unless there was somewhere an authority for making laws binding upon all the inhabitants of a given territory. The true achievement which lay in this recognition of the need for a central government has been obscured by the struggle over the control of such a government. It was forgotten that it was necessary first to create a government before the question of its control could even arise. And it was furthermore forgotten that this question of control could arise earlier in England than in France, because Tudor absolutism had consolidated previous efforts to establish an effectively centralized bureaucracy at a time when France was in the grip of an extended civil war. From this civil war the crown emerged with a considerable army at its command, which made it possible to crush the *Fronde,* while Cromwell's Model Army triumphed over the royal forces in England. This military ascendancy of the French crown, stimulated as it was by the possibilities of foreign invasion, delayed the outbreak of the struggle over the control of the government for one hundred and forty years. But the usefulness of the concept of sovereignty in providing a symbol for national unification and for the monarchical governments which destroyed feudal localism did not outlast its time. It was in the preconstitutional period that "sovereignty" was destined to play its most significant role. The word itself served as a symbol for concentrated power, deriving from the word "sovereign," connoting the holder of such power. Since under constitutionalism there is not supposed to exist any such concentrated power, sovereignty as a conception is at variance with the logic of constitutionalism,[14] and all constitutional regimes have shown a marked tendency to resist its use. Even under a constitutional democracy this is true. The notion of "popular sovereignty" — a confused expression at best — needs to be supplanted by that of the "constituent group." For this group is not the holder of concentrated power, but exercises the revolutionary, residuary, constituent power of establishing a new constitution. Most of the time other groups exercise intermediary powers of decision, such as amending the constitution, legislating, and so forth.[19]

The problem of responsibility · As long as rulers were effectively influenced in their conduct by the moral teachings of the church — a united church with universal claims of obedience — the problem of responsibility could remain obscure. Modern secularized methods of securing responsibility through electoral controls and the like has tended to make us forget that through long ages responsible conduct had to be brought about by other means, and that even today much remains of these ancient ways. Historically speaking, we find that responsible conduct of power holders has been enforced not only through secular, political, administrative, or judicial sanctions, but through religious sanctions as well.[20] In fact, such religious responsibility has bulked larger than any of the others. Medieval constitutionalism was largely built upon that sanction. When a religious ethic prevails in a community (and it does not inherently matter what particular religion it is), the possibilities of producing responsible conduct in terms of that religious spirit are on the whole more promising than any of the secular devices. Since responsibility presupposes logically a set of norms or standards in terms of which conduct can be evaluated, the actual prevalence of a believed-in set of such norms makes responsibility of conduct almost automatic, as long as the faith lasts. It would be instructive to analyze the workings of Chinese bureaucracy in these terms, but even our own civilization has relied upon religious sanctions for long periods. As might be expected, there exist two primary forms corresponding to the two primary patterns of Christian ethics, the Catholic and the Protestant. Yet they have much in common. Under both creeds, the person who is supposed to be made responsible for his acts is made responsible for his acts to God. In practice this means, of course, responsibility to the clergy who legitimately interpret the will of God. The only thing a prince can do to escape clerical censure as long as he accepts the faith is to conform as nearly as possible to the religious ethic. Luther's notion that the prince himself could function as the head of the church, if spiritually guided by an ecclesiastically unencumbered clergy, made the clerk sufficiently subservient to the government to make it increasingly ineffective as an instrument for securing responsible conduct. The result was either civil war, as in England, or absolutism, as in the various German principalities. The career of Archbishop Laud stands as an example of the unmistakable tendency within the clergy to extol the principle positions for the sake of ecclesiastical support.

Basically, the position and approach of the Catholic Church was not dissimilar. Throughout the Middle Ages, the increasingly independent and highly effective administrative organization of the Catholic Church had run into bitter conflicts with the secular authorities. In these conflicts the secular authorities gradually gained the upper hand. The appearance of the concepts of "state" and of "sovereignty" marked the ascendancy of the secular authorities. At the same time, the secular authorities now became themselves "clericalized" in the sense that their offices were being surrounded with a quasi-religious halo and sanction. It proved impossible in the sequel for the ecclesiastical authorities to recapture the medieval position in the Counter Reformation. Like the Protestant clergy, the Catholic authorities were obliged to concentrate on maintaining the loyalty and support of individual princes by every available means.

But as soon as the compelling standards of a divinely ordained faith faltered, a prince and his administrative following were able to emancipate themselves from the restraints which a religious conviction had imposed on them. Just as responsible conduct had almost completely disappeared from the republics of Renaissance Italy, so it now tended to disappear from the Northern kingdoms. The doctrines of the agnostic pagans for whom Machiavelli had spoken spread throughout Europe. The clash of his doctrines with the earlier religious notions of responsible government produced the doctrine of "reason of state."

Reason of state • Since religious responsibility means that a man has to account for his actions in terms of transcendant ethical norms, it involves particular pitfalls for the ruler and official who seeks to be guided by it. Situations are bound to occur in which such norms conflict with the exigencies of the conduct of government. The proverbial saying about ambassadors that they are men sent abroad to lie for the good of their country epitomizes this difficulty. The ruler or official who obeys the moral law may lose out to his rival. To have observed and described such situations with corrosive frankness was one of Machiavelli's achievements. He challenged much "conventional wisdom" about government. His own resolution of the difficulty was to make the state the highest value and the source of all human virtue. He could then blandly claim that no real conflict existed, because to build and maintain a state was man's highest achievement, his greatest work of art. This his frankly "ancient wisdom," derived he thought from Greek and Roman historians, was of course, unacceptable to most of his Christian contemporaries. They had to try and reconcile the requirements of state-craft with Christian morals. The result was the doctrine of reason of state.[21] It is actually merely a specific form of the kind of rationality which places organization requirements (an operational code) above a moral code.

It is no accident that a Catholic priest, Giovanni Botero,[22] attempted to fit Machiavellian statecraft together with a Christian pattern of thought. His attempt at constructing a particular ratio status or governmental rationality was not especially successful, but it pointed the way. Generally speaking, it served to reinforce the absolutist monarchy's claim to paternal authority over its subjects, based upon the divine right of kings. Some writers develop the idea that every form of government has its proper "reason of state," and that meant "acting in conformity with the essence and form of that state." At this point, we are face to face with a special "constitutional reason of state," that is to say, "the means which are opportune for ordering or pre-serving a particular kind of constitution."

Constitutional reason of state[23] in its subtler, modern form raises the question: how can one, how must one, deal with declared enemies of the constitutional order, *any* constitutional order, when such men are as citizens entitled to the protection of that constitution? Are they entitled to enjoy the fundamental rights and civil liberties? The answers range all the way from completely denying any such rights of "subversive elements" to fully vindi-cating them for "enemies of the constitution." Security and survival of the state, or more especially of the good state, of the constitutional, civilized political order, has challenged the ingenuity of the best constitutionalists, from Locke to Hegel and into our own time. But no entirely satisfactory answer has been found. Constitutional reason of state is, in the last analysis, a matter of ever-more effectively ordering its internal and external relations. If constitutionalism is based upon the belief that the most fundamental of all its rights is the right of a man to his conviction, his faith, the hard core of man's dignity, then its very survival is at stake in its protection. To make his innermost self secure is more vital to the security and survival of a constitutional order than any secret. It defines the boundary beyond which no expedient measures can be permitted to go in safeguarding the system's survival.

Developmental administration: core of the state · Constitutional rea-son of state is a far cry from the original, absolutist conception which was preoccupied with war and the growth of the state. In the age of absolutism, public policy was dominated by *mercantilism* — a body of thought which its ablest expositor has called a "system of power."[24] Mercantilism, though usually associated with the idea of protectionism, was committed to internal freedom of trade. Internally, it was an economic corollary of the monarchical policy of centralization and unification. "Domestic tolls, local privileges, and inequalities in the system of coinage, weights and measures, the absence of unity in legislation, administration and taxation, it was against these that the mercantilist statesmen struggled. They therefore opposed everything that . . . obstructed trade within the boundaries of the state." Thus Eli F. Heckscher has characterized the mercantilist position. It was a particular branch of mercantilism, which the so-called "cameralists" expounded.[25] They developed the practical implications of mercantilism in terms of government action. They thus became the expositors and theorists of administration. For no matter how keen the statesmen of mercantilism, men like the Cecils in England and Colbert in France, might be about *freedom of trade*, they found themselves confronted with innumerable existing restrictions *in* trade which had to be removed. Willy-nilly they had to undertake governmental intervention; in other words, they had to interfere with interferences.

It was the intention of the mercantilists, then, to enhance — along with the wealth of the nation — the *power* of the government, that is to say, its strength and resources, regardless of the effect upon individuals. To put it another way, they believed in government and in administration. They looked upon the "state" as a creative agency. In this outlook they differed completely from the times preceding and following theirs. When Thomas Jefferson said that that government is best which governs least, he formulated a political outlook diametrically opposed to that of the mercantilist admirers of the "creative state." On the other side, many mercantilists had little else than scorn for the medieval constitutionalism which their centralized administrative systems supplanted. They believed in centralization and in administrative action, none more so than Francis Bacon, whose thinking was really a theoretical projection of Tudor absolutism. As we have already remarked, English developments were more than a century ahead of Continental ones, so that we find thinkers like John Locke combining constitutionalist and mercantilist views. This fact has tended to veil the parallelism between the two; from the standpoint of economic and constitutional development, Cecil, Colbert, and Frederick William I are "contemporaries." Although one worked in the sixteenth, one in the seventeenth, and one in the eighteenth century, they were each responsible for consolidating one of the modern power systems. They were each responsible likewise for consolidating an administrative service, a bureaucracy, which a succeeding generation could then subject to controls and thus convert into a constitutional system.

Such a bureaucracy had, of course, existed at other times. The great despotic empires of Asia had developed considerable administrative machinery, and so had the Roman and Byzantine empires. In discussing the "political systems of empires," a learned sociologist has recently interpreted them as "bureaucratic societies."[26] He is able to show that recurrently some of these bureaucracies developed a kind of "service ideology," even though the stress on service to the rulers remained strong. Since bureaucracy will be discussed at greater length in the next chapter, it suffices here to add that these bureaucracies underwent in all the modern states a striking development from personal servants of the ruler, in the late feudal stage, to carefully trained public servants.

Constitutionalism · In the preceding discussion, the ideology of constitutionalism and more particularly its link with Christianity have been discussed, its function (objective) has been indicated as that of safeguarding each member of the political community as a person, and the chief means, namely dividing power, has been mentioned. It is high time that this central concept and its referents be more fully explored. For even though a complete analysis cannot be given until later (ch. VII ff.), a sketch of constitutionalism's historical evolution presupposes a general grasp of what it is, or is taken to mean here. Constitutionalism by dividing power provides a system of effective restraints upon governmental action. In studying it, one has to explore the methods and techniques by which such restraints are established and maintained. Putting it in another, more familiar, but less exact way, it is a body of rules ensuring fair play, thus rendering the government "responsible." There exist a considerable number of such techniques or methods, and they will receive fuller treatment at the appropriate place.

In this general historical sketch, the question confronts us: how did the idea of restraints arise? And who provided the support which made the idea victorious in many countries?[27] There are two important roots to the idea of restraints. One is the medieval heritage of natural-law doctrine. For while the royal bureaucrats gained the upper hand in fact, the other classes in the community who had upheld the medieval constitutionalism, the barons and the free towns and above all the church, developed secularized versions of natural law. At the same time, they clung to residual institutions, such as the *parlements* in France. After the task of unification had been accomplished, and the despotic methods of absolutism could no longer be justified, these elements came forward with the idea of a separation of power. Both the English and the French revolutions served to dramatize these trends.

But why did the same not happen in Germany and Italy? Remembering that the centers of medieval universalism were Empire and Papacy, we can readily understand that they would stay intact much longer, both institutionally and ideologically, in the countries which constituted their core, that is to say, in Germany and Italy. Political organizations and systems of government disintegrate at the periphery first; hence Sweden and Britain were among the first to evolve national unification and emancipation from the medieval system. Indeed, both countries never fully belonged to the universal structure of medieval Europe. They developed their own *imperium in imperio,* and hence their transition from medieval to modern constitutionalism was interrupted by only a comparatively short period of absolutism. This English absolutism, moreover, never went so far as it did in the countries nearer the center of medieval universalism.

The other root of the idea of restraints is shared by medieval and modern constitutionalism, and is peculiar to some extent to Western culture.[28] It is Christianity, and more specifically the Christian doctrine of personality which has already been discussed. The insistence upon the individual personality as the final value, the emphasis upon the transcendental importance of each man's soul, creates an insoluble conflict with any sort of absolutism. Here lies the core of the objection to all political conceptions derived from Aristotelian and other Greek sources. Since there exists a vital need for government, just the same, this faith in the worth of each human being is bound to seek a balance of the two needs in some system of restraints which protects the individual, or at least minorities, against any despotic exercise of political authority. It is quite in keeping with this conflict that the apologists of unrestrained power have in all ages of Western civilization felt the necessity of *justifying* the exercise of such power, a necessity which was not felt elsewhere. Bacon and Hobbes, Bodin and Spinoza, and even Machiavelli insisted that some sort of inanimate force, reason, natural law, or enlightened self-interest would bring about what their constitutionalist opponents would embody in effective institutions: restraints upon the arbitrary exercise of governmental power.

Turning to the question of who provided the effective support which made the idea of restraints victorious in various countries, the answer must be that it was essentially the mercantile middle class who did. The bourgeoisie, as it has come to be called, furnished everywhere the mainstay of political support for constitutionalism. This fact is noteworthy, but should not be overemphasized. In recent times, organized labor has stepped into the role of the bourgeoisie in many countries, for the simple reason that it, above all other classes in the community, is an exposed minority. To be sure, the class-war doctrine of orthodox Marxism took exactly the opposite line, but two things should be kept in mind. First, in the countries most deeply permeated by constitutionalism the Marxist doctrine never gained a substantial following, except amongst intellectuals. Second, the terrible persecution of the labor class in Fascist countries produced a "crisis" of Marxism[19] amongst its most ardent upholders. It is undeniable that the economic problems of our industrial society have generated strains which are taxing established constitutional systems to the breaking point. But the evils of totalitarianism have so rapidly become manifest that the most diverse groups, classes, and nations throughout the world are seen banding together for the reconstruction of constitutionalism on a new social and international basis.

The preceding sketch of the genetic forces which produced constitutionalism still leaves the question of what these restraints are somewhat open. Starting from the notion that a concentration of power, such as the classical doctrine of state and sovereignty had called for, inevitably produced absolutism, constitutionalism, evolved from the classical notion of a mixed government — the *politeia* Aristotle had praised as the best regime — into the idea of a careful, legally prescribed separation of the powers of making laws (rules), executing and administering them, and settling disputes arising over their interpretation. And since this kind of basic order requires establishing, the idea of a distinct power of making and amending the constitution also became part of the total syndrome of constitutionalism. At an early date, during the English revolutions of the seventeenth century, the need for formulating in greater detail what constitutes the personal sphere to be protected and guaranteed also made itself felt and produced a number of bills of rights.[29]

England's leadership in constitutionalism · Although the idea is firmly rejected that constitutionalism is somehow the result of a mysterious English national character which has more recently been expanded into Anglo-Saxon or even Anglo-American tribal character to placate the Americans, it is nevertheless true that the English-speaking peoples have developed their political traditions more steadily in a constitutional direction and have thereby become the leaders of modern constitutionalism.[30] Why? We do not know. But the fact is incontrovertible. Probably many different factors combined to make possible this steady deepening and expansion of political culture among the English-speaking people. Some features have already been mentioned. The English revolution came so early that it practically transformed the medieval constitutionalism of king and estates, of "the king in parliament." Ever since, British constitutionalism has been more traditionalist than rationalist in its foundations. Although Sir Edward Coke, when he glorified Magna Charta, basically reverted back to a feudal charter, he was a typical representative of the commercial middle class. This commercial middle class had been behind Tudor absolutism during the sixteenth century, because

Henry VIII and Elizabeth had been engaged in breaking down the feudal privileges of barons and church; they were building what has been called by economic historians the metropolitan economy (see below, p. 91 f.). But once these feudal powers had been weakened sufficiently, the rising commercial interests felt no longer the need of royal absolutism. For two full generations, from the accession of James I to that of William and Mary, the revolutionary struggle went on, finally producing the constitutional order that has been developing uninterruptedly in England ever since. During these two generations the whole range of political issues, from absolutism in Hobbes to anarchy in the Levellers, was explored, fought over with word and sword, and finally settled in favor of a division of power between king, lords, and commons. This order, while it sounded medieval and traditionalist, was in fact modern in that the real foundation of this division was the electorate behind the Commons, rather than the ecclesiastical authorities and feudal land owners behind the Lords. It was the Commons who from now on were to restrain the exercise of the Crown's power, reinforced by independent courts. After the Commons had, in the eighteenth century, become the real core of the government, the division was maintained through the recognition of the opposition, the basis of the party system.

The English system of free institutions aroused a great deal of interest in other countries in the course of the eighteenth century. The eyes of all those who were disgusted with absolutism turned toward Britain. But not only theirs; the eyes of kings, too, looked at the home of liberty to be sure that things would not turn out that way in their own realms. Frederick the Great of Prussia, in one of his political testaments, advised his successors not to allow the development of the office of Prime Minister; he rightly recognized in him the leader of the popular forces. The movement of Enlightenment preached to the absolute rulers the necessity of rationally conducting their office so as to forestall constitutionalism. Even so enlightened a spirit as Voltaire would rather educate Frederick of Prussia than build a constitution. So unique appeared the British system that Montesquieu built his entire discussion of *The Spirit of the Laws* around the contrast between Britain and France. Though he was behind the time in detail, he generalized effectively the importance of the separation of powers as the essense of the constitutionalism which Britain had produced.

The spread of constitutionalism • The pride which the British themselves took in their constitution must have been very general. It runs through the writings of an ardent Tory like Dr. Johnson; it was encountered by travelers, even when they were preoccupied with very different matters, such as Casanova, who tells at length about it. Bentham and Burke, though worlds apart in general outlook, share this sense of achievement. Since British wealth and power were, at the same time, continually on the increase in that period, it was natural that the old ideas about absolutism should be viewed with increasing scepticism everywhere. But what is more, in France and elsewhere the rising middle class, just as in England a century or more earlier, no longer felt the need of royal aid in combating the local power of church and nobility. The French crown had effectively destroyed the power of local authorities. The middle class, grown strong and wealthy, increasingly resented the privileges of those classes in the community which no longer served any vital function. Against these privileged groups, the idea of the equality of all men was pitched and was gaining ground steadily through the years.

But there was another side to British constitutionalism. In the Empire's North American colonies, populous settlements of white men had developed a new sense of independence.[31] Many of them were Englishmen; they claimed with insistence the rights of Englishmen for themselves. When the Commons refused to heed such voices, they finally sounded the bugle call of universal constitutionalism. In spite of the grandeur of the French revolution, it should not be forgotten that it was once again in the English tongue that this all-embracing constitutionalism was declared. "We hold these truths to be self-evident, that all men are created equal, that they are endowed by their Creator with certain inalienable rights, that among these are Life, Liberty and the Pursuit of Happiness. . . ." At the time, these famous phrases seemed to most of the powerful an empty challenge of a small crowd of rebels sure to be defeated. In actual fact they heralded the irresistible forward march of constitutionalism during the nineteenth century. In America, this constitutionalism struck deeper root than almost anywhere else on earth, except England and Switzerland. The American fight for independence foreshadowed the constitutional development of the British Empire. As Lloyd George once said when speaking under a statue of Washington: "He taught us how not to run an empire." The very fact of their revolting against England protected the American constitution makers from committing the error of copying, or rather trying to copy, the English constitution.

The landmarks of the spread of constitutionalism in the eighteenth and nineteenth centuries are, summarily put, the American war of independence and adoption of the constitution, 1776–1787; the outbreak of the French revolution in 1789, followed by numerous constitutional experiments in France; the reforms of Baron Stein in Prussia, 1806–1809; the Restoration in France in 1814–1815; the establishment of the German Union (*Bund*) in 1818; the French revolution of 1830, followed by a revolution in Belgium and elsewhere; Lord Durham's famous *Report* in 1838, which eventually led to the creation of the Dominion of Canada in 1867; and finally the revolutions of 1848, including the abortive effort of the Germans to achieve both constitutional government and national unity at the same time. It testifies to the strength of the movement that even such "Machiavellians" as Bismarck and Cavour could unify their countries only through the adoption of a constitution.

The steady spread of constitutionalism followed pretty definitely the curve of industrialization. This is only natural, since it was the commercial and professional middle class which carried forward not only the industrial revolution, but the demand for constitutional government as well. The bourgeoisie, to repeat, unquestionably furnished the minds and the men for this politico-economic revolution. But it is quite another matter whether the leadership stayed with them. Even the term "middle class," quite appropriate at an early stage in the evolution of modern society, gradually loses its distinctness in the course of the nineteenth century. This broadening at the base will be dealt with presently.

Industrialization brought with it one feature peculiarly favorable to constitutionalism, and that is the progressive cheapening of the printed word. For the modern press, the channel of mass communication, was everywhere in the vanguard of advancing constitutionalism.

The living constitution · All the foregoing goes to show that a constitution embodies a system of power relationships which has been effectively institutionalized. No "countervailing power" or other amorphous influence, no matter how effective, satisfies the requirements which the concept of a constitution is meant to denote. The ideological justifications for such a system, as well as the thoughts associated with its practice, embody the meaning of constitutionalism. Although some of these ideological and behavioral projections have treated a constitution as a static given, as something which never or very rarely changes, a constitution is, on the contrary, a *living* system. To be sure, the basic structure or pattern may remain even though the different component parts may undergo significant alterations. How very different is the American Congress today than it was after 1787; how profound are the alterations which the British Parliament has undergone during the same period! And yet, both still constitute vital parts of the evolving constitution.

Some of the conventional arguments about constitutions, such as whether it is rigid or flexible, written or unwritten, and so forth, appear rather artificial in the perspective of the living constitution. The concept of a living constitution makes short shrift of such conventional notions as that of a recent text which suggests "The Constitution" to be "a selection of the legal rules which govern the government of that country and which have been embodied in a document." Not only may the living constitution be embodied in many documents, but in good measure any functioning constitution is, like the living law of which it is a part, embodied in convention and customs, in ways of acting which may eventually become fixed, as did the pocket veto of the American President, or which remain "understood" without such fixation.[32]

It would, of course, be a grave mistake therefore to belittle the making of fixed rules. There is obviously at times great need and patent advantage in having offices and powers explicitly framed and maintained over long periods. They are, if the simile may be permitted, the bony skeleton of a deliberately adopted constitutional order. But like a skeleton they do not make a living constitution live; they give it structure and stability. All these matters will be taken up again, and at greater length, below. Here we need to mention briefly one other critical point.

It has at times been suggested that an emphasis upon the limiting role of a constitution, a stress laid upon the restraints which it establishes, negates the more important function of organizing the government of a country for effective political action. There can be little doubt that this mistake has at times been committed. But this is only true when the restraints are so structured as to impede action. It was the alleged fault of the Articles of Confederation, and the American constitution was deliberately designed to remedy the fault. Events have vindicated the expectation, so vigorously expressed in the *Federalist*, especially when discussing the presidency.

This problem of organizing an efficacious government is also the reason why a sound amending procedure is of great advantage. Of course, as we have seen, a constitution may be changed in many more informal ways, but still, there are often explicit rules which may be in need of amendment. Custom and convention are of great value in shaping the office, but the President's four-year term could only be changed by formal amendment, and when a President disobeyed a custom not to seek a third term, a formal amendment was considered necessary to prevent it in the future.

Constitutions have, as was noted at the outset, been adopted in many of the countries emerging from colonial rule. Often these constitutions were in fact promoted by the colonial power for various reasons. In country after country serious difficulties have been encountered in making such Western schemes work. Nor is this really surprising, when one remembers that Western constitutional democracy is rooted in and to some extent dependent on basic religious and ethical convictions which are not part of the developing country's culture. Even the thought processes, like Aristotelian logic, which are associated with Western constitutionalism may be alien to such a new nation.

As we pointed out already, this does not mean that constitutionalism necessarily will not work, but it does mean that its working may be exposed to peculiar difficulties, stresses, and strains. We shall deal in our concluding chapter with some of these difficulties and possible ways of coping with them. At this early point in our analysis, it merely remains to remark that the emphasis on cultural determinism is apt to lead astray. It is unlikely that a particular constitution can be distilled from any cultural tradition, except possibly in regard to man's personal sphere, where the prevalent values and beliefs are at issue. For the rest, a sound, operative, viable constitutional order may well be built out of a considerable variety of cultural givens, in the light of the very considerable experience which is already at hand.[33]

The broad tradition of constitutionalism has in this century been projected onto the world plane.[34] The Covenant of the League of Nations and the Charter of the United Nations are both embodiments of this international constitutionalism. Quite in keeping with the constitutionalist tradition, a Universal Declaration of Human Rights was adopted after vigorous debate by the United Nations in December 1948; but no enforcement machinery has been set up, except for the weak supervisory machinery provided for dependent territories. Indeed, it is very doubtful that any such enforcement could at present be implemented. International constitutionalism is not a mere facade; but the very fact of the participation of totalitarian regimes makes it inevitable that this constitutionalism partakes to some extent of the character of totalitarian constitutionalism. That such constitutionalism is imperfect, that it does not restrain the governments operating under it to any significant degree, is obvious. That it may nevertheless become the basis for gradual implementation, and thus the starting point for the achievement of genuine constitutionalism, is the hope of many. Such hope may find some confirmation in the past history of constitutionalism.

Democratization of constitutionalism · Constitutionalism, both in England and abroad, was at the outset not at all democratic, but rather aristocratic. In spite of the fact that the *Declaration of Independence*, and the *Rights of Man* of the French revolution, had proclaimed the equality of all men, dominant political practice remained sceptical. The *Federalist* has not much love for the mass of the common people; it has much to say about the "gusts of popular passion" and the like. Throughout the nineteenth century, intellectuals in England and elsewhere were highly critical of democracy.[35] What is more important, democracy, in requiring the universal suffrage of men and women, the equal participation of all classes, especially the labor class, in political life, and the elimination of racial and religious discrimination — democracy in this sense spread slowly throughout the nineteenth century, and has not yet reached its culmination.

The milestones in the process of democratizing constitutionalism in the nineteenth century were: Jackson's presidency; the Reform Act of 1832; the revolution of 1848 in France; and the Civil War. Although none of them, obviously, realized democracy, they each contributed a significant forward step. Jackson's presidency provided the first effective frontal attack upon government by the elite; through the Reform Act of 1832, and the other great measures of reform which accompanied and followed it, a broad breach was made in the system of government by the privileged, as exemplified in rotten boroughs and vote restrictions. The revolution of 1848 in France challenged the power of financial and industrial capital, and while its premature, radical experiments with socialism led to the Bonapartist reaction, it nevertheless heralded the coming of labor into its own. Farther east beyond the Rhine, the revolution precipitated an unsuccessful attempt to unite Germany by popular movement, after having swept away the system of Metternich. In Italy a similar initiative failed. But in spite of the fact that popular forces proved too weak to unite and free nations, the idea of self-determination took root. Finally the Civil War in the United States destroyed slavery after four formidable years of armed conflict. In the course of this struggle, the leader of the antislavery forces of the North, Abraham Lincoln, formulated some of the most hallowed tenets of democratic faith. Nowhere has the progressive spirit of democracy found more eloquent expression than in the Gettysburg address: ". . . that government of the people, by the people, for the people shall not perish from the earth." The ideals which inspired this speech are still far from having been realized.

Every one of these milestones marks an element in the process of democratization which in spite of many setbacks is still going forward. The successive extensions of the suffrage, eventually embracing women's suffrage, as well as numerous social and governmental reforms, carried on the work that the Reform Act of 1832 began. Likewise in the United States, many administrations in this century have extended and deepened the control over concentrated economic power and monopoly. France, in successive phases of the Third and Fourth Republics, realized part of the program of the revolutionaries of 1848, while in Germany the Weimar Republic gave a first token of what a fully democratized and socially conscious German people might contribute to a democratic world order. For here, for the first time, *social* democracy was taken up in earnest. The Fascist reaction there and in other countries of Europe meant a desperate attempt to stem the tide of advancing democracy. By exploiting all the stresses and strains of a new social pattern, Fascism managed to install itself, and then, by the ruthless employment of every known method of violence, to maintain itself until the inner tensions and strains resulting from such desperate repressive efforts embroiled the Fascist dictators in foreign wars that spelled their doom. But even the dictators found it necessary to make continuous bows toward the people, thus acknowledging the fact that democracy alone offers legitimacy, an acceptable ground for the exercise of political power.

This increasing recognition of popular majorities as the only basis of legitimate government naturally has led to a fading of the monarchical tradition. Kings, not having been popularly elected, could rarely stand up against a leader of the people. The reign of Queen Victoria is most interesting in this respect. Time and again her monarchical sense of responsibility clashed with the parliamentary responsibility of successive prime ministers. Continental crises may have been more dramatic outwardly; they brought revolution and reaction in their train. But the deep roots which constitutionalism had struck in English thinking make the slow fading of royal prerogative worthy of detailed attention. The story of the bedchamber comedy is characteristic. Peel would not form a cabinet unless, as evidence of the Queen's confidence, he should be given the right to nominate the ladies of her household. The Queen refused. The Queen thought that she would be "supported by my country who are very enthusiastic about it and loudly cheered me on going to church Sunday." The basis of this conflict was the fact that court gossip still played a significant role in the forming of a government. That was in 1839. It was not long before the idea of the politically "sovereign" people had taken root to such an extent that only the parliamentary support of a man could determine his leadership. The kings and queens just faded out of the picture.[36]

Socialism and constitutionalism • The revolution of 1848 projected, as has been said, a new issue: socialism. Though there is no inherent logical reason for it, the demand for socialism became the primary goal of the rising labor class. The *Communist Manifesto* had by one year anticipated the revolution of 1848. It has remained a radical challenge ever since. It had denounced some of the very weaknesses which contributed to the failure of "utopian" socialism as represented by men like Proudhon. More particularly, the *Communist Manifesto* rejects any possibility of cooperation between the revolutionary socialist proletariat and other classes in society. Consequently, the *Manifesto* denies completely the central idea of constitutionalism. It combines an advocacy of force and violence during the revolutionary and postrevolutionary period, a ready acceptance of dictatorship, with a belief in a vague anarchical type of democracy after all classes except the labor class have been destroyed.[37] The *Communist Manifesto* and all orthodox Marxists who followed it revived the belief in the creative possibilities of violence; they expounded the concept of a transitional dictatorship in the name of the proletariat. This is not the place for entering upon an analysis of the Marxian view of society, to discover the underlying reasons for the Marxist rejection of constitutionalism. It seems a curious paradox in the light of the fact that the working class constituted and still constitutes a minority, since constitutionalism is designed to protect the minorities against arbitrary action by the government, even when supported by a majority. But this paradox disappears when it is remembered that Marx expected the evolution of industrialism to turn the labor class into a majority. His predictions in this respect, though striking, were basically erroneous. Quite contrary to his views, the growth of the middle class, the managerial, professional, and clerical workers, together with the inability of the Communist antiproperty view to gain a substantial number of adherents among the farmers, provided mass support for the Fascist reaction.

A sense of these realities and the strength of the constitutional tradition combined to keep English and American labor largely hostile to Communism and its doctrine of violence. Even in those European countries where Marxism became powerful, Socialist parties found themselves in practice obliged to soften the rigor of the doctrine. Sharp conflicts raged which led to an increasing recognition of the desirability of working within a constitutional context. After the First World War, the Socialists entered a number of governments and proceeded to apply their general policies under constitutionalism. But owing to their failure to face the issues involved in a combination of socialism and constitutionalism, very serious strains developed. Germany, Italy, Sweden, Czechoslovakia, France, all these and many others, experienced dangerous crises which in a number of cases proved fatal. The advent of the Labour party into power in Britain in the twenties was somewhat less disturbing, but provided no real test because of its lack of a majority. In the meantime, the dominions of New Zealand and of Australia have been governed for some time by Socialists under a constitution.[38]

It is a curious fact that the two countries with the most distinctively democratic constitutional tradition, the United States and Switzerland, have not participated in this experimentation. Some said, of course, that Franklin D. Roosevelt and more recent American Presidents were socialist in outlook. There is no need here to go into these partisan arguments; the fact is that neither Roosevelt nor many of his followers, let alone his successors, ever acknowledged a theoretical attachment to socialism, not to say Marxism. To this extent they certainly differed from their continental counterparts.

But while there has been no participation of professed Socialists in these two democracies, the socialization of the economy, that is to say, the extension of governmental participation in the economy, has gone forward apace in both these as in all other countries. The constitutional systems of the United States and Switzerland have often creaked under the load, but they have not broken down. In both countries, though, some grave warnings have been voiced.[25] Basing their analysis upon the "state" concept, these writers have urged that a continuous expansion of the state was bound to destroy the individual and hence the free society of "capitalism." As a result there are quite a few today who would hold that constitutional democracy requires "capitalism" or "free enterprise" for its operation. These slogans are rarely carefully defined. A realistic view reveals that words like "free enterprise" and "free competition" refer to conditions which have never actually existed.

Since the Second World War, the social-democratic movements in the leading countries of Europe have increasingly stressed constitutionalist views, and all major new constitutions, like those of France, Italy, and Germany, are cognizant of the need for regularized restraint. To be sure, the first French constitution, rejected by the voters in 1946, was radically unrestrained in its concentration of most power in the hands of a parliamentary majority, as is indeed the constitution of East Germany, as well as the draft constitution for all of Germany, published by the German Communists. In contrast, the Social Democrats of Germany, as well as the Socialists of other European countries to some extent, are sharply opposed to such corruption of the constitutionalist position. More especially do all moderate elements now perceive the importance of a firm guarantee of fundamental human rights or civil liberties. At the same time, the British Labour governments have proved wrong those prophets who freely predicted a collapse of English constitutionalism at the time the Labour party would attempt to institute socialism.[39] The crucial point is unquestionably this: that socialism can be realized gradually enough, in the view of these Europeans, to become compatible with constitutional democracy in the process, by extending participation.

Without pretending to pronounce final judgment in the matter, it would seem, in the light of present evidence, to be quite probable that constitutionalism is combinable with a considerable variety of economic systems. Constitutionalism rests upon a balance of classes in a society. But this balance is not a hard and fast one, it is not an equipoise of mechanical weights, but rather a moving equilibrium of a kaleidoscopic combination of interests. The government, through the parties, operates as the balancer of these combinations. In a wider and deeper sense, the introduction of the "state" concept distorts the outlook of constitutionalism. For, when socialism is interpreted as "state" socialism, "state" and "society" are confronted as if they were two mutually exclusive corporate entities. Constitutionalism is built on the simple proposition that the government is a set of activities organized by and operated on behalf of the people, but subject to a series of restraints which attempt to ensure that the power which is needed for such governance is not abused by those who are called upon to do the governing. There is no apparent reason why a greater or lesser amount of such governmental activities should be incompatible with effective restraints, provided the concentration of power in one group or one man is guarded against. "Social democracy," one of its ablest historians has said, "is not a miracle which comes to life at a particular moment and then continues to function automatically, but it is rather a political task upon which it is necessary to work continuously."[40] Change, as we pointed out at the beginning, is not something to be feared and avoided, as Aristotle thought, but is of the very warp and woof of modern constitutionalism.

Conclusion · There are two issues which confront constitutionalism today: socialism and the international or world order. In spite of the fact that internationalism and socialism are linked in many minds, the two issues are intrinsically distinct and perhaps even liable to suggest conflicting solutions. For to the extent that socialism implies planning, it impedes the progress of internationalism, since planning is more complicated on an international plane. It is a striking fact of contemporary life that convinced adherents of constitutional democracy usually split on the issue of the relative urgency of these two tasks. Fortunately, from a more comprehensive viewpoint, the conflict resolves itself. The history of the past thirty years suggests that constitutional democracy in order to function effectively on a national plane needs an international framework. An international pattern of constitutionalism is clearly indicated for all that part of the world which is democratically governed. The League of Nations, no matter what its faults, and they were many, nevertheless represented a first decisive effort to extend constitutionalism to the world at large. It was a projection of the aspirations of the Declaration of Independence. Whether the United Nations will prove to be more viable remains to be seen. Its greatest advantage over the League is that the United Nations really encompasses most of the world.

The world-wide tasks of constitutionalism should not be allowed to obscure the many unfulfilled tasks of democracy at home.[41] Even in the most democratic countries, the process of democratization has stopped short of some of the most obvious issues, racial, social, and others. The need for a responsible government service is widely felt; yet the methods best adapted to fit such services into a constitutional democracy are as yet untried. The fear of the bureaucracy, inherited from a monarchical past and enhanced by a totalitarian present, remains a powerful factor inhibiting bold solutions. The role of public opinion and propaganda is casting a shadow over the conventional formulas of "the will of the people" and "the belief in the common man," which have been axiomatic in democratic constitutionalism.

Even more disturbing are recent trends, engendered by the concern over security, which are weakening the tradition of basic civil rights, including academic freedom. Investigatory and intelligence functions, believed necessary to cope with the enemies of constitutionalism, are dangerous activities in themselves. They are firmly rooted in "reason of state," and in the traditions of government in the preconstitutionalist period. Yet, the collapse of constitutional systems has raised the issue of how to deny the protection of constitutionalism to its avowed enemies. Any analysis of constitutionalism today would be incomplete if it did not attempt to assess recent efforts made to cope with the dangers which the rise of totalitarian dictatorship has created.

The Developmental Core: Bureaucracy*

Introduction · In discussing governmental development, we called the body of servants devoted to the prince a "bureaucracy." We might have called it officialdom, magistracy, government service, or even civil service, as long as it is clearly understood (1) that we are talking of a group of human beings, not some mysterious superentity such as is suggested by the word "state," and (2) that these human beings perform definite functions which the community at large considers worthwhile. In primitive agricultural communities, these functions are directly attached to the possession of the land; they frequently become hereditary. Such was the foundation of the feudal system. Hereditary offices attached to the land offered the most promising means of securing a certain amount of law and order over widespread areas under primitive conditions of communication. It was a very inefficient system, allowing wide latitude for personal abuse and great variations from one locality to the next. To cope with the attendant evils, the royal overlords sought to extend their personal estates through marriage, escheat, and various other means which the feudal law placed at their disposal.

As the royal domains grew, it became of vital importance that a central body of direction be created to prevent new disintegration at the center, a process which took place in England, France, Spain, Prussia, Austria, and other realms. The only serious competitor to the princes in their determined efforts to concentrate power in their own hands was the church. In many

---

* Besides this broad sketch, important aspects of bureaucracy are dealt with later; the general functions of the developing administrative services of modern governments are treated in chs. III–VI, while ch. XVIII takes up executive leadership, and ch. XIX, the modern governmental service with particular reference to the question of responsibility.

38

ways the church became the example of secular rulers. In no respect was this more true than in that of the techniques of administration. More amply provided with literate personnel, the church developed, during the Middle Ages, the rationalized techniques of administration which the princes were quick to follow, at the suggestion of clerical advisers. These central bodies of royal servants are the beginnings of our modern administrative systems.

The elementary or basic aspects of bureaucracy: England • Conventional English and American history-writing has so exaggerated the role of Magna Charta and Parliament that the administrative core of British institutions of government has been obscured. Out of a justifiable pride in later developments, constitutionalism and democracy, the myth has grown up that the origins of modern government in Britain and America were different from those in Continental Europe, that constitutionalism came first and the administrative services afterwards. Such a view is not only contrary to the facts, but it obstructs a real understanding of the strength of constitutionalism itself. Constitutionalism comes as a restraining, civilizing improvement; there must, in other words, first be government before it can be constitutionalized. That is why we suggest the study of administrative government, of bureaucracy, as the necessary preliminary of a full grasp of constitutional government. A comparison between the English and Prussian development, one very early and the other very late, will be instructive, though other countries, such as France and Spain, could serve equally well, since the development in the early phases is very similar throughout Western civilization, notwithstanding the great divergencies in the coming of constitutionalism.

A number of English historians, outstanding among them T. F. Tout,[1] have in recent decades brought to light the main outlines of early administrative history. The great Stubbs already had shown that the administrative system was set up in the days of the later Norman kings and found its first full development in the reign of Henry II (1154–1189). But to him "the Angevin administrative system was important, not so much in itself, as because he regarded it as the source of the parliamentary organizations of later times." His main interest "was in the origins of our modern constitution." It is the more striking that he should have stressed the early administrative system. But of course the great administrative departments kept on developing, and it is not too much to say that without that continuous development the government could not have succeeded in uniting the nation, which enabled it to undertake the task of constitutionalizing the centralized system. In the Middle Ages, Tout has rightly observed, when legislation was small in amount and largely declaratory in character the administrative side of government activity bulked immensely larger. To be sure, administrative, legislative, and judicial functions greatly overlapped, and not until the fourteenth century was the differentiation of these functions begun in earnest.

The administrative system of the Norman and Angevin kings, while set within a strictly feudal pattern of society, nevertheless showed the decisive elements of modern rationalized administration. Its most important task being the centralization of the realm, we find a corresponding centralization of supervision and control. Under Henry II this was carried out through the king's council, the *curia regis*, and the exchequer. In the course of time, the law courts and the chancery were separated from the council, while the exchequer's control of financial business was divided between the exchequer, the wardrobe, and the machinery for the collection of parliamentary grants. Among these several bodies, the council was the over-all controlling and coordinating body. But it was not administrative in the strict sense. According to Tout, the central administration of England centered around the exchequer, the chancery, and the household offices. This pattern we find in all the developing European governments: household offices become transformed into public functions as the king's rule expands and takes root.

Records and files have become so much a matter of course today that we tend to forget that a great deal of determined effort went into their development. If the administrators in England had not on the whole been so conscientious in keeping these records and files, we could not know what we do know about the establishment and execution of their task. Even a cursory survey of the sources which a study of the medieval administrative system calls for reveals the astounding mass of carefully preserved records. There are striking differences between the household offices, and the chancery and exchequer. The officials of the former often took their archives away with them, considering them strictly secret. Time and again regulations were directed toward working out the details of this keeping of records, and official keepers were appointed at an early date.

Space does not permit even the sketchiest outline of the development of the several functions and departments of administration. Throughout the twelfth, thirteenth, and fourteenth centuries we can observe a continuous process of differentiation of functions, with various aspects of financial business becoming distinct, as the exchequer, the wardrobe, and other offices struggle for their respective spheres of influence. Though only detailed study can offer convincing proof, all evidence points toward the conclusion that the differentiation of functions resulted largely from such struggles for power of the different departments in the administration, and the need of defining their respective competencies. After the granting of Magna Charta, this interdepartmental conflict was broadened through the efforts of the barons to control at least part of the administration. Yet "it would be rash to maintain that constitutional and political considerations played an important part in bringing about the division of the task of ruling England between a national alminstration, controlled by the chancellor, and a court executive, controlled by the clerks of the wardrobe."[2] It was primarily a matter of expediency, as the government became more complex and more modern, that produced the "imperative necessity" for greater differentiation of functions.

Qualification for office is another aspect of rationalized administration which progressed slowly throughout these centuries, as trained clerks took the place of nobles. The king's interest in freeing himself from baronial pressure aided mightily in making him seek for acceptable personnel elsewhere. Clerics were, of course, the most obvious source for such personnel throughout the Middle Ages, apart from legally trained men to staff the courts. Elsewhere in this volume, the particular and highly significant development of the legal profession in England is briefly outlined. Eventually, with the coming of humanism, inroads into the clerical monopoly on higher education were made by men trained in the humanities. The role of humanism in strengthening Tudor absolutism has never been thoroughly investigated. Some brilliant men, like Bacon and the Cecils, are associated with this movement. It is characteristic of England, no less than of other countries, that royal absolutism, in its desire to free itself from the influence of the feudal constitutionalism of the estates, especially of the barons and the church, found a mighty ally in these *literati* educated to admire the spirit of classical antiquity. The development of such a central bureaucracy was checked in England by the Puritan revolution and the subsequent ascendancy of Parliament. The price Britain paid for the uninterrupted retention and effective transformation of important elements of medieval constitutionalism was a corrupt administrative service. British administration at the beginning of the nineteenth century was honeycombed with nepotism and political patronage to an extent which contrasted painfully with the bureaucracies of absolutist governments. The thoroughgoing reforms of the fifties recaptured, however, all that had been lost and more, and gave Britain an administrative service superior in integrity and ability to that of any of the bureaucratic Continental governments. The qualification for office could, by that time, be determined in a truly modern scientific spirit by a system of competitive examinations based on professional training.

Bureaucracy in Brandenburg-Prussia[3] · Since Brandenburg-Prussia forms in many respects a complete antithesis to British institutional history, the parallels in her evolution, as far as the administrative establishment is concerned, are the more striking. Since Brandenburg worked out a centralized government almost five hundred years later than England, developments which took generations were telescoped into a few decades.[4] We are well supplied with documentary evidence. In 1598, when Joachim Friedrich became Elector of Brandenburg, absolutism was unknown in his lands. Under his predecessor, Brandenburg was ruled by the Estates (Parliament). But Joachim Friedrich wanted to create a rule by officials (*Beamtenregiment*), a bureaucracy. Since most educated people sided with the Estates, he resolved to draw upon foreigners, men brought to Brandenburg from other territories (they were, of course, Germans) and made into a Council by the order of 1604. This document, together with one amending it in 1651, shows again, in embryo, the vital constituent elements of a government service, or bureaucracy. Admitting openly that he was motivated in this step by the example of other states (presumably France), Friedrich through this order sought to centralize control, where a great confusion of councils had prevailed before. In general it made the following provisions: The councilors should be allowed to speak and vote freely, and, for the sake of order, the votes should be counted. So that the transactions might be remembered, the prince's private secretary should keep records, and produce them when needed. All these records should, however, be kept strictly secret. In accord with this secrecy was a further provision regarding the mails. The prince's chamber secretary was to bring all the letters unopened to the prince, who would read them and decide upon the answer either with or without consulting the councilors. The provision that every councilor who was given a letter for answering should make out a receipt for it points to the fact that many letters were lost by being taken away from the office. We have here, then, full confirmation of four elementary constituents of a bureaucracy: (1) centralization of control and supervision; (2) safeguards for the independence of judgment of each member of the organization; (3) maintenance of records and files; and (4) secrecy.

In the succeeding decades, certain difficulties appeared which had to be dealt with if the bureaucracy was to triumph over the Estates (Parliament). These arose from the acquisition of additional territories, which in turn caused a multiplication of functions. The unification of a number of territories and provinces under one princely house was for Prussia, as it was for Austria, the most powerful impulse toward the development of an efficient bureaucracy (as it had been in France and England earlier). The aim was to make Brandenburg-Prussia strong, to win respect for her abroad, and to make her prosperous and progressive. By the ordinance of 1651, the authority of the privy council was extended to all the different parts of the realm. Moreover, each councilor was assigned certain definite and specific functions which he must perform in the name of the prince. In accordance with this differentiation of functions, each councilor was to receive the mail which referred to his functions, read it, make comments, and then submit it to the prince and the other councilors. When the business at hand was familiar to all, council was to be held. In the council, the councilor especially in charge had the first vote and the votes were registered; but the ultimate decision was reserved for the prince. When we inspect the list of duties or functions, we also find a beginning made in the direction of distributing functions according to the qualification of the several councilors; court work was assigned to lawyers, diplomatic work to high nobles having experience therein, and so forth. We note, therefore, (1) the differentiation of functions, and (2) qualification for office, two or more aspects of a rationalized government service. The parallelism with the much earlier English development is therefore striking. All the later documents merely reaffirm and expand these elementary aspects, and all these factors or aspects could be as readily shown to have appeared in other governments — France, Spain, Sweden, Austria; they all went through a parallel development.

American colonial bureaucracy • In spite of the fact that the American revolution was explicitly waged against the royal bureaucracy, or perhaps because of it, the view is often expressed that "bureaucracy," that is, the administrative service, is not the core of modern government in the United States. "The Mayflower compact men, the framers of the constitution, and others, could start from scratch, creating their new institutions with an awareness of other countries' experience . . . having little need to accommodate their new ideas to a continuing institution like bureaucracy."[5] Such a view, though persuasive, is nonetheless untenable. One might be satisfied with pointing toward the bitter denunciations of federal bureaucracy in the period of the Jeffersonian and Jacksonian assault upon the Federalist knee-breechers. But it was not merely a partisan matter. The colonial governor, who in the course of the one hundred and fifty years of colonial development emerged as the key official in American government, reveals clearly the fact that the organization of the executive power must precede the constitutionalizing process. Until there was a rationalized and coordinated government, there could not be any efforts at restraining it and subjecting it to popular influence, if not control.

The American administrative system crystallized, of course, still later than that of Prussia. Nor did it achieve the rationalized forms which Prussia's absolutist rulers could give it. Indeed, the colonial governor found himself hamstrung by the conception that had sprung up in British administration, as we noted. Colonial offices were treated as plums to be handed out to deserving party followers, many of whom preferred to stay at home and let their office be administered by an agent. The resulting inadequacies were admittedly an important factor in creating that sense of dissatisfaction in the North American colonies which eventually led to revolt. This American experience created a permanent suspicion of executive power which has stood ever since in the way of developing responsible government service in the United States. It gave color to the facile contrast between democracy and bureaucracy which asserts that a government can give satisfaction without adequate administrative staff work. Carl Russell Fish, in tracing the evolution of the civil service, commenced his searching study by pointing out the extent to which George Washington had emphasized qualification for office. This remained the major bone of contention throughout; for the differentiation of functions was so well recognized by the time Washington's administration was organized that there was no need for him to grope for such elementary distinctions as administrators had done in the days of Henry II. This shows us more clearly than anything else that American constitutionalism *presupposes*, as does all constitutionalism, that the core of modern government, a functioning bureaucracy, had already been brought into existence. The rich experience of British administrative genius had already been at work in creating the framework of a government service into which the constitutionalizing forces merely had to put new men to carry on. All the elements which we have noted and which had been discovered by trial and error and the survival of the most suitable techniques were thus made readily available. At times some of these insights were lost, as when central supervision and control by the governor was dissipated in the wake of democratic enthusiasm; but after some unhappy experiences, a later generation readily returned to a recognition of their worth.

More recently, Leonard D. White, in his searching study of the establishment of the federal government service, has shown how inadequate is[6] the view, which imagines a society governed only by economic laws, readily overlooking the extent to which modern business and corporate organizations had themselves learned the lessons of a rationalized bureaucracy. People looking at America through such spectacles failed to see that the rationalized methods of modern business administration are merely elaborations of techniques which the governmental bureaucracy had first developed. Rightly did Carl Russell Fish observe that "as long as the controlling element in the country (namely, business) manage their private affairs in a careful systematic manner, we may expect the government to conduct its business on approximately the same principles."

Functional and behavior aspects · The six elements of a bureaucracy brought out by this analysis fall naturally into two groups. Three of them order the relations of the members of the organization to each other (namely, centralization of control and supervision, differentiation of functions, and qualification for office (entry and career aspects), while three embody rules defining desirable habit or behavior patterns of all the members of such an organization, namely, objectivity, precision and consistency, and discretion. All these elements are familiar enough to the modern science of administration. But it is sometimes forgotten that they were originated by men of extraordinary inventiveness who were laying the basis of a rationalized society by these inventions.[7]

Turning first to the relations of the members of an organization, we find that they are elaborated and defined with reference to the functions to be performed. We may therefore call this group of elementary aspects functional criteria. These simple functional criteria, while underlying elaborate modern rules and regulations, as far as governments are concerned, still are far from being fully carried out. Practically all modern governments have struggled time and again to revamp their administrative pattern in terms of these basic functional relationships, but whether it be the *Report of the Hoover Commission* (1949), the *Report on Administrative Management* (1937), or the *Machinery of Government Report* (1918), there are always many vested interests ready to resist such simplification and reform.

When we come to the second group of criteria, dealing with behavior, we find a similar situation. In fact, these criteria contain normative elements which are puzzling. They are really striking instances of the intimate connection between fact and norm which is characteristic of political science concepts. As in other cases, the normative aspect is dominant when individual conduct is examined in the light of the concept. An official who is indiscreet is immoral. But these criteria are rules of expediency founded on experience when an organization is examined in relation to the concept; organizations which fail to maintain discretion among their staffs usually fail. Let me first consider the functional aspects.

The differentiation of functions · The first two functional aspects, namely, centralization of control and supervision, and differentiation of functions, are in a sense related; for the centralization of control and supervision is itself a kind of differentiation of a particular function, viz., the function of control and coordination. Central supervision is necessary only when a differentiation has previously existed. This is why centralization stands in close relation to integration. They both coordinate diffuse functions. But while centralization coordinates spatially diffused functions, such as the feudal age bestowed upon early modern times, integration coordinates technically differentiated functions, such as arose from the early differentiation of functions at the center.[8] The differentiation of functions means that offices or functions are distributed carefully and rationally among the members of a given organization, like a government service, and are then arranged into an integrated whole, thus producing a more or less elaborate system of competencies or jurisdictions. This differentiation seems such an obvious prerequisite of an administrative task of any magnitude that it is frequently given only the most cursory attention. This is perhaps also due to the fact that the "division of labor" which it implies is generally accepted as a matter of course in modern life. And yet, literally hundreds of years of the history of modern government were consumed in evolving even the most elementary distinctions, and in discovering by trial and error that, all things considered, functional differentiation is superior to regional differentiation, though a certain amount of both are always necessary. Furthermore, the process of differentiation is a continuing one. To be sure, every modern government has a separate ministry (department) of foreign affairs, of finance, of commerce, of labor, and so forth, and what cannot be readily classified is thrown into the ministry of the interior. But here the simplicity ends. There are the greatest variations between the several governments when we go into further detail. Students of administration are wont to consider the problems which arise under this heading as those of departmentalization. In reality the problem is intimately related to the broader questions of constitutional framework. In the United States, for example, tariff problems occupy not only the Department of Commerce and the State Department (handling foreign affairs), but also a special Tariff Commission which owes its existence to the separation of powers. In European countries where the separation of powers has not developed along the same lines, we do not find such a body. Brief reflection upon this and many other similar items will show that a rule embodying the principle of differentiated functions is more frequently pronounced in general terms than put into practical effect. Constant experimentation and change are necessary in order to keep the differentiation of functions of a government service abreast of developing communal needs. For example, every government in recent years has had to struggle with the problem of a distinct air force. In every case, the established services have strenuously resisted the differentiation of that function. Everywhere they have yielded in the end. In the United States the issue was resolved only partially in the face of the war, in 1941. Even the establishment of the Department of the Air Force after the war has not wholly settled the matter. Likewise, the vast problems of the public-welfare field have raised very difficult differentiation issues.

Centralization and integration · The technical differentiation of functions, as we have pointed out, may be complicated by a regional differentiation. Under such regional differentiation, which is often spoken of as decentralization, all kinds of governmental functions are assigned to an individual or to a body having jurisdiction over a territorial subdivision, such as a province, a department, a county, a town, and so forth. The functions of such local authorities will invariably overlap to some extent the functions of technically differentiated central authorities. For this reason, some supervision and control are invariably found necessary, and are usually vested in ministries of the interior (France, Italy, and so forth), but may be lodged elsewhere for historical reasons (England: Board of Health). This central authority then acts as an intermediary seeking to integrate technically and regionally differentiated functions. This often causes a great deal of red tape when the central authorities themselves have widely scattered local representatives. It might be very much easier for the local assessors to deal with the field staff of the treasury, but apart from personal contacts they are dependent upon some central authority, like a ministry of the interior, for effective coordination. This shows vividly the close relationship between functional differentiation and central supervision and control. For when we pass from the top level of offices in a large organization, say the treasury, to the next lower one, the differentiation must be carried forward into the regulation of activities of individual officials on that level. Each official's sphere of competency is smaller, and comprised within a higher official's competency along with that of several other officials. There is, then, a double differentiation, namely (1) a technical differentiation on each level, and (2) a differentiation between more routine and more discretionary activities, as we go up and down the line in each organization (or chain of command, as the armed services like to call it). Because of its peculiar significance for the development and rationalization of a government service, we must isolate this type of differentiation as a distinct process. Historically speaking, functional differentiation commences at the top, and gradually is extended downward, limiting in its course the sphere of regional differentiation, or, as it is usually called, local self-government (home rule). But as it proceeds downward, such differentiation raises problems of integration with regard to differentiated functions, and problems of centralization with regard to functions not yet technically differentiated, but regionally dispersed. These problems of integration and of centralization, of supervision and control, may be lumped together under the heading "hierarchy."

The hierarchy • Nowhere is the impact of ecclesiastical experience upon administration more apparent than in the term "hierarchy." Indeed, the word has such definite associations with the Catholic Church that it might be well if we had another term. But since none is readily available, we will say that hierarchy is the pattern of subordination by which the several levels of command and obedience are defined. The hierarchy is a concomitant of the rational distribution of functions. As soon as an organization grows to any size, the large number of officials who exercise partly conflicting functions stand in constant need of integrating and coordinating leadership. This seems obvious enough, and yet the implications of administrative leadership have received rather inadequate attention, except in connection with private business management. The urgency of such administrative leadership springs from two related and recurrent problems. On the one hand, the detailed and specific functions of the "lower-downs" need constant reinterpretation in terms of the larger objectives which they presumably serve. On the other hand, the obstacles and difficulties encountered in the exercise of these detailed and specific functions require consideration with a view to the possible improvement or alteration of these larger objectives or purposes. Even so general a statement shows that the semimilitary, authoritarian nature of a government service is by no means a gratuitous invention of petty autocrats, but is inherent in the very nature of the processes which form the essence of all administrative services. This point hardly requires emphasizing in an age which exhibits examples of such authoritarian, hierarchical control on all sides, since large-scale business corporations, trade unions, and many other organizations are conducted on precisely this pattern.[9]

The need for administrative leadership explains to some extent why monarchies have been so successful in developing a high-class government service. If the powers of control and coercion connected with the various offices and functions are arranged in more or less concentric circles which become smaller as we ascend to the higher levels, a single individual or bureau acting as a unit would presumably have ultimate control and power. Moreover, such an individual or group must be himself a part of the hierarchy, though not necessarily chosen from among it. This unitary central control characteristic of a fully developed hierarchy may, of course, be quite effectively exercised by elective officials, provided there is a sufficient amount of continuity and agreement between successive officeholders as to the conduct of governmental activities. The English cabinet in the second half of the nineteenth century succeeded in building up a remarkable public service corps; it may be well, however, to keep in mind that the English Prime Minister has often been called a practical dictator once he has entered No. 10 Downing Street with a safe majority in the House of Commons.

Even though a trend toward unitary leadership be inherent in the hierarchical aspect of bureaucracy, or of effective government service, it seems undesirable to overemphasize this point. Hierarchy in our opinion should describe more generally any determinate system of distributing the powers of control and coercion. Hierarchy subordinates officials performing very specific and tangible functions to other superior officials, who supervise and direct a determinate number of these subordinates; the superior officials in turn may be supervised and directed by a still more limited number of "higher-ups." Nor need this scale of subordination and control be restricted to individual officials. A hierarchy may subordinate one group of officials to another group of officials acting together as a unit. Or individual officials lower down may be subordinated to a group superior higher up. The Swiss (Executive) Council, American administrative commissions, and practically all judicial systems are of this structure. In English-speaking countries, although the power of specific coercion of the higher courts to determine the decisions of lower ones is limited, the power of reversing decisions produces a similar effect crystallized in the rule of *stare decisis*. This rule narrowly limits the discretion of lower courts. An element of discretion remains, however, and this fact has led some writers to overemphasize the difference between courts and administrative bodies. In terms of actual conduct, the difference is quite small; for although the hierarchical principle seems to imply flawless subordination, the extent to which any given hierarchy conforms to that standard is limited by other competing principles which are essential for its life, such as the principle of differentiating and distributing functions. A higher official will hesitate to reverse the decision of a lower official when he feels, as is often the case, that the lower official has a better knowledge of the facts in detail. The question of whether judicial or administrative action should be provided for is only to be answered in respect of the purposes or objectives to be achieved. There is nothing inherently beautiful in either. Both are techniques for accomplishing certain purposes, as we shall show further on. And both are comprehended within the governmental services or the bureaucracy, as that term is here understood. These processes can be fully grasped only if the rule of anticipated reactions is taken into account.[10]

Discipline and morale • Almost all administrative hierarchies have well-defined rules of discipline, according to which acts of alleged insubordination are judged. Some rudimentary discipline is inherent in any hierarchy.[11] The rigor of the discipline should be studied by the political scientist in relation to the purpose for which the administrative setup has come into existence. If the purpose of the particular hierarchy is kept in mind, a better understanding will result. A purpose which is likely to be defeated by delay in execution will produce a more rigorous discipline than one which is not imperiled by being postponed. An army at war and business enterprises in highly competitive fields offer good examples of rigorous discipline, while much ordinary government service, in peacetime, and business enterprises in distinctly monopolistic fields offer examples of rather relaxed discipline. Sometimes the operations are intrinsically fraught with danger, as they are in the railroad business. Then even a monopolistic business may show high disciplinary standards. A further condition making for variation is the general state of public morale. The student of the history of administration is struck with the extent to which discipline is initially very severe, but is gradually relaxed. As the service becomes well established, organizations with poor discipline are likely to be outdone by their rivals, whether in business or government. The comparatively static condition of most governmental activities during peacetime has made it possible to subject all disciplinary action to fairly elaborate judicial procedure; its main purpose is to protect the official against arbitrary exercise of the disciplinary power. His punishment and removal cannot take place until he has been accused, indicted, examined, and pronounced guilty, either by a regular court or by a court composed of his peers.

The discipline of an administrative organization is intimately related to its morale. Where morale is high, the problems of discipline are reduced considerably; they stand in inverse relation to each other. The task of maintaining morale has always been of central concern to military men, and they have developed an elaborate set of techniques for maintaining it. It is obvious that morale enhances the chance for effective cooperation. It may be defined as "group persistence in the pursuit of collective purposes." Evidently it depends upon the sharing of purposes or ends, and therefore everything that assists in securing loyalty to common purposes or ends is relevant to him who would deal with morale, either theoretically or practically.[12] A potential danger to good morale lurks in excessive discipline. The annals of warfare are full of it. The techniques suitable for peacetime may be disastrous when applied to troops shaped in the crucible of war. Likewise, every administrator worth his pay knows that disciplining his subordinates can never be an effective substitute for securing voluntary cooperation, which is the equivalent of good morale. Hence modern students of administration have given increasing attention to cooperative techniques of administration. This is largely a matter of making sure that the subordinates understand the reasons for taking certain actions or for making certain policy decisions. The effective management of morale here impinges upon the problem of communication. Successful administration under democratic, that is to say, cooperative, conditions will seek to broaden the range of participation on the part of all members of the organization.

Qualification and training for office · Our third functional criterion, the qualification for office, has received so much attention from students of public administration in the United States that the problem of government personnel is treated by many people as identical with that of qualification for office. The great movement for the establishment of the merit system was focused upon qualification for office. Nor can there be any question that the rationalization of the bureaucracy finds its most significant expression in provisions for such qualifications. There have been marked national differences in the past (see ch. XIX, p. 409 ff.), but at present they are gradually being supplanted by a universal drift toward "technical" qualifications in the strict sense. What is meant by that is the tendency, particularly in this country, to select men in the light of their training for some technical specialty, such as civil engineering, banking, or animal husbandry. Speaking very broadly, such requirements may be called a unique expression of our technological civilization. Altogether the emphasis upon special intellectual achievement and promise in technical fields, as contrasted with literary skill (China) or with other personal aptitudes and character traits, is a peculiarity of the modern age. Only very recently has the perfecting of psychological tests opened up new avenues to the problem of how to select the person best qualified for a particular office.

In view of the preoccupation in the United States with the problem of qualification, it is curious that the cognate problem of training for the service did not for many years receive more than cursory examination. Yet the system of public schools and universities traditional in Europe originated to a considerable extent in the requirements of the government for well-trained officials. Speaking broadly, such a system of public schools and universities fulfills the function of coordinating educational facilities with the differentiated hierarchy of official functions through an elaborate system of standardized examinations. If such coordination is effective, it becomes possible to consider the degrees from the several educational institutions as constituting, at least in part, satisfactory evidence that the person passing such examinations and holding the corresponding degree is qualified for a certain function in the hierarchy. Civil Service Commissions, as we find them in the United States, could possibly be an effective substitute for such a system of coordinated schooling if they made a persistent effort to bring about a mutual adaptation of the required qualifications for service and of the training which is given to acquire them. This has only recently been recognized. European governments in days gone by could not rely upon such a coordinator, because there were few schools to coordinate, and so they undertook to organize schools and universities themselves. Schools and universities in this country are being increasingly influenced in their programs by the requirements of the government services. The numerous governmentally financed training programs sharply increased these trends. In England, not to speak of Continental countries, there has been worked out a close correspondence between service training needs and school programs. Not only the so-called administrative class of higher officials, but also the lower ranks, are recruited in accordance with their schooling. Thus the clerical class is recruited through an examination framed with reference to the standard of development reached at the end of the intermediate stage of a secondary school course.[13] In the United States there used to be a marked contrast in the upper range of the service. But in the twentieth century it has become more and more clear that broad qualifications for the task must be asked of all public servants. Presidents since Roosevelt have been more and more concerned with the expertise of men appointed even to the top rank of the government service.

Publicity · The foregoing analysis of the functional aspects of a developed bureaucracy would be incomplete if we did not discuss briefly a feature which these several aspects gradually acquire to an ever-increasing extent. This is the feature of determinateness and publicity.

It will be recalled that we found all the elementary aspects present in the embryonic bureaucracy of the Brandenburg councils of the seventeenth century. What they then lacked was determinateness and publicity. In a sense, it is possible to assess the stage of development of a given bureaucracy by examining the extent to which its functional aspects are determinate and publicly known. We must link determinateness with publicity, because determinateness is never insured unless full publicity enables any reasonably intelligent and interested person to judge for himself whether equality of treatment is safeguarded, and favoritism, nepotism, arbitrariness, and so on, are excluded. Under a popular government, the governmental services will attract that high caliber of personnel which is an essential prerequisite for its ultimate success only if public scrutiny enables the citizenry to have confidence in its public service. Publicity is very difficult to achieve because it is the natural tendency of officials to be secretive. Indeed, even in relatively democratic countries, the public is not able to find out important facts. Questions in Parliament and investigations are heavy tools to bring into play. Perhaps the most advanced system among all modern governments is that of Sweden, where a long tradition of making official files available to the interested citizen has provided full publicity for the transactions of most of the services (foreign affairs is, of course, excluded). In some ways, however, the United States has been a pathfinder in this field, especially through the development of the regular press conference of high officials where they answer relatively freely questions put to them by duly accredited correspondents.[14] One branch of the government's work, however, has been conducted in most countries within public view for a long time, and that is judicial business. In this field the need for rationalized procedure is particularly urgent.[15]

Objectivity and impartiality • Having examined the functional aspects of bureaucracy, we may comment briefly on the three behavior aspects of bureaucracy; that is, traits of the administrators. It is not possible to examine them in detail.

What was called "objectivity", or perhaps "impartiality," in the administrator is both an ideal and, within limits, a distinguishing trait. It is closely related to *expertise,* and is usually found in persons who possess such *expertise.* No one can be a good craftsman, nor indeed a craftsman at all, who does not acquire the capacity and inclination to think in terms of objective needs; in terms, that is, of what the particular job in hand requires. Thus an administrator, if he needs to hire a secretary or any other subordinate, will ask: How good is she? What experience has she had? and so forth. A politician, on the other hand, will be more inclined to give consideration to who recommended her, whom she knows, etc. There is something to be said for both points of view, but obviously the relative weight to be assigned to each will depend upon how difficult and technical the tasks, how much depends upon them, and how expensive are the services. The same difference in viewpoint permeates all other fields of action and decision. Evidently, an adminstrator will be successful to the extent to which he is capable of being impartial, taking the word "success" in the sense of real achievement, of course, not in that of "making a career." For it is unfortunately a fact that subserviency to the views of a superior, and hence lack of impartiality, often helps an official to advance. Much of the most searching thought on administrative management has gone into discovering methods for preventing that sort of deterioration in the service. Some of these methods will be discussed in a later chapter.

Objectivity has often been belittled in English-speaking countries. Behind it there seemed to lurk the danger of autocratic disregard of public opinion. And yet the British civil service today yields to none in its attachment to the needs of the service. Some American federal agencies also have achieved an enviable tradition of objectivity and impartiality. It is true, of course, that the expert inclines toward dogmatism. The very fact that he knows more than most others with regard to a certain matter induces him to be satisfied with his particular views. He is likely to disregard the "broader" considerations, that is to say, those points at which his particular problem links up with others concerning which he is no expert at all. Since we have to work with finite minds, this issue has become increasingly aggravated as the complexity of our industrial society has increased. Government public relations officials have battled with this problem for some time now. The final integration of will and understanding, of decision and knowledge, of man's laws and of nature's laws (which are always enforced), cannot be accomplished once and for all. It is a continuing process, and the administrator's penchant for objectivity plays a vital role in bringing about a sound balance. His craftsmanlike pride in actual achievement, as contrasted with make-believe, derives its satisfaction from the admiration it arouses in fellow craftsmen rather than in the public at large. It is unlikely without long training in the social sciences (including the law); for only such knowledge enables a man to develop objective standards and an awareness of the limits of his knowledge.[16]

Precision and continuity · The effective administrator usually is precise in what he says and steady in what he does. This is generally recognized and perfectly sound. Imprecision in speech and writing leads to faulty communication, with the result that the subordinate does not understand what he is being asked to do, while the superior does not understand what has been reported to him. Vacillating action obviously is undesirable; it bewilders subordinates, irritates associates, and endangers the achievement of lasting results. Both precision and continuity are so evidently desirable that the observations concerning them might be considered trite, were it not for the fact that much public indignation over red tape and other rigidities in the behavior of administrators results from precisely these two traits. An intimate knowledge of a certain field of public policy or governmental activity is a prerequisite to rendering an informed judgment concerning administrative actions. The routine which seems annoyingly rigid to the occasional citizen may be the result of long efforts and repeated trials of alternative procedures. Private organizations of any size are bound to develop the same rigidities in dealing with outsiders that governmental organizations do. It is only too often forgotten by all of us that a large organization is an amazing achievement of human cooperativeness, and that it is possible only through the making of *rules*. Exceptions to such rules require decisions by higher-ups who cannot always be readily consulted. The good administrator must abide by his rules in most instances. If he makes exceptions too readily, particularly to rules which have been made with regard to other rules over which he has no control, he is likely to throw the whole organization into confusion. It is somewhat like the difference between driving an ox-cart and an express train. The ox-cart driver can stop to chat with a friend; the engineer of the express train cannot. It is, of course, easy and only too common among administrators to fall into the opposite error of refusing to adjust the rule, even when its application is evidently unreasonable. It is the great merit of constitutionalism that it provides machinery for the airing of any complaints that may arise. In discussing the use of questions in the British Parliament, an attempt is made to suggest the operation of that corrective. Such a forum for venting complaints has the added advantage of offering an opportunity to the skillful administrator to explain necessary rules and regulations to a wider public, and thus to gain support and understanding of the need for precision and continuity as essential features of a functioning administration.

Discretion versus secrecy · Many writers on government and administration might object to including secrecy as a main behavior aspect of a functioning bureaucracy. The word, like bureaucracy itself, has a derogatory connotation. But a realistic view of the facts obliges one to recognize the undeniable importance which rules and regulations looking toward secrecy have played in the history of administrative organizations. The documents concerning Brandenburg and Britain are apt illustrations of what could be documented down to this very day as a major concern of administrators, both governmental and private. There is no use in closing our eyes to the facts; the determined efforts of all organizations to secrete their more important evidence in controversial and competitive matters show vividly that such secrecy is functional. In thus insisting upon the importance of secrecy, are we not contradicting ourselves and what we said in our discussion of publicity? The apparent contradiction resolves itself when we recall that publicity has come with the growth of constitutionalism. The range of what is to be kept secret has been more narrowly circumscribed, different services showing marked variations. Thus foreign and military affairs, even in the most highly developed democracies, have been much more widely recognized as entitled to a broad measure of official secrecy. However, the progressive inclusion of more and more aspects of industrial production under the term "military affairs" has once again extended the area of required secrecy. In a crisis this led to a very broad definition of "official secrets" in the Official Secrets Act (1939), passed in Britain just prior to the outbreak of the Second World War. In the United States, too, the problem of "security," after being highlighted during that war, has been further aggravated by the problem of nuclear weapons. Fear of Soviet spies, heightened by the presence of Communists, has not only led to the exclusion of members of this party and its sympathizers from government work, but to more and more elaborate policing by highly secretive organizations, such as the Federal Bureau of Investigation. The Espionage Act (1917) and the Alien Registration Act (1940) highlight this development, but Soviet espionage and the atomic-war problems have produced the even more stringent National Security Act (1951).

As a trait of the administrator, this aspect of secrecy is appropriately spoken of as "discretion." Though an essential trait of administrators of all kinds, it has not received much attention, except where its excesses have been attacked. The secrecy of the bureaucracy under monarchical absolutism was a source of continuous irritation to the liberal forces contending against them. It also served as a convenient target. In the discussion of the press and censorship below, these issues are more fully developed. The sympathy which most of us feel with that outlook, the revival of complete secretiveness in the totalitarian regimes, and the general human dislike of secrets which one cannot share, all combine to make difficult a recognition of discretion; that is, the ability to keep a secret. Disgusted at the secrecy which shrouded governmental transactions, reformers in the past have tended to assume that anything which is secret is *ipso facto* bad.[17] They too easily overlooked the practices of their own organizations, or assumed that their own secrecy was merely the result of having to deal with opponents who practiced secrecy. While this is understandable enough, it bars a realistic insight into the requirements of a well-functioning bureaucracy. For while discretion can be abused, its ubiquity is due to the real needs which it serves.

There are many details of human relationship which, if bandied about, would make such relationships more difficult. A supervisor reporting on his men should be able to speak with complete frankness; but if his views are not kept confidential, he will not be able to do so, since he has to continue satisfactory working relationships with the men. An administrator engaged in tracking down some violations of rules and regulations would be likely to find such investigation impossible if what he was doing were publicized and thus brought to the attention of the violators. Occasions of this sort are numerous; they occur wherever conflicts arise in the work of government and administration. Of course the most noted instances, often emphasized to the exclusion of the mass of minor cases, are found in the field of foreign affairs; the conflict between nations adds drama to the issue of secrecy, as the "secret services" of the several governments carry on their efforts to wrench from a hostile power the information which is being guarded by diplomats and staff officers.

While the public and its representatives incline to frown upon secrecy (although the secrecy of Congressional committee proceedings makes American Congressmen more willing to defend a measure of secrecy), administrators often incline in the opposite direction. They consider matters secret which are or could be known to everyone. A well-known scholar and adviser of the State Department used to tell a story, the gist of which involved a vigorous protest to him from the Department concerning a confidential matter he had mentioned in a public address. In his reply he dryly remarked: "I do not blame you for considering matters secret which have been published in the *Congressional Record*." This secretiveness of certain officials and departments often is quite innocuous, but when it takes the form of forbidding high officials of the government to express in print their views on matters of grave public concern, it is unequivocally contrary to the public interest in a constitutional democracy. Since these officials are, or ought to be, the leading experts in their respective fields, the public is clearly entitled to share their knowledge. This is not the place to enter into all the arguments brought forward on both sides of this issue. But it is the place to say that this tendency among officials to broaden the sphere of "official secrets" to include matters of *public* policy is both common and harmful. The case of the civil engineer whose sound analysis of the consequences of governmental land-grant policies lay buried in the files for fifty years, while the country went the predicted road toward destruction of its soil, provides a poignant illustration.

The foregoing discussion shows, it is hoped, two things: (1) secrecy is an inherent feature of all governmental administration, and discretion a carefully cultivated trait of administrators; and (2) the sphere of applicability of both is dependent upon the nature of the tasks in hand, the conditions under which the task must be executed, and the governmental framework, whether democratic or autocratic. We know too little about the probable limits of discretion and secrecy to formulate precise hypotheses concerning the sphere of applicability. But this fact should not mislead us into denying the great importance of secrecy and discretion as parts of bureaucratic behavior, regardless of whether we like what the particular bureaucracy is doing.

Conclusion · We have sketched the nature of a government service or bureaucracy in broad outline. All realistic study of government has to start with an understanding of bureaucracy (or whatever else one prefers to call it), because no government can function without it. The popular antithesis between bureaucracy and democracy is an oratorical slogan which endangers the future of democracy. For a constitutional system which cannot function effectively, which cannot act with dispatch and strength, cannot live. Fortunately, both the Swiss and the British have shown that an effective, responsible bureaucracy is quite compatible with vigorous constitutionalism (see below, ch. XIX). British constitutionalism, like all constitutionalism, developed as a system of controls imposed upon a vigorous bureaucracy. The early unification of England made her one of the pioneers in developing administrative techniques for modern government. But the trend is universal throughout the Western world. In the course of this analysis, six primary criteria of such bureaucracies have been identified: (1) the differentiation of functions; (2) qualification for office; (3) centralization and integration of control and supervision; (4) objectivity; (5) precision and consistency or continuity; and (6) discretion. They are found in a small administrative council at the beginning of Norman England, and they pervade a vast administrative machine such as the British Empire. As administrative organization unfolded, an increasing amount of publicity could and had to be given to governmental activity. Such publicity, though often bitterly resented and opposed by the bureaucracy, really contributed powerfully to its devolpment by making it more determinate and institutionally stable. The effective working of such responsibility and publicity depends upon a viable constitutional system. Therefore constitutionalism, though historically opposed to monarchical "bureaucracies," actually reinforced and aided the full development of bureaucracy — a process which is still going forward.[18]

Security and the Military Establishment

III

Introduction · British navy and Continental armies · Size of armies and the development of arms · The evolution of arms and science · Government control of universities · The provisioning of armies · The problem of revenue · Commissioners and the emergency power · Civil and foreign war · The military aspect of the Fascist rise to power · Limitation of armaments · Conclusion

Introduction · The conditions which form the background of modern government are closely related to its central objectives. In fact, if they were not related to such objectives, they could not form conditions for the development of these governments. For such is the nature of human and social, as compared to subhuman and inorganic, life that many of its most essential conditioning factors must and do pass through the forge of human consciousness where they are wrought into willful purpose.[1] Thus the geographic factor exerts its most powerful influence where a determinate will for territorial expansion exists. This desire for territorial expansion is deeply rooted in human history; for long periods the control of land was the primary basis of all power. Feudalism had been altogether built on it. The process of territorial unification was at first almost exclusively directed toward the extension of the royal domain. The great kings of Europe who built modern governments were in a sense land-hungry farmers.

When several such "farmers" live in close proximity, the question of security at once arises. Everyone has heard the ancient tales about the peasant who in the depth of night goes out to his field to shift the stone which divides his field from that of his neighbor. The peasants can go to court. But not the "sovereign" princes. Where there are no courts to decide the quarrel, armed conflict will be the only method of settling the dispute. Thus the idea of security arises as a corollary to the will for territorial expansion; the dread of foreign invasion haunts those who dream of territorial acquisitions.

Rare are the occasions when a government has admitted blatantly its intentions of territorial conquest, except in the colonial sphere, even in the stark days of the seventeenth century. Louis XIV, Frederick II of Prussia, and Napoleon are among the few who have dared to speak out frankly and admit the brutal facts. And even they sought support for their aggressive schemes in the records of the past, like Louis XIV citing Caesar and Charlemagne. Usually each government insisted upon its own pacific intentions and its need for security, as they do to this day. But when the scientific observer places the various declarations side by side and compares them with the actual behavior of their authors, he clearly perceives that armed conflicts, and hence insecurity, result from the policy of territorial expansion. Each of the contestants seeks to increase his armed strength. Thus an expansion of the military establishment became the obvious corollary objective of those who sought territorial expansion and talked of security.

It would be incorrect to attribute the evolution toward vast military establishments alone to the passion for territorial conquest innate in the land-hungry kings. The tendency toward ever-increasing armaments also received great impetus from the onslaught of the conquering Turk. After the Reformation had swept away the halo of a united religion which had sanctioned the medieval empire, the Hapsburgs found in their struggle against the huge armies of the Moslem a new justification for asking the united support of the German princes.[2] Military and administrative methods were deeply affected by these struggles. The military successes of the Ottoman Turks hastened the abandonment of feudal, and the adoption of modern, bureaucratic methods; the standing armies of the Sultans forced the organization of similar troops in the Hapsburg realms. The Hapsburgs learned, of course, also from the parallel experience of the Spanish predecessor kings in their fight against the Arabs. Once a central bureaucracy had consolidated the scattered Hapsburg dominions and organized them for the support of a large standing army, it did not take long to repel the Turkish power, at the beginning of the eighteenth century. A similar, though slower, evolution can be traced in the rise of Russia against the Tartars. It is noteworthy that the military establishments of each of these powers, Spain, Austria and Russia, became of decisive importance.[3]

British navy and Continental armies · There has been a tendency to overlook the parallelism of English and Continental development. England was at least as aggressively expansionist as other European governments. Finding her road to European conquest blocked by the consolidation of the French kingdom, she limited herself on the Continent to balance-of-power diplomacy (see next chapter), and turned her attention to conquest overseas. For this reason her military development is predominantly naval.[4] But the needs of this royal navy engendered, as was remarked before, the same administrative problems as did those of the army in other European countries. The decisive turn came, as might be expected, during the reign of Henry VIII — a natural sequel to his policy of expansion and rivalry with the Hapsburg and Bourbon princes. In 1546 he established the Navy Board as a central administrative body. Naval development continued unchecked through the reign of Elizabeth, but under the Stuarts the increasing hostility of Parliament made it impossible for the kings to get the necessary funds. The rapid development of naval organization during the Commonwealth period strikingly illuminates the dependence of modern military development upon unimpeded executive leadership, such as the dictatorship of Cromwell afforded. It is well known that the decisive defeat of the Dutch in 1653–1654 was of crucial importance to nascent British imperial aspirations. The victory would have been impossible without the rapid expansion of the naval forces under the administrative leadership of the Cromwellian Navy Commissioners. Ever after the navy remained the mainstay of English centralized administration, just as the army did in France. Hence, the search for territorial expansion overseas led in Britain, as elsewhere, to the typical military establishment.

At the same time, it was a most important circumstance for the growth of constitutionalism that this should have been so. For a navy is very much less dangerous to the freedom of the citizen than an army. G. M. Trevelyan has stressed this point. "The possession of a royal navy does not enable the monarch to hold down his subjects as a royal army may do. In England, there was no royal army, and in the Civil War of Charles I, the royal navy actually took the side of Parliament." Trevelyan even ventures to suggest that had the British fought the Spanish Armada as an army carried by a fleet, "in all probability the character of such a military effort would have diverted English society and politics in a martial and monarchical direction." Perhaps this is going a bit far. A remarkable Swiss writer of the eighteenth century, J. L. de Lolme, argued in his book on *The Constitution of England* (1775) that "the crown, in England, does not rely for its support, nor ever has relied, upon the army of which it has command. From the earliest times, — that is, long before the invention of standing armies among European princes, — the kings of England possessed an authority certainly as full and extensive as that which they now enjoy . . . they began to derive from the civil branch of their regal office that secure power which no other monarchs had ever possessed, except through the assistance of legions and praetorian guards. . . ." The truth is that there is to be noted an interdependence between the growth of constitutional liberty and the absence of a standing army which decisively influenced the British development.[5]

Size of armies and the development of arms · Nothing shows more vividly the trend of the development than the bare figures of the size of the several armies.[6] In medieval days armies were small — people were astounded at the French army of 32,000 men at Crécy in 1346. Four hundred years later, in 1750, Austria, France, and Prussia had armies of 297,000, 182,000, and 190,000 men respectively. Nor were these armies collected temporarily and for a specific purpose as was the French army at Crécy; they were permanent standing armies which had to be fed, clothed, and sheltered all the year round. Soon this matter of provisions became the touchstone of victory. To revert once more to the Hapsburg victory over the Turks, Prince Eugene of Savoy has been described as "a provider and husbander of resources, as well as a leader of armies," and that "he set to work with a firm hand to organize the finances which he found in the worst possible condition with debts of enormous proportions. . . ." Similarly, the attention of the Great Elector and his Prussian successors was concentrated to a considerable extent on building up an effective administrative machine to safeguard once and for all the financial and provisional rear of their big armies. Toward this aim, the French and later the English Treasury contributed on a large scale; indeed, it would have been utterly impossible for Brandenburg-Prussia to maintain such a large army on its own resources. In a sense, the Prussian army of the eighteenth century gave Britain a mercenary standing army on the Continent.

Along with the constant growth of the size of the armies, there took place a constant improvement in the effectiveness of the arms which these armies employed. If the Middle Ages were on the whole an epoch in which defensive weapons were stronger than aggressive ones, that relative superiority was now reversed. To be sure, fortresses continued to play a decisive role in the East, where the Turkish onslaught broke under the walls of Vienna, though even here only after outside reinforcements under a Polish king made a successful counterattack against the beleaguering forces. But usually the force of attack was strengthened more by the new weapons of firearms than was the force of defense. The trench warfare of the First World War seemed momentarily to give supremacy to defensive techniques — only to be broken once more by the advent of the tank and poison gas. The history of the Second World War is one of striking superiority of the means of attack, especially of the airplane; once air supremacy was achieved on a battlefield, all defenses caved in.

The relative strength of defensive and aggressive weapons is of great importance in shaping government and politics. The superiority of defensive weapons strengthens the chances of local resistance, and therefore entails a dispersion of political authority. Aggressive weapons, conversely, strengthen the chances of successful attack by growing units, and therefore help the concentration and centralization of political authority. This has been true since the dawn of civilization, when tribes of horsemen, equipped for successful attack by their greater swiftness, first succceded in building large territorial dominions. But while these horsemen, and later similar conquerors down to the bombarding battleships and aircraft of modern imperialism, fell upon alien civilizations, the curious and striking aspect of modern army development in Europe was a constant parallel forward march of a group of competing countries, each at once ready to adopt a new device introduced by one of its opponents, and by its civilization fully equipped to do so. This is as true of the spread of Swiss compact infantry technique in the fifteenth century as it is of the firearm and the gun in the sixteenth, of rapid troop movements in the seventeenth, of the goose step and sudden cavalry attacks in the eighteenth, of the loose infantry technique evolved by the *levée en masse* of the French revolution and its attendant compulsory military service (the nation in arms), of the ironclad, the machine gun, the airplane, poison gas, the atomic bomb, and so on in more recent years. Here is a long list of some of the most remarkable achievements in the development of modern weapons and military techniques, each of them signifying a new impetus to potential aggression.[7] During the Second World War one small country after another was vanquished by the Germans, until the technical superiority of the United States eventually triumphed over them in turn. But the decisive blow came with the atomic bomb released over Japan. Until that event occurred, there was still some lingering doubt as to whether an island might not provide adequate defensive support under modern conditions. Since then, the terrifying aggressive potential of this new weapon has led to a protracted effort for achieving international control of its use. This has at once greatly enhanced the need for and the willingness to accept world-wide government and the difficulty of achieving it under present conditions. A sharp conflict has developed between the two dominant powers, the United States and the Soviet Union, over the methods of control to be employed, each naturally insisting upon the adoption of a plan in accordance with its own governmental and political pattern of organization and thought.[8] These negotiations have been greatly complicated by the appearance of two "outside" nuclear powers, France and Red China.

The evolution of arms and science • If we consider this evolution in retrospect, we see at once that it is intimately linked to modern science, and thereby to the whole context of modern industrial civilization. Every great discovery, we find, has its counterpart and concomitant effect in new engines of destruction.[9] So intimately are the two related to each other that if governments and peoples should resolve tomorrow to abandon armaments, they would face a major economic crisis. If they wished to mitigate it, they would have to place orders on a large scale for peacetime products to be made by the armament factories. The close link between bathtubs and mortars, between the progress of civilization and science and the intensification of warfare, has received inadequate attention.[10] A German professor's invention of synthetic nitrogen during the First World War solved a raw-material problem which otherwise might have led to the defeat of the German government at a much earlier date. Synthetic gasoline and rubber played a similar role in the Second World War. This and many similar "achievements" illustrate the close connection between man's struggle with nature and with his fellow men. Is it too much to hope that a time will come when science can progress without giving new tools to the warmakers? Does science need this stimulant? Now that our industrial society has reached maturity, may not science carry forward on its own momentum?

It is the hope of those who are seeking to establish, if not world governmen, then at least an effective United Nations, that the time has come for science to progress without the continued stimulus of war and its requirements. Now that modern industrial technology has reached so advanced a stage, this disappearance of war as a stimulus to the progress of science might conceivably slow down this progress. It has been argued that such a slowdown may be even desirable. For scientific advance has been so rapid that social and governmental institutions and policies have failed to keep up with it, and controls tend to become antiquated. But these are but hopes, whereas the present situation is characterized by a fierce armaments race, especially in terms of atomic and air weapons. At the same time, the shift to competition in the "conquest of space" is replacing war as a stimulant of science and industry.

Government control of universities · As long as a strong connection exists between science and the engines of war, governments are bound to take a decisive interest not only in science but in the institutions where it is developed and taught. That is one of the reasons why war-minded European governments have always controlled universities and other institutions of higher learning. While formerly neglected in the United States, the relationship between government and the universities has become a subject of increasing concern as well as inquiry. Not only the government's control of science, but also the scientists' share in preparing governmental decisions and procedures, are involved in the discussion.[11] Naturally, the greatest importance must be attached by the government concerned to insuring the loyalty of the inventor. This is much easier when the inventor is an official of the government, as all state university professors are. The chances of winning a war are of such decisive importance to expansionist governments that large amounts of purely "academic" work might well be supported with a view to the gambling prospect of a major discovery of that kind. For this reason, research work is closely associated with the military techniques evolved by governments seeking expansion and security. This link has vastly and characteristically expanded in the United States during and since the Second World War.

Other associated techniques, such as taxgathering and the stimulation of trade and industry, will be treated in a separate chapter (see ch. V). Their development also serves modern government's second major objective, namely, the fostering of prosperity, and their importance and ramifications are so considerable that the thread of our argument would be lost if we were to consider them at this point. But we must briefly discuss one aspect, namely, the provisioning of the armies.

The provisioning of armies • Arming, feeding, and clothing soldiers acquired only slowly the prominence which it occupies in the military program of modern governments. In medieval days every soldier, knight as well as hired mercenary, had to bring his own arms and clothes, had to buy his own food.[12] Heavy guns made a first dent in this system; cities and princes commenced to set up armories from which to supply their troops. Soon it was discovered that other arms, too, might be secured on advantageous terms and rented out to the mercenaries, deducting fees from their pay. Similarly, the purchase of clothes wholesale made possible considerable savings; standardization of these clothes into *uni-forms* readily suggested itself as the next step. Regarding food, a mixed system prevailed for a long time. But as armies grew, troop commanders found themselves shouldered with the task of providing canteens where the soldiery might secure food at reasonable prices. Graft and corruption were difficult to avoid. Therefore it seemed imperative, particularly to princes with a sense for economy, to take over entirely the feeding of troops, particularly after the general draft got under way. Perhaps the early beginnings of this system of governmental provisioning must be sought in countries with a considerable navy. It was palpably impossible to let sailors do their own buying of food. Therefore in maritime nations like the English, governments entered at a very early date into the "retail business" of feeding their navies.

During the Second World War, the United States military establishment took full measure of the importance of food for morale, and succeeded in making its army and navy the best fed in the world. Scientific insight into dietary problems is brought to bear upon this problem; at the same time the advantages of centralized purchasing are carried to the point where "rations" are determined for all armed forces, so that for months ahead the menus of hundreds of thousands of military personnel are "planned" day by day.

The problem of revenue · It is apparent that for all these activities of organizing and keeping intact arsenals and armories, of collecting, storing, and distributing foodstuffs and drinks, and of purchasing, storing, and handling uniforms, considerable administrative organizations had to be set up.[13] For a time, attempts were made to handle these problems within the context of the medieval constitutional order by multiplying council and boards, partly under royal, partly under parliamentary, direction. Incredible confusion resulted. Where a strong and capable administrator-king attempted to take the necessary measures without consulting the "estates," his activities encountered very serious difficulties. Since the levying of additional taxes was in varying degrees subject to the consent of such estates (in England called Parliament), the princes had great difficulty in securing the necessary revenue. Debasing the currency was a temporary expedient often resorted to. The chartering of colonial trading companies helped some governments, but the returns were much less considerable than was commonly hoped for. The seizure of church lands helped the Protestant princes. Both transactions were obviously of a predatory nature. It has never been determined how much the government of Holland or the king of England gained from their chartered companies, because these princes were not regular stockholders. Whatever they were able to extract from organizations like the East India Company they received in the form of charter fees, loans, and so forth. What benefit kings derived from the confiscation of church lands, and the like, is almost as difficult to determine. But a very rough estimate, based on extant sources and probably representing a minimum, suggests that these confiscations yielded Henry VIII £1,890,500 between 1524 and 1547. The military significance of such loot can roughly be gauged by comparing it with the cost of a medium-sized man-of-war such as the *Ark Royal,* the flagship for which Queen Elizabeth paid £5000. Had these sums been used by the English kings to organize and equip a sizable army, as Charles V and his Hapsburg successors in Spain and Austria did with their American gold, they might well have triumphed over the parliamentary forces. But since the road to territorial expansion lay overseas, they concentrated on the navy, and as colonial revenue was slow in coming into the royal treasury, they had to wrange with a Parliament which was quite aware of the dangers of allowing the king to build up military support.

Estates' assemblies on the Continent were, of course, no less alive to the threat which any rapid expansion in royal military forces contained for their own position. But the immediacy of dangers from abroad made it difficult, if not impossible, for them to refuse to grant the revenues which the prince demanded, and in any case proceeded to collect, if the Estates were slow in making the grant. In other words, the continual imminence of foreign invasion gave to Continental monarchs the entering wedge for expanding their revenues.[14] They could appeal to the "emergency power," a power always recognized even in England as part of the royal prerogative. This royal prerogative appears to have been a decisive factor which might explain why Continental Estates did not often proceed to expand their armies along the lines of Cromwell's Model Army. It was quite common in the sixteenth and the first half of the seventeenth centuries for representative assemblies to maintain their own military establishments. But they were seldom as ably led as the Model Army, and if they attempted to take the field against an oppressive prince, as happened in Bohemia after 1618, the civil war at once embroiled them in foreign complications and actual invasion. In the course of such intervention the monarchical cause could more surely count upon support from foreign princes than the Estates. Thus the battle on the White Hill (near Prague, 1620) was lost because the Bohemian Estates and their elected king could not secure adequate foreign support. Would the Parliaments of Cromwell and William III have fared better if they had needed such aid? Where the estates did expand their military forces, as in Poland, the consequences were disastrous.

Commissioners and the emergency power · Estates and princes alike were dependent upon a host of intermediary officials, commissioners or commissaries, as they were called. The princes could much more effectively employ such agents on account of their claim to "emergency power" under the prerogative.[15] Such commissaries often appeared with the armies in the field and collected money, grain, horses, and what not from the unfortunate local populace, claiming simply that it was needed. Thus constant deprivations of the civilian population, particularly of the peasantry but also of the cities, took place because of an alleged impending threat to peace and security. Such commissions varied greatly in scope; some commissioners, as in the cases just cited, were merely sent to do one particular errand, others had more or less plenary powers to accomplish a certain result, such as quelling disturbances and re-establishing the authority of the prince. But in all these cases, the decisive point was a specific need requiring immediate or, as it is nowadays often called, "direct" action. It is an interesting and striking fact, and one well illustrating the persistence of political techniques within a given culture pattern, that with the advent of the dictatorship of the proletariat in Russia and the innumerable occasions for direct action (the legal order having for the time being vanished), the commissary at once appeared on the scene as the People's Commissar — an agent of the revolutionary leaders and the mass behind them. The same thing had happened during the French revolution. This technique is inherent in the very situation requiring direct action. Thus we may say in conclusion that direct or emergency action is an important concomitant technique of modern military evolution (see ch. XXV and below).

Civil and foreign war · There is a kinship between civil and foreign warfare, between internal and external armed conflict, which is of broad significance.[16] The unrealistic quality of much nineteenth-century political thought is revealed in the fact that it failed to perceive this close kinship. In fact, in recent times the group which has shown a distinct propensity toward foreign war is the modern nation and the princes under whose leadership it arose. Religious and class interests are more likely to get embroiled in civil war. Thus the position of the Chinese Communists preaching the doctrine of class and race warfare turns out to be merely opposition to one kind of war in order to be better able to fight another kind, like a government which keeps its peace with one adversary to concentrate all its force upon crushing the other.

The bellicose spirit of militant Communism raises not only the specter of civil war, but difficult questions regarding the prospects of lasting peace in a fully socialized world. Self-contained empires such as Russia might in such a world be pacific since they possess all they need. But recent events, especially the reliance upon military force in the rising conflict between the Soviet Union and Red China, raise serious doubts on this score. Furthermore, the very exclusiveness of Communist governments with their trade and production monopolies augurs ill for international cooperation. New causes for war seem to be lurking in the struggle for raw materials and markets. One should remember also that the attitude of British labor, or at least sections of it, toward Egypt and India has at times in the past been rather imperialistic. There is, then, no certainty that a family of socialist nations might not become engaged in armed conflicts as fierce as those fought between expansionist monarchies. The mere adoption of socialism will not abolish or even minimize the danger of war. No matter how considerable might be the solidarity of the labor class when confronting their employers, this solidarity weakens when the labor classes of various countries confront each other. The Soviet Union for many years played the Communist parties of the several countries against each other.

The military aspect of the Fascist rise to power · We have seen how the exigencies of external pressure facilitated the monarchs' military ascendancy. We have seen how the prince in times of release from external pressure could broaden his military ascendancy into a general political ascendancy. He became a monocrat, almost a despot. When, in the course of events after the French revolution, this central control was wrested from the princes and appropriated by the "people" through its representatives, the control of the military establishment passed into the latter's hands. Maintenance of this control has always seemed of vital importance to those who reflected upon the conditions of successful constitutional government. It is a striking confirmation of their views that the collapse of constitutional orders in Europe after World War I occurred where that monopoly of control over the military was not or could not be maintained. Germany, Italy, Spain, Austria, Rumania, and Hungary all suggest the trend of development in countries where the government surrenders this monopoly of military power which the autocratic governments of seventeenth- and eighteenth-century Europe labored so persistently to establish.[17] In Russia, too, the Kerenski government allowed itself to be so misled by Entente diplomacy and the liberal doctrinaire's indifference to the vital condition of effective control over the military forces, that it continued an increasingly unpopular war and thus hastened the disintegration of the regular army. Trotsky expressed it well: "The mass of the soldiers shaken by the revolution was looked upon by Kerenski as clay with which he could do as he pleased. . . . He ordered a new offensive (in June). . . . It soon was clear that no 'democratic army' stood behind Kerenski; . . ." Lenin and Trotsky knew that they must strike while the army was defunct. Foreign observers have agreed with reactionary generals in making the same point.[18] In Germany, the Communists were unable to employ similar tactics, because the moderate Socialists immediately made peace. A sufficient body of the army and police remained loyal to cope with the situation. But owing to these services the army was able to entrench itself sufficiently to escape from all serious efforts at effective democratization. In this endeavor it was greatly helped by the provisions of the Treaty of Versailles, which forced Germany to reduce her army to a small professional force; a liberalist indifference toward military problems of government common among the new leaders of the democracy did the rest. As a result, the democratic leaders later were placed at the mercy of generals who were admittedly quite indifferent to the fate of the Weimar regime. "Private" armies, both Communist and National Socialist, scheming for the overthrow of the "system," were allowed to grow up alongside the rather puny army of defenders of the new constitution. For a time, each of these "armies" numbered about 100,000 men, red fighters, Brownshirts, Steel Helmets, and National Banner men. They balanced each other, with the official army and the police endeavoring to keep the "peace." But when the Steel Helmets made common cause with the Brownshirts, and the official army was won over, too, the democratic and constitutional forces found themselves cornered and without the support of adequate armed force, let alone a "monopoly" such as the maintenance of government is claimed by many to require.[19] In Italy, where the situation was somewhat obscured by the gradual emergence of Mussolini's power, the "humiliations" of the peace treaty had undermined the position of the parliamentary leaders in the popular mind. The army was profoundly affected. It is significant that the proclamation of the Fascists after their March on Rome stated, first of all, that the march was not made against the army. What is more, the government's intention to declare a state of siege was thwarted by the king's refusal to sign such a declaration and this refusal was motivated by urgent advice given the king that "the army would not fight." These situations suggest that a constitutional government's loss of superiority in military force heralds its imminent collapse. Lenin in Russia, Hitler in Germany, Mussolini in Italy have all shown by their later actions that they were most anxious to remove the weakness which had given them success. Their military policies showed a clear realization of the dangers to which a government is exposed which does not rest upon a firm basis of military support. On the other hand, the remarkable resiliency shown by the United States upon the occasion of both the First and the Second World War in putting very large armed forces and vast equipment into the field in a relatively short time is striking evidence of the dormant reservoirs of military strength which a cooperative society contains.[20] But it must not be forgotten that these reservoirs could only be activated because the United States was given two full years in which to mobilize its resources and manpower. It is a key task of effective strategic planning and the foreign policy resulting from it to keep this advantage of time until effective world organization can be achieved.

Limitation of armaments[21] · As part of the struggle against militarism carried on by the democratic and pacific nations, the idea of disarming the "aggressor" has come to be generally accepted. It has more especially been adopted as a policy toward those countries dominated by the Fascists which were held responsible for the Second World War. Such "demilitarization" is, of course, hopefully viewed as the beginning of a general disarmament. But how can disarmament, or even the limitation on armaments, be accomplished in a world faced with revolutionary movements preaching violence?

There is a paradox involved in all these schemes which proposals for "unilateral" disarmament bring out, though they do not solve it. The paradox of this situation reveals that "disarmament" can only mean a pooling of armed forces and military establishments. This may indeed mean a reduction of the total contingents required; it may even make an agreement against the spread of nuclear weapons possible; but it is a transfer of arms, rather than their abolition. It may eventually lead to an international or supernational army (or police force, as it is often euphemistically called).

Armaments do not "cause" wars; military establishments are the governmental instrumentalities for realizing the territorial objectives: expansion, security, defense. As long as these objectives remain, the close connection between the progress of civilization, science, culture, and military undertakings will make it inevitable that disarmament turn into a change of armaments. Nor, in a world-wide industrial society, can the abolition or limitation of certain types of weapons in use at present ban the specter of wholly new weapons. It is, in other words, not the possession of arms, but the disposition to use them for expansionist and aggressive purposes, which must be uprooted. Such a change in outlook and purpose can only come about gradually, as territorial questions recede in importance. That they will disappear seems more than doubtful, in light of the universal appeal of the territorial imperative which recent researchers have shown to be a potent factor in animal life too.[22] In 1866 the several German states, Prussia, Bavaria, and the rest, were fighting each other, and the victorious Prussians appropriated large amounts of territory, including the entire kingdom of Hanover. Fifty years later such a proceeding seemed to most Germans hard to imagine. The problem of the country's territorial divisions had largely become a question of administrative expediency. If a civil-war situation flared up between Bavaria and the Reich in 1923, it was not over territorial questions, but concerned the political organization of the whole country, the problems of monarchy, socialism, and so forth. The territorial objectives had been minimized, if not eliminated, by creating a government comprising the several German states. This does not mean that the conflict over boundaries may not be a bitter one — attempts to change state boundaries in the United States show that; but they can be settled within an international framework by decision of the people affected. Modern military techniques, with their predominantly aggressive potentialities, afford the most persuasive argument for government as the only effective guaranty for lasting peace between nations, because only such government will reduce the passions engendered by territorial issues and make them arbitrable. Even the chances of civil war would be somewhat decreased in such a larger context. Size reduces the possibility of frictions developing into fighting because of the pressure from the remainder of the community which is not involved in the controversy. These considerations apply to supranational government, even if such a government does not comprise the entire globe. This is one of the key arguments behind the emerging European Community.

Conclusion · The increasing determination of people the world over to be rid of war has raised for many the problem of how to discover a "moral equivalent for war," as William James put it in a celebrated essay. Proceeding from the assumption that the sacrifices required by fighting and dying for a cause bring out some of the finest qualities in man, various ideas for comparable joint efforts have been advanced. It was just mentioned that the efforts at conquering space do provide such an "equivalent" in fact. The war against microbes has also been suggested as a sufficiently powerful unifying objective — the health work begun by the League of Nations and continued by the United Nations representing a first vanguard engagement. Economic crisis may also call forth supranational organization of a government type; it too had its beginnings in the League and is now being developed by the Economic Commission of the U.N. and by the EEC and comparable organizations in Latin America and Africa. But all things considered, these promising seedlings are likely to be crushed if the existing territorial rivalries continue to engender a feeling of violent insecurity and a consequent determination to remain armed. When, as at present, these territorial rivalries are embittered by ideological conflicts, the "spheres of influence" become more rigid, and symbolized in phrases like the "Iron Curtain" and the "Cold War."

From a careful consideration of the facts of military force in relation to government, political science is justified in concluding that the military establishment is a necessary concomitant of all government, that it transcends territorial objectives and ultimately is rooted in the general objective of security. Its basic paradox, so baffling to Hobbes and other political philosophers, that man, seeking peace, makes war, is rooted in one of life's basic aspects: where there is life, there is death. When man feels that his life is threatened, he gets ready to kill. Hobbes was wrong in making the search for security from fear of violent death the only, or at least the dominant, objective of man. He was right in stressing its persistence. Especially in revolutionary periods fraught with civil war potentialities, this fear and this search reassert themselves. For group dissensions within a community also can reach the point where violence flares more readily than more stable periods are willing to allow. The people of the United States, whose most dangerous wars have, like the Civil War and the Second World War, involved revolutionary situations, may be expected to be alert to the lessons which this experience implies. But neither should the United States become oblivious to the tremendous risks to a constitutional order which a large military establishment may become if its leadership loses confidence in the viability of the constitution. The military, like other experts, should be on tap but not on top, as a popular phrase has it. One way to keep them there is to make sure that the military remain dedicated to freedom. It is one of the toughest problems of contemporary constitutionalism.

Peace and Diplomacy

_____IV

Introduction · Diplomacy and war · The art of negotiating · Foreign and domestic affairs · The language of diplomacy · The system of ambassadors · The "social" functions of the professional diplomatist · Technical experts abroad · The foreign service as an organized administrative service · The international civil servant · The balance of power · Peace and foreign policy · Conclusion

Introduction · The living together of modern nations seems to be a continuous warfare, interrupted by brief periods of relaxation caused by utter exhaustion. Contemplating the history of Europe during the last four hundreds years, a gloomy philosopher would certainly be tempted to reiterate Heraclitus' sinister phrase that war is the father of all things. Still, most of the time the inevitable friction resulting from territorial and other maladjustments has been successfully reduced by the methods of diplomacy. Diplomacy, the textbooks tell us, is (or at least was) "the application of intelligence and tact to the conduct of official relations between the governments of independent states" (Satow). Notwithstanding Napoleon's mocking sally to Talleyrand that "treaties might be signed by diplomats, but they are made by soldiers," war would thus appear as the breakdown of diplomacy, since it is the application of brute force. Appearances to the contrary, diplomacy, by reducing the friction which is inevitable between governments striving toward conflicting objectives, such as territorial acquisitions, tries to avoid war, while yet realizing a maximum of a government's purposes. Contested territories, like Alsace-Lorraine, are the classic source of international conflict. But the expanding industrialism of the modern age has added many others, such as raw materials. Whenever a government reaches beyond its boundaries, diplomacy comes into play.

Diplomacy and war · The proposition that diplomacy strives to avoid war is often questioned on the supposedly realistic ground that the diplomacy of a Louis XIV, a Napoleon, or a Bismarck was more concerned with preparing for war than with avoiding it. This is undoubtedly true, and if it had been asserted that it was the objective of diplomacy to avoid *all* war, the objection would be well taken. But when the diplomacy of certain aggressive statesmen was employed to isolate a particular enemy so as to facilitate his defeat, the diplomat's task in effecting such isolation consisted in an effort to maintain peace with the enemy's potential allies. The failure of Louis XIV's diplomacy is generally admitted; his inability to prevent the great alliance which was formed by England, the Netherlands, and the House of Hapsburg resulted in his being checked by the series of wars which ended in the Peace of Utretcht (1713–1714). Likewise Frederick the Great was almost crushed beneath the combination of Russia, France, and Austria which Maria Theresa succeeded in bringing together against him; a brilliant strategist and army leader, this extraordinary Prussian king was handicapped by his ineffective diplomacy. Napoleon Bonaparte, another remarkable soldier, also affords a striking illustration of how superior military strength will suffer defeat if not aided by skillful diplomacy. The alliance of almost all of Europe, led by England, Russia, Austria, and Prussia, proved too strong even for Napoleon's military and administrative genius; diplomacy, such as Talleyrand had advocated, would have anticipated this alliance and tried to prevent it. The success of Bismarck's diplomacy, on the other hand, lay precisely in his careful elimination of potential allies of whoever happened to be his particular opponent. In Prussia's war with Austria he succeeded in keeping out France, England, and Russia (1866), while in Germany's war with France (1870–1871) he similarly kept peace with Austria, Russia, and England. It is small wonder that after the brilliant victories which his diplomacy had prepared, he spent the rest of his days haunted by the specter of coalitions which might be brought together against Germany. It was in an effort to prevent such coalitions that Bismarck became so interested in maintaining peace throughout Europe; the catastrophic consequences of the failure of later German governments to follow his lead are well known. Throughout all these great clashes of modern history, a tendency can be observed: the dominant objective of successful diplomacy is the reducing of friction between governments, and, if possible, the maintaining of peace. These efforts at eliminating the friction engendered by the conflicting interests of the various countries must be continuous. Diplomacy would be perfect if through mere art in negotiation it could realize the maintenance of peace, while at the same time securing such advantages as are demanded by the people, a prince, big business, or whoever happens to determine the policy of the particular government.

The art of negotiating[1] · Unfortunately, the so-called "sovereigns," whether princes, peoples, or interest groups, are and have been in the habit of demanding things which no diplomat, no matter how skillful, could secure without the ultimate use of armed force. We have here confronting us a paradox which has puzzled the students of diplomacy, both of democratic and of autocratic governments. There is the desire for peace, and the concurrent insistence upon things which cannot be had without recourse to war, because someone else's vital interests are involved. This suggests the need for differentiating between goals of foreign policy and the negotiations involved in realizing them.[2] Apparently, when talking of diplomacy as a method of government, one considers it mainly in terms of the art of negotiation. The goals, and their realization through negotiation, however, are often fused in reality. One of the goals of British foreign policy, in the days of Palmerston and Gladstone was "free trade." The prevailing trend in Continental Europe and the United States was to resist British commercial supremacy by protecting tariffs designed to shield infant industries and achieve a measure of equality. No art of negotiation could hope to eliminate the basic conflict of interests, as conceived by the several powers. Indeed, in the course of negotiating trade policies, British goals themselves gradually changed, until eventually "imperial preference" emerged as an alternative policy, or goal. Many similar examples could be cited, especially in recent American diplomacy, for example, the Marshall Plan and the Atlantic Pact. There is a tendency at present to conceive of foreign policy as some kind of fixed and static pattern, similar to the pattern of agricultural or labor policy. But what John Locke in a rather picturesque phrase called "the design of foreigners" provides an ever-shifting need for alternative solutions. Hence the cases just cited show that the distinction between goals of policy and the negotiations required to realize them is a rather difficult one to maintain. A closer analysis of reality reveals that the actual negotiation generates a policy, and a given policy imposes certain and peculiar methods of negotiation. To say, therefore, that we wish to consider diplomacy largely as the art of negotiation means defining our standpoint and method of approach.

The interrelation between objectives and techniques, between goals and the negotiations directed toward achieving them, constitutes the quintessence of what goes under the title of "foreign policy." Recurrent panaceas are offered under this head, often under formulas which pretend to be "solutions" to the problem of a "sound" foreign policy for a particular country. Actually, such plans never explain how acceptance is to be gained from a divided and confused public, nor how the "design of foreigners" is to be dealt with. It stands to reason that any particular "foreign policy," if firmly stated as such, will elicit adjustments on the part of other powers with divergent interests, which would in turn necessitate readjustments, and so forth indefinitely. What these disquisitions usually boil down to is either a series of goals for a given country; or vague and unquestionable "principles" such as the one that a country should not try to "overextend" itself; or, finally, critical comments upon the particular conduct of foreign affairs, either in terms of the persons responsible for foreign policy, or of institutional arrangements, such as legislative control. These are all important issues, but they do not, in the nature of things, yield to general solutions. In any event, such arguments as whether a country like the United States should or should not make "peace" its major goal are not scientific problems, but preachments presumably addressed to the general electorate in the hope of persuading it to the writer's view. A coherent "foreign policy" is probably a marginal case, occurring only at rare intervals under unique conditions and exceptional leadership. The rest of the time, and especially in democratic countries, it is more "realistic" to speak of "foreign affairs" rather than foreign policy. Foreign affairs may be understood as the complex manifold of policies, relationships, and negotiations which in retrospect yield to the analyst some coherent pattern as a result of the emergent realities.[3]

Foreign and domestic affairs · To delimit the field of foreign affairs is not as easy as the constant use of the phrase would lead one to believe. The various human activities involved in carrying on the relations between nations can be fairly clearly illustrated by examples: De Gaulle making a speech on Franco-German relations; the British Parliament ratifying the Rome Treaty; the German ambassador calling upon President Kennedy; a conference held at The Hague; a clerk in the State Department decipering a message from one of the embassies; these and many similar situations suggest themselves. Perhaps the phrase "foreign relations" would be more indicative of the true nature of these activities; together they constitute the relationship through which nations and their governments are bound together. Nations at any rate are not truly independent in any factual sense, even though governments may be. Yet legally their relations are treated *as if* they were independent of each other. This leads to many difficulties, both in learned analysis and in popular views. The United States provides a particularly easy example for those who have been and are inclined to treat foreign relations as if nations were in fact independent of each other, thus making the fatal mistake of treating as a fact what is a legal fiction. Even to treat foreign relations as a separate thing amounts to committing a similar mistake; for the distinction between foreign and domestic affairs is to some extent a fiction also.[4] Is there under modern industrial conditions any such thing as a purely domestic concern when speaking of major policies? Laws may treat the tariff, the restriction of immigration, the regulation of various fields of production, governmental subsidies, and similar measures of governmental policy as strictly domestic, but are they in fact? Matters of governmental organization likewise are anything but domestic, unless they concern minor details. Were the rise to power of the Nazis, of the Fascists, of the Communists, purely domestic matters? How could the United States have insisted upon the disappearance of monarchy in Germany if governmental organization had no bearing upon foreign relations? Similarly, did not the question of maintaining monarchy inject itself into the League of the Three Emperors and the Holly Alliance? Searching students of foreign relations and diplomacy have always known that foreign and domestic affairs constitute a whole which one is bound to discover if one digs deep enough. One of the great turning point of European diplomacy before 1914 was the conclusion of the Franco Russian alliance (1894);[5] historians have shown how powerful a role Russia's need of large loans played in her shift from Germany to France. Important shifts occurred in 1933, when the emergence of the Hitler government led to a realignment of the powers and to the accession of the Soviet Union to the League of Nations; a similar turn came with the Communist accession to power in China. From this vantage point one perceives the difficulty of maintaining the time-honored principle of the "primary [priority] of foreign over domestic policy"; the two are so much part of one pattern or web that the meaning of the principle is obscure.

The language of diplomacy · The supposed failure of diplomacy to eliminate war has made people forget what a great advance over earlier conditions its carefully-worked-out and subtle methods represent. There is an oft-quoted wisecrack that ambassadors are honest men sent abroad to lie for the good of their country. It is less than a half-truth. Many statements which to the average lay reader of diplomatic documents would seem to be "lies" or pretenses are in fact conventional phrases which carry to the informed recipient precisely the meaning they possess in the mind of the person who uttered them.[6] When the President of the United States, in his letter of credence for the American ambassador to Mexico, speaks of "the desire to cultivate to the fullest extent the friendship which has so long subsisted between the two governments," he obviously is not "lying," and when the ambassador on suitable occasions repeats such phrases, his candor cannot on that account be questioned. Formally amicable relations between two governments constitute a "friendship" in the soothing language of diplomacy. It was, therefore, an extraordinary breach of diplomatic tradition when the government of the Soviet Union announced that it would teach unfriendly powers "to keep their swinish snouts out of our potato patch." Such language is very dangerous in the intercourse between powerful nations. It has been the purpose of diplomatic etiquette to avoid these dangers by carefully prescribed traditional restraints in conduct and language. The British Foreign Office "was aghast," we are told, at the breach of diplomatic etiquette which one of their ministers committed when he quoted the text of messages and instructions exchanged between the Soviet government and their representatives in Persia and India which had been intercepted by the British Intelligence Service. The Foreign Office was aghast, not because the statements were untrue, but because "never, even in the most embittered diplomatic controversy, had information thus obtained been cited as evidence." In other words, governments maintain a secret service to spy upon their "friends," but they will never, never admit it. Yet labeling as deceit this falure to admit such a generally recognized practice would be little short of absurd.

The development of diplomacy, that civilized form of intercourse, parallels, therefore, the general development of constitutionalism. The recurrent breaches of diplomatic etiquette, indeed the wholesale abandonment of the methods of diplomacy by the totalitarian governments, is the manifestation abroad of their nonconstitutional conduct of government at home. But this decline in manners cannot be blamed entirely on totalitarian dictatorships. A democratic age is given to rougher language, and the elected representatives of the people the world over have committed breaches of etiquette. It pervades the meetings of international bodies, too, when the rival conceptions of government clash.

The system of ambassadors · The elaborate system of ambassadors and other plenipotentiaries which one is inclined to take for granted today is a major achievement of the evolution of modern government. The practice of sending such representatives originated with the medieval church and from it spread first to the city-states of Renaissance Italy.[7] From there it was taken over and developed, as were so many other practices, by the monarchical governments north of the Alps. Yet regularized practices developed very slowly. Ambassadors were often given a discourteous reception, if they were not actually maltreated. Many protracted struggles arose over questions of eitquette, and the prestige connected with them. How imperfect the arrangements still were at the end of the Thirty Years' War, toward the middle of the seventeenth century, can be seen from the fact that almost four years were consumed in clearing up innumerable questions of eitquette before the peace conference could commence to sit at Muenster and Osnabrück in 1645. Nor were the succeeding negotiations easy: they lasted for fully three years. The development in the subsequent hundred and fifty years brought into existence a tradition of diplomatic conduct which was codified by the Congress of Vienna in 1815. This was some twenty-five years after the professional diplomat had almost accidentally made his debut. That happened in France, where, after the revolution had swept away the titled ambassadors of the old regime, the conduct of affairs had been left in the hands of their secretaries. The latter were mostly commoners who had acquired a semipermanent professional status by the force of custom and circumstance. To be sure, seasoned and quasi-professional diplomats had existed in the monarchical service wherever a man held his post for a considerable length of time, but the service as a whole was amateurish, except perhaps that of the Catholic church and the Republic of Venice. Even a casual reading of the instructions handed to French ambassadors of the period will reveal that fact. These instructions often sound like an introduction into the nature of the relations of the two governments concerned. Only during the nineteenth century did a professional bureaucracy take hold of the field of foreign affairs. It is perhaps worth passing notice that with the exception of the French service under the Third Republic and of course that of the United States, these services even in the nineteenth century were dominated by titled noblemen; the diplomatic service, like the corps of cavalry officers, was considered the exclusive province of the upper crust of society. Just the same, or perhaps as a result of this circumstance, the diplomatic corps developed certain characteristics which bear scrutiny beyond that given the officialdom which carries on the government's work at home.

The "social" functions of the professional diplomatist · Great importance is attached to social etiquette in the conduct of international negotiations. It has been shown how deeply this regard for etiquette and procedure is embedded in the intensity of the power struggle; its sensitizing effect and its heightening of the feeling for all questions of prestige has also been shown. In private life, people are apt to smile about someone who makes a great fuss over who should go first to the dinner table. But where each person is a public person, representing a nation jealous of its prestige, this is no small matter, and the salutary effects of etiquette are seen in the rule of seniority, which ranks each representative according to the length of time he has been accredited to the particular government. This custom attests to the fiction of equality between all the states, great and small: no balance of power intrudes itself into the dinner parties.

The importance of social functions is closely linked with the tasks of diplomacy. Countless memoirs, written by distinguished diplomats such as Sir Cecil Spring-Rice and Walter Hines Page, attest to the fact that much of their most important information is gathered at social functions of one sort or another. Since the seventeenth century, the houses of distinguished diplomats have been the center of a brilliant social life. Is the glamour of this past which often draws young men into the foreign service. They forget that it, too, has been sullied by the smoke of the machine age. Most members of the foreign service spend a large proportion of their lives in relatively small and remote cities, often not even capitals of unimportant countries. But even in the great metropolitan centers of London, Paris, and Berlin, it is not today a matter of court intrigues and cabals of the high aristocracy, but rather dull dinner parties for press magnates and industrial tycoons with an occasional journalist or parliamentarian to brighten up the atmosphere.[8] Even so, no person can make a success in the foreign service unless he is able to handle social relations effectively. This fact, too, differentiates the professional diplomat from other officials. Since social grace is acquired more easily by those who grow up in wealthy surroundings, the predominance in the diplomatic service of the nobility, later shared with the upper-middle class, is quite understandable, though not necessarily beneficial for the service.

Technical experts abroad · What has so far been said concerning qualifications remained very largely true until the First World War. But since that time, considerable change has come about. The creation of the League of Nations, and constant international conferences widely participated in by governmental officials outside the foreign service proper, set the stage for intergovernmental relationships of a technical sort in the many fields which require international action, such as communications, transportation, and health. Such technical contacts have multiplied since the Second World War and fiscal, agricultural, cultural, labor, and many other issues are the concern of specialized agencies. In these fields, the old "secret" diplomacy is no longer the acknowledged method of handling business. The administrative technique of bureaucracies within federal systems has taken its place. This technique is characterized by solicitude for the opinion of every member of the group. Since it is impracticable to coerce a recalcitrant member of the cooperating group, every effort has to be made to avoid the possibility that any member may become recalcitrant. Naturally, such cooperative efforts are rendered considerably more difficult when the members belong to different nations proud of different cultures. Yet the fact that such cooperative undertakings were commenced long before the First World War in specific fields, such as that of the Universal Postal Union, shows conclusively that their rapid development after the First World War and under the aegis of the League was by no means gratuitous; the U.N., as the League before it, merely affords a convenient administrative device for coordinating the various activities.

In view of the central importance which the bureaucracy has had for the growth and development of modern government, this expansion of administrative services into the international field is very important. The more advanced industrial countries consequently send more and more permanent experts abroad whose task it is to follow the developments in their particular fields.[9] They are attached to the legation, and hence are called *attachés*. As these activities have grown, diplomats have found themselves surrounded by commercial, agricultural, and labor experts who were in direct communication with their corresponding ministries at home. The presence of such experts frequently has been the cause of considerable friction in the foreign legations. Independent and often conflicting points of view are at times held and expressed by these experts on issues of international significance, particularly within their own bailiwicks. Thus a commercial attaché may favor the lowering of tariff rates at a time when the representative of the foreign office considers such a plea very inopportune. From the point of view of integration, the complaints of the professional diplomat are undeniably justified. But from the point of view of governmental growth, the independent initiative of the expert may open up new avenues of international progress, just as in centuries past expanding technical services served, we have seen, as the vanguards of national unification.[10]

The foreign service as an organized administrative service · If we apply our analysis of bureaucracy we find that the three functional criteria, namely, differentiation of functions, centralization and integration of control (hierarchy), and finally qualification for office (professionalization), are found in all modern diplomatic services. The differentiation is partly along geographical and partly along functional lines. It varies from government to government, as one country or another looms large in importance. Thus Germany appears of greater significance to France than to the United States, South American countries more important to the United States than to the Soviet Union. Sometimes policy trends are discernible in these arrangements, as when the United States State Department sets up a separate office for Germany and Austria outside its European Division. Functional differentiation appears when such sections as the legal, the commercial, and the cultural are organized as separate units in the foreign office, as is now generally the case. As far as the commercial work is concerned, foreign services have for a long time recognized a distinction between the consular and the "diplomatic" service, though the tendency to separate these two services as careers is now generally criticized as unsound. In reorganizing their foreign service, the British have recently abolished the distinction, as has the United States. Field services, in turn, are sometimes distinguished from the work in the central foreign office (Department of State in the United States), but again without differentiating the career. Even in the arrangements for these field services, policy trends can be shown. After the Franco-Prussian War, the French abandoned a number of consulates in Germany. After the First World War, Great Britain, France, and Germany changed their missions in the ABC states to embassies, thus recognizing the enhanced power of the new world. With the steady increase in the number of states, there is now a fairly general trend to multiply ambassadors.

As far as integration and centralization of control are concerned, the foreign services present problems distinct from other services. The great distance between the central directing office and the field offices necessitates a large measure of autonomy, even under modern communication conditions. Not only ambassadors, but consuls as well, are still their own masters in all matters not specifically directed from the central office. While the embassy in a large country like the United States may have general direction of affairs, it is not exclusively the hierarchical superior of the various consulates in its territory; they may and often do communicate directly with the home office.

Within the last fifty years, clearly defined professional requirements have become established in all the major countries, with the United States following suit by the Rogerts Act (1924). Each country, in its own way and in keeping with its peculiar traditions of preparing and testing for the administrative services of the government, has set up its own system. It is unnecessary to describe the detailed provisions here. Suffice it to say that the higher ranks of the service (except for political appointments in the top rank of the United States service) are, in all the leading countries, manned by men and women possessing some type of academic university training.

Besides these functional criteria, we have seen that certain behavior patterns are essential to effective administrative services. Objectivity, continuity, and precision, as well as discretion — these, of course, are also essential aspects of a good diplomatic service. Therefore, a good diplomatist is, in the words of one of them, "indifferent to public applause, has devoted some thirty years to the study of foreign psychology, is unaffected by vanity, dislikes controversy, eschews all forms of publicity, and is not subject to acute time pressure or overwork. In addition, as a trained expert in a common science working with other experts, he is intent upon producing a piece of work which will satisfy his own professional standards." According to the same author, "a man who has spent some thirty years in the diplomatic service acquires, inevitably, an international frame of mind."[11] He comes to have a kind of fraternal sentiment for other diplomatists and to feel that parliamentary and public opinion is foolish and ill-informed. While the latter attitude is often found among professional administrative officials in national services as well, it seldom is held with as much show of good reason. There are always citizens who know as much as any government officials about particular governmental tasks, though most citizens do not, but there are rarely, if ever, citizens who have a full grasp of all the implications of a given decision in the field of foreign affairs. (See below, p. 358 ff., for a discussion of parliamentary control.) This "international frame of mind" is subtly adjusted to a rapid, though careful, calculation of the effects which a given move will have throughout the network of international relationships. This chess player's attitude often results in a neglect of underlying trends of long-range significance, particularly of social and economic forces. But the diplomatist is, on the other hand, acutely aware of the balance of power at any particular moment, and highly sensitized to the prestige connected with certain developments.[12]

The international civil servant • As international organizations develop, the officials employed by them become more numerous. Their relations with the foreign services of the several governments represented in these organizations constitute a problem of great complexity. Ideally, the international civil servant should be completely devoted to the organization he serves and quite neutral with regard to the wishes and preferences of the national government which speaks for the nation to which he belongs. Actually, the United Nations, like the League of Nations, administers an oath of office which embodies this ideal. Nevertheless, human beings vary in their ability to rise to so unusual a challenge. What is more, governments vary in the extent to which they will permit their nationals to serve with "instructions." The Soviet Union, to take an extreme example, would hardly condone a Soviet citizen's stepping out of line; anyhow the official's self-interest tends to combine with various other factors to keep the official linked to his homeland.

In spite of the aforementioned drawbacks, the international civil service is constantly expanding and gaining in prestige and influence. Generally speaking, the secretariat of the United Nations is a stronger, more active body than its predecessor, the League secretariat, though splendid work was done by it. But the emphasis in the League was on research and informational activities, whereas under the United Nations and associated international bodies such as the World Bank, the International Monetary Fund, and the International Children's Emergency Fund, a high degree of executive and administrative skill is required. The same is true of the several technical branches of the United Nations which call for and command a highly specialized and technically trained person, whether it be in aviation, communications, or shipping. The continued expansion and consolidation of these specialized services means, of course, that once again the process of establishing a responsible bureaucracy is building the core of a governmental system, this time of world-wide scope. There is undoubtedly coming into being a devoted corps of international civil servants whose loyalty and devotion transcend national and cultural boundaries. This does not mean a loss of national identity, for it is generally agreed that a person without deep roots in his national community is apt to be handicapped in negotiating the compromises which the international community involves. But they do not think in terms of the struggle for power all the time, as the professional diplomat is trained to do. Though many come from the diplomatic service, and may even return to it, they are becoming more international in outlook.[13] This trend is particularly pronounced in the large bureaucracy of the Common Market, which has lately therefore acquired the name of "eurocracy."

The balance of power · The phrase "balance of power" since the sixteenth century, when it was first used by Guicciardini and other Florentine historians, has been a euphemistic description of any particular distribution of the power among nations which happened to be acceptable to the person using the phrase. The French, after 1871, said they wished to *restore* the balance of power in Europe which the unification of Germany had disturbed. The Germans held that they must *maintain* the balance of power which the French desire for revenge threatened. These observations were reversed after the First World War. Thus it can be seen that the balance of power does not necessarily refer to the maintenance of the *status quo;* it may also be the basis for arguing that this status be changed. Since the phrase describes any kind of distribution of power, the history of the balance of power is largely identical with the history of foreign relations.[14]

Whatever the actual balance or distribution of power may happen to be, the idea affords a ready argument in international negotiation, and presumably even a foundation for international law. As such, it has had its greatest vogue when it was a question of checking the tendency toward concentration of power in the hands of a single government. The desirability of "redressing the balance of power" was thus invoked against the Hapsburg world empire by Francis I during the first half of the sixteenth century. It was, in turn, brought forth against Louis XIV by William III. Maria Theresa used it against Frederick the Great, the tottering French monarchy against the British Empire under George III and Pitt, everybody against Napoleon I. In the course of the nineteenth century, the scope of its application was widened. The United States, by the Monroe Doctrine, forbade the extension of balance-of-power politics to the American continents, and thereby maintained its own supremacy with considerable success. In the twentieth century, the notion of regional balances of power spread rapidly. There is talk of a balance of power in the Balkans, in the Near East, in the Far East, in Latin America, and more recently, around the Pacific and in Africa.

There has been a *balancer* behind each balance. The power equilibrium has never worked when it was merely looked upon as a dead, material equipoise of power. Henry VIII of England once said: *"Cui adhaereo, praeest,"** when it was a matter of who would become emperor. It was a boast rather than a fact, but the claim is characteristic. It shows that the *balancer* is playing one power against another in order to prevail himself. Hence, the balance of power carries us beyond diplomacy in the strict sense. It is foreign *policy*. Peace, or at least the avoidance of war, may be the immediate objective, but security and national aggrandizement are behind it. The balancer is substituting the balance for military methods.

The Fourteen Points enunciated by President Woodrow Wilson in 1918 undertook to banish the balance of power from the world. No longer were people to be bartered about from sovereignty to sovereignty, as the balance-of-power diplomats had done; instead all nations were to determine their own status under an all-embracing League of Nations. But even had the League become truly all-embracing, and even had the treaties terminating the First World War been negotiated on the basis of the Fourteen Points, the balance-of-power argument would not have disappeared. The problem of the balance of power is almost as pressing in a federation as it is in a family of nations. How could Wilson, an American and a Southerner, have failed to perceive this? Had he forgotten the lesson of the Civil War? Was not the whole story of the genesis of that baneful conflict a tale of balancing the power of slave states against the others, till the final rupture occurred? Had not the same happened under the Swiss Confederation in 1847, and under the German Union in 1866? The failure to reckon with the continuance of balance-of-power politics within the League contributed its share to the League's difficulties. At the same time, we should not forget that both the League and the balance are mechanisms for conducting internal negotiations. Who would question that the League or the United Nations offer the superior technique if for no other reason than that such an organization contains within itself whatever is useful of the balance of power? It became apparent soon after the First World War that there was much need for considering the balance of power within the League, and successive international crises brought the balance of power within the League, and successive international crises brought out the importance of it. The problem forced itself to the fore much more rapidly after the Second World War in the

* Whoever has my support, prevails.

United Nations. Every problem faced by the U.N. is affected by the shifting balance of power between the U.S.S.R. and the Western powers. Whatever the future of international organization, the problem of the distribution (balance) of power will remain a matter of prime concern to all professional diplomats, and we shall very probably continue to use the concept as a convenient standard or idea in terms of which to discuss the shifting scene of international power relationships. On the other hand, the recognition of a continuing effort at maintaining a balance of power within the U.N. must not blind us to the fact that this organization possesses distinct advantages. It constitutes a framework, and it thereby elminates the need for a "balancer." All those members who are "neutral," relatively speaking, in a given controversy tend to operate as "balancers." This fact was clearly apparent in the role the United States and the U.S.S.R. played in the Security Council regarding the issues raised by the Suez crisis of 1956. The substitution of such an international *organization* for an intermittent balancer is, in a sense, merely a specific instance of the general feature of all constitutions; any constitutional system seeks to balance various governmental powers and organizes a balance of interests, including classes, in the community.

Peace and foreign policy · In a study some years ago, Walter Lippmann wrote mockingly that we must ask ourselves "whether peace, as so many say, is the supreme end of the foreign policy." And he answered this question with an emphatic "no," alleging that survival is, or should be, the supreme end, and that "the logic of peace as the supreme national idea leads to absurdity."[15] This view, or some version of it, has impressed many Americans who are in search of a "realistic" foreign policy. It is argued persuasively in terms of a conception of pure power politics among states that must conduct their foreign policy on the basis of their actual power resources. There is, many feel, a tendency for the United States to overextend itself in regard to ideological concerns, and more especially in the search of peace. The weakness of this reasoning is revealed when it is applied to revolutionary states. Particularly such ventures as the defense of anti-Communist regimes against internal threats have involved the United States in highly controversial undertakings. As the confrontation with Hitler had shown, or was believed to have done, a policy of compromise and partial retreat did not result in "peace in our time," as the slogan then had it. The policy of containment, however, has engendered a series of small wars. Some of these conflicts have been very risky and involved what at one time was ironically referred to as "brinkmanship," because the then-Secretary of State had allowed himself to speak of the threat of "massive retaliation" even if it involved getting to the "brink of war." The most dangerous situation arose, however, afterwards, when President Kennedy had to handle the Cuban missile crisis, in the course of which he managed to force the Soviet Union to liquidate a forward position under threat of nuclear war.[16]

No other country, though committed to a policy professedly directed toward the maintenance of peace, has since the Second World War had to face quite as many warlike emergencies. Yet, when the British and French government sought to force the reopening of the Suez Canal by supporting the war Israel was waging against Nasser's Egypt, failure of the United States to back this venture foredoomed it to failure. Similarly, several emergencies in Africa and Latin America could, in spite of a considerable amount of sanguinary fighting, be settled before they developed into a regular war.

If one were to accept "survival" as the supreme test of foreign policy, the obvious conclusion would be to wage a preventive war to destroy any revolutionary state while it can be done. But the government and the people of the United States continue the "absurd" logic of peace as the supreme national ideal, partly because too many Americans fear that they might not be the ones to survive as individuals. American diplomacy has been engaged in a tough program of containing the Soviet Union and the revolutionary forces which it sponsors throughout the world without war. It is a calculated risk, but, in terms of constitutional democracy, it is a lesser risk than that of becoming an aggressor in the name of "national survival." Recent experience in no wise invalidates the established theory, based upon long observation, that security is primarily the objective of military establishments (even international police forces), while the objective of diplomacy and foreign policy is peace. Yet that objective is forever placed into jeopardy because, as Raymond Aron has recently reasserted, international relations constitutes a distinctive chapter of political theory, because it treats "of relations between political units of which each claims the right to seek justice by and for itself and to remain master of the decision as to whether to fight or not."[17]

Conclusion • In the long run, friction between governments is unquestionably reduced by administrative internationalism; for each participant becomes in time a bit more internationally minded. He perceives that the most diverse cultural backgrounds and personal habit patterns may be combined with high achievement in a given specialty. This is true to such an extent that the resulting situation has given rise to the query whether the regular, old-fashioned diplomatic service is needed any longer at all. The answer is that the regular old-fashioned diplomatic service is not at all old-fashioned, if it is good. The modern diplomat will look upon himself as a liaison officer who will promote cooperation and understanding on all sides.

He will induct experts into the general setup of a foreign country, will furnish them introductions as well as an adequate meeting ground, will smooth out difficulties wherever he can; in short, he will act according to the first paragraph of the general instructions of the American Department of State to foreign service officers: "He creates good will and common understanding, and, with restrained and critical leadership born of mature experience and profound knowledge of men and affairs, he uses these as instruments for enhancing international confidence and cooperation among governments and people." A man of this type is a far cry from the honest fellow sent abroad to lie for the good of his country.

In keeping with this outlook, the foreign policy of all constitutional governments, but more especially constitutional democracies, will be directed toward peace as its primary objective and chief end. For it is the quintessence of political wisdom that the moral imperative that "there shall be no war" is reinforced by the "realism" of the basic objectives of human beings in politics.[18] Two insights, (1) that constitutionalism needs peace for its survival, and (2) that only a world-wide constitutionalism will provide an eventual guarantee of lasting peace under law, are the culmination of constitutional theory and practice in Europe and America.

Prosperity, the Police, and Legislation

V

Introduction · When considering expansion as an objective of modern government, the stimulation of trade and industry was discussed briefly. But while the governmental activities were related to the tax resources and hence to the provisioning of armies, they were undertaken also in pursuit of a distinct, though related, objective: general prosperity. It has been claimed that prosperity was wanted solely because it facilitated the maintenance of armies and navies, and therefore territorial expansion. May it not reversely be claimed that territorial expansion was sought because of the added opportunities for insuring prosperity, particularly in the case of colonies? As has been suggested before, all the objectives are interrelated. But prosperity was sought by many governments as an end quite in itself. Indeed, mercantilism was, in the first place, a doctrine concerned with how this might be accomplished. The marvel of the Dutch wealth in the seventeenth century was, in a way, the cause of all the speculation about commerce which mercantilism comprises.

Growth of the community would seem to be the drive behind territorial expansion and prosperity. At certain times, communities undeniably tend to grow. The ultimate whys and wherefores of such growth are rather obscure. But what the mercantilists sought to discover were the causes of making a country grow rich and powerful, on the assumption that that is what they all wanted to do. Governments, they believed, can do a lot to bring such growth about.[1]

The organismic fallacy · The recognition that countries grow in wealth, power, population, culture, and so forth, gave rise to the organismic fallacy.[2] The mercantilists were amoral in the sense that they did not interest

89

themselves in the moral issues that might be involved in such governmental action. Many of the medieval restrictions were the result of such moral considerations; the new outlook on power discouraged them. The mercantilists extended to all society what the doctrine of "reason of state" had claimed specifically for government: that whatever was necessary was justified by that necessity. This organismic view of society and its government (the "state") survived mercantilism and became a major ideological weapon in the hands of those who desired to oppose *laissez-faire*. Seeley in England and Treitschke in Germany are leading examples of European thought on this subject, while the manifest-destiny school of historians provided America with similar notions. In order to buttress their view that governments do tend to grow, such writers have gone further and asserted that governments, or rather states, are organisms. From the time of John of Salisbury in the twelfth century, writers have reveled in relating various parts of the government to various parts of the human body. The prince was said to be the head, his councilors the nerves, the army the hands and feet, and so forth. Even to this day, these analogies survive in speaking of the president of a country as its head. It is easy to ridicule this "organic" concept, particularly in its more extravagant forms, and to point out that governments are composed of human beings, each with his own will and consciousness. Since nobody has ever seen the entity apart from these separate human beings, it is indeed doubtful whether it exists in the same way as the body of an animal exists apart from the cells composing it. Yet, on the other hand, these human beings composing the government are living human beings, and there is no very tangible reason why we should not assume that the government and the nation live too. If they do, they will tend to grow for a certain length of time, as all living things do. The whole controversy over the "organic" nature of governments, communities, "states," comes down in the last analysis to an argument over what meaning should be attached to the word "organism." If an organism is defined in terms of an organic system, then a political order surely more nearly resembles such a system than a mechanical one. Hence one needs to discard the crude analogies, yet understand it as a whole consisting of several parts that are distinct and different from each other, bearing a definite functional relation to one another which establishes a mutual dependence of these parts upon each other so that the destruction of one entails the destruction of the whole.[3] It is clear, or ought to be, that such a system is not inherently "expansive"; but may quite as readily be self-contained or cooperatively interacting.

Prosperity and government expenditure · Prosperity appeared to be an intrinsically desirable state of affairs to all those princes who looked upon their countries in the same way in which a proprietor looks upon his estate. This desire for good husbandry may be motivated by a love of lavish expenditure, as we find it in France, in Austria, or during the Restoration in England. Nor ought we merely to scoff at these extravagant masters; for much of the enjoyment of later generations is derived from the masterpieces of art, architecture, and music which the prodigal expenditures of these courts called forth. As the cathedrals of the medieval church were lifted skyward upon the backs of serfs, so the castles and picture galleries of Europe were born of the extortions of vainglorious princes. Mozart and Beethoven were made possible by the autocratic Austrian government, no less than Raphael and Leonardo by the tyrants of Renaissance Italy.[4]

But, of course, this desire for lavish display was really a minor *motif*, though a very palpable one. The incessant labor of a Cecil, a Colbert, a Frederick the Great, was dictated by no such considerations. Prosperity was clearly an objective of primary importance in making the country more powerful. Hence much revenue was expended by the government to provide capital for new industries, to develop trading companies, and to build up shipping, mining, roads, and forests. They thought of the economy as an enterprise to be planned and promoted for the betterment of all. The word "paternalism" was quite appropriate. But it is not true that this paternalism was primarily restrictive. Indeed, the liberty of commerce was one of the main slogans of Colbert. At the same time, as he put it in a famous letter: "Trade is the source of public finance, and public finance is the vital nerve of war." And, as I added some years ago: "victory in war was seen by him and his contemporaries in turn to be the basis for aggrandizement and power."[5]

Police or administrative action • A whole welter, then, of different "policies," was initiated by these incipient modern governments for the purpose of fostering prosperity at home. These policies were carried into execution by administrative officials who took a strong hand in enforcing them.[6] Again, this enforcement must not be considered primarily a matter of restrictions, but rather of instigating private initiative. It is no accident that the word "policy" is so intimately related to that of "police." Both derive from the old French *policie*. The Oxford Dictionary tells us that the general connotation of "police" is "civil administration," which is charged, of course, with the several courses of action adopted by the government (policies). The second connotation of "police" is "public order" and that of course is to be maintained by these several policies. It is, therefore, hardly surprising to find early modern governments preoccupied with the problem of police. After our modern industrial society had gotten well under way, and we had begun to reap the profits of the manufactures and the commerce which these governments had initiated, it became the fashion to decry their attitudes and techniques as paternalistic. It was easy to forget what governments had done and to assume that the entire industrial revolution had been a work of "nature." It was an easy step from such an assumption to the belief that any organized effort of the community or its government to take a hand in industrial development would be an "interference." But if we use a homely analogy, the interference appears to be no greater than that of a gardener who, having sown vegetables, proceeds to pull up those which he finds too thickly grown. It is by no means an accident, but a revival of ancient precedents, if in the United States the "police power" is so often called upon to interfere in the industrial sphere.

Early legislation · Administrative action, however, was not enough. A great many ancient customs stood in the way of the desired development of manufacturing industries. Under time-honored charters given to cities in a period when urban handicraft was predominant, craft guilds had entrenched themselves as exclusive and monopolistic associations. To break their resistance, new rules had to be worked out and established. Both general and special legislation, in other words, were needed to clear the way for infant industries. It was this need, more than anything else perhaps, which contributed to the appeal of Bodin's famous doctrine of sovereignty.[7] For this sovereignty consisted of all but constitutionally limited legislative power; in other words, the power to make laws without regard to any previous laws already existing. Without such a power, Bodin and his contemporaries argued, there was no real government at all. In medieval times, by and large, the oldest law was considered the best law; and when popes, emperors, and kings sought to overcome the confusion of local customs, they had recourse to the Roman law, as we have seen before. Certainly insofar as the government was there to work out and apply *policies* which would enhance the *general* welfare, the power to make general rules was essential. We are thus compelled to recognize legislation, or the purposeful making of new rules, as a second method of modern government in its pursuit of prosperity. This association of the legislative with the police power seems startling nowadays, for we have come to look upon the police as engaged in strictly administrative action, and under the separation-of-powers doctrine it is customary to differentiate sharply between administrative and legislative activities. It has been pointed out that the division of powers is the essence of constitutionalism. It will be seen later that this differentiation could not take place until power had been concentrated in the hands of autocratic princes: under the Tudors in England, under Henry IV and Louis XIV in France, under Frederick William I and Frederick the Great in Prussia. All these autocrats were, economically speaking, "progressive." They pushed mercantile progress through legislation. When their successors slipped into "unprogressiveness," they were overthrown, through either revolution, or war, or both.

The ordinance • The formal method of police action and legislative reform, its legal instrument, was often the same, at least on the Continent of Europe. It was the royal ordinance. The ordinance was not only employed for specific action, but for broad legislation as well. In fact, much of the most important early economic legislation of France is found in the *Ordonnances du Roi*, and the same is true in other countries. Even in England, under the Tudors and Stuarts, much actual legislation of paramount economic and social significance is embodied in royal ordinances and decrees. But here the subservience of Parliaments under Henry VIII and Elizabeth often made it easy and advisable for the prince to "pass the buck" to the representatives of the "people." This policy had the great advantage of keeping Parliament "in the picture." The mercantilist reforms of Elizabeth, such as the Statute of Artificers, were carried through as regular statutes.[8] On the Continent, by contrast, the Estates' assemblies became, in the course of the sixteenth and seventeenth centuries, economically reactionary bodies. They represented too definitely those classes in the community whose interest lay in preventing economic, and more specifically, industrial progress. The royal emissary or intendant, carrying out an ordinance to accomplish some definite purpose, was resisted by these Estates, which in France and other countries had remained on a local basis. Thus the ordinance was also an instrument of centralization.

There are some curious parallels between those ordinances of early modern times and the recent emergence of rule-making activities on the part of executive or administrative authorities in America. In Continental countries, where monarchical government is less remote, such law-making ordinances have continued to be recognized as part of the executive's work. They have achieved a new and growing significance in Gaullist France, as will be shown later. This same trend is notable in England, though with parliamentary authorization. In America such measures have developed as instrumentalities of federal centralization and legislation. To describe them as "quasi-legislative" disguises only thinly the true nature of the instrumentalities of central government intervention. They are, as they were earlier in Europe, accepted as instruments to produce desired economic change.

Increase in wealth the central goal • Turning now from the forms of government activity again to their specific content: What things did these governments do in order to bring about what they conceived to be prosperity? The various undertakings of centralizing governments were all directed toward increasing the wealth of the country. They believed that wealth could be increased in a number of different ways. They were primarily concerned with two closely interrelated economic problems: commodities and money.

In view of their policy of stimulating the growth of industry, the governments inclined toward a protectionist policy. Their attitude toward goods or commodities was that of producers: they "feared" goods and wanted to protect their countries against wasting their wealth by buying goods abroad.

But what was this wealth they were wasting? It was essentially money, in their view. Montchrétien, a French exponent of this school, wrote in 1615: "We live not so much from trade in raw materials as from gold and silver." And in *The British Merchant* (1713) it was said that all countries with whom England traded "contribute to the Prosperity and Happiness of this nation" in proportion as England's trade with them yielded a balance of gold and silver.[9] Just as a simple farmer measures his wealth by the number of coins he has stowed away in his chest, so the princes of those days and the governments which they directed looked upon the actual gold and silver in their treasuries as the only reliable measure of prosperity. Their entire policy was aimed at increasing these treasures, or at least preventing their decrease. During this period various devices were worked out to satisfy this craving for money, in the most primitive sense of "coin." Apart from simply prohibiting the export of precious metals, a device which goes back to the Middle Ages, we find that governments groped their way toward a well-defined monetary policy calculated to assist their struggle to attract as much precious metal into their coffers as possible.

The trade balance and tariffs · The governmental activities which were directed toward promoting industry and commerce may be divided into the granting of privileges and monopolies and the attendant regulation on the one hand, and into measures affecting the trade balance on the other. It is from this preoccupation with the trade balance that the whole system derived its name: mercantilism.[10] The fact that England first abandoned mercantilism has led to our forgetting that she also probably first consciously embraced it. At any rate, England practiced mercantilism like all other European governments. For mercantilism was not merely an economic theory, and a wrong one at that, it was a very powerful formative force in the growth of modern government. In fact, there are those who would claim it as the cradle of modern government. Now, the effort to interfere directly with the flow of trade took, as we said, the form of impeding or prohibiting certain imports and exports. This policy was carried out by means of general legislation, as in the Navigation Acts, and tariffs were employed on a very considerable scale. It is impossible to say at what point commercial tariffs commenced to develop out of the older fiscal tariffs. It seems that they emerged more or less gradually as people found that the manufacture of goods subject to a fiscal tariff, that is, a tariff for revenue purposes only, offered a margin of protection against foreign competition. Certain it is that at the time of Colbert these ideas were fully worked out and that the greatness of this remarkable minister of Louis XIV lay rather in the zest with which he pursued the policy than in his discovery of it. The French tariff of 1581 was certainly a protective tariff. Protective tariffs dominated throughout the seventeenth and eighteen centuries, and the commerial treaty negotiated in 1786 between France and England made the first real breach in the system. Such a tariff policy consisted in placing high duties upon the export of raw materials and unfinished products, and high duties upon the import of finished products, while at the same time facilitating the export of finished products and the import of raw materials. It is easy to see why the contemporary trend of economic nationalism is sometimes called "neomercantilism."

The stimulation of trade and industry through monopolies • This direct method of affecting the balance of trade favorably was complemented by the policy of stimulating industry and commerce through the granting of more or less extensive monopolies. Such grants were usually in the form of specific action, rather than of general legislation. Every American knows that the Massachusetts Bay Company received a charter from the king of England. Few have stopped to consider what this meant with regard to the growth of modern government. The granting of charters was a device carried over from medieval days, when it was the legal method for bringing municipal corporations within the context of a feudal order.[11] In the period when modern governments emerged from the medieval context, such charters were turned to the rather different use of licensing corporations for diverse commercial purposes. These were the regulated companies of the English of the seventeenth and eighteenth centuries. The device of creating such corporations and granting such privileges was employed on so vast a scale as to revolutionize the whole economic life of the several poples. Naturally, administrative authorities had to be developed to supervise and regulate these undertakings, at home and abroad. The multiplication of central authorities in England, France, Austria, and other states is directly related to the rapid expansion of trade and manufacture under governmental guidance and supervision. Ministries of commerce and boards of trade developed everywhere, and local commissioners were sent out to break down the resistance of old-fashioned craft guilds. The development of such industries would keep the money at home. The arts and manufactures must be promoted, according to the preamble of the Edict of Henry IV of 1603, "for they are . . . the only means of preventing the taking of gold and silver out of the kingdom and thus enriching our neighbors." Therefore he sent out his intendants to discover what industries might be started and where, and to find persons interested and able to undertake such efforts.

Enforcement · It is obvious that this policy of stimulating trade and commerce entailed regulation and supervision of industrial and business life on a large scale.[12] There was no point in decreeing tariffs unless the border control was made effective for dealing with smugglers. Nor was it worthwhile to grant a manufacturing monopoly to a particular enterpriser unless an effort was made at the same time to set up authorities to enforce that privilege. The English government, which granted many trading monopolies to colonizing companies, solved the problems of enforcement by delegating governmental authority to the commercial corporations themselves. This transfer of government authority was the basic premise of Edmund Burke's fight against the practices of the East India Company. Adam Smith protested against this transfer of governmental authority to the company. For by this policy the government really allowed the establishment of a separate government which in course of time might elect to declare itself independent, as the American colonies did. After this experience, the British changed their policy and commenced to reabsorb the great commercial corporations into the government. At home, governmental authority was more readily retained and central administrative bodies continued to regulate and supervise the economy until the full-grown industrial society could dispense with most of these restrictions.[13]

The process on the Continent was quite similar, except that it lagged behind England by several generations. In fact, in the countries east of the Rhine the governments never quite released their grip on industry and commerce; or, to put it another way, industry and commerce could never quite get along without the support of the government, English competition being too powerful. Consequently, all these countries inclined to look with greater equanimity upon governmental restrictions, and even acquiesced in collectivism on a comprehensive scale. As the breakdowns of industrial society have made men eager for remedial action, opinion in Continental European countries is once more predisposed toward some variety of socialism, or *étatisme* as the French put it; that is, of governmental direction of the economy. The trend is world-wide.[14]

Stable money • The amassing of gold and silver being, as we saw, closely related to the central goal of mercantilist governments, it was only natural that they should also attempt to affect the flow of precious metals by a suitable monetary policy. Perhaps it is a travesty to call the activities in which early modern governments engaged a monetary policy.[15] Certainly they had little in common with the subtle and complicated operations which are today comprehended under that term. Nor can they be said to have been very successful at the outset. During the Middle Ages, the purchasing power of the early monetary units (pound, shilling, penny) had declined along with a constant decrease in their metallic weight. For example, in England a silver-penny's weight in troy grains fell from 22 to 12 between 1300 and 1464. This fall continued during the sixteenth and seventeenth centuries. The utter confusion into which such handling of the monetary units plunged trade and commerce caused the city of Florence, the forerunner of so much that is significant in modern government, to establish as early as 1252 a stable monetary unit, the florin, later adopted by Edward III for England but not maintained stable by his successors. Not until the eighteenth century did England get a monetary unit with a fairly stable metallic content. This followed upon the rapid deterioration of silver coins during the "clipper period" at the end of the previous century (from 1672 to 1696, when all silver was recoined). In other European countries, the decline continued all during the eighteenth century. Yet there can be little question that an ordered fiscal economy was impossible as long as such uncertainty as to the monetary units prevailed. With rising prices, tax returns were bound to fall below the requirements, even though the salaries of the officials were not adjusted to the rising price level. This consideration alone would show that a modern government with its extensive purchasing of materials and supplies must seek to maintain a stable monetary system. Yet for the longest time the temptation of getting something for nothing by making the coins smaller was irresistible. Fundamentally it was inflation, of course. Consequently, inflation cropped up time and again as a "policy" (see next paragraph). All inflation aids the debtor class, and that meant it aided industry wherever industrial establishments had been newly set up with capital from either the government or others. But the effects monetary policy had in this direction were certainly quite unintentional. Nor was all of the weight decrease intentional, as a matter of fact. Certain scholars, at least, have argued that technical inefficiency in the coining of money had a good deal to do with it.

Minting coins was a very complicated process which made certain variations in weight difficult to avoid. This fact was seized upon by shrewd men who discerned a chance of making money by sorting the coins. In the language of an Englishman of the late seventeenth century: "But tho' all the pieces together might come near the pound weight or be within remedy; yet diverse of 'em compared one with the other were very disproportionable; as was too well known to many persons who pick'd out the heavy pieces and threw 'em into the Melting pott, to fitt 'em for exportation or to supply the Silver Smiths. And 'twas a thing at last so notorious, that it 'scap'd the observation of very few."[16] Once all the heavier pieces had been withdrawn from circulation, the inducement to coin at the lower level was obviously great. Since, according to Gresham's Law, this poorer coin forthwith commenced to invade adjoining countries and to drive the better coin off the market (by making the latter desirable for hoarding), the governments of those countries would willy-nilly be driven to debase their coins also. This was particularly true as long as money consisted of metallic coins, and the governments looked upon wealth in terms of the amassing of precious metals. They were not in the happy position of the American government after the war, which could cheerfully let Europeans hoard American dollar bills, since they were nothing but paper representing the credit of the government. On the other hand, the peculiar dangers of that situation in case the government's credit collapsed were much less pronounced under the earlier conditions, as has since become amply manifest.

On the whole, governments were pretty helpless in dealing with monetary conditions. The more extravagant courts, like those of the Hapsburgs and the Bourbons, were almost always heavily in debt, and they often had recourse to quite dubious practices in order to escape the burden. The most notorious of these was the huge stock swindle into which the French government allowed itself to be persuaded around 1720 by the Scottish adventurer John Law. This man had the notion that the government's debt might be taken care of by forming a colonial corporation and selling its stock to the public. When the ensuing speculative boom collapsed, the idea of paper money, implicit in it, was utterly discredited, though with sound handling it might have made history. About the same time, the English government made the first very tentative steps in that direction through the organization of the Bank of England, which issued notes to the amount of its capital (£2,000,000). These notes were at first issued in very large denominations (£20), and constituted hardly more than 2 per cent of the total currency. Even in 1796–1797, there were only approximately £10,000,000 available, or about 10 per cent. Yet a significant beginning had been made here, soon to be followed by other governments. The Bank of France was established by Napoleon in 1800 and followed the English example. In the meantime, methods of coining had been steadily improving, and by the beginning of the nineteenth century governments were already on the road toward effective management and control of this difficult technique, so vitally important for real prosperity.

Colonial policy • Though colonial policy is usually treated as a part of foreign policy, it exerted the profoundest influence upon the growth of the modern economy and its government, and it formed an absolutely essential part of its mercantilist scheme. As we have said before, colonies made it possible to safeguard markets for a country's industrial products and, what was even more important at first, to control sources of raw material supply.[17] Gold, around which mercantilist policy has been found to revolve, was brought back from America in large quantities by the Spanish *Conquistadores*, and its impact upon government was so decisive that one writer has gone so far as to say that "modern government emerged from the silver mines of Mexico and Peru and from the gold mines of Brazil" (Sombart). This is of course meant only as a necessary, not as a sufficient, condition: without such an abundant production of precious metals, modern government could not have blossomed forth as it did. For one thing, the arms of Hapsburg would not have been nearly as potent against the popular forces in Germany without American gold. Likewise, it is quite imaginable that the Stuarts might have triumphed in England if the North American trading companies which they had chartered had discovered gold, instead of land for colonists. It is interesting that Charles I tried to capture part of the rich India trade, but he only succeeded in throwing the East India Company's rich traders behind the Puritans and Pym. The wealth of the traders thus reinforced constitutionalism, and England was forced to travel the slower road of converting an agricultural society into an industrial one. This gave superior strength to the great commercial families (Whigs), and strengthened the aristocratic rather than the monarchical forces. But as American gold was claimed by the *Conquistadores* for the royal chest of Spain, so the agricultural produce of the colonies was restricted to London merchants. The Navigation Act of 1660 (1. Charles II, c. 18) well expresses in its Article XIII the prevailing temper of the time: "No sugar, tobacco, cotton-wool, indigo, ginger, fustic, and other dying wools, of the growth or manufacture of our Asian, African, or American colonies shall be shipped from the said colonies to any place but to England, Ireland, or to some other of His Majestys said plantations, there to be landed."

Much of this tale is very familiar to Americans, since these policies stand at the threshold of their national history. Yet it seems desirable to recall the facts here, in order to show how profound a relation they bore to the early growth of modern government. Besides the policies already mentioned, colonial mercantilism prohibited colonies from manufacturing those products which the mother country produced, claimed a monopoly of transportation to and from the colonies for the mother country, and imposed duties between the several colonies and between the colonies and the mother country. This entailed a vast amount of additional governmental activity, and ministries for the colonies became a settled part of the great colonizing nations. Since these colonies consisted almost invariably of conquests beyond the seas and were hotly contested, they required very considerable military forces, both land and naval, but particularly the latter. Here, then, is another vital point of contact between the mercantilist policy of furthering prosperity by governmental action, and the absolutist policy of territorial expansion, the one involving administrative and the other military efforts on an unprecedented scale.

These colonial policies constitute "the old colonial system."[16] This system was justified in terms of mercantilism, but was of primary advantage to the merchants. There is little exaggeration in the judgment of Adam Smith when he declared: "Of the greater part of the regulations concerning the colony trade, the merchants who carry it on, it must be observed, have been the principal advisers. We must not wonder, therefore, if, in the greater part of them, their interest has been more considered than either that of the colonies or that of the mother country." Thus the colonial policies grew in this period out of the objective of prosperity, rather than of territorial expansion. "What England primarily looked for in the colonies was neither extension of territory per se, nor overseas aggregations of Englishmen, but goods and markets." It was the belief that commodities could be secured without loss of precious metals which underlay the "old colonial system," — an outlook markedly different from later colonial imperialism.[19]

Conclusion · In conclusion, the question may be raised as to whether the mercantilist economic policies were basically economic or governmental in origin. In one view, they were definitely governmental. Much effective support came from those classes in society which were benefiting from the policies. It was the primary fallacy of the *laissez-faire* outlook to assume that the economy is a system of nature rather than a system of methods used by men in the pursuit of whatever ends they have in view. Mercantilism was a system for unifying the country and increasing its power as well as for increasing its wealth. The increase in wealth was sought through manipulating both commodities and money. The builders of modern administrative government believed in the ability of government to do all these things, and they believed this in England no less than on the Continent. But the industrial revolution which they set in motion proved too much for government to handle. The social classes which rose with it, the commercial and professional middle class, eventually recognized that greater prosperity could be achieved through limiting governmental, i.e. administrative, participation. But this historical limitation should not blind us to the achievement of the governmental administrators who built the modern "state." This is the more true since recent breakdowns of free enterprise have brought a new development of governmental administrative participation in the economy.

Justice and the Judicial Function

Introduction: justice and government · Rival conceptions of law · "Artificial reason" of the law · The views of Hooker, Locke, and Rousseau on the importance of laws · The judicial process · The rule of precedent and the judicial process · Judicial organization in Continental Europe · Bench and bar and the Act of Settlement · The judiciary and the rule of law in Prussia: a contrast · Judicial restraint as the beginning of constitutional government · Administrative law · The *Conseil d'État* · French administrative justice and American problems · Conclusion

Introduction: justice and government · "Justice is the end of government," *The Federalist* noted. "It ever has been and ever will be pursued until it be obtained, or until liberty be lost in the pursuit." Justice has often been expounded as the primary, or even the only, "ideal" purpose of government. This is the view of Plato, especially as stated in *The Republic*. That marvellous dialogue, perhaps Plato's greatest, bears the subtitle: "or about the just." But do Plato and *The Federalist* mean the same "justice"? Plato himself makes it quite clear that he is not talking about "states as they actually are," but about an ideal commonwealth, perhaps realizable with great good luck, but certainly not then in existence. Careful reading soon shows that what Plato meant by "justice" includes a large part of morals. That government should be conceived and carried on with the objective of making its citizens "good men" is an idea which Christian thinkers such as St. Augustine and Thomas Aquinas rejected. It seems to modern man questionable primarily because of the totalitarian implications of employing the force of governmental power for such ethical purposes. In any case, justice as an objective of modern government, in the sense in which objectives are taken here, is a more limited concept. It is neither identical with law, nor entirely transcending law:; nor is it the subjective quality in the individual which makes him try to achieve justice. The ancient Aristotelian conception of justice as related to equality distinguished between corrective and distributive justice. Distributive justice is concerned with equal distribution of goods among members of the community; corrective justice with the righting of wrongs. If a contract has been broken or a tort has been done, then corrective justice seeks to provide adequate compensation to the wronged party; if a crime has been committed, then proper punishment is meted out to the wrongdoer. In Aristotle's view, injustice occurs when the established equilibrium in the community is disturbed. Aristotle's notion of equality is related to such an equilibrium. "The law looks only to the difference created by the injury and treats the men as previously equal, where the one does and the other suffers injury, or the one has done and the other suffered harm," a leading jurist has summed up the position.[1] Thus justice as a primary objective of modern government is concerned with two things: to insure that all persons are put in a position to get what they are entitled to under the law, and to insure that no one is injured, that is to say, suffers injury to life or limb, as old phrase goes, unless he has infringed the law. But the phrase "the law" must not be taken to mean merely the positive enactments of legislative authorities; it encompasses standards of fairness, reasonableness, and the like, which the judge must bring into play at certain points.[2]

A large part of the task of settling the problems connected with this objective of justice arises in disputes between private parties. From the governmental standpoint, this means that the maintenance of justice is closely related to the task of maintaining internal peace. Unless people could be reasonably certain of securing their "rights" through a process of adjudication, violence would often flare up. Hence one of the most ancient governmental functions is unquestionably that of settling disputes between members of the group. Among the several methods and techniques developed to fulfill this function, the most permanent are judicial. Far back in prehistoric times, verdicts were pronounced and punishment meted out to the evildoer in accordance with traditional customs.[3] The legendary Germanic chieftain, with a long beard, sitting under an oak tree and performing this crucial function, is not peculiar to one racial group, as the Romantics once imagined; he could be duplicated in practically every other land. This tribal chieftain, if successful, eventually emerged as a king surrounded by a group of elder statesmen, a council of wise men, the Witenagemot of Anglo-Saxon times. Its members were counselors of the king, the bishops, the ealdormen, and the thegns. Besides exercising many other functions of government, this great council sat as a high court of justice over all persons and causes. The function of a high court was later inherited by Parliament, or rather by the king in Parliament, as the ancient phrase goes. Throughout the Middle Ages, judicial work was the central function of Parliament. It is one of the most significant developments of modern government that this function was ultimately differentiated from the lawmaking, the legislative, function, and allocated in large part to separate organs and officials. Indeed, from the legal point of view, the most significant feature of modern government is this differentiation of the judicial process. This was clearly stated by Montesquieu, who, generalizing from English practice, considered an independent judiciary the essence of constitutional government. In the *Spirit of the Laws* he observes: "There is no liberty yet, if the power to judge is not separated from the legislative and executive power. . . . In the majority of the kingdoms of Europe, the government is moderated, because the prince leaves the exercise of the judicial power to his subjects." Montesquieu's idea of a moderated government corresponds, in general, to the notion of a constitutional government.

Rival conceptions of law · Differentiation of the judicial function could not commence, of course, until the idea of "making" laws had become distinct. In the Middle Ages there existed, broadly speaking, no such idea. Law was assumed largely to be something already in existence, fixed and immutable. All that was thought necessary was to find out what this law was, to interpret and determine it (*jus dicere*). Custom was supposed to be the fountain of this law. But custom is local, and the inconveniences which resulted from the great variety of rules seriously troubled medieval governments. One ideal weapon, the Roman law, was available against this multiplicity of local laws. It fitted in with the prevailing notion that law is something immutable, and had the further advantage of stemming from a single source. The Roman law was, however, patterned on the needs not of a feudal, but of a highly civilized society, built on commerce and industry. It was, to that extent, a welcome instrument to the commercial and industrial classes in their conflicts with the feudal landowning classes. Emperor, pope, and king, in so far as they relied on the urban classes against their feudal aristocracy, alike sought refuge and relief in its provisions. However, the struggle between royal and papal authority, which was so significant an aspect of the later Middle Ages, made national kings insist increasingly on their own authority. More particularly in England, a common law, expounded by the king's judges, rapidly amalgamated the more useful ideas of the Roman law with the broader principles of Germanic customs. This development is most strikingly illustrated by the work of Bracton (1216–1272). As a result, England already possessed a substantial body of common national law at the time when elsewhere the Reformation, by eliminating most of the ecclesiastical jurisdictions, for the first time made possible the consolidation of national systems of law. On this law judges could base their decisions in opposing the royal claims to supremacy in the field of lawmaking, which Bodin's sovereignty had so ingeniously vindicated for the royal authority. Coke's famous claim that the king is *under* the law assumed a significance which it could not have had when no national low was extant.[4] In the course of the century from 1520 to 1620 (the Reformation), it became increasingly clear that in England parliamentary statutes were laws made by the king in Parliament. Legislation became an acknowledged fact; but it took quite some time until it was generally recognized. To be sure, Sir Thomas Smith in his *English Commonwealth*[5] distinctly speaks of a legislative function apart from the judicial function of Parliament. Sir Edward Coke's entire work on the common law is also permeated by this distinction, which is implied in his celebrated dictum that "the common law is more worthy than the statute law." Yet it is not easy to fix with any exactness the beginnings of the legislative activity which has become one of the main characteristics of modern parliaments, or to assign the causes of its growth (McIlwain).[6] Probably the many statutes consequent upon the Reformation and involved in the separation of the Church of England from the Catholic Church represent a first genuine outburst of legislation in the modern sense. Here was a genuine rupture in the community, and whatever was done in the form of parliamentary enactment could not but appear in the light of man-made law to those opposed to it. Sir Thomas More was executed because he would not take an oath established by parliamentary "legislation." And when, under Mary, the opposing faction gained the upper hand, and repealed a good many statutes, only a blind man could have failed to perceive that laws were made and unmade by human beings. Yet the older idea constantly recurs. "King Henry VIII," Bacon recalls, in suggesting the making of a Digest of English Law to James I, "was authorized by Parliament to nominate thirty-two commissioners to purge the canon law, and to make it agreeable to the law of God, and the law of the land." This idea that all laws should be related to the "fundamental law" of the land gained ground constantly. In Dr. Bonham's case, Sir Edward Coke, then Chief Justice of the Court of Common Pleas, claimed "that in many cases the common law will control acts of Parliament and sometimes adjudge them to be utterly void." The difficulty in extracting the true meaning of this statement lies in the fact that "acts" of Parliament could, in that period, refer to judicial decisions as well as to legislative enactments. At the trial of the Earl of Strafford, in 1641, a member of Parliament declared that if any question arises concerning either a custom or an act of Parliament, "the Common Law of England, the First, the Primitive and the General Law, that's the Rule and Expositor of them, and of their several extents," must be decisive. In other words, the common law was supposed to contain within itself broad basic principles regarding the procedure and limitation of governmental organs which no one of them could undertake to change. To this day, the "common law" tradition has retained something of the older notion in the emphasis placed upon court decisions.

Bacon's attempt to supersede this idea of a fundamental law (which he recognized as judge-made law) by resuscitating the Roman doctrine of a law of nature as the rule of right reason failed utterly. This is striking and significant, since natural-law doctrines were so very successful on the Continent as pathmakers for monarchical absolutism. Bacon wanted to place the law of nature above both common law and statute law. By the "law of nature" he meant, of course, the rule of right natural reason. This encountered the fierce opposition of Sir Edward Coke, who in answer evolved the doctrine of the "artificial reason of the law." This peculiar notion has been of decisive significance in the development of the judicial process.

"Artificial reason" of the law • The doctrine of the "artificial reason," then, grew out of an argument as to whether the king was or was not above the law. Sir Edward Coke had been restricting the jurisdiction of the ecclesiastical Court of High Commission. He was asked to discuss the matter with the clergy in the presence of King James November 13, 1608, and he roundly asserted that he would not be able to accept the Romanist interpretation of the clergy. James, taking exception to this dogmatic view, declared that he was the supreme judge, and that under him were all the courts. To this Coke replied: "The common law protecteth the King." "That is a traitorous speech," King James shouted back at him in great anger; "the King protecteth the law, not the law the King. The King maketh judges and bishops." He then proceeded to denounce Coke so vehemently, shaking his fists at him, that Coke "fell flat on all fower" before the king, and humbly begged his pardon.[7] But the matter did not long rest there. In 1616, a similar quarrel ensued over whether the king could stay a court proceeding which he considered contrary to his prerogative. Under the leadership of Coke, then Lord Chief Justice of King's Bench, the judges had claimed such a proceeding to be contrary to law. To this claim James answered that although he never studied the common law of England, yet he was not ignorant of any points which belong to a king to know.[8] Therefore his idea that "natural reason" unrelated to a knowledge of the law of the land could be employed in interpreting statutes was rejected by Coke in the most explicit form. "Reason is the life of the law, nay the common law itself is nothing else but reason; which is to be understood as an artificial perfection of reason, gotten by long study, observation and experience, and not as every man's natural reason . . . by many successions of ages [the law of England] has been fined and refined by an infinite number of grave and learned men, and by long experience grown to such a perfection, for the government of this

realm, as the old rule may be justly verified of it, that no man out of his private reason ought to be wiser than the law, which is the perfection of reason."⁹ Thus reason is clearly not a standard, philosophical or otherwise, brought to the law from outside, but the essence of the law itself, acquired in the process of learning the law. This notion is not only historically significant, but has a certain general validity. For it is only when general rules, embodied in legislative enactments, are transformed into detailed statements applicable to everyday life that they become part of the living law.

The views of Hooker, Locke, and Rousseau on the importance of laws • To show the strong sentiment regarding the importance of laws and of legislation as the process of making such laws, it may be well to cite here three leading constitutional theorists, Hooker, Locke, and Rousseau. Rousseau describes the fundamental nature of a republic in terms of law: "I therefore give the name 'Republic' to every State that is governed by laws, no matter what the form of its administration may be: for only in such a case does the public interest govern, and the *res publica* rank as a *reality*."¹⁰ Likewise, Locke's discussion of the forms of a commonwealth is based on the conception of law as the essence of a commonwealth: ". . . for the form of government depending upon the placing the supreme power, which is the legislative, it being impossible to conceive that an inferior power should prescribe to a superior, or any but the supreme make laws, according as the power of making laws is placed, such is the form of the commonwealth."¹¹ And Hooker concludes his first book of *The Laws of Ecclesiastical Polity* thus: ". . . of Law there can be no less acknowledged, than that her seat is the bosom of God, her voice the harmony of the world: all things in heaven and earth do her homage, the very least as feeling her care, and the greatest as not exempted from her power: both Angels and men and creatures of what condition soever, though each in different sort and manner . . . admiring her as the mother of their peace and joy."¹²

The judicial process • To the judicial *function* corresponds a distinctive *process*. This process is typically that of deciding what is just in a controversy between two or more contending parties. It is a refined form of a much more basic and universal process, that of dispute settling. In a sense, the settling of disputes is the primordial internal function which a political order has to perform, antedating the making of rules and the application of such rules. In the broadest, most general sense, the process of dispute settling always involves at least three: the accuser, the accused, and the settler. A developed judicial process presupposes an additional element, namely a system of law in terms of which the dispute may be settled.¹³ The decision may be rendered by one man, or by several men acting as a body. Characteristically it offers the contending parties an opportunity to state their case to the best of their ability, either stating it themselves or through a representative (counsel); such statement may be cast in terms of more or less formalized law, but the judicial process when fully developed presupposes some kind of rational basis (law) in terms of which all arguments, including the decision of the judge, are cast. It is conventionally called "adversary procedure."

This basic pattern of the judicial process can be elaborated and refined in many different ways; each system of law is apt to have some features that are distinctive. The knowledge of these is vital to anyone who wishes to "practice law" under that system. This fact may raise very difficult problems if an attempt is made to constitute a court composed of judges trained in different systems of law, as happened at Nuremberg in connection with the International War Crimes Trials. But such difficulties can be composed, provided there is agreement on the basic aspects of the judicial process.[14]

Increasing sophistication concerning all rationalizations and the emphasis on semantics as a "tyranny of words" have tended to produce a facile cynicism concerning the judicial process. Wisecracks about the judge at the breakfast table have their value; for they call attention to the human failings of judges. In spite of these, the significance and value of the judicial process is great, even though the propositions contained in legal judgments are not seen as eternal truths. Such generalizations may be as important and influential as absolute and immutable laws once were. Even though one appreciates the irrational forces which affect judicial conduct, the traditional beliefs, acquired convictions, and the deep-rooted prejudices which mold the judge's interpretations of the law, he continues to realize the essential service which is rendered by the man who seeks to find the just decision in the light of all the available facts and rules. For even if the fabric of the law be considered a huge web of effective make-believe, the life of the community and the maintenance of government are dependent upon it.

The rule of precedent and the judicial process · The artificial reason which permeates the judicial process is, in turn, so firmly grounded in the tradition of *stare decisis*,[15] that is, the idea that the courts must abide by rules set up in previous decisions, that some consideration must be given to this important technique of the judicial process. Rules set up by previous decisions are called *precedents*. That judges are guided by such precedents is hardly surprising. "It takes effort and time to solve problems. Once you have solved one it seems foolish to reopen it. . . . Both inertia and convenience speak for building further on what you have already built; for incorporating the decision once made, the solution once worked out, into your operating technique without re-examination of what earlier went into reaching your solution." In other words, the following of precedent is firmly rooted in human experience, and characteristic of all human activity. It is the governmental equivalent of what, in the community at large, we know as folkways, and of what, in the individual, we know as habit. As Justice Cardozo once put it, "the power of precedent . . . is the power of the beaten track." And even if the judges were willing to discard their previous decisions, the lawyers at the bar pleading their cases are constantly reminding the judges of these former decisions, and thus keep the courts conscious of such precedents. What is more, the precedents not only stabilize and unify governmental practices, but they make available to the inexperienced newcomer the accumulated experience of the past. Perhaps they also heighten the sense of responsibility of the judge who confronts an unprecedented situation, since he knows that the precedent which he sets may become the guiding star of many judges following him. It would, however, be foolish to assume that all cases can be decided by precedent. As a matter of fact, precedent makes for change as well as stability. How? Essentially through the use of two rather contradictory views of precedent which one might call the strict and the loose view. According to the strict view, the judge must make certain just what it was that the precedent decided, he must confine the case to its particular facts. This view is applied to unwelcome precedents. It is the technique for freeing the lawyer and the judge of precedents. The loose view, on the other hand, maintains that the court has decided any or all points on which it chose to rest a case, no matter how broad the statement. This loose view accordingly provides lawyer and judge alike with a technique for capitalizing welcome precedents. The doctrine of precedent is therefore two-faced, and if applied to the same precedent at the same time, it yields contradictory results. It is apparent how this equivocal "rule" provides for both stability and change, by offering a technique for getting rid of previous rules, as well as for bringing in previous rules. Broadly considered, it is a most extraordinary make-believe calculated to maintain the continuity of the legal system and to bind the new judge to the experience of the past.

Judicial organization in Continental Europe • On the European Continent, the ingenious make-believe of the rule of precedent does not prevail.[16] Do Continental judges then fail to follow precedent? Of course not. Precedent, we saw, is so much a reflection of general human experience with law that we find it wherever human beings pursue the same tasks for any length of time. But European judges call their following of precedent by a different name, namely *usus fori*, that is to say, the "usage of the Court."

Continental practice focuses attention on the corporate activity of the courts rather than on individual pronouncements. There are no "dissenting opinions." The decisions themselves are much less elaborate in most jurisdictions. The judges are, in fact, considered a species of government officials. Organized into a distinctive group, quite separate from the practicing lawyers, or "members of the bar," the judges are members of a hierarchically organized bureaucracy. Into this bureaucracy men enter after appropriate training and remain in it for the rest of their lives. Until recently, at the top of the system there was a ministry of justice which supervised the system, attended to promotions, and in general acted as a directing force in making judicial experience available to the legislature. As a consequence, ministries of justice have been the spearhead in promoting the recurrent great codifications of Continental law, of which the French *Code Civil* is the most striking instance, although the Prussian and Austrian codes preceded it. A prime motive for the individual judge in following the precedents in the interpretation of these codes is the ministry's influence upon promotions.

Under the Fourth Republic, the French Ministry of Justice lost much of its power over the nomination and promotion of judges to a Superior Council of the Judiciary, appointed half by the President of the Republic and the Council itself and half by the Assembly. In the Constitution of 1958, however, the Ministry regained its power to suggest nominations to all but the higher judicial posts, while the Superior Council retained the right only to "give its opinion" on these nominations and to propose nominations for the higher offices. Nevertheless, this Council, now appointed by the President, two members directly and seven from lists drawn up by judicial bodies, has, it is claimed, succeeded in reducing the number of political appointments.[17] The Germans have likewise retained the system of ministerial control of all but the highest judges, restricting only the removal of judges and proclaiming them "independent and subject only to the law" (Article 97).

Thus we find that the two most important practical objectives of the doctrine of precedent, (1) to bridge the gap between experience and inexperience, and (2) to maintain relative continuity of the legal system, are here achieved through administrative devices, to wit, an adequate apprentice training and a judicial career leading to the higher judicial positions. The dangerous potentialities of this method of bureaucratizing the judiciary were revealed in the extent to which judges in Germany and Italy betrayed their judicial trust under Fascist inflence.[18]

The contrast in judicial organization and precedent between the European Continent and common-law countries is in keeping with the general lines of differentiation between the political traditions of England (and America) as compared with those of the Continent. In England (and

America), reliance is placed upon believed-in traditional groupways resting upon common consent as compared to authoritarian, administrative devices. In order to understand better the cleavage which underlies this differentiation in the judicial process, it will be helpful to describe the particular group with whose ways we are here concerned. In England and America judges usually are appointed from among the practicing lawyers, so that there does not exist any distinct judicial profession. Instead, judges are included in the lawyer's guild.

Bench and bar and the Act of Settlement • The lawyers' guild in English-speaking lands is one of the most ancient and honorable professions. It goes back to the thirteenth century.[19] As we have seen, England had acquired centralized institutions and was in the process of acquiring a national common law as well. This common law was being developed by royal judges and drew extensively on custom for its sources. Since the universities (under ecclesiastical guidance) taught Roman and canon law, the practice grew up of teaching the common law in fraternal organizations, of which the four so-called Inns of Court were the most important. The education given at these Inns was primarily of a practical nature; it was an education which trained students for their work both at the bar and on the bench. In connection with this development, the custom grew up that the judges must be taken from among the practicing lawyers, rather than from the universities where the Roman and canon law was taught. Eventually these Inns of Court acquired the exclusive right to call men to the bar, through calling them to the so-called bar of the Inn. Thus legal education became a monopoly of the professional class itself, uniting as it did in one body both judges and advocates. This development of an all-inclusive professional guild was of the greatest political consequence. At first, and well into the sixteenth century, the common lawyers constituted a force strengthening the monarchical position in its struggle with the Catholic Church and the local feudal lords. But their allegiance shifted gradually as the apologists for royal power and prerogative in the field of government, such as Bacon and King James, began to expound truly Romanist pretensions as far as the law and its adjudication were concerned. Thus the position taken by Sir Edward Coke that the king is under the law is a consistent expression of the traditional groupways which the legal guild had developed in the preceding age.

It is only against this background of a consolidated legal profession, priding itself upon its mastery of the "artificial reason" of the law, that the emergence of judicial "independence" can be evaluated. Truly communal control effected through the lawyers' guild had become so well established and "independence" from autocratic governmental control served the dominant interest of the community so well, that it was not challenged until the reform movement of Bentham and the Utilitarians began to press the neglected interest of the town laborer. The role of the judiciary in protecting exploitation and injustice was mercilessly portrayed in the novels of Charles Dickens. But the reformers sought the remedy in changed legislation, rather than in making the judiciary dependent upon politics, as was done in the United States. Here, in many local jurisdictions, the election of judges was the "democratic" answer to an excess of conservatism on the bench. In England, it would seem wisely, reliance has been placed upon the control which professional standards and judgments tend to exert. The same is true, of course, for the higher judicial positions in America. Without adequate consideration of this collegiate control, judicial independence would indeed spell judicial "tyranny." The irresponsibility of such a tyranny is avoided by the fraternal community of bench and bar. It continues to make the English and the American judge highly sensitive to the criticism of his brethren off the bench. As long as judges held office during royal pleasure, they were in some difficulty whenever "the royal pleasure" ran contrary to predominant lawyers' sentiment. Coke made the common law, as we have seen, the basis of his attacks upon James's conception of the prerogative as of divine right. Is it surprising that James's instinctive feeling toward lawyers should have been hostile? On the other hand, it was rather natural that the legal brotherhood should have felt that the royal displeasure should only be displeasure with the conduct of judicial business, according to the established law of the land. Hence, the demand arose that judges should hold office during good behavior, or, as the ancient phrase goes, *quamdiu se bene gesserint.* This aspiration was realized in the Act of Settlement, which thereby supplemented the Bill of Rights in a very important regard. But what does "good behavior" mean? The standard of conduct implied by that phrase is set by the collegial and fraternal organization of bench and bar. The compelling force of professional ethics was thus given governmental recognition.

The judiciary and the rule of law in Prussia: a contrast · The different situation on the Continent is strikingly illustrated by the famous case of the miller Arnold which occurred under Frederick II of Prussia, in 1779–1780.[20] A technically correct, but in substance unjust, decision led to the summary dismissal and imprisonment of six judges. They had incurred the royal displeasure, because they did *not* employ the rule of right reason, but followed the artificial reason of the law, and rendered a judgment which favored the wealthy landowners to the detriment of a simple peasant-miller.

Frederick's despotic, yet popular, action was widely acclaimed throughout Europe; yet in Prussia it had the unhappy consequence that direct complaints to the king were pouring in from all sides. The king himself was profoundly worried, lest he had punished an innocent man. It was so affirmed after the king's death. Perhaps the most striking result of this case was the king's perseverance in having a general code prepared. This code was to be based upon reason and the Prussian common law. It was, in other words, conceived in the same terms as Francis Bacon's celebrated proposal for the codification of the laws of England. But whereas Bacon's plan foundered upon the solid rock of opposition of the lawyers' guild, the Prussian code was completed in 1794, and thus became the first of a long series of codifications which characterize the law of European constitutional governments in the nineteenth century. These codes mark, broadly speaking, the passing from the arbitrary government of absolutist monarchy to the "government according to law" which followed it. But the codes are, at the same time, striking expressions of a conception of government that subjects the judicial process to general rules.

In disposing of the case of the miller as he did, Frederick II followed his father, Frederick William I, who had been filled with a deep distrust of the courts. He looked upon them as the last refuge of feudal privilege and patrician intrigue. The upper classes were so strongly entrenched in these local courts that Frederick William saw no other escape than to develop separate jurisdictions where judicial functions would be exercised by his own administrative officials. His endeavors in this direction closely parallel the development of the Court of Star Chamber and the Court of High Commission under the Tudors in England. But whereas England was already a united realm with a strongly developed judiciary expounding a national common law, the kingdom of Prussia consisted of scattered fragments in each of which the established courts attempted to maintain a local law. They consequently lost ground constantly to administrative officials. This conflict led to the demand for a common law. The consequent return to a system of strictly judicial procedure was the prime object of the reforms of Samuel von Cocceji.[21] Under his influence Frederick the Great decided to submit himself and all his administrative officials to the law. Thus, in 1748, he decreed that "the judicial boards should decide the case according to the written law." And even though later certain cases were exempted from this general instruction, and were declared suable before administrative tribunals, it was provided that in all these cases the same procedure should be used as that employed in the ordinary courts; in other words a measure of due process of law was guaranteed. We have here, together with the recognition of some kind of "rule of law," the emergence of the idea of administrative law. The idea of administrative law is rooted in the Continental notion of a royal or public domain, of the public needs in military, tax, and police matters, and of a code of behavior for the official hierarchy itself.

Judicial restraint as the beginning of constitutional government · A generation ago, administrative law was the occasion of a heated controversy in which A. V. Dicey maintained that such law was utterly alien to English and American legal traditions, and that any growth of it must be viewed with profound alarm. In his statement of the problem he harked back to the time-honored argument that law when administered by administrative agencies becomes arbitrary and bureaucratic. It is the fundamental problem of how to enforce responsibility. Though a king cherish the noble sentiment that he is the first servant of his state, it is not enough if he is left to himself in determining whether he has lived up to this standard. Now the least objectionable method, from the point of view of monarchy, appears historically to have been the proposition that the king is bound by the law. We have seen how this rule was insisted upon by Sir Edward Coke in his struggle with James I, and how it underlay the judicial reforms of Cocceji. But the question immediately arises as to who is to say what the law is. In other words, the problem of who determines the personnel of the courts is politically the decisive question. Just as the control of many courts by the Catholic Church had seemed an unbearable situation from the point of view of national monarchies in the late Middle Ages, so the control of the courts by the patrician classes represented in parliaments and diets had carried with it economic and social implications which aroused bitter struggles. Since the patrician classes were quite prepared to interpret the law in their own favor, their control of the courts was resented not only by the king, but by the common people as well. This issue is related, therefore, to the conflict of various groups in the community, each attempting to secure supremacy.[22] The common man cannot be said to have been on the side of judicial supremacy at a time when courts were closely linked to the patrician class. And yet, the era of modern constitutional government commences with the establishment of judicial restraints upon the executive branch of the government. This is due to the fact that such judicial restraints mark the beginning of a division or separation of power in the community which the advocates and builders of absolute monarchy had denied. They, like their modern brethren advocating dictatorial forms of government, were persuaded that nothing but a complete concentration of power could hope to overcome the grave disorders which religious disunity had produced.

Administrative law • From this point of view, administrative law, that is, the administration of certain bodies of law by administrative agencies, is undoubtedly a step in the direction of concentration of powers.[23] It is, therefore, bound to be welcomed by all those who have a leaning in the direction of dictatorial methods, provided it is employed in support of objectives which they approve. Since, broadly speaking, the expansion of governmental activities is the goal of reformers or "progressives," we find these groups actively supporting the expansion of administrative jurisdiction. But it should be apparent that efficiency, expediency, and utility are formulas which can be diverted to various ends, as nothing is inherently and ultimately efficient, expedient, or useful. It all depends finally upon what you want to do or have. On the other hand, it cannot with any show of factual evidence be claimed that the appearance of administrative law, that is, the exercise of judicial functions by administrative agencies in limited fields, heralds the disappearance of the "supremacy of law" or of constitutional government. On the contrary, the devolpment of administrative law in France and elsewhere is a definite achievement of the constitutional era. For it does not signify the supremacy of administrative officials over the law, but its exact opposite, namely, the regularization of all administrative conduct in terms of legal rules. The central concern of administrative law has been the legal limitation of administrative "discretion." Thus the first principle of administrative law is that no administrative measure which imposes a burden upon anyone can be taken without legal authorization. Through this principle, "discretion" is enclosed within the narrowest possible limits. It may be claimed, in fact, that the exercise of judicial functions by administrative officials, which so thoroughly alarmed Dicey, is, when seen in historical perspective, an indication of the fact that large areas of formally administrative activity are actually judicial in nature, or are in the process of being judicialized. The failure to develop truly judicial bodies and techniques in England and America has occasioned criticism, and at times violent criticism. It is difficult, however, to arrive at a balanced judgment. Such a judgment is well expressed by Harold Laski: "If administrative tribunals are to command public confidence it may be suggested that their membership must satisfy certain historic canons on which public confidence appears to depend. Their composition must be stable in character. The minister or department head must not be able to change their membership at his discretion or to overrule their findings on issues of fact. . . . The men appointed to such tribunals must be known and chosen for their competence in the theme of their particular jurisdiction. Such tribunals should moreover always contain a legal element. These canons are in fact satisfied by the French and German systems; it cannot be said that they have yet been satisfied in the tribunals which the necessities of the modern state have led Great Britain and the United States to erect."

The Conseil d'État · It may be well to examine a bit more closely the apex of the French system, the *Conseil d'État*.[24] It is a common mistake to describe the French Council of State as primarily, if not exclusively, a judicial body. In fact, this council combines its judicial activities with very important administrative functions, particularly in the field of ordinance-making (*réglements* and *décrets*). The judicial functions constitute the work of merely one section of the Council. The regular members of the Council, a total of about one hundred and seventy councilors, masters of petition, and auditors, are the only ones to participate in the work of this judicial branch of the Council. The majority of these members are career men who have entered the Council as assistant auditors (*auditeurs de seconde classe*) on the basis of a competitive examination, and have been promoted on merit. Councilors and masters of petitions taken from outside the Council are not spoilsmen without preparation; usually they are career officials and university professors who, the French believe, add a valuable element of flexibility to the Council's work. To the extent that the *Conseil* is a court, it is objectionable that even the regular members of the Council hold office at the pleasure of the government. It is argued that since the Council is engaged in administrative as well as judicial work, tenure during good behavior is rather impracticable. It is, as in the case of administrative commissions in the United States, a question of the right balance of advantages and disadvantages; for the loss of administrative experience may not be sufficiently balanced by the gain of complete judicial independence. Certainly thorough familiarity with many branches of administration (the regular members rotate from section to section) is no mean gain to men who are called upon to settle judicially contentions or disputes (*contentieux*) which arise over administrative activity. Though many such disputes are raised and settled in ordinary courts, even in France, the bulk is brought before the Council of State. Administrative law, therefore, cannot be defined in terms of the jurisdiction of the Council of State — a tendency which is ever-present in common-law countries. It is much more comprehensive, and includes, in the language of Professor Hauriou, that branch of public law which regulates (1) the organization of public administration and of the several administrative officers, (2) the powers and privileges which these administrative officers possess in order that they may operate the public services, and (3) the exercise of these powers and privileges through the prerogative, specially through the procedure of official action (*action d'office*), and the disputes which result therefrom. In considering these questions of administrative adjudication under the Council of State, we must keep in mind, then, that administrative law comprises a broader sphere, and that the Council has administrative functions other than those of adjudication. Furthermore, in the opinion of a leading scholar in this field the Council of State is more than an administrative court. It not only maintains judicial control of Public Administration, but participates both directly and indirectly in the administrative process itself and also influences government policies by advising the legislatures on legal matters. These administrative and advisory semi-legislative functions of the Council constitute unique and significant aspects of its activities which must not be neglected.[25]

French administrative justice and American problems • Perhaps the greatest difficulty which arises in connection with a separate set of administrative courts is that of a conflict of jurisdiction between such courts and the ordinary judicial courts. In France that problem is settled by the organization of a separate court of conflicts (*Tribunal de Conflits*). This *Tribunal de Conflits* is essentially a court interpreting the constitution, since the whole separation of administrative adjudication rests upon the French doctrine of the separation of powers (see below, ch. X). There is no reason why in the United States this sort of problem could not be settled by the Supreme Court, which is the interpreter of the constitution anyway. A case concerning an alleged conflict of jurisdiction can only be raised by an administrative court, because according to the French conception it is a matter of protecting matters involving the government against interference by the ordinary courts. In the United States, it would undoubtedly be more in keeping with constitutional traditions if that question could be raised by ordinary courts as well. But there is another side to the development of truly judicial bodies in the administrative field, which is equally fundamental, and which seems to stand in the way of building up a high administrative court on the French model, as has been suggested. The French administrative courts have grown out of what is known in France as consultative, as contrasted with active, bodies of administration. This idea of consultative, advisory bodies goes back to the *Ancien Régime,* was retained during and after the revolution, and remains a significant feature of French as well as of other European administrative systems. The personnel of these consultative bodies is considered a sort of passive administrator. In the United States, consultative bodies are of very minor significance, though the Governor's Council in Massachusetts shows the persistence of these older (monarchical) forms. What is more, these consultative bodies have not been active in usurping the growing amount of judicial work which modern administration entails. In keeping with the tendencies of the federal government, many administrative boards and commissions with quasi-judicial as well as quasi-legislative functions have been created. Their work is quite uncoordinated. In France, where such a consultative body existed at the center of the government, it offered a personnel which was at once conversant with administration and yet not actively involved in the administrative decisions. It could, therefore, lay claim to a position of neutrality and impartiality such as a judicial body must possess if its decisions are to be accepted. French writers are correct in emphasizing the fact that the Council of State and the lower administrative courts are *public* bodies, and thus clearly distinguished from the secret working of any kind of appeal to active administrators. Even though the latter device through long periods of history has proved a satisfactory instrument for the maintenance of political order (Catholic Church), there can be no question of comparing such an appeal with any sort of appeal to an independent administrative judiciary. The procedure before the Council of State is essentially that of an investigating commission; that is, the case is conducted by the judges themselves. This is the final point of real difficulty in applying the remarkable experience of the French Council of State to American problems; for this kind of procedure does not satisfy the standards of the American constitutional tradition. But "administrative law," whether we like it or not, is on the march. Casting aside the outworn legal rule that "the king can do no wrong," we can see and describe the growth of administrative law as an application of the judicial methods to the work of the government. This is necessary in order to keep abreast of the ever-widening sphere of administrative activities entailed by the expansion of our industrial civilization. In the eloquent phrases of William A. Robson, the ablest expositor of administrative law in England, we may assert: "The judicial power which has been given to administrative bodies will be exercised wisely, and the results are likely to be good. . . . I am convinced that Administrative Tribunals have accomplished, and are accomplishing, ends which are beyond the competence of our courts of law as at present constituted. Furthermore, those ends seem to me socially desirable ones which compare favorably with the selfish individual claims based on absolute legal rights to which the formal courts are so often compelled to lend ear. I believe that administrative law as it has developed in modern England is filling an urgent social need which is not met by any other branch of the law; and that there is no inherent reason, if due care and foresight are exercised, why it should be unfitted to take its place side by side with the common law and equity and statute law in the constitutional firmament of the English governmental system."[26]

Conclusion · In conclusion, it may be said once again that the judicial function is one of the basic functions of government. In its more general form, as the process of dispute settling, it is so basic that government cannot be imagined without it. "Tribes without rulers" depend upon it.[27] The methods employed to fulfill the judicial function are of central importance in any political system. A full appreciation of the contrast of Anglo-American and Continental political development is impossible without taking into account the great differences in the position assigned to judicial bodies and the techniques employed by them.

The extension of judicial methods is a concomitant of civilized government. Judicial methods, especially in the matter of the taking of evidence, are, or at any rate ought to be, akin to the spirit of science and the search for objectivity characteristic of science in the broad sense. That, basically, is the meaning of the rationalized procedures of a modern judiciary.

The view, often heard at present, that the judicial function is at variance with the requirements of democracy is unsound. Only an unrestrained democracy and an arbitrary judiciary conflict with each other. A constitutional democracy finds one of its important institutional expressions in a judiciary *serving the law*.

Existing courts usually resist the extension of judicial methods, and hence at present seem hostile to administrative justice. This must not deceive us; administrative justice represents another step in the evolution of modern government. Constitutionalism is in a sense the application of judicial methods to basic problems of government; administrative justice, extending this application, attempts to employ judicial methods in the wider sphere of activities which government is handling today. It is, therefore, an extension of constitutionalism itself.

PART 2

THE PATTERN

OF CONSTITUTIONAL

GOVERNMENT

The Constitution as a Political Process
VII

Introduction · Five nonpolitical concepts defined · The functional concept · The development of Anglo-American government · Restraint a question of degree · Medieval constitutionalism · The dilemma of Cromwell · The constitution as the decision regarding the organization of the government · Free speech and free assembly · The constituent power and the right of revolution · Locke's view restated scientifically · Conclusion

Introduction · A certain Senator from the South, when told that a measure he defended was unconstitutional, expostulated in reply: "When the Constitution comes between me and the virtue of the white women of South Carolina, I say: To hell with the Constitution." Autocrats and revolutionaries of all ages have spoken in a like vein. By doing so they have revealed their common opposition to restraints placed upon political and governmental action. As a political process, the constitution can be described as analogous to the rules of a game insuring fair play. This is the meaning of the word "constitution" in its functional, political sense, as distinguished from its meaning in law, in history, and in medicine. The political scientist inquiring into the process of constitutionalizing a government must study the technique of establishing an operating government and yet maintaining effective restraints on its political and governmental action. How do such restraints function? He must not allow himself to be sidetracked by the many senses in which the word "constitution" is used.

We may recognize as outstanding *three* nonpolitical concepts of a "constitution," the philosophical, the legal, and the historical. The first of these is a general concept, the other two particular. The historian may speak of the Constitution of Athens, the Constitution of Medieval England, and the Constitution of the United States, and by each mean something particular or specific, found only at the time and place with which he is concerned. Similarly, the constitutional lawyer in America, England, or France is talking about *the* constitution when he discusses the particular constitution with which he is familiar in terms of a whole "system of law." Philosophical concepts of the constitution, on the other hand, are usually generalizations from several such historical or legal constitutions with which the author happened to be acquainted. European philosophers have usually arrived at their concepts of a constitution by contrasting the meaning commonly attached to the word "constitution" (*constitution, Verfassung*) in their own country at the time of their writing with what the Roman law and Aristotle presumably suggested as being the meaning of "constitution" in classical antiquity.

Five nonpolitical concepts defined · Long lists of such "meanings," historical, legal, and philosophical, can easily be compiled. It seems more profitable to summarize such an inventory in terms of a few dominant concepts. Aristotle's concept of a constitution — or rather his concept of *politeia,* which is commonly translated as "constitution" — refers to the whole order of things in a city. Hegel, who so profoundly influenced the nineteenth century, entertained a very similar idea. Akin to this conception is the notion that the constitution describes the actual organization of the government in broad outline, so that we can speak of a monarchical constitution, a democratic constitution, and so forth. Finally there is found the idea, current among lawyers with a philosophical bent of mind, that the constitution is the basic law; that is, embodies the basic legal conceptions of the community, their outlook on life, insofar as it can be embodied in general legal rules. It is obvious that these three descriptive, general concepts of what a constitution is apply to all political communities, to a Fascist and Communist dictatorship just as much as to the United States or England.

Besides these general descriptive concepts of a constitution we find two concepts which are based upon a formal aspect. Of these, one maintains that a constitution must be *written* in order to be a constitution, that it must be embodied in a document.[1] Superficial though this view may seem to us today, it was widely held during the age of constitution makers in the past century and a half. This may be called documentary, or code, concept. It was bound to be challenged by adherents of the English political system like James Bryce; for English law makes considerable use of the concept of a constitution without having a written document to argue from. One argued about it in terms of a "rigid" and a "flexible" constitution — words carrying a distinct value implication. Why not rather speak in terms of "firm" and "fluid" constitutions? But apart from such an evaluation, it is true to say that a constitution embodied in a distinct written document *is* in some important respects different from one which is not, and hence the documentary concept is valid.

The other concept stresses the requirement of a distinctive, especially a popular, mode or procedure of amendment. For such a procedure implies the recognition of a distinct constitution-making power. If these are recognized, then the problem as to how to guard the constitution against violations becomes paramount. This concept may be called "the procedural concept." In sum, the five concepts which we have so far enumerated may be labeled philosophical, structural, legal, documentary, and procedural. They are all valuable within their respective contexts, but none of these concepts is concerned with the political *function* of a constitution and what it is supposed to accomplish.

The functional concept • In the course of the development of modern government, it has become increasingly clear that a political order may be organized in such a way that power may be wielded effectively and yet be restrained in its exercise. Growing out of earlier notions that government ought to be conducted according to law, the belief gained ground, especially in England but also elsewhere in Europe, that the task of constituting a government well called for its several functions or powers being clearly delimited. Constitutionalism came to mean this conviction, and to constitutionalize a government meant to subject it to such regularized restraints. It was, of course, always understood that such restraints must not prevent the government from operating well. Hence the elementary structural notion was no more abandoned than was the philosophical or the legal. But they were in a sense restricted, so that it became possible to talk of a constitutionalist constitution, such as that of the United States, and a nonconstitutionalist one, such as that of the Soviet Union.[2]

The definition given at the outset of this chapter said that to render a government constitutional required the establishment and maintenance of effective restraints upon political, and more especially upon governmental, action. It is the function of a constitution in this sense to organize such a restrained government. Why should we insist that the restraints must be effective? What is this standard of effectiveness? It should be evident that the existence of formally legal restraints is in no wise an indication of the existence of a constitutional order in the political sense. The Roman republican constitution in the first century before Christ had become a facade for an aristocratic absolutism, with power concentrated in the hands of the Senate. Similarly, the formal separation of powers under the Soviet constitution does not alter the fact that power in the U.S.S.R. was concentrated in the hands of the Communist party. On the other hand, a restraint might be very effective and thoroughly regularized, without necessarily being embodied in positive law unless "law" is very broadly defined as including all custom. Thus, what is perhaps the most important restraint of the English constitution, namely, the protection of the opposition and hence the alternation of government between two or three parties, is quite effective. From what has been said it can be seen that the problem of effectiveness involves a factual situation and an evaluation and existential judgment of that situation. If no one has "absolute" power, if in actual fact there exists no sovereign who holds unrestrained power in a given community, then the restraints may be said to be effective.[3]

At this point it becomes necessary to introduce another important qualification. Unless such restraints are regularized, they cannot be said to have value as constitutionalizing factors. Madame Pompadour scolding the king at her bedside, or a Brownshirt rebellion against Hitler, while possibly very effective checks upon the arbitrary whims of an autocratic ruler, cannot be classed as even rudimentary constitutional devices. The restraint which they produce is wholly irregular; it is also entirely unpredictable. Obviously, it is not always easy to determine what is a regularized procedure. A practice which at one time is wholly irregular, and at another fully regularized, will, for a certain period, be hard to classify. But it is enough that we can readily determine when a procedure is fully regularized. In the United States, a decision of the Supreme Court ordinarily marks the point of ultimate regularization, as happened with the presidential pocket veto.

The development of Anglo-American government · To this functional concept of a constitution, it may be objected that it is a generalization derived from English and American political development. But while it is true that English and American constitutional development afford some admirable illustrations for the abstract concept, actual developments in England have at times largely veered toward a scheme of powers concentrated in the hands of a landed aristocracy, aided by other big property owners.[4] When Sir Edward Coke waged his historic battle with James I, he did it, to be sure, in the name of the constitution. He took the constitution to mean the basic legal notions accepted by the community. He alleged that only the acceptance of this constitution provided the "rule of law" to which England had been accustomed since time immemorial. The king's claim that the royal prerogative was beyond the law he flatly denied. Coke would, however, allow Parliament to exercise the power which he withheld from the king in the name of the law. Thus the particular importance of his struggle lay, admittedly, in his insistence upon the exclusive right of Parliament to change the laws of England, his vigorous opposition to the claim of any right, even by the king himself, to change the law of the land. Thus the constitution, the fundamental law, restrained all but the organized people speaking through Parliament. But while Coke still meant by "Parliament," the "king in Parliament" — that is, the ancient body politic composed of kings, Lords and Commons — a decade or two later that medieval aspect of Coke's thought was forgotten. Parliament emerged clothed with unrestrained power. Once parliamentary supremacy was established, it was not long before a new opposition developed to restrain parliamentary absolutism, ending in the dictatorship of Cromwell. After this collapsed, a return to the former constitution based upon a separation of powers between king and Parliament provided an unstable equilibrium. This equilibrium was only temporarily disrupted by the conflict issuing in the Glorious Revolution. During these decades of controversy, the constitutional issues exposed the shifting balance of political power between the two classes in the community struggling for supremacy: the landowning squirearchy allied with the church, and the mercantile classes. In the course of the eighteenth century the latter gained increasing ascendancy as the formal constitution of divided powers was superseded by a new concentration in the hands of parliamentary leaders. This emergence of "parliamentary government" under Walpole eventually brought on the American revolution and the Reform Bill (1832). Both were fought by new classes in the community who sought to establish an effective and regularized restraint. From this sketch it can be seen that what appears to the legalist or the historian as an unbroken period of constitutionalism (simply because men in authority called it so), must in terms of the functional concept of a constitution appear as oscillating between constitutional and nonconstitutional periods. It also makes it easier to recognize basic rights or civil liberties as patterns of restraint. This means that they are variable in correspondence with the shifting class structure of society, rather than God-given or nature-given absolutes. Thus the personal rights recognized in eighteenth-century England differ markedly from those adopted later in America. They were the rights which mattered most to the landed gentry and the mercantile aristocracy ruling the land. Beyond the class conflict, they represented an "area of agreement" for most people. In short, such restraints depend for their maintenance upon a balance of classes in the society to which they apply.[5]

Restraint a question of degree • Upon further reflection, it will be apparent that no government, in the light of the preceding discussion, can be described as strictly constitutional. Nor will a completely nonconstitutional order be discovered amongst the governments known to us. Like all true functional concepts, the notion of constitutional government is essentially descriptive of two poles: very strong restraint and very weak restraint. Between these two poles, all actual governments can be ranged. The unreal limits are "complete restraint" and "no restraint," thus:

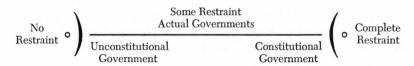

No Restraint ○) — Some Restraint / Actual Governments — (○ Complete Restraint

Unconstitutional Government — Constitutional Government

For rough descriptive purposes, governments near the no-restraint pole could be classed as nonconstitutional; governments near the complete-restraint pole as constitutional. In the middle there would remain an area of uncertainty. Thus the Soviet Union today would be in the first class; the United States in the second; Prussia in 1860 (before Bismarck's usurpations) might be put into the third along with England before 1832. As we have seen, the maintenance of all restraints depends in the end upon a balance of groups and classes in the community to whose government they apply. But whatever the classes, there are certain recurrent forms.

The functional and qualitative analysis of the constitution as the process by which governmental action is effectively restrained can be pushed much further. In the first place, it is possible to describe the several restraints which have actually proved effective in the historical experience of mankind. This task will be undertaken with some care in three later chapters (X, XI, XII). There is also the problem of who decides what restraints shall be employed and under what conditions; finally, there is the question of how such a system of restraints is generally related to various forms of government. Each particular form of government has its particular tendency toward concentration of power, and the so-called "pure" forms of Aristotle are all characterized by such a concentration of power in the hands of one, a few, or the many, as the ancient formula goes. No actual government ever conformed to these pure types, though a good many of the Greek city-states seem to have come perilously close to being completely unrestrained and hence nonconstitutional in the functional sense.

Medieval constitutionalism · Even in the Middle Ages, the governments of Western civilization tended toward the constitutional pattern.[6] This tendency may justly be attributed to the *Christian* concern for the individual and his personal salvation. Attempts by nationalist historians to claim that Germanic folk traditions or English national character are responsible for it are unconvincing. For the tendency is universal throughout Christian lands, though continually under pressure from one quarter or another. Newly emerging classes and vested interests have each in turn clamored for restraints to prevent the abuse of power by their opponents. Hence the development of political institutions in our civilization has been continuously concerned with discovering effective restraints. The authoritarian aspects of Catholicism must not blind us to the fact that throughout the Middle Ages the church was the bulwark of effective restraints, and hence of a kind of constitutionalism. It is no accident that the rights of the "people" to a voice in government were persistently defended by church writers. It was in the course of the thirteenth century that the earlier military feudalism became transformed into the government by estates epitomized in the phrase "the king in Parliament." The curious dualism of this *Ständestaat* underwent many transformations and shows marked differences in different countries. But from England to Hungary, from Spain to Poland and Sweden, we find charters, resembling Magna Charta, which provide for restraints upon the princes and a division of governmental power between the several states, i.e. groups or classes, in the community. The story of Magna Charta shows as clearly as any of the charters that the church officials, the bishops, prelates, abbots, and others, played a vital part in developing these systems. In most countries the rise of the burgher class, of merchants and professions and craft guilds, also was an important factor. But the church's role was central. Hence, the eclipse of the ecclesiastical power during the later Middle Ages and upon the advent of the Reformation paved the way for absolutism, first in England, later in France and other Continental countries. The efforts made and the techniques employed in restraining emergent absolutism often brought on revolutionary upheavals. While France, Germany, and other lands went through the religious wars, only England, of the large countries, saw these revolutionary efforts succeed.

The dilemma of Cromwell • In England the problem of a constitution had to be squarely faced in the age of Cromwell. It is well known that two plans called *Agreement of the People* which the more radical followers of Cromwell in his Model Army submitted to him in 1647 and 1649 were not accepted. But even though these prophetic documents with their strongly democratic bias failed to become the first English "constitutions," Cromwell was haunted by a sense that his arbitrary exercise of power needed a sanction.[7] This sanction he sought to obtain from several Parliaments which were elected in rapid succession. Yet, since they endeavored to restrain him as well as to sanction his rule, they were dissolved one after the other. A constitution was at last produced, the Instrument of Government (1653). The long-drawn-out story of Cromwell's conflicts with his several Parliaments serves as an admirable illustration of the fact that once the *de facto* government, controlling power by force of arms, seeks to secure the approval of the community, it may find itself confronted by demands for effective restraint.

The constitution as the decision regarding the organization of the government • While there is a close relationship between the constitution as a political process invariably concerned with the technique of establishing effective restraints and the constitution as the fundamental decision about the form of government, the two must be clearly distinguished. Defining the constitution thus is misleading. The decision of an all-powerful tyrant to maintain his tyranny cannot be called a constitution without rendering the meaning of the term highly equivocal. However, the establishing of such restraints does invariably *imply* the choosing of some form of government. We may therefore say that every constitution implies such a decision, but not that every such decision necessarily implies a constitution. Thus, if it be clearly understood that nonconstitutional government is excluded, we can even speak of the constitution as the basic decision about the organization of the government.[8]

Who, it may now be asked, will make such a basic decision? It used to be customary to answer: the people. Yet, did the electorate which stood back of the Commons in England during the seventeenth century constitute more than a fraction of the people? It did not; and still in common parlance we speak of the Glorious Revolution as one seeking to set up a constitutional government, and the stricter language of political science cannot deny that a constitution in our functional sense was in the making in Britain at that time. To be sure, the Act of Settlement's guarantee of judicial independence was another very essential step. But the Glorious Revolution certainly aimed at setting up restraints on governmental action, and therefore at constitutionalizing the government. That only a fraction of the governed participated in the process does not alter this fact. Therefore all that we can say in answer to the question: By whom is the decision made? is "By not too few." "Not too few" is a less ambiguous if vaguer statement of the actual facts. But this numerical description is not all that we can offer regarding the makers of constitutions. To make the constitutional decision genuine, it is also necessary that it be participated in by some of those who are being governed as contrasted with those who do the governing. This differentiates such a constituent act from the *coup d'état*. The participation by some of those who are being governed, that is, the politically less active members of the community, does not necessarily mean democracy. It does mean, however, that an effort will be made to restrain governmental action. Therein lies the importance of the participation of these less active members. Any decision arrived at solely by the governing bodies is not likely to be directed toward defining methods of restraining governmental action. Cromwell realized this vaguely, and therefore persisted in his efforts to secure parliamentary and popular approval. But since he was unwilling to allow restraints on his power in concrete instances, he found himself obliged to scrap the charters one after another. He could not shake off the idea, so characteristic of all absolutist governments, that opposition was rebellion.

In speaking of a decision, when dealing with the process of constitution making, it is important to remain aware of the limitations of decision making in politics. Decisions are not, as decisionist and existentialist writers have pretended, intrinsically arbitrary. The alternatives are limited and prescribe a framework; reasoning and discussion are basic parts of the decision-making process.[9] It is easy, in any case, to overestimate the importance of deciding upon courses of action in politics, especially in highly rationalized modern government. People think they push, when they are actually being pushed. In politics, as in other realms of living, many actions are repetitive or adaptive, shaped by tradition and custom. No one who has studied with care the records of constitutional conventions can help but be impressed with the degree to which what appears as decisions is actually ritualistic repetition.[10]

Free speech and free assembly • Decisions do not occur in a vacuum, least of all constitutional decisions. They presuppose extended argument and discussion, if they are to be right. Hence there exist important conditions which must be fulfilled, in order to render the constitutional decision genuine: the decision must be reached after the mature deliberation of those who participate in the decision. Confusing *opposition* with *rebellion* prevents the mature deliberation of those who participate in the decision. Thus no genuine decision results. Whether or not free speech and free assembly are "natural rights," they are necessary concomitants of constitutional decisions. For mature deliberation of an issue by any number of people who are to act collectively presupposes an exchange of views on the issues involved in the decision. If that opportunity is not available, nothing can be decided. This is the reason why plebiscites, so popular with dictators from Cromwell to the present day, fail to have the legitimizing effect which their initiators often hope for. Though they seem to offer an opportunity for collective approval of a government, their effectiveness in accomplishing that purpose is quite small. They carry little persuasive force in the community, because in the absence of free discussion and deliberation, few of the participants feel any responsibility for the action taken.

The constituent power and the right of revolution • We are now ready to designate the group of human beings which we have broadly characterized in the last two paragraphs. No matter how large or small, it is a very decisive group which it is here proposed to call the constituent group wielding constituent power. Political thinkers during the seventeenth and eighteenth century were deeply concerned with this power, and we owe to them a great deal of our elementary insight. A thorough analysis of their views belongs to a history of political theory, where they are commonly discussed under the heading of "the right of revolution." These early thinkers were preoccupied with the question of rights. A descriptive political science does not ask whether people have a right to make a revolution, but rather what are the conditions under which they do make it. Those early writers, however, in their efforts to vindicate a right of revolution, brought out with much learning what the conditions of revolutions were. The traditional doctrine of the "right of revolution" contains at least this kernel of scientifically valid generalization. Thus Calvinist theorists, like Althusius and Rutherford, pointed to the many revolutions recorded in the Old Testiment as proof of the fact that God permitted and even commanded revolutions, provided such revolutions were directed toward restraining the government in accordance with the command of God as interpreted by the priests. This argument the church had already used extensively in the Middle Ages. Still others, like Hotman and Buchanan, had likewise emphasized the historical fact of revolution as a valid part of their national history, whether French or Scottish. This earlier scientific interest in revolutions as manifestations of a constituent power was obscured by the moralist turn which this problem was given by Locke, and more emphatically by Rousseau. But the more realistic analysis supporting it continues to be the mainstay of the argument.

Locke's view restated scientifically · In his *Second Treatise of Civil Government* (¶ 149), the great English myth maker remarks: "For no man, or society of men, having a power to deliver up their preservation . . . to the absolute will and arbitrary dominion of another; whenever anyone shall go about to bring them into such a slavish condition, they will always have a right to preserve what they have not a power to part with. . . . And thus the community may be said in this repect to be always the supreme power, but not as considered under any form of government, because this power of the people can never take place till the government is dissolved." On the basis of our previous discussion, we should rewrite this statement, as follows, in order to fit it into the hypothetical form of scientific thought: "For a considerable number of men (who constitute the more intelligent and energetic part of the community at large) have a tendency to maintain their freedom (of decision) . . . against the unrestrained and arbitrary decision of others; whenever anyone shall go about to bring them into a constrained and dependent condition, the presumption is that they will try to escape from it even at considerable sacrifice. . . . This more intelligent and energetic part of the community may be called 'the constituent group'; it does not operate *under* any government, because their power can never come into play except to dissolve the established government and set up a new constitution." This transcription shows that Locke's juridical statement contains the kernel of two important scientific generalizations: (1) there tends to exist a residuary and unorganized power of resistance in the community which seeks to restrain the government; and (2) this constituent power can only come into play when the government fails to function satisfactorily. This second proposition is important in differentiating the constituent power from the constitutional amending power, discussed in the next chapter, for which provision is made in most modern constitutions. To be sure, the amending power is set up in the hope of anticipating a revolution by constitutional change, and therefore provides an additional restraint upon the government. But should the amending power fail to work, the constituent power may emerge at the critical point. It was part of the optimism of rationalists like Locke to assume that the revolutionary group necessarily and always employed its power to *establish* a constitution. This is not the case. Events in our time, as well as Cromwell and the Napoleons, have shown that such revolutionary groups may set up an autocratic system. When they do so, groups are not a "constituent power" in the sense here suggested.

Conclusion • The word "constitution" has, then, for modern political science, a very distinct meaning, namely, that of a particular organization of the government. It is understood as the process the function of which it is not only to organize, but to restrain. In spite of the fact that the word "constitution" has a variety of other meanings, it seemed best to define it in this political sense. Perhaps it would be less ambiguous not to speak of this process as the constitution at all. But as long as the word "constitution" is understood to refer to this process, the possible ambiguity may be excused so as to retain the superior suggestive value of the word "constitution." There is another reason for this way of putting the matter. The total complex of effective restraints which makes up the "constitution" of a given community will necessarily crystallize into more or less familiar word patterns, such as "legislative, executive, and judicial power," "states' rights," "due process," "fredom of speech," and so forth. These word patterns gradually become symbols of order, and thus the constitution becomes itself a political force.

The Constituent Power, the Amending

Power; and Revolution

VIII

Introduction • Revolutions are successful rebellions. If they have failed, their makers have with rare exceptions been executed for treason. An attempt to overthrow the established order is commonly understood to be treason. And since the constituent power can only come into operation when there is no established order, the decline and the eventual breakdown of an established order will be heralded by the multiplication of treasonable acts. All the significant constituent acts of recent years, such as the establishment of the Fourth and Fifth French Republics, the Italian and the Federal Republic of Germany, the Republic of India, and of other new and emergent nations, have been preceded by a revolutionary period in which acts of treason became not only numerous but honorific. The traitors and criminals of one regime are the heroes of its successor.[1]

Hence it is true to say that the constituent power bears an intimate relation to revolution. To be sure, not all revolutions are made by a group that seeks to establish a constitution. We have been witnesses in this century of a whole series of revolutions which sought to destroy a constitution rather than establish one. But every time the constituent group becomes active, a revolution (or at least a rebellion) will take place.

This constituent power, as we have seen, is exercised by a group of persons. They must be not too few and they must include some of the governed. After the existing order has been overthrown, a measure of free speech and free assembly is established so that the constituent group can work. The suppression of free speech and free assembly thwarted the constituent group in Cromwell's time as well as in our own. National Socialist, Fascist, and Communist revolutionaries are united in their opposition to free speech. It is but natural, therefore, that no real constitution should have been established in countries ruled by these groups, but only a facade. Since the need for popular approval is still felt, totalitarian leaders tend to employ the plebiscite as a substitute. They act as if they felt that a constituent group should have brought them into power. They do not appear satisfied with merely having usurped the absolute power of government. Therefore they seek the plebiscitary semblance of wide popular acclaim. Cromwell, the two Napoleons, Mussolini, Hitler, and many others since have employed this technique.

Cromwell and the Puritan revolution · Cromwell's *Instrument of Government* of 1653 provided in its Article XII that the officers supervising the elections to Parliament under this instrument should obtain from the electors a written acknowledgment "that the persons elected shall not have the power to alter the government as it is hereby settled in one single person and a Parliament."[2] This provision contains the notion of an implied consent of the electorate, and is a characteristic device for escaping the need for an effective constituent group. Yet, no sooner had this Parliament assembled than it commenced an extensive debate on the constitution. This provoked Cromwell (after locking up Parliament) into making a speech to justify his demand that each member of Parliament sign a statement similar to the one just cited. In the course of his speech, the Lord Protector made it quite clear that he perceived a constitution to be a fundamental law basically concerned with restraining arbitrariness. During the Long Parliament there had been, in his opinion, a definite drift toward parliamentary absolutism. "And so the liberties and interests and lives of people not judged by any certain known Laws and Power, but by an arbitrary Power; which is incident and necessary to Parliaments. By an arbitrary Power, I say: to make men's estates liable to confiscation, and their persons to imprisonment, — sometimes even by laws made after the fact committed; often by the Parliament's assuming to itself to give judgment both in capital and in criminal things, which in former times was not known to exercise such a judicature. . . ." For that reason he claimed the dissolution of the Long Parliament had been necessary. But Cromwell did not wish to take over the absolute power thus revoked. In bringing together the Little Parliament, popularly dubbed Barebones Parliament, he had another end in view which he himself claimed to be his greatest end, namely, "to lay down the power" which was in his hands "in which unlimited condition" he "did not desire to live a day." In other words, he wished them to draft a constitution. But they despaired of the task and decided "to deliver up unto the Lord-General (Cromwell) the powers we received from him." Upon the failure of these representatives to exercise the constituent power, the Instrument of Government was drawn up by some of Cromwell's supporters in the army and elections were called with the proviso cited in the beginning of this paragraph. After Cromwell's exhortation, most of the members signed the pledge not to propose or give their consent "to alter the Government as it is settled in a Single Person and Parliament"; yet immediately upon reconvening they returned to constitutional controversies. Cromwell's admission that in every governmental charter "there must be something Fundamental, something like a Magna Charta, which should be standing, should be unalterable," and therefore in this "establishment there are some things which are Fundamental," others which "are Circumstantial," had left an avenue open for such a discussion of constitutional issues. To be sure, Cromwell had himself outlined three fundamentals of the *Instrument:* (1) "that Parliaments should not make themselves perpetual"; (2) that there should be "Liberty of Conscience in Religion"; and (3) that the army "should be placed so equally that no one party neither in Parliament nor out of Parliament have the power of ordering it." Each one of these will readily be recognized to be a measure of restraining the government. When Parliament kept on debating about the constitution, instead of attending to its constitutionally appointed task, Cromwell dissolved it, and thereafter governed as a military dictator — a constituent group had not emerged in England, and Cromwell's rule collapsed with his death. The implied consent of the plebiscite of 1653 had remained a futile gesture.

Napoleonic plebiscites · Cromwell's failure was not considered by the two Napoleons when they sought to sanction their rule by plebiscite. After the first Napoleon had staged his *coup d'état* (November 1799), he proceeded to draft a constitution which centered all power in the first consul and submitted it to a plebiscite. Here, then, the consent was not implied, but explicitly asked for — and overwhelmingly given. The same thing happened again in 1802 when the consulate was bestowed upon Bonaparte for life. It is, however, important to realize that these "constitutions" contained no provisions for the effective restraint of the government, and were therefore not constitutions in the functional sense. It is noteworthy that Louis Napoleon should also have had recourse to the plebiscite. After his *coup d'état* of December 2, 1851, the third Napoleon demanded from the people that they sanction his authority and that they delegate to him the necessary powers for making a constitution along the general lines of a proclamation he had issued. Again, the plebiscite was accepted by an immense majority, which is hardly surprising in view of the wording of the plebiscite: "The French People wants to maintain the authority of Louis-Napoleon Bonaparte and delegates to him the necessary powers for making a constitution. . . ." The voter could either accept or reject this proposal, but was not given any positive alternative. Practically the same tactics prevailed about a year later when the imperial office was re-established as the result of a plebiscite modeled on the precedent of the first Empire. The restraints established by these charters were quite weak, and even the more liberal constitution of 1870, also submitted to popular plebiscite, was definitely monarchical. That no effective constituent power came into play through their adoption was emphasized by a speaker who wished to see the constitutional laws of 1875 submitted to popular approval. On the 28th of January, 1875, M. Naquet said in the Assembly: "I believe that a constitution must be ratified by the whole people. By affirming that, I merely return to the tradition of our great (revolutionary) assemblies; for the Constitution of 1793 and the Constitution of the Year III were submitted to direct ratification of the people. . . . We do not have to abandon this right merely because the Empire has abused the plebiscite, the right derived from an appeal to the people. . . . There is an immense difference between the imperial plebiscites which posed the question *a priori* (*ex post facto*) and made it one between some solution and pure negation, and an appeal to the people destined to ratify the charter voted by a national assembly after long and serious deliberations."[3] In this concluding sentence, we find a clear recognition of the necessary conditions of the functioning of a constituent group, as we have here depicted it: not only participation of some of the governed, but also free speech and free assembly.

When seen in this perspective, the plebiscites of Napoleon were gestures. Wholly different were the circumstances of the adoption of the Constitution of the United States. Here wide popular discussion, even heated controversy, preceded the ratification of the constitution. Likewise the Constitution of Switzerland of 1848 owes its existence to the work of a genuine constituent group.

Constituent and amending powers • The rather orderly procedure which led to the adoption of the Constitution of the United States must not mislead us into thinking, however, that the constituent power can itself be brought "within the four corners of the constitution."[4] To be sure, since a constitution is by definition a technique (or a set of techniques) for the organizing and restraining of the government, acts of arbitrary and tyrannical violence are much less likely to occur under a constitutional government.

Moreover, a well-drawn constitution will provide for its own amendment in such a way as to forestall, as far as is humanly possible, revolutionary upheavals. That being the case, the provisions for amendment form a vital part of most modern constitutions. The value of such provisions was, however, by no means realized in the early days of modern constitutionalism. The several Cromwellian constitutions did not contain any adequate provisions for their own amendment. In fact, the clear recognition and deliberate organization of the amending power was an achievement of the American revolution. The Philadelphia Convention *invented* it. Contrariwise during the French revolution people came only with much delay to see the importance of amending provisions. Thereafter, constitutions were rarely made without some thought being given to this problem. But no matter how elaborate the provisions for amendment may be, they should not be assumed to have superseded the constituent power. The relation and the difference between the amending power and the constituent power is brought out with particular vividness by the constitutional history of Switzerland. In 1848 a new federal constitution superseded the federation of cantons which had broken down and given rise to a civil war in 1847. This federal constitution was adopted by a constituent assembly, submitted to the people of the several cantons for ratification, and accepted by a considerable majority. In 1874, this conservatively liberal constitution was entirely overhauled and democratized, but the draft failed to secure the necessary majority of cantonal ratifications as provided in the amending provisions of the constitution. Thereupon the draft was remodeled and in the same year adopted in accordance with regular amending procedure. The constitutional amending power proved sufficient to make the necessary changes. The potential constituent group worked through the amending power. But that does not mean it is identical with it. For the constituent group in the exact sense is to be understood as that part of the community which is capable of wielding the *de facto* residuary power of changing or replacing the constitution of an existing political order by a new constitution.

Constitutional change without amendment · The constitutional history of England is less simple. Formally speaking, her constitution dates back to the Glorious Revolution of 1688. That constitution was enacted by a genuine constituent power. But since that time the English constitution has gone through a number of profound changes without there being any explicit decision on the part of anybody.[5] These customs — called conventions in England — have grown up from precedents. Thus Walpole's way of conducting the government created a series of precedents which became the basis and form of parliamentary government. In turn, the nineteenth century saw that same parliamentary government transformed into a cabinet government by a similar slow evolution. The masterly analyses of writers like Bagehot and Jennings come at the end of such a development; it all happens without any but the men who are "insiders" quite understanding what is going on. English constitutional change is more informal anyway, on account of the fact that the amending power is vested in a parliamentary majority. This arrangement is reinforced, however, by the convention which calls for a new election in case the opposition should stress the importance of the issue. But the fact remains that the basic changes have been quite gradual. They have been accretions or growths, often occurring without explicit decision. All this merely goes to confirm our earlier statement that revolutions often take place without any constituent group coming into play. The seemingly unrestrained power of Parliament, or of the oligarchy whose interests and ideas it voiced, was restrained by the evolution of the two large parties, and the firm, if unwritten, convention of their regular alternation. This constitutional device was institutionalized as "Her Majesty's Loyal Opposition."

The British case raises a very general problem. When one talks of a constitution as the basic decision regarding the political organization of a community, the impression is conveyed that all is settled once this decision has been made. The constitution is represented as absolute. But we know already that all restraints are matters of degree. What is more, even a carefully considered and widely discussed decision is subject to certain inherent limitations. Human language is anything but unequivocal. The working out of human relationships is difficult to forecast. The actual conditions of human society change. These three inherent limitations of all human decisions affect constitutions profoundly. Some of the subsequent changes may be made by using a supple amending power. But others will be made by those who govern, and they usually will be acquiesced in by those who are governed. They very often take the form of constitutional interpretation, not only by the courts, but by all departments of the government. The relative importance of such constitutional interpretations depends upon a number of factors, including the clarity of the constitutional document itself and the nature of the formal amending process. If the process of formal amendment does not respond readily to any widely felt need for change, the change may be accomplished through interpretation. In the United States, where the formal process is rather cumbersome, many constitutional adjustments have taken place through such interpretation, and constitutional usages or conventions are numerous. Under the First German Republic, which merely required a two-thirds majority of the two chambers of the legislature, constitutional amendments were frequent, and usages of the constitution were few and of minor importance. Again, the Swiss procedure of amending the constitution by popular referendum has lent itself rather readily to formal changes. In the period from 1893 to 1924, the referendum was used twenty-three times; eighteen of the proposed amendments were passed. In some of the American states where the amending process functions more smoothly than legislation — or, to put it another way, where determined minorities can more readily gather a popular than a legislative following — the constitutional amendment is employed for a great deal of legislation (see below, p. 146 f.).

The other important factor is the relative simplicity or complexity of a constitution. The American constitution is more complex than the constitution of the Third French Republic; for it contains a federal system and a bill of rights. The German republican constitution of 1919 was even more complex than the American constitution; for its bill or rights was based upon conflicting political and social philosophies, liberal, Catholic, and socialist, and was therefore in many respects quite equivocal. If one provision of the constitution seemed to set up a separation of church and state, another forthwith denied it by implication. Which of the two interpretations was a court to enforce if a controversy came before it in which one of the litigants based his case upon one interpretation, the other upon its opposite? The development of the due-process interpretation by the American courts since the adoption of Amendment XIV offers another striking illustration of the opportunity which equivocal provisions of a constitution provide for constitutional interpretation. Even more significant is the role of interpretation in connection with the whole welter of complex provisions through which the American constitution attempts to settle the relation between the federal government and the states. Undoubtedly a certain measure of such difficulties and complexities are inherent in any constitution embodied in written documents.

Flexible versus rigid constitution · These two factors, easy process of amendment and inherent complexity, together constitute what is often discussed as the relative flexibility or rigidity of a constitution.[6] The argument is usually extended to include the English system of government, where no distinction is made between the legislative and the amending power, or, to put it another way, where no fundamental distinction is admitted between constitutional and other law. Such a system seems more flexible than any other. But we have already seen that the traditional device of a two-party system embodies an effective restraint, the more so when, as in Britain, the government in power feels obliged to appeal to the electorate on any major issue. Such fundamental changes as would involve a repeal, let us say, of a principle established and set down in the Act of Settlement, like the tenure of judges during good behavior, could not, it is held, be enacted by a government unless it had fought and won an election on it. (But see below, p. 144 f., for illustrations to the contrary.) When in 1911 the Liberals wished to curtail the power of the House of Lords, they had to carry the issue to the voters. From a political point of view, therefore, the amending power is recognized in Britain as belonging to the electorate. Only an election which amounts to a referendum can sanction constitutional change. But that means a bare majority of the electoral districts, which may not be a majority of the people. The discussion of the relative advantages and disadvantages of rigid and flexible constitutions is equally inconclusive.

The great and outstanding advantage of a flexible constitution is the smoothness with which it can be adapted to new conditions and altered conceptions in the community. This advantage is particularly apparent, of course, in times of rapid change. An oft-cited example is afforded by legislation regulating the conditions of labor under modern industrial conditions. In England the introduction of new rules prohibiting child labor proceeded apace and unincumbered by constitutional provisions regarding freedom of contract. It is, however, obvious that such flexibility presupposes a nation steeped in traditions and by nature opposed to change, or the whole political structure will easily become the object of attack from restless and irresponsible groups. An illustration of the great dangers inherent in an easy amending process was provided by the events of March 1933 in Germany. Here a bare majority of Nationalist and National Socialist deputies abused its legislative power to bar part of the opposition (the Communists) and then proceeded to "amend" the constitution by giving the government absolute power to change it. This "Enabling Act" was a procedure which had never been sanctioned by a majority of the electorate.[7]

The overthrow of the German constitution "from within" brings to light the great advantage of a "rigid" constitution. In fact, it would be better to call such a constitution "stable," because the epithet "rigid" prejudices the case. A stable constitution seeks to provide effective safeguards against what one might, with de Tocqueville, term majority tyranny. It seems for that reason better adapted to a community which is not firmly rooted in tradition, or one in which the people are deeply divided by religious, racial, or class conflicts. If, moreover, the form of government is new and untried, a stable constitution lifts it somewhat above the party struggle, while a soft and pliable charter would be tossed about by the shifting currents of party strife. A stable constitution, by making constitutional amendments more difficult, obliges advocates of such changes to concentrate upon the essentials and to build up solid popular sentiments behind them. If such support has been secured, however, the changes will be swift and decisive. This conclusion is amply supported by the history of constitutional amendments in the United States. Accordingly, American policy, in promoting democratic constitutionalism in Germany, stressed the need for a constitution protected against too-easy changes. There have been a number of changes in the Basic Law, but these have required building a consensus between the two major parties.

The American federal amending process · The American federal amending process, while cumbersome, has turned out to be less of an impediment to change than was at one time assumed. In spite of the great impact of "interpretive" customs and usages, this American procedure deserves attention. Its drafters had clearly grasped the conclusion that certain amendments to a constitutional document are unlikely if the power of amending the document is vested in an official or a group of officials whose own power might conceivably be curtailed by such an amendment. Article V provides four methods for amending the constitutional document, thus making it impossible for either Congress or the state legislatures to block a constitutional amendment. In keeping with this idea it has been decided by the Supreme Court that neither the President nor state governors have any veto power over amendments. In practice only one of the methods has, however, been used so far, namely, that which requires the collaboration of Congress and the state legislatures. Amendments have originated in Congress, on the approval of two thirds of both houses, and have been ratified by the legislatures in three fourths of the states. But if Congress wished to avoid calling upon the state legislatures, it could insist upon special conventions in the states. If, on the other hand, a widespread movement for amending the constitution got under way, and Congress would not respond to it, the legislatures of two thirds of the states could demand that a national convention be called. Such a move was contemplated before the repeal of the eighteenth amendment; it has also been advocated in connection with broad programs of constitutional reform. It will be noted that the American constitution does not admit an initiative on the part of the "people," as does the Swiss constitution. (Since no amendment has been added to the Swiss constitution by that process, it may be doubted whether the loss is serious.) At any rate, no governmental authority has a monopoly of the amending power, as is the case wherever the power of amending a constitution is vested in a legislature alone. It may, however, be asked whether the process need be as elaborate as it is in the United States; the provisions of the United States Constitution have been subjected to serious criticism. It was estimated at one time that some 3000 amendments had been proposed in Congress. Some years ago the resulting indignation led to suggestions to amend the amending process, permitting future amendments by a majority of both houses of Congress, to be ratified by a majority of the voters in a majority of the states. Such plans have so far failed. Since that time, several amendments have been passed. Particularly the repeal of Amendment XVIII has inclined people to feel that the constitutional amending process is probably sufficiently responsive to popular demands for change as well as for progress.[8]

Conditions for formal amendment · Interpretation and formal amendment of a constitutional document are not, however, simple alternatives. In spite of the great changes which interpretation and practice may produce, certain specific changes may be quite impossible with a formal amendment. This is sometimes forgotten by those who would have us rely entirely upon informal change. The American federal structure, the division of the country into states, could not be altered without a formal amendment, nor could the explicit distribution of functions. Still, it is extraordinary how far interpretation and practice may go under favorable conditions. Thus intrastate commerce, which for a long time was held to be a matter which the federal government could not regulate, has now been interpreted as subject to federal regulation if it "affects" interstate commerce. In view of the close interdependence of all economic factors, it seems almost impossible to draw a line between *intra*state commerce which *does* affect and *intra*state commerce which does *not* affect *inter*state commerce (see ch. XI). It all seems to depend upon how imperative the need for federal regulation is. Where the pressure of need is small, and the formal and human obstacles are great, changes are not likely to be brought about by interpretation, particularly if gradual measures are out of the question. Thus the equal representation of the states in the United States Senate cannot be interpreted away. Similarly the coequal power of the House of Lords in matters of taxation had to be formally abolished. A further reduction in the power of the House of Lords has been on the Agenda of the Labour party. In other words, matters about which English written law itself is reasonably explicit usually are explicitly changed. If the formal process is too elaborate, the constitutional structure may in the course of time be very seriously warped. As long as limitations of time and resources are not important, such warpings may be endured. The years of effort and the millions of revenue lost in the struggle to put through the amendment allowing the American federal government to levy graduated income taxes may have failed to arouse the wealthy American nation; the Germans were not equally patient with the difficulties arising from their federal system after the First World War. When the amending provisions fail to work in adjusting the constitutional document to altered needs, revolution may result. This is quite generally admitted at present. But in addition, it is now realized by many that even a process of amendment which responds to the need for widely felt change cannot completely protect the constitution against revolution. For revolution may be made by others than those who would constitute a constituent group. Just the same, the fact that all men must die does not dispose of arguments in favor of a doctor.

Holland, England, and France · An interesting combination of the English procedure of constitutional amendment by simple legislative enactment, and the American emphasis upon the more basic importance of constitutional changes, is found in the Dutch constitution.[9] This constitutional kingdom requires first a dissolution of the chamber and a new election, and then a new vote by a two-thirds majority. Through such a provision the amending power is vested in the representative legislature, and the new election insures the truly representative nature of the parliament enacting the change. In making this arrangement, the Dutch have put into practice what Dicey wished to see adopted in England. The principle he advocated was that no far-reaching changes in the governmental system should be made until the voters have had a chance to pass judgment upon the proposed amendment, at a general election. This has, indeed, usually been the case. Thus in 1832 the Liberal majority secured a mandate from the electorate to carry out electoral reform; but lacking a majority before, it could not have done otherwise. More significant is the instance when in 1910 the Liberal government, possessing a stout majority in the Commons, went to the electorate with a plan for reform of the House of Lords. But in contrast to this move, the enfranchisement of women and other changes in the electoral system were adopted in 1918 by a Parliament elected eight years before; similarly the Irish Free State was created in 1922 without consulting the voters.

In the French Third Republic, no appeal to the people was required for enacting a constitutional amendment. In keeping with traditional conceptions of parliamentary government (see below, ch. XVIII), the two chambers, after separately accepting the proposal of a constitutional amendment from the cabinet, would go to Versailles, where in a joint meeting of the two chambers they would proceed to ratify the amendment, thus marking the solemnity of the proceeding. This arrangement was a clever device for combining the recognition of a distinct amending power with the parliamentary system. In keeping with the postwar disenchantment with the parliaments of the Third Republic, the French have moved away from strict parliamentarism toward a conception of the constitution as higher law, proceeding from the people rather than the Assembly. Accordingly, the constitutions of 1946 and 1958 have gone considerably further in recognizing an amending power distinct from the ordinary process of making laws. It is now provided that a constitutional amendment, after being passed by a majority of both the National Assembly and the Senate, has to be submitted to popular referendum unless both houses, meeting together, have adopted it by a three-fifths majority (Article 89). These procedures were, however, disregarded by the President of the Republic when in November 1962 he adapted Article 11 to the purpose of amending the constitution. This article simply provides for the submission to referendum of "any government bill dealing with the organization of public authorities." The first revision of the 1958 constitution, allowing member nations to become independent yet remain in the Community, also avoided the regular processes of amendment. It was carried out under Article 85, which concerns changes in the *functioning* of Community institutions, but not changes in the fundamental *nature* of the institutions themselves. It is interesting in this connection to recall that M. Michel Debré, presenting the draft constitution to the *Conseil d'Etat* in 1958, condemned the parliament of the Fourth Republic for its disregard of the constitution, "under the pretext of sovereignty, not of the Nation (which is right) but of the Assembles (which is fallacious)." "The creation of the 'Constitutional Council,'" he continued, "demonstrates the will to subordinate the law, that is the decision of Parliament, to the higher rule decreed by the Constitution."[10]

Limitations on the amending power • Where the constitutional amending power is vested in the legislature, limitations are usually imposed upon it. In France, an amendment of 1884 provided that the republican form of government should never be made the subject of a proposed revision.[11] A similar provision is still found in the constitution of the Fifth Republic, as well as the present Italian constitution of 1948. The makers of the Basic Law of the Federal Republic of Germany have gone a good deal further and have exempted not only the form of government, but the basic aspects of the federal system and the principle of basic rights as such (not particular ones) from constitutional amendment. English constitutional lawyers have argued that Parliament cannot abolish itself, for that would mean binding its successors irrevocably. In the United States, the states cannot be deprived of their equal representation in the Senate without their own consent. Whatever the ultimate validity of such provisions and arguments, they make violent revolution more likely by limiting the chance of effecting "revolutionary" changes gradually. For example, Poincaré, in arguing the binding character of the French inhibition just cited, insisted that any revision which would have for its object the substitution of the monarchical system for the republic would be illegal and *revolutionary*. By thus forcing those who might constitute an emerging constituent power to have recourse to a violent revolution, such inhibitions would have the political effect of depriving the amending power of some part of what is its essential function, viz., to forestall the revolutionary emergence of the constituent power. That is the sound kernel of the objections raised to such provisions by those who insist that they are merely declaratory and cannot bind the "will of the people" — a remark repeatedly made in the French Chamber. But the "will of the people" is too broad a term. It has often been a cloak for revolutionary groups endeavoring to destroy the constitution and the constituent power. Therefore, such limitations also have the effect of inhibiting revolutionary upheavals which are admittedly or secretly opposed to the continued existence of any constitution or constituent group. For as we have seen, revolutionary movements opposed to free speech and free assembly are quite frequent. They are politically possible in communities where the constituent group is atrophied for diverse reasons. A determined gang is then able to seize power and reorganize the government in its own interests and without consultation with the governed.

Nonfundamental constitutional provisions · Many modern "constitutions," that is, documents containing a real constitutional system of restraints, will, along with this system of restraints, contain what are in fact legislative provisions. Ordinary legislation within the confines of a "constitution" is particularly notorious in the state constitutions of the United States. The constitution of Oklahoma, we are told, contains eleven pages of legislation relating to the subject of corporations alone, besides much more ordinary legislation relating to homesteads and exemptions, banks and banking, insurance, the employment of children, and education. It forbids plural marriages, fixes the maximum rate of interest, abolishes the so-called fellow-servant doctrine, and regulates the use of the contributory-negligence and assumption-of-risk doctrines as defenses in certain suits for damages, establishes the eight-hour day on public works and coal mines, and determines the test for the purity of kerosene oil. The constitution of Oklahoma is an extreme instance, but the tendency is manifest elsewhere. The German constitution of 1919 abounded with constitutional legislation about railroads, schools, and other phases of community life. Now it is clearly unreasonable to place a provision like the one that Germany is a republic, or that all power emanates from the people (Article I), on the same footing as the provision that all children graduating from normal school shall receive a copy of the constitution (Article 148). Similar contrasts, though perhaps not quite as extreme, can be found in the Constitution of the United States. Yet nowhere have the amending provisions been organized in such a way as to take account of this difference.[12] The simplest technique for coping with the difficulty would seem to be a provision that parts of the same constitutional document might be amended by different methods. A process requiring much deliberation and delay might be provided for the basic parts of the document, while constitutional provisions of a legislative nature could be amended by a simpler and more rapid procedure. This would seem a sound plan; the "fundamental" parts of the document would thereby be marked as the basic constitution. Oklahoma and Virginia have attempted something of this order. It must be considered doubtful, however, whether their example will be widely emulated; the reasons for this difficulty result from the constitution also being a symbol, and hence political force. Under the alternative scheme of leaving the amending of the constitution to the legislature, as in England, reliance is placed up public opinion for maintaining the "fundamentals." The idea is that since revolutions turn upon these "fundamentals," their emergence cannot be prevented by a constitution anyway.

Limited and unlimited revolutions • Revolutions may be limited to the political, governmental sphere, or they may be not so limited, and thus be unfathomable, incalculable, and incomprehensible to all but those who have been "seized by the spirit."[13] While the deeper impulses remain unfathomable, except to the initiated, the pattern of these revolutions seems to be rather uniform. Crane Brinton, taking the English, French, American, and Russian revolutions as the material for a comparative analysis, has sketched a convincing set of generalizations. To be sure, they are strictly inductive, and it is quite possible that the pattern is limited to our culture and to that type of revolution. But within these limits, it is an enlightening analysis.

So far as the signs of an approaching revolution are concerned, they are not very distinctive. They seem largely to be an intensification of the sort of strains and stresses that are always found in society. Nor is there anything very definite to be said about the work of revolutions; they leave society changed, but there seems no distinctive pattern to the change, except a measure of exhaustion. But there is a definite succession of stages, a rhythm, to revolutionary upheavals of this "unlimited" variety. In the first stage the revolutionaries, full of the "new spirit," engage in an orgy of revolutionary perfectionism. They set to work in the conviction that the millennium is at hand. But this honeymoon does not last very long. The practical tasks of carrying on the government have to be faced, and a split develops between the moderates and the radicals. (By the way, Brinton brings forward plenty of evidence that "revolutionaries" are no particular kind of people, that "it takes almost as many kinds of men and women to make a revolution as to make a world.") Their conflict ends in the failure of the moderates, the rise of the extremists, and the *concentration of all power* in their hands. This concentration of power then is followed by the terror. It is a desperate attempt to make earnest with the revolutionary purposes by force and violence, and it is soon followed by a strong reaction. This is the *Thermidor*, to use an expression the French revolution coined. "Thermidor comes as naturally to societies in revolution as an ebbing tide, as calm after a storm, as convalescence after fever, as the snapping-back of a stretched elastic band." Thermidor brings a tyrant or dictator, a man who speaks the revolutionary language but refuses to act upon it, who is preoccupied with practical problems of how to restore "order" and organize administration. Old habits of daily life reappear, though restricted by the dictatorship. The revolutionary symbols, now become devoid of psychic appeal, lose their hold; as time goes on the dictatorial power appears increasingly naked, and the road is paved for a "restoration" which seeks to re-establish the old regime. But the changes wrought in the society by the revolution are too profound, and a new pattern emerges.[14]

While the features just outlined, following Brinton to a considerable extent, are clearly discernible in the case of the English and French revolutions, it is not possible to discover more than faint resemblances to them in the case of the American revolution. For the moderates, not the extremists, won out; there was no terror, no concentration of power, etc. Nor does the pattern fit the Glorious Revolution of 1688, nor the German revolution of 1918, nor yet the numerous limited revolutions which have produced a change of government time and again. Indeed, it may be doubted whether the two great revolutions in England and France are not a very special case, intimately related to the dynamics of Western Christian culture. One characteristic of these great cultural upheavals in the Western world is certainly that they were associated with the idea of a "constitution." The revolutionary groups were seeking to establish a constitution. They thought of themselves as fighting against absolutism. Hence the concentration of powers in the hands of a dictator involved the revolution in a self-contradiction. Cromwell, as we say, more than any other revolutionary leader struggled with this paradox, but in vain.[15]

The most typical instances of limited revolutions in the modern world are to be found in Latin America. Bolivia is reported to have had sixty-eight revolutions in the first sixty-five years of her existence as a state. This is of course an extreme case. But a compilation by the State Department listed 106 changes of chief of state in Latin America between 1930 and 1965 by other than constitutional means, out of a total of approximately 270 such changes altogether. Thus about 40 per cent of the changes were brought about by revolutionary violence. There is little question many of these revolutions must really be classed as *coups d'état;* yet there are a goodly number of real changes of regime among them. A leading student of Latin America has therefore with some irony claimed that stability cannot be denied to a region in which revolution is the normal way of rotating the executive[16] (K. H. Silvert). A similar fluidity seems to have been characteristic of many of the Greek cities, hence the theory of revolution, or rather turnover (*stasis*), which Aristotle developed in his *Politics*. It stressed the class character of these conflicts and suggested that clashing notions of justice were intrinsic to them.

Unlimited revolution and amending process • The distinction between limited and unlimited revolutions has important consequences. Limited revolutions afford a safer field for scientific inquiry. At the same time, the transcendental, metaconstitutional nature of the constituent power is nowhere so clearly seen as in the great spiritual upheavals. A wisely drawn constitution can anticipate the revolutionary potentialities of the constituent power by so constructing the amending process that sustained pressure would be able to produce sweeping changes in the system of governmental restraints. But even the most supple provisions for amending the constitution may fail when wholly different ideas or a basically altered economy make their appearance. Assuming, then, a more resistant amending process, the forces opposed to the "new spirit" are bound to appeal to the fundamentals of the "constitution" in their struggle to stem the rising tide of impending change. By doing so, they force this new spirit to attack and often to destroy the constitutional morale. Sometimes, as in Germany after 1918 or in France after 1958, a new constitution will be built to take the place of the old. At other times, no constitution results, but a government without restraint will attempt to realize the new spirit by force. An amending process broad enough completely to revamp as well as to amend the existing constitution is an extremely difficult thing to construct. The Swiss, as we have already shown, accomplished a change approaching a fundamental one in 1874. The English did it in 1832. Walter Lippmann at one time argued, in his *Method of Freedom*,[17] that England and the Dominions, America, Switzerland, Holland, and the Scandinavian countries were in the process of revamping their governments so as to make room for the "socialist" right to work. It is happening. Much undoubtedly depends upon the rapidity with which the demand for these changes develops and culminates. Much also depends upon the prevalence of that intelligent view which looks upon the constitution as a human creation subject to change, rather than as a divinely ordained thing of primordial perfection.

It is easy to exaggerate the dangers which spring from an amending process facilitating change. While it is undeniable that such a process might be used for destroying the constitution as a system of restraints altogether, it is not as likely as some writers would have us believe. There are people who might be tempted to cite the overthrow of the Weimar Republic as evidence to the contrary. Did not the German parliament abdicate its own powers and hand them over to a dictator? Might not Congress do likewise, if the amending power were vested in it? The answer is that the German parliament did not abdicate. In order to get parliament to do his bidding, the Hitler government first purged it of many Socialists and all Communists. This purge terrorized many of the remaining deputies. It is significant that constitutional lawyers apologizing for the National Socialist government have themselves shown convincingly that the constitution of the republic was not only violated but actually abolished, when a considerable group of deputies was excluded from parliament. These opposition leaders were prevented from participating in the session of March 21, 1933, which voted to invest Hitler with absolute power. It was by revolutionary force, by a *coup d'état*, that Hitler came into power.[18]

By contrast, the radical change, revolutionary in retrospect, by which the Fifth French Republic came into being was accomplished entirely by means which could be interpreted as legal and constitutional. What brought on the constitutional crisis? There certainly was fairly universal agreement that the constitution of 1946 had been unsatisfactory. Many proposals for reform had been aired, and parliamentary committees had been busy trying to devise corrective improvements in specific respects. But these criticisms were not, during the first ten years of the Fourth Republic, of great moment; indeed those parliamentarians working on constitutional reform found themselves not only without much popular support, but even without any real assistance from their parliamentary colleagues. Given the sceptical turn of the French mind, these criticisms did not seem to exceed the healthy amount of griping to which any government in a democracy should be subjected. To be sure, there was a serious lack of constitutional allegiance in large sections of the populace, but the operations of the government were not seriously impaired by it. The crisis developed over the disintegration of the French colonial empire in North Africa, and more particularly over the prospect of the loss of Algeria. Algeria had been an important part of Metropolitan France, rather than a colony; yet a large part of its electorate was disenfranchised — not completely deprived of participation, but given must less voting strength than the minority of European settlers. This had led to a bloody and costly war with an insurgent minority of the indigenous Arab population which conjured up the threat of a total loss of Algeria, since these insurgents demanded independence. The governments of the

Fourth Republic, pushed by strong public sentiment, found themselves obliged to take ever-more-vigorous action without achieving total victory. Eventually, a rebellion of the military leaders, in conjunction with the settlers, put the authority of the government in jeopardy. By May 13, 1958, it became clear to all that the government had ceased to function, and the President compelled the reluctant Assembly to summon De Gaulle to the premiership.[19]

Negative revolutions · The peculiar conditions of Europe after the Second World War have produced a series of quasi-revolutionary upheavals which may be called *negative* in character. By this we mean to suggest that they were motivated not so much by any positive enthusiasm for a presumably splendid future as by a negative distaste for a sordid past. The French constitution of 1946, the Italian constitution of 1947, and the (West) German constitution of 1949 are of this negative type. Rejecting totalitarianism, whether it be Fascist or Communist, as well as the individualistic liberalism of industrial capitalism, the political outlook of these negative revlutions revolved around four major focal points: 1) reaffirmation of human rights; but 2) efforts to restrict these rights in such a way as to make them unavailable to the enemies of constitutional democracy; 3) stress upon social goals and their implementation through planning; but 4) efforts to circumscribe the goals in such a way as to prevent the re-emergence of totalitarian methods.[20]

In the case of France, the driving force came from the resistance groups which were radically antagonistic to the Third Republic, as well as to the Vichy regime, and repeated efforts of the Radical Socialist Party to have the Third Republic revived were roundly rejected. Yet, as the preamble of the constitution of the Fourth Republic clearly showed, the draftsmen of this document were looking back to the glorious traditions of the great French revolution and its philosophy as expressed in the Rights of Man. The resistance clearly constituted a constituent power in the sense of this analysis, but its constitutional ideal was conservative; the earlier draft, rejected by the electorate, was somewhat more radical, though far from being a Soviet constitution. The constitution of the Fifth Republic is likewise the result of this negative spirit. Since it was widely felt that the constitution of the Fourth had failed to give France an effective government, the new constitution was, as we have seen, written by a group of "experts" under the direction of the then-Minister of Justice, who had been a leading and bitter critic of the Fourth Republic. Plebiscitary approval was given *faute de mieux*, and without enthusiasm.

The Italian constitution bears the same hallmark of the negations associated with the violent overthrow of the Fascist government. In the case of Italy, too, the first draft was more radically Rousseauistic and "democratic" than the constitution finally adopted. But while it is quite true, as has been said, that the new republican constitution represents the first deliberate effort by the Italian people as a whole to guarantee their freedom and common welfare within a constitutional framework, it is equally true that the Italian people only received this opportunity at the hands of conquering armies of the United States and Great Britain. English and American democrats considered themselves liberators of the Italians, and were eager to see them undertake the task of giving themselves a constitution. Many of these democrats were pleased when the Italian people by referendum abolished the monarchy so unhappily associated with the Fascist regime. A constituent group undoubtedly came into being in the course of the three years between 1944 and 1947. That there were relatively only a few who participated in the group is not decisive. But it is important to be clear about the "negative" aspect of the revolution which begot the "constituent power." It was the victory of foreigners over an unconstitutional system which cleared the road for the reassertion of constitutionalism. It is a lukewarm revolution at best.[21]

Even more extreme is the situation in Germany. Here no pretense was made at liberation; foreign conquerors imposed "democratization" as the essential condition of their own security. In using this term, the Western powers meant, as events were to prove, democratic constitutionalism of one kind or another, while the Soviet Union meant as much proletarian dictatorship as could be achieved in "cooperation" with the West. In their own zone, the Soviet Union eventually developed facade "constitutions" which looked as innocuous on paper as her own "constitution" of 1936. They were actually modeled on the pattern of the French constitution of 1946, rejected by the French voters; like this draft constitution, they placed concentrated powers in the hands of a majority of parliament. Such a constitution is, of course, very workable as a camouflage for one-party control, if the realities of politics are handled with the support of a secret police and an occupying army determined to suppress any divergent political activities. But just how free and democratic, how genuinely "constitutional," were the developments in the Western zones? This anxious question was a source of persistent worry to genuine constitutionalists and "democrats" among the personnel of the Western occupying powers. In the first place, and at the start, the "negation" was that of the occupying powers; they were unequivocally determined to destroy the Fascist dictatorship in Germany. Denazification was the concrete policy directed toward this end, and an elaborate system of eliminating former Nazis and militarists from all positions of influence was inaugurated and at least partially carried out. This "cold revolution" had its parallel in the "epuration" procedures by which Fascists and collaborators in both France and Italy were criminally prosecuted. But unlike these processes, which were highly selective and focused attention upon the most responsible individuals, denazification, especially in the American zone, went very far in concentrating upon the little party member. The results of this process were rather unfortunate. Many cases have since been tried by German courts; they have been complicated somewhat by the "dual jeopardy" limit and more recently by superannuation.

In spite of this cold revolution imposed from above — some writers have argued that a real revolution from among the people was thereby prevented — there are some indications that a constituent power did develop among the Germans themselves. The parties, quite clearly linked to the parties of the Weimer Republic, soon entered upon vigorous discussions of the constitutional issues and organized special commissions to prepare drafts. By the time the Western Allies, in June 1948, reached agreement on what kind of constitution to ask the Germans to prepare, their agreement resembled in broad terms the probable compromise between the several positions the parties had taken. Although the drafting process proved very difficult, due to the determination of the constituent assembly (parliamentary council) at Bonn to find viable compromises between the Christian and the Social Democrats, eventually 80 per cent of the assembly voted for the Basic Law, thus giving it the approval of a majority of the German people.* Thus a broad constituent group did in fact crystallize, but it was not so much animated by any enthusiasm for democracy and constitutionalism as it was prepared to reject the totalitarianism of right and left. The Basic Law is a negation of dictatorship. One would like to think that General Clay was right when he reported to the Congress of the United States on his return, in May 1949, that the siege of Berlin, its blockade, and the airlift had lighted "a flame of freedom." He said he saw in Berlin "the spirit and soul of a people reborn." And he expressed the belief that some of that spirit had "spread throughout Germany," and that "the German people have responded. The Germans have cast their die for a government which stands for the dignity of man as an individual." And as the general spoke, the Germans in the Eastern zone under the Soviet terror rejected the Soviet and Communist solution of German unity in sufficiently large numbers (over 35 per cent) to reinforce his belief that Germany may be part "of a new European concept devoted to common economic effort and to a common love of freedom."[22]

---

* Eighty per cent of the Western zones constituted about 55 per cent of all of Germany, leaving Berlin out of account, which would actually somewhat swell the percentage.

There has always been a degree of negativism associated with the rise of constitutionalism. Human beings are more alert to the "blessings of liberty" after they have had a good dose of autocratic abuse of power. In the seventeenth, eighteenth, and nineteenth centuries revolution spelled great hopes for the future. Yet, the more enduring constitutions, especially the American constitution, were made by men who entertained much doubt about their viability. Perhaps the scepticism accompanying the new constitutions in Europe augurs well for their lasting value.

Conclusion · In conclusion it may be said that the course of revolution, though vitally related to the making of constitutions, and therefore of decisive importance for an empirical theory of constitutions and constitutional government, has so far been only partially analyzed. We know something, though far too little, about the working of plebiscites and amending processes. We have large-scale metaphysical interpretations of history asserting generalities concerning the implied political change. We have Aristotle's presumably empirical theory of revolutions in the Greek polis. But a welter of more or less detailed questions and facts present themselves with which we have not as yet effectively coped. Even after we discard "causes" and limit ourselves to the more modest inquiry into concomitant variations of interdependent variables, we are at the present moment only able to advance certain very tentative hypotheses. One deviation from the Aristotelian view is fairly certain: when the revolution is carried out by a constituent group in the modern sense, the end is not the seizure of complete power by the revolutionaries. The end being the making of a constitution, such a revolution aims at a separation of powers.

The Constitution as a Political Force

Introduction · The evolution of human rights · Civil liberties · Social rights and freedoms · Constitutional reason of state · Conflicts of principle · Preambles · Two basic cleavages · Cultural disunity overcome · Switzerland · Contrast between Germany and Great Britain · Symbols and stereotypes · Conclusion

Introduction · According to Rousseau, the most important of all laws "which is not graven on tablets of marble or brass, but on the hearts of the citizens" is embodied in what he calls "the real constitution." It "takes on every day new powers, when other laws decay or die out, restores or takes their place, keeps a whole people in the ways in which it was meant to go, and insensibly replaces authority by the force of habit."[1] In this curious passage, reminiscent of Burke and other traditionalists, the great Swiss revolutionary is, according to his own words, "speaking of morality, of custom, above all of public opinion; a power unknown to political thinkers, on which none the less success in everything else depends." Since the days of Rousseau, political scientists have, however, been much occupied with this important power, although not infrequently neglecting its relation to custom and to the constitution. On the other hand, Professor Holcombe stressed the connection when he said: "The fundamentals of state governments are predetermined outside of the conventions by public opinion. . . . Insofar as this is true, and written constitutional charters set forth the accepted moral standards, customs and public opinion, they themselves constitute a political force of great influence. In a sense this is obvious; for were it not so, there would be little sense in making constitutional charters." Among these basic principles, the guarantee of rights has always been paramount. Indeed, together with the barriers to a concentration of powers, the protection of a personal sphere against interference by the government and other powers has constituted the core of the restraints which constitutionalist thought has evolved.

The evolution of human rights[2] · When President Roosevelt proclaimed the "Four Freedoms" in 1941, he accepted a new conception of human rights far removed from the natural rights of the seventeenth and eighteenth centuries. The conception of rights which inspired the British Bills of Rights (1689), the Declaration of Independence (1776) and the Declaration of the Rights of Man and Citizen (1789) is grounded in simple natural-law notions.[3] Man was believed to have a fixed and unalterable nature, to be endowed with reason, which gave him certain rights without which he ceased to be a human being. These natural rights, summed up in the Lockean formula of "life, liberty, and property" (later broadened to include the pursuit of happiness),[4] were largely concerned with protecting the individual person against governmental power. Each man was seen as entitled to a personal sphere of autonomy, more especially of religious conviction and property; the inner and the outer man in his basic self-realization and self-fulfillment. These rights depended in turn upon the still more crucial right to life — that is to say, to the self itself in terms of physical survival and protection against bodily harm. This right to life was believed immutable, inalienable, involable. Locke exclaimed at one point that no one had the power to part with this right, and hence no government could ever acquire the right to violate rights derived from it.[5]

Natural rights gradually were transformed into "civil liberties," the range of activities of the citizen. This transformation was, of course, closely linked to the forward march of democratization, and a marked shift in the assortment of such rights occurred as the right to vote and participate in government and public-policy formation became generally recognized and extended to the underprivileged and to women. The freedom of religion became broadened into one of conviction; and academic freedom, the freedom to teach and to learn, was recognized even in countries like Germany and Austria-Hungary, where such participation was restricted. In the more advanced democratic countries, those rights which served the political function of better enabling the citizen to participate — freedom of the press, of assembly, and of association, often summed up in the general freedom of expression — moved into the foreground of attention, while the right of property was subjected to restrictions and limitations arising from the widely felt need for greater social control and for restraining the concentration of economic power.

Civil liberties · Civil liberties, vigorously advocated by progressive forces, often seemed to transcend the individual and his personal interest to such an extent that groups were brought into being, such as the American Civil Liberties Union, which lent their organized support to the defense of individuals otherwise unable or unwilling to protect themselves. Civil liberties were the key issue of such writings as John Stuart Mill's *Liberty* – the classic statement of the libertarian doctrine in terms of social utility. Liberalism in its broadest connotation was the belief in these civil liberties and in the need for constitutionally protecting them.[6] This belief became, of course, associated with a great many more specific issues, political, economic and social, and it is therefore possible to see these rights merely as rationalizations for a class interest, as Marx was inclined to do. Such an interpretation underlies the conception of rights in Communist states, as shown below. As against this one-sided analysis – for it contains an element of truth – the notion of civil liberties was grounded in the conviction that freedom required social and political organization which would overcome both natural and man-made obstacles to the realization of individual freedom. Bentham's view of democracy, as the way to have all individuals participate in shaping the conditions of such freedom, influenced (as it represented) a widespread belief.[7]

Freedom of independence was being crowded by freedom of participation. This freedom of participation was actually the older of the two. In the Greek cities it was this freedom rather than that of a personal sphere which had inspired such noble utterances as Pericles' Funeral Oration. The freedom of self-determination of "peoples" which the Draft Covenant of the Human Rights Convention of the U.N. proclaims in its Article 1 (though it is not included in the Universal Declaration) is a modern version of this ancient freedom of classical Greece: the freedom of each man to live under a government belonging to the same national group as his own, as well as to participate therein. One must not allow oneself to be misled by the collective form of this freedom to exclude it from the civil liberties. It is the civil liberty *par excellence*,[8] and closely related to the freedom of participation and its collaterals. That this freedom may collide with and at times even negate other freedoms is undoubtedly true. But there are and always have been conflicts of principle between different liberties. The interpretation of constitutional provisions concerning rights by judicial bodies has had to weigh and balance conflicting claims of priority. Unless one were to construct a rigid hierarchy of these rights, or liberties, culminating in one highest and most important one, any broad recognition of rights will have to accept their pluralism, the fact that their relation and interdependence will evolve as concrete situations are confronted by courts and legislatures. Yet the right of self-determination is seen by many persons as a paramount right which is placed ahead of all personal rights.[9]

Social rights and freedoms • The civil liberties, including the right of self-determination, have, however, in the twentieth century been rivaled not only by the older personal rights, but also by the *freedoms* suggested in the Rooseveltian proclamation and embodied in quite a few of the postwar constitutions as well as the United Nations' Universal Declaration of Human Rights.[10] These new freedoms are rights of an economic and social character which characteristically involve collective, and more especially governmental, effort. Among them are the right to social security, to work,[11] to rest and leisure, to education, to an adequate standard of living, to participation in cultural life, and even to an international order ensuring these rights. Some of these rights which have come into prominence in the twentieth century actually appeared among other "natural" rights at an early date. Thus the French declaration of May 29, 1793, declared in its Article 22 that "education is the need of all and society owes it equally to all its members." This declaration also clearly faced the need for government action; in its Article 24 it asserted that the national sovereign (i.e., the people) must guarantee their enforcement. But the emphasis at that time, and especially after the revolutionary fervor had subsided, was upon the rights *against* the government and, as the nineteenth century progressed toward democracy, upon the rights *within* the government.[12] Only in the twentieth century has the full significance of these social and economic rights become manifest. Such rights are obviously not protecting the individual *against* the government or other power wielders, but call upon the public powers to see to it that such liberty as man possesses by himself is implemented by another set of freedoms which in contrast to those of independence and participation may be called "freedoms of creation." They are rights which provide man with the freedom from fear and the freedom from want; that is to say, they liberate him from restrictions and inhibitions which hinder his full development as a human being. While radically different from the older freedoms, they are nonetheless rightfully claimed for all men *qua* men. It is no longer permissible to brush these rights aside as less basic than the earlier ones, or to question them because of the difficulty of effectuating them. All rights contain norms, and all norms fall short of their enforcement — if it were otherwise, why would norms be needed? No one insists that the law that all men must breathe be enforced by appropriate enactments. It is unwise to ridicule these economic and social rights because at times the drafters of such bills are carried away by their humanitarian enthusiasm and provide for "periodic holidays with pay" or for "enjoying the beauties of nature."[13] Such extravaganzas are recurrent in the elaboration of principles. The constitutions of American states offer many illustrations. The validity of a principle is not invalidated by its overextension, although such *reductio ad absurdum* is a favorite tool of political oratory.

Nor is it true to say that these rights are propounded by enemies of the established order, that the social rights, especially those associated with the freedom from want, are "Communist" or "Un-American." Actually, Marx and Engels had little use for the tradition of natural or any other rights, which they considered a bourgeois prejudice. The adoption and incorporation of them in the "constitutions" of Communist states is part of the general function of such constitutions: to provide a facade of principles. All constitutions have, of course, this function to perform, and there is no gainsaying their role as myth. Still, the elaboration of these social rights in traditional constitutions was and is the result of protracted struggles by particular groups and minorities for equality and freedom. These rights, far from being "Communist" or "Un-American," represent a response to a new and different situation of men frustrated by technological innovation and the like. Numerous American state constitutions contain provisions granting one or another of these economic and social rights.

Therefore, to claim that these rights be considered "Communist" inventions is historically untrue and philosophically and legally unsound. The right to work goes back to the Great Revolution in France; a number of these rights, as just mentioned, have appeared in constitutions of the American states; and they are found in many constitutions of the period after World War I, more especially the Weimar constitution.[14] Indeed, it has recently been argued that the formulation and enforcement of these newer human rights is a central concern of Western as much as Eastern, of nonsocialist as well as socialist, societies. Thus both Italy and the Federal Republic of Germany have included in their recent constitutions most of the economic and social rights which the Universal Declaration contains.

Recognizing these rights as true rights must not prevent their being seen as different from the older rights. In order to appreciate fully this difference between the three sets of rights, as evolved in the history of the last three hundred years, it is necessary first of all to determine what they have in common. If one takes these three rights, the right to one's religious conviction, the right to vote, and the right to work — three rights which illustrate the freedom of independence, the freedom of participation, and the freedom of creation, invention, and innovation — one finds that like the corresponding freedoms, these rights are all related to enabling a human being to become a rounded self, a fully developed person. Not to be allowed to believe what one does believe, not to participate in choosing one's ruler, not to be active in the sphere in which one could produce and create anew — every one of these deprivations is readily recognized as dehumanizing, as crippling the man so afflicted and preventing him from being a person in the full sense. That it may be difficult to implement such rights, even after they are proclaimed, does not invalidate them, any more than the failure to claim a right makes it disappear. Rights have an objective existence; they flow existentially from the recognized nature of man, as do the freedoms which correspond to them. For these freedoms are the manifestation of the power of human beings, of their capacity to put them to some account. There no doubt exists, as far as capacity goes, a wide range of difference between individual human beings; but all men are capable of religious conviction, of voting, or working — to stay with our illustrations. The fact that each of the rights may be expressed as a capacity, as a power of man to achieve self-realization, is the hard core of all rights. Hence we may say that the most comprehensive right is this right to self-realization which has also been simply called "'the right to freedom."[15]

Constitutional reason of state · In all Western countries, including the United States, novel problems have arisen in connection with the activities of anticonstitutional, subversive groups and movements. The crucial question is: To what extent can a constitutional democracy afford to grant the protection of its civil liberties to those who employ them for the purpose of undermining and eventually destroying the constitutional order? The annals of the Nazi movement prior to seizure of power are strewn with incidents where Hitler and his lieutenants made the greatest possible use of freedom of speech, of the press, and of assembly and association for the furtherance of their subversive activities and purposes. Similar things happened in France and Italy. The German Basic Law is rather explicit in seeking to prevent a repetition of such use; it contains provisions which are of course also directed against the Communists. Thus Article 18 states that "whoever abuses the freedom of expression of opinion, in particular the freedom of the press, the freedom of teaching, the freedom of assembly, the freedom of association, the secrecy of mail, post and telecommunications, property, or the right of asylum, in order to attack the free democratic basic order, shall forfeit these basic rights. The forfeiture and its extent shall be pronounced by the federal constitutional court." The provisions obviously suggest various dangerous potentialities; it is a hopeful sign that a judicial interpretation may prevent police action of an arbitrary sort. No similar provision is found in the French constitution.

A further striking proof is the British Public Order Act of 1936. It was the purpose of this act "to prohibit the wearing of uniforms and the maintenance by private persons of associations of military or similar character, and to make further provisions for the preservation of public order on the occasion of public processions and meetings in public places." It was the view of chiefs of police that the wearing of political uniforms was the source of special provocation. Section 2 of the act prohibited organizations from training and equipping men for the purpose of enabling them to usurp the functions of the police or of the armed forces. Other sections gave the police power to control processions, dealt with the use of abusive or insulting language or behavior, and the interrupting of meetings. The act was hotly debated in Parliament, but it was the general opinion back of this act that all were willing to recognize the need for protection of their liberties against antidemocratic influences, and thus to protect the democratic system itself. All were agreed that the *government* must proceed to check action calculated to destroy existing liberties.

In the United States, restrictive legislation of various sorts has been adopted from time to time. Some of the most radical provisions of this kind were included in the Alien Registration Act (1940). At the time, because of its title, most people believed that it was a statute concerned with the fingerprinting of foreigners and similar matters. Zechariah Chafee, Jr., wrote a little later: "Not until months later did I for one realize that this statute contains the most drastic restrictions on freedom of speech ever enacted in the United States during peace. . . . The act gives us a sedition law for everybody, especially citizens of the United States."[16] Like the German provisions, the law is directed against those who seek the overthrow of the government of the United States, but it restricts itself a great deal by including only the *forcible* overthrow. However, the American method of making a particular kind of conduct punishable is certainly sounder than the German one of permitting the "suspension" of "inalienable rights" in case of such conduct. That the Germans, in light of their experience, should be particularly concerned with the problem of subversive activities is not surprising. Actually, the Germans also provided constitutional sanctions against subversive elements, and in Article 143 made it as near a serious crime as they could (having abolished capital punishment) to incite, attempt, or threaten to change, or to actually change by force the constitutional order — in fact they provided penal servitude for life.

This argument about security and survival raises an issue which may properly be called that of "constitutional reason of state,"[17] a complex and difficult matter. It is troublesome in all constitutional democracies because of the challenge of totalitarian movements. Their camp followers and sympathizers are enemies of any and all constitutional order, and yet they are regularly employing the rights made available *by* the constitutional order to its loyal citizens for the purpose of destroying the constitutional order itself. For a constitutional democracy either to allow them to do so or to outlaw them may become self-destructive. If such enemies of the constitutional order were only individuals acting for themselves, one could well afford to adopt the noble stance of Jefferson, who in his first inaugural said: "If there be any among us who would wish to dissolve this Union or to change its republican form, let them stand undisturbed as monuments of the safety with which error of opinion may be tolerated where reason is left free to combat it."[18] Would it were only a matter of opinion, or that reason were free to combat it. Unfortunately, we have to deal with the agents of revolutionary world powers. They operate on the basis of a more deadly form of reason of state, namely, the "reason of party," which is grounded in a presumed certainty beyond all argument, dialectical materialism. How to cope with these challenges is a problem which no sentiment expressive of the early days of the republic will enable us to solve. But neither will it be solved by more or less desperate appeals to a comparable reason of state on our own behalf. Since the protection and elaboration of human rights is the core of the constitutional order, its very reason for existing, every infringement of such rights ought to be justified by clearly stating the overt acts which constitute a clear danger and demonstrate its presence beyond the peradventure of any serious doubt. The hysteria of the McCarthy days violated this principle in gross and indefensible fashion. An alerted citizenry will insist that such a breakdown of American tradition will not occur. What this calls for is that not only judges and legislatures, but the learned professions of political science and the law, devote much more effort than they have in the past to reaffirming and strengthening public understanding.[19]

Conflicts of principle · If constitutional rights express the ideas dominant in the community regarding the desirable relations between the government and individual citizens, such rights must necessarily undergo considerable alterations when these dominant ideas change, as was just shown. For as new interests arise in the community, they will clamor for recognition as soon as they become sufficiently weighty to arouse a sizable group of people to rally to their support.[20] The resulting need for adjustment creates sharp tensions. The threat of revolution arises and calls for compromise. And since compromises are well-nigh impossible between mutually conflicting fundamental positions, such compromises often assume a very peculiar form. Two mutually exclusive, conflicting clauses or formulas may be inserted into the constitutional charter, each expressing the outlook of one of the rival groups. The American federal constitution contained very few if any such clauses until the enactment of Amendment XVIII. The courts could settle the conflicts with older rights which arose out of the enforcement of this amendment by maintaining the ancient principle that the later rule of law supersedes the earlier. There are, however, indications that Amendment XVIII was approved by an electorate which was only dimly aware of the implications of its principle and their effect upon the older rights, and that the movement for the repeal of this amendment gained momentum as these implications became apparent. But what would be the attitude of a court or other official when the original constitutional charter embodied such compromises in the form of contradictory clauses? The German constitution of 1919 was drafted and enacted by what later became known as the Weimar Coalition, a conjunction of Liberals, Catholics, and Socialists. These parties had been united in their opposition to the monarchical government of Germany. But had they enough in common to draw up a constitutional bill of rights? Even a casual inspection of the second part of the Constitution of the German Republic would incline one to reply with· an emphatic "no." These "Rights and Duties of Germans" contained Liberal, Catholic, and Socialist principles in a motley assortment. Such questions as church and state, the schools, and economic life reveal the indecision of the makers. Private property rights are declared to be inviolable, except where laws provide otherwise — which means that private property rights are not inviolable. The church was excluded from control of the schools, but a majority of the parents were given decisive influence — which meant that the Catholic Church would nevertheless control the schools wherever it predominated, and so forth. Nor is the German constitution singular in this respect. Many of the postwar European constitutions contain a mixture of liberal and socialist principles. It was the comparative unanimity of the American Constitutional Fathers in matters of general principle, all of them being more or less liberal in their outlook, which gave the American constitution its great inner coherence. The present German and Italian constitutions are much more satisfactory than the previous ones in these respects. Their statements of basic rights are forthright and on the whole they avoid the artificial compromises of the Weimer constitution. In fact, the Basic Law tries specifically to prevent the destruction of such basic rights by legislation, where such legislation may under the constitution restrict it (as is the case with property, for example). Such restrictions may in no case affect the core of such a basic right (Article 19 (2)).

Preambles · Preambles of constitutional charters are of considerable weight as an indication of the values and beliefs to which a particular constitution owes its force.[21] The well-known American preamble is characteristic: "We, the people of the United States, in order to form a more perfect union, establish justice, insure domestic tranquillity, provide for the common defense, promote the general welfare, and secure the blessings of liberty to ourselves and our posterity, do ordain and establish this Constitution for the United States of America." It may be contrasted with the preamble of the French constitution of 1946 and of the German Basic Law, both of which stress peace and social progress; the French, in fact, goes so far as to proclaim that the French Republic "accepts the limitations of sovereignty necessary to the organization and defense of peace." The Germans provide similarly in their Article 24. As previously noted, the French preamble contains the entire bill of rights; after solemnly reaffirming the traditional rights of man as stated in the epochal revolutionary Declaration of the Rights of Man, it recites the more recent rights: equality of women, health and old-age protection, child care and education, as well as those rights noted in the preceding paragraphs. Interestingly enough, it couples with these rights the community's right to control any "national public service or monopoly." In many ways, the French preamble is a legal anomaly; for such a preamble must needs have more than declaratory force. The stress laid upon peace and social progress is indicative of a new spirit, and one which would doubtless express itself forcefully in the preamble of any American constitution written today. It is, therefore, often maintained that the *real* constitution of the American people is no longer fully expressed in the written document. On the other hand, the preamble of the constitution of the Soviet Union sets forth some ideas which are as yet quite generally rejected in the United States.

In the light of the foregoing, brief mention might be made of an argument which has recurred in the annals of constitutionalism. It is the question as to whether such a preamble possesses any enforceable legal principles or rules. Does, for example, the commitment to "the general welfare" reinforce the welfare clause in the constitution? In the French constitution of 1946, a kind of declaration of rights was included; did it have validity as substantive law? The prevailing notion among positivist jurists has been to deny such validity and assert that preambles have, as in other laws, merely declaratory value. But why "merely"? In all law the declarations of intent, disclosing the purpose of an actor, are of significance for interpreting his legal acts. Thus the fact that the preamble of the Basic Law of the Federal Republic of Germany declares that it is "the will of the German people to maintain its national and political unity," anyone dealing with the great majority of the Germans living in that republic would disregard at his peril. At the same time, the statement conjoined with it that the Germans wish "to serve the peace of the world" offers some reassurance that the determination to seek the reunification of their country will not be attempted by the use of arms. "Very well," say the jurists, "but is that a proposition enforceable in a court of law?" The answer must of course be "no." But the further comment is permitted that not all legally relevant propositions are enforceable in court, as the United States Supreme Court has always recognized in refusing to deal with what it considers "political questions." The propositions contained in preambles are preeminently such political questions.

Two basic cleavages • The two most formidable cleavages which divide modern nations are the cultural, and the social or economic groupings.[22] People are willing to go to war and to die for a national culture or for the working class. If we accept this willingness to die as the final test of effective allegiance, any citizenship which is divided by such loyalties would seem to be distinctly heterogeneous. The relative size of these heterodox groups is of great importance. The significance of heterogeneity would be small if the ratio were 9 to 1; it would be very great if it were 1 to 1. Countries like old Austria or contemporary Canada and Belgium, which include large numbers of people who are sentimentally attached to other national cultures than that of the majority, or who even strive for complete independence, would seem to be so constituted that constitutional popular government can at best maintain no more than a very precarious existence. Especially perplexing is the case of India. However, as the case of Switzerland shows, such heterogeneity can be resolved in a higher unity: the real attachment to the basic principles of constitutional democracy can overcome national cultural divisions, as it has overcome religious and other cleavages in the past. The case is different when the disagreement turns upon the basic institutions of constitutional democracy itself. Countries which, like Weimar Germany, had a large, organized Communist or Fascist party were equally or perhaps even less likely to maintain such a system of government. This was simply the result of there being anticonstitutional forces which not only were ready to destroy the existing constitutional order but were opposed to establishing a new one. Arnold Brecht, in writing of his experiences as a high official of the Weimar Republic, rightly stressed the fact that there was no majority supporting Weimar's democratic constitution after 1920. Hence "the astonishing thing was not that thirteen years later democracy collapsed, but that this did not happen much sooner."[23] In short, an effective constituent power was nonexistent and the constitution was not real enough to become a political force.

The making of culturally united nations has been a long and arduous process wherever it has been carried through, as in England, France, Holland, Denmark, Sweden, and Norway.[24] In these countries, unification was accomplished before the rise of the international labor movement added a new element of dissension and disunity. Hence, the leaders of the labor movement in these countries were imbued with a sense of national loyalty even after they had begun to admit a higher allegiance to the international labor community. In Italy and Germany, where national unity was achieved only with difficulty and *after* the rise of the international labor community had already commenced to take hold of their working class, the conflict remained unresolved. The intensification of nationalist emotionalism during and after the First World War led to a violent reaction against all popular constitutional government. Fascism here, National Socialism there, proceeded to attack ruthlessly the flourishing internationalist labor movement. Determined to achieve national unity at all costs, these movements went far beyond the methods which were in vogue in the sixteenth and seventeenth centuries under the autocratic monarchies of England and France, and which had started those countries on the road toward their unitary national culture. Once united, the British and French nations in two bloody revolutions had long since vindicated their right to rule themselves. There was something strangely atavistic about the Fascist position, and yet there was good reason for placing Mussolini and Hitler in parallel to Cromwell and Napoleon. All these men radically coerced national unity in an autocratic fashion after a period of confusion attendant upon a revolutionary upheaval. It remains doubtful whether national unity can be achieved under a genuinely constitutionalist regime in which powers are divided and restrained and human rights effectively guaranteed.

Cultural disunity overcome: Switzerland • Those who maintain that such a multinational constitutional system is inconceivable should examine the case of Switzerland.[25] Here popular constitutional government has achieved great stability, though it rests upon three very distinct national cultural groups. To aggravate the difficulty, each of these constituent elements of the Swiss people belongs to one of three most powerful national cultures on the Continent; French, German, and Italian are the three official languages of the little mountain republic. Nor are the Swiss linked by a common religion. But these three distinct cultural groups are united by a long tradition of common political customs which through centuries separated them from the surrounding monarchical governments. The partly democratic, partly aristocratic member states, today called cantons, were uniformly republican and very proud of it. Protected to some extent by natural geographic conditions, and long surrounded by the halo of their startling victories over much more powerful princes, the Swiss Confederation profited by peace and afforded an asylum to victims of the religious persecutions. Though each of its cultural groups stuck with tenacity to its own language, customs, and habits, none went far in attempting to proselytize the others. The leading French Swiss canton, Geneva, was kept away from France politically by its stern protestantism, and neither Germany nor Italy possessed a united national government to which their Swiss brethren could have rallied on the basis of common national sentiment. Thus a tradition of common political destiny welded the culturally divided cantons into a united whole.

In important respects, the sentiment of nationality in Switzerland resembles that in the United States. The racial and cultural elements which play the decisive role in England and France are supplanted by a kind of secular religion: the free political traditions common to different and distinct racial and cultural groups. The shared experience of fighting for these traditions, both spiritually and materially, builds up a common store of memories which finds poetic expression in symbolic paintings and in holidays such as Columbus Day which emphasize the distinctive contributions. As far as the United States is concerned, there is no more vivid epic depicting the saga of such joint endeavor than Stephen Vincent Benét's *John Brown's Body*, with its panoramic view of races and peoples.

Switzerland most strikingly illustrates the weight of a common tradition rising from a joint past as the procreator of that *real* constitution which transforms a written charter into a political force of lasting importance. Burke has well stated the need for real unity in favor of a common government as a necessary prerequisite. In his *Appeal from the New to the Old Whigs* he said: "The power of acting by a majority . . . must be grounded on two assumptions; first, that of an incorporation produced by unanimity; and secondly, an unanimous agreement that the act of a mere majority . . . shall pass with them and with others as the act of the whole."[26] Now this unanimity at the start of an association or a group (what Burke calls an incorporation) must, in the case of so extensive and complex a group as that which constitutes the citizenship of a modern country, be built upon a fairly long period of living together or upon an overwhelming sense of the need for association, such as existed at the start of the American federal union.

Contrast between Germany and Great Britain • It was not pusillanimity, as the radicals charged, when Friedrich Ebert sought to retain the monarchy, but a sound sense of the fragile foundation of German political tradition. Germany having been united under one government for less than fifty years, the time was not ripe, according to Ebert, for overthrowing the monarchy without jeopardizing national sentiment of unanimity and cohesion. That sense for the need of continuity found expression in the curious phrase of the preamble of the Weimar constitution ". . . to renew and strengthen *their* Reich . . . ," as well as in a lengthy debate over the retention of the word *"Reich"* itself. There is a great contrast between the use of the word *"Reich"* in this preamble and the meaning given to it in the preamble of the imperial constitution of 1871. There it was said that "His Majesty the King of Prussia . . . His Majesty the King of Bavaria, His Majesty . . . and so forth [enumerating all the ruling German princes and the governments of the free cities of Hamburg, Bremen, and Lübeck] . . . do conclude an everlasting union for the protection of the federal territory and of the rights valid therein, as well as for the furtherance of the welfare of the German people. This union shall bear the name of the German Reich and shall have the German constitution." In this preamble, then, the term *"Reich"* is nothing but the name for the union of monarchs ruling in Germany, who even insisted that the emperor be merely "German Emperor" and not "Emperor of Germany." Those members of the republican constitutional convention were doubtless right who maintained that the term *"Reich"* referred to the monarchical past.[27] But when they contended that the term *"Reich"* should be eliminated in favor of the term "German Republic," Friedrich Naumann and others urged that the word *"Reich"* was a symbol of German national unity, that it embodied much more than the Bismarckian preamble allowed one to infer, and that it should be retained. The contrary conclusion was reached by the Western Allies and by the Germans who drafted the Basic Law of 1949. The word "federation" or *"Bund"* has replaced the *"Reich"* of Weimar days. Whether this is the last word remains to be seen. Britain and the United States are more fortunate. Their slow evolution has enabled them to handle their symbols of national unity more effectively. It was a stroke of genius when Lord Balfour, in search for a symbolic formula around which sentiments of underlying traditional unanimity of British people could rally, hit upon the expression "British Commonwealth of Nations."

Symbols and stereotypes · The traditionalism of the British in matters of politics has always manifested itself in a strong sense of the importance of symbols. Skillful handling of symbols is as important for constitutionalism as for other forms of government. The symbols can be of many different types. Picturesque customs, such as surround the conduct of judicial business in Britain, have a definite symbolic value. Special celebrations greatly aid in strengthening the sense of community; practically all modern nations have special holidays of their own, none more so than the Americans. These patriotic occasions, while often irritating to the more sophisticated (note such deprecatory expressions as "Fourth of July oratory"), symbolize allegiance to the community, whether local or national, or even supranational.* The ritual of the flag, so consistently observed in the United States, is an everyday illustration of how the symbols of communal unity are instinctively hallowed in a democracy. In recent years, the problem of symbols has received more general attention from political scientists than it used to. Searching inquiries into the nature of nationalism focused attention upon the important role which flags, national anthems, and the like play in rallying mass sentiment.[28] All this is by no means new; for unless shrewd, practical

---

* Europe has developed a flag, stamps, etc.

men had been aware of these effects, such symbols would not have been created. But what is new is a clear recognition of the bearing these psychological factors have upon the government of men. It is, however, quite easy to exaggerate the manipulative side. Thurman Arnold, in his *Symbols of Government* (1935) and his *Folklore of Capitalism* (1937), advanced the extreme proposition that most scientific word usages constitute folkloristic ceremonials. In thus making light of all the analytic elements contained in modern economics, jurisprudence, and political science, he finds himself without any coherent analytic terminology. As a result, both his books end on a note of plaintive preaching. Harold Lasswell, in his *Politics: Who Gets What, When, How* (1936), stated a similar view, but without the factual case material which reveals Thurman Arnold as a lawyer impatient with the make-believe of his symbol-laden trade. The charge has been made against such opinions that they represent a new Machiavellianism. Maybe they do. But the more important question seems to be: Are these analyses accurate, are they realistic, as they certainly pride themselves on being? For if they are, no highfalutin name-calling will dispose of them. Unfortunately, the answer to such questions leads beyond arguable evidence; certainly their underlying assumptions are different from those of the present study. They are, we believe, also different from those underlying the Western constitutionalist tradition. For their metaphysics is deterministic; it is the metaphysics underlying Freud and the psychoanalytic approach. The human being is seen as motivated largely by drives beyond his control. Charles Merriam has called these aspects the "credenda" and the "miranda" of power. There is a great deal of make-believe in social intercourse, and especially in politics. The "constitution" tends to become a symbol, and its provisions become so many symbols in turn. It is this symbolic function of *words* which makes the constitution a political *force*. It is no longer possible for us to look upon traditions and customs as God-given or natural, as was done by Burke and many of his contemporaries and predecessors. We know that even the most hoary tradition has been created by men, that all such traditions can be manipulated, and, in short, that propaganda permeates our existence on every side.

It is readily apparent how this "disenchantment" with ideas and sentiments through exposure to the glaring searchlight of modern psychology, how this "debunking" of ideals once held to be sacrosanct as "natural rights," shatters the foundations of the unanimity which has been held to be an essential prerequisite of a constitutional order. If all ideas and ideals are merely shrewdly designed veils hiding special interests in their sparring for position, where is that underlying unanimity to come from which can give a constitution lasting force? Are modern communities bound to dissolve into a free-for-all in which the most ruthless will eventually win out by imposing their will, trampling the common men underfoot? Or are there traditions and customs which, though admittedly created by men, yet do represent habitual preferences and patterns of behavior in certain communities? These questions are more easily raised than answered at this stage of our inquiry. We shall later return to them. (See below, ch. XXI.)

It is highly doubtful that a political order could endure without effective symbols — not only symbols for its myth, but also for its ideology and the values and beliefs upon which such ideology rests. As for the symbols of government, and more especially the founding of a political order, take the following statement: "However you reduce the functions of your government to their utmost simplicity, yet symbolism remains. . . . You abolish the etiquette of a royal court, but at official receptions you ceremonially shake the hand of the Governor of your state. Just as the feudal doctrine of a subordination of classes, reaching up to the ultimate overlord, requires its symbolism; so does the doctrine of human equality require its symbolism."[29] Here presumably the symbolism consists of "doctrines," i.e., ideatic embodiments of value preferences. But it would seem doubtful that the handshake referred to is symbolic in any precise sense. There has been a considerable danger of depriving symbols of their distinctive role in the political order by thinking that "almost all human conduct is symbolic."[30] Like the notion that all believed-in ideas are "myths," this theory signifies a corrosion of the true symbols of any political order. Symbols are signs for meanings transcending the empirical content; symbols therefore refer to something else, usually by simplifying a complex and absent person or thing. The coat of arms of a landowner, the flag of a country, the signature of a writer — these are typical symbols of considerable political relevance.

Conclusion · The constitution, then, which *is* the process by which governmental action is effectively restrained, *functions* also as the most effective symbol of the unifying forces operative in a community. Our insight into social motivation owing to modern research enables us to distinguish fairly well between the system of institutional safeguards, patterned in many different ways but always designed to prevent the concentration of power, and the congeries of symbols, expressive of communal traditions and general agreements. Through recognizing this, one can avoid the cynicism which springs from a naïve rational search for close correspondence between such symbols and the things they refer to. It is equally important to recognize the need for continual change. An appreciation of the symbolic value of the "constitution" need not obscure the dynamic, changing nature of the traditions and agreements which it symbolizes. That is the meaning behind Lincoln's famous remark that "Any people anywhere being inclined and having the power, have the right to rise up and shake off the existing government, and form a new one that suits them better. This is a most valuable, a most sacred right ... More than this, a majority of any portion of such people may revolutionize, putting down a minority ... It is a quality of revolutions not to go by old ideas or old laws. ..."[31]

The Separation of Powers and Functions

X

Introduction · The theory of mixed government · Importance of institutional background · Cromwell's *Instrument of Government* · Locke's view · Montesquieu's reinterpretation · American problems · Fusion of powers in England · The judiciary · The French *Charte Constitutionnelle* of 1814 · German constitutions · Weakness of monarchical executive · Sweden's unusual separation · A modern theory of divided powers · Practical aspects: checks and balances · The party as the integrator · Conclusion

Introduction · The entire history of government shows that substantive restraints embodying the opinion and customs of the community, its way of life, rest upon a tenuous foundation unless reinforced and backed up by procedural restraints of one sort or another. True constitutional government does not exist unless procedural restraints are established and effectively operating. Such restraints involve some division of power; for evidently some considerable power must be vested in those who are expected to do the restraining. Such a division of governmental power under a constitution has largely taken two forms: the functional division such as that into legislative, executive, and judicial, and the spatial (territorial) division, embodied in federalism. Though federalism and the separation of powers have been thus intimately related, their theoretical and practical connection has often been overlooked. Leaving federalism to the following chapter, we shall be primarily concerned in this one with stating a modern, rational theory of separated powers which is only a more scientific statement of views well established in classical antiquity and elaborated down to Montesquieu. This contention can be verified, in a sense, by the fact that totalitarian theory and practice are solidly opposed to any institutional division of power. Efficiency and planning seem indeed to call for a concentration rather than a division of power. A line of argument that runs back through Marx and Bentham to Hobbes makes the practitioners of concentrated power and their theoretical apologists contemptuous of any separation of powers. Typical is the view of Bentham and his friends: "If the power is being used for good, why divide it; if it is being used for evil, why have it?" The constitutionalists' reply ought to be: "Who is the judge of what is 'power for good' and what 'power for evil'?" To organize the answering of that question well is precisely the task of good government.

The theory of mixed government • The Roman republican constitution affords a particularly striking example of carefully divided powers. When Polybius came to analyze the Roman constitution in terms of the classification of forms of government evolved by Plato and Aristotle, he must have been baffled by the discovery that several forms were skillfully combined. He thereupon constructed his theory of mixed government, which exerted a considerable influence down to modern times.[1] Political theorists in the seventeenth century evolved from it the theory of the "separation of powers." Particularly English theorists, during the civil wars, tended to generalize from the experience and the institutional pattern developed by medieval constitutionalism. It is too-little realized that we owe to this approach the theory of the separation of powers which forms so vital a part of modern constitutionalism. Political thinkers undertook to analyze political processes from a functional point of view and thus they discovered the distinctive features of certain basic functions or "powers." This pattern of thought found its clearest theoretical expression in James Harrington's *Oceana* (1656). Reverting to thoughts on Roman constitutionalism, Harrington undertook to answer the question of how a commonwealth comes to be an empire of laws and not of men. Harrington candidly recognized that men are predominantly governed in their decisions by interest rather than reason, and he therefore felt that unless one can show how different men can be restrained, one will not achieve a government of laws. The crucial point, according to Harrington, is that of achieving a balance between various orders. There are two main orders, the "natural aristocracy" and the common people. These must concur in order to make a law. Together they constitute the legislative power. Of necessity there must be a third "to be executive of the laws made, and this is the magistracy," magistracy then meaning the judiciary primarily. Once this balance is achieved, you have a commonwealth, or government of laws: the commonwealth consists of "the senate proposing, the people resolving, and the magistracy executing."[2]

Importance of institutional background • In the explicit form which Locke gave the theory of the separation of powers,[3] it was an attempt to generalize the results of the struggle of the English Parliament for an equality of status with the Crown. As is usual in political theory, it was the product of a long evolution of political organization, and by looking primarily to theoretical precursors we mistake the theory for something largely divorced from practice. Nothing is further from the truth. English political thinkers would never have evolved the theory of the separation of powers from that of mixed government if the institutional evolution in England had not pointed in that direction. The function of interpreting the law in a high court of Parliament was transformed by a very gradual process into the function of making the law. Early statutes were conceived of as stating what the old law was rather than as creating new law. From the time of Fortescue, who in the fifteenth century praised the rule of law as the outstanding feature of English government, this function of creating the law became increasingly important. Through that function, the position and power of Parliament were necessarily increased. Not content with the skillful manipulation of members of Parliament as practiced by Henry VIII and Elizabeth, James I undertook to challenge explicitly the supremacy of the law as interpreted by courts and sanctioned by the "king in Parliament." He claimed this as reasonable, because the law was rapidly becoming man-made legislation instead of eternal custom. But his efforts caused violent opposition. Sir Edward Coke, though often medieval in his outlook on law and highly partisan in his guild-spirit as a lawyer, came to claim absolute parliamentary supremacy. The rapid succession of royal and parliamentary absolutism, Cromwellian dictatorship, and a return to royal absolutism, which marks the several phases of this struggle, impressed upon English minds the need for some harmonious balance between those who make the law and those who execute it. This harmony the Glorious Revolution of 1688 tried to achieve, and in the fashion of the age, Locke's essay gave it the halo of general and eternal truth.

Cromwell's Instrument of Government · Yet Cromwell's *Instrument of Government* (1653) had already made a first attempt to distinguish and separate the executive and the legislative power.[4] In Article XXIV it provided "that all Bills agreed unto by parliament, shall be presented to the Lord Protector for his consent; and in case he shall not give his consent thereto within twenty days . . . that then . . . such Bills shall pass into and become laws, although he shall not have given his consent . . . ; provided such Bills contain nothing in them contrary to the matters contained in these presents" (the constitution). Again, in Article XXX it was provided "that the raising of money . . . shall be by consent of parliament and not otherwise. . . ." The great importance which Cromwell himself attached to these separate legislative powers can be gleaned from his speech on dissolving the Parliament elected under the *Instrument*. Cromwell, deeply disgusted at their debating constitutional issues instead of making laws and granting money, told them that they had wasted their time instead of attending to their duty, which was to make "those good and wholesome laws which the people expected" of them. His opening speech, in which he had outlined the necessary legislation much as the American chief executive does in his inaugural address, he had concluded by saying: "I have not spoken these things as one who assumes dominion over you; but as one who doth resolve to be a fellow-servant with you to the interest of these great affairs, and of the people of these Nations." When he finally dismissed them, after their injudicious palaver, he told them more explicitly that the government was limited and divided between a single person as chief executive and a Parliament. "This was thought most agreeable to the general sense of the Nation; — having had experience enough, by trial, of other conclusions; judging this most likely to avoid the extremes of Monarchy on the one hand, and of Democracy on the other . . ." he exclaimed, thus showing the connection between the separation of powers and mixed government in the minds of practical politicians of the day. It never did, however, seem acceptable to Cromwell to provide for his own popular election, and so English constitutional development turned back to hereditary monarchy as the safest method for securing the chief executive.

Locke's view · Locke's view of the system is briefly this. He distinguishes the legislative power, that is, the power which makes general rules, from the executive and federative power. The latter is concerned with foreign affairs and security. But he does not at all attribute the legislative power to Parliament, and the executive and federative power to the king, as is often in the light of later developments supposed. Rather he divided the legislative power itself, attributing it to the king in Parliament, as orthodox English constitutional law provided. This is also the system which we have just found to underlie the Cromwellian *Instrument of Government*. The difference lies solely in how the chief executive is created, a point not germane to the theory of the separation of powers proper. The division of authority between the king and Parliament with respect to the legislative power is not, however, balanced by an analogous division of authority in the executive and federative power. These are solely attributed to the king and his council. An explanation for such concentration of power is given only in the case of the federative power. The conduct of foreign affairs requires expedition and cannot be bound by general rules because it depends too much upon the changing international situation. This division of authority and the separation of the executive and legislative powers is justified and explained by Locke as by Harrington before him on the well-known ground that it is necessary for the maintenance of liberty; liberty suffers when the same human beings make the laws and apply them. This view was canonized by Blackstone in his *Commentaries on the Laws of England* (1765): "In all tyrannical governments, the supreme magistracy, or the right both of *making* and *enforcing* the laws is vested in one and the same man, or one and the same body of men; and wherever these two powers are united together, there can be no public liberty."[5]

Montesquieu's reinterpretation · When Montesquieu came to rewrite Locke's doctrine, the Act of Settlement of 1701 had already, in ¶ 3, undertaken to guarantee to English judges tenure during good behavior. Montesquieu was, of course, equally concerned with liberty. Granting that as a starting point, he was next primarily interested, as a result of the contemporary situation in France, in the problem of how to secure, or rather to maintain, an independent status for judges. What could be more natural for him, therefore, than to rename Locke's "executive power" and to call it "the judicial power"?[6] The executive's function, as described by Locke, had been to execute the laws, in any case. This transformation of Locke's executive power in the analysis of Montesquieu was accompanied by another equally significant though misleading change in terminology, whereby Locke's "federative power" became "the executive power" in Montesquieu. By emphasizing the importance of maintaining internal as compared to external peace, and by thus assimilating the police functions to the functions of defense and foreign policy, Montesquieu constructed the modern executive power. This executive power included also the prerogative which English lawyers had always carefully kept apart for special purposes. It will be seen that through these changes Montesquieu assimilated the core of modern government, bureaucracy as it had developed on the Continent, to the English doctrine, which had emphasized legislation or the power to make general rules. It is therefore not surprising that the theory had much wider appeal in the form which Montesquieu gave it. Men of affairs throughout Europe recognized in Montesquieu's executive power the type of government with which they had been familiar.

Montesquieu's argument was, as a matter of fact, incidental to his discussion of the English constitution in book XI entitled "Of the Laws Which Shape Political Liberty in Its Relation to the Constitution." The argument is curiously tortuous and not informed by a clear philosophical conception. This basis was furnished by Immanuel Kant. He was the first to observe that the distinction of powers or functions corresponds to the pattern of a practical argument or syllogism. Such a syllogism is divided into a major premise, a minor premise, and the consequent. The separation-of-powers doctrine is thus linked to Aristotelian logic, which is perhaps the reason it is unique to Western culture. The resemblance of the distinctions underlying the pattern of separation of powers and that of a syllogism is related to the fact that powers imply decisions, and decisions in turn imply judgments. A practical syllogism is composed of the three basic kinds of judgments.[7]

American problems · It was of the greatest moment that this theory happened also to fit the political experiences of most of the American colonies, where a governor, a distinct colonial legislature, and a fairly independent judiciary had come to constitute the essential organs of government.[8] After the Declaration of Independence had severed the bonds with the mother country, a brief experiment with legislative supremacy in some of the states had led to what seemed to many majority tyranny, and had thus made people ripe for an application of the celebrated theme. Nevertheless, in many of the state constitutions which contain an express statement of the doctrine, the older English emphasis upon the importance of general laws remains intact. The most famous and perhaps the most succinct statement of that doctrine is contained in the constitution of Massachusetts, which declares that the reason for the separation of powers into a legislative, executive, and judicial branch is to make sure that this will be "a government of laws and not of men." The federal constitution, too, though abstaining from stating the doctrine, puts the legislative power first and therefore, by implication, foremost. In spite of the silence of the constitution regarding the doctrine, the Supreme Court has repeatedly called it a "fundamental tenet." Many who in recent discussions have belittled the separation of powers seem unaware of the fact that their clamor for efficiency and expediency may lead to dictatorship. Fortunately, the one-party dictatorships in many countries have gradually awakened a realization of where the fusion of power leads. In the words of a renowned jurist and judge: "The flexible scope of the Constitution and the qualities of statesmanship demanded for its construction are illustrated by what is often alleged to be the greatest defect of the Constitution, namely, the doctrine of the separation of powers. That doctrine embodies cautions against tyranny in government through undue concentration of power. The environment of the Constitution, the debates at Philadelphia and in support of the adoption of the Constitution, unite in proof that the purpose was, not to avoid friction, but by means of the inevitable friction incident to the distribution of the governmental powers among the three departments, to save the people from autocracy. As a principle of statesmanship, the practical demands of government preclude its doctrinaire application. The latitude with which the doctrine must be observed in a work-a-day world was insisted upon by those shrewd men who framed the Constitution." Europeans, and not only Europeans, have been little inclined to adopt constitutions which closely resemble the American system. Among the aspects they object to, perhaps the most important is the American form of the separation of powers, implying presidentialism.[9] The most important argument advanced against this point of view is derived from what is alleged to be the nature of parliamentary government in England. There an increasing fusion of executive and legislative powers does not seem to have destroyed the foundations of free government.

Fusion of powers in England · Though the problems of parliamentary government will receive more careful treatment later on, it is necessary to deal here in a general way with the so-called "fusion" of the legislative and executive branches in England. The relative absolutism which this fusion appears to have created has been endurable because of a constitutional safeguard which no one clearly envisaged until after Montesquieu's time: the institutionalization of the opposition and the regular alternation of two large parties in controlling this broad power.[10] These parties represented a slow growth, for in most cases they went back to the "town and country" divisions prior to and after the Glorious Revolution when political groups, growing out of the earlier conflicts of the civil wars, had formed in each local district. It is this traditionalism which accounted for a good deal of the aristocratic, gentlemanly character of British politics throughout the nineteenth century. To the beginning of this century, the remnants of aristocratic organization retained by English society exerted a profound influence upon the political life of the nation. The lack of this traditional aristocratic basis of the English parliamentary government has had a good deal to do with the failure of European systems presumably modeled after the English pattern. In addition, of course, the confusion of small parties fails to respond to the recurrent popular demand for clearly recognizable leadership. In some countries this confusion contributed to the development of one-party systems. Under the pressure of threats of a Communist takeover, which is so freely advocated by the adepts of a proletarian revolution, the public at large accepted a real fusion and concentration of powers without the constitutional custom of a recognized opposition as we know it in England. In any case, the growth of parliamentary and eventually of cabinet government as a system of consolidated power as it occurred between 1740 and 1940 certainly seems to have obliterated the separation of powers, as envisaged by eighteenth-century doctrine. This change must be seen, however, against the background of party development. If, as happened in England, there is a genuine development of a constitutional custom of party alternation, if there is fairly general recognition that, leaving aside the judiciary, the elected representatives debate and "propose," in Harrington's phrase, while the people resolve through general elections, then that basic conception of a balance and counterpoise is effectively preserved. It is important to realize that there are many ways of arranging regularized restraint. What appears, then, as a fusion of powers in modern England is really a different and more subtle division of powers. Still another pattern is represented by the "constitutional monarchies" of nineteenth-century Europe.

The judiciary • As already pointed out, before this fusion of powers occurred in England, a new and crucial "separation" had taken place, namely the separation of the judicial from the legislative power (see pp. 111–112). Montesquieu was aware of it, and in light of the situation in France, where the *parlements* had become high courts, had stressed it (p. 176). This separation holds, of course, in England as elsewhere, except that it has not been carried to the extent of giving courts the right to question the legality of acts of Parliament. We shall leave that special issue apart which springs from the recognition of the constitution as a basic law different from other laws and of a consequent amending power. It will be discussed below when we are dealing with the guardianship of the constitution. The general principle of the independence of the judiciary has come to be universally accepted as a basic tenet of constitutionalism and government according to law. Once this patent fact is taken into account, it becomes clear that the alleged "fusion" of powers is quite partial. For as far as the legislative and executive power are concerned, their close interrelation is counterbalanced by the recognition of the opposition as a "potential" power, and the judicial power is separated, though ministerial control often jeopardizes judicial independence.

The French **Charte Constitutionnelle** *of* **1814** • It is often forgotten that the constitutions of nineteenth-century monarchies in Europe were in fact almost as much built upon Locke's and Montesquieu's theories of the separation of powers as was the American constitution.[11] These constitutions were at the same time dictated by a deep-seated mistrust of the theory itself, which was supposed to be inextricably related to the rights of man and of popular government. This had actually been the case in the ill-fated constitution of 1791, in which the principle had made its debut in Continental constitutional law. In Title III, which deals with the "Public Powers," it is provided that the legislative power is delegated to one national assembly, that the judicial power is delegated to judges, and that the executive power is delegated to the king in order to be exercised under his authority by ministers and other agents. But all these powers were said to be ultimately derived from the people. On the other hand, the *Charte Constitutionnelle* of Louis XVIII (1814) is built upon a separation of powers in fact and a denial of the separation of powers in theory. To quote the relevant passage: ". . .

although all authority in France resides in the person of the king, our predecessors have not hesitated to alter the exercise thereof in accordance with the change of times . . . that only the supreme authority can give to institutions which it establishes the strength, permanence, and majesty with which it is itself invested . . ." In these words the preamble of the Restoration Charter reasserts the doctrine of monarchical absolutism. But it should not be overlooked that the preamble speaks of "authority" rather than "power." In the same spirit the charter is granted: "We have voluntarily and by the free exercise of our royal authority, accorded and do accord, grant and concede to our subjects, as well for us as for our ancestors forever, the constitutional charter which follows . . ." But when we come to the actual organization of the government, we find that the separation of powers — though not of authority — is recognized. Like the American constitution, the *Charte* implied the separation of powers; it does not enunciate the doctrine. Its articles reveal a close analogy with the pattern of government in England after the Act of Settlement, and before the evolution of parliamentary cabinet government had commenced. Nor was it long before a similar evolution commenced in France, gradually reducing the king to a neutral and moderating role. The provisions of this charter soon became the model for a considerable number of other constitutions, especially those of Belgium, Holland, and Bavaria.

German constitutions · In Central Europe, however, the actual separation of powers was carried even further, while general declarations which seemed to maintain the absolute authority of the monarch were rigidly maintained.[12] For here the separation of powers became in time the bulwark behind which the executive establishment, directed or presided over by the monarch, entrenched itself against the rising tide of legislative pretensions. Thus the constitution of Bavaria (1818) states in the preamble: "Maximilian Joseph, by God's Grace king of Bavaria . . . the present constitution is the work of our *free* and firm will, drawn up after mature and extensive consultation." Similarly, Title II, 1 provides that the king is the head of the government (state), unites in himself all rights of government (state power), and exercises these powers according to the provisions of this constitutional document *given by himself*. What is here asserted, namely, a concentration and fusion of powers in the person of the king, is not borne out by the later provisions of the constitution, which confer the essential legislative and financial power upon the Estates' Assembly (Diet), set up a relatively independent judiciary with jurisdiction even in constitutional matters, and finally bind the king by a solemn oath upon this constitution. It will be noted that this document has nothing to say regarding the responsibility of ministers, a matter which was only regulated formally after the uprising in 1848, in Bavaria, as in other German states and in the Netherlands. We have here, then, a rather strict separation of powers between king, Estates, and judiciary. It is a characteristic of these Germanic countries that they continued to use the expression "Estates" for parliament. The word is symbolically reminiscent of medieval constitutionalism. Already in the fourteenth and fifteenth centuries the government of some of the great and almost independent cities, like Strasbourg, had evolved a fair separation of powers between three councils, each charged with more or less distinct functions, following the practice of Italian cities like Florence. But since the territorial governments which superseded these free cities concentrated the powers in the prince and his council, Continental theorists adopted the theory as doctrine only when it came to them from England. The examples of France and Bavaria are indicative of the general pattern of monarchical constitutionalism on the Continent. It is important to recall this phase of European development, because the later adoption of a republican and democratic system has obscured the essential features of these constitutions.

Weakness of monarchical executive · Constitutional monarchies proved weak and unstable. They encountered great difficulty in maintaining a separation of powers intact; in spite of the grandiloquent proclamations of their preambles, the king usually lost control over the ministers as the result of a gradual broadening of the power of elected parliaments. Though at first glance the French king under the *Charte Constitutionnelle* seems to be considerably stronger than the President of the United States, he did not prove so in practice. That he shared in the legislative power to a larger extent tended to weaken his position rather than strengthen it. What is more important, tenure based upon heredity proved inadequate when pitched against the popularly elected parliament. The American President as leader of his party possesses resources of reserve strength which were utterly lacking to these constitutional monarchs. If they did not wish to submit to the dictation of their parliaments, they had to assume absolute power and by a *coup d'état* break the constitution. This happened in Prussia under Bismarck in the period of conflict, 1861 and the years following. When, at that juncture, the Prussian parliament sought to maintain its position and extend its authority, Bismarck retorted: "Prussia's kings have not yet fulfilled their mission. Prussian kingship is not yet ripe enough to form a purely ornamental trimming of the constitutional system, it is not yet ready to become a dead piece of machinery in the mechanism of parliamentary rule."* For

---

* Today, what strikes one most in this remark of Bismarck's is the unquestioned assumption that parliamentary constitutionalism is coming.

more than fifty years after, Germany, under the leadership of Prussia, held out against parliamentary government under a constitution which separated the powers much as they had been separated under the *Charte Constitutionnelle* and other monarchical constitutions. During this period the same drift toward parliamentary supremacy which had tranformed the English and the French constitutions manifested itself in Germany, but before it could culminate, the First World War broke out, Germany was defeated, and her constitutional evolution was revolutionized after 1918.

Sweden's unusual separation · A unique development occurred in Sweden. Here parliamentary as well as royal absolutism was tried during the seventeenth and eighteenth centuries. This experience led to the elaboration in 1809 of a constitutional system based upon a unique dualism of king and representative assembly; even the coming of cabinet responsibility to parliament did not supersede this unusual system. In a sense, administrative power became separated from the executive power.[13] While the executive power of the crown is conducted, according to the system of parliamentary responsibility, the great public services, like the post office, are conducted with considerable independence, "according to law." Their responsibility is enforced through judicial boards especially concerned with complaints against administrative action, and these complaints are facilitated by throwing all the files open to public inspection. In other words, if a Swedish citizen believes that he has been arbitrarily mistreated by an official, he can and frequently does request permission to look over the files which deal with that particular matter. To buttress further the responsibility of these very independent administrative services, a solicitor-general, elected every year by the parliament, has the right to prosecute any employee who has failed to discharge his official functions properly. Since the duties, competence, and organization of these boards and offices have been outlined by permanent instructions, issued by the executive, no considerable difficulties are encountered. Without any theoretical recognition of the fact, the American federal government tends in the same direction of differentiating between strictly executive and purely administrative functions.

A modern theory of divided powers · Differentiating between executive and administrative functions brings us once more to a discussion of the theory of separated powers. However, we shall not consider it any longer from the historical point of view, but shall ask ourselves instead what truth it contains from the scientific point of view here expounded.[14] The general doctrine has an implicit double meaning. On the one hand it contains a generalization, theory, or hypothesis; on the other hand it contains a practical suggestion, a proposal for the organization of government in the interest of individual liberty. For the doctrine declares that governmental powers can be separated into three categories: executive, legislative, and judicial. Is this generalization concerning the division of power valid? What are the grounds for it? On the other hand, the doctrine also holds that the exercise of these same powers should be entrusted to three separate bodies or persons. Is it essential, is it feasible, is it expedient that these powers be attributed to different bodies for attaining the purpose?

The idea that there are three major types of governmental power would seem to be a valid generalization and one in accord with the operations of the human mind. As we saw, Kant had analyzed this aspect. It needs now to be clarified and refined, in order to provide a basis for a generalized theory. It should, however, be remembered that quite apart from such theorizing, the three functions involved in the theory, namely, dispute settling, rule making and measure taking, are found, by an empirical inquiry into government throughout the ages, to be constant and ever-recurring aspects of how men are ruled.[15]

Decisions are of two elementary types, which might be illustrated by the following examples. A man seeing a hat lying about may say to himself: "I will pick up that hat," a decision which is direced toward one particular instance. On doing so, he may continue by resolving: "I shall never allow hats to lie about," a decision which involves an indefinite number of instances. It is evident that if two basic types of deciding can be distinguished, powers admit of a corresponding classification. Specific decisions are the realm of the executive power, general decisions the sphere of the legislative power. The latter is for that reason often called the rule-making power. Analogously, the executive power may be called measure-taking. As to the judicial power, it will now be apparent that it stands between the two; for it transforms a general into a specific decision. When a general decision has been made, that is, a rule has been established, there still remains the further decision involved in applying the rule. If I have resolved never to let any hat lie about, I may be obliged to decide whether a particular object, for example, a cap, is a hat and therefore falls under my general rule, or whether a hat placed on an anteroom table is "lying about." This kind of decision is related to the general decision in that it cannot arise without a rule having previously been established; it is related to the specific decision in that it is itself a specific decision. Evidently this kind of decision, and the judicial power which makes it, is more intellectual, less active than the other two. This analysis also shows that most of the time we are our own judges; for whenever we decide to do or not to do something because the law demands or forbids it, we are applying that law by subsuming the particular situation with which we are confronted under the established legal rules. Ordinarily, it is only the doubtful and controversial points of law which are brought up before the courts. It is indicative of the truth of this typology of decisions that the so-called "independent" commissions, like the Interstate Commerce Commission, have developed the same differentiation of powers or functions. Although combining legislative, executive, and judicial functions, they have been organizing the exercise of these functions according to the established pattern, providing distinct procedures for each. Thus in the ICC administrative decisions are made by one commissioner, quasi-judicial decisions by three, and quasi-legislative decisions by the entire commission. Clearly, then, the "separation of powers" reappears at a lower plane,[16] differentiating the functions according to the nature of the decision. Those who incline to criticize the doctrine of the separation of powers have rarely shown any appreciation of these sound underlying observations. The reason for this lack of discrimination is that the theoretical aspect is seldom clearly distinguished from the practical proposal of attributing these several powers to different bodies. But while the distinction contained in the classical doctrine is sound, there is nothing sacrosanct about it. There are other ways of distinguishing powers or functions — for example, by reference to their technological content. Thus the power over commerce or that over coinage may be distinguished; they have been so distinguished in the American constitution, of course.

Practical aspects: checks and balances · The classical doctrine, we said, held that these powers, as distinguished, should be allocated to distinct bodies. But let us correct a false impression. It was never proposed that the exercise of all of each power be entrusted to one person or body. On the contrary, the doctrine of checks and balances requires that after the main exercise has been allocated to one person or body, care should be taken to set up a minor participation of other persons of bodies. Budget and impeachment, judicial review and pardon, are examples of this sort of check. Moreover, we have already seen that everywhere in Europe the separation of powers was in practice always and foremost a separation or division of the legislative power between the king and parliament, and that this separation was clearly demanded by Locke, if not by Montesquieu. When seen in this light, there is nothing peculiarly impracticable about the proposal contained in the doctrine. It makes no sense to fulminate against it on the ground that a complete separation is not expedient or practicable. Whether such division of power, however, will effectively restrain governmental action, as the doctrine maintains, depends upon other considerations as well. Checks and balances reunite what has been separated according to what may be called the first part of the doctrine. To the modern mind, and indeed in terms that are meaningful from a scientific viewpoint, the notion of checks has greater validity than that of balances. To be sure, equilibrium analysis has had considerable vogue, but it presupposes measurable, quantitative givens. Such givens are not available when we are dealing with entities such as executives, parliaments, and courts, except in terms of their internal operations, where votes can be counted and decisions analyzed. But the proposition that one power checks another is demonstrable in terms of the actions taken or avoided. It is therefore quite meaningful to say that the constitutionalist quality of the present French regime is in doubt, because of the lack of effective checks upon the president, although it is wrong to say that there are none, as is the case in totalitarian regimes. In spite of the frequent assertions to the contrary, checks have been multiplying in modern constitutional systems. Many of them will be described and discussed in later chapters of this book. As the pluralism of democratic societies has become more pronounced, informal checks have been added to the formal ones, and an ever-more complex system of interacting equilibriums has been created.[17] John Adams, the great expounder of the theory of checks and balances, would indeed be gratified with the political reality of contemporary constitutionalism.

The party as the integrator · It is often said that the reason the separation of powers has worked in the United States is due to the party leadership of the President.[18] The party bosses of both executive and legislative power are said to have reintegrated them and brought them together for fruitful action. Of course, whenever either house of Congress has a majority belonging to another party than the President's, this argument does not hold. Yet unquestionably the emergence of the modern mass party has introduced a new factor. It does not obliterate the separation of powers, but it certainly softens it. At the same time, as has been shown already, the alternation of two parties itself constitutes a regularized restraint which consequently reduces the need for a rigid separation. In any case, there is a danger here of getting involved in the following contradiction. Writers like Woodrow Wilson in his *Congressional Government* and W. Y. Elliott in his *Need for Constitutional Reform* have emphasized and deplored the extent to which the Congressional majority and the President are working at cross purposes. The cases in which one has blocked the other are too numerous to mention. But if we thus insist that the separation of powers does incalculable damage, we can not then turn around and argue that it does no longer operate, as a result of the growth of our party system. The fact is that the majority party, usually led by the President, controls its own members of Congress only very partially, that most of them give primary consideration to their own constituencies, while the President must look toward his own larger constituency, that is, the nation. This has so often been a fact that it is hardly possible to treat it as an exception. An established two-party system helps in maintaining a constitutional separation of powers intact. Wherever one-part rule establishes itself with any degree of permanence, as it did in England during the better part of the eighteenth century, and as it now prevails in some of the American states, the separation of powers is weakened too. It may actually fail to operate as an effective restraint upon governmental action. As a result, the government may drift in the direction of parliamentary supremacy, as it did in England. Or it may lead to one-man rule and dictatorship, as was the case in Louisiana. A single party at times contains sufficiently powerful factions to prevent such an outcome, as it has done in Wisconsin. The Wisconsin case reveals with great clarity the interrelation between party and class structure and the deeper significance of dividing powers. Such division is a method for making it difficult for any one class or group in the community to seize all the power and then exercise such concentrated power for the complete subjugation of other classes or groups. Even though class lines are fluid in America, this is an important objective in any "free" society. If we consider the history of the institutional development of divided powers, it is very clear that such division has facilitated the maintenance of an equilibrium between various rival groups and claims, not a stable equilibrium, but a moving one which continuously adjusts itself to the shifting balance of these groups as they evolve.

Such entrenchment, however, will never afford real protection to the weaker of the two opponents, unless there is somewhere a fairly neutral arbiter. John Adams' view that a balance of powers in the constitution itself will be able to control the parties and thus keep them in check can no longer be accepted.[19] To be sure, a carefully-worked-out balance of separated powers is a first step in the direction or controlling party ascendancy, but a mere mechanism can never defend itself against the lust for power of organized human beings. It needs a guarantee (see below, ch. XIII).

Conclusion · In short, the doctrine that the making of rules and their application and the adjudication of controversies regarding the applicability of such rules in the main should be entrusted to different bodies is still valid. We have shown that it rests upon a broad logical and psychological foundation. At any rate, governmental powers in a constitutional system should be divided between several relatively independent bodies or persons. It may be wise to modify the threefold scheme by charging a separate body or person with the representative function and therefore with foreign relations as well.

If so, the distinction between the executive and the administrative functions will have to be clarified and perhaps broadened. The recognition of a governmental (executive) function exercised in common by the legislative and the administrative branches would insure the degree of integration which must be maintained for the safety of the political order as a whole. Anyway, against the advocates of a dictatorial concentration of power in one leader, the case for a separation of powers may be allowed to rest upon much broader grounds than are suggested by the limited doctrines of Locke and Montesquieu. Lack of historical sense prevents the prophets of absolutism from perceiving that their allegedly *new* form is a very ancient and primitive form: the tribe at war led by its chieftain amid the shouts of the multitude. The difficulties resulting from divided powers are great. But the consequences of concentrating powers are disastrous. Hence, it seems of paramount importance that an effective system of divided powers should continue to operate; a scheme suitable, on the whole, to the needs of an industrialized society.

Federalism and the Territorial

Division of Power

XI

Introduction · Federalism in historical perspective · Federation versus empire · Federalism as a dynamic process · The problem of autonomy · Federalizing: a territorial dividing of power · Federalism and democracy · The common objectives of federations · Federalism and nationalism · The structural pattern of federal systems · The distribution of legislative functions: a matter of expediency · Participation of the component units in the amending process · Federal executives · Federalism and opposition · The constitutional judiciary · The former British Dominions and the Commonwealth · India · The French Community · The union of Europe · "Cooperative" federalism · Admission and association · Decentralization · Conclusion: strength and weakness of federal structures of government

Introduction · The rise of modern constitutional government has been accompanied by the establishment of an increasing number of federal schemes. The parallel is so striking that federalism must be considered one of the most important aspects of constitutionalism. Federalism, when spoken of in general discussions, is used rather vaguely to mean any kind of association of autonomous units. The word may therefore refer to a league or federation of states, as well as to a federal system, such as the United States. Not only this country, but Switzerland, Germany, Canada, Australia, the Union of South Africa, Brazil, Austria, India, Nigeria, Malaysia, and many others have evolved a governmental structure of this federal type. The organization of the world at large into the United Nations points in the same direction, and so does a united Europe, though both are at present loose leagues or federations of states. Many of the more close-knit federal systems developed their structure out of a preceding league.

The realistic study of the political nature of these federal schemes has been handicapped by an exceptional amount of formalistic, juristic argument. Having first posited that all "states" possess an indivisible "sovereign," jurists have strained human ingenuity to discover such a "sovereign" in a federal "state." But, as a critic remarked, even the incredible learning of a German scholar could not find something which was not there. The following discussion will not be concerned with these controversies about "sovereignty" and the "state." Instead, it will discuss federalism as a process for institutionalizing a composite community and thereby providing a territorial form of dividing political powers under a constitution.

Federalism in historical perspective · From a pragmatic viewpoint, an effectively centralized government, a decentralized government, a federal government, a federation, confederation or league of governments, an alliance, an alignment, a system of "independent" governments, and finally completely "independent" governments (such as those of Rome and China in the time of Caesar), all these could be represented as differences of degree in the relation of government to the territory affected by it, between two extremes, complete unity and complete separateness. An inordinate amount of interest has centered upon the point at which we pass from a federal government to a federation or league of governments, for it seems at this point that we pass from unity (no matter how organized) to multiplicity. But this is an illusion; for a federal government is as hard to distinguish clearly from a federation of governments as it is to distinguish it, at times, from a thoroughly decentralized government. Federal schemes, generally speaking, seek to combine a measure of unity with a measure of diversity; usually the diversity follows a territorial pattern, such as French spoken in Western Switzerland, German in Eastern Switzerland. Federalism is the form of political organization suited to communities where this territorially diversified pattern of values, interests, and beliefs and traditions can be effectively implemented by joint efforts in the pursuit of common values and interests, and the cultivation of common beliefs and traditions. Whether the particular federal structure is best described as a single federal government, or as a federation of several governments, may sometimes be difficult to determine. The same observation holds true for all territorial divisions of government power. When the particularistic local objectives are sufficiently strong and compact to hold together the territorial subdivisions of the more comprehensive group, sustaining them as or molding them into autonomous groups, then the adequate political pattern is federational. On the other hand, the federal organization comes into existence when conflicting objectives (interests, traditions, values) are not as yet, or are no longer, sufficiently strong to sustain autonomous units. The contrast between the federal and the federational type of organization must not blind us, therefore, to the great similarities between them. Communities pass readily from one into the other. For federalism must be seen as a dynamic process, and not merely as a static design.[1] Any particular design or pattern of competencies or jurisdictions is merely a phase, a short-run state of continually evolving political reality. This fact has only in recent years become recognized. Classical theory was concerned with the design and tended to juxtapose the several possible designs, and the arguments revolved around the question as to which of these designs was the one *genuine* federal system of government. All this theorizing, political and juristic, unfolded, so to speak, the potentialities of the process by discovering the phases of its successive designs or patterns. A sketch, even in outline, of this evolution of federal theory is a rather complicated affair, since this theorizing is intertwined with the evolution of general political theory.[2] It runs from Althusius to Proudhon, and includes such illustrious masters of political philosophy as Grotius, Montesquieu, the *Federalist*, Rousseau, Kant, and de Tocqueville. The earlier thought down to the end of the eighteenth century was preoccupied with the problem of how to safeguard the component units of a federal system against encroachments, and it stressed the contractual nature of the federal bond, as did Proudhon. The great turn comes with the *Federalist* and the innovations hammered out at the convention in Philadelphia; there and from then on the preoccupation of the theory of federalism is with how to organize an effective unity and thereby allow a federal order to become a "state." It should be added that from the very beginning and throughout its history, federalism has been seen as a concomitant of constitutionalism; indeed, its very first modern theorist, Johannes Althusius, juxtaposed a federal conception of the state as a cooperative association to the unitary and imperial view of Bodin. The theory presented in the *Federalist* embodies the successful surmounting of the practical difficulties and the beginning of modern federal theory.

Federation versus empire · Federation is the alternative to empire. It is this because the power wielded in a federation is predominantly consensual, while that of empire is coercive. In light of that analysis, it is hardly surprising that an empire may be converted into a federation, and a federation into an empire. The British Commonwealth and the Holy Roman Empire provide interesting instances of the first process, the Roman Republic of the second. Either of these structures is exposed to the danger of such transformation. But not to accomplish such transformation may also prove fatal, as it did in the case of the Hapsburg Empire.

The most interesting example of a gradual substitution of a federation for an empire is, of course, the transformation of the British Empire into the Commonwealth of Nations. This feat was accomplished over a long stretch of years during which the British were giving "dominion" status to former colonies. A dominion today is a nearly independent state, tied to

Britain by bonds of common political tradition as symbolized in a common crown, though Ireland and India, while associated with the Commonwealth, do not acknowledge this symbol.[3] In this case, we observe the "federalizing" of a once centrally controlled political system to the point of near-dissolution. By skillful bargaining and pragmatic compromise the British have succeeded in holding the Commonwealth together. They have provided the essentials of federal equality of the component units while avoiding all formal constitution making. Such institutions as the Commonwealth Prime Ministers' Conference have operated effectively as instrumentalities for designing common action; whatever predominance of the British homeland continued to exist was retained by actual weight of active contribution and operative know-how rather than through any formal procedures or explicit principle and doctrine. Even so vast and independent a world power as India has remained associated with the Commonwealth, though the ties are extremely tenuous and in some ways do not even have the force of a firm alliance. Similar in many ways is the case of Ireland. These extreme instances of loose confederation suggest the intrinsic potentialities of the process. Who would be prepared to answer unequivocally the question: Is India more firmly tied to the Commonwealth than to the United Nations?

The disintegration of the French Empire was more sudden and accompanied by much bloodshed and violence. It has ended in virtual dissolution, rather than a loose federal system. When General de Gaulle sought to recapture the allegiance of the disintegrating empire by establishing what on paper appears to be a near-approach to genuine federalism, in the form of the *Communauté Française,* he discovered that it was a rope of sand which dissolved soon after it came into being.[4] Even this federal scheme was somewhat defective. In any case, it did not succeed in transforming the French Empire into a commonwealth; for as has been rightly observed, "the French government favored federation because it hoped to maintain through it the levels of political control on all important issues." De Gaulle himself spoke of "association" rather than "confederation";[5] the magic term "community" was finally conjured up to designate what was intended as a grouping of autonomous states. Since the Community freely permitted secession, however, it seemed the most convenient road to independence, and the several African countries entered it only in order to leave it again. The hopes that federations might in turn be formed by some of these territories have not so far been fulfilled, though a loose federal unit has been formed by these and other African states for the purpose of associating themselves with the EEC.

More common than centrifugal federalizing is the occurrence of the federalizing process for the purpose of bringing together hitherto wholly separate and even hostile states. It appears as an alternative to unsuccessful attempts to accomplish a common order by the establishment of an empire. Thus in Europe, both the imperial conquests of Napoleon and of Hitler were so completely unacceptable to the conquered nations that their empires collapsed within a few years of their establishment. Indeed, Hitler met defeat in the course of the very process of imperial expansion. In lieu of such imperial efforts at unifying Europe, there has now set in a process of accomplishing this objective by building a federal system. While still in its early stages, this process became manifest in the setting up of several "communities" with specific objectives, the Coal and Steel Community, the European Atomic Energy Community and the European Economic Community (Common Market).[6]

A curious blend of empire and federation occurred in the case of Germany, where the unification was accomplished by warlike conquest on the part of Prussia, which transformed Germany into a quasi-federation; the German Empire resulted from this conquest. The federalizing process, set in motion by these partly coercive beginnings, has continued and produced the German Federal Republic, a fully integrated federal system.[7] A parallel endeavour on the part of the Hapsburg monarchy to solve the problems posed by the increasing resistance of subject nationalities to its imperial dominion met with failure.[8] The difference between the two developments is, of course, to a considerable extent due to the centrifugal forces of the culturally divergent nationalities of the Hapsburg lands as contrasted with the centripetal forces provided by a common German "nation." But the federalizing process played its part.

India, when confronted with a similar problem after the disappearance of British imperial control, also sought to solve it by federalizing its political order. This policy was successful, except for the predominantly Mohammedan parts of British India. In this instance, religious, as contrasted with national, differences proved an unsurmountable obstacle to federal union. As a consequence, two separate states were formed which have been on a rather hostile footing, India proper and Pakistan. But inside both of these states the federal pattern was adopted to cope with their further difficulties of linguistic and nationality differences. It is not possible at the present time to draw any very clear conclusions from these undertakings. More especially in India there has been a steady evolution in the direction of regional differentiation, and prophets of doom predict an eventual breakup of the Indian political order. One need not agree with such counsels of despair to recognize that the last word has not been spoken about the clash of centrifugal and centripetal forces.[9]

All these examples and many more that could be cited suggest that a broader theoretical approach than the customary one is needed. Federalism has to be seen and understood not only as an alternative to empire, which it surely is, but also as the institutionalizing of a very general process of politics operating on every level of political ordering. This process is on the higher levels intimately linked to constitutionalism because it presupposes the rule of law and the "sanctity" of contracts.

Federalism as a dynamic process • None of the major theories of federalism have given, though occasionally they have hinted at, an adequate interpretation of this complex political phenomenon, primarily because of their static approach. A federal system should not only be considered statically, i.e., in terms of a fixed pattern of a particular and precise division of powers between governmental levels. Instead, "federalism" seems the most suitable term by which to designate the process of federalizing a political community, that is to say, the process by which a number of separate political organizations, be they states or any other kind of associations, enter into arrangements for working out solutions, adopting joint policies, and making joint decisions on joint problems; or, reversely, the process through which a hitherto unitary political community, as it becomes differentiated into a number of separate and distinct political communities, achieves a new organization in which the differentiated communities, now separately organized, become capable of working out separately and on their own those problems they no longer have in common. But it is not only a matter of decision making, but of the entire range of power and its exercise. The federalizing process accompanies, so to speak, the communal development as its organizational counterpart. If values, interests, and beliefs exhibit a stable and structured pattern in which the commonly shared values, interests, and beliefs are counterbalanced by values, interests, and beliefs that are not shared, though territorially distributed, then a federal development becomes possible. Take, for example, trade unions, which have formed extensive federations in all industrialized countries, such as the American Federation of Labor and the British Trade Union Congress. Each competent unit at first had its own interest, associated with distinctive values and beliefs. But these unions soon discovered that they shared not only values and beliefs, but also broader common interests. Federation then was indicated and was not slow in coming, challenging and eventually eliciting the organizing ability of the leaders of the component units. The same holds true for churches and many other groups. Whenever such groups cannot, or rather do not, wish to merge, because of their distinctive values and beliefs, their self and identity, yet need to unite for the accomplishment of common objectives, usually springing from common needs, federation is indicated. It is essentially the fact that unity is combined with diversity in such a fashion that there coexist spheres of autonomy for the inclusive and the exclusive community, that there coexist spheres of loyalty for both, and that a distinctive characteristic, whether it be living in a particular territory, belonging to a particular church, or practicing a particular trade, can be made the basis of assigning persons to the exclusive as well as the inclusive communities.

The federalizing process may indeed commence in the forming of a league, such as the Council of Europe, the North Atlantic Community, or the confederation which preceded the forming of the United States of America. Or it may lead to such loose association as that of the British Commonwealth of Nations. But always there is the problem of how to combine local autonomy with comprehensive unity. It is, of course, the crucial issue in world organization, except for those who are prepared to accept the imperial design.

The problem of autonomy · Autonomy is here taken in its original meaning as signifying the power and authority, as well as the legitimate capacity, to govern oneself in those matters which form the basis of the community. Such autonomy is actually the basis of individual rights and was so interpreted for individuals in the constitutional order by its greatest philosopher.[10] In other words, the autonomy of no entity or being, whether individual or social, is considered as impaired by participation in a wider and more inclusive community, provided the sphere of power of the wider community is instituted, maintained, and altered only with the effective participation of the component communities, as likewise the autonomy of the inclusive community is considered unimpaired if its sphere cannot be altered without its effective participation.

Such firm protection of the autonomy of both against the encroachments of either level of the political order obviously cannot be achieved unless embodied in law. That is why this sort of political order can only be accomplished within the context of a constitution. In fact, it is precisely such embodiment of the territorial division of power in legal constitutional rules which distinguishes a federal from an imperial order. For empires have often not only permitted but sponsored a large degree of regional (as well as of local) autonomy; indeed it may well be questioned by the political theorist comparing the ancient empires with modern federal structures whether the regions of such empires as the Ottoman Empire or ancient China or India did not have more substantive autonomy than the components units of federal America or Switzerland. But the difference is that such autonomy might at any time be invaded or indeed wholly obliterated by the whim of the central imperial authorities, while the constitutionality protected autonomy of a unit in a federal system, limited thought it may be, is protected against such arbitrary intrusions upon its sphere by suitable constitutional procedures.[11] This crucial point also is involved in evaluating the Soviet-type federalism. Although Soviet public law insists upon the relevance of federalism to the government, and indeed has built its claim for multiple representation in the United Nations upon this federal structure, it would seem that the autonomy of the several Soviet republics, such as the Ukraine, was not and is not adequately protected. Soviet constitutionalism is merely a facade for the political reality of Communist party control — a centrally directed body of rigid hierarchical form. From this point of view, the Soviet Union appears to be an unitary structure in which the central sovereign — according to Communist orthodoxy the Soviet people, of course — speaks through the Communist party of the Soviet Union, and that means through its leadership; in fact, those controlling the hierarchy have "the last words."[12]

In short, we can properly speak of federalism only if a set of political communities coexist and interact as autonomous entities, united in a common order with an autonomy of its own, of course. Such federalism is incompatible with the traditional concept of sovereignty.[13] No sovereign can be discovered in the federal system; autonomy and sovereignty exclude each other in a political order. At least that is true unless such autonomy is itself designated as "sovereignty," as is in fact done in America, where the states are described in the constitution as "sovereign." That such a usage constitutes a perversion of the classical meaning of sovereignty is evident. The same may be said of all notions that the component units "transfer" part of their sovereignty to the higher level; for such transfer implies divisibility of him who "has the last word." The attempt to escape from this difficulty by arguing that the constitutional amending power becomes the sovereign is rather misleading; for this power is intermittent and constitutionally circumscribed in its operation, as are all other uses of power in such an order. The only theoretically clear and admissible way of putting the matter is to admit that instead of being directed by a sovereign power, a constitutional system rests upon the constituent power.[14]

Federalizing: a territorial dividing of power • A federal system then is a particular kind of constitutional order. The function it is supposed to serve is to restrain the powers wielded by the inclusive community, *as well as* those of the communities included within it. It is, as we have just said, a kind of division or separation of powers, but applied on a territorial basis.[15] This function of restraint may be and often is hidden by the motivation which leads to the establishment of a federal system. When the need for cooperation is uppermost in the minds of those who establish a federal system, they may think of the restraints purely in terms of concessions to the more reluctant participants. This oversight is less apt to occur in the reverse process of federalizing a pre-existent community. Here the need for restraining at least the central power is a driving motivation; the federalizing process is set in motion by the desire on the part of the divergent subgroups to take over and govern themselves in all but a few select spheres of joint interest and joint need. In either case, the restraint of power is the crucial objective; in governmental organization, for which territory is of central significance, only territorially delimited communities have been able to achieve such a pattern of mutual restraint and joint operation on a limited scale.[16] The very fact that this pattern of restraints is the organizational manifestation of a peculiarly structured pattern of values, interests, and beliefs suggests that spheres of joint interest and joint belief, as well as those of divergent interest and divergent belief, are likely to undergo a steady evolution. This evolution is apt to be both quantitative and qualitative, and the history of every federal system has a distinct tale to tell. In a recent comprehensive review of several federal systems in terms of distinct fields of operation, such as commerce and the like, it was possible to show the variegated pattern of development.[17] Consequently, every federal system evolves in response to such evolving needs, by governmental (administrative, judicial, legislative) interpretation, as well as by formal amendment. Such changes are related to the very basis of the federalizing process itself, and it is therefore important not to confuse the process of federalizing with particular divisions of power which may be characteristic of a federal system under some particular circumstances of time and place.

A great many of the arguments and controversies over whether a particular political order is federal or confederal result from precisely this neglect of process as contrasted with structure. They have bedeviled the politics of European unification. They are now troubling other federalizing processes, including those in Africa, the Caribbean, and the world at large. The real problem, politically, is whether the federalizing process is in progress and whether the institutional structure as it evolves facilitates the changes required by it. Even the much-argued issue of supranationality, important as it is as a way station in the progress toward federal union, does not compare in importance with the task of setting the federalizing process in motion.

Federalism and democracy · The relation of the federalizing process to the functioning of democracy is of great importance. If democracy is understood in terms of the absolute and unrestrained rule of the majority of the members of a given political community, as was done by Rousseau and many others, then a stark and unresolvable conflict between federalism and democracy must be acknowledged.[18] Curiously enough, Rousseau does not seem to see it thus, although a radical democrat in his outlook. The reason is not difficult to detect: He treats federal arrangements as a static structure of lasting *foedus*, rather than as a process of intercommunal growth; his very hostility to representation prevented a better understanding of the issue. Absolutist democracy is incompatible with federalism, because it does not permit an effective division of power. This aspect probably explains in part the general penchant of radical democrats all over Europe, such as the British Labour party, to be wary of European federalism. For there can be little doubt that the "sovereign will" of the British electorate might be thwarted, if it has to adjust to what other electorates prefer or reject. More specifically, socialism may become more difficult of achievement if it has to be worked out on a European plane.

These difficulties can be resolved, if a constitutional democracy, instead of an absolutist one, is taken as the basis of theoretical analysis and of practical operation. All that is then required is to recognize that every member of the inclusive political order is part of, that is to say, a citizen of, two communities operating on two levels, the regional and the national (federal). A given group of persons, A1, A2, A3 . . . , and another group, B1, B2, B3 . . . , "belong" not only to community A or community B, but also to community AB, which includes them both and is therefore a composite community. The participating decisions of these persons, their "will" in the old-fashioned terminology, shape communal action through effective participation in the communal decisions of AB as well as either A or B. The inclusive community as well as the included community being politically organized, democracy, far from clashing with federalism, now is seen to require it whenever a composite community exhibits more than one level of effective communal existence in terms of distinctive values, interests, and beliefs.

The relation between federalism and party structure presents highly significant issues which have been receiving increasing attention in recent years.[19] The comparative analysis of party systems has highlighted the fact that in federal regimes parties tend toward paralleling the government set-up. American parties are seen as essentially federations of state parties; similar trends may be observed in other federally organized countries. Political science has recognized for some time that the organizational structure of parties tends to correspond to the governmental pattern under constitutional democracy. This is only natural, since it is one of the purposes of parties to gain control of the government; therefore, if the government is federally structured, parties must adapt themselves to such a structure. In Germany and Switzerland, there is stronger cohesion in the national party organizations than in the United States, corresponding to the tighter federalism in these countries. But the Land and Kanton parties display a much greater degree of autonomy than do party subdivisions in unitary states such as England.

Before we explore these issues in somewhat greater detail, it is worth noting that the interaction between governmental structure and party organization is also to be observed in authoritarian regimes based upon a single party. Only here it is the government which responds to the centralizing impact of the party. Notably in the Soviet Union the formal federalism of the governmental structure is superseded and transcended by the integrating force of the CPSU. This does not mean, as is often asserted, that the federal system has no significance in the Soviet Union; it is, as indicated before, a formalized system of decentralization. But it cannot resist the centralizing impact of the single party. For this to happen, there would have to be at least two parties so that in some of the component units the "other party" than the one being in power at the center could render effective the local autonomy under some such slogan as states' rights. Even so, deep-rooted local differentiation may reinforce the local party organization, as was the case, for example, in the Ukraine and in Georgia, which have long traditions of resistance to central Russian predominance.[20]

But there is another force which increasingly shapes the interaction between government and party and transforms the federal system through its impact on party, and that is the policy aspect. There is increasing need for a fully integrated national policy, and this need has been taken care of primarily by party effort. It is, to speak of the United States, simply not true that only presidential elections help to federate local parties into a national body; the need for an integrated foreign and defense policy has become an additional and ever-present factor (as contrasted with the intermittent presidential elections). The creation of national policy committees which occurred in the fifties is expressive of this trend. Even the much-sloganized "bipartisan foreign policy" has its role to play in this syndrome of interacting factors, even though it clashes with the tradition of the two-party politics of countries like the United States. For a policy field that must ever seek to transcend party controversy surely involves federal integration. Therefore, this universal trend, manifested in Europe in the insistent demands for an effective coordination of foreign policy, makes any plan illusory which presupposes a distinctive foreign and defense policy for a member state, even if it is merely an associated state, of a federal system. What it does call for is adequate procedures of consultation and participation in decision making which will render such integrated policy fully "democratic."[21]

The difficulties of effectuating such central coordination are indeed formidable, on account of the inner divisions within parties, reinforced by local issues. In the United States, both parties contain an international and a nationalist (isolationist) wing which can by no means be identified with the progressive and conservative wings in both parties. Comparably in the Federal Republic of Germany, the parties contain elements that differ sharply on such crucial matters as European unification, cooperation with France, and the Cold War. A local leader may be an exponent of a divergent position which his federally reinforced party position may enable him to give additional weight. Switzerland has always been troubled in maintaining its traditional neutrality when the sympathies of French-speaking, German-speaking, and Italian-speaking Switzerland become entangled in the rivalries of the neighboring great states. It is one of the marvels of Swiss federalism that it has been recurrently able to overcome these tensions through the deep loyalty of all Swiss for their traditional order.[22] In cases such as Belgium and Canada, the parties have had to respond to divergent sentiment, possibly aggravated by foreign policy issues. Belgian conservative elements of the Flemish persuasion have traditionally leaned toward Germany, even to the point of imperiling the national foreign policy. French Canadian sentiment, though by no means favorable toward "laicist" and "godless" France, has been hostile toward a vigorous maintenance of a foreign policy of close cooperation in the British Commonwealth of Nations, and is apt to become more radical in this respect. Under such circumstances, parties may have to provide the real battlefield for the reintegration of policy when the formal federal arrangements foster division and disunity. It has been rightly observed that there has been a tendency to treat in cause-and-effect terms this interrelation between party and constitutional structure, when it is actually a matter of circular interaction.[23] It is therefore right to conclude that in a federal system decentralization and lack of cohesion in the party system are based on the structural fact of federalism, but the degree to which these become the dominant characteristics of the distribution of power within the political parties is a function of a variety of other governmental and social factors which are independent of the federal structure or are merely supportive of its tendencies. It is therefore necessary to turn to the exploration of some of these "other social factors" which constitute the social substructure of a federal system.

The common objectives of federations • If it be now asked, in keeping with our general theory, what are the common objectives arising from common interests and needs, as well as the common beliefs and values, the answer is that they are different for different federations. But there appears usually to have been involved the common objective of resisting some outside pressure or threat of a military nature, a possible conquest even, to which all of the potential member communities are exposed. Australia is one of the few exceptions.[24] The same holds true conversely: common defense needs will hold a group of differentiating communities together long after other interests have become diversified. If some of the communities entering the federalizing process have formerly been hostile and engaged in sanguinary conflict, this may prove to be an added inducement in face of a greater threat.[25] It is to be expected, in any case, that there may remain security problems (insecurity feelings) between political communities which formerly were rivals on the international scene. The same kind of problem arises also (in other types of organization). A federation of churches may be troubled at times by the continuing effort of each of them to secure new converts, and a federation of industries by the competition between member enterprises or groups of them.

A significant problem impeding the federalizing process may be the fear of weaker members that they would be overpowered and absorbed; in their eyes this process may appear as a kind of peaceful domination by the stronger units. In a sound federal system, such fears have usually turned out to have been unjustified, except for the smallest units. Thus the extended controversies in the Philadelphia Convention over the issue of the large versus the small states proved largely irrelevant in the sequel; the size of states, while of importance in the workings of American federalism, has not become a significant threat to the smaller among them. Likewise in the case of Germany, it is Prussia, the largest state, which has disappeared, along with the minute states, such as Lippe-Detmold, rather than even so small a state as Bremen (less than a million inhabitants). Nor was this disappearance of Prussia wholly a result of the Hitler war, though it was decreed by the victorious Allies; it was already being envisaged by the reform of the federal system of the Weimar Republic which was impending at the time of the National Socialist seizure of power.[26] It would therefore seem that the security of the three small states, Belgium, the Netherlands, and Luxemburg, within the Community of the Six is also reasonably protected by the close balance of the three larger states, France, Italy, and Germany's Federal Republic; these three are so nearly equilibrated that the predominance of one among them, though a factor in political oratory from time to time, is not likely to become a major problem.[27] The pressing problem is external defense, as the *Federalist* already argued.[28] As is well known, the first articles of the *Federalist* are devoted to this problem.

Another major objective resulting from the common interest in prosperity has been the field of commerce and industry. Indeed, this objective is likely to prove in the long run the more lasting underpinning of a structure that might at the outset have been motivated by the need of common defense.

A comparative study of various national and international federal systems, even as loose a one as the European Community, but certainly the United States, Germany, and Switzerland, as well as Canada and Australia, shows that a large market, permitting correspondingly large productive enterprises, eventually became of primary importance. The development of a multitude of common interests associated with such markets and production facilities usually weaves an increasingly dense network of interpersonal relations, from mere verbal communication to *connubium* as the ultimate sign of established community. At this point, the analysis of Federalism merges with that of nation Formation. The patterns of communication provide empirical evidence for the the march of the Federalizing process.[29]

Federalism and nationalism • The relation of federalism and nationalism is a complex one. For whereas on the one hand an existing nation has at times been able to overcome the obstacles resulting from its division into several political orders, at other times the existence of nations has slowed down, obstructed, or even prevented the federalizing process from taking its course. Again, in the inverse process, developing national communities may help to federalize a formerly unitary structure, or on the contrary a powerful national sentiment may obstruct or prevent such regional differentiation. For the first of these situations, one might cite Germany in the nineteenth century; for the second, Europe at the present time; for the third, the British Commonwealth serves as an illustration; whereas the fourth is in part responsible for France's difficulties in the Saar, Algeria, and elsewhere. Many more examples could be given to show that nationalism and federalism are neither naturally linked nor naturally opposed to each other. It all depends upon the structure of the political communities involved. To the extent that nationalism is the most powerful factor in political community building, it always affects the federalizing process by strengthening either the inclusive community or the component ones, and thus operating either to build nations or to dissolve them.

American experience, reinforced by German and Swiss experience, is by contrast the most telling in showing what a federal order can accomplish in facilitating the growth and the building of a nation. In sharp contrast to the forcible uniting of disparate elements by the monarchical rulers of medieval Europe, American federalism provided a chance of linking unity with diversity as the democratic alternative. Federalism thus provides the only voluntary approach to the task of coordinating disparate national elements. It is being experimented with all over the world, in India as well as in Nigeria and the Congo, and finally in Europe. The issues are similar, but usually contain a specific and unique element. Thus in India, the federalizing process encompasses an entire culture, in many ways more complex than that of Europe, more diversified in religion, language, and social customs. In Nigeria, similar complexities are compounded by the absence of an over-arching tradition such as the great literature of India provides for the cultural elites in many parts of the country. The key issue is whether a national sentiment can become associated with the federal order of things.[30]

The most difficult issue which endangers such entities as India and Europe is whether it is possible to cultivate two rival nationalisms alongside each other. Much thought on loyalty tends to stress its exclusiveness, since divided loyalties are patent sources of conflict. And yet, human experience is familiar with divided loyalties of all kinds, in interpersonal relations of family and profession. Analogies suggest themselves which we cannot develop here, except to hint that for most men the loyalty to wife and mother have to be effectively coordinated and integrated. Under democratic conditions, unfortunately, the potential conflict situation offers a rich source for demagogic exploitation. Dr. Johnson's poignant observation that "patriotism is the last refuge of a scoundrel" has its apt relevance to the agitators for nationalist causes in the twentieth century. Federalism, by providing channels for inter-group communication, by delaying precipitate action and offering a stage for intergroup compromise, seems to be one of the political instrumentalities for negotiating the problem of a divided loyalty, by affording both integrative and differentiating forces some room to operate in. But the Canadian instance shows that it may not do so, if unwisely constructed. There is evident need in the Canadian case for a looser bond in the case of the French Canadians than for the rest. Only the most skillful deployment of "federal behavior" would seem capable of coping with these difficulties.

At this point, it may be well to add a reflection on the built-in contradiction of nationalism as it is now understood. In contrast to the traditional divisive nationalism of Europe which is being mirrored in the corresponding divisions of Africa and Latin America, as well as the Middle East, both India and China have been inclined to speak of their very inconclusive cultural communities as "nations." They have done so in spite of profound differences in language and other manifestations of culture; for the common written languages of Mandarin and Sanscrit correspond to Latin in medieval Europe — they are literary vehicles of cultural communication beneath which a rich variety of vernaculars provide the means of interpersonal communication. One should therefore perhaps rather speak of "culturism" than of "nationalism" in dealing with these comprehensive cultural communities, and the same applies to the emergent European Community and other broadly defined areas.[31] It is in these areas where marked diversity is combined with a common framework of culture that political federalism seems to be particularly appropriate as a form of political order. Such vast federal structures may become the eventual building blocks of a viable world order.

The structural pattern of federal systems • There is a typical pattern which such composite federated communities, whether national, supranational, or perhaps eventually world-wide, develop; it seems the form best suited to the organizing, dividing, and restraining of powers. These structural features are intimately bound up with the fact that the federalizing process, when it unites formerly separate communities, or, rather, organizes their inclusive community, begins with a league or other kind of intergovernmental association. It was so in a number of Western countries, in Switzerland, in the Netherlands, in the United States, and in Germany. It is proving the same in Africa, Asia, and Europe as a whole at the present time. In view of this circumstances, it is not surprising to find that typically the organizational features of a league are found prevalent in the governmental structure of federated communities. In a sense, it could even be said that the institutional pattern of a league survives in a federal system. It shapes the structure of a federation and of a federal "state" in the direction of "organized diversity." Hence the theory of federalism calls for a sketch of the institutional pattern of a league. It is a recurrent pattern and consists of three elements, namely: (1) an assembly of representatives of the constituent communities, which, after instituting the league, usually by way of a charter or treaty, amend it, when necessary; (2) an executive establishment of some sort to carry out the decisions of the assembly; and (3) an arbitral or judicial body, interpreting the treaty in its bearing upon the relations between members of the league and between them and the league as a whole, thus seeking to eliminate the recourse to arms.[32]

It is evident that this pattern corresponds to the basic functions of the concrete political order, namely the settling of disputes, the making of rules, and the taking of measures, while the process of establishing a league by the conclusion of a treaty or the adoption of a charter is composed of those processes which constitute the founding of a political order. It is therefore hardly surprising that the task of common defense should be a primary function of a league and that the development of parties and of traditions should prove as vital to a league as to other kinds of political order.[33]

The distribution of legislative functions: a matter of expediency • Federal legislative assemblies present some interesting general problems which are treated later on (see p. 319 ff.). Typically, they are composed of two chambers, one of which represents the people at large, the other the states, as we have said. Owing to the variety of possible origins, every federalism is likely to be different from every other. The composition of federal representative assemblies may well startle the student by the wealth of heterogeneous forms. The distribution of their legislative functions is even more complex. Many federal constitutions contain long catalogues of what the federal legislature may do; the American constitution is relatively simple as compared to the German Basic Law. It goes without saying that such divisions of the "competencies," that is, the sphere within which each may operate, must and will vary according to time and space. Economic and social life, the military and geographical factors, all will play their role in determining the particular arrangement. From a political standpoint, no distinctive generalization or principles can be derived. It is a question of more or of less; if the functions of the central government are increasing at the expense of those of the local governments, the federal government may become dominant. Jurists have stressed the difference between a central government with powers specifically delegated to it, such as that of the United States, Switzerland, and Germany, and one in which the powers are specifically delegated to the provinces, as in the case of Canada. The existence of residuary powers has been held to constitute the decisive test of "statehood" for the component units. In reality, such residuary powers are an illusion, if the powers or functions delegated to the central government are practically all-embracing, as they were in Weimar Germany; broad delegated powers would mean more "local government" in actual practice than such a "residue" of "genuine self-determination." In either case, the only guaranty for whatever distribution of functions there is, delegated or residuary, is the constitution which determines the governmental structure as a whole.

In sum, a comparison of the several federal constitutions shows that certain matters, such as foreign affairs, customs, money and currency, posts, and national defense, are invariably attributed to the federal authorities. On the other hand, certain matters, such as education and cultural affairs, the police, and local government, are usually left to the component units. But the focal point of modern life, namely, the economy in all its ramifications of technology, welfare, and taxation, is handled with the widest variation. Whether by judicial interpretation of the commerce clause, or by amendments broadening the scope of federal jurisdiction, we find that the United States, Switzerland, and all the other federal systems display the most varied distribution of functions and competencies.

Participation of the component units in the amending process · Another important question as far as functions are concerned is this: Do the local units — states, cantons, *Länder,* provinces, dominions — actually participate as such in the process of amending and altering the constitution, either through their representatives in the federal representative assembly, or directly, or both? Every federal system of government we have examined provides for the participation of the local units in the amending power. The particular provisions in the American and Swiss constitutions we described in an earlier chapter when we discussed the general problems of this power and its relation to the constituent power. In America, as in Switzerland, the provisions for a constitutional amendment developed quite organically from those of a preceding federational compact. In fact, we probably could trace the importance attached to the amending process and the practical procedure for it to the federational origin of these constitutions. Certainly before the adoption of the Constitution of the United States the need for adequate amending provision was not distinctly perceived.[34] On the other hand, the various federations of an earlier time all had to face this issue of changing their charters, usually through the action of instructed delegates. The United States and Switzerland, it will be recalled, both provided for participation of the local units as such in the amending process. In both countries the component states' representatives in the federal representative assembly as well as the component states themselves assent by qualified majorities. In the United States (in the process usually employed) the local legislatures or special conventions have to "ratify" the amendment as proposed by the Congress; in Switzerland amendments proposed by the federal legislature (or by a popular initiative) must, like ordinary laws, be ratified by a majority of the cantons as well as by a majority of the voters at large. To be sure, disagreements sufficiently wide to make the national majority and cantonal majorities vote opposite are rare (among thirty-two amendments, there was only one such disagreement), but this is hardly surprising, since the upper house already represents the cantons.

In Germany, under the Empire, under the Republic, and now under the Basic Law of 1949, no direct participation of the territories (*Länder*) or their electorates in amendments was required. Though natural enough under the Empire, under the Republic this omission was an indication that federalism was on the way out. A weak remnant was the provision that two thirds of the *Reich* Council's votes had to be cast in favor of constitutional amendments. If it refused thus to "ratify" the amendments proposed by the *Reichstag,* they were to be submitted to a popular referendum. Though never actually invoked, this provision shows that constitutional amendments could be put through without the consent of even an ordinary simple majority of the states. The amending power under the Weimar constitution was cer-

tainly not very federalistically organized. The Basic Law provides an amending process similar to that under the Weimar constitution, but eliminates the
referendum.

Federal executives · The second organizational feature of a federation
is the federal division of the executive-administrative sphere.* The local
units as such either have a part in selecting the federal executive or in conducting the executive work for the whole or both. The federal structures in
the United States, Switzerland, Germany, and the Dominions all satisfy this
criterion. To be sure, in none of them (except the German Empire) have
the local units more than fragments of the power of selecting the federal
executive. Thus, in the United States we may say that voting by states in
the electoral college is a partial recognition of the states; for the President
is not elected by a majority of the whole people, but by a majority of state
majorities. Another fragment of state participation is the constitutional right
of the American Senate to advise on and consent to presidential appointments. Out of this has grown the rather important tradition of "senatorial
courtesy." It is a kind of *liberum veto,* and means no more than this: that
while the Senate will not suggest particular nominations, it expects that the
President, in naming certain local officeholders, will choose persons satisfactory to the Senator or Senators of the President's political party from the
state in which the officers are located, or from which the appointees come.
"The strength of the pack is the wolf, and the strength of the wolf is the
pack."[35] At times the President has been inclined to disregard this rule in
the case of Senators who, though formally of his party, did not acknowledge
his leadership. However, the President's desire to hold certain states in line
for renomination affects his policies, as well as his appointments, and the
Senate's regional sensibilities insure to the citizens of all the states a certain
measure of "opportunity." Another more formal recognition of the same type
is the civil-service rule according to which each state is given a certain quota
of appointments to the service. It is difficult to assess the relative advantages and disadvantages of these practices.

In Switzerland, the members of the executive are elected by the two
houses of the legislature; hence the cantons have a decisive voice. The
strength of local autonomy is recognized in certain customs: Bern and Zürich
are always represented in the executive, and seats are evenly distributed
among the other cantons. This means primarily that the French and Italian
cantons get at least one or two members. The executive councillors elect
the president from among themselves for one year.

*This discussion is only concerned with the federal aspect; for the executive in general,
see below, ch. XVIII.

Under the Basic Law of the Federal Republic, the federal element is formally weak in the executive sphere. To be sure, state legislatures are given a share in the election of the president, but he is largely a figurehead. The chancellor is appointed by him on recommendation of the majority of the *Bundestag* without any references to the Federal Council. But the reality of politics provides a somewhat greater scope to federalizing tendencies, largely as a result of the federal structure of German parties. To be sure, they are not the loose confederacies which American parties are; but nonetheless, the several *Land* party organizations play a significant role. This aspect remained somewhat hidden under the strong leadership of Adenauer, but it became apparent when his control of the party disintegrated, and even while it lasted, a man like Kiesinger could after falling out with the chancellor go back to his *Land* and build up an effective following there. It is also quite evident that federal balances play a considerable role in the composition of the cabinet, and the position of a leader like Strauss rests basically upon his local Bavarian following.

All in all, in many ways the most crucial task to solve, if the forming of a league is to initiate a progressive federalizing process, appears to be the establishment of a workable joint executive. It was so understood in the setting up of the European Coal and Steel Community and of the Common Market; its absence has frustrated the Council of Europe. Historical evidence in support of this general proposition is abundant. This is not to say that the creation of such an executive establishment guarantees the forward march of the federalizing process; obstacles to such a development, that is to say, divisive forces, may be too strong for real progress, in which case such an executive merely insures the effective operation of the league. The history of the United Nations to date amply corroborates this conclusion.[36] But for all federal systems in their early stages the executive is crucial, because rule making is restricted to the making of the original treaty and its amendment, except for such interpretative implementation as its application calls forth. The advantages of a developed and responsible bureaucracy thus accrue to and tend to advance the inclusive community and its federal structure. Naturally, such an executive will be influenced by the nature of its tasks, military, economic, or more broadly political. In the selection of the executive, the stage of federalizing will be reflected: the further developed in the direction of a unity a political order is, the more completely will the executive be a function of the inclusive community and its representatives.

Federalism and opposition · If we assume that, in judging federalism's operation as a pattern of opposition,[37] we might employ certain criteria suitable for determining whether a political system increases the chances for the realization of constitutional democracy, we can state the following hypotheses: Federalism (1) increases the opportunities for dissenting minorities to make their views known to other citizens and policy makers; (2) multiplies the opportunities for citizens to participate in political life; (3) enhances consensus in political discussion in the sense that solutions are sought that will reduce the size, resentments, and coercion of defeated minorities, as well as of permanent minorities who cannot hope to become majorities; (4) greatly improves the chances of the peaceful resolution of conflicts; (5) aids the solving of urgent policy questions by providing an opportunity for experimenting with solutions on a limited scale; and (6) enhances confidence in and loyalty to a constitutional polity.[38] On the other hand, it appears doubtful whether federalism reduces "political violence," but does opposition necessarily do so? The empirical evidence is contradictory. Federalism also would appear to increase, rather than decrease, the chances that policy decisions are effectively made by minorities, rather than majorities, of citizens, voters, and elected officials, although this is not necessarily so. Whether the rationality of political discussion and decision making is greater or not seems more difficult to determine; sometimes it would seem to be so, at other times not. But the validity of this criterion appears in any case rather dubious, considering the uncertainty as to what is rational;[39] and is it correct to say that a system is more *democratic*, when it is more *rational?* If, then, these issues are left aside, we may examine each of the others in turn in an effort to assess the value of federalism as a pattern for broadening the opposition's role.

The more interesting problems, at least from the viewpoint of the student of opposition, are presented by temporary opposition. By temporary opposition I mean an opposition which on the personal side is carried forward by men who consider themselves an integral part of the general constituency and therefore expect to become the government, that is, to convert their minority following into a majority. On the impersonal side, it is an opposition whose values, interests, and beliefs may well become those of the majority of the population. Both these aspects results in such an opposition being dynamic, rather than static; in opposing, it strives to change the political situation so as to enable it to govern rather than oppose. A dynamic opposition will therefore marshall all the resources of persuasion and propaganda for the achievement of its central goal. A federal system greatly enhances its chance of doing so. For by becoming first the government in one state, *Land,* or canton, it achieves the authority and secures for itself the resources and tactical advantages which a government naturally possesses. Party history in the United States provides many interesting examples for this federally conditioned rise of oppositional elements, especially within parties. The radical progressivism of midwestern republicanism in the era of Senator LaFollette is of course the most striking illustration, but the so-called Bull Moose movement of Theodore Roosevelt is another one. And who would deny that the New Deal of Franklin Delano Roosevelt did not have its experimental beginnings in his governorship of New York State? The dangerous potential of this kind of local experimentation lies in the opportunies a federal order provides for destructive movements of opposition to instal themselves and thus achieve an operating base. Here the most famous — or should we say infamous? — instance is provided by the history of the National Socialist movement. The conquest of Thuringia and other small *Länder* gave the Hitler movement the chance to "prove" its capacity to participate in German government.[40] It is, however, possible that in mature democratic societies, this danger could be minimized by providing, as do the American constitution (Article IV, 4) and the Basic Law of the Federal Republic of Germany (Article 28, 1 & 3), that the component units must maintain a constitutional democratic order. Thus opposition would be restricted to parties and formations that do not attack the basic principles of the popular consensus.[41]

If one considers now the specific form available to the opposition for the exercise of its oppositional capacities on the federal level, it is evident that situations may arise in which the opposition party may secure a majority in a majority of component units and thereby be enabled to make its opposition more effective. A special case is provided by the qualified majorities, usually required for constitutional amendment. Switzerland has had some dramatic experiences in this connection, especially in the field of foreign affairs. Her entry into the League of Nations eventually turned upon the winning of sufficient support in some of the small rural cantons, and a veritable avalanche of potent national figures in politics and university life was unloosed upon the electorate to debate the issue. Similarly, the re-establishment of the armed forces in Germany's Federal Republic required constitutional amendments which enabled the oppositional Social Democrats, who controlled enough votes in both houses, to exact important concessions in connection with the essential compromises, such as the esetablishment of a civilian commissioner charged with providing the necessary liaison and advising on military developments. It is generally true to say that the federal government must be closely concerned with the elections in the several *Länder*, especially when the balance in the Federal Council is a close one. Then the winning or losing of a *Land* election may vitally affect the government's entire legislative program and general policy.

The foregoing observations raise one final issue, and that is the fact that federalism requires relative stability in the executive. It has for some time been argued that a federal regime is hard to combine with a parliamentary executive of the British cabinet type. It is so combined in Canada, Australia, and the German Federal Republic. But considerable difficulties result from the fact that the relation between the opposition and the government is thereby given an almost uninterrupted chance of erupting into an electoral struggle. For under conditions of traditional parliamentary dependency of the cabinet, elections may be called on the national as well as the local level at any time, and the resulting multiplication and unpredictable timetable of elections become all the more unmanageable as the number of component units increases. If in a country like the United States, with fifty states, they were organized according to classical parliamentarism, elections would be taking place almost continually. Wherever they carried implications for the national government, because of its own dependency upon parliamentary support, such elections would elicit national participation. This consequence has led to a widespread demand in Germany that the local elections be synchronized with the national ones; but such synchronization presupposes that elections should occur at regular intervals, in other words, that the traditional parliamentarism be abandoned. There is a further complication on the national level which points in the same direction. A federal regime presupposes a bicameral representation, since the component units are and must be represented in a separate body, be it senate or council. The cabinet can then be made dependent upon the confidence of either one house or the other, or both. If one house is chosen, it is necessarily given a predominant position which is apt to endanger the federal balance; if both are chosen, extreme instability results. As a consequence, it would seem that a federal regime is greatly benefited by, if it does not actually necessitate, a stable executive. It is, however, debatable whether it is then more desirable to have local elections so arranged as to coincide with the national one, as is largely the situation in the United States, or whether it would be better to have them arranged for a date halfway between or in some other way, as is true for some states in the United States. We shall not here review all the arguments, but the role of the opposition locally and nationally would suggest that different dates are desirable so as to avoid the submerging of local issues in national issues, and the carrying of local candidates on the wave of popularity of a national leader, as has often been observed in the United States. Certainly the operative range of the opposition would thereby be enhanced.

The constitutional judiciary · The executive's unifying role is usually greatly aided by some kind of arbitral or judicial body. Such a body can settle disputes concerning the meaning and interpretation of the treaty, charter, or constitution which the other federal authorities, especially the executive, are not able to compose. Again typically, the extent of the participation of the component communities in the selection and dismissal of such a body and its members is determined by the degree of federal diversity. Both in this and the case of the executive, quantitative studies might throw considerable further light on the extent and degree of proportionality. Such participation may be restricted to that in the treaty making or legislation under which the judicial or arbitral body operates, as in the Federal Republic and Switzerland, or it may assign to the component units a substantial share of the appointing power. Such share may be indirectly exercised, as in the United States, where the Senate, representing the states, has to "confirm" appointments to high federal judicial office; or it may be directly exercised, as in the European communities, where the member-governments do the appointing themselves; or an intermediary system might be chosen, as in Switzerland, where the highest federal judiciary, the Federal Tribunal, is elected by the federal assembly in one house of which the component communities, the cantons, are represented *qua* cantons. It is evident that the mode of election of such a body will be a subject of controversy between those persons seeking to accelerate the federalizing process in whichever direction and those seeking to retard it. In a differentiating process, a judicial body may be the last operative bond, as was and is the case in Britain, where the Privy Council exercises judicial functions over Dominion constitutions.

However constituted, such arbitral or judicial bodies are characteristically an instance of last resort, and whether or not they will forward the federalizing process, in either direction, will often depend upon circumstances of personal predilection or party politics, as the history of federal judiciaries clearly shows. Their operations must be seen in the light of the general propositions which apply to dispute settling to which they are largely subject, of course. The prevalence of arbitral, as compared with judicial, procedues will roughly speaking depend upon the state of the federalizing process: the more closely knit the federal system, the more formally judicial will these procedures become.[42]

A judicial body for the settlement of disputes between the central and local authorities, as well as between the component units, one finds in most federal systems. In the United States the Supreme Court, of course, is charged with this duty. Though on the whole favoring the federal government, it has not followed a consistent course. The same can be said of such federal judiciaries as those of Switzerland, Australia, and India. The Court was nationally minded under Marshall, and several of his most famous decisions, like *McCulloch v. Maryland* and *Gibbons v. Ogden*, asserted doctrines which favored the central government. Later on, the Court in the course of the slavery controversy shifted toward a states' rights position which culminated in the ill-starred *Dred Scott* decision.[43] After the Civil War, the Court turned back to its national orientation in some important economic fields, especially through the steady expansion of the interstate commerce clause, but it regrettably did not maintain the federal authorities in the civil rights field. In 1883, the Supreme Court held the Civil Rights Act to be beyond the power of Congress. Justice John Marshall Harlan's vigorous dissent prophetically asserted at the time that "not only the foundation upon which the national supremacy has always securely rested will materially be disturbed, but . . . the rights and freedom and American citizenship cannot receive from the nation that efficient protection . . ." which they deserve.[44] The Supreme Court has, admittedly and radically, reversed its position in recent years. Since it decided in *Baker v. Carr* in 1954 that segregation of American Negroes was a denial of their equal protection under the constitution, and afterwards in 1963 disallowed the unlimited freedom of state legislatures to manipulate the apportionment of the electoral districts, the Court has resumed its vigorous defense of federal authority.

In Switzerland, where the court has no right to review the constitutionality of federal legislation, it is noteworthy that provisions about the administration of federal legislation by the cantons have not resulted in serious complications. This is probaly owing to the fact that not a single canton is large in relation to the federation as a whole, that the cantons have not been sharply divided by partisan issues (neither Communism nor Fascism assuming serious proportions), and that the central government has practiced marked moderation in employing force, relying rather upon persuasion and other kinds of pressure. The situation is rather different in the Federal Republic of Germany. This new and increasingly important Federal Constitutional Court has gradually become a champion of the *Länder*, "to enhance their position on the federal system."[45] The work of the court has been distinguished by the assumption of a degree of discretionary power in its decisions involving federal relationships, and more particularly its views on "federal loyalty" (*Bundestreue*). There can be little question that an eminent specialist is right in summing up the development as characterized by the "effective judicial recognition of the states in the federal system."[46] Whether one favors judicial "activism" or judicial "self-restraint," there can be little question that in effectively functioning federal systems, the umpiring of such a system by a constitutional court is of the essence.

The former British Dominions and the Commonwealth · Federalism has played a significant role in the development of a number of former colonies of Great Britain. In all these vast territories, a demand for self-government arose in time. Thus effectiveness in dealing with the mother country rather than resistance to outside pressure became the common objective, along with the economic and national considerations, in the federating of groups of colonies in Canada, Australia, and South Africa,[47] as well as in India, Nigeria, Malaysia.

These federal structures, while self-generated in the colonies, received encouragement from Britain. The earlier constitutions were embodied in an Act of Parliament. Canada was the first to enter upon this development. Out of the Union of Upper and Lower Canada (1840), which was inspired by the far-sighted report of the Earl of Durham (1838), grew a broader federalism which eventually comprised all of British North America. The original federal union, established through the British North America Act of July 1, 1867, comprised only Upper Canada (Ontario) and Lower Canada (Quebec), New Brunswick, and Nova Scotia. But soon after, the western territories were added. It was at once a matter of uniting in the face of the rapidly growing United States and of overcoming the cultural cleavage which divided English and French Canadians. Lord Durham had felt that the cultural division was threatening Canada's future; the united provinces would, he believed, show more homogeneity through the dominance of the British element. His expectations seemed for a time fulfilled. But the double division of race and religion has produced serious strains in recent years.

Australia's federal union, though obvious in view of her insular unity, did not come into existence until 1901, after more than ten years of trial and error and intense agitation. Australia's original impulse was in some measure national defense. After the withdrawal of British troops in 1870, it soon becamse apparent that some measures for the common defense would have to be adopted. As early as 1889, Australia's defense problem had been analyzed by a military expert who suggested a federal setup. It was in keeping with this background that Australia was the first English-speaking country to adopt universal military service in peacetime, in 1911. The Australian Federal Commonwealth, composed of the six provinces, called states, of New South Wales, Victoria, Queensland, South Australia, Western Australia, and Tasmania, and one territory, the Northern Territory, operates under a constitution which is a blend of English and American elements. It is patterned on the Constitution of the United States in its provisions for equal representation of the component units in a senate, its requirement of state participation in constitutional amendments, and its judicial power of constitutional interpretation. On the other hand, it vests executive power in the governor-general, representing the Crown, and in an executive council, presided over by the leader of the majority party. This prime minister, dependent upon parliamentary majority, is of course the real executive, and hence we have a parliamentary system of government. This system is ill-adapted to a federal parliament with two houses; difficult conflicts arise when the majorities in the two houses differ from each other, as has happened repeatedly in Australia. The legislative power is formally vested in Parliament, consisting (according to the time-honored formula) of the king (represented by the governor-general, in turn represented by the prime minister and his cabinet), the Senate, and the House. In fact, the tendency toward cabinet government (see below, ch. XVIII) has rendered obsolete the distinction between legislative and executive power in this traditional sense.

The Canadian system was conceived as a more centralized one, since the national government possesses all the residuary powers not specifically assigned to the provinces. In point of real issues, this arrangement has not proved important. But the problem of executive power, as between the governor-general and the prime minister, issued in a constitutional crisis in 1926. The prime minister, having suffered defeat in Parliament, wanted to dissolve that body and hold an election. The governor-general insisted upon appointing the leader of the opposition; but when an election became necessary, a few weeks later, the former party was returned. It was assumed that this result established the principle that the governor-general, like the king in England, is bound by the advice of the prime minister. At the same time, it should be noted that the upper chamber of the Canadian Parliament has no role in this scheme of parliamentary responsibility. The dependence is solely upon the confidence of the House of Commons, with the result that the Senate has gradually lost in importance (see for these problems Ch. XVII, below).

It does not seem worthwhile at this stage to review the experience in some of the new federal states, such as Nigeria, Malaysia, and the Caribbean, except in order to note that in these countries with a weak constitutional morale, federalism has encountered formidable difficulties. The case is different in India. All these former Dominions and colonies are novel experiments in government through their effective combination of federalism with parliamentarism. Whether that combination could be successfully worked without the benevolent neutralizing influence of a distant "crown," remains undetermined. The British Commonwealth of Nations, composed of the United Kingdom and the self-governing Dominions, has been evolving into the loosest kind of confederation. While before the First World War it might have been argued that the Commonwealth was still a federal structure of government, it has since in fact been described as a "League of Nations."[48] The Dominions have separate military establishments, and they possess separate diplomatic representatives and membership in the U.N. The difference between the Commonwealth and a federal setup such as the American one is striking. In fact, it has been cogently argued that only the belief in a common crown holds it together formally. The impersonal nature of the Crown and its complete dependence upon the several parliaments through parliamentary responsibility of its ministers makes such "personal union" precarious. Pragmatically speaking, the Commonwealth became a league when the Irish claimed the "right" of secession.

The Commonwealth possesses no functioning common government; there are various meetings of officials high and low, from the prime ministers on down. In a way, the Commonwealth has a confederal representative assembly in its imperial conferences, in which the local governments, Great Britain, and the Dominions are recognized as equal in law. The meetings of these imperial conferences, now called Prime Ministers' Conferences, are too infrequent, really, to call it a representative assembly. Much collaboration takes the form of "consultation," which is acclaimed as the magic formula for strengthening the bonds between the several Dominions and Great Britain.

Returning to the executive branch, we find the local units at an earlier stage shared in it. From 1904 until the Second World War, an Imperial Defense Committee united in a rather informal way various cabinet members in Great Britain and the Dominions, as well as other officials, around a permanent secretariat; this committee took a definite hand in military questions, though in a purely advisory way. During the First World War its functions were greatly expanded, and it became a "War Council," coordinating the war machine of Great Britain and keeping elaborate records. In the words of Lord Balfour, the Committee of Imperial Defense provided "a continuing instrument of consultation within and without the Government Departments, the ministers responsible to the British Parliament, and, when they desire it, the ministers responsible to the Dominion Parliaments. But nowhere and under no conditions can it modify or limit parliamentary control or ministerial responsibility." It was not re-established after the Second World War.

There is finally a judicial body. For some years there existed the Commonwealth Tribunal as well as the Judicial Committee of the Privy Council. Of these, the latter interpreted the several Dominion constitutions in relation to the law of the mother country by serving as a court of last appeal in dealing with the interpretation of these constitutions, while the former settled justiciable disputes between the governments of the British Commonwealth. The tribunal is not a permanent court, but rather it provides the framework for the arbitral settlement of each dispute; its use is discretionary with the disputants, and membership is determined anew in each case. Students of the British Commonwealth are inclined to consider this setup another feature of a still somewhat confederate Commonwealth, because it keeps the Dominions from appealing to the Permanent Court of International Justice. In sum, the Commonwealth is bound together by common traditions, but possesses no organizational structure.

India · India's federal experiment is particularly interesting, because of its increasing differentiation, due to the diversity in languages and economic development. While originally it was hoped by its creators that India would become monolingual in the course of a few years, it has actually proved necessary not only to accept multilingualism, but also to restructure the country's effective divisions in accordance with diversified cultural and linguistic ambitions. It might be objected here that the issues India presents are not, properly speaking, related to federalism, since many Indian scholars insist that India is not a federal system, but "a unitary state with subsidiary federal features."⁴⁹ But apart from the fact that such arguments are usually based on too narrow a conception of federalism, excluding the "unitary federal state," India is clearly undergoing a federalizing process in the course of which federal diversity is increasing. It is, as has been shown a number of times in this study, a recurrent process that in the course of the democratizing of a society, regional and linguistic-cultural communities become more articulate and demand recognition in the form of a set of political institutions, including safeguards for the identify of the particular community. India is as much a case in point as are Belgium, Canada, Cyprus, and the rest.

It stands to reason that at first after independence had been won and British imperial rule had been replaced by local authority, unitary sentiment should be very strong, especially after one of the major subdivisions, namely, the Muslim community, had broken away into a separate Pakistan. Yet, even though the federal scheme of the constitution of 1935 had proved unworkable, there was virtually no sentiment for the establishment of a constitutional unitary state;⁵⁰ but there was powerful sentiment for giving the central authorities sufficient power to combat the centrifugal tendencies in so vast a country with a rich diversity of cultures, languages, and religions, and it is submitted that the extent of these formal powers cannot be made the measuring rod of the force of regionalism and federalism in India. The consolidation and regrouping of the original subdivisions — largely the result of dynastic conquest in the princely states and of British administrative expediency in the rest of India — into fairly large units of unilingual homogeneity has increased the weight of the states considerably.⁵¹ As a leading Indian scholar put it recently: "It would be rash to assume that the federal system in India has definitely settled down to the acceptance of central dominance. The growth of regional consciousness has only just begun and new problems based on it are coming to the surface despite the weight of law, custom and habit on the side of the Center."

Altogether, India's federal system is probably the most complex ever devised by the mind of man. All of the factors needed for setting the decentralizing process in motion were present in India in 1946. It has been observed that "the makers knew that they were making a federal constitution for India, but the Constitution never used that word,"[52] for their inclination was to create as much unity as possible, after Pakistan had broken away. There is much difference of opinion among Indian scholars as to the strength of federal union. On the basis of our own conception, India is certainly far from being a fully federalized state. For the existence of the component units is at the mercy of the central authorities. Their competence is very limited, and the central legislature can and does invade this limited sphere. In the executive sphere, one finds that the governors are appointed by the president and are subject to his removal; furthermore, the federal authorities may at any time upon their own estimate of the situation substitute an emergency regime under their own control for the state government. Finally, although judicial safeguards are provided, these are readily circumvented by large political encroachments. In short, provincial autonomy is very limited indeed, if it exists at all. Large-scale planning for economic development as well as numerous other forms of direct interference serve to make it possible for the national government to "plan" India into a unitary system. A leading scholar has expressed the fear that "there will be a persistent tendency on the part of the Centre to encroach upon the Units until they become mere administrative units. . ." The constant friction which this arrangement entails "will weaken the solidarity of the country much more than a real federation with greater provincial autonomy could have done."[53] In sum, India's federalizing process may be persistently centripetal, but the weakening of the Congress party may change the trend.

The French Community · A development comparable to the British Commonwealth was initiated, with somewhat less success, by France in relation to her empire. The French Union, as it was called in the constitution of the Fourth Republic, or the French Community, as it appears in the constitution of the Fifth, has undergone considerable evolution since its inception in 1946. The French Union under the Fourth Republic was never a true federal system, but rather mute testimony to the inability of French leaders to understand federalism. It was almost impossible for an organization consisting of two bodies, both restricted to consultative and advisory functions and both containing a predominant French element, to have aroused the enthusiasm of peoples kindled by the nationalist sentiment stirring Asia and Africa. The French, however, saw any move toward decentralized, federative control as a scheme for total secession. Their ideal of complete assimilation in a republic "one and indivisible," their lack of a deep common tradition with the peoples under their rule, and their conviction that France's status as a great power depended on the retention of control in her colonies, led the French into tragic wars in Indochina and North Africa. Only in 1956, when Morocco, Tunisia, and the Indochinese states had already won their independence, did the French National Assembly vote reforms giving the member states considerably more autonomy within the union. By then it was too late. Two years later, under pressures caused by the progress of colonial wars and colonial policy, the Fourth Republic collapsed.

The constitution of the Fifth Republic provided for a French Community in which the member states were to "enjoy autonomy . . . administer themselves and manage their own affairs democratically and freely" (Article 77). It established a representative Senate, a common executive in the President of the Community (the President of the Republic), and the Executive Council and a Court of Arbitration. It allowed any member state to attain total independence on condition of withdrawing from the Community. (This provision excluded Algeria, which was not a member state but an overseas department and therefore an integral part of France.) By 1958, however, the African states were suspicious of a federal solution and desired complete independence. They voted to join the Community on the original terms, but chose independence as soon as France allowed such status within the Community. Since that time Algeria has become fully independent and has, with certain other former members, opted to leave the Community altogether, while retaining economic and cultural ties with France. Those states still within the Community (Senegal, Gabon, Congo, Chad, the Central African Republic, and the Malagasy Republic) have the same independent relationship with France as those outside it. The formal institutions of the Community — Senate, Executive Council, and Court of Arbitration — have ceased to exist and have been replaced by periodic meetings of heads of states. The President of the Republic continues to function as President of the Community, with the aid of his Secretariat General for Community and African Affairs, an office which includes representatives from the member states of the Community. But the present system is little more than a loose alliance of soverign states, some formally outside the Community, linked with France by bilateral treaties and accords. These accords provide the new states with considerable economic assistance and give France a dominant military position in her former empire.

Within the French Republic itself, which still contains four overseas departments and seven overseas territories, there may be a chance for the federalizing process to set in. The departments, while governed in most respects like those in the home country (see below, p. 239 f.), now possess their own constitutions; and the territories, though moving toward self-government, have some potential for developing flexible federal ties with France. Such a process has in fact commenced among some of the former French colonies in Africa for whom France negotiated a special position in the Common Market. They became associated in a loose federal scheme for this purpose, and they may well turn toward closer ties to consolidate their economic position.[54]

The union of Europe • The loosening of the ties of the British Empire has contributed positively to the developing program of a union for Europe. The idea of a United States of Europe is an old one. It has always had a certain appeal, but until recently it seemed a utopian proposal considering the sharpness of national rivalries on the European Continent and the extent of Europe's overseas empires and commitments. The late twenties brought a very tentative proposal by Aristide Briand, fashioned in the hope of saving Europe from another war. But the movement did not really get under way until 1946. The most active and energetic leadership came at first from Britain and France, although the British have been divided among themselves as to how far they could afford to go in light of their empire and Commonwealth commitments.

The movement was greatly promoted by the danger of the Soviet expansionism; this provided the "external" stimulus so vital to federalization. It was also considerably stimulated by United States economic aid under the European Recovery Program, and the same power's military aid, both actual and potential, under the Atlantic Pact. Both of these programs were, of course, in turn intimately linked to the first factor, Soviet expansionism. Security and prosperity, in short, the ever-recurring objectives of modern government, are once more at the center of the whole development.

United Europe, or more specifically Europe in the process of federalizing the relations among its members, presents some very special issues to the student of federal and regional relations. One of the industrially advanced regions of the world (except for some retarded entities, like Sicily and Ireland), it represents the greatest conglomeration of people within a small territory. Its population of several hundred millions (the exact figure depending upon what is included) is living on a territory not much larger than Texas. Formerly the "hub of the universe," it is now being united not only by its defense needs, but by the economic problems which the disintegration of its several colonial empires has created. At its core, France, Germany, Italy, and the Benelux have formed the Community of the Six, so called, the primary focus of which is the Common Market, a treaty-based confederation for the purpose of developing a united economic policy. Many more states are loosely associated in the Council of Europe, which preceded the Common Market, having come into being in 1950. Great Britain, the Scandinavian countries, and a number of other smaller states participate in this international union. It has primarily promoted some general patterns of cooperation through conventions in the social and cultural field, including the setting up of an arbitration procedure for alleged violations of an agreed bill of human rights;[55] unfortunately some important powers, notably Great Britain, have so far not ratified this convention. These two organizations of a federalizing Europe are implemented by a special union in the military field, the Western European Union, brought into being in the sequel of the failure to agree on a European Defense Community; it has not played a very vital role, since its functions overlap with those of NATO. Significant mostly as a forum and means for promoting all-European economic cooperation is the Organization for European Economic Cooperation, which renders valuable service also in the field of banking and currency.

As a result of these and other specific functional ties, it is extremely difficult to define the European federal relationship at the present time. Special issues, such as that of supranationality, meaning the question whether any of these functional bodies have an authority transcending the authority of the national governments which cooperate in them, are rather artificial in view of the fact that the formal juristic situation is continually being superseded by specific developments in particular fields of custom and usage. But there can be little question that the lack of a unifying and integrating *political* organization is causing very serious difficulties. Numerous proposals for creating such an organization have been put forward in recent years, and men of great experience, such as President Hallstein of the EEC, have often stated it as their conviction that an economic cooperation cannot hope to succeed without adequate political organization to back them. But none of the plans and proposals have so far succeeded, or even come near doing so. The most advanced of these proposals, the draft of a constitution for a European Political Community, fashioned by an *Ad Hoc* Assembly in the winter of 1952–1953, may be considered a high-water mark which Europe is now farther from reaching than ever. Yet, even this "advanced" mechanism was far from adequate as a framework of European political unity, and it was only meant to apply to the Community of the Six.[56]

If the question is asked, why the federalizing process has been so slow and has recently been retrogressive, the answer is not simple. Personal factors, such as President de Gaulle's hostility toward any kind of supranational authority, undoubtedly have played a considerable role and continue to do so. But they could not have done so if support for a federal union in Europe were stronger in the respective constituencies; a France truly committed to European unity would withdraw its support from a leader who refused to participate effectively in this task. The more powerful factors feeding European disunity are both economic and political ones, while the cultural field has seen a much greater readiness to shape a European future. Among the political factors, the varying intensity of apprehension concerning the aggressive designs of the Soviet Union is very important. Such fears have varied not only between periods; they have also been much more intense in Germany than in Britain, more intense among farmers and workers, and so forth. Under these circumstances it can hardly be considered surprising that initiative promoted at one time and by one power falters at a succeeding period of thaw, or *Entspannung*, and so forth. It is more than doubtful that this situation will change noticeably in the years to come.

Even so, the Common Market continues to attract states, seeking both membership and association, and Switzerland has joined the Council of Europe after many years of hesitation.[57] There can be little doubt that the European Community is a growing one; numerous informal bonds are being created through the multiplication of human contacts in business, in cultural relations, and so on. There are today developing in Europe intimate working relations between parties, research institutes, publications and other communication media, that were rare in the interwar years. At the grass-roots level, communes are developing special links, the so-called *jumelages,* through which French, Italian, German, Belgian, and Dutch, and indeed British, local governments cooperate in promoting a European "togetherness" and a belief in the potentialities of solving common problems jointly. From all these different sources, in themselves small, spring activities which presuppose an eventually united Europe with a common citizenship and foreign and defense policy. Indeed, certain nationality problems which have plagued European states, such as the Belgian and Italian ones, will become attenuated.

Admission and association • All federal systems are confronted with the problem of admission of new members and the related one of secession.[58] It is evident that the looser a federal community, the more readily will it admit new members and allow old members to secede. Former theory therefore inclined to make secession the test as to whether a composite political order was federal or confederal. The American Civil War as well as the Sonderbund War in Switzerland were waged to prevent secession of units which had rejected a key policy decision expressive of a broad value preference on the part of the majority; abolition of slavery in the United States, economic liberalism in Switzerland. But in spite of these sanguinary conflicts, the problems of admission and secession cannot be said to be decisive from either a theoretical or practical viewpoint. At one end of the federalizing process, the ability to secede regardless of the formal right will obviously exist. It will decline and tend to disappear as the inclusive community is extended to ever-widening spheres of the common values, interests, and beliefs, so that at the other end, neither admission nor secession is likely to occur. Exceptions must be recognized, however, under particular circumstances, such as the admission of formerly dependent colonial territories into a federal union. The cases of Hawaii, Alaska, and Puerto Rico come readily to mind. They also illustrate another significant difference. For Puerto Rico's greater cultural separateness, as expressed in her Spanish language preference, has produced a new form of "admission," namely, that of free association.

Free association is, as a matter of fact, a new dimension of federalism suggesting that there could be an inner and outer group of participating communities, such as is developing in the process of European unification. Free association is also the form in which West Berlin is able to participate in the Federal Republic. It is likewise provided for in the constitution of the Fourth and Fifth Republics of France, but without having been actualized.[59] The idea that an autonomous, self-governing community might be an "associated" member of a federal system is difficult to interpret, unless federalism is seen as a process. Once federalism is thus understood, association is comprehensible as an institutional device for organizing a relationship which is close enough for a loose federal tie, but no more. This is the case with Puerto Rico. Or a closer tie may be prevented by outside pressure as is the situation of Berlin.[60] Or again, the closer tie may be objected to by allies or confederates, as was the case with Britain's entering into the European Community.[61] Whatever the cause, association constitutes the potential beginning of a federalizing process. The same phenomena that characterize it under more normal conditions are to be observed, and hence there exists always the possibility that it will end in actual federal union, once the obstructions have been removed or worn down by time.

To illustrate with the case of Puerto Rico, the specific form of its association with the United States is rather a close one. It makes the individual citizen of Puero Rico an American citizen, obliges him to serve in the United States armed forces, commits him to United States foreign policy, subjects him to all those laws which the United States Congress decides to make applicable to Puerto Rico — in consultation with a Puerto Rican representative in Congress to be sure — but it also makes him, as a citizen of the Commonwealth, more autonomous; for the Commonwealth is more self-governing than the average state, with its own constitution and laws more fully protected.

"Cooperative" federalism · Even though the federal division of powers is a mainstay of free constitutional government, it should not blind us to the

fact that all governmental units share in the common task of accomplishing the "will of the people." Since the thirties, the conviction has gained ground that "an emphasis on separateness or rivalry tends to forward the least desirable developments in American government today."[62] To put it thus may be to belittle the constitutional importance of divided powers; yet there is great merit in the view that "the sphere of government is increasing in its relation to life and there is a growth in both federal and state functions along a wide front." In short, there has grown up a wide area of effective cooperation between the states and the federal government which is mutually advantageous and not necessarily destructive of the broader constitutional division of powers. The federal government stands in need of the more intimate contacts with local problems in such fields as social security, while on the other hand the local authorities in the poorer sections of the country may require the financial aid of the national government. The forms which such cooperation between the federal and state governments may take are many. Grants-in-aid, federal tax credits, cooperative use of personnel, as well as agreements and formal compacts, have been employed. In recent years there has been an increasing amount of dovetailing of legislation, examples of which include making federal laws contingent on state activities, suggesting model statutes, and protecting through federal legislation one state against the unfair competition of another. There is, of course, forever present a fear that fiscal aids by the federal government may turn into means of compelling state action contrary to the preferences of the people's majority in the state. Even the fact that a state has sought federal aid under such conditions is no conclusive argument against the presence of compulsion. However, a measure of pressure such as we find in the fields of agriculture and education is probably desirable.

The trend toward concentration of economic power makes such cooperation well-nigh inescapable in the United States at present. Those fields of necessary regulation which the courts have withdrawn from the federal government's authority, in spite of the fact that the economic conditions make it inaccessible to the state authorities, may be handled by cooperative effort. The marketing of agricultural products is an outstanding example here. Although a number of objections are raised against the federal government's use of state personnel for the administration of federal legislation, the trend has been persistently forward in that direction.

The broadening scope of effective cooperation between state and federal agencies obscures the difference between a closely knit federal setup and an effectively decentralized government such as that of England — so much so that years ago one could foresee the day "when the character of a state is changed or modified into a kind of administrative unit to carry out federal plans and policies." The pressures and exigencies of a compact and highly industrialized national economy may eventually force the United States to abandon federalism. While this would undoubtedly weaken the constitutional restraints in one important respect, it need not spell the end of constitutionalism. As the example of Canada (if not of England) shows, there are other methods available. A government — even a constitutional government — has to function effectively if it is to last.

The Second World War, probably the most dangerous war the United States has so far fought, brought in its train a great many additional centralized activities. The draft, price and many rationing controls, as well as many of the directed production problems immediately growing out of the requirements of procurement for the armed services, all but swamped the American federal structure. This is perhaps nowhere as clearly visible as in the weight of the federal budget as compared with that of the states. Recently state and local governments have seen a rapid increase of their expenditures, due not only to price and wage increases but also to expanded functions. It would be a mistake, however, to declare federalism in the United States dead; in some areas the states have recaptured some of their power through more vigorous insistence upon their participation in the federal administration. As the late Professor Grodzins rightly commented, the American federal system is principally characterized by a federal-state-local sharing of responsibilities for virtually all functions. He added that the functions cannot be reasonably divided without "drastically reducing the importance" of the states (and localities). He went on to say: "The rhetoric of state and national power becomes easily and falsely a rhetoric of conflict," conceiving the two as "adversaries."[63] American federalism has, in other words, become cooperative federalism, and in this, much more nearly resembles Swiss and German federalism than was formerly the case. This development in no wise conflicts with the advantages of divided power; the powers remain divided, even as they cooperate. The point has been well put in a Senate report on intergovernmental relations. "'Cooperation' and 'coordination' are the key needs if we are to make federalism work under modern conditions . . . we are engaged in the task of assigning roles in the governmental processes."[64] It then spoke of new procedures and a "hidden dimension," all adding up to "the improvement of cooperative devices designed to enable each level to share in the whole government activity." All this makes good sense only if the federalizing process rather than some static design is seen as constituting its enduring nature.

Decentralization · Local self-government had throughout the nineteenth century been a battle cry of the progressives in nondemocratic countries, such as Prussia, whereas the more conservative forces have been inclined to support it under democratic conditions. These political slogans should not prevent one from recognizing decentralization as part and parcel of free institutions. In England a long series of statutes, beginning with the Poor Law Amendment Act, for many years enlarged both the powers and the duties of local authorities. Through these statutory reforms, local authorities were transformed completely, until the semi-feudal justices of the peace of before 1834 had given way to what is a system of effective civic participation in numerous matters of immediate local interest, such as health, sanitation, schools, housing, and so forth. While it is not possible here to treat of these matters at the length which they deserve, let us note the large extent to which England and other countries modeled on the English parliamentary pattern have relied upon this device so as to escape from a deadening centralism in administration. However, in this century British local self-government has undergone a steady process of weakening, due to the central government's expansion. Since 1939, more and more functions have been transferred to national authorities. It is generally agreed that local government structure must be radically reformed if this trend is to be reversed. One leading authority has asserted that the reorganization of the local government structure "is fundamental to the survival of local government."[65] He added that "few people appear to understand the essential role of local government in the welfare states." "Nearly everyone in Britain agrees," another has added, "that some reform of local government is overdue." But actually not very much progress has been achieved so far.[66]

In the United States this issue is of real significance within the states. There is great variety throughout the union, local authorities being subject to state law. In fact, in some states the centralizing tendency of the state government has been marked. That two towns in Massachusetts should not be able to merge without an act of the legislature seems unfortunate. That the voting on liquor regulations should be done in Vermont towns contrary to the best judgment of town officers, because of a state statute, seems hard to believe. Federal authorities have encountered all kinds of unreasonable restrictions in securing the effective cooperation of municipal authorities because the state was found watching jealously over "its" local powers. As both state and federal powers expand in response to various novel tasks, it seems important that more effective decentralization accompany the new federalism if the citizen is to retain a measure of participation in the government. If one reads the *Federalist* or Jefferson's writings with this in view, one sees that the state a hundred and fifty years ago was to the citizen what at best the town or city can be today.

If, from this vantage point, one were to contrast federalism and decentralization, one would find the conclusion equivocal. As long as unitary government is thought of as centralized government, there is no great difficulty in distinguishing between it and a federal structure. But what if the unitary government should be decentralized, as it has been in England? Are there no distinctions between such a decentralized government and a federal one, as one distinguished scholar has recently asserted? It is merely a matter of "the territorial composition of the state"? Can "no issues different in kind" be raised in regard to one or the other? The preceding discussion ought to have shown that the answer to these questions is in the negative, and not only in terms of "the time-honored divisions of Federalism and Local Government." The difference is precisely this, that federalism affords a constitutional sanction to the territorial division of governmental powers. On account of that sanction, the change of this division is beyond the reach of the central government. Of decentralized England it has been said that "the British system is nevertheless dominated by the idea that all legislative power is presumed to lie in the first instance in the king in Parliament and all executive power in the Crown — a twofold constitutional principle which represents the very apotheosis of centralization."[67] All that is centralized is the power over the constitution and general legislation. But even if elements of decentralization should be supported by a formal constitutional sanction, as they are in many American states, we do not have federalism unless the local units are presented as such in the representative assembly which changes the constitution (and legislates), and unless these units' powers are safeguarded by adequate arrangements for a constitutional judiciary. There is no object in laboring the distinction, however.

Conclusion: strength and weakness of federal structure of government
The foregoing shows that federalism is intimately related to modern constitutionalism, as may be suggested by its rise alongside of it.[68] There is nothing in the distinction between federalism and decentralization which would imply an inherent superiority of one over the other; their advantages and disadvantages can only be contrasted in terms of the peculiar conditions of the time and place under which a particular government is supposed to operate. Federalism is an integral part of modern constitutionalism. A federal governmental structure provides a spatial or territorial, as distinguished from a functional, division of powers. Such a division operates as a rather effective restraint upon the abuse of governmental powers by the central as well as the local authorities. Indeed, in many situations it is likely to be more effective than a functional division; for this, as we have seen, can be more readily overcome by an effective party organization. In other words, what federalism does is to mobilize firmly entrenched local powers in support of the constitution, and to offer them protection under the constitution

as well. Localized groupings are treated in a manner analogous to the treatment of the individual citizen, to whom a sphere of relative independence, of civil liberties, is likewise guaranteed. Besides these constitutional considerations, there is a great advantage in providing an opportunity for limited experimentation in one or more of the component units.

However, federal structures of government share with all formalized constitutionalism the difficulty of adjusting a relatively rigid scheme to the shifting exigencies of a dynamic industrial society. Under modern conditions areas of friction are bound to develop where technological change radically alters the conditions under which government has to be conducted. If competencies are divided between the central government and the local governments, as they are in the United States, governmental functions emerge which can only be performed by one of these units, and for which no constitutional provision has yet been made. The particular difficulties in the United States are at present believed to be solvable by delegating specific functions to the state governments and by making the central government one of residuary powers, but it would be a mistake to assume that the problem would thereby be solved permanently. There would presently appear situations in which the local (state) governments alone could act, and yet, under the new constitutional arrangement, only the federal government, with its residuary powers, would be constitutionally able to act. In other words, the rigidities which arise from a division of powers are inherent in the federal scheme and are the price which has to be paid for the advantages set forth above. In this respect the spatial division of powers does not differ from the functional division. In both cases a measure of inefficiency is the price for the measure of freedom which such constitutional restraints afford.

Local Self-Government Democracy:

Basis of Constitutional Democracy

XII

Introduction · Political philosophers on the best size of towns · A pragmatist's approach · Growth of local government functions · The British
tradition · Alternative patterns: (1) Great Britain, (2) France, (3) Switzerland, (4) Germany, (5) United States · Metropolitan problems ·
Middletown and *Yankee City* · Conclusion

Introduction · The violent upheavals of our time have revived interest
in the local community. Its importance for the functioning of constitutional
government is common knowledge. The local community has often proved
surprisingly resistant to the pressures of totalitarian government. When
Hitler's armies conquered France and the central government of the Third
Republic was swept away, the tradition of French democracy found refuge
in the villages and small towns, where intimacy of personal contacts enabled
people to know friend and foe. Again, when the conquering armies of the
West had completely destroyed the government and party of Hitler, an older
and better German tradition re-emerged in the local communities. Local
government turned out to be more disasterproof than the broader, more far-
flung structures of state and nation.

During the turmoil of the last great depression, a phrase became popular
which was meant to express that aspect of local government and the local
community: grass-roots democracy. It was often used with conservative
implications; as contrasted with the swiftly changing scene of national politics and the popular majorities which were presumably supporting these
policies, "democracy at the grass roots" was supposed to represent the steady
and persistent outlook of Americans in the local community, especially in the
rural community with its settled ways.

Perhaps the most striking document of our time describing the rediscovery
of the "small town" was written by a literary critic of distinction who had
been deeply sympathetic with the outlook of Marx and Marxism. Granville

Hicks, in *Small Town,* has recorded his experiences as a national and world-minded "intellectual" in trying to participate effectively in the self-government of a village in upstate New York. He concludes it with a highly significant reminder that self-government constantly demands that one make concrete what, for the "intellectual," is general and abstract: "As I write this, I think of the meeting of the board of fire commissioners that I must attend in a few hours. The outcome may be good or bad; all I can predict is that a considerable amount of time will be wasted in unnecessary talk. However it appears to be my job as much as it is any man's. . . . As a matter of fact, I expect to enjoy parts of the evening, as I have enjoyed parts — and rather large parts — of the whole experience with which this book has dealt." This outlook is part of the perspective, the slant, that this intellectual acquired when he learned that the resistances to proposed changes are not the product of stupidity. "People take what they can use without surrendering their way of life."[1]

Any thorough analysis of the way in which the "common man" participates in common concerns of the community will disclose that he hesitates to assent to what he does not understand. Hence his inclination to vote for persons, rather than policies, when it comes to national and international affairs. There are recurrent important exceptions, but as a general propensity it holds true in all Western countries. At the same time, a great similarity characterizes local government functions everywhere. This fact has made it possible for local government authorities to band together for the defense and advocacy of their interests even on an international level. When the European communes decided to do so, a famous French mayor, Eduard Herriot of Lyons, stated the matter: "When I step down from the state to the local community, I come close to human beings. If I talk with an English mayor, or a German or Russian one, I discover that we have the same pre-occupations . . . That is why I believe that the bringing together of the local communities is the best condition of the bringing together of men."[2]

As a matter of fact, though, these common preoccupations allow for a good deal of variety in their handling. Genuine local autonomy permits such variety; one community stresses public parks and other kinds of landscape beauty, another stresses schools, still another public safety. All these objectives have to be given some attention in every modern community, but there is considerable leeway as to emphasis. Whether to extend the town water line down in a certain direction and gain the added fire protection will be of vital concern to all citizens, for it will affect the future growth of the town. The decision they make may seem unwise from the standpoint of the expert town planner, the architect, the engineer — but if so, the citizens will discover it in time and they may learn a vital lesson in self-government.

Popular government includes the right of the people, through their majority, to make mistakes.

These statements hold true primarily for the small community where the electorate is reasonably familiar with the practical tasks in hand; in communities over 100,000 it proves impractical and has led to many breakdowns. Then the drift will be in the direction of central decision making, while what Banfield, following Lindblom, has called social choice, where various influences are brought to bear upon the policy-making process, will deteriorate.[3] To some extent, districting has modified these difficulties, but on the whole only the small town is able to make good use of the right to govern itself. It is in fact often forgotten that the notion and practice of local self-government was developed at a time when few cities had over 100,000 inhabitants. The small town therefore can be, though often is not, the "school for democracy" that Bryce and others have claimed it to be.[4]

Political philosophers on the best size of towns · Discussions about the optimal size of a community have been part of political philosophy since Plato and Aristotle. In keeping with their attachment to the city-state or polis of classical antiquity, these philosophers talked in terms of an independent community or state. Believing that a well-governed polis must rest upon a foundation of common beliefs, of shared convictions regarding what is right and wrong, and that such sharing presupposed leadership of the personal intimacy which the modern world has come to associate with churches, both Plato and Aristotle believed that the community, for good living, should be quite small. It should be small enough for everyone to know everyone else, Plato pointed out in his *Laws,* and he urged a regular system of festivals and rituals in order to acquaint the citizens with each other and to teach them a sense of mutual obligation. On the basis of such knowledge about each other, sound decisions could be arrived at concerning who should serve in public offices and similar matters. Both he and Aristotle suggested that 1000 citizens, i.e., about 6000 inhabitants, would be the best size; only in his *Laws,* in which generally, as an old man, he makes concessions to practicality, is Plato willing to go as high as about 5000 citizens, i.e., 30,000 inhabitants.[5] Growth of a city which goes beyond this, as had that of Athens in the fifth century B.C., when it reached perhaps 300,000, Plato condemned as disruptive of sound communal life and order. This figure seems to have been more or less standard in Roman times as a basis for planning new towns first in Italy and afterward throughout the empire, although of course politically the position of such dependent cities within the Roman realm cannot, in spite of their autonomy, be compared with the problems of an independent city in Plato's Greece. Certain it is that the enormous growth of cities, especially Rome, caused considerable concern in antiquity, and many would have agreed with a leading writer of our own day that Rome "remains a significant object lesson of what to avoid," namely "megalopolitan elephantiasis."[6]

The discussion of the best size for a city was resumed in the later Middle Ages, when the works of Aristotle were studied anew. Philosophers like St. Thomas seemed inclined to follow Aristotle's lead, in spite of the fact that the modern territorial state was in the making, containing many times the inhabitants Plato and Aristotle had thought right. In the Renaissance, the city-states of Italy, the Low Countries, and Germany played such a vital role that their size, not too different from that of the city-states of classical Greece — Florence had perhaps 40,000 inhabitants in 1470; Cologne had about 30,000 at the same time — seemed to support the contentions of the ancient philosophers. Toward the end of the sixteenth century, writers like G. Botero, J. Bodin, and J. Althusius became increasingly realistic about describing the growth of cities in relation to their location, but continued to stress the importance of keeping size under control. During the succeeding century, when the large territorial kingdoms definitely became the communities in terms of which the Western nation-state was conceived and governed, philosophers tried to find a basis in nature and reason for abstract law which was to regulate the relations between individuals as well as with the government. The close community corresponding to the old city was that of the monarchical court — but in contrast to these trends under absolutism England preserved the local autonomy of its towns and counties sufficiently to serve as a basis for her growing representative institutions. It was the French philosopher Montesquieu who clearly recognized and appropriately stressed the importance of this English tradition for the viability of her constitutional system. According to him, the intermediate powers moribund in France under her despotic government, were the taproot of freedom and constitutionalism. Following him Jean Jacques Rousseau, citizen of one of Switzerland's small cantons, Geneva, dogmatically asserted once more, like Plato and Aristotle, that a "state" in order to be free and popular must be as small as a Swiss canton.[7]

A pragmatist's approach · John Dewey, after exploring the decline of democracy and the eclipse of the public, turned to the local community as the place where both might be reborn. For the troubled pessimism of Walter Lippmann's *Phantom Public* (as well as earlier studies), John Dewey sought to substitute a pragmatic ethic of neighborly cooperation in *The Public and Its Problems*.[8] Dewey thought that the democratic public, still largely inchoate and unorganized, could not adequately resolve its most urgent problem:

to find and identify itself. Perhaps it would be more in keeping with historical facts to say that this public is "increasingly" inchoate; it certainly was less so in earlier times than in mid-twentieth century America. If that is borne in mind, Dewey's entreaty that "democracy must begin at home, and its home is the neighborly community," has a rather unpragmatic ring. For more than two thousand years, as we have just seen, philosophers have urged that the community should be small; yet for some centuries now, communities have been growing larger and more inclusive — having done the same in classical antiquity. At the very time of Aristotle's plea, the territorial dominion of Alexander the Great was superseding the small city-state, to be succeeded in turn by the Roman Empire.

But regardless of the homily, Dewey is undoubtedly right, if not very original, when he insists that only in the intimate contact of the neighborhood can the public, that is, the mass of common men and women, become articulate. If this neighborly community is to be revived, it is important to understand the causes of its decline. The ideal which Dewey and other philosophers have portrayed is far from being a true description. In many American localities, hard-bitten machines are run by county sheriffs and town assessment boards. Fear and greed often play a greater role in the small community, with its weapons of social ostracism and personal discrimination, than in the more inclusive communities. Certainly Lord Bryce was rash in simply correlating the growth of party machines to the size of cities. Genuine democratic constitutionalism calls for disagreement, open expression of conflicting views, and responsiveness to divergent interests. The overemphasis on agreement which the philosophic partisans of the small community from Plato to Rousseau and Dewey have indulged in corresponds to boss rule rather than constitutional freedom. But whatever one's view concerning this aspect of the problem, the question as to the causes of the decline remains.

Unfortunately, several of these causes are so intimately linked with the development of modern industrialism that only very determined efforts to counteract them will have the desired result. If we agree with Dewey that "there is no substitute for the vitality and depth of close and direct intercourse and attachment," we have to ask how we may resolve such complex problems as the following: How can we induce the metropolitan cities to devolve into many smaller communities? How can we provide adequate substitutes for the deep attachment which life-long membership in a local community gives, but which present-day mobility prevents; how can we counteract the constant expansion of central (federal and state) functions, impinging on every side upon the local autonomy? In view of such questions and in view of present trends, quite a few students of these problems incline toward abandoning any such attempts at reviving the dying local community, and instead tend to recognize the professional group, the trade union, and similar associations as providing that "direct and close intercourse." In this view these units are the "living communities" of twentieth-century man.[9]

In any case, the insistence upon the importance of direct intercourse is based upon the conviction that "the essential need is the improvement of the methods and conditions of debate, discussion and persuasion." Often the belief in this need rests upon the unqualified belief in the *rationality* of the citizen. At the same time, it is easy to exaggerate the amount of intelligence and ability which may be required to judge the bearing of expert knowledge upon common concerns. Dewey and others have pleaded for doing away with secrecy, prejudice, bias, misrepresentation, and propaganda. The plea appeals to the idealism of the troubled democrat, but is it pragmatically based upon an understanding of how human relations actually work? Is it really true that all we need is greater publicity? How are we to get it? More concrete studies, such as *Small Town, Middletown, Yankee City,* and *The Lonely Crowd,* suggest that a more realistic understanding of the actual working of local communities calls for a reassessment of such rationalist appeals. Too much has been taken for granted in regard to the actual working of "democracy at the grass roots." New institutional safeguards are needed to reinforce the legal and constitutional position of the local foundations of the constitutional order. But only a survey of what the comparative situation is in various constitutional systems will provide a firm ground from which to start efforts at reconstruction.

Growth of local governmental functions · The recognized growth of governmental functions at the national level has tended to obscure the parallel development of ever-wider local governmental functions. Actually, the technology of modern industrialism has produced many wants and needs which are of peculiar importance to local government. Thus, the rapid improvement in all kinds of motor-driven vehicles has challenged local communities by making available superior fire-fighting or snow-removal equipment. These matters often become simply problems of dollars and cents, comparatively. Thus, the increase in the tax rate resulting from the acquisition of such fire-fighting equipment may be balanced or outweighed by the reduction in fire insurance rates which the householders have to pay, with a net saving for the citizen-owner. While the saving in automobile repairs which may be traced to more efficient snow-removal equipment may be more elusive, it may yet appeal to a community alert to technical progress.

Generally speaking, there has been a rapid increase in the number and quality of local functions, though in many countries, notably Britain, this increase has been associated with a decline in local independence and judgment. In larger cities, unfortunately, these technical complications have led to increasing apathy on the part of the average citizen, with the consequence that special interests, boss rule, and corruption have become rampant, at least in the United States. The corrective has been, both in the United States and elsewhere, increasing bureaucratization and central decision making combined with planning.[10] Obviously, the increase in technical services means that local self-government is of vital concern to the average citizen. Water supply, fire protection, sanitation, welfare, roads, gas and electricity, parks, libraries, building regulations and town planning, housing, and transportation are certainly matters which concern the daily well-being of everyone. If to these are added, as they must be in the United States, education and police functions, it is clear that active citizen participation in all these matters means tangible, concrete self-government.

The great problem is how to maintain local control over these varied services. Here the availability of adequate financial resources is of vital importance. The student of constitutional government has cause to regret the rigidity characteristic of most modern constitutional systems in this matter. In many American as well as European communities, the property tax on real estate is overworked and has caused the blight of central urban areas which provide many services for out-of-towners from the surrounding areas and countryside. This in turn has given rise to various artificial devices, often highly undesirable from a social standpoint, such as sales taxes and other kinds of consumption taxes. These taxes fall with almost equal weight upon rich and poor alike. Yet so simple a device as a percentage addition to the state income tax is "constitutionally" prohibited.

Related to this problem of fiscal autonomy is the problem of optimal size. Functions are related to size. While a community of 10,000 inhabitants may be able to acquire a bulldozer for snow-removal purposes, a community of 2500 may not be able to do so. There has been a tendency in European countries, for example in Britain, to decree alterations in size by legislative fiat. The Local Government Boundary Commission, an administrative body which in recent years exercised this discretionary legislative authority delegated to it by Parliament, which retained vague supervisory control and could act on appeal (it was abolished in 1948), was reported to favor local government units of approximately 200,000. Communities of this size are clearly too large for effective sharing of experience. It is both characteristic and a bit alarming that the criteria which this body stresses are efficiency and economy; the problems of democracy and constitutionalism are placed in the background. Effective cooperation of several local communities through joint boards is more cumbersome, but it is probably sounder when effective citizen participation is considered.

The British tradition • Ever since Montesquieu wrote his praise of British constitutionalism and stressed the importance of the "intermediate powers" of local authorities, it has been customary to think of Britain as the home of local self-government. Yet in the strict modern sense there was very little self-government in the local sphere in Britain from the end of the Middle Ages to the nineteenth century. In towns and counties, in parishes and districts, the local gentry shared with the nobility and the patricians the privilege of government, largely upon appointment by the Crown. To be sure, the Crown chose these local authorities from among the local gentry, a natural thing considering that the basis of parliamentary bodies was the corporate entity of county and town (the towns being greatly underrepresented). Yet the fact remains that their authority, whether judicial, military, or ecclesiastical, was closely linked to the king and his ministers. It may be quite wrong to say, as has been done, that "the Justices of the Peace . . . exercised a benevolent dictatorship," for what these justices of the peace and other local officers could and did do was based strictly upon parliamentary authorization.[11] Yet the crucial characteristic of modern self-government, namely, the election of local officials by local popular vote, was restricted within narrow confines and was in any case only participated in by the property owners of substance.

Nevertheless, this British tradition of entrusting the local concerns to members of the local squirearchy was self-government in an aristocratic sense, especially after the Crown, in the eighteenth century, became increasingly identified with the parliamentary majority through the development of the cabinet system of responsible government. There is a vital difference between such a system and the bureaucratic system of Continental Europe, where officials unconnected with the local scene are sent out from an administrative center to handle local affairs. It is this system, in the France of Richelieu and Louis XIV, which Montesquieu believed to be the basis of potential despotism.

It was only in conjunction with the great reforms of the nineteenth century that democratic local self-government was adopted in Britain. But the older "self-government" laid the basis for a striking feature of the British local government tradition which is at variance not only with practice in those states in the United States where home rule prevails, but also with Continental practice. Rudolf Gneist, in his justly famous study of English local government, noted that the concept of local self-government had never been clearly defined by statute or judicial decision. Yet he found it a stable and firmly structured whole in the mid-nineteenth century. This is the way he described it: "Legislation has regulated the exercise of governmental power since the days of *Magna Charta* in such a way that the responsible offices of internal administration are conferred upon locally resident

persons and committees [of such persons] as *honorary offices* in accordance
with statutory enactments [defining the authority] in county, town and
parish. Likewise the funds required are raised by the *association of neighbors* [local community] according to legally established rates. Self-government appears thus as a mandate for [the carrying out of] the local governmental functions, through a relative distribution of the personal and tax
obligations among the social classes in the neighborhood association which
are suited [for these tasks]. Looked at from the local end, self-government
is an administrative system of the [local] community which is regulated by
legislative norms in such a way as to represent the government's authority
[*Staatsgewalt*] when it is locally active; and since this obligation is at the
same time recognized as the right of the community, self-government constitutes the legal constitution of county, town and parish in England." What
this means is that the British local self-government tradition makes one and
the same institutional structure a system of internal (national) administration as well as of local constitutionalism.[12] This emphasis upon local government *according to laws*, that is to say, in line with parliamentary and judicial
authority on the national level, constitutes the significant contrast to Continental Eurupe (except Switzerland). It has led to the British tradition of a
local government of enumerated powers, that is, a local government empowered to do only what Parliament has authorized it to do, in contrast with the
United States, France, Germany, and other countries.

In view of the tendency to "idealize" British local self-government it may
be well to conclude these observations on the British tradition by a statement made some years ago by Sir E. D. Simon, considered by many the
most eminent British authority on local government at that time. Commenting upon local government in Stockholm, he found that "it was on about the
same level as that in Manchester, that is to say, it is honest and fairly competent, without much energy or imagination; and there are few signs of any
general or deeply felt sense of responsibility among the citizens for the
government of their city."[13] The same would, I believe, turn out to be the
conclusion of a candid observer in any of the countries we shall presently
describe.

Alternative patterns · Patterns of local self-government are quite
numerous. There is not only the obvious need to shape the pattern in such
a way as to fit it into the broader constitutional pattern of each country, but
even within a given country, numerous alternative patterns are found. If the
constitution should be a federal one, as in the United States, the determination of local self-government law may be left to the several component units.
If the constitution is a unitary one, traditional differences in different locali-

ties may be permitted to exist, as in Britain, or several possible alternative solutions may be offered the local communities for organizing themselves, as in Massachusetts. It is obvious that we cannot attempt here to give a complete survey, even in outline form; nor would any useful purpose be served by such a bare sketch. The following subparagraphs are intended merely to provide an opportunity for highlighting a few striking and instructive aspects of the several national traditions.

(1) *Great Britain.* The key aspect of the British local government pattern is a popularly elected council, supported by a professional civil service. It exercises both administrative and legislative functions, but as previously noted cannot do anything which has not previously been authorized by either a general or a special act of Parliament. The British like to think of this relationship as a partnership between the national and local authorities, but recent trends make it seem something of an euphemism. These elective boards, with their reasonably well-defined territorial jurisdiction, are a creation of the nineteenth century; they superseded a welter of overlapping boards and commissioners, dealing with welfare, highways, health and so forth, and created *ad hoc* when the justices of the peace proved incapable of handling the multiple tasks resulting from the industrial revolution. First, in 1835, councils were established for the towns or boroughs; then, in 1888, for the counties and cities (called county boroughs); and last, in 1894, for the districts and parishes. A succession of local-government acts, down to the present, has dealt with assignment and reassignment of functions. Most important, from an American standpoint, is the fact that the control of education is not local, but a national concern.

The elective councils give a considerable uniformity to British local government. Concerned as they are with making ordinances, fixing the budget, determining such "policies" as are still left to them (not many) and working out their application, as well as selecting and appointing the permanent officials, the councillors are the mainstay of local democracy. Their qualifications, since 1945, are the same as for members of Parliament and are no longer tied to property and real estate. In the smaller units all councillors are popularly elected, while in the larger units, one fourth of the councillors are co-opted and serve for six years rather than the three years which are customary for elected councillors. Through staggering the elections, continuity is preserved in these councils in the larger local communities.

The mayors of British cities are elected by the councils from among their midst, serving usually for one year; in other units of local government a chairman is chosen. Ceremonial occasions, surrounded with the customary British pomp and circumstance, are deceptive in that they suggest a position of leadership which these chairmen and mayors rarely occupy. They resemble the president of Switzerland and the rector of a Continental university.

In recent years, the local sphere has increasingly become a battlefield of the national parties. The "welfare state" (see below, ch. XXII) has proliferated programs calling for close cooperation of national and local government, and therefore the political parties have injected their party programs into local elections. This has served to heighten interest in these contests, which were formerly a matter of indifference to large sections of the electorate, participation falling at times as low as 5 per cent. This is scarcely a pattern suggesting emulation in countries to be democratized (see below, (d)). Opinions differ widely as to the people's interest in local affairs; the pattern seems too impersonal to arouse popular interest and concern. The councils are large, thirty on the average, but running as high as one hundred, and their work is broken up into committees. These committess have a tendency to depend upon the permanent civil service engaged in the work they control. Considering the complexity of technical work, it is only natural that these civil servants should carry great weight, but since they are appointed and paid by the council, the responsibility is clearly to the council. There are more than a million of these professional civil servants employed by local governments, and their general competence is high; in fact they escape the elitism which is characteristic of the "administrative class" in the national government. The standards for many officials, notably teachers, are set by the national government.

The most important of the permanent officials in British local government is the town clerk, a general administrator coordinating the several special services. The British are inclined to consider this official a most valuable feature of their local government (and hence undertook to export him to British-occupied Germany). It is doubtful whether such a permanent official is really as desirable as the British think; he tends to legalize and thus to "bureaucratize" the local government, and thus stultify local democracy.

Even before the return of the Labour party to power in 1946, the growing need for town and country planning and their effective coordination led to the establishment in 1943 of a separate ministry to deal with these problems. Its tasks are defined as "securing consistency and continuity in the framing and execution of national policy with respect to the use and development of land throughout England and Wales."

(2) *France.* The pattern of French local government is radically different, due to the fact that true local self-government has never been accepted in France. All the constitution is willing to concede is that "the territorial units of the Republic are the communes [municipalities], the Departments, the Overseas Territories. . . . These units shall be free to govern themselves through elected councils and under the conditions stipulated by law." (Arti-

cle 72.) This sounds as if there were to be established a system somewhat similar to the British, but such is not the case. In the next paragraph, the constitution takes it all back by announcing the traditional centralist French doctrine that "in the departments and the territories, the Delegate of the Government shall be responsible for the national interests, for administrative supervision, and for seeing that the laws are respected."

These "delegates" of the national government are the prefects, appointed one for each department, and directed by the ministry of the interior. They are assisted by subprefects for each district (*arrondissement*). Of the prefects, twenty-one carry, along with their departmental duties, the responsibility of coordinating several adjacent departments into one administrative "region" for puposes of defense, policing, and economic development. A significant reform in 1964 gave the regional prefect even greater supervision over other agents of the central government. (This "deconcentration," whereby local agents of the central government acquire considerable power in and for their local units, has replaced the original postliberation effort to establish genuinely autonomous regions for purposes of decentralization.)[14] Local government revolves around the prefect.[15] Not only does he coordinate the agents of various ministries, but he appoints most of the local officials and may suspend mayors, council presidents, and councils. The prefect may even add to the local budget expenses he believes the laws make mandatory. Under the prefect, the elected councils, as well as their chairmen (called "mayors" in the communes and "council presidents" in the other units), play a decidedly subordinate role, except for the mayors of a few big cities who, like Gaston Defferre, may achieve such national prominence as to gain personal independence. This subordination is manifest in their lack of financial resources; the mayors and council presidents have no solid basis for taxation, they must provide for many activities in accordance with national legislation, and, when they fail to do so, are subject to administrative discipline by the prefect. But the councils cannot request the transfer of a prefect.

The prefects are administrative politicians, or political administrators. While no longer dismissed with changes in party control at the top, they have many tasks which might properly be described as those of a political agent, and their instructions from Paris are numerous and detailed. While the prefect is no longer the sole head of the department, the president of the council having acquired somewhat more the status of a local executive, the prefect still plays a predominant role. But all in all, the French pattern is one of central administrative control and direction to such an extent that the often-cited right of French local authorities to initiate anything they wish without having to wait for national authorization, as in Britain, is largely illusory, as a result of lack of funds. As a matter of fact, throughout the nineteenth century, France maintained extensive prohibitions against certain municipal and local activities in order to protect a *laissez-faire* or free-market economy. Under such regulations the communes could not enter any field where they would compete with private enterprise. These prohibitions are now gone. In fact, socialism is widespread in local government, and in some communities the Communists take a large and growing part in local administration.

(3) *Switzerland.* At the opposite pole from France is the local government pattern of Switzerland. Here much the most important protection of communal democracy is found in the constitution, which gives the cantons, as members of the confederation, not only a clearly defined sphere of local autonomy but actually all residual power which the constitution does not specifically grant to the federal authorities. The cantons themselves are so small (see above, ch. XI) that the further local self-government granted by them under their cantonal constitutions to the municipalities, towns, and villages are merely a further reinforcement of the marked localism of Swiss government. This localism is rooted in ancient traditions and feeds the relatively strong interest in local politics which has often been stressed by students and observers.

Constitutional provisions and statutes vary from canton to canton, as does local government law in the American states, but the broad outlines of the pattern of government in the municipalities are similar throughout Switzerland. In the smaller of these "resident communes" (*Einwohnergemeinden*) the pattern is that of a town meeting, which decides upon broad questions of policy, passes ordinances, adopts the budget, fixes the tax rate, and elects the officials; in short, it operates very much like the New England town meeting. Again, like the board of selectmen, a communal council (*Gemeinderat*) usually numbering from five to nine members, handles the administrative tasks. The council, presided over by a chairman (president), acts as a body in more important matters; this council is chosen by the town meeting. In larger communes (cities of considerable size), this council is chosen by popular vote and handles all but broad issues of policy, which are submitted to popular referendum. There may be a smaller executive committee (*Stadtrat*) to supervise the administrative work, which the members sometimes divide among themselves as heads of departments. Finally, and again resembling New England, the town meeting elects some of the officials, while others are appointed by the council. Both councillors and officials serve for four years but they are often re-elected and reappointed.

It is evident that this system is truly democratic local self-government in a sense much more nearly in keeping with democratic constitutionalism than is either the British or the French. As a leading British student of local government has commented: "As regards village or city government, it seems to me that there can hardly be any doubt that this system is far superior to our British system . . ." and again ". . . not only is democracy in Switzerland based on the commune, but so also is culture . . . most villages have their art, their singing, their drama. . . ." The last remark coincides with the judgment of Professor Robert C. Brooks: ". . . the devotion of the Swiss goes out to his own canton, valley, or commune. . . ."[16] It is local self-government truly grass-rooted and supported by the citizen.

(4) *Germany.* It is perhaps the most striking feature of Germany's total collapse that self-government reasserted itself first on the local level. To be sure, Allied and more especially American policy was explicitly committed to building "democracy from the ground up" and thus making it secure. But there is little doubt that the same thing would have happened without Allied promptings. As a matter of fact, local government in rural as well as in urban areas tended to resume its pre-Nazi form upon the entry of Allied troops.

Unfortunately, some grave errors were committed as a result of an inadequate grasp of pre-Nazi German local government. Americans took the fact that German local government officials were charged with carrying out and enforcing state (*Land*) legislation to mean that they were lacking in independence, in spite of the fact that this situation is characteristic not only of Britain but of Switzerland as well. British occupation officials and policy makers, on the other hand, felt that the managerial position of the *Bürgermeister* was undemocratic, and that the office should therefore be made elective, supported in professional administrative work by a town clerk of civil-service status; this was felt in spite of the fact that the city-manager movement in the United States had for years been promoted as the most promising pattern of administration under democratic conditions, provided this manager was responsible to and controlled by an elected council — which was precisely the German situation. As a result of these two assaults upon the traditional German pattern of local self-government, we find today a perplexing dichotomy.

The "traditional" pattern, prevalent under the Weimar constitution and derived from those under the monarchies, varied to some extent in the different states, as it does now under the new state (*Land*) constitutions, since local self-government is a state prerogative. However, the Basic Law guarantees to the communes (*Gemeinden*) the right to decide on their own responsibility upon all matters of local concern within the framework of the laws, and it provides for popular representative bodies, based upon universal, free, equal, and secret elections,[17] unless the commune wishes to assemble in its entirety, that is, hold a town meeting. In other words, the Basic Law returned to the "traditional" pattern of Weimar, under which local self-government was composed of three tiers of authority, all derived from the people: (1) the popularly elected assembly; (2) the assembly-elected council (*Kreisausschuss* in the counties, both rural and urban) or executive board (*Magistrat* in the cities); and (3) the chief executive (*Bürgermeister* or *Oberbürgermeister* in cities, *Landrat* [also other titles] in the rural counties) to be chosen by the council or executive board or sometimes by the assembly. However, in the name of democracy, the British and Americans insisted that the chief executive be popularly elected, the British demanding that this be counterbalanced by the creation of a town clerk (*Stadtdirektor*). Furthermore, the Americans tried to have all delegated administration eliminated, or at least reduced to a minimum. As a result, local self-government was twisted out of shape. A deeper insight into German tradition would have shown what was admittedly needed to make local government less bureaucratic and more responsive to popular views, thus also permitting it to serve more effectively as the proving ground of grass-roots democracy. On the whole, German local governments have steadily progressed toward more democratic procedures. Where the *Bürgermeister* (mayor) is elected, the electorate has shown a surprising amount of independence.[18] It is also clear that the British, if their purpose was to promote democracy, made a mistake in persuading the Germans to adopt their town clerk, in Germany called *Stadtdirektor;* for this office has served as a rallying point for the traditional bureaucratic forces. The success of German cities in mastering the vast tasks of reconstruction is in many ways just as impressive as the widely acclaimed economic miracle, indeed, it has been an important conditioning factor. The Social Democrats have played a primary role in making this success possible; the major German cities, Berlin, Hamburg, Cologne, Frankfurt, Munich, and Stuttgart, as well as the cities in the Ruhr, are all Social Democratic strongholds.

(5) *United States.* The characteristic feature of American local government is the "extreme freedom enjoyed by American municipalities, especially in the home rule states."[19] Considering the ever-tighter central control in Britain, local freedom may well seem "extreme," but in terms of the analysis of constitutional democracy given here, this freedom is appropriate and sound. It resembles the situation in Switzerland.

Under "home rule," the voters have a varying measure of freedom to adopt their own pattern of local government by referendum or even by initiative. While the several states have varying programs, the prevailing tendency is toward several basic patterns or "plans" among which local units may choose. There is more of this freedom for cities than for counties, but in New England, where the unit of effective local self-government is the town rather than the county, such freedom includes towns. Without going into the details, it is worth remarking that American cities and towns are governed according to three primary patterns. The first and oldest is mayor-council plan, under which both mayor and council are popularly elected (as are the judges and other officials); this plan is conceived in analogy to the broad pattern of American state constitutions, with their governor and state legislature operating in accordance with the traditional doctrine of separation of powers. The second pattern is the so-called commission plan, under which a small elected body combines executive and legislative functions, each commissioner heading a department for administrative purposes. Finally, there is the manager plan, under which all administrative responsibility is centered in a manager who is a cross between the town clerk in Britain and the *Bürgermeister* in Germany. The manager is responsible to and controlled by a council presided over by a mayor or chairman (in rural counties). There is sharp disagreement among Americans as to which of these patterns is the most desirable, but expert opinion leans toward the third alternative, provided popular referendum and initiative afford an opportunity for the citizen at large to participate in deciding the more important issues.

A special pattern is presented by the small New England towns with their town meetings, to which the entire citizenry foregathers once a year (and more often, if necessary) to vote the budget and the taxes, elect town officers, and decide broad issues of town policy, usually in conjunction with an appropriation. In these towns, many small administrative officers are elective, including such ancient "honors" as "surveyor of fences." But the administrative nub of the town is the board of selectmen, usually three in number. The selectmen may meet once a week in the evening to handle current issues connected with the administration of the town's various departments. They may also head up one or more of the administrative departments, although these are more often in the hands of another elected official (the selectmen, however, appoint some). Town meetings, like other forms of American local self-government, often suffer from a lack of interest on the part of a majority of the voters, participation falling as low as 10 per cent. This shows the limited importance of forms; in Switzerland, local self-government of the town-meeting type in commune and canton is the mainstay of democracy, and participation is lively and continuous. The problem remains how a comparable "school of democracy" may be set up in the vast metropolitan areas or even in the large cities with which the United States is dotted today.

Metropolitan problems · In any event, the great metropolitan areas represent a most perplexing range of problems, technologically, economically, ecologically, culturally, and, last but not least, governmentally and politically. Efforts to solve these problems have been made in all major countries. They have taken three forms, governmentally speaking, all aiming at securing a workable pattern of over-all direction and control. These three approaches are (1) the creation of special boards or commissions to handle particular aspects, like the London Metropolitan Water Board, New York's Port Authority, or Boston's Metropolitan Transit Authority; (2) the consolidation of many smaller units into one larger unit; (3) the federation of the central urban core with the outlying suburban towns. Of these, the first appeals to the engineering-minded specialist, the second to the power-conscious politician and the efficiency-preoccupied administrator, but only the third offers an opportunity of combining the essential popular controls with the intimacy of close community contact which is necessary for effective local self-government.[20]

While these efforts and plans have been widely advocated and discussed, they have, except for the first, been mostly programs rather than realities in England and America. The strong democratic tradition and local autonomy and independence, and the extent to which these sentiments make themselves felt in legislative bodies called upon to authorize any proposed action, make it essential that public opinion be developed to provide a firm democratic foundation for both the establishment and the maintenance of metropolitan government. No program of simple annexation will meet the inherent requirements of this situation, as experience in Boston and elsewhere shows. In the second half of the nineteenth century, several immediately adjacent towns were annexed by Boston, but then the movement stopped; local resistance became too strong. Nor will a program of administrative bodies controlled by a national or state legislature meet the situation. Boston has had such a body, the Metropolitan District Commission, dealing since 1919 with metropolitan sewers, water, and parks. But while this commission has done very acceptable work, it has no broad popular base, and hence lacks the democratic support which would enable it to function aggressively as a metropolitan authority ready to expand into new fields.

Federalism, as we have seen, is the modern governmental technique for combining the effective management of common concerns of several communities with the continued separate existence of these communities, each attending to the management of their several local concerns. Constitutionally speaking, federalism ranges all the way from a loose confederation of separate units agreeing by compact to establish a joint agency for the handling of common tasks, to the closely integrated federal union of such components into one joint government, with only residual powers remaining as the task of the united communities. These distinctions are not hard and fast; rather they should be seen as stages in an ongoing process of federalizing a community, as has been shown in the preceding chapter. Whether, in a given metropolitan area, one or the other of these federalisms should be adopted or can be secured is a pragmatic question of political prudence and expediency. Generally speaking, however, the history of federalism shows that it is wise to begin with a confederation, and then allow it to grow into a federal community with its federal government if the centripetal forces are strong enough. It is at the same time more likely that the communities to be joined in such a federation will agree to do so if their local autonomy remains intact in all but the palpably common concerns calling for joint management.

In cities such as Boston and New York, it would seem best to organize a metropolitan authority to exercise those joint functions which are clearly metropolitan in nature. As a body politic it would provide the central organs of a federation of cities and towns in the area. Such a federal solution of the metropolitan problem could well be combined with the city-manager type of governmental pattern. A representative council, based upon federally united local communities as electoral units (federal principle), would adopt the budget, make the basic policy decisions in the enumerated fields of the metropolitan authority, defend these policies before the electorate, and generally provide the political leadership in the metropolitan community. The manager, too, would have the usual functions, being elected and discharged by the council. While the cities and towns would retain their separate entity and autonomy, a measure of reduction in municipal activities and expenditures would take place, and the tax dollar would go farther than under the chaotic conditions of the present time. In any case, however, both the problems of the large community of the metropolis and those of the neighborhood community would be attended to on a strongly democratic basis. Much of the corruption which afflicts metropolitan communities is due to the failure to organize the government in such a way that the people can control it.[21] In light of experience in Switzerland, as well as in the United States, it would seem desirable to explore fully the possibilities for utilizing referendum and initiative for certain very basic decisions affecting the metropolitan community at large. This would apply especially to decisions in the planning field involving preferences of the individual citizen. For example, one of the most elusive problems of metropolitan planning at present is how to spend the available funds in the metropolitan transport field: whether to expand rapid transit lines and other forms of public transportation, or whether to develop superhighways and great parking areas, linking the metropolitan core with the outlying communities. This problem cannot be answered except in terms of the preferences of the inhabitants of the area for use of public conveyances as contrasted with use of private automobiles. It is the kind of problem which, if conscientiously handled, might be most helpfully decided by the electorate itself.

Referendums have the additional and important advantage of arousing citizen interest in the area of their application. Since it will remain a very real problem how to secure that interest in the vast metropolitan areas of modern countries, the referendum may serve to keep citizen interest alive, and not restrict it to the infrequent use of the ballot. In addition, it may well be very desirable to organize advisory committees of citizens for each major field of metropolitan activity; such committees might be drawn from the civic associations and interest groups active in the particular sphere. To these might be assigned the role of shaping and recommending policies and program; they could work with the planning and programming unit in the metropolitan authority.[22]

Just before the Second World War, W. A. Robson presented a study of the government and misgovernment of London. In it he sketched the perennial struggle with London's vast urban problems. In spite of the fact that London is the capital, its problems have been inadequately attended to by Parliament — in fact, Robson speaks of "neglect." Like Washington, London is too much controlled by men who are not responsible to the inhabitants of the city — a common source of metropolitan ills. After critically assessing the irresponsible and undemocratic *ad hoc* boards and commissions and outlining a "regional authority" like the "metropolitan authority" discussed above, Robson points up his argument by the following general observations: "If we wish to preserve and strengthen democracy in this country, it is obvious that we must reject expedients of these kinds and acknowledge the necessity for a directly elected regional council for Greater London as the only type of institution which is satisfactory from a democratic view. . . . This aspect of the matter cannot be regarded as of secondary importance at a time when our democratic faith, and the institutions in which it is embodied, have acquired a new and enhanced significance in a world of competing creeds and hostile authoritarian doctrines. Democracy on the national scale can function in a healthy manner only if it is supported and nourished by democratic local government. It will be a disaster if the reform of the essential structure of London government is delayed and evaded by the introduction of piecemeal expedients without regard to their undemocratic or antidemocratic character. . . ."[23] Unfortunately, this timely warning went unheeded, and years later, Robson noted with some bitterness that the opposition of local officeholders and other pressures had prevented the necessary changes.

Middletown *and* **Yankee City** • The difficulties encountered in realizing such programs as have been developed by reform groups for the rebuilding of metropolitan communities are to a considerable extent due to lack of knowledge about these communities.[24] It is, as a matter of fact, easy to realize that something on the order of the detailed information contained in studies like *Middletown*[25] would be vital for anyone desiring to bring about comprehensive reforms on a democratic basis. But that would be a gigantic undertaking for a metropolitan area of several million people. It is rather interesting that the two most striking studies of urban life have dealt with small cities, but not with the close-knit, intimate community. In the very small community, and especially in the rural community, the interviewer-investigator encounters difficulties in establishing the necessary basis of confidence. The neighborly qualities of small communities makes them very suspicious of outsiders asking "impertinent questions."[26] On the other hand, the metropolitan community staggers the potential inquirer by the range and complexity of its problems, as well as by the sheer mass of data to be gathered and analyzed.

Actually, there are some crucial methodological issues involved in both *Middletown* and similar studies such as *Yankee City* and *Plaineville*. The investigation in these cases was set up on the assumption that such an inquiry could be conducted without any value judgments being implied. In the usual terms, it was assumed that these inquiries could be "completely objective," "without any bias," "strictly scientific" and so on. They were, in other words, conceived as "demonstrating" what the authors as sociologists and anthropologists cherished as a desirable goal of scholarly studies of this kind. Anyone reading these books who happens not to share their particular ideas ("prejudices," these writers would call them) can readily identify the unexplained major premises in each case. In the case of *Middletown,* the antireligious, antibusiness, antibourgeois notions of the analysts stick out all over; in the case of *Yankee City,* the determination to find "classes" led the authors to discover them, when as a matter of fact the data merely supported a vague general recognition of "higher" and "lower," while no class consciousness or ability to act cohesively as a result of such consciousness could be demonstrated. These critical observations are not intended to belittle the significance of either *Middletown* or *Yankee City.* But they serve to contrast them with studies like *Small Town, The Lonely Crowd,* or *Political Influence,* which are conceived in a different spirit. In terms of our present concerns, it appears that the clearly apparent urgency of revitalizing constitutional democracy calls for intensive inquiries into the various factors involved in the blight of local self-government, both in the United States and abroad. There is little to be gained by anguished outcries or sermons imploring us to take greater interest in arrangements which do not interest us. For this task, past studies provide striking challenges which the student of constitutional democracy may use as steppingstones for the more clearly directed inquiry into the why and how of the functioning of local self-government, into the government and misgovernment of local communities. Banfield's and Dahl's studies represent important beginnings, although neither is preoccupied with the functioning of constitutional democracy as such. Dahl's primary concern in his study at New Haven appears to have been an inquiry into the extent to which small elites control the policy decisions in a medium-sized city.[27] His answer: They do not, to anywhere near the extent that is often assumed by those who talk about "boss rule" and "pressure politics." His findings have not gone unchallenged, but even if correct, they answer only partially the question as to the functioning of local self-government, and leave unanswered the question as to how typical the case may be.

Conclusion · Even so swift and general a survey as the preceding one provides many suggestions for needed thought and action in the field of local self-government as an essential part of the pattern and functioning of constitutional government. As the world is groping toward a federal organization for large regional communities and even world community, it is becoming increasingly evident that any such further broadening of government upward and outward will have to be accompanied by the extension of the federal principle downward and inward. In Europe, particularly, the unification movement, vigorously supported by many local government authorities, has raised these questions.[28] Students of this field have felt that there is need for federating adjacent communities for effective joint action where the constituent communities are too small for handling needed community services; that there is need for federating many communities which have become part of a metropolitan region; that there is need for giving local government in general more nearly the autonomous status of component federal elements, comparable to the cantons of Switzerland, with firm constitutional guarantees for such local communities. Every one of these several federalisms can contribute to the "territorial division of power," and can thereby reinforce the stability of the constitutional order, while at the same time providing room for the democratic working of the local community as the "proving ground of democracy."

The Guardianship of the Constitution:

The Issue of Judicial Review

XIII

Introduction · Medieval precedents · The supremacy of Parliament · The impact of federalism · Constitutional interpretation and partisanship · Due process · "Manifest Tenor" · Judges and propertied interests · Disinterestedness and representative quality · Universality versus partisanship · European constitutional tribunals · Representative quality of judiciary · Conclusion

Introduction · A constitution, if it is to be maintained, needs a guardian. But who is to be the guardian has remained controversial throughout history. Each of the main powers recognized by its doctrine, as well as a separate and distinct neutral power, have had their advocates. Benjamin Constant, in his famous *Reflections on Constitutions and Their Guarantees* (1814), proposed to make the monarch the neutral arbiter over and above a balance of separated powers. If the three powers of Montesquieu interfere with each other, disturb each other, or impede each other, it is necessary to have a power which puts them back in their place. This conception of the royal as the neutral power is closely akin to the English prerogative which, in the words of Dicey, is "the residue of discretionary or arbitrary authority which at any time is legally left in the hands of the Crown."[1] It is, therefore, the final security of the subject against abuse by ministers, politicians, and pressure groups. While it was difficult for the king to maintain this prerogative against a prime minister backed by a compact parliamentary majority, it remains in the background to be used in an emergency. When, in 1931, the weak Labour cabinet fell apart, the king stepped into the breach by authorizing Ramsay MacDonald to form a coalition cabinet, after his Labour cabinet had resigned. It was at the time claimed that a breach of the constitution by the king had occurred, but the course of succeeding events seems to have vindicated the exercise of royal authority in this instance. It would in any case be contrary to fact to call the English king a guardian of the constitution. Whether he could, for example, effectively oppose an attack upon the independence of judges may be doubted.

Under the Weimar constitution of Germany, it was hoped by some that the president might become such a neutral arbiter and guardian of the constitution. His powers were typically those of a constitutional monarch. In the exercise of these powers, he was bound to the countersignature of a minister responsible to the parliament. But owing to the confusion of parties, and to the state of emergency which arose, the German president inclined toward assuming wider and wider powers of actual government. From a representative head of the government, he became its executive center. Thereupon he lost the neutrality which would have been essential for a guardian of the constitution. Under their new constitution, the Germans have tried to take advantage of this experience by (1) stripping the president of the excessive emergency powers which he had under Article 48 of the Weimar constitution, and (2) by establishing a constitutional court with broad powers to interpret the constitution and review legislation. In short, the new German constitution is turning toward the American system of a high court as the neutral power and umpire.

More recently, the constitution of the Fifth Republic has revived the idea which Benjamin Constant proposed. The president is made explicitly the guardian of the constitution; he also insures the "continuity of the state," whatever that may mean (Article 5). As I wrote some years ago: "He (the president) is above the government, and yet somehow immersed in it . . . Very similar was the position of the king under the constitution of 1830."[2] President de Gaulle has, with the help of the article on the emergency powers (Article 16), become so clearly the chief executive that it is impossible to call him a "neutral power," however. Yet he claims the right to interpret the constitution and has thereby shown once again how dangerous it is to entrust the guardianship to the executive.

But in a number of European states, as in some Latin American ones earlier, constitutional courts have been developed, mostly since the Second World War, charged with the guardianship of the constitution. This is, of course, the American solution to the problem. More than a hundred years earlier, the drafters of the American constitution had clearly perceived that it is highly improbable, if not impossible, that a neutral guardian will be secured by election. As Hamilton, building on Montesquieu, wrote in the Federalist, No. 78: ". . . the judiciary, from the nature of its functions, will always be the least dangerous to the political rights of the constitution . . ." But of course, no power is ever absolutely neutral, or it would not be any power at all, because unrelated to the values and beliefs of the community.

Medieval precedents • Hamilton's view that a high court of justice affords the best protection of a constitutional system[3] was a political restatement of the famous dictum of Sir Edward Coke that "Magna Charta is such a fellow that he will have no sovereign." In the days of Justice Coke, to be sure, it was the king in Parliament who seemed to threaten this "supremacy of the law." But in Hamilton's time the English Commons had pretty nearly achieved parliamentary supremacy. It therefore seemed apparent to him and to many other Americans that what was needed were limitations upon the legislative authority, irrespective of whether it was being exercised by a prince or by an elective body. A "tyranny of the majority" had loomed up in some of the states, and the makers of the constitution sought to restrain it. The development of the function of the courts to interpret the constitution is closely related to the doctrine of the separation of powers; yet the doctrine did not originally include it.

The origins of the idea of an independent judiciary interpreting *the* law are to be found in medieval England. As we saw (in ch. VI, p. 106 f.), Coke and other seventeenth-century expounders of the supremacy of law claimed the right of the courts to interpret acts of Parliament according to the common law.[4] Coke's most signal conflict with King James originated in his belief that the high courts of England had the right to decide whether an act of Parliament was "legal" or not. However, this view did not triumph in England. Lip service was paid to it, though, until the end of the eighteenth century, just long enough to influence American juridical thought. By combining the constitution as the fundamental law of the land with the common law, a great deal of common law has been worked into the American legal fabric in the course of a century and a half of judicial "interpretation" or "construction" of the constitution.

The supremacy of Parliament • In England the supremacy of law merged with the supremacy of Parliament. As a result, English legal historians have been inclined to minimize unduly the importance of Coke's position. Certainly Cromwell and his followers were, as we have seen, deeply convinced of the need for some fundamental law limiting the power of Parliament. Sir Francis Bacon, Coke's opponent on the king's side, stressed the fact that English law "is grounded on the law of nature." The idea of such a relation between natural law and parliamentary legislation, stemming from Bracton,[5] continued down to the end of the eighteenth century, and is clearly stated by Blackstone. But it became a rather empty formula after the evolution of cabinet responsibility in the eighteenth century. That the lawyers in England never placed any considerable obstacle in the way of this development had, as is justly argued by Professor Holdsworth, very important consequences for the English constitution and English law. There was, nevertheless, a great accumulation of judge-made law in England, and it was against this power of the judges that Bentham uttered his vigorous polemics in favor of statutory legislation. The issue of law making, by whom and for whom, was involved in the American struggle for independence. Although Americans were explicitly challenging the supremacy of Parliament in their cry against "taxation without representation," the anger with which people turned against the royal judges in the colonies was a clear sign that the issue of judge-made law was likewise involved. The whole issue evidently rested upon one of those principles of a fundamental nature which Coke and his contemporaries sought to except from parliament legislation. As Professor McIlwain has convincingly shown, justifiable doubt could be entertained by conscientious men as to the constitutionality of these acts of Parliament.[6]

It was natural, therefore, that the framers of the American constitution should have been divided on the issue of legislative versus judicial power. While the conservatives, that is, authoritarian members, were particularly sensitive to the chances of arbitrary usurpations of power by a legislature, the progressive, that is, democratic, ones were disturbed about the judicial usurpations. On the conservative side, the magistral John Adams is full of thoughts on this subject, which were shared to a greater or less degree by his contemporaries. To these men, Hamilton's doctrine was most palatable, and Justice Marshall's famous decision of *Marbury v. Madison*, reasserting it, was equally so.[7] The issue flared up into open conflict in the famous struggle between Jefferson and Marshall when Jefferson sought the impeachment of Marshall. Were these issues appreciated in Europe by those who were inspired by American constitutionalism? On the whole, very little. On the Continent, people seem always to have been greatly concerned with securing bills of rights, but to have cared little about securing sufficient legal guarantees of their enforcement. The idealists who continued to cherish the French revolutionary ideals lacked the practical judgment to appreciate the importance of institutional safeguards, and in France itself suspicion of the ultraconservative courts both before and after the revolution prevented any concerted attempts to give them powers of judicial review. European lawyers and jurists, accustomed to looking upon government and politics in terms of "the state" and of "sovereignty," began to evolve the vacuous theory of "state sovereignty." Later formalists and positivists alike denounced the natural-law tradition as incompatible with this "state sovereignty." How indeed could institutional safeguards against the "sovereign state" be conceived? The Continental tradition is that of settling questions of principle by express statutory enactment. It calls for extensive codification of such principles as freedom of speech, of assembly, and of the press; it does not favor judicial development of practice from broad constitutional rights. It has only recently been challenged by the development of constitutional courts.

The impact of federalism • In the discussion of federalism it has been shown that a constitutional judiciary is an integral part of any federal structure. If there is to be a division of powers between the central and local authorities, conflicts over the respective spheres of authority are bound to arise, and a procedure for their settlement is obviously needed. Generally speaking, this need is analogous to the need for an arbiter between authorities dividing powers functionally under some kind of separation of powers. Therefore, it is not surprising that federalism should reinforce the idea of a guardian of the constitution, along with the idea of a judiciary interpreting the constitution, which embodies "higher" law than ordinary legislation. Though judicial review of legislative acts has disappeared completely in the English constitutional tradition; it has become an integral part of federalism in several of the Dominions, even though these Dominions are governed by cabinets responsible directly to a parliament. In Australia, judicial interpretation has developed important constitutional principles and resembles the American tradition most closely. Significantly, Australia is the most markedly federal of these Dominions.

It is, of course, possible to keep such a constitutional judiciary over federal-state controversies entirely separate and distinct, as are the constitutional courts of Austria, Italy, and Germany. By contrast, the Supreme Court is "the ultimate organ . . . for adjusting the relationship of the individual to the separate states, of the individual to the United States, of the forty-eight states to one another, of the states to the union and of the three departments of government to one another."[8] Short of constitutional amendments it is the ultimate federal constitutional authority, and since federalism could be maintained only with difficulty without such a constitutional judiciary, it is likely to remain so. Switzerland, by contrast, failed to establish so comprehensive a judicial control, the guardian of the constitution, although the courts review cantonal legislation. But the inherent logic of the situation was so compelling that proposals for the outright recognition of judicial review over federal legislation have become more and more insistent. Such efforts are rooted in part in a desire to curb the collectivism which Swiss democracy has increasingly adopted. It is doubtful whether a judicial body can serve as the moderating influence between rival groups and classes if it is thus recognized as a partisan instrument. Even so deep-rooted a federalism as that of Switzerland may be insufficient to insulate such a judicial body against the more apparent forms of partisanship.[9]

Constitutional interpretation and partisanship · It would, of course, be vain to pretend that the American courts, and more especially the Supreme Court, had not in fact been partisan. The whole setting predisposes them toward a conservative position. To this setting must be added the distinct policy of conservatives, initiated by Adams and Marshall, to maintain control of the Court. In this century the great property interests have certainly been more alert to the Court's extraordinary importance in affecting the balance of interests and classes than have been the progressives. As William Howard Taft once wrote, in justifying his staying on the Court: ". . . I must stay on the Court in order to prevent the Bolsheviki from getting control . . ." At another time Taft said (in the presidential election of 1920): ". . . there is no greater domestic issue than the maintenance of the Supreme Court as a bulwark to enforce the guaranty that no man shall be deprived of his property without due process of law."[10] The Court has in the past been on the conservative side. Recognition of this fact must be coupled, however, with the further recognition that the public at large believes the Court to be relatively nonpartisan. This belief is part of the belief in the constitution which makes the constitution a political force.

There are three levels of political insight into the constitutional and political function of a high court: (1) the court interprets the constitution, the norms of the constitution being as clear as a mathematical equation (popular view); (2) the Court is an instrument of party politics, it decides according to the political views of the judges, it is antidemocratic (political view); (3) the Court is the high priesthood of the faith in constitutionalism, it rationalizes the new norm in terms of the old and thereby maintains continuity, if not consistency; in short, it arbitrates between the fundamental and ever-present rival forces under a constitutional system. It is this third level of insight which recognizes fully the function of a high court as a guardian of the sacred word symbols that hold many men and many minds together in one organized community. As Mr. Justice Jackson put it, when he was still attorney general, "the Court keeps the most fundamental equilibriums of our society, such as that between centralization and localism, between liberty and authority, and between stability and progress."[11] At any rate, the Court *should* keep such an equilibrium. There is ever present the danger that its members become ensnared in their own logic, and in the effort to maintain the sacred words attempt to throttle life and life's progress. The Court at such times shifts from a conservative to a reactionary position. When it does, the future of constitutionalism is in jeopardy.

Due process · In the decades prior to 1937, the Court had been inclined to find ways to narrow some of the powers conferred by the constitution upon the federal government, and more particularly Congress, such as the tax power, while at the same time it broadened the meaning of limitations such as "due process." Due process provides in many ways the most interesting illustration of the working of constitutional interpretation. When the constitution was adopted, its meaning was strictly procedural: in compelling public officials to act in accordance with established rules of procedure, it served a clear constitutional purpose; it prevented arbitrary imprisonments, seizure of possessions, and the like. It was not until after the Civil War that due process began to assume the substantive meaning which it has been given since. First through *obiter dicta* and dissenting opinions, finally in the decision of *Lochner v. the People of New York,* "a constitutional doctrine contrived to protect the natural rights of men against corporate monopoly was little by little commuted into a formula for safeguarding the domain of business against the regulatory power of the state."[12] In vain did Mr. Justice Holmes register his famous protest that a "constitution is not intended to embody a particular economic theory, whether of paternalism . . . or of laissez-faire . . ." But the wonder is not that business interests were given verbal protection under the constitutional roof, but that the protection was so vague and insecure. For the real forces molding the evolution of the doctrine of due process were generated by the development of large corporations, vast economic powers which found themselves challenged by a government whose decisions a democratic ideology seemed to make legitimate beyond dispute. The conservatism of the law held out against these forces of a new industrial revolution; forever it remained troubled by the old doctrines which gave government sweeping powers over public safety, public health, public morals, and public welfare. These powers are deeply rooted in the established objectives of modern government. Far from frankly espousing the revolutionary forces which challenged these ancient governmental powers, the Court continually sought to hold back, to conserve and balance, the old and the new. It was only in our own day, when the Court became dogmatic about the doctrine of due process which it had so hesitantly evolved, that it threatened seriously to upset the equilibrium. But when President Roosevelt poignantly reminded them of the fact that their position was no more than what the constitution and the laws, that is, the people, made it, the judges beat a hasty retreat. Soon after the Reorganization Bill was introduced in 1937, the Court began to reverse its dogmatic stand by holding the National Labor Relations Act constitutional (almost too soon for dignity's sake). It confirmed the quip of Theodore Roosevelt: "I may not know much about law, but I do know one can put the fear of God into judges." In the period since then, the Supreme Court has not only allowed Congress considerably greater latitude, but has become itself an activist power, forcing the executive and legislative powers into lines of progressive policy in the field of civil liberties, and more especially race relations, as well as popular representation. Equality, when taken literally, is thus becoming once again the revolutionizing principle that it had been earlier. Due process has not been employed to hold legislation unconstitutional which limits property rights. "Since 1937," one leading authority remarks, "due process has been more frequently the basis for holding interferences with civil liberties invalid than in any previous period of our history."[13]

"Manifest Tenor" · In his famous treatise on the common law, Justice Holmes wrote many years ago: "The life of law has not been logic; it has been experience. The felt necessities of the time, the prevalent moral and political theories, intuitions of public policy, avowed or unconscious, even the prejudices which judges share with their fellowmen, have had a good deal more to do than the syllogism in determining the rules by which men should be governed. The law embodies the story of a nation's development through many centuries, and it cannot be dealt with as if it contained only the axioms and corollaries of a book of mathematics. In order to know what it is, we must know what it has been and what it tends to become."[14] That would be a beautiful statement of the deeper insight into the function of courts and judicial interpretation, if the first phrase read: "The life of the law has not *only* been logic . . ." for surely a great role has been played by logic in the life of the law, and nowhere is this more apparent than in the constitutional role of a high judiciary. Indeed, the judges' main claim to being a superior guardian of the constitution is the higher rationality of their argument. As a matter of fact, the courts are often admonished to make *better-reasoned* decisions.

Constitutional interpretation is not limited to the courts; other departments of the government, though less highly placed in the priesthood of constitutionalism, share in this important function. To illustrate, the American pocket veto resulted from inaction on the part of the President; the Senate pressed for and the President conceded Senatorial influence over appointments, known as the "Senatorial courtesy." The important Congressional role has been the subject of a searching inquiry. Rejecting the notion that either the Congress *or* the Court must be presumed to interpret the constitution, the learned author asked: "But is it a simple either-or choice? There may be factors that require that Congress supplement the Court in the consideration of constitutional questions."[15] Very true; but it remains nonetheless correct to say, as his insistence upon a *supplementary* role implies, that there is, and can be, only one guardian. The very idea of guardianship implies it. Hence the question we are here concerned with primarily is that of judicial review of legislative acts, viewed as a technique for preventing such legislative "interpretations" from going beyond a reasonable point. By judicial review, in other words, the judicial sanction is denied to measures, even of the legislature composed of the representatives of the people, which according to the manifest meaning of the constitution are void. The crucial question, however, is that which inquires: "To whom is this meaning of the constitution manifest?" The answer must be: "To no one, but judges are more likely to possess the authority to make it seem manifest."

The institution of judicial review substitutes the judgment of judges for the judgment of the elected representatives of the people whenever doubt exists regarding the full meaning of a constitutional provision. It is *not* often a question of the *manifest tenor,* as Marshall maintained, but on the contrary a question of the doubtful meaning of various constitutional provisions, or the actual lack of any provision.[16] As Professor Sutherland has recently written, in commenting on Judge Chase's resolve never to declare an Act of Congress unconstitutional unless "in a very clear case" that it "forecast, like other constitutional utterances of the eighteenth century Justices, difficulty which still abides among us. The language of the Constitution is more precise in some clauses than others; the Seventh Amendment prescription of a jury . . requires less judicial interpretation than the due process clause of the Fifth . . ."[17] Courts have been in the habit of obscuring the bare truth of this statement by arguing about the "intention of the framers." But doubt usually has arisen where no intention was indicated in the debates. Indeed, how could the framers of the constitution in the horse-and-buggy age possibly have had any intention concerning interstate commerce as it has developed in the age of railroad, steamship, automobile, and airplane? A striking case of this kind is the welfare clause in the American constitution. That clause provides that "Congress shall have power — To lay and collect taxes, duties, imposts, and excises; to pay the debts and provide for the common defense and general welfare of the United States." In view of the semicolon, the courts have construed this clause narrowly, and on the whole have shied away from admitting that the taxing power might be used for the "general welfare." "It could not have been the intention of the framers . . ." ran the argument. Recent historical research, however, has brought to light the fact that the text of the constitution which Washington signed had a comma and that the semicolon was entered by a clerk afterward. What, then, was the intention of the framers? Or take the case of the delegation of legislative powers to the executive departments. Under the National Industrial Recovery Act of 1933, the power to prescribe rules of conduct was delegated to the President and the representatives of various enterprises; this was later held to be a violation of Article I, 1 of the constitution, which forbade the delegation of legislative power. The Court, in sustaining this argument, observed that there existed an old maxim of the Roman law that *potestas delegata non potest delegari,* that is, that a delegated power must not be delegated further. Since the legislative power, the argument runs on, is delegated by the constitution-making power to the legislature, the legislature cannot delegate it further. But were the framers of the constitution aware of this maxim of the Roman law? And has this maxim any application to a constitutionally delegated power, when it was originally evolved to maintain the hierarchy of Roman officials intact? These questions the courts do not ask, and do not answer, except by the cryptic statement that there is nothing to indicate that the framers did not intend it thus.

This type of "reasoning" is not very helpful in dealing with distinctly *new* problems of a social or economic type. They require a scientific attitude of mind which is not authoritarian, but antiauthoritarian; which does not seek guidance from the past, but distrusts it. In support of precedent it is further urged that any new departure must be supported by a good show of supporting reason. This, however, is equally true of scientific work. Still a more or less public exposition of the reasons which led a court to decide as it did helps to settle the controversy by appealing to the reason of the losing litigant. It also serves the important legal and political function of holding the legal rules together so that they are something more than isolated bits, even if they do not, from a realistic point of view, constitute a coherent system. These two functions of legal reasoning are more or less impaired if judicial language becomes highly technical and incomprehensible to anybody but a trained lawyer. It will be found that the very great lawyer-judges, like Marshall, have usually been distinguished by a very lucid style. This lucidity may hide serious logical defects, but it serves the political functions just the same, as long as these defects are not discovered by any but very astute minds.

Judges and propertied interests · Those who, from Jefferson to La Follette, have attacked judicial review have argued that judges are conservative folks, and that the judicial attitude of mind is ill-adapted to the solution of problems that require striking out along new paths. Judges sitting on the high courts are advanced in years. Though some brilliant work has been done by very old men, it is natural that a man should think in terms of a society with which he is familiar. If society is undergoing rapid change, it is apt to put an elderly judge behind the times. It has often been pointed out by more radical reformers that judges are, through their training and upbringing, closely linked with the propertied interests. This may have thrown them on the side of the revolutionary middle classes in the days of Coke, when these classes were battling the king and his feudal landowning aristocracy. For many years, it put them with the big-business interests opposed to the reforms desired by farmers and workers. Recently, however, a frank recognition of this problem has produced a marked change. No one familiar with the personnel of the United States Supreme Court in 1948 would charge them with excessive partiality to property.

Judges whose primary function it is to settle controversies between contending private parties when they disagree about the meaning of the law must in the nature of things be very careful to be consistent, lest the community feel themselves subjected to quite arbitrary rulings. All judicial systems are, therefore, careful in observing precedents at least within their jurisdiction. This practice in itself acts as a conservative force. It generates a habit of mind which turns to the past for guidance and counsel. This *need* not lead to conservatism, however. In the face of an executive and legislature who were reluctant to deal with racial discrimination, the Supreme Court since 1954 in a number of dramatic decisions, beginning with *Baker v. Carr,* undertook to remind the country *and its government* that the egalitarian principles of the constitution were being neglected and called for stricter enforcement than had been accorded them in the past. The same reasoning also applies to reapportionment. In this issue the Court faced up to the fact that practice had more and more patently been violating the intent of the makers of the constitution and its spirit. Hence it demanded a review of all forms of gerrymandering. Indeed, the Court's hostility toward property interests has led to sharp criticism in some conservative comments. In writing *In Defense of Property,* a learned author has, harking back to Jefferson, insisted that freedom is inseparable from property. Feeling that freedom is declining in America because property rights are increasingly curtailed, he argued for the "original intention" of the framers, who thought that "a restriction of majoritarianism facilitates the protection of private property and is conducive of progress, order and justice."[18] But is it wise for a Court to look back to what was conducive to progress in a society long left behind by that very progress?

Disinterestedness and representative quality · As noted earlier, the judicial and scientific attitudes have one very important aspect in common, their "disinterestedness," or rather, their effort to be disinterested. It is admittedly easier to be detached when the issues are not of the human sphere. An economist studying the incidence of a certain tax and a judge deciding a case involving the conflict of interests between management and labor must both strive to detach themselves from their own personal bias.[19]

This they can only do by realizing what that bias is presumably going to be. If they find themselves habitually on the side of management, they must be particularly suspicious of any conclusion which seems to favor management. To accomplish this is admittedly a great moral as well as intellectual achievement, and many, if not all, judges and social scientists fail at times to live up to this standard. The extent to which they do so, and are believed to do so, profoundly affects their political role. The willing acceptance of judicial review in the United States has been due to the fact that the community has had faith in the comparativeness of the judges composing it. This faith gave the Supreme Court a truly representative character, even though, or perhaps rather because, it was not elective and therefore not so obviously partisan. In countries where the courts do not possess that representative quality, they cannot readily assume the guardianship which is based upon arbitral function of interpreting the constitution.

From this standpoint, the tendency of the Europeans to make their new constitutional courts either elective *by* or outright committees *of* the legislature must be viewed very critically. In France, there is only a "constitutional council" which decides, on the request of the president of the republic, the prime minister, or the president of either assembly, whether laws are in conformity with the constitution (Article 61).[20] In Italy, a constitutional court is provided for, with the authority to declare laws unconstitutional (Article 137). Its personnel is chosen by the legislative, the executive, and the judicial power, each electing five judges. In the Federal Republic likewise, the legislative bodies are centrally concerned with the election of some judges to the constitutional court. In Austria, the same notion has prevailed since 1920, when their constitutional court was established. Behind all these arrangements is the distrust of judges and the suspicion that judges are not capable of dealing with political issues. The United States Supreme Court has dealt with this problem by excluding what it considers "political" issues, but that solution presupposes a rather narrow conception of what is political. Europeans have rather been inclined to solve it by making sure that some of the judges are politicians.[21]

Universality versus partisanship · When the case between a court and a legislature is put on the ground that one is elected by the people and the other not, as is still done in most French and English textbooks, the elected legislature appears to be "representative," the courts "aristocratic." But once the legislature is viewed as divided into parties, its representative quality is seen to be of a more limited kind; for such majorities change, and the more universal and lasting aspects of community life may well require additional symbols. A court composed of the highest legal talent in the community may often be quite representative of the community's beliefs as to what is just in a more real and universal sense.

But why should the ordinary courts be entrusted with this particular duty? Would it not be more in keeping with all aspects of the problem if a separate body were set up to handle these thorny questions? The great French revolutionary politician, Abbé Siéyès, thought so, and accordingly expounded the idea of a constitutional jury in his famous speech before the Convention on the 2nd of *Thermidor* of the year III.[22] The distinction between the amending power and the legislative power requires, he held, a guardian of the constitution. But this guardian cannot be the judicial power; it must be a special political representative body. "I demand," he said, "a jury of the constitution . . . or constitutional jury. This jury must be a real body of representatives which I demand should have the special mission (function) of judging all protests against any infringement of the constitution. . . . If you wish to give a safeguard to the constitution, a salutary curb which keeps each representative action within the limits of its special function, then establish a constitutional jury!" But no one heeded his advice then. The Italians, in their 1949 constitution, adopted this view. It was, of course, extreme in its rationalist disregard of political reality: the partisanship of the members of elected bodies. The idea of a constitutional jury was supposed to be realized in the form of the *Sénat Conservateur* of the year VIII. But of course its functions as the guardian of the constitution remained on paper under the autocratic rule of the first Napoleon. In a sense, Siéyès' notion is still powerful in Continental European constitutionalism. In any case, it certainly posited the problem of a neutral, nonpartisan arbiter and guardian.

European constitutional tribunals · The idea of a special body charged with safeguarding the constitution had already gained much adherence in countries engaged in establishing new constitutions after the First World War. In republican Austria, Germany, and Czechoslovakia, special courts were set up under the constitutions to examine the constitutionality of legislation. In Germany this court was primarily concerned with conflicts over jurisdiction between governmental authorities. The European concept of a "public corporation" offered, however, an entering wedge for extending the jurisdiction of these courts. Thus in Germany, parties were admitted as litigants before the Court of State in contesting an election procedure, and elections in certain states were actually held null and void because the election procedure did not correspond with the requirements of the national constitution. In Austria, under the constitution of 1920, revised in 1929, a constitutional court was organized to deal with the constitutionality of laws, while the ordinary courts only had the authority to examine the formal aspects of proper publication, etc. Article 140 provided that the constitutional court might "suspend" laws which violated the constitution. In other words, the law was not declared null and void, as in the United States, but while contrary to law yet was legally binding until so suspended. This meant that only certain paragraphs might be so suspended, and that the suspension might be fixed for a later date than that of the court's decision. These provisions strikingly illustrate the different approach of Continental jurists to the entire problem of law and judicial review. If an individual litigant raises the issue or a judge questions the constitutionality of a legal norm, he submits the question to the constitutional court. The Italians largely followed this model, but by looking upon their constitutional court primarily as guardian, they have raised it above the judiciary proper. The German constitutional court, on the other hand, admits individual and private corporate litigants. Although reluctant to accept fully the notion of a distinct amending power — the parliament still amends, albeit with a qualified majority — Article 79 makes it obligatory for parliament to amend the constitution explicitly. But what is really important is that the Basic Law goes beyond most modern constitutions by withdrawing from such amendments four crucial matters, as pointed out above (p. 145 f.). Obviously only if there exists an independent guardian, will the parliamentary majority, and especially a broad consensual, one of more than two thirds, abstain from disregarding these basic restrictions. They are, of course, the result of a strong reaction against totalitarian autocracy. As far as providing for judicial protection of these provisions is concerned, it should be remembered, however, that both the Prussian and Bavarian constitutions of the Weimar period had contained provisions for the judicial guardianship. In fact, the arguments go back to the constitution of 1848–1849.[23]

But while we thus find an increasing acceptance of the general idea of judicial guardianship, and more particularly of the notion of protecting the citizen in his rights against legislative inroads, the practice of judicial review is quite different from the American tradition. For it is not linked to the idea of the unity of the legal order — the constitutional courts are *specialized* courts; they are not supposed to integrate the legal order, as is the case with the United States Supreme Court. Besides the constitutional court, bodies such as the supreme judicial and the supreme administrative court function in all three countries as courts of last appeal in their particular jurisdictions.

It is noteworthy that the Christian Democrats have been the protagonists of the broadening of judicial powers in France, Italy, and Germany. The efforts of the MRP during the 1946 constitutional convention in France were directed toward the establishment of something that might have been a genuine supreme constitutional court. But, as one writer puts it, the Socialists were obsessed by the memory of Roosevelt's struggle with the Supreme Court, [and hence] were determined to avoid any mechanism which might obstruct future social and economic reforms. It may seem strange that what happened under an eighteenth-century individualist constitution should worry anyone concerning the future policies possible under a twentieth-century constitution for a planned economy (*économie dirigée*), but it testifies to the continued absence of any real grasp of what has been called the "most characteristic, the most unique political institution" of the United States.

Representative quality of judiciary • Broadly speaking, it can be said that the question of how representative a judiciary a country possesses is a question of fact. The more deeply the community's respect for the courts is rooted, the less dangerous it is for such courts to assume the arbitral function of ultimate constitutional interpretation. This is particularly true if a workable amending process offers hope to the discontented that they may alter provisions in the constitution which irk them. The courts do not enjoy an unqualified respect in those areas of Europe where the Marxist labor movement is strong. For according to Karl Marx's class-war doctrine, the courts are nothing but camouflaged exponents of the bourgeois class aiding in the exploitation of the toiling masses. In other words, they dispense class justice, instead of mass justice. It is evident that whenever such opinions have wide currency, general confidence in the "disinterestedness" of the judiciary will decline.[24] If courts under such conditions are called upon to decide cases which involve the "interpretation" of constitutional provisions, which may be partly socialist and partly not, the ensuing controversies will further undermine their position, no matter which way they decide. If, moreover, many of the judges are held over from a previous regime, and kept because of the principle of judicial tenure during good behavior, the loyalty of the courts to the new government may also become suspect. Such a situation developed in the United States when the Supreme Court declared a series of New Deal statutes unconstitutional. The issue was brought out into the open when Roosevelt proposed legislation to alter the composition of the Court. Violent partisan passions were aroused and conventional party lines collapsed as conservatives amongst Democrats as well as Republicans arose "to defend the Constitution." The President was accused of seeking "to pack the Court." A hallowed symbol of constitutional government appeared to be under attack, and many foes of the President's reforms saw clear proof of "dictatorship." So the plan was defeated; yet it had served the *political* purpose of calling attention to the Court's *political* position. Once the community had become conscious of the social and economic cleavage which divided it, the Court's representative quality was impaired by the mere fact of its identification with one side of partisan controversy. This reaction, however, was temporary. The country soon settled back into its traditional acceptance of the Supreme Court as the ultimate arbiter of its constitution, the more so since Roosevelt was able to alter profoundly the actual composition of the Court through entirely legitimate replacements. Since 1937 the Court has been rather partial to economic and social reform. Thus the crisis of the Roosevelt era has taken its place alongside many another political storm which the Supreme Court has weathered.[25]

We have mentioned the economic class conflicts first among the conditions depriving courts of their representative quality because they happen to be in the foreground of popular attention today, and they appear wherever modern industrialism prevails. But other basic cleavages can have the same disruptive result. Thus national minorities will rarely accept the decision of a court manned by the majority as rendering "disinterested" justice. They will always suspect partisanship on the part of a judge of the other nationality. Therefore a supreme court could not hope to be the effective guardian of a constitution which undertook to guarantee minority rights. None but an international tribunal or a mixed arbitral body containing members of their own nationality will be able to satisfy such a national minority. In other words, the actual disunity of the political community cannot be neutralized by even the most liberal-looking constitutional provisions or by stringent judicial safeguards.

Both these examples, but more particularly the economic class division, indicate that the political scientist is really confronted with a problem quite distinct from that outlined by Hamilton in the *Federalist*. There the entire emphasis is on which of the three powers will be least likely to extend its authority on its own initiative. Hamilton's conclusion has stood the test of a century, and there is not much actual fact which would oblige us to question it today. Hamilton, of course, in the fashion of his day, did not consider the function of parties under popular government. Yet, it is well known that the contest between the executive and the judicial power did not commence until the party issue was injected under Jefferson and Marshall. At that time, too, it was a matter of economic group interests. Marshall was an exponent of eastern business and manufacturing interests, while Jefferson fought for the southern and western farmer. However, the issues and the conflict were kept in bounds. These group interests did not crystallize into dogmatic and mutually exclusive positions. Nor have they done so in America at the present time. Still, the Court is believed to be divided (as, of course, it actually is) into progressives and conservatives, and their respective balance is a matter of public controversy and great political pressure, as it used to be before the Civil War in connection with proslavery and anti-slavery members. Under such conditions the confidence of the community in the Court is considerably shaken. A wise Court with a sound tradition will seek to check that decline in public esteem by avoiding extreme positions on the most controversial issues. It may cease to perform the function of being guardian of the constitution when it accepts the "interpretation" of the legislature. Counterbalancing that, the legislature may try to avoid enacting measures which are too palpably beyond any conceivable "interpretation" of the existing constitution.

Conclusion • The problem of the guardianship of a constitution is the touchstone of its efficacy as the basic law of the land. While in a sense all authorities are called upon to protect the constitution, as expressed in their oaths of office, there needs to be an individual or a body which has the "last word." Constitutional experience points to the judiciary, and more specifically, its apex, as the least objectionable choice for such guardianship.

However, the political technique of judicial review can be employed only where considerable confidence in the integrity of the courts is generally entertained by the people at large. On the other hand, no "constitutional jury" other than such a judiciary will be sufficiently neutral and detached to exercise effectively the functions of a guardian of the constitution. We must conclude, therefore, that in the absence of a constitution deeply rooted in tradition, such as exists in England, Switzerland, or Sweden, a judiciary capable of exercising judicial review will be required if a constitution, in the political sense of a set of techniques for restraining the actions of government, is to be established. Only through the neutralizing and rationalizing influence of such judicial interpretation will the various interests, groups, and classes in the community be kept sufficiently balanced. Even such a judiciary may not be able to accomplish it. It is a wholesome sign of the strengthening of constitutionalism in Europe that the new constitutions in Western Europe all endeavor to establish some sort of judicial review of legislative acts. The extent of these efforts seems to stand in inverse relation to their experience with totalitarianism. In light of the history of the institution, it seems natural enough that those who have felt most intensely the results of the loss of constitutionalism should be most concerned with securing it against future undermining by anticonstitutional forces.

PART 3

THE FUNCTIONING

PROCESSES OF

CONSTITUTIONAL

GOVERNMENT

The Problem of Representation
_____ XIV

Introduction · Late appearance of representative bodies · Representation and responsibility · Representation in Hobbes · In Rousseau · The dual nature of representation · Responsible representative conduct · Defining political representation · Election and legitimacy · Representation and legislation · The power of the purse · Representation and constitutionalism · Conclusion

Introduction · Representation is one of the basic aspects of modern government. It has, of course, always existed. But men were only dimly aware of its political importance. The Greek philosophers did not see it. Plato and Aristotle hardly touched on the subject. Indeed, there was no word for it. It is a commonplace that the Greek failure to build representative institutions left them helpless in the face of large-scale political orders, and that the Romans, walking in the footsteps of the Greeks, lost their freedom when Rome grew into a large territorial state. The change came in the Middle Ages.

Gierke has told us that "the political theories of the middle ages made considerable use of the idea of representation in the construction of the Church and the State . . . they borrowed from corporation law . . . the theoretical formulation of the idea, current in the middle ages though unknown to antiquity, of the exercise of the rights belonging to a community by a representative assembly."[1] This idea is, of course, rooted in the theological notion that the head of the church represents God, the ruler of the universe, on earth. This idea of making someone present who is the real ruler, because he is not able to take care of the task himself is, in the modern mind, linked to the notion of election or deliberate choice. It may therefore be called "voluntary" or "willed." Behind such voluntary representation, and often associated with it, is, however, the notion of a presentation which flows from the mere fact that one is made present by another? A Frenchman traveling in the United States "represents" his country, though never selected for this purpose, and he does so even if he would prefer not to. Similarly, the President of the United States represents all Americans, even though nearly half of them did *not* wish him to. This kind of representation, springing directly from the existence of human beings who are linked in the minds of others by features which they are supposed to have in common, may therefore be called "existential representation." The direct opposite of such existential, involuntary representation is the explicit mandate, often called "imperative mandate," by which a person is instructed to do or say something. Some writers have wanted to draw an absolute distinction between such a mandate and representation; but while there are important and politically relevant differences between mandatory and general representation, that is, between specific and unspecified mandates to a representative, they both are truly representation as is indeed the existential representation which is completely without mandate.

Late appearance of representative bodies · Representative schemes arose as part of the medieval constitutional order when that order assumed proportions which forbade any direct action. In the first place, the unitary organization of Western Christendom within the Catholic Church necessitated representative assemblies, the great councils, in which all the Christian people were believed to be present. It was natural to apply the same idea to the representation of monasteries and cathedral chapters within a secular feudal order. And when the cities and towns reached a place in the sun in the course of the thirteenth century, and had to be reckoned with as centers of wealth and power, a further extension of corporate representation of these municipalities was clearly indicated.[2] Was it a matter of peculiar genius, or of pure accident, that Simon de Montfort, in calling the Parliament of 1265, issued a summons to the knights of each shire, as well as to the burgesses? It has been suggested that the exigencies of the English crown, hard pressed by unruly and powerful barons, gave the minister of Edward I this idea as a matter of electoral strategy. At any rate, the shires were corporate entities, capable of representation by analogy to the towns. Apparently in all these cases the corporate spirit of solidarity was sufficiently developed to render the group willing to exercise its influence through agents or representative persons. Where personal attendance is practically impossible, and the result is considered more important than personal participation, such corporate solidarity will appear. In classical antiquity the situation was quite different; personal attendance was quite possible in the small city-states, and the result was rarely considered more important than personal participation of the citizenry. In fact, the prevalence of slavery placed the citizenry in the position of a small leisure class who enjoyed the daily gossip in the market place. This necessity for personal participation became fatal whenever such a city-state reached larger proportions. The attempts at solving this problem through a federal organization foundered upon the inability of the ancients to work out a representative scheme. Ingenious as were the arrangements of the Romans for their Latin Federation, they could not get away from the idea of embodying the citizenry of each city in the Roman citizenry, with the result of swelling its numbers so unduly that eventually they had to abandon this practice altogether.[3] As we have seen when discussing federalism, its embodiment in an effective political order has to await the completion of a representative scheme under which the whole people as well as the people of each component unit can be given a certain influence upon the federal affairs, and a firm and uniform federal authority can thus be established.

Representation and responsibility • From a historical standpoint, the effective securing of responsibility in government is the central objective in all the various schemes of representation. In strongly religious epochs the notion that the king represents God on earth may be a most powerful impulse toward making him and his officials responsible. But when such faith declined, the most arbitrary tyranny might and often did grow out of such a scheme of representation. Modern government can in some respects be interpreted as an effort to produce the responsible conduct of public affairs without religious sanction and without the standards supported by these sanctions. In the place of such standards, mutually acceptable interests, public interests, so called, become the basis for evaluating the actions of officials and other public authorities. But who is the final judge as to whether governmental action corresponds to the public interest? The orthodox answer is: the public. In modern countries the public cannot, of course, foregather in the market place, like the Athenian citizens of old. Hence the only possible method of securing adequate controls is some scheme by which a small selected group of citizens acts for the whole body. Such action is representative. Conflicting interests require compromise. Compromise results from argument and discussion. Through such argument and discussion interests become articulate; they are rationalized. When the representatives thus are exposed to full public view, it becomes increasingly desirable that the methods by which they are chosen be likewise "rationalized," so that favoritism and other personal motives would play only a minor role. The long struggle for parliamentary reform in England was fought over this issue; rotten boroughs, patrons, and all the paraphernalia of aristocratic nepotism became unacceptable. In spite of Burke's eloquent defense of irrational traditionalism, Bentham and his insistence upon rational standards prevailed. In the modern world, direct general election has been generally accepted as the most rational method for choosing representatives. There are, however, important exceptions. Courts, for example, are manned by a different method, which may be more rational, and probably is more effective. Their selection is based upon a relatively objective standard: legal competence. It could be argued that legislatures should be similarly selected. Their representative quality would not necessarily disappear; it might in fact be heightened. Burke, in his discussion of parliamentary representation, insisted that even the elected representative must conceive of himself as a guardian of national interests. Parliament, he said, was not a congress of ambassadors from different and hostile interests, but a deliberative assembly from *one* nation, with *one* interest, that of the whole; these representatives ought to be guided not by local purpose, but by the general good. Such an idealistic conception of the function of a parliament evokes the ridicule of moralists and cynics alike; they would maintain whatever a parliament ought to be, it is in actual fact a congress of ambassadors from different and hostile interests. Actually, Burke's view is not wholly mistaken, but is true only of the noblest Congressmen and M. P.'s — the cynical popular view is also partly wrong in that it applies only to the basest representatives.

Representation in Hobbes · It seems strange to us now that representation should at one time have been one of the most important ideas brought forth in the defense of absolutism. No writer offers a more striking case than Thomas Hobbes in his *Leviathan*. Hobbes's entire conception of the state, or even of a community, rests upon the idea of representation. According to him: "A multitude of men, are made *one* person, when they are by one man, or one person, represented. . . . for it is the *unity* of the representer, not the *unity* of the represented, that maketh the person *one*. . . . *unity*, cannot otherwise be understood in multitude."[4] Political writers in more recent times have often paid too little attention to the crucial significance of this notion when considering Hobbes's idea of the state. His notorious doctrine of the governmental compact, according to which every man covenants with every other man to make one man or assembly of men their representative, is rooted in this conviction that the unity of the state can in no other way be understood. And why can it not be understood? Because each individual composing the multitude is a being utterly apart, like a particle of matter, moving through time and space in search of "power after power unto death." Therefore, only the superimposition of one such individual over all others can bring unity and order out of multitude and chaos. It is quite evident that such a point of view was eminently fitted to the age of monarchical absolutism. The modern idea of representation is different, indeed. Avoiding the mysticism of Rousseau's general will, the modern conception is built upon the idea that the many specific interests in the community — local, professional, commercial, and social, to mention only the more important divisions — can by argument and discussion be coordinated and compromised, by public scrutiny and criticism be scaled down to become compatible if not identical with the public interest, that is, the interest of the community as a whole. It is the task of the popular representatives thus to coordinate and criticize. The necessary unity does not logically follow from the unity of the representer, as Hobbes would have it, but must be created and constantly re-created through a political process of dynamic activity. This process consists mainly of parliamentary action and elections. Since both involve multitudes of persons, those with relatively similar interests form parties, that is, groups of people with common interests and ideals. Therefore parties are of great importance in any discussion of representation.

In Rousseau • But what about Rousseau's mysticism of the general will? In Anglo-Saxon minds the idea of representative government is firmly linked to that of democracy. It is, therefore, worth noting that Jean Jacques Rousseau, the most ardent and influential expounder of democratic ideas, rejects representation in the field of legislation in the broad sense as contrary to the very essence of sound, legitimate government. In his *Social Contract* he asserts that as soon as public affairs cease to be the primary occupation of the citizen, the state is bound to perish.[5] In such a condition, if it is a question of going to battle, the citizens prefer to pay mercenaries and stay at home themselves. If it is a matter of going into the assembly, they appoint deputies and stay at home. From indolence they allow paid soldiers to tyrannize the fatherland and "representatives" to sell it for profit. Therefore sovereignty cannot be represented, and for the same reason for which it cannot be surrendered: the sovereign should express the general will. The deputies of the people are, therefore, not its representatives, but merely its commissaries; they cannot give a definite decision. Every law which the people have not approved is null and void; it is no law at all. It is obvious from these remarks that Rousseau was misled by giving too much weight to the experience of the ancients. Where the active citizenry had been able to foregather in the market place, as in Athens or Rome, their failure to do so did indeed spell disaster to the commonwealth. If Rousseau were correct, it would, in fact, make it impossible to organize responsible popular government in our modern countries with their millions of people. Rousseau, to be sure, does not bar the choice of professional magistrates to *administer* the law. But he does insist that legislation as an exercise of the "sovereign" power must be adopted by the people themselves. In truth, his arguments constitute the *reductio ad absurdum* of the idea of "sovereignty" in a democratic society. There is no good reason for singling out the making of general rules (laws) and saying: This only the people themselves can do. In legislation as in other concerns, where many people have the same right or interest, it is often absolutely necessary for them to agree upon one person to represent them lest their interest be neglected for want of unity in urging it. Nor is there any reason for drawing a hard and fast line between representatives and the agents, curators, and mandatories, as Burke did. They all are related types of human relationship recognized by every more highly developed legal system. Rousseau's hostility to any kind of representative scheme was no doubt stimulated by the fact that his great antagonist Hobbes gave it such a prominent place in his political system. Moreover, the small self-governing cantons of his native Switzerland provided a living model for active participation of the citizenry, which persists to this day.

The dual nature of representation · As was said above in introducing the subject, representative assemblies developed in most European countries in the course of the later Middle Ages as an important part of the medieval constitutional order. Very often the three "estates" were composed of nobility, clergy, and the merchants of the cities (the burgesses).[6] But the greatest variations existed in this respect. The most important of these assemblies is undoubtedly the English Parliament, where the higher nobility were joined with the higher clergy in the "Lords Spiritual and Temporal," while the knights together with the burgesses constituted the Commons. Thus the more important groups in the community — nowadays often referred to as "classes" — were represented and called together by the king through his "minister" for the purpose of securing their consent to extraordinary taxes or levies. This was necessary because the undeveloped state of central administrative systems and the absence of effective means of coercion rendered the collection of such levies impossible without local cooperation. Quite naturally, these representatives when gathered together undertook to bargain for their consent to such grants of money; they presented complaints and petitions which the Crown had to heed in order to secure what it wanted. These, then, were not national representatives, but agents of local powers acting under special instructions or mandates. It was true, however, only as long as they acted separately. When the king and the two houses of Parliament acted together, after having settled differences and reached a compromise, they were taken to *represent* the whole body politic. More particularly, they were supposed to represent all of the realm of England when acting as a high court, which was taken to be their most solemn function down to the seventeenth century. Historically, then, one cannot draw a hard and fast line between agents with definite instructions or mandates, and representatives empowered to attend to a general task. An elected body may and usually will be both a set of agents from different interests, and a representative group determining the common interest. Therefore, to use the terms suggested by Burke and cited above, a parliament is both: a deliberative assembly from *one* nation, with *one* interest, that of the whole, and a congress of ambassadors from different and hostile interests.

Older definitions of representation have tried to escape from this dualism, which lies deeply embedded in the political reality of representative schemes. But political thinkers, being philosophers or lawyers, sought some *logical* unity. Thus Hobbes, on the basis of his general theory about man propelled by fear of violent death and greed for power (the latter springing from the former), argued that man will seek to escape from the desperate plight in the state of nature into a commonwealth. In order to do that, "a multitude of men are made *one* person, when they are by one man, or one person, represented," as long as it is "done with the consent of everyone of that multitude in particular." For Hobbes, it is "the unity of the representer" that is decisive. It is the only way unity in a multitude can be "understood." It is evident that such a "definition" is much too broad. It neglects the conflict of interests and values, not only between groups, but within the individual himself. Hobbes's view was, it has been claimed, revived in the contemporary Fascist and Nationalist Socialist doctrines of leadership and implied in the Communist claim to represent the proletariat. This interpretation overlooks the collectivist tendency of modern totalitarian thought, which posits the unity of the collective, precisely what Hobbes had denied. Such self-appointed guardians of alleged proletarian or nationalist interests would in the last analysis be basing their claim upon some kind of religious or inspirational sanction. Marx, Mussolini, Hitler, Stalin — all have been made to serve as inspired guides. The cult which grows up around such individuals places them into parallel with the demigods of old.

Responsible representative conduct • Whether the basis is religious or political, representation is, as we saw, closely linked to responsible conduct. If A represents B, he is presumed to be responsible *to* B, that is to say, he is answerable to B for what he says and does. In modern parlance, responsible government and representative government have therefore almost come to be synonymous. As our example shows, secularized political responsibility is conceived in terms of a relationship between human beings. There are two basic ways of securing such responsibility. One is the administrative, and the other is the political or electoral, form of responsibility. But in either case responsibility is measured in terms of service to interests determined by the preference of another. This means that responsibility always implies communication between human beings. Human beings will disagree as to what are their interests, and in the ensuing argument, the services are rationalized through which these interests are realized. All rationalizations are bound to be more or less incomplete. Comprehensive notions, such as that of a "national interest," certainly lack definite content, and the conduct of officials in terms of them is therefore only vaguely rationalized. Such notions possess rather the nature of a believed-in standard of value, and this is not at all surprising in view of the fact that nationalism developed into a sort of substitute for religion. Even much more specific interests cannot be thoroughly rationalized. How are we, then, to solve this problem of holding the several interests together and giving them a common direction, of integrating them into a more or less consistent whole? How, in other words, can the discordant private interests be converted into a common public interest? Authoritarians have always presumed to answer this question in an authoritative way. From Plato to Marx and Hitler, they have been ready to say: I know! Leave it to me and all will be well. The classical doctrine of democracy answers: By the will of the people. But how is the will of this somewhat vague entity, the people, to be found? With the development of modern means of communication and the vast scale of propaganda, the "will of the people" has lost its magic. When smart public relations men can substantiate the claim of changing the public's mind on basic questions, the belief in the common man, which was at one time such an obvious aspect of orthodox constitutionalism, must be restated to accord with the new reality. This is the second reason for seeking a new basis for responsible government. The problem, however, is not entirely new.

In a celebrated speech to his electors at Bristol, Burke enunciated the idealistic conception of political representation and responsibility, to which reference has already been made more fully, thus: "My worthy colleague [his opponent for the seat] says, his will ought to be subservient to yours. If that be all, the thing is innocent. If government were a matter of will upon any side, yours, without question, ought to be superior. But government and legislation are matters of reason and judgment, and not of inclination; and what sort of reason is that, in which the determination precedes the discussion; in which one set of men deliberate, and another decide . . . ? To deliver an opinion is the right of all men; that of constituents is a weighty and respectable opinion, which a representative ought always to rejoice to hear; and which he ought always most seriously to consider. But *authoritative* instructions; *mandates* issued, which the member is bound blindly and explicitly to obey, to vote and to argue for, though contrary to the clearest conviction of his judgment and conscience; these are things utterly unknown to the laws of this land, and which arise from a fundamental mistake of the whole order and tenor of our constitution." And then follows the sentence already cited, that "Parliament is not a *congress* of ambassadors from different and hostile interests; which interests each must maintain, as an agent and advocate, against other agents and advocates; but parliament is a *deliberative* assembly of *one* nation, with *one* interest, that of the whole; where not local purposes, not local prejudices ought to guide, but the general good." These justly famous sentiments stated the ideal of a representative assembly with a general mandate from the electorate to legislate in the public interest, but they do not describe how such an assembly actually behaves. Yet Burke pushes the argument a step further and into the realm of existential representation. Drawing upon religious thought, Burke asserted that the reason a representative ought not to "sacrifice" his convictions to any man or constituency is that it is a matter of conscience. "His unbiased opinion, his mature judgment, his enlightened conscience, he . . . does not derive from your pleasure; no, nor from the law and the constitution." Whence then do they stem from? "They are a trust from Providence, for the abuse of which he is deeply answerable."[7] This normative, indeed idealistic, concept of representation has since Burke's time become a staple of European constitutions, which repeat phrases like "the deputy is only responsible to his conscience." It is a conception that accords neither with constitutional realities, the living constitution, nor with notions of democratic responsibility.

For the conflict of various interests and their possible relation to a more comprehensive public interest is the realistic issue. Ideally conceived, of course, a special mandate cannot be admitted, since it would make the members of representative assemblies into mandatories for special interests. But there is a vast difference between a special mandate and a broad indication as to the general line of policy to be pursued. The obvious question to be asked of Burke is: "Who decides whether you, Edmund Burke, have carried out this trust from Providence?" To which Burke could only answer: "The electors of Bristol!" "Very well," his cross-examiner would continue, "what about the well-known quip about representatives that after having become a deputy, a man need have but one essential preoccupation, to remain a deputy? Will it not be true that unless a representative does obey the mandates and instructions of his electorate, or of groups of them, he will fail of re-election?" Such thoughts are now common among people who consider electoral responsibility; for the actual behavior of most elected representatives belies the lofty sentiments of Edmund Burke. Even in Burke's own day, many a listener to his speech must have chuckled inwardly as he reflected upon the complete subservience of most members of Parliament to the great aristocratic landowners, who did not even have to issue instructions, so assiduously did "their" members study their every wish before each vote in Parliament. As realistic students of political behavior we must conclude, therefore, that Burke's doctrine of reason and conscience as applied to representation and electoral responsibility was an untenable idealization even in his own day. Burke's argument is most persuasive, but it is built upon the false assumption that the major decisions in politics are purely reasonable when often they are not even partially so. Only to this partial aspect would his argument apply.

Defining political representation · If then we stick to actual experience with representation, we find that the scope of political representation can well be indicated by adopting a rather unpretentious definition.[8] Representation is the process by and through which the political power and influence which the entire citizenry or a part of them might have upon governmental action is, with their express or implied approval, exercised on their behalf by a small number among them, with binding effect upon the whole community thus represented. Some aspects of this definition deserve further comment. We speak advisedly of *influence* rather than participation or control, since the large number of citizens is not very likely to participate in or effectively to control governmental action. The general expression "governmental action" is needed rather than "legislation," because all kinds of governmental activities might be representative and subject to popular influence. By suggesting, further, that influence of a part of the citizenry, as well as the whole, may be represented, we recognize the representative quality of such bodies as the American Senate. Group representation is more ancient than the representation of the whole people, in any case. Finally, the most essential part of this descriptive definition of the process of representation is contained in the phrase: "with their expressed approval." This approval may be generic, and is then expressed presumably in the constitutional provisions regarding representative institutions — the particular institutions of that constitutional order, as well as the general principle. In short, it is in this phrase that we recognize the constitutional setting of all such representation. The authority of the representatives is not only created by the constituent power, but it is subject to change by the amending power under the constitution. But express approval may also refer to the specific approval of the voters in electing a particular person or set of persons to represent them. By that act, these persons acquire "representative quality." The representative acts which such persons may take in the place of those represented then have their "implied approval." Some constitutions permit a challenge to such acts and provide for initiative and referendum to confirm the action.

Election and legitimacy • The modern tendency has been to identify representation with election. The reason is that popular approval as expressed in the vote for a person or a measure is believed to be the only ground of democratic legitimacy. If "legitimacy" is understood as a ruler's right to rule, recognized by the ruled as such, then this proposition may also be stated as saying that only the assent of a popular majority in a given constituency or electoral district can provide a representative with the title to speak on their behalf.[9] To discover the "will of the people," elections must take place at regular intervals to give the people a chance to express their approval or disapproval of the stewardship of key officials. The large masses of individual will that are merged in this collective concept of the popular will have been personalized and symbolized, at least in America, in the normative idea of the "common man." So familiar have these notions become, and so generally are they accepted in the United States, that it is sometimes forgotten that a process of elections is not the only process for creating representatives and representation. Representation is a matter of existential fact. Elections, when seen in this context, appear to be a method of finding persons who possess this representative quality. But usually the persons so found also have to perform specific and often difficult tasks; for these may not be the best qualified. Apart from the electoral method of selection, representatives may be chosen on the basis of technical achievements. The representative quality of the Supreme Court and other judicial bodies rests in part upon this foundation. There is also the older method of having the officials of constituent corporate bodies be *ex-officio* members of a larger representative body. This method is genuinely used by the United Nations, where the foreign ministers of various nations or their deputies are usually members of the assembly or the council or both. The German Federal Council also belongs in this category. Various economic councils, such as the French, the German, and Czechoslovak councils, were likewise composed of this type of representatives.[10] Another method of considerable historical significance is inheritance of the office. Older representative bodies, such as the House of Lords in England and some of the French upper chambers, rested upon this base. Inheritance as a basis of election has become anachronistic for representative purposes. Election has superseded it almost completely.

If the election is envisaged as a method for securing people adequate for purposes of representation, it by no means follows that all those whose interests are to be represented should participate in the selection as such. The representatives may be dealing with the interests of children and imbeciles, yet most people nowadays readily admit that every voter should be able to read and write. Such requirement is desirable, indeed, in a voter, who should certainly be capable not only of reading about what his representative is doing and saying in Congress, but also of writing to him concerning it (though some Congressmen might at times wish that there were fewer letter writers in their constituencies). We may witness a considerable extension of such qualifications for the electorate.[11] In the days when the American constitution was made, property qualifications were often justified on the ground that they ensured a better education on the part of the voter. Democracy has found the answer to that argument by providing free public schools for all. The firm belief in the common man's judgment which democracy presupposes has thereby been given a firmer basis. Schemes of multiple representation have been advocated from time to time. It might conceivably provide a solution of the problems confronting democracies in foreign affairs. No such constitutional provisions would in and of themselves render a representative scheme less representative. But any advocates of such a proposal will have a hard stand against the ingrained equalitarian presumption that each citizen should have one vote.[12] Election — popular election — has become the most widely accepted basis for legitimate representation.

Representation and legislation · How can we explain the fact that legislation came to be considered the peculiar province of representative, popularly elected bodies, when in fact medieval representatives had little or no concern with legislation? Because ever since the sixteenth century, legislation was believed to be the most striking manifestation of political and governmental power. Legislation entailed the making of rules binding upon the whole community. Bodin maintained that this power was the peculiar characteristic of a state.[13] As we have seen before, the medieval notion of law as eternal custom, as something already there and merely to be discovered by learned men, was giving way to a realization that laws are man-made, that they are essentially decisions as to what ought to be rather than as to what is. The shift, of course, was merely one in emphasis. The High Court of Parliament had changed the law in the process of finding it, and so had the other courts of the realm. This relation of general rules to religious, moral, and other principles was the other pillar upon which men's preoccupation with laws and legislation as a manifestation of governmental power rested. The underlying idea is that human beings cannot be forced in matters of principle, and more especially in matters of religious conviction. A specific act of government may be justified in terms of a specific emergency, but no general rule ever can be so justified. This leads to the important if elementary consideration that the making of a rule presupposes that there is a series of events which have certain aspects in common. In other words, there must be a "normal" situation. This means that time is available for deliberation to determine what had best be done regarding such a situation.

Representative, deliberative bodies require time, obviously, and therefore legislation seems to be peculiarly the task of such bodies. Some writers on the Continent have thereby been led into linking parliamentary deliberation to the romantic passion for everlasting conversation, a generalization which is as glittering as it is uninformed. For parliamentary deliberation is entirely focused upon and organized with a view toward action, the enactment of a general rule. The history and practice of parliamentary procedure proves this beyond doubt. But the enactment of such a general rule requires careful coordination of conflicting viewpoints. Really effective compromises must be reached. Such compromises are justified, because any considerable group of people in a given community possesses the capacity effectively to resist the enforcement of certain rules which they do not, or which they cannot, approve.

The power of the purse • This preoccupation with law and legislation must not blind us to the fact that representative bodies are not usually limited to that activity. At the very outset, representative institutions were brought into existence, as we have seen, by the ability of nobles, clergy, and townsfolk to resist the royal tax collectors, to assert their right of being asked for their consent to new or exceptional levies. The influence which one part of the citizenry, the nobles, and then another, the burgesses, actually possessed gave birth to representative institutions for the exercise of that influence. The purely negative power of resistance could thus be converted into the positive power of affecting the conduct of government through petitions, complaints, and so forth. This celebrated "power of the purse" has remained one of the cherished activities of parliamentary bodies, although the English Parliament has delegated all detailed control to the cabinet.[14] Closely related to this power is the power to determine the expenditures of the government. In the beginning the two were joined; Parliament granted specific levies for specific tasks. Today, the expenditures of the government are, under a representative scheme, fixed through an annual budget. Since many of these expenditures are the direct outgrowth of legislation, however, the lines of distinction cannot be clearly drawn. A final aspect of fiscal influence exercised through representative bodies in civilized countries is the accounting control usually carried out by some kind of independent officer or "court" directly responsible to the popularly elected body, such as the comptroller-general in the United States, or the *Cour des Comptes* in France (see below, ch. XIX, p. 424). Their relation to the representative bodies is rather formal.

Representation and constitutionalism • In our discussion of the separation of powers and federalism, we showed that the problem of restraint is indissolubly connected with the problem of dividing governmental powers. Such a division can take different forms, of which the most important are the functional separation of powers, in the traditional sense, and the territorial division through some sort of federalism. For both purposes, representation is of vital importance. Distinct divisions of the electorate, created and maintained under a constitution, require the selection of distinct sets of representatives between whom the several functions of government may be divided. The same is true under any kind of separation of powers. We have shown how in England the legislative power was divided between king, lords, and commons, and how the judicial power was separated from all of them. Likewise in the United States the separation of powers presupposes a variety of representatives for different constituencies. Looked at from this angle, these schemes for dividing "power" really amount to dividing the people in a number of different ways, and then giving these several subdivisions a voice through different representatives who are kept from abusing their power by holding each other in check. Such a plan could not have any effect unless the community were *actually* divided into a number of groups or classes, one of which might have a majority in one constituency, while another has it in another. We thus speak of farm states, Catholic states, and Negro districts, of a governor who is the farmers' man but who battles the Senate dominated by a utility, etc. Without representation, such balances could not establish themselves.

This fact has given rise in recent years to demands for some kind of new corporative body to represent the various class and interest groups in the industrial society. Such occupational representation was offered after the First World War as the panacea for the admitted shortcomings of territorial representation. Occupational representation, based as it is upon the idea that man's true community in an industrial society is his professional or occupational group, such as his trade union, has great difficulty in determining clearly the actual size and conformation of a constituency of this sort on account of the overlapping and the difficulty of assigning appropriate weight to each organization selected. How do housewives compare with musicians? It also has been found difficult to cope with multiple representation of individuals belonging to several such groups. The tedious history of the efforts to carry out the mandate contained in Article 165 of the Weimar constitution shows clearly how extraordinarily complicated these issues are.[15] The Economic and Social Council established in Title X of the 1958 French constitution represents employers and employees, producers and consumers, industry and agriculture, Metropolitan and overseas France. Its considerable influence, however, derives partly from the fact that it is only an advisory body.

Proposals to make it a senate with the power of decision have so far failed because the question of representation has proved insoluble.

Conclusion · In any case, neither in Europe nor elsewhere has the idea of representation been significantly advanced since the time when proportional representation was set against majority representation — unless one wishes to consider the declining support for proportional representation an advance. Occupational representation, which continues to claim some adherents, still founders upon the difficulty of finding the proper "constituency." It is generally agreed that the traditional method of basing representation upon territorial subdivisions is quite artificial since no genuine community corresponds to them any longer, especially in the great urban conglomerations. Yet no one has succeeded in discovering a really workable plan for a change that would take account of the transformation of communal bonds. While an old established democratic system might adapt itself through various devices, such as legalizing interest groups and the like, it is doubtful whether such devices do more than attentuate the decline in representativeness of the territorially based representatives. The success or failure of efforts to re-establish and reform representative government will turn upon the finding of adequate techniques of representation through decisions. Else the fragmentized mass, feeling lost and unrepresented in the processes of would-be democratic government, will follow a "leader" of the inspired kind who sets forth a claim of representativeness on nonrational grounds of a transcendental community, whether of class or of nation.[16]

Electoral Systems in Theory and Practice

Introduction · The English system · The proposals for proportional representation · Bagehot's view: the functional approach · John Stuart Mill's view: the individualist approach · The problem of "justice" · Gerrymandering (electoral geometry) · The different functions of proportional systems · Practical applications · Recent trends · Assessment of past experience · Conclusion

Introduction · Tom, Dick, and Harry trotting to the voting booth enact the most distinctive process of modern politics. There have been kings, revolutions, constitutions, and vast bureaucracies since time immemorial, but the mass voter is something quite recent. To the Greeks, democracy meant that the vital decisions were made by the assembly of the whole citizenry in the market place. To us it means that the whole citizenry goes and elects representatives, after having read about their platforms and other views in the newspapers, listened to them in a meeting or over the radio. As we saw in the last chapter, elections are not the only possible method for securing representatives. They are, however, considered the most democratic method. What does "democratic" mean in this connection? Should all those whose interests are to be represented participate in the selection of representatives?[1] A considerable number of people are quite obviously unqualified to *select* a modern legislator. To admit that obvious truth does by no means imply a plea for government by intellectuals. On the contrary, the real backbone of an elective system are the cautious, steadfast men and women of common sense who can see the forest rather than the trees. It is one of the recurrent errors of intellectuals to make light of the sound sense of the average citizen. It has recently been reaffirmed on the basis of careful statistical data in a study by V. O. Key.[2] The electoral methods which have been in use are part of the trouble. A comparative estimate of electoral methods, therefore, is one of the most urgent concerns of the political scientist, as well as of the practical reformer.

The English system · Parliamentary government in England rested for a long time upon a strictly traditional system of elections. It had grown out of the corporational basis of early Parliaments. Until the Reform Act of 1832, it abounded with the most abnormal situations.[3] Districts which had once been populous centers, and therefore entitled to separate representation in Parliament, retained this representation after all just claims had gone. One such "rotten borough" actually had been swept away by the sea. On the other hand, in the industrial north of England, thriving cities had grown up which had no member in Parliament at all. During the nineteenth century a series of parliamentary reforms undertook to cope with this problem. At first the expedient was used of giving several representatives to one district. This system lasted down to 1884–1885, when the single-member constituency came into general use. Since that time, elections in England have been held on the basis of what is known as the system of plurality, that is, relative majority. This means that the candidate who secures the largest number of votes (but not necessarily an absolute majority) wins the seat. At the same time, the elections are now secret. Formerly they were public and took place by a showing of hands. As a result, polling was an occasion for much brawling and merrymaking. "Rivers of beer were set flowing; bribes were openly offered and accepted; organized bands of 'bludgeon-men' went about intimidating and coercing electors; non-voters thrust themselves joyously into the fray; political convictions were expressed in terms of rotten apples and dead cats; heads were broken and a generally riotous time was had by all" (Ogg).[4]

Yet there is something to be said for an open election. As John Stuart Mill pointed out, the right to vote is a public trust, and should therefore be exercised in such a fashion as to give the public a chance to see how it is used.[5] What is more, under proper conditions of free assembly, it develops in the citizenry that most desirable quality of civic courage which does not shrink from standing up for one's convictions. Unfortunately, economic pressures have introduced a new element into the situation which obliges us to forego these advantages in order not to deprive a large body of citizens of their "right of suffrage." Since 1855, then, England has adopted secret balloting under a system of single-member constituencies. The purpose of these constituencies is to elect a Parliament, which in turn will be ready to support a cabinet, which in turn is to govern the land. In other words, the English electoral system is clearly directed toward the goal of dividing each constituency, and thus all England, into two halves, the majority to govern and the minority to criticize. This may mean permanent voicelessness for a man who belongs to a perpetual minority. As Walter Bagehot told his readers many years ago: "I have myself had a vote for an agricultural county for twenty years, and I am a Liberal; but two Tories have always been returned, and all my life will be returned. As matters now stand, my vote is of no use.

But if I could combine with 1,000 other Liberals in that and other Conservative counties, we might choose a Liberal member."[6]

The proposals for proportional representation · The foregoing statement sounds like a criticism of the existing English electoral system; in fact, it constituted part of a reasoned defense of that system against those who had just brought forward the plan known as proportional representation. To be sure, Thomas Hare's scheme, first expounded in 1857, cannot claim to be the first exposition of the idea of proportional representation.[7] The idea appeared in the French National Convention in 1793, without leading to action. It was further elaborated by the mathematician Gergonne (1820), and developed independently by an English schoolmaster, Thomas Wright Hill, whose son took it to Australia (1839). At about the same time, in 1842, the idea gained a foothold in Switzerland when Victor Considérant proposed a proportional-representation system to the Council of Geneva. Two years later Thomas Gilpin set forth another plan for proportional representation. Finally, another twelve years later, a Danish minister of finance, Carl Andrae, worked out a system resembling the Australian plan, but using ballots. The following year Hare published his tract. From this rapid survey it can be seen that proportional representation was "in the air" during the first half of the nineteenth century. It has been debated and experimented with ever since.

The underlying idea of all the various systems is to secure a representative assembly reflecting with more or less mirrorlike exactness the various divisions in the electorate. Why should such divisions be reflected? They should be "represented." The voice of minorities should be heard. Justice requires that no votes be lost, that the Bagehots be able to get together and send a representative to Parliament. A man of the eminence of John Stuart Mill extolled the virtues of the scheme in his *Considerations on Representative Government* and called it one of "the very greatest improvements yet made in the theory and practice of government." Proportional representation shifts the basic meaning of representation. An important part of representation, we saw, is to represent the citizenry as a whole, not the divisions among them. Representation means the exercise of the people's influence through a smaller number acting in their behalf. Proportional representation, on the other hand, looks upon the divisions in the electorate as the only entities to be represented; in the last analysis it looks upon the individual as the representable element or unit.

Proportional representation has been a subject of heated controversy for more than a hundred years now. It has been the inspiration of civic groups, such as the Proportional Representation Society in England, to which men of great ability and standing have devoted much time and effort. And yet, it is a curious fact that in the English-speaking countries (except Eire, which presents a special case), proportional representation has not made any substantial headway in spite of the fact that these countries are the home of representative government. Is this due to the greater resistance of established ways to any innovation or to some inherent defect in the plan which reveals itself to the good sense of peoples with a sound political tradition? or to conditions, such as greater homogeneity in the electorate, which would make proportional representation less urgently needed? These and related questions will be answered very differently by different observers, depending upon their general convictions concerning proportional representation. This fact suggests that broader political and moral issues are involved in this apparently technical problem of political machinery.

Bagehot's view: the functional approach • When two men of the ability, insight, and experience of John Stuart Mill and Walter Bagehot disagree sharply, in spite of their belonging to the same party, the issue is likely to be a deep one. They were both liberals and they were both economists, but while Bagehot was a liberal of the right, Mill was a liberal of the left. In spite of his socialist leanings, Mill was an ardent individualist. His adherence to proportional representation clearly reveals this. The real core of the disagreement between Mill and Bagehot can be found in the former's distinctive emphasis upon the rationalist aspects of the problem, as against the latter's insistence upon the functional aspects. Bagehot asked:[8] What will proportional representation do to the functioning of Parliament as we know it? Bagehot's great achievement anyway was to spell out what everyone "knew in practice," namely, that the function of Parliament was twofold: (1) for the majority to support the cabinet in its conduct of the government; and (2) for the minority to criticize the actions of the government. The combination of action and criticism enables Parliament to represent the people as a whole both toward itself and toward the outside world. Of the two functions, Bagehot naturally considered the first more important than the second, and therefore he argued that no matter how great the gain on other accounts, proportional representation must be rejected if it seriously threatens the government's capacity for action.

Bagehot considers the basic difference between election by majority and proportional representation the fact that proportional representation makes the constituency voluntary; in other words, each voter individually is able to choose his own constituency in accordance with his personal preference. He votes as a voluntary member of a group which has no other common ties. A constituency being the group or segment of voters who are entitled to send a member to Parliament, this is indeed the basic point, although the language of proportionalists often obscures it. To put Bagehot's point another way, all proportional schemes say to the electorate: if so-and-so many among you can agree upon a candidate,* that candidate shall be elected. The majority system by contrast says: so-and-so many among you shall constitute an electoral district or part of the whole people, and whomever the largest number among you elect shall be one of the members of Parliament. As Bagehot pointed out, the temptations of the idea of a voluntary constituency are very plain. "Under the compulsory form of constituency the votes of the minorities are thrown away. In the city of London now, there are many Tories, but all the members are Whigs; every London Tory, therefore, is by law and principle misrepresented: his city sends to Parliament not the member whom he wished to have, but the member he wished *not* to have. But upon the voluntary system the London Tories, who are far more than 1,000 in number, may combine; they make a constituency and return a member. In many existing constituencies the disfranchisement of the minorities is hopeless and chronic." "Again, this plan gets rid of all our difficulties as to the size of constituencies." "Again, the admirers of a great man could make a worthy constituency for him." Yet Bagehot saw defects in the scheme which overbalanced and outweighed these merits. Essentially, under the voluntary system, so-called central party organizations would acquire an overweening influence. "The crisis of politics would be not the election of the member, but the making of the constituency. . . . The result of this . . . would be the return of party men mainly. The member-makers would look, not for independence, but for subservience — and they could hardly be blamed for so doing. They are agents for the Liberal party; and, as such, they should be guided by what they take to be the wishes of their principal. The mass of the Liberal party wishes measure A, measure B, measure C. The managers of the registration — the skilled manipulators — are busy men. They would say: 'Sir, here is your card; if you want to get into Parliament on our side, you must go for that card; it was drawn up by Mr. Lloyd; he used to be engaged on railways, but since they passed this new voting plan, we get him to attend to us; it is a sound card; stick to that and you will be right.' Upon this (in theory) voluntary plan, you would get together a set of members bound hard and fast with party bands and fetters infinitely

---

* The required number varies greatly. The following prewar list will give an idea.[9]

Austria	39,500	Ireland	20,000
Belgium	40,000	Netherlands	70,800
Bulgaria	20,000	Norway	17,650
Czechoslovakia	45,400	Poland	61,200
Denmark	22,500	Sweden	26,100
Finland	17,125	Switzerland	20,000

tighter than any members now. . . . The full force of this cannot be appreciated except by referring to the former proof that the mass of a parliament ought to be men of moderate sentiments, or they will elect an immoderate ministry, and enact violent laws. But upon the plan suggested, the House would be made up of party politicians selected by a party committee and pledged to party violence, and of characteristic, and therefore immoderate representatives, for every 'ism' in all England. Instead of a deliberate assembly of moderate and judicious men, we should have a various compound of all sorts of violence. The voluntary plan, therefore, when tried in this easy form, is inconsistent with the extrinsic independence as well as with the inherent moderation of a parliament — two of the conditions which, as we have seen, are essential to the bare possibility of parliamentary government." It seemed desirable to quote this memorable passage at such length, because its conception has always remained dominant in England, in spite of persistent agitation for proportional representation over the last fifty years. What is more, it foretells in the most extraordinary manner the experience which we have been able to observe where such systems have been put into force. On the other hand, these arguments by no means exhaust the problem. They are applicable only to a parliamentary government. And what if the divisions or cleavages of the people have reached proportions where any electoral system would be abandoned which did not give these warring groups adequate representation in national affairs?

John Stuart Mill's view: the individualist approach • Had John Stuart Mill[10] thought of it in terms of this function of Parliament, the function Bagehot later called the "elective" one? Obviously not. Mill was preoccupied with the issue of "representation." After briefly outlining Hare's scheme of proportional representation, Mill sets forth a number of reasons which in his opinion constitute "transcendent advantages." "In the first place, it secures a representation, in proportion to numbers, of every division of the electoral body: not two great parties alone . . . but every minority in the nation . . . Secondly, no elector would be nominally represented by someone whom he had not chosen. Every member of the House would be the representative of an unanimous constituency." He stresses the strong tie, the complete identification, the weakening of localism (N.B.!), the higher intellectual qualification of the representatives and avoidance of "collective mediocrity." Finally, Mill sees is as a check on "the ascendancy of the numerical majority" by offering "a social support for individual resistance . . . a rallying point for opinions and interests which the ascendant public opinion views with disfavor." Characteristically, in this enthusiasm, Mill finally calls proportional representation *"personal representation,"* offering a refuge to the "instructed elite." No objections of real weight could be discovered by Mill, though in his usual judicious manner he examines a few, but finds them wanting. He did not consider the function of Parliament. He also failed to examine his major premise, namely, that there can be no representation of the whole without a representation of each of the whole's individual parts.

The extreme individualism of Mill's approach is further illustrated by an unexplained premise concerning *justice*. As the title of his chapter suggests, Mill was concerned whether Parliament represented all or only a majority. Unless it did represent all, it was not "truly" representative; it was false democracy. But since traditional constitutional law had always claimed that Parliament represented all, Mill's challenge had to be based upon a new view of what constituted representativeness. "There is a part," he wrote, "whose fair and equal share of influence in the representation is withheld from them; contrary to all just government, but above all, contrary to the principle of democracy...." Now we must remember that the word "democracy" did not at that time in England spell the almost universal approval which it today elicits in England, and even more in America. It was a symbol of the radicals. Parties have usually argued their interest in terms of justice, and so in Mill's thought the issue is a question of justice. "The injustice and violation of principle are not less flagrant because those who suffer by them are a minority, for there is not equal suffrage where *every single individual does not count for as much as any other single individual* in the community." This phrasing somewhat obscures the issue, since the minority in one constituency will be the majority in another, but this very obscurity is highly revealing. It shows that Mill is thinking of the particular *individual* who finds himself without a representative. The whole, seen as a compound of all these particular individuals, is therefore not "represented" if all the individuals as individuals are not represented. Is this true? The answer to this question turns upon a problem of "justice."

The problem of "justice" · No functional arguments will meet the moral and philosophical issue raised by Mill. Bagehot might well have been charged by his illustrious opponent with shifting the ground. "Nothing is more certain than that the virtual blotting out of the minority is no necessary or natural consequence of freedom; that far from having any connection with democracy, it is diametrically opposed to the first principle of democracy, *representation in proportion* to numbers." And again: "Real equality of representation is not obtained, unless any set of electors amounting to the *average number of a constituency wherever in the country they happen to reside* have the power of combining with one another to return a representative." What kind of concept of justice and democracy is this? Clearly it is one in which the individual is treated as unrelated to family or any other local attachments, so that "the people" are not seen as a whole, a distinctive entity, created out of smaller but vital groups. Rather, the people are merely the sum of the individuals composing it, atomistic units which require each their own representative. But is representation possible on such assumptions? Is not this kind of reasoning subject to the *reductio ad absurdum* which Rousseau's denial of the possibility of representation foreshadowed? Furthermore, is this view of the situation realistic? It is significant that the intellectual Mill dwells at length upon the advantages to the intelligentsia of sending their own ilk to Parliament. Were the numerous professors in the German *Reichstag* much help to the German republic?* The intellectual elite are, by their work and profession, the most individualized lot. Unlike workers, farmers, and other simple folk, they possess a high mobility and little attachment to any particular locality. They usually speak a highbrow, national language, untainted by much local color. All this is part of their function in contemporary society. If one belongs to this elite, one should beware of generalizing from one's own natural propensities, and of constructing institutional devices for society at large on that basis. Such uncritical disregard for what most people are really like is likely to cause great difficulties in the end. Can anything be just which does not work?

But let us assume for a moment that representation through a person elected by the majority of your fellow townsmen is "unjust" to some minority, and that this can be remedied by giving this minority a chance of combining with others constituting a similar minority elsewhere. If there were only one such minority, it would simply mean that there would be more men in parliament to criticize than before. This would mean less action, rather than different action. If there were many such minorities, so that no group any longer had a majority, it would mean complete inaction over long periods. In either case, is it not a question of competing claims? Why should the problem of what is just to a minority be given precedence over what is just to the majority? Admittedly the majority wants action. Such action is, through Proportional Representation, being delayed or altogether prevented. What is the justice of that? It would appear that Mill, in his concern over the minority, had neglected the majority. Problems of justice in politics are problems of adjustment between conflicting claims. The election of representatives therefore always involves the paring down of *some* claims; justice can only be achieved if these claims are equitably adjusted. Presumably the

---

* The British formerly made allowance for the professorial elite by providing a dozen special seats in Parliament for the great universities. This survival of medieval corporate representation, although serving a modern purpose, was abolished in the Representation of the People Act of 1948, which took effect in 1950.

majority's claims are weightier than those of any minority. Representation is a broad thing; representatives are elected so that many participate indirectly in the essential tasks. The majority participates through acting, the minority through discussion and criticism. If the majority fails to be presented adequately, because its representatives are unable to act, the injustice is just as great, or greater, than if the minority fails to be represented adequately, because its representatives cannot talk as much as they would like to. It is not a question of justice, then, but of more adequate representation of minorities. This may or may not be a desirable thing. But it should be considered on its merits. A skeptical French political commentator wrote some years ago: "In proportional representation . . . the power will go to the party which is in fact the strongest; and this power would then be just . . . For what is justice for the parties? It is a just rule to ascertain who will govern, to know who will determine France's fate, realize his utopia, inflate his pride and give jobs to his nephews . . ."[11]

Gerrymandering (electoral geometry) · Besides providing for the representation of important minorities, proportional representation possesses the merit of getting rid of the difficulties as to the size and structure of constituencies. As long as the population shifts, periodic readjustments of the boundaries of electoral districts are necessary if gross injustices such as the rotten boroughs are to be avoided. In the United States that problem is a familiar one through the recurrent struggle over reapportionment. Some time ago a somewhat agitated controversy was raging among statistical scholars regarding the right method of such reapportionment.[12] It is this difficulty which affords many of the illustrations of those who argue for proportional representation. Unequal electoral districts are not of the essence of the system of plurality elections, but it must be conceded that this system does, *usually*, show considerable maladjustments in the size of electoral districts. In the United States, the Supreme Court had to step in.

What is worse, under adverse conditions of unscrupulous party politics, the determination of electoral districts lends itself to the practice of gerrymandering, so called after a former governor of Massachusetts who perceived the potentialities of affecting the electoral result by manipulating the geography of the constituencies. Since all a party needs to gain a seat is a small majority (or in three-cornered fights a mere plurality) of votes, you can draw the boundaries of your electoral districts in such a way as to crowd large percentages of your party opponents into a few districts, and then divide the rest in such a way as to give yourself a majority. What you are thus doing is merely artificially creating conditions which resemble those which arise in course of time through the shifts in population. To give a

concrete illustration, suppose you had an area which had to elect ten representatives for 100,000 voters. These voters are divided between party A and
party B in such a way that party A is adhered to by most of the city dwellers,
whereas party B is counting most of the farmers as its partisans. There are
three cities in the territory, one of 20,000 voters and two of 15,000 voters.
If party A were in power and undertook to gerrymander this territory, they
would want to get about 7000 of their supporters into seven districts, thus
giving them a clear majority in the representative body. They would do this
by constructing mixed country and city districts, leaving the rest of the voters
in solid agricultural areas. But the managers of party B also would want,
if they were in power, to construct mixed districts, but in such a way as to
leave some strictly urban districts. The two pictures would compare thus:

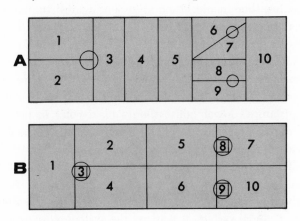

The districts under the gerrymander of A would be:

(1)	A	7000	B	3000	(6)	A	7500	B	2500
(2)	A	6500	B	3500	(7)	A	7500	B	2500
(3)	A	6500	B	3500	(8)	A	7500	B	2500
(4)	A	0	B	10,000	(9)	A	7500	B	2500
(5)	A	0	B	10,000	(10)	A	0	B	10,000

The district under the gerrymander of B would be instead:

(1)	A	3500	B	6500	(6)	A	10,000	B	0
(2)	A	3250	B	6750	(7)	A	2500	B	7500
(3)	A	10,000	B	0	(8)	A	2500	B	7500
(4)	A	3250	B	6750	(9)	A	10,000	B	0
(5)	A	2500	B	7500	(10)	A	2500	B	7500

These samples illustrate in a typical fashion how the same *total* electorate
may give entirely the opposite result if divided along opposite lines. Many

American states show the most extraordinary shapes for electoral districts, shapes which are much more exotic than the "salamander" to which the "gerrymander" was supposed to be related. But even if party managers do not stoop to such tactics, it would be too much to hope for party managers to change electoral districts when the social forces have produced effects akin to our example but quite independent of any manipulation. The malapportionment eventually became so extreme that the Supreme Court felt obliged to step in. The decision has been loudly criticized by traditionalists, who deplored not only the bad reasoning in the case, but also objected to the "activism."[13] The Court, it was said, was getting involved in legislative and very political questions. But since the artificiality of apportionments not only distorted the party strength, but also gave excessive weight to rural as against urban electorates, there could be no argument against the basic proposition that such malapportionment violated, if not the spirit of the constitution, then certainly the notion of equality. It may be extreme to demand that "one man" have "one vote," but some rough approximation to this surely is called for. The decision and its sequel have led to a flowering of radically proportionalist proposals, such as that made in Illinois that each representative in that state legislature's lower house should have votes in proportion to the number of votes he received from the electorate. In consequence, a man receiving twice the votes of another would presumably have double the vote in the legislature too.[14] It seems a very ingenuous suggestion, to make the "one man, one vote" principle fully workable. On the other side, it has been asserted in the dissent in *Baker v. Carr* that "it was not the English system, it was not the colonial system, it was not the system chosen for the national government by the constitution, it was not the system exclusively or even predominantly practiced by the States at the time of the adoption of the Fourteenth Amendment, it is not predominantly practiced by the States today." These assertions are widely shared and often quoted. But while they are true, and while the "one man, one vote" principle is disputable, a rejection of it does not suffice to justify the extremes of malapportionment which legislatures have allowed to develop over the years. When one learns that the imbalance between the most and the least populous voting district was 682:1 (Connecticut House) or even 296:1 (California Senate), he cannot help thinking of England's rotten boroughs. But quite apart from such extremes, only fourteen of the ninety-nine state legislative chambers showed a discrepancy of less than 3:1 by 1950.[15] These discrepancies result whether population or valuation of property — the two major bases — are used for comparison of potential and actual apportionment. In a study for Georgia, for example, it was found that Fulton County, which had three representatives in the state legislature totaling 205, would have had 29 seats if seats had been assigned on the basis of population, and 48 if based on valuation. Representation of the 103 smallest counties, on the other hand, rural to be sure, which had 103 representatives, would have been reduced to 48 on the basis of population, and to 28 on the basis of valuation.[16] There are in fact six ways of apportionment employed in American state legislatures,[17] but the details are not of interest here. What matters is that either deliberately, or through population shifts and changes in industrial location, serious mal-apportionment has been common in the United States. It is being remedied gradually. The long-range consequences of giving an increasing weight to urban electorates is hard to predict, especially in light of racial problems. One cannot but agree with the sane statement in a study by Alfred de Grazia: "Provided that the courts do not force apportionment systems of the country into a rigidly egalitarian mold, the government of the states, localities and nation can and should explore new methods of representation."[18]

The situation in England throughout a large part of the nineteenth century was quite similar. The English reforms undertook to redistrict the country, and eventually in 1885 divided the whole realm into a fairly even number of single-member constituencies, probably because the more conservative Liberals, like Bagehot, could not see eye to eye with proportional representation. On the other hand, the German Social Democrats, who had advocated proportional representation under the Empire, stuck to their conviction after the revolution of 1918, and adopted a thoroughgoing system of proportional representation. This they did in spite of the fact that it would have been to their distinct advantage as a party to redistrict the country and hold elections in single-member constituencies.

The different functions of proportional systems · Unquestionably, Bagehot put his finger upon the central objection from a governmental standpoint.[19] But he did not formulate it in the most persuasive fashion. It is more important that a majority system of elections oblige the voter to *decide* between two or more alternatives than that the constituency be compulsory. The need of a decision is paramount when the representative body has over and above everything else the function of constituting either the executive or the government which is to hold office as long as the representative body is willing to support it. As everyone knows, such a system of parliamentary government makes the executive dependent upon and responsible to a majority in the representative assembly. For, if the assembly becomes divided into so many factions that there cannot be found a stable majority for the executive's support, all governmental activity becomes paralyzed. Impressive documentation has been assembled to show how in country after country precisely this paralysis crept in. Eventually the people lost hope that effective action would ever be produced, and "parliamentarism" became a by-word for inefficiency and inaction.

England resisted the lure of proportionalism. Sticking to their traditions, most Englishmen, including the Labour party, rejected P. R., recognizing it as the most important function of the English Parliament to support the government. For a long time this function was obscured by the doctrine of a separation of powers, particularly since such a separation prevailed in the United States. Parliament was looked upon as a legislative assembly. But while the legislative function is quite important, it is not *as* important as the maintenance and functioning of the government itself. The influence of the whole electorate upon this executive management must become focalized into a few clear alternatives. For large numbers of people cannot decide between any but two or three very simple alternatives.

But what if the elected representatives do not have this function of constituting the executive? It is, after all, by no means a foregone conclusion that the function of the representative assembly should be a decision as to who shall govern. Not only in the United States, but in Switzerland and in prewar Germany, the main function of the representative assembly is supposed to be legislation. Such legislation, particularly modern economic and social legislation, touches the everyday interests of all citizens, and the divisions of interest between them are fairly persistent. It cannot, for example, reasonably be expected that the employer and capitalist would be persuaded to hand all profits over to his workers, nor can we hope that the workers will readily yield to those who expect them to be satisfied with the joy of work, and be content with long hours at starvation wages. Legislation touching these and many similar issues between the various groups in the community must be framed as an acceptable compromise in which all relevant views are voiced with a vigor approximately comparable to their actual strength in the community. A representative assembly, then, whose primary function is the framing of such legislation, would greatly benefit from a well-thought-out system which would bring into it the various groups in the community in rough proportion at least to their strength. But there must still be an effective majority ready to support a fairly coherent policy. The difficulties in the way of achieving that purpose are great under the American presidential system even without any multiplication of parties such as proportionalism envisages and engenders.

For no matter what the variations in detail, the fundamental principle of P. R. is always the same: to secure a representative assembly reflecting with more or less mathematical exactness the various divisions in the electorate. Now, there are two predominant ways of achieving that purpose, the single transferable vote advocated by Thomas Hare, and the list system of proportional representation widely used in Europe. The first scheme gives the voter leave to indicate first, second, and third choices (and more if there are more candidates in the district). Thus the voter continues to choose between individual candidates. The second scheme, on the other hand, asks the voter to choose between lists of candidates which contain as many names as there are representatives to be chosen. The particular form which P. R. has been given in various countries is often combinations of the two basic types. A detailed study would offer an opportunity for an understanding of both. The most radical application of the list system of proportional representation was found in the Weimar Republic, whereas the single transferable vote is used in the Republic of Ireland. More or less mixed plans are in operation in Belgium, Denmark, the Federal Republic, the Netherlands, Norway, Sweden, and Switzerland (among others).

Practical application · The oldest system of proportional representation for national elections is that of Belgium. Here the voter has to choose one of the several party lists, but at the same time he is entitled to indicate his preferences within the list.[20] It is noteworthy that under this system of proportional representation, a remarkable stability of party strength at first gave the strongest party, the Catholics, long periods of undisputed leadership. But more recently Belgium experienced marked ministerial instability, which undermined the long-felt satisfaction with proportional representation in that country.

Very similar in its conception to the Belgian system was the Dutch electoral plan, which was adopted in 1917 after very extensive deliberations and inquiries over many years. In the Netherlands, however, the entire country was constituted as one single electoral district. The Dutch system also led to a remarkable stability of party strength, and, on the whole, public opinion was satisfied. It is noteworthy that Holland as well as Belgium has a parliamentary system of government. It seems that the tendency toward a multiplication of parties was held in check by the very fact that parliamentary government renders small parties ineffectual.

The three Scandinavian kingdoms, Sweden, Norway, and Denmark, also combine parliamentary government with proportional representation. Their systems are each different from the other, but both Sweden and Norway have list systems, whereas Denmark has tried to work out a complicated plan of combining single-member constituencies with proportional representation. In Sweden and Norway the voter has the sole voice in the rank order of the candidates on the lists. There are considerable variations in the extent to which the voters of the several parties exercise their own judgment in the matter of individual preferences. While the social-democratic electorate (labor) is very loyal, the conservative and liberal groups are more ready to bolt. In spite of these elements of flexibility, the Swedish electoral system has been considerably criticized in recent years, and occasional voices have been heard which demand the return to some kind of single-member constituency. The main point of attack has been the power of central party bosses and the lack of connection between the voter and the elected representatives. However, neither in Sweden nor in Norway does there seem to be any inclination to abandon proportional representation, and the same thing is true of Denmark. To be sure, Denmark has worked out a peculiar plan according to which the voter elects representatives in single-member constituencies, with certain complicated provisions for the transfer of his vote to adjacent constituencies combined into districts. The remainders are distributed nationally on the basis of the proportional vote for each party. The main objection to the Danish system is its complexity, but it does not seem to perturb the Danes, who are operating parliamentary government under its aegis with considerable success; whatever difficulties were encountered in connection with forming a workable ministry were not attributed to proportional representation.

Switzerland, without a parliamentary executive, has a federal system. Elections to the lower house of the federal legislature did not become proportionalized until 1919, and experience with this system is therefore limited. The Swiss system is another variant in the list system, made more flexible by giving the voter entire freedom in making up his list, as in Norway and Sweden, and adding the opportunity of voting twice for the same candidate. By the Swiss method an almost mathematical reproduction of the existing views in the community is achieved in the legislative body. The considerable division of parties under this system cannot, however, endanger the conduct of the executive government, since the Swiss Executive Council does not feel obliged to resign if the vote in the legislature is adverse to its recommendations. Instead, it sets to work on the preparation of a measure more in keeping with the wishes of the representatives. Though there are many complaints heard about the hardening of parties into class-interest pressure groups, to date the Swiss representatives seem to have performed effectively their one essential function, that of legislation.

Whereas Switzerland is on the whole a country famous for its moderation in politics, Ireland is noted for the violence of its political partisanship. Yet proportional representation seems to have taken root there without much friction. Indeed, it is claimed that the very intensity of political animosities necessitated a proportional scheme, because the lack of unity might have led the party defeated by an ordinary plural system to resort to violence. Be that as it may, the Republic of Ireland has adopted the single-transferable-vote system of proportional representation which the British Proportional Representation Society has so long been advocating. Each voter has only one vote, but if a candidate should receive more than his share of first choices, the second choices of his ballots are distributed among the other candidates to see which then gets the highest number. Although the parties may instruct their followers as to which candidate to put first, they usually content themselves with urging their voters to vote for the men on their list — or so it is asserted. At any rate, the voters can do as they please. The relative stability of party strength at the start prevented the extereme oscillations in the policy of the government which a new country with such passionate partisanship might otherwise have experienced. Since the necessary minimum quota of votes cannot readily be reached by groups which are too small to command solid support in at least one district, the number of parties is not exceptionally large. It seemed for a time that the breaking-up process had commenced; in the general elections of 1948 no party received a majority and Ireland had to form a coalition government composed of all the minor parties. However, the Fianna Fail was able to achieve an absolute majority in the election of 1957 and has been able to maintain a predominant position since, even though obliged to seek coalition partners.[21]

From the Republic of Ireland we must finally turn to the ill-fated German Republic of 1919, where proportional representation according to the list system was carried to its logical conclusion, and by some is held largely responsible for the collapse of the republic. In contrast to the small or dependent states which we have so far considered, Germany was, even after the First World War, a large power with a complicated foreign policy of its own. Such responsibility for foreign affairs on a large scale broadens a government's political tasks, and enhances the importance of stability.

The German system was rather simple in its conception. The country was divided into thirty-five electoral districts. Each party prepared a list of candidates for these districts, the larger parties usually containing as many candidates as there were seats to be filled in the district. For each 60,000 votes this ticket received, one of its candidates was elected, and exactly in the order in which they appeared on the ticket. Remainders were transferred to regional and national tickets. The voter could make no changes; he really voted for a party, rather than a canidate. This was supposed to make it possible for national leaders to return to the parliament without undergoing the exertion and sordidness of an election campaign. Actually these lists provided safe berths for the party managers and wire pullers behind the scene. It also kept them well insulated from the people, thereby increasing the chances of a demagogue like Hitler. The very irresponsibility, or rather lack of responsibility, encouraged extremism in the electorate; for the electorate did not learn, through the competition of responsible parties, what the realities of Germany's political situation called for and what the available alternatives were. Consequently, and to make things worse, the radical wings hostile to the constitutional system gained at the expense of the more moderate and responsible parties and leaders.

The system adopted after the Second World War and sketched below has not produced comparable results, but on the contrary has led to a continuing trend toward consolidation of parties. Since it still is somewhat proportional — a mixed scheme — it suggests caution about generalizing on proportionalism. Other factors in the situation may outweigh it in the shaping of the party system.

Recent trends · If men were rational, P. R. would have been adopted only in countries prepared to work out a constitutional system which would not make the government dependent upon stable party support in the representative legislative bodies. People would generally have recognized that P. R., whatever its pros and cons — and that, as we have seen, is a complicated problem — leads to the fragmentation of parties and fails to give clearcut decisions by the electorate, and therefore forbids the use of a parliamentary system. In spite of that, France, Italy, and Germany after 1945 adopted a parliamentary system of making the executive dependent upon the parliament and provided for proportional representation besides. When this failed in France, the Fifth Republic in 1958 reverted to a single-member-constituency system combined with the traditional double-voting, or run-off, elections.

Before 1958 in France, proportional representation lists were allowed on a district (department) basis only, but the voter, as in Belgium and Scandinavia, was enabled to change the order of candidates on the list, that is, express a personal preference. (Only 1.7 per cent of the voters made use of this privilege in the election of November 10, 1946). This compromise was expected to contribute "to the growth of a new political pattern, with four or five strong party machines replacing the undisciplined and flexible formations of prewar days." However, the divisive tendencies of P. R. prevailed and the resulting fragmentation of parties greatly contributed to undermining public confidence in the Fourth Republic's system. Men like the then-senator Michel Debré continually attacked the system as vicious along lines suggested in our own analysis.

Even more disruptive than the effect of any single electoral system have been the frequent changes in France from one kind of electoral system to another. Some fifteen times in the last one hundred years, and three times since the war, the electoral system has been completely overhauled to conform to a new majority's concept of justice. Sometimes the changes (from a majority system to P. R. and back; from two ballots to one and back; from large to small constituencies) appeared to have been inspired by considerations of political advantage. In 1951, for example, it was claimed that the new system of electoral alliances or *apparentement* had been introduced for the purpose of depriving the Communist and Gaullist parties of a number of seats in the Assembly proportional to their votes. It is difficult to predict, however, the exact effect of any particular system.[22] In 1958, France's return to a single-member constituency with double ballot was expected to favor established politicians with strong local following and hinder the relatively unknown candidates from the new Gaullist party. But the result was a Gaullist landslide. In spite of the possible therapeutic effect of such occasional mispredictions, the long-run effect of constant electoral manipulation has been to reduce public confidence in the justice and representative character of the system. By doing so, it tends to undermine the general confidence in democracy itself.

In the opinion of Professor Einaudi, in Italy "the usual fateful consequences of proportional representation were avoided." Others are less optimistic. As in France before 1958, proportionality applies primarily to the districts; for the senate, there is provided an opportunity to be elected on a single-member district basis for those who can secure 65 per cent of the votes: the others are handled proportionally. In any case, Italy has stuck to the parliamentary system and is being governed accordingly. Due, however, to the exceptional threat of Soviet domination, the Christian Democrats, the Communists' main opponents, achieved for a number of years an absolute majority in the important lower house. More recently, such a majority has been lacking and the usual barter between a number of parties for the formation of a coalition has weakened the Italian government.

The Germans, too, have modified P. R. somewhat. Abandoning the list system of Weimar days in the *Länder,* where a variety of electoral systems have been used, including a British-imposed straight-majority system, the Germans have instituted two major innovations. One is the exclusion from all representation of a party which fails to receive a specified percentage of the total vote. In Bavaria this percentage is as high as 10 per cent, in others, 5 per cent. Obviously, such a provision deals the death blow to small splinter groups, but it has been attacked as not democratic. The electoral law, while excluding parties which receive less than 5 per cent, seeks to combine majority and P. R. by providing that half of the representatives are to be elected by plurality in one-man constituencies, the other half on the basis of party lists, put forward for the parties in each *Land.* Each *Land* is given a certain number of seats to fill. It is a hybrid which fails to give either the clear decision of the majority system, or the "just reflection" of the P. R.

system. Under this scheme, which has been changed in minor ways several times, the electorate of the Federal Republic has become increasingly polarized into two dominant parties, the Christian and the Social Democrat, with a small Liberal party surviving to date as in England. In recent elections, the trend has been clear; the two parties have consistently gained both in national and local elections. Consequently the demand has been growing for abandoning the present system and substituting a majoritarian system for it. It is thought — overlooking the British case — that one would then get clear alternatives, leading to a definite majority for one or the other party. This would, so Germans think, eliminate the Liberals and would thus prevent them from exerting an excessive influence in the bartering over coalitions with them. The recent emergence of nationalist extremism is also cited as a reason for substituting a majoritarian for a proportional system.[23]

Assessment of past experience · The P. R. system of the Weimar Republic was subjected to searching criticism by both theorists and practitioners. The most thoroughgoing student of this entire controversy arrived at very negative conclusions and goes so far as to assert that proportional representation "caused" the collapse of the Weimar Republic. Maintaining that democracy can reconcile liberty with authority only by subjecting the minority to the will of the majority, he finds that "certain fundamental tendencies are created by proportional representation which make this compromise impossible, replacing it by the kind of constitutional deadlock which is the ideal preparation for dictatorship." The expression "proportional representation" here refers of course primarily to the list system. But what were these "certain fundamental tendencies"? Perhaps most important was the fact that the list system not only stratified existing party organizations, but created new ones. It was much easier to found a new party under the German system than under a majority system. What is more, the parties under such a list system are controlled by the party bosses, who determine who is placed where on the lists. Experience has essentially borne out the predictions of Bagehot as to the rigidity of party lines and the disregard for the marginal voter; it has shown further that the political consequence of that emphasis upon regularity, dogmatism, and creed was the rise of radical extremist parties. Hence the homogeneity which parliamentary government needs is not only not created, but is actually destroyed. Yet, curiously enough, this emphasis upon dogmatism has not banished the impact of special interest groups. On the contrary, each moderate party in Germany tended to become identified with some particular one of these interests, and some interests actually organized parties of their own. The result of such a combination of entrenched interests on the one hand and radical dogmatism on the other was a recurrent deadlock when it came to making up a cabinet. Under such a system, there is rarely any clear "decision" at the polls in terms of which a cabinet could be set up.

Internally, relations between members and leaders tend to become rather authoritarian. It is next to impossible for the party membership to dislodge entrenched leaders. The overweening position of the party bureaucracy was further enhanced by the size of the electoral districts under the list system, which makes personal contacts difficult, if not impossible. While a small constituency depends upon the cooperation of local volunteers for much of the work, such large constituencies allow the party to pay a permanent secretary and to become quite independent of genuine membership cooperation. Unlike the man who seeks election, such party functionaries remain unknown to the electorate, and dissatisfied groups in the party following are unable to make themselves heard. This oligarchic and bureaucratic trend naturally also molded the relations between the rank and file of the representatives and the top men. Having no personal backing in the electorate, they had to look toward the party for support.

Where seats are personally contested under an electoral system, a man seeking election must be able to wage an effective contest; he must be a "vote getter." This brings forward men of the "leader" type. Under the German list system, with its emphasis upon party regularity, a man seeking election had to conform; this brought forward the bureaucratic type. In the German parliament there were many excellent specialists on technical matters, but leaders were decidedly lacking. What made matters worse was the premium such an arrangement places upon older men. Young men find it surprisingly difficult to break into the ranks of all but the most radical parties. Many more detailed demonstrations of the evil workings of the list system of proportional representation could be given, but it ought to be quite clear from this summary that it greatly increases certain defects in the democratic process. In short, the proportional scheme which makes the whole country one constituency and bases its proportionality upon votes for unalterable party tickets (lists) has been found wanting and incompatible with parliamentary government.

As to systems which allow the voter greater freedom to choose between individual candidates, the case is not clear, especially in a system which clearly divides legislative from executive and administrative responsibility, such as that of Switzerland. For here the main concern of the representative body is legislation. While a multiple-party system entails some difficulties, the adequate representation of all important groups in the community is in many respects desirable, particularly when social and racial differences are clear cut and well known. In the second place, under conditions of marked stratification of the social structure, that is, fixed political diversity in the community, proportional representation may be the only system acceptable to the larger minorities. The decisive question here would be how permanent these minorities are. Racial and religious minorities frequently have this rigidity which distinguishes them from traditional English and American conditions: they are quite permanent yet can never hope to grow into a majority. Where such minorities exist, and have reached a state of self-consciousness, they may feel the need for an electoral system which assumes stratified diversity. Yet even here it should be borne in mind that P. R. reinforces such stratification whereas the majority system tones it down.

An interesting case is provided by Austria. Although proportional representation has been in use here for many years, the country has developed a clearly polarized two-party system. This system in turn produced, under the stresses of foreign occupation after the Second World War, a coalition regime of the two parties with the consequence that there was no real opposition. The situation has changed recently, and the Christian Democrats, commanding a small but absolute majority, have now formed a government, with the Socialists in opposition. It is difficult to see what difference a change to the majoritarian system would make under such circumstances.

Proportional systems of representation have given reasonably acceptable results in a number of other small European countries, notably the Scandinavian kingdoms, the Netherlands, and Belgium. Protracted crises in connection with the breakdown of coalitions have not been unknown, but on the whole these countries have enjoyed fairly stable government. In all of them, a special factor plays a stabilizing role, and that is the monarchy. In Belgium, Holland, Sweden, Norway, and Denmark monarchy has survived in a form more nearly resembling older constitutional forms than is true in England. While these governments are parliamentary, in the sense that they must find support in parliament, the royal head of the government still exerts a certain influence in the selection of the candidates, and his moderating tendency is often apparent. It is obvious that the very smallness of these countries allows for an intimacy between Court and parliament which would be hard to maintain in larger countries. In connection with this monarchical tradition, it is important, especially in Holland and Sweden, that traditions have been developed in the administrative field which effectively neutralize a large part of the executive establishment and thus limit parliament largely to the legislative function, as in Switzerland under a separation of powers. None of these countries are great powers. Their foreign policy depends on that of the greater powers. They all strive for neutrality, accepting internationalism as their natural course. When totalitarian aggressiveness, particularly Hitler's, rendered this policy impractical, they all encountered serious difficulties. While proportionalism can scarcely bear the sole responsibility, it certainly did not aid in producing an effective integration of the electorate and thus a clear decision. Since the Second World War, these countries have either continued neutrality, as Switzerland and Sweden, or have vigorously participated in international organizations, or both. Proportionalism does not seem to have significantly weakened the large consensus which the public has formed on these issues.

Conclusion • All this goes to show that the prevalent English and American opinion against proportional representation is traditional. There are special conditions which might mitigate this conclusion. Yet the proportional representation enthusiast, who would argue from the relative success of proportionalism in some small countries that we should try it in Great Britain and the United States, goes wrong. Although in the United States the constitutional order is based upon a separation-of-powers scheme, the President as chief executive must be elected by a simple plurality. While this might act as a deterrent to the development of minor parties, certain religious, class, and race cleavages might, in the course of time, emerge and plague us by their intransigent attitude. The appeal of P. R. lies in the promise it holds out for breaking up corrupt machines. There can be no question that P. R. starts out by doing this quite effectively. But after the machine politicians have caught their breath, they are quite skillful in "taking over" proportional representation. Since proportional representation in the long run strengthens, rather than weakens, party, and that means machine, control, the bosses return with another rampart added to their fortress. Some cities have tried it, and the results are not encouraging. Here is what an experienced American wrote in light of one of these experiments: "We have groups of all sorts and kinds, formed around religious, racial, language, social and other contentious distinctions. Proportional representation invites these groups to seek to harden and intensify their differences by bringing them into political action where they are irrelevant, if not disturbing. A wise election system would invite them to forget these distracting prejudices."[24]

Within the framework of most Continental European countries, the case is again not so clear. For apparently the divisive cleavages of the people often are of such an intensity that any electoral system which does not give these warring groups adequate representation in the legislative process would be unacceptable. Yet, there is more vigorous opposition to P. R., to some extent influenced by the fact that the Communist parties throughout Europe have been firmly supporting it.

At any rate, electoral systems must be seen and studied in relation to the whole constitutional order, as well as to the social and other conditions of the country concerned. Popular government requires the working out of a system adapted to the peculiar needs of the country.

Parliaments as Representative Assemblies
XVI

Introduction · John Stuart Mill's position · Representation as integration · The importance of party structure for the work of parliaments · Procedure and parties · Social composition of membership · Professionalization · Second chambers · Federal representative assemblies · The representativeness of representative assemblies: early studies · Conclusion

Introduction · Parliaments until recently have been the institutional core of modern representative government. At present the executive, particularly when representing a majority party, is forging ahead and is tending to become the heart of representation, as will be shown in Chapter XVIII. Parliaments held the center of the stage until the First World War for many reasons. As election came to be looked upon as the primary basis of legitimate authority and hence of representative qualifications, the position of parliaments was enhanced. The emphasis upon legislation as a man-made body of rules helped to strengthen parliaments, because their public deliberations were peculiarly well adapted to the legislative process. Finally, the doctrine of the separation and balance of powers, particularly as applied to constitutional monarchies strengthened the claim of parliaments, as the representatives of the people, to offer a counterpoise to the Crown. There is a difference between the procedure of such parliaments, and legislatures in Switzerland or the United States, where constitutional provisions made executive and legislative authorities independent of each other. Yet it is difficult to appraise correctly the effect which this difference has had upon the inner working of parliamentary bodies; it seems that the effect is less marked than one might be led to expect. But an effect there is; the contrast in the position of the speaker in the Commons and in the House of Representatives is perhaps the most striking illustration. Whatever the difference, all these elected bodies have in common representative and deliberative functions which, though related, are quite distinct, and hence should be considered separately. They are the specifically political functions, as contrasted with legislative and such like functions. The representative and deliberative functions are in turn related to the integrative and educative functions; for to represent a multitude means to integrate it, as we have seen; and to discuss and argue public policies means to educate the public concerning them. These functions are but very imperfectly performed by representative bodies in a totalitarian, one-party state, such as the over-all congress of soviets in the U.S.S.R., or the Fascist Grand Council. Such bodies, while still representative, serve as sounding boards for the party leadership; the deliberative and educative functions are crippled in favor of an integrative symbolism.

John Stuart Mill's position · Probably the best-known work on representative assemblies is John Stuart Mill's *Considerations on Representative Government*. Written in 1860, it contains much more criticism than consideration of representative government. Highly normative in outlook and treatment, it continues the long-established preoccupation of the Utilitarians with the reform of established institutions, rather than their description and analysis. It is therefore only in passing, so to speak, that Mill concerns himself with the problems of representation as such. The meaning of "representative government" for him is, he tells us at the beginning of the chapter on the "proper functions of representative bodies," that "the whole people, or some numerous portion of them exercise through deputies periodically elected by themselves the ultimate controlling power, which in every constitution must reside somewhere." And he adds for good measure that "this ultimate power they must possess in all its completeness." The scientific student of modern politics would be inclined to ask: "Has there ever been representative government where this requirement is fulfilled?" And looking at it from the other side, he might add: "Would not governments like that of the Soviet Union claim to be 'representative' in your sense?" The discussion of the functions of representative assemblies in light of this inadequate characterization is surprisingly negative. Thus Mill argues that although representative assemblies are supposed to vote taxes and generally control fiscal matters, "in no country does the representative body prepare the estimates." Recalling that the Commons grant money only on the proposition of the Crown — a principle by no means as universal as he assumes — he concludes that "the sole power it [Parliament] possesses is that of refusal." He thinks that the principles involved in this constitutional doctrine are "a guide to the limitation and definition of the general functions of representative assemblies." But are they? What about the American Congress and state legislatures, none of which accept his doctrine? Mill first of all insists that it is everywhere agreed that "representative assemblies ought not to administer." Principles of good government and sound business forbid it. Yet in spite of it, representative assemblies have managed to administer; they have done so with the help of the device of a committee under a strong chairman. A popular assembly is still less fitted, he claims, to administer or dictate in detail to those who have charge of administration. While true up to a point, American and European assemblies have done a good deal of such "dictating in detail," and, again with the help of committees, have done a fairly good job. "The proper duty of a representative assembly in regard to matters of administration . . . is to take care that the persons who have to decide them will be the proper persons." But even here he has doubts. Since it has never been thought desirable that Parliament should nominate even the members of a cabinet, this function of selection is limited to and concentrated upon the selection of the top few who will do the rest. Carrying his critique further, Mill then surprises us by declaring that "a numerous assembly is as little fitted for the direct business of legislation as for that of administration." The business of making laws is only for "minds trained to the task by long and laborious study." In arguing this proposition, Mill vigorously attacks the English tradition of lawmaking by amateurs, and pits his intellectual elitism against the rising tide of democratic egalitarianism. No belief in the discrimination of the common man mitigates Mill's rationalization of the aristocratic tradition which the British constitution had so effectively institutionalized.

Mill would, however, grant that while a representative assembly is "radically unfit" to govern, its proper office, its true function, is "to watch and control the government; to throw the light of publicity on its acts; to compel a full exposition and justification . . . to censure them . . . and, if the men who compose the government abuse their trust . . . to expel them from office, and appoint their successors." Hence we can sum up Mill's argument as saying that the functions of a representative body are (1) selecting a chief executive, and if need be (2) replacing him, and (3) controlling and supervising him. But only the third of these has been the function of American representative assemblies, while legislating and administering, including more especially budgeting, have been central. So Mill's British-based theory lacks a sufficiently broad empirical base. It has, however, great value by showing us that it may be a function of a representative assembly to choose the top executives, though this function is not inherent in its representative position, whereas legislating, political education, and integration are inherent in its very existence.

Representation as integration · Traditionally, legislation is considered the peculiar province of representative assemblies. Representative assemblies are in fact referred to as *"the* legislature," although it is always at once conceded that these assemblies do not have exclusive control over legislation nor are they concerned only with legislation. Nevertheless, legislation is traditionally looked upon as their primary function. Such a view is formal rather than political. Politically speaking, the function of making laws is nowadays at least as much carried on by the central bureaucracy, which drafts all important bills in England, France, and other European countries, and to an increasing extent in the United States.[2] The political function of representative assemblies today is not so much the initiation of legislation as the carrying on of popular education and propaganda and the integration and coordination of conflicting interests and viewpoints. The representative must be a master in the art of compromise. Parliaments and parliamentarians appear as integrating agencies through which the policy of the government and the claims of the various interest groups are expounded to the larger public with a view to discovering a suitable balance. At this point, the representative and the deliberative function are linked. There can be little doubt that the educational function is highly significant. The average citizen needs to have the pros and cons of pending proposals dramatized for him. The clash of argument in representative groups helps this greatly. The drama of the filibustering Senator, though often arousing indignation, helps the citizen to appreciate the implications and significance of new legislation. The consequences of the lack of such contact between the government and the citizen are very apparent in totalitarian regimes. A great many measures of the government, which may be intrinsically necessary, meet with sullen indifference if not with hostility from the people merely because they are not understood. Occasional rhetorical outbursts on the part of a few leaders are not sufficient.

Integration is not, however, automatic, but highly dependent upon the structure of thought and outlook, feeling and interest, of the electorate. Hence the pious formula that representatives are not bound by mandate, that they are subject only to their conscience and are supposed to serve the common weal, which is repeated in so many European constitutions, while significant as a norm, may lead to differentiating as well as to integrating results. As in mathematics, so in politics, differential and integral functions are interrelated. One of the most dramatic instances of recent years in this field occurred in many countries, but more especially in the United States, just before the outbreak of hostilities of the Second World War. Popular sentiment became increasingly polarized as interventionists and isolationists in and out of Congress propagandized and educated the public to the dramatic issue of peace and war. Two large national organizations, the Committee to Defend America by Aiding the Allies (William Allen White Committee) and the America First Committee, spearheaded the contending forces. But while the sharp conflict — which was almost an even one, judging by the financial resources of each side — seemed to differentiate to the extent of almost dividing the American people into two halves, a broad integrating process was taking place on a deeper level. Both groups, and the many minor ones associated with them, were represented in the Congress; many Congressmen sought hard to maintain a middle ground and effect a compromise. The underlying integrating factor appears in the title of both organizations: "America." For what happened in the course of the struggle between the contending parties, both seeking to represent America, was to arouse the American people to the need to *defend* America. As was pointed out in the discussion of representation, it is the elected assembly as a whole which represents the people. Majority and minority acting jointly, therefore, have a powerful integrating effect. When, at the outbreak of war, all but a few act together in supporting the government, the unity of the people is strikingly represented, and integration reaches a high point. National emergencies can have the same effect. No single executive, elected by a majority, can be as integrating as such a joining together of opponents.

We have seen in an earlier chapter that representation and responsibility are closely linked. Representatives of the people are intended to be responsible to those whom they represent; in turn such responsible conduct enhances the representative quality. In fact, it is not too much to say that systems of representation developed out of the need of insuring constitutional responsibility. More especially elections, by permitting a recurrent review of the actions of representatives at regular intervals, are supposed to be the most rational method of establishing responsible government. This review was facilitated by the development of parties; they both differentiate and integrate. While trying to integrate as many voters as possible, they succeed in integrating perhaps half of them, the other half being integrated by a competing group of leaders. Such polarization of the electorate into two focal differentiations is characteristic of the major system of representation, while the proportional system, as we have seen, produces multiple differentiation. Which of the two systems will more nearly facilitate over-all integration of the community for purposes of constitutional government depends upon circumstances; we have seen that the social composition and structure of an electorate, such as class, religious, and cultural groupings, are important in this connection. The problem is also intimately linked to the pattern of executive-legislative relationships, which are discussed below in chapter XVIII.

The importance of party structure for the work of parliaments · The organization and structure of parliaments is profoundly affected by party organization. A two-party system divides the house into two more or less equal parts. In line with this fact, the English House of Commons is divided into two halves facing each other. One half is supposed to be occupied by the party supporting the government, the other half by His Majesty's Opposition. In the American Congress, both Senate and House, the representatives are scattered according to seniority and personal preference. The committees in the American Congress are composed of members of both parties, but the chairman is of the major party, as is the Speaker of the House. This may tend to obscure political realities; in the United States, the genuine battle line is frequently that between conservatives and progressives, rather than between Republicans and Democrats. Hence the administration cannot "count" on the committees staying in line. Another difficulty in the United States arises from the strength of sectional-interest and local-interest representation, especially in the Senate. Again, we see the impact of party organization here: Senators and Representatives are put forward by state party organizations.

Following the French tradition, a multiple-party system may range from conservatism to radicalism. Again, as in the German parliament of the Weimar Republic, it may possess a cluster of moderate groups at the center, surrounded by groups of radical extremists who might be either reactionary or revolutionary, or both. The seating arrangements in parliaments often are expressive of the innate structure and relationship of the groups contained in it.[3] Thus, if the conservatives sit on the right side of the house and the radicals on the left, as was the case in the French Constituent Assembly of 1789 and has been the case in France ever since, it is possible to speak of the "right" or "left" in a symbolic sense. It is a tribute to the force of French ideas that these expressions are now used in countries like England and the United States where no such seating arrangement is actually found.

It is obvious that the work methods of representative assemblies will be different, depending upon who sits in them. If each shade of public opinion is set off in a separate party, debates will tend to become a series of speeches, each speech representing one of those parties. Appointments to committees will be determined by party membership, since care must be taken that each party is represented, and so forth.

Procedure and parties · One may ask what effect a certain procedure has upon party development. We have already, in several connections, referred to the famous protection of the minority under English parliamentary procedure. Authorities are agreed that the several devices provided for this purpose greatly aided the Irish Nationalists in developing their party organization. In the French Third Republic, the practice of providing for the election of the all-important committees by arbitrary divisions of the Chamber, the so-called *bureaux,* checked the development of real parties by emphasizing the individual member of parliament. In Germany, where the system of proportional representation adopted under the Weimar Republic produced many small splinter parties, a rule was introduced according to which only parties represented by a certain number of deputies could claim seats on the committees. This was done in order to discourage the election of representatives of such small parties by making it impossible for such representatives to accomplish anything. In the United States Senate, the loose procedure for closure only in extreme emergencies, as Lindsay Rogers once showed, has greatly aided the maintenance of "independents" and other opposition groups.

In England many new and vexing questions arose after 1919 when the Labour party tried to carry on the government as a minority party with the "support" of the Liberals. Procedure in the House of Commons has in more recent times been developed in response to the system of a cabinet responsible to the majority of the House of Commons. This procedure proved very ill-adapted to the needs of a minority government, and it may well be questioned whether the Labour party was wise in agreeing to form a government without insisting upon sweeping changes in the rules of procedure. The difficulties became quite apparent during the very first debate on the Address to the Throne in 1929. The Labour government could not get preference for government bills, being opposed on this vital issue by Conservatives and Liberals alike. It is conceivable that it might have made this very issue a question of confidence; for here was the test as to Liberal "support."

While a Conservative attempt to force a commitment on the protective tariff was defeated with the aid of the Liberals, a Liberal effort to secure the repeal of the Home Rule for Scotland Bill (passed by the preceding Conservative government) was defeated with the support of the Conservatives. In other words, the Labour government was at the very outset shorn of real "leadership," such as Bryce had claimed existed in the House of Commons, because it did not command a majority. English procedure, developed for a two-party system, was unfit for the new situation (for which the procedure of the Swedish *Riksdag*, for example, is preferable). As a consequence, procedural handicaps prevented the Labour government from doing any real work and measurably discredited it with the people. But that situation has now come to appear "marginal." The situation after 1931 returned to the "normal" two-party arrangement, except for the wartime coalition. Before 1939, the Labour party, and since 1945, the Conservative party, have played the traditional role of His (Her) Majesty's Loyal Opposition. In 1950 the Labour party met its first *real* challenge as a majority government facing a general election. Thereafter English parliamentary procedure was put to a difficult test after the election of 1963, when the Labour party had a very slim majority of only a few seats. This situation once again made Labour depend upon Liberal support, even though the party was small. But by skill-ful leadership and vigorous discipline, the party managed until a general election could give it a much broader base of operations.[4]

Social composition of membership • Even more important, perhaps, than the party system is the social composition of the representative assembly. There can be little doubt that the aristocratic backbone of the English Parliament which persisted throughout the nineteenth century was of great importance in giving to that body a certain homogeneity of outlook and a code of "gentlemanly" conduct which materially affected its mode of proce-dure.[5] What is more, the willingness of the English aristocracy to absorb new members who distinguished themselves in public affairs added a power-ful social sanction to whatever conventional restraints were suggested by such a code. The reverse side of this gentlemanly tradition was described by George Bernard Shaw, albeit with typical satirical exaggeration, when he wrote: "It is the secret of our governing class who, though perfectly pre-pared to be generous, humane, cultured, philanthropic, public-spirited, and personally charming, in the second instance, are unalterably resolved in the first to have money enough for a handsome and delicate life, and will, in pursuit of that money, batter in the doors of their fellowmen, sell them up, sweat them in fetid dens, shoot, stab, hang, imprison, sink, burn and destroy them in the name of law and order."[6] In France and Germany, where parlia-ments arose in opposition not only to the monarchy but also to the exclusive hereditary aristocracy which supported it, professional men, particularly lawyers and to a lesser degree journalists, predominated in elective bodies at the outset. However, in more recent times, the peculiar feature of French parliaments has been the relatively large number of farmers (and estate owners), with a fairly even distribution between other professional groups. The two outstanding features of the German and other parliaments of the 1920's were the numerous representatives of economic interest groups (the so-called *syndics*, lawyers for trade associations, and the trade-union offi-cials) and the surprisingly large number of public officials; there were be-tween one hundred and one hundred and fifty such officials in the parliament of the Weimar Republic. Their entrance into parliament had been facilitated by the constitutional provision which allowed them to attend parliament irrespective of their administrative duties.

The same situation is developing again. In the assembly to draft the Basic Law of 1949 sat forty-three officials out of a total of seventy, or roughly 60 per cent. The percentage has since declined; the German *Bundestag* elected in 1965 contained 163 civil servants out of a total of 518 deputies, or 31 per cent. This is interesting in view of the opposition made to the attempts of

American and British occupation authorities to have such an arrangement abolished as incompatible with "democracy." These efforts foundered upon the counterclaim of the German Social Democrats, who declared that to bar such officials would be undemocratic. Many other Continental Europeans would say the same. Among these officials there is a fair sprinkling of university professors, a group which is notably absent from American legislatures. The socialist parties have found among the lower officialdom men reasonably well-suited for parliamentary work, but such men are of course not willing to sacrifice their tenure and pension claims for anything as temporary as a parliamentary seat.[7] The situation in France is roughly similar, though in France deputies are forbidden not only to be concurrently in government service, but to have held certain positions within six months of running for office. Yet civil servants can contest local elections and sit on local councils so long as they do not occupy posts which are dependent on, or connected with, the councils in question. Civil servants cannot sit in parliament while remaining active in the service. They can, however, contest a seat while remaining in active service. There are only a few exceptions to this: thus prefects — who are direct agents of the government — may not stand for election within the area of their prefecture (nor may they stand there until after they have left the area for six months). Civil servants need not resign from the service once elected; they become *detachés* and must be taken back into active service, if they so desire, when they lose their seat.[8] It is a difficult problem in view of the steady expansion of officialdom with the growth of the "welfare state."

Studies of the social background of representative bodies have multiplied in recent years, and one wishes it were possible to report on all of them. One of the most interesting and elaborate is that carried through for Italy. The learned researcher studied not only the social background, but such other factors as age, geographic origin, class level, and education. On the latter point, it was surprising to find that over 70 per cent of the elected deputies of the four national representative assemblies studied (a total of 1,358 deputies) have a university education, and that over half of these are graduates of a law school. A breakdown by parties shows that the Communist party, in contrast to other socialist parties, has a substantially lower percentage of university-educated deputies.

A breakdown according to professions which does not highlight the part officials play shows that the liberal professions have 34 per cent, teachers 16 per cent (university 6 per cent, high school 9 per cent, primary 1 per cent), business 14.8 per cent (divided half and half between entrepreneurs and managerial personnel), journalists 4 per cent, and workers 1.3 per cent — a truly amazing figure in light of the strength of leftist parties in Italy —

while the remaining 22.8 per cent (7.1 per cent of nondesignated apart) belong to what are called "professional politicians," divided into 13.9 per cent who are party professionals, and 8.9 per cent who are trade-union professionals. If we take also into account that 27.2 per cent of the liberal-profession category are lawyers (*avocats*), the "professionalization" and the bureaucratization of the Italian parliament appears striking. The study proceeds to a breakdown of these figures in terms of party, and while there are some considerable deviations, the pattern as a whole seems to suggest that the Christian Democrats, with percentages roughly paralleling the over-all figures, appear reasonably typical. There is one striking contrast: the Communist party deputies are largely (64.6 per cent) professional politicians; they too have only 1 per cent manual workers. After discriminating remarks concerning the vagueness of the term "professionalization," the author finally offers statistical evidence to show that from session to session the professionals have increased, the non- and half-professionals decreased, in number. Even so, the author warns against definitive conclusions, even though clearly his results resemble those in other countries of Europe.[9]

In all these parliaments, there has however occurred a steady increase of members who formerly were workers. Almost all these so-called workers are, unlike the traditional farmer in American representative assemblies, not men who come directly from the factory, but men who have risen through the trade-union bureaucracy and are therefore actually trade-association officials when they go into parliament. Still, the inclusion of labor representatives is an important democratic gain and one in keeping with the forward march of constitutionalism. The only real drawback is that it (along with other developments) has contributed toward a gradual increase of the heterogeneity of parliaments. This social heterogeneity has multiplied frictions and complicated parliamentary work.

Professionalization • The problem of the professionalization, and in fact bureaucratization, of parties and parliaments has been a subject of concern to political scientists and political sociologists for quite a few years. Especially some leading German and Italian scholars have offered analyses in this field of study.[10] Leaving aside for later treatment the party aspect of the problem, it is important to be clear as to what is meant by these terms. At least four meanings may be distinguished when speaking of professionalization and bureaucratization.[11] First, there is a functional sense, which involves the specialization of representatives in terms of particular fields of competence, such as agricultural or fiscal policy. Second, there is the sense in which elected representatives acquire particular operational skills after years of service in legislative assemblies. Third, there is the sense in which professionalization, or perhaps rather bureaucratization, brings with it an increasing distance from those represented, makes the representative less "representative" in an existential sense. This in turn and *fourth* means that the representative has only the profession of being a politician; he "lives" politics. This of course also means that he lives "off politics," i.e., he makes his living by attending to politics. That such a person is far removed from what Mill had in mind when he denied the capacity for legislation and fiscal policy to a representative assembly is obvious. That such professionalization, especially in the fourth sense, but based on the first and third sense, promotes the formation of permanent committees is obvious. Such professionalized committeemen often possess greater knowledge of precise detail in budgetary or agricultural matters than the minister and his subordinates. Their representative quality may at the same time have changed, as they come to think of themselves as representatives of agriculture or labor, rather than of the nation at large.

Second chambers · Since the Parliament Act of 1911, the question of whether or not there is a place for the continued existence of the House of Lords within the modern constitutional machinery has never ceased to command popular interest. The Conservatives favor its retention, even its extension, while many Liberals and the Labour party demand its radical change or abolition. This view is partly the result of partisan considerations: the House of Lords with its several hundred peers has always contained a large Conservative majority. In spite of the very wide use made by the Liberal party after 1905 of the Crown's prerogative to create peers, and a further use made by the Labour party after 1945, there were in 1954 only one hundred and nineteen Liberal and Labour peers out of a total membership of more than eight hundred. This development may be dated from 1886, when Gladstone split the Liberal party over the issue of Home Rule for Ireland; a great many members of rank and position went over to the Conservatives as "unionists."[12]

The Labour government, while at one time committed to the abolition of the House of Lords, has so far only reduced the period that the Lords may delay legislation. This is no doubt due in part to the large Conservative majority in the Lords showing a marked degree of self-restraint. There exists, for example, a traditional rule that the Lords should not negate any policy for which the government has a mandate from the people.

The problem of the House of Lords revolves around the question of representativeness. From the standpoint of electoral majorities, the House of Lords is merely an anachronism; "it represents," as one wit has remarked, "nobody but itself, and therefore enjoys the full confidence of its constituents."[13] But representativeness is not necessarily insured by an election, by a simple counting of heads. It may be based upon objective achievement, and a variety of other believed-in qualifications, such as birth or the possession of property. Such qualifications may be wholly illusory. As Benjamin Franklin once remarked, to pick legislators on the basis of heredity is just as sensible as to pick professors of mathematics in that fashion. But elections by electoral majorities may also fail to produce representatives, as we have seen in our survey of electoral methods.

It is a curious but noteworthy fact that the voices demanding the abolition of the House of Lords have declined in number and vigor. Indeed, the express purpose of the Parliament Act of 1911, which stripped the Lords of their ancient prerogatives to a very considerable extent, namely, to pave the way for giving the second chamber a "popular basis," has not been the focus of the reforms effectuated since then. The Parliament Act of 1949, the Life Peerages Act of 1958, and the Peerage Act of 1963 have rather sought to make the second chamber more useful than to abolish it. One writer suggests that after 1945 "the volume of government work was so great that a Second Chamber could hardly be dispensed with."[14] Some defenders of the Lords go a step further and speak of the "dangers of single-chamber government." The arguments in support of this contention are familiar and, federal states apart, not very convincing, except in terms of ideological conservatism. "Moderation and restraint," "continuity and tradition," and similar terms refer to real values and interests, but it is more than doubtful that only a second chamber can secure them. It is the same as with the argument over the conservatism of courts; courts may become actively engaged in promoting social change, and a House of Lords may become similarly occupied, unlikely as it seems. Certainly the decision of the House of Lords after Labour came into power in 1945 to accept its radical proposals for the nationalization of much economic activity, because they had a popular mandate for doing so, exhibited a self-restraint which meant abdicating the "moderating and restraining" which are to serve "continuity and tradition."

Even so, the delay which an adverse vote of the House of Lords can now cause a bill adopted by the Commons is only one year. Other than that, the 1949 act left the Lords as before because the talks broke down on the issue of what are the proper functions of a second chamber. Obviously, these functions ought to determine on what basis to choose the Lords, if it is generally agreed that "a hereditary legislative chamber is an anachronism in a modern democratic state."[15] But without altering the functions, the Life Peerages Act of 1958 empowered the Crown to bestow the title of a lord upon any commoner (or peer) for distinguished service and thereby enable him to participate in the work of the Lords. Reversely, the Peerage Act of

1963 made it possible for hereditary peers to renounce their title for their own lifetime and thus enable them to participate in the more vital branch of the representative body. But the problem of functions remained in abeyance.

The classic statement by Bryce in his Report of 1918 on the Conference on the Reform of the Second Chamber is still a good guide.[16] He described the Lords' work in terms of four functions, (1) the examination and revision of bills, (2) the initiation of noncontroversial bills, (3) the delay in the adoption of bills, and (4) full and free discussion of broad questions of policy. There is little question that these functions could be better performed by a body of lifetime peers than by a hereditary chamber. Yet, not very many such lifetime peers have been created, forty-five by the end of 1963. Clearly the Life Peers Act could be an effective instrument to create a chamber of experienced men and women who could explore in depth the problems of public policy which agitate the nation. But so far it has not happened. This is partly due to the fact that there are other ways, such as advisory committees and the like, which more nearly are in keeping with contemporary technical trends than a broadly based representative assembly. Still, the debate over the "reform" of the House of Lords goes on.

All such proposals for change assume that a second chamber is intrinsically worthwhile and desirable. As was shown in the discussion of federalism, such a body is important because it provides the basis for a balancing group of representatives, one house representing the whole people, the other the federated units. But there is also the question of a second chamber as a check upon the first. While such a check has appealed to some, it is this check upon the popularly elected majority which has brought forth the most virulent attacks as well. The *Labour Speakers' Handbook* declared in 1923: "Abolish the Second Chamber altogether; any second chamber would be a reactionary body. . . ."[17] This is practical politics rather than sound theory; a second chamber composed in large part of the representatives of organized labor would evidently not be reactionary. But Labour's view is in the tradition of Benthamite radicalism, pure and unadulterated; a second chamber Bentham regarded as "needless, useless, worse than useless." His objection was based strictly on logical grounds. Since the end of government is "the greatest happiness of the greatest number," a legislative assembly should be based on universal suffrage. There is no room for a second chamber. If it represents the general interest, it is useless; if it represents only a particular interest, it is bad. If the first chamber has not produced the proper kind of legislation, the right check is to turn it out (or to improve it), but not to establish a second chamber. This argument apparently holds only as long as one accepts Bentham's rational view of human beings. If all human beings acted rationally and farsightedly, there would be no sense in a second chamber except under federalism. But since they do not, such chambers may fulfill a variety of useful functions. The House of Lords does fulfill some such functions, through thorough debate of nonpartisan issues. While a large number of the members are of no use in either legislation or other matters, the limited group of genuinely interested lords (and these, incidentally, are much more nearly balanced between the parties) brings a degree of detachment, experience, and leisure to the discussion which is lacking in the House of Commons.

Bentham's line of reasoning also disregards the time factor. For it might happen, as it did happen in France in 1851, or in Germany in 1933, that "it is too late" for any turning out. Accordingly, the previously mentioned parliamentary committee agreed that it is desirable to interpose "so much delay (and no more) in the passing of a bill into law as may be needed to enable the opinion of the nation to be adequately expressed upon it. This would be especially needed as regards bills which affect the fundamentals of the Constitution or introduce new principles of legislation, or which raise issues whereon the opinion of the country may appear to be almost equally divided."[18] It is not really so much a matter of expression of opinion, as of crystallization. The cabinet governs in accordance with the general mandate of the majority, but there are issues upon which more than a majority may be desirable. As far as representation is concerned, it is all a question of who should be represented in the particular community. If persistent subdivisions entitled to separate representation are contained in it, or if certain interests are recognized as of paramount importance from a government viewpoint, two chambers may be desirable. It is undeniably true that such dualism raises grave complications, but these may be offset in part by the gain in providing for a reasonable and convincing division of powers, thus aiding the maintenance of a constitutional order.

Federal representative assemblies · All three, the United States, Switzerland, and Germany, provided for participation of the component units in the formation of general policy and legislation for the whole commonwealth. Each organized a scheme of representation for the whole which is a compromise between a federational scheme, in which the representative assembly is exclusively composed of representatives of the component units, and a unitary scheme, in which national representation is based upon legislatively determined subdivisions of the whole.[19] Thus in the Congress of the United States the Senate represents equally the people of each state while the House of Representatives represents the people in the districts as determined by Congress. Traditionally, this difference finds expression in the claim that the

Senate represents the states, the House the people. Actually (see below, ch. XIV), the Congress as a whole represents the people as a whole, and each individual member his constituency. Similarly, the Swiss Council of Estates, representing the cantons, contrasts with the National Council, representing the several districts on a numerical basis. This sort of compromise, dividing as it does the legislative power, provides a rather effective constitutional restraint, and one which appears reasonable. It is, however, important to keep in mind the mounting criticism which has in recent years been leveled at the American Senate as "unrepresentative" of the people. What this means is that the federational equality of the component units within a federal structure conflicts with the "democratic" equality of the citizens within the federal whole. The Senate, it is claimed, distorts the popular "will." Each voter of Alaska has seventy-four times as much voting strength in the Senate as has each voter of New York, because Alaska has 226,000 inhabitants, and New York has 16,782,000.* Similarly, there are sixteen states with less than 1,000,000 inhabitants, giving them (with a total population of a little over 10 million inhabitants) thirty senators, as compared with only two senators for California, which has a greater population (15,717,000) than these sixteen states combined. In certain matters over which the Senate has a large measure of control, such as foreign or agricultural policy, this difference may be of considerable consequence, because region is often arrayed against region. During the thirties, the prevalence of isolationist sentiment in rural unpopulous states probably forced upon the country a more cautious course than might otherwise have been necessary. Certain writers have therefore argued that a maintenance of a federal scheme in the United States will require a consolidating and regrouping of the component units. "The states as at present geographically constituted have lost all reality as economic units. Even as rough boundaries of cultural unity and traditional loyalties, there are few of them that possess enough vitality to resist the inevitable march toward federal centralization."[20] This view is hotly contested by some people, and not only states' righters; those strongly in favor of centralization feel, too, that such larger component units would be objectionable, because they would throw greater obstacles in the path of the central authorities. Whatever the merits or demerits of such a change, the United States would still retain a federational representative assembly composed in part of representatives of the component units. In view of this fact, it may be well to consider whether the divergencies are not being exaggerated when we compare Alaska with New York. After all, Alaska and New York together contain less than 10 per cent of the population of the United States. If we

---

* These figures are based on the Census of 1960.

list all the states in order of their population, we find that, with the exception of Alaska on one end and California and New York on the other, they constitute a series, few elements of which are more than 20 per cent apart, and the mean difference between them is such that they approximate a statistical continuum.

The Swiss have likewise provided strict equality of the component units, called cantons, in their Council of Estates. Further concessions are made to their federational past by leaving the election and tenure of these representatives (two for each canton, and one for each half-canton) to the cantons themselves. Unlike the Senate of the United States, the Swiss States' Council is on an even keel with the popular National Council, as far as functions are concerned; it has neither more nor fewer. Once the members are elected, they are, however, no longer dependent upon the cantons; legally, they cannot be instructed regarding their vote. Actually, there is between them and their electors the usual interplay. In most cantons today, the members of the States' Council are elected by the people; but in some of them election is still by the cantonal representative assembly. In recent years, the principle of equal representation has been attacked, and efforts have been made from time to time to introduce a system which would take account of the differences in population. For in Switzerland, too, the differences between the weight of votes are quite striking. A citizen in the canton of Uri, with 23,000 inhabitants, has thirty times as much influence upon federal legislation through the States' Council as has a citizen of the canton of Bern, with 690,249. However, no such efforts have thus far been successful. In spite of these divergencies, Swiss cantons are roughly like American states in that they can be arranged in a series in which no two consecutive elements differ excessively from each other. Their population figures, too, form a fair statistical continuum.

Germany has always had a distinctive pattern of representative institutions. Due to the strength of bureaucratic authoritarianism in the monarchies which were united into a federal empire in 1871, the federal representative assembly was combined with a "council" of administrative officials, representing their several princes. The two federal republican constitutions followed this scheme; both in 1919 and 1949 a similar council was retained, so that the German legislative organ is composed of two somewhat separate bodies. The popular chamber is a typical parliament, a deliberative assembly representing the nation at large. The other body is composed of the minister-presidents of the several *Länder;* most of the time, however, they delegate their authority to other ministers and lower officials. Thus to this day, the Council has remained a "congress of ambassadors" in which each *Land* speaks as one, even though it has several votes.

The persistence of the German tradition was demonstrated after the Second World War. Although a strong movement for the establishment of a true second chamber of the senate type made itself felt, especially among the Social Democrats, the Basic Law of 1949 resuscitated the *Bundesrat* or Federal Council. To make doubly sure that this council would not evolve in the direction of a senate, that is to say, to make sure that votes by party would be excluded, the constitution provides that each *Land* is obliged to vote as one. Due to the relatively similar size of the eleven *Länder,* it would have been easy at least to provide for equality of representation by giving each *Land* one vote. Instead the votes are made somewhat proportional to size, with three, four, and five respectively. This has proved significant from a political and party standpoint, because the majorities in the *Bundestag* may and have differed from those in the Council, especially the qualified ones required for constitutional amendments. The functions of this council are limited, but they pertain to both legislation and administration. The government's bills must pass through the Federal Council. What this means, even though a limit of three weeks is set, is that all federal government bills, before being introduced, come to the attention of *Land* governments, which thus secure the valuable opportunity to object. Without going into details, it should be noted that the Council also has considerable powers of delay, through veto and otherwise, but can be overruled. What is more, constitutional amendments require approval by two thirds of the Council. The Council also participates in the making of administrative ordinances and has an important part in the fiscal procedures and powers of the federal government. The retention of the council type was probably a mistake. The chamber type of federal representative assembly seems to be better adapted to popular government, because it responds more readily to the party system without which popular government cannot be successfully operated.[21]

Austria, by contrast, adopted the senate principle in its original American form, but without admitting equality of the *Länder.* The complicated compromise between strict equality and strict proportionality produced (in 1945) a variation from three to twelve (Vienna), and a total of fifty members of this second chamber, called the Federal Council. The election is by the parliaments of the several *Länder,* on the basis of proportional representation, with some exceptions, and these representatives lose their mandate when the mandate of the parliament which elected them ends. The Austrian representative assembly is relatively weak, as is its German counterpart. It may initiate laws, it ordinarily has the right to object to proposed laws, and sometimes its consent to such laws is required; a third of this council may force a referendum on a proposed constitutional amendment.[22]

The representativeness of representative assemblies: early studies •
We have so far considered parliaments as representative assemblies in terms
of certain institutional devices and social conditions which these parliaments
have developed in the past. It is, however, possible to study the representativeness of elected representatives and the behavior of such groups in terms
of the statistical picture which their votes offer to the investigator. Years ago
Stuart Rice made a very interesting attempt along these lines. He analyzed
the votes in selected American representative bodies in the hope of throwing
light upon two moot points regarding such bodies. It is often assumed that
a legislator is representative because voters tend to select men of their own
"kind" to office, even though similarity in kind may be based on the voter's
"identification" of himself with the social, economic, or intellectual attributes
of the officeholder. Related to this is the second notion that such a legislator
is representative because he responds to legislative issues on the whole in
about the same manner as would his fellow group members in the constituency. In order to verify these assumptions or hypotheses, Rice undertook to
correlate the "progressiveness" of Minnesota legislators with the "progressiveness" of their districts. The *indications* were that such a relation did exist,
although the coefficient of correlation was no higher "than could be reasonably expected." This tested the first assumption; other studies along this line
have been made since. In terms of our prior hypothesis it may be found that
the assumptions should rather be that a legislator is representative because
he effectively correlates with existing notions legislative issues brought forward by special interest groups and is successful in selecting those for attention which, through education and propaganda, he can "put across" to his
fellow group members in the constituency. In other words, he is a specialist
in diagnosing group opinion in his constituency, and knows just how far to
go in order to strike a balance between the pressure from various special
groups and the resistance (passive pressure) from the group as a whole.

Now as to the first point, that voters tend to select men of their own
"kind," Rice selected as the social factor the representative's *nationality*.
He had already explicitly excluded as possible factors, wealth, legal and
political training, and possibly education generally. In order to determine
the influence of nationality, that is, to find an answer to the question of
whether voters tend to select as representatives persons of their own nationality, Rice studied the members of both houses of the legislature in Minnesota and Wisconsin for several years. These legislators were selected, he tells
us, on the basis of availability, of personal familiarity with these states, and
an arrangement of legislative districts generally conforming to county lines
(which is the unit used by the census). More than a hundred of these

legislators were born in foreign countries. A quotient which Rice called "the ratio of nationality excess" was calculated for each district in terms of its representative to determine whether there was a higher percentage of that nationality in the district than in the state at large. He found that there existed "a well marked disposition on the part of the foreign-born voters to elect men of their own nationality to the legislature." While this is probably true, the data examined do not justify so explicit a conclusion, but rather the more modest one that there existed a well-marked disposition on the part of districts with an excess of voters of a certain nationality to elect a representative from that nationality; for as to who voted no data were examined at all. It must be remembered that where such an excess was found, a greater probability existed that men from that nationality would be available for election to a representative assembly. It would be highly desirable, if many more such explorations could be undertaken, to trace out the extent to which and the conditions under which the assumption from which Rice started is correct.

Comparative and historical material of a less quantitative though of a sufficiently definite sort suggests that under different social and political conditions the impact of nationality is even more pronounced than would appear from Rice's analysis. In Switzerland, for example, it is a matter of course that the French-speaking cantons elect French-speaking representatives, the Italian-speaking cantons Italian-speaking representatives, and the German-speaking cantons German. Of course, in most of these cantons there would appear a high "ratio of nationality excess."[23] Again, in prewar Germany, the Poles elected Polish representatives. Czechoslovakia offered another interesting political arena of a similar sort, where the antipathy of nationalities toward each other was at times so profound as to make election of a representative of the other nationality utterly inconceivable. Germans, Slovaks, Hungarians, Ruthenians — all these struggled against the Czechs and against each other with such intensity that the nationality issue was of paramount significance, whereas in Minnesota and Wisconsin it is a minor factor. Again, Czechoslovakia and Switzerland have proportional representation, which favors the separate representation of distinctive groups; thus in Czechoslovakia such subdivisions as German, as well as Slovak and Czech Socialists, were found. The situation is, of course, more complex in some of the developing countries, such as India.[24] Various factors, in other words, may carry different weight, depending upon the electoral system. Here would be a "political" condition, as contrasted with the previous "social" condition, affecting the weight of the nationality factor. What is true of the nationality factor is, of course, equally true of the factor of "class," for example. Restating the first assumption of Rice, and in keeping with our general analysis of representation, it might be better to say that a person is representative because voters tend to reject men who do not possess certain traits which correspond to dominant objectives and prejudices of the voters themselves. These traits could probably be arranged in an order of relative weight, such ratings presumably being subject to variations under differing social and political conditions. It is doubtful whether the distinction between rational and irrational objectives, interests, prejudices, and so forth, would serve any useful purpose in this connection. Rational interests, such as a trade union's interest in higher wages, may take precedence over any irrational prejudice against a representative of a foreign nationality, or vice versa. Stuart Rice opened up a rich field of enquiry bearing upon the representativeness of representative groups.[25] Unfortunately, the subject has not since then been as extensively researched as might be expected.

Conclusion • After pointing out that parliamentary assemblies had become the core of modern representative government in the course of the nineteenth century, we showed that their prime function is not so much the initiation of legislation or the making of laws as the carrying on of popular education and propaganda, and the integration and coordination of conflicting interests and viewpoints. Parliaments and parliamentarians, it was said, appear as integrating agencies through which the policy of the government and the claims of the various interest groups are expounded to the public, with a view of discovering a suitable compromise. It was shown how important party structure is for the innner workings of such bodies, and the role which the social composition of members plays in their work. The progress of professionalization and the consequences for the representativeness of representatives was noted. The problem of second chambers was shown to be intimately related to the structure of the community, and to whether any permanent subdivisions required separate representation. The most important of these possibilities is provided by federalism. Basing our argument upon the general treatment of federalism, a comparison of the representative federal chambers in the major federal systems was offered, showing the basic importance of the principle of equality. All such institutional studies of past practices require, it is submitted, implementation by statistical analysis of present practices as manifested in the voting behavior of representative groups under the most varied conditions, socially, economically, politically. Quite a few studies along such lines have been made since the pioneering researches of Stuart Rice. They seem to suggest that the general assumptions underlying the present study, concerning representation and the function of elected bodies of representatives within the modern constitutional order, are in keeping with the facts. But much further inquiry is indicated.

Ultimately, the representative function of elected assemblies depends upon the general recognition that not the majority alone, but majority and minority together, represent the nation. As Jennings has put it, in concluding his work on *Parliament:* "The one permits the other to govern because the second permits the first to oppose, and together they lead their parties in the operation of the constitutional machine. The 'National' Government is truly national because it has a National Opposition and the people are free."[26] In short, majority and minority together *represent* the people.

Parliaments as Deliberative Assemblies
XVII

Introduction · Modern parliaments not only represent the "will" of the people, they also deliberate. Their political function is a double one: as representatives they integrate the community through periodic appeals, based upon a continuous process of education and propaganda; as a deliberative body they endeavor to solve concrete problems of communal activity — to do or not to do, that is the question. While the two functions are closely intertwined, they may, from the standpoint of political science, usefully be distinguished, as the present chapter will attempt to show. A parliament, it will be seen, deliberates upon many questions and decides many issues upon which it does not and could not consult the "will" of the people, nor does it attempt to develop such a will by education and propaganda. On all such occasions, publicity is unnecessary, often even undesirable. Procedural devices have been developed to guard the confidential nature of such deliberations.[1] In the age of Dr. Johnson no person with as much as a pencil was allowed within the halls of Parliament. An anecdote told of Johnson well illustrates this point. In a tavern, friends were discussing the quality of parliamentary oratory when one amongst their number recited verbatim a speech of the elder Pitt as an example of beautiful English diction. Upon turning to Johnson to hear his opinion, they were told that he himself composed that speech while working for a London paper, basing it upon a brief report by one of the attendants in Parliament! Only in the last quarter of the eighteenth century were reporters allowed, and regular publication of the debates followed. For a time the peculiar conditions of English electoral politics made possible a continuation of the deliberative function of Parliament in the full daylight of publicity, but under the impact of democratic forces, Parliament in England gradually became less of a deliberative body; at the end of the century critics began to describe it as a "voting machine." It became, in the words of Finer, purely a "will-organization," and ceased to be a "thought-organization." This is probably an overstatement. The opposition still makes very vital contributions in the course of the deliberation of bills, not just in the whole house. How the English Parliament has undergone this transformation, and how it and other parliaments have tried to escape this transformation, will be the central topic of this chapter. Closure and committees are the two battle cries. For the rest, it will be shown that fiscal and administrative supervision by a parliament are entirely dependent upon the fact that it continues to be a deliberative body. Technical as these matters may seem, they are vitally related to the future of parliamentary institutions.

General problems of procedure · Procedure, intrinsically a rather technical subject, is in its broad outlines essential for an understanding of the work methods of parliaments. Josef Redlich, in his celebrated treatise on the history of British parliamentary procedure, has done more than anyone else to show this vital relationship.[2] In the earlier period prior to the reign of Elizabeth I, the fundamental procedural device of legislation by bill rather than by petition had been worked out. The later development can be roughly divided into four periods. During the time when Parliament was engaged in its struggle to curb the Crown, it was essentially a question of preventing the exertion of undue influence by the Crown's ministers over the deliberations of the House. Perhaps the most important achievement of this period was the establishment of each member's full right as an individual participant in the debates and decisions. It is to this period also that we owe the gradual separation of the Speaker's office from the Crown, as well as the development of separate readings. The provisions insuring the opposition a fair share of the time of the House, the famous protection of the minority, while begun earlier, were carried forward in the second period, when, after 1688, the House was divided by the two aristocratic factions which governed the country rather oligarchically, particularly after the accession of Walpole. In this period, the great conservative speaker Arthur Onslow and his colleagues thoroughly developed the institution of His Majesty's Opposition by the consistent refinement of various technicalities. Among the technicalities may be mentioned the employment of the committee of the whole for the debate on all bills, the use of the same for all budgetary questions, and the many different techniques which make it possible to bring up any subject at any time. All these and many other provisions were meant to encourage the participation of members in the debate, which was often lagging. Since the whole Parliament was an instrument for the maintenance of aristocratic government, there was not much inclination on the part of the opposition to use its power for purposes of obstruction, nor did the majority care to do violence to the minority. Considering this, Redlich believes that the period from 1688 to 1832 could almost be called the golden age of the English Parliament.

Oligarchic rule evolved parliamentary responsibility. During the period after the Reform Act and down to the late seventies, when the Irish obstruction began, Parliament faced very different problems. The House of Commons was then the real core of the governmental system, as Bagehot showed in his famous treatise. Two fairly evenly matched groups were pitted against each other in the House under the able leadership of such men as Palmerston, Disraeli, and Gladstone. As industrial, social, and imperial problems multiplied, procedural reforms were concerned with expediting necessary business and preventing debate from being merely the occasion for the display of brilliant rhetoric. To this period, therefore, we owe the rules of debate and the elaborate system of questioning. It has remained of considerable importance ever since. A recent assessment could however conclude that "the really significant feature . . . is not that there has been an increase (in the number of questions), but that the increase, however measured, has been so small,"[3] which is due primarily to the limited time available and the increased limitations of ministerial responsibility.

After the Irish obstruction arose, it became increasingly apparent, in the period from 1880 to the First World War, that the ministry was dependent not so much upon parliamentary as upon electoral support. In other words, as party organization and the caucus supplanted parliamentary control, the dominant task of procedure became this: how to insure to the government as leaders of the majority party efficient control of the business of Parliament. To this period, therefore, we owe the development of closure and various other techniques for expediting parliamentary discussion.

It must be remembered that the obstructionist tactics which engendered closure and such like tools are expressions of the fact that the community is rent by violent conflicts — conflicts which obstruct the maintenance of the community, and consequently of its representation. One way of escaping from the difficulties involved in such social cleavages is to reduce the representative importance of a parliament. Under the American constitution, federalism and the separation of powers make Congress just one cog, though a central one, in the total setup of representative organs, with the result that the burden of national representation does not only fall on Congress. The impact of the (absolutist) ideas of sovereignty and the consequent hankering after unitary representative decisions are correspondingly weakened. Stimulated by the confused developments during and after the First World War, there has developed in Britain a demand for the curbing of this overweening governmental leadership. But as a matter of fact, the "national" government after 1931 seemed at times to proceed on the assumption that the opposition was no longer part of the parliamentary system; indeed, it was claimed by some that such opposition was merely factionalism. This tendency to discount the validity of party conflict is akin to the Fascist intolerance of opposition and democracy. Yet we must beware of rash comparisons. Throughout history, the perversions of institutional development are exaggerations of persistent general trends, and thus useful change often appears akin to the revolutionary and reactionary extremes. "The mother of parliaments," W. I. Jennings has written, "has discovered that the secret of perpetual youth lies in the ability to adapt the technique of its practice and procedure to meet the problems of new generations."[4] To cope with the current trend toward the excessive power of the majority, some have urged the strengthening of parliamentary committees, as will be shown further on. But as yet their influence does not extend very far toward the control of the ministry. But before we consider these developments, we must further explain rules of procedure.

Bentham's views, their influence and results · Bentham's writings constitute, in the opinion of leading authorities, the only attempt at theoretical clarification of the immense mass of procedural detail which could then be found in the practice of representative assemblies. They are also worth considering on account of the influence they have exerted, on the Continent if not in England.[5] The first impact of Bentham's ideas came through his brief sketch of the English procedure which he furnished Mirabeau as a model for the procedure of the French constituent assembly in 1789. But more important was the effect of his *An Essay on Political Tactics* (1816). This treatise undertook to fit the mass of detailed rules of procedure, particularly of the English Parliament, into a rational pattern; as a result, it greatly enhanced the general appeal of English procedure on the Continent. Through its Genevese editor it entered Switzerland. It also exerted some influence upon French parliamentary ways down to the present day. It helped to shape the procedure of the German National Assembly in 1848, and from there its influence spread over Central Europe while the French procedure was molding Belgian, and later Italian and other, parliamentary practices.

The central purpose of the rules of procedure, according to Bentham, is to produce a majority and thus to discover the true will of the assembly. That the proceedings should be public is now generally conceded.

Bentham considered legislation the primary function of a parliament. He consequently lists as inconveniences inaction, useless decision, indecision, delays, surprise and precipitation, fluctuation, quarrels, falsehoods, decisions which are defective in form, and others which are defective in substance. Ultimately, all these "inconveniences" come down to two: not reaching a good decision, when it might have been reached, or reaching a bad decision. Who is to judge what decisions are good? This question did not concern Bentham; he simply answers that good decisions are those which promote the greatest happiness of society. Such a reply recommends itself by its simplicity, rather than its adequacy. Yet Bentham's view of procedure aroused considerable enthusiasm when it was first expounded. English radicalism, with its faith in the rational nature of man, took it to be the final word. The more sophisticated, almost Machiavellian debating primer of W. C. ("Single Speech") Hamilton was condemned as "the wickedest book in the English language." Its failure to consider the general good earned it the most outspoken condemnation of Bentham himself. Yet intrinsically, Bentham's own *Tactics* does not lack a touch of Machiavellian preoccupation with pure *technics*.

The main shortcomings of Bentham's work result not so much from the general ethical purpose which he posits, as from the neglect of certain factors in the real situation. In England, these omissions were perhaps not very serious, since the reader could supply them from his own experience. But wherever Bentham's theories were taken as realistic guides, as was the case among Liberals on the Continent, the effect was serious and has contributed its share to the breakdown of parliamentary politics. In considering it the main business of deliberative assemblies to make laws, Bentham had failed to recognize that it was as much a matter of fighting the opposition party. To be sure, he recognized the necessity of parties; but at the same time he viewed with indignation Hamilton's notion that "Parliament [is] a sort of gaming-house; members on the two sides of each house the players; the property of the people . . . the stakes played for; . . . what course will be most for the advantage of the universal interest, a question never looked at, never taken into account. . . ." He knew the fact, then, but he condemned it. Despising party strife, he would give as little consideration to it as possible in developing a theory of procedure. By doing so, Bentham fell into the error of neglecting the real value which attaches to securing effective party support. As a consequence, he failed to perceive the significance of the cabinet's responsibility to Parliament, which was just then emerging. Debating laws *and* supporting the government, not debating laws *or* supporting the government, would seem to have provided the right approach to the problem. Since Bentham's time the need for governmental leadership in debate has caused sweeping changes in parliamentary procedure, such as closure.

In addition to minimizing the procedural significance of party struggle and governmental leadership, Bentham also misjudged the possibilities of organized obstruction. In many benign sentences, scattered through his *Tactics* and too long to quote here, he expressed his doubt as to such methods ever gaining a foothold. He considered them self-defeating. A permanent minority like the Irish Nationalists lay beyond the confines of his experience. In fact, parliamentary procedure everywhere has to some extent been affected by organized obstruction; the filibusters of small minorities in the American Senate are perhaps the best known, but the Irish Nationalists developed great skill in availing themselves of every conceivable procedural advantage. All such tactics have undoubtedly contributed much toward discrediting parliaments. The writings and reminiscences of politicians of an antiparliamentary outlook in Italy, France, and other countries are filled with critical observations. Bentham could not conceive of parliaments willfully discrediting themselves, because he never considered that popular forces might arise which would be out of sympathy with representative assemblies. Through one of the paradoxes so frequent in institutional history, his radical views contributed toward the adoption of unrealistically rationalist procedure in countries where parliamentary government has since had great difficulties in taking root. Under this influence, Continental parliamentarians failed to consider the problems of procedure in terms of the party system. A considerable number of minor absurdities crept into parliamentary practice in France, Germany, and elsewhere, because procedures well-adapted to the English two-party system as it existed in England in the time of Bentham were adopted in countries where very different conditions prevailed, such as a multiple-party system, permanent national minorities, and class-conscious groups.

Presiding officers: the English Speaker · If the effectiveness of a procedure is to be measured by results, perhaps the most important question is how to provide adequate leadership for a legislative program. Such leadership is in the United States in the first instance given by the President. But he cannot "run" either Senate or House directly, but only through others. This leadership is provided by the Speaker or the floor leader as presiding officers, with the aid of the Committee on Rules. Other representative assemblies, following the theories of Bentham, adopted the idea of a neutral presiding officer. Curiously enough, at the time of Bentham's writing, the strictly neutral position of the Speaker in the House of Commons had not yet been perfected. Bentham really anticipated developments. His very success in forecasting the English evolution bolstered his authority elsewhere. Consequently, Josef Redlich could rightly conclude his discussion of the speakership with Bentham's dramatic statement: "Throughout the whole business, the grand problem is to obtain, in its most genuine purity, the real and enlightened will of the assembly. The solution of this problem is the end that ought everywhere to be had in view. To this end, everything that concerns the president, ought of course to be subservient. — The duty and art of the president of a political assembly is the duty and art of the accoucheur: *ars obstetrix animarum* . . . — to assist nature and not to force her — to soothe upon occasion the pangs of parturition; — to produce in the shortest time the genuine offspring, but never to stifle it, much less to substitute a changeling in its room. It is only in so far as it may be conformable to the will of the assembly, that the will of this officer can as such have any claim to regard. . . . Any influence whatever that he possesses over the acts of the assembly, is just so much power taken from the assembly and thrown into the lap of this single individual."[6] This statement is not a descriptive generalization; it is a norm realized in the British House of Commons, but only because actual leadership comes from the cabinet, and not from the "real will of the assembly," as Bentham would have us believe. Where something like British cabinet leadership does not prevail, the presiding officer cannot and does not assume such a neutral role; if he tries to, the result is chaos.

It is quite significant that the neutrality of the Speaker in England developed right along with such cabinet leadership. The first great example of a neutral Speaker, Arthur Onslow, falls into the period of Robert Walpole's and his successors' power and influence. Before his time, the Speaker had been oscillating between being an instrument of the Crown (More, Coke, Finch, Sir John Trevor) and the spokesman of the parliamentary party (Lenthal and others). Stubbs has shown how Sir Thomas More ran the House of Commons according to the directions of Wolsey. This remained so throughout the Tudor reign. In the words of Redlich: "There can be no doubt that the absolutist domination of parliament by Henry VIII and his successors found its main support in the position of the Speaker as a servant of the crown and as a representative of the crown's interests." In other words, as long as the British constitution was built upon the medieval separation of powers between the king and the houses of Parliament, effective leadership in the House of Commons had to come from the Speaker (just as in the House of Lords it had to come from the Lord Chancellor). In this period, the Speaker usually held a position under the Crown, as, for instance, Sir

Edward Coke, who was Solicitor General. Such a position was unendurable once the government (the cabinet) became a party government. Once the majority in the House of Commons supported the cabinet, there was an urgent need and a profound reason for developing the speakership as a judicial office mediating between the majority party and the opposing minority. Just as the judiciary itself in the course of the eighteenth century became independent of the party struggles and removed from the influence of both Crown and Parliament, so also this "moderator" and judge presiding over parliamentary proceedings became neutral and more and more effectively insulated against partisan influences. His decisions are "rulings," they "apply" the precedents of parliamentary law and custom according to legal logic, and whatever discretionary authority he possesses closely resembles the type of authority of a judge, and is derived from a skillful use of existing precedents. "Just as the immense, and many-meshed net of the common law binds the judge a thousand times in his decisions, but also offers him a thousand times the opportunity to develop the law through the employment of the stored-up precedents, and to create new law, in just the same way the Speaker faces the parliamentary law and customs. Here too vast fields extend beyond the limited line of positive norms, the vast field of parliamentary practice developed through hundreds of years as it is recorded in the proceedings." To develop new law is the highest function of the English Speaker. This state of affairs, however, must not blind one to the fact that ultimately Parliament itself is the sole judge of its procedure. By making a positive rule, it can eliminate whatever precedent may have grown up. Parliamentary supremacy is not subject to judicial fetters in this area any more than in other fields of legislation. No law behind the law can be appealed to.

Since the reform of Parliament, the independent judicial position of the Speaker has been generally recognized. Not only inside of Parliament, but outside of it as well, he must observe the strictest neutrality. According to prevailing practice he is not opposed in his own electoral district and makes no speeches nor even visits his former party club. He has an official residence, and is on all sides surrounded by the repressive pomp of royalty. His salary is £8500, and on his retirement he is made a peer and given a liberal pension. In every respect he resembles the highest judicial officer in the land. On account of this elevated position, reinforced by many ceremonial details inside of Parliament and out, the Speaker is enabled to maintain that high order of efficiency and dignity which characterizes the proceedings of Parliament. He can, with the aid of the sergeant-at-arms and the Metropolitan Police, arrest any person, whether a member of Parliament or not, and deliver him into jail. There is no appeal against his decisions. This plenary power contrasts strongly with the helplessness of the president

of the French chamber or those of other Continental countries, whose ultimate weapon, suspension of the sitting, is precisely the aim of obstructionist
groups. Inside Parliament, all speeches are addressed to the Speaker, and his
direction of the debate and other proceedings is beyond appeal, for, as
Speaker Lowther once remarked: "The Chair, like the Pope, is infallible."
If Parliament was once a court, today there is a judge that presides over
Parliament, and that judge is as absolute, as final in his decisions as any in
the realm. Only through such a device does the British constitution manage
to combine great dispatch of all kinds of legislative and budgetary business,
embodying the policy of the majority party, with an adequate protection of
the minority's opportunities to speak and express their vigorous criticism.
His Majesty's Loyal Opposition remains a recognized part of the government,
even when it is as small a minority as it was between 1931 and 1935, when
the combined opposition had only 59, as against the National Coalition's 556
votes. As Jennings has put it: "Care of the rights of minorities is evidenced
by the deliberate exaltation of the office of Speaker. . . . As often happens in
British institutions, the Speaker's authority is greater than his power." The
reason this can be so is that the Speaker is the representative of the unity of
the House (and hence of the nation). His qualities must be representative
qualities, that is, character will be more important than intellectual brilliance.
It has been said: "The qualities required of a Speaker are not really very
high, and so great is the prestige of the office, and so careful are all parties
to maintain his independence and authority, that any reasonable man can
make a success of the office." This is true only if by "qualities" are meant
merely intellectual gifts. A Speaker, to be a success, must be an embodiment
of those qualities of moderation, fairness, and gentlemanly conduct which
are expressive of British tradition.

The American Speaker · Very different is the position of the American
presiding officer in the deliberative assemblies — just the reverse, in fact, of
that advocated by Bentham.[7] Everyone knows that party leadership in the
House of Representatives is provided from the chair, whether occupied by
the speaker or by the floor leader. Allusion has already been made to the
underlying major factor explaining the complete difference between British
and American practice. As James Bryce, in *The American Commonwealth*,
pointed out, "a deliberative assembly is, after all, only a crowd of men; and
the more intelligent a crowd is, so much more numerous are its volitions; so
much greater the difficulty of agreement. Like other crowds, a legislature
must be led and ruled. Its merit lies not in the independence of its members,
but in the reflex action of its opinion upon its leaders, in its willingness to
defer to them in minor matters, reserving disobedience for the issues in which

some great principle overrides both the obligation of deference to established authority and the respect due to special knowledge." Another writer elaborated this by saying that what was wanted was "a centralized, responsible authority, like the Cabinet of the British Government or of Canada, which will determine what laws are to be considered, and cast aside without mercy the mass of trivial and irrelevant bills that now discredit our legislative records. . . ." The presiding officers in American legislatures have often attempted to fulfill such a function. It was the explicit purpose of Speaker Carlisle, who considered it the duty of the speaker to have a legislative policy and "to take every means in his power to secure its accomplishment." That view was continued and carried forward by his successors, Reed and Crisp. Each in his turn at the end of the last century made his particular contribution toward strengthening the power of the speakership, until at last in 1909–1910, revolt rose against their system as personified by Speaker Cannon. Robert Luce rightly observes that the epithet "Cannonism" was rather undeserved, as Cannon merely carried on what others had done before. It is curious that Carlisle himself, after having done so much to strengthen the power of the Speaker, should have attacked the system upon leaving the chair. He felt it to be an inevitable scourge. "Under any system of rules that can be devised, the presiding officer in a body so numerous as the House of Representatives will necessarily have more power than ought to be entrusted to any man in this country." Numbers alone hardly suffice as an explanation; for the British House of Commons is much larger. It is a question of the confusion resulting from lack of effective party leadership.

Leadership is the central task of the Speaker. Several devices, such as the absolute discretion as to whom to recognize, prearranged schedules for the debate and what should be taken up therein, extensive control over committee vacancies, all these contributed their share to the indignation which in 1910 led to the overthrow of the Speaker. A coalition of the Democrats, then in opposition, with insurgent (progressive) Republicans took away from the presiding officer much of his discretionary power; they enlarged the Rules Committee, provided that it should be elected (by the two caucuses in the ratio of 6 to 4), and deprived the Speaker of a seat on it. A little later, it was further provided that all committees should be elected by the House. "Amid cheers for 'the fall of the Czar' and the end of 'despotism,'" C. A. Beard tells us, "a dissipation of leadership was effected." Yet, as Beard shrewdly remarks, this revolution did not destroy leadership.[8] Concentration of power has remained. However, there is a certain distribution: leadership shifts about between the Speaker, the Rules Committee, the Chairman of Ways and Means, the floor leader, and the "steering committee" of the majority party. The resulting uncertainties have recurrently raised the demand for more effective leadership; in certain quarters the President is favored as the effective leader in Congress. Powers such as that of dissolution, the item veto in the budget, and so forth, are favored as desirable modifications to bring about such a change. If such presidential leadership were to become a reality, the Speaker of the American Congress could travel the road of the English Speaker, retire from active political leadership and make himself an impartial umpire or moderator for the House. Such was his position at the outset, but as long as measures vitally important to the majority party were delayed or even defeated by opposition tactics, the Speaker in conjunction with one or more of the other directing forces would be obliged to assume a measure of leadership. Such is his political function within the American setup, and what is true of the federal Congress is largely true of the states as well, though the Speaker in Massachusetts, for instance, is much more nearly an impartial moderator than the Speaker in other legislatures.

The chief whip • To refer to James Bryce once more, he commented extensively upon the lack of any recognized leaders in either the Senate or the House.[9] How can such a statement be squared with the previous discussions? Was Bryace unaware of the existence of the Speaker, the Committees on Rules, and so on? Had he never heard of the floor leader at all? Curiously enough, Bryce himself calls the Speaker "almost the leader" of the House; the importance of the floor leader he tended to overlook. The American Congress (and the same is true of American state legislatures) carries on most of its work in committees, and the votes in the whole House largely ratify the committee reports. Nor does the position of the majority party in the House depend upon any particular vote. Only during the last few days of the session do conditions requiring something like the English parliamentary strategy prevail, and for these few days it is relatively easy for the caucus to keep members in hand. What Bryce was admittedly looking for was the "whip." It is desirable for a complete understanding of the contrast between the English Parliament and the American legislatures as representative assemblies to know what these whips are. Bryce considered them a "vital, yet even in England little appreciated, part of the machinery of constitutional government." The term, taken from the hunting field, denotes the men aiding the government in Parliament. The government party in the House of Commons appoints certain of its members as officials, nominally, whose real function it is to direct the party forces of the majority. The chief whip is the First (Patronage) Secretary of the Treasury, the others are mostly Junior Lords of the Treasury. Viscount Gladstone, chief whip himself from 1899 to 1905, claims that the office of the government whip originated about 1836, that is, after the Reform Act, and that the whip became *ex-officio* Patronage Secretary of the Treasury in or about 1845. This meant that he kept his machine running by handing out jobs, titles, and other favors. More recently, the favors have changed in accordance with the rise of the "social service" state. Furthermore, the "peerage" has been protected by providing for review by the Privy Council. In a planned economy, effective contact with the planning center would be more valuable than most of the earlier "favors."

Under the direction of the cabinet, the chief whip, with the help of the assistant whips, lays out the plans for the parliamentary session, prepares a schedule, determines what opposition leaders are proposing to do, tries to arrange a fair distribution of work, and keeps the cabinet informed of important developments in the party. He may also smooth out difficulties between several leaders. Lloyd George, for example, claimed that the rift between him and Asquith would not have developed if the Liberal whip had not died and thus deprived the party of a skillful moderator. We are also told by Bryce that "a ministerial whip is further bound to 'keep a house,' that is, to secure that when government business is being considered there shall always be a quorum of members present, and of course also to keep a majority. . . . Without the constant presence and activity of the ministerial whip the wheels of government could not go on for a day, *because the ministry would be exposed to the risk of casual defeats.* . . . Similarly the Opposition . . . finds it necessary to have their whip or whips because it is only thus that they can act as a party. . . ." From these remarks it should be clear that the institution of the whip is clearly linked with the position of the English House of Commons as the supporter and critic of the cabinet. The role of the government whip and the opposition whip are quite far apart. The opposition chief whip is more interested in work outside the House of Commons to prepare for victory in the next election. He collaborates with the party agent in giving financial assistance to candidates, in recommending and discovering suitable candidates, in keeping local organizations in running order, and so on. It has been pointed out that most American legislators would strongly resent any such control and, furthermore, that the power of American whips as they have functioned since 1900 is much more limited, and that all we want and ask of them is that they shall incite members to be on hand at moments of party importance. And indeed, if any American were to be compared with the English government party's whip, he would be a representative of the President. It used to be the Postmaster General under many administrations, but more recently "special assistants," whose task it is to deal with Congress, have handled these problems.

Speech and debate • Speech is the essence of parliamentary activity; it is the very lifeblood of parliament's corporate body politic.[10] But just as blood has to flow through well-encased channels in order to fulfill its salutary function, so speech has to be circumscribed and regulated in Parliament. Not the bedlam of a multitude of voices, but the balanced and ordered procedure of speech and reply, of argument and of debate, is "speech" within Parliament. The privilege of "freedom of speech" is not an absolute privilege of the individual member, it is a relative freedom compatible with the freedom of others. In the words of the Marquess of Hartington, uttered when discussing closure in the House of Commons in 1882: ". . . the privilege of speech is a privilege which the House permits to be exercised for its own instruction, for its own information, in order to form its own opinion, and . . . [is] not a personal privilege to be used irrespective of the convenience and the efficiency of the House. . . ." He could, in the same vein, insist that the business before the House, and nothing but the business before the House, determined the rules and limitations of debate. When all relevant arguments have been advanced, debate ought to come to an end. But who is to say when this is the case? Modern English and American practice has given the decision to the majority party. This naturally raises the problem of constraint of the minority. But filibustering, "talking against time," and similar practices in turn raise the problem of constraint of the majority. As in other political arenas, so in parliaments a certain measure of constraint is inherent in the situation. Effective political engineering needs to be directetd toward achieving a minimum of such constraint. At the same time, it has been argued by none other than the late Professor Zachariah Chafee, Jr., that freedom of debate is a basic right, citing the constitution's clause: ". . . and for any Speech or Debate in either House they [the Congressmen] shall not be questioned in any other Place." Tracing the issue back to the Middle Ages, the learned author makes it amply clear that what he is really talking about is a privilege, "the privilege achieved in the long English struggle . . . of members to be tried and punished by their fellow-members and not by any outside tribunal."[11]

The eighteenth century was occupied with the development of rules guarding against the restraining of private members; in the period of the Irish obstruction it became a matter of guarding against the restraint placed upon the majority by a recalcitrant minority. Still other problems have been raised by the fact that there may be no majority party, have hardly been faced, except by academic discussions. But throughout these different phases certain ironclad rules have persisted which crystallized so early that their beginnings are obscure. Without going into detail, certain important general practices might be mentioned. In order that there may be a debate, a definite proposal, called a motion, must ordinarily be before the House. Whatever anyone may say ought to be and ordinarily is germane to the subject matter of this motion. At any rate, no new motion can be introduced until the old one is disposed of. After those who wish to speak have each had their opportunity to do so, "the question is put" and a vote is taken. A proposal, a discussion of the proposal, a decision regarding the proposal — these are the ironclad stages of an orderly parliamentary transaction. It is evident that speech is the essence of it.

Questions and interpellations · One of the important tools in the hands of members of Parliament today is the question. As private-member bills in the course of the nineteenth century were replaced by government bills, and as the government's administrative activities increased, private members — that is, members not connected with the government or the ministerial opposition bench — began to ask more and more questions. While at first intended to secure information, they have today become instruments for securing redress from administrative errors, as well as important occasions for embarrassing the government. A question may become the starting point for extensive newspaper discussion, leading in turn to governmental and parliamentary action. Only the more important (starred) questions are nowadays answered by the minister, orally, and even these only when there is time. But the fact that the questioner and others have the right to ask supplementary questions, if the first answer does not satisfy, makes the question hour a chess game, and many oratorical questions are brought forward to dramatize a point which the opposition wishes to bring up. The right to ask such questions greatly strengthens the hand of the ordinary M.P. when asking a minister to look into a complaint of a constituent; for the minister who neglects to attend to such matters is likely to find himself embarrassed by a question in the House. At times, particularly during war, members will ascertain beforehand that a question will not embarrass the government in a manner contrary to the general interest; the minister may take an M.P. into his confidence and persuade him to withdraw the question.[12]

The English system of questions cannot lead to a debate unless the questioner couples the question with a motion for an adjournment. Hence a question cannot ordinarily become the occasion for a vote of nonconfidence. In many Continental parliaments this was different. In these parliaments an institution known as "interpellation" was developed to do just that, and numerous French ministries went down to defeat after having thus been interpellated. Indeed, three fifths of all ministerial defeats were due to interpellations. In its individualistic implications, the interpellation was the expression of the multiple-party parliaments of pre-Fascist Europe. It enabled the individual representative to challenge the government to an explanation of its policy in a particular branch of activity and to provoke a general debate in the course of which antiministerial sentiment could crystallize to the point where the assembly was ready to overthrow the government. In the French parliament the total number of interpellations between 1924 and 1928, which actually consisted of a discussion followed by a vote of confidence or no-confidence, was 152. The interpellation was revived in France and Italy after 1945, but not in Germany. The underlying conception is "control of the administration." But while the ever-present threat of such an interpellation certainly kept the ministries on the alert, in France and elsewhere, it has been rightly observed that "it cannot be good for Ministers to be in hourly peril of fall." The interpellation, when not offset by the cabinet's power to dissolve the representative assembly, too readily produces impulsive reactions and sudden decisions taken under the sway of effective oratory and without regard to the broader long-run results. The interpellation often produced brilliant debate; it precluded sound deliberation. The new French constitution thus provides for questions only one day a week (Friday). Because the constitution was unclear as to whether these questions could be followed by a vote, the Constitutional Council was asked to settle the matter. It decided against the vote, agreeing with M. Debré that the government should not be faced every Friday with an implicit vote of confidence.

Closure • Even an ordered debate has to come to an end at some time. In order to bring this about, certain rules are needed. Short of the presiding officer "putting the question," the classical form for achieving this purpose of terminating the debate is a motion for adjournment.[13] There were essentially three such motions, adjournment to another day (fixed adjournment), adjournment without naming another day (indefinite adjournment), adjournment until after something else has been done, such as securing certain necessary information (relative adjournment). Each one of these motions became a tool in the hands of a determined obstructionist opposition. For as on each of them a vote (division) would have to be taken, and as these votes consumed a great deal of time, much delay could thus be effected. In other words, motions for adjournment could be employed much as the roll calls are being used in American legislatures. These motions for adjournment, as well as the inevitable extension of debate in a very numerous House of Commons, produced in course of time a demand for procedural devices which might be effective in expediting business. In France and in the United States such devices have had a longer history, but even in

England, the Speaker has for a long time had the right to bring the debate to an end by putting the question. This sort of closure, however, was not regularly used unless and until everybody appeared to have had a fair hearing. Only the crisis brought on by the obstruction of the Irish Nationalists in 1881 induced the then-Speaker, Brand (later Viscount Hampden), to discard the ancient restraint and by putting the question to bring to an end a debate which had lasted forty-one hours. He explained his procedure in a short statement. After stressing the intolerable delays (five full days of debate) caused by the obstructionist tactics of a small minority, he declared that "the dignity, the credit, and the authority of this House was seriously threatened, and it is necessary that they should be vindicated. Under the operation of the accustomed rules and methods of procedure, the legislative powers of the House are paralysed. A new and exceptional course is imperatively demanded; and I am satisfied that I shall best carry out the will of the House, and may rely upon its support, if I decline to call upon any more Members to speak, and at once proceed to put the question from the Chair. I feel assured that the House will be prepared to exercise all its powers in giving effect to these proceedings." The action of Speaker Brand had been taken with the understanding that the government (Gladstone) would at once proceed to alter the procedure in the House of Commons.[14] This was done and, amended by minor innovations later, closure was introduced so that any member of the House may, with the support of one hundred members, move that the question be put.

In the train of these reforms, even more coercive forms for limiting the debate were soon adopted, the so-called guillotine, and the closure by compartments. The former provides that after a set time, the question is brought to a vote, no matter what the state of the discussion; the latter, that a bill may be divided into sections (items), and a certain amount of time, agreed to beforehand, allotted to the discussion of each of these section. Finally, in 1911, the so-called kangaroo type of closure was added, which permits the presiding officer to declare which of a number of amendments proposed shall be debated. When impartially employed, this type of closure can be highly beneficial. Yet it discourages active participation by members of the House. What is equally serious, it undermines confidence in the deliberations of the Parliament. If measures of the highest importance can be put through without even a word of debate, the deliberative function of such assemblies becomes a farce. This in turn weakens their representative position.

The markedly partisan exercise of the closure rules in the American House of Representatives is more readily endured because this assembly is not at all taken as the sole national representative. Speaker Reed, who did as much as any man to strengthen the control of the majority over the debates in Congress, voiced sentiments much like those of the Marquess of Hartington, cited above, when he said that the purpose of a parliamentary body was action and not the stoppage of action. Hence he felt that if anybody undertook to obstruct the orderly progress of business even by regular and permitted means, it was right for the majority to refuse to have such motions entertained and to cause the public business to proceed.[15] He and his successors were instrumental in bringing about the implied majority control by making it possible to discard motions, by forbidding speeches exceeding one hour except by unanimous consent, by allowing motions for putting the "previous question," and by placing the power of arranging legislative business at the discretion of the Committee on Rules, controlled by the majority. Since the American Senate admits closure only on the basis of a special vote by a qualified majority, measures fostered by the majority party will more readily meet an adverse vote in the Senate than they would in the House of Representatives. From this fact, Lindsay Rogers has rather persuasively argued that "with responsibility divided and confused, the check which is on occasion exerted by senatorial obstructionists is of great value. . . . Only the American Senate can act as a 'teaching apparatus' or bring about a 'catastrophe' of obstruction. . . . The Senate can help the country to form opinions and by its eternal vigilance . . . act as the 'real balance-wheel' of the Constitution."[16] The absence of closure in the Senate, which many people so bitterly resent, does not prevent a reasonable amount of business from being attended to; but of course the Senate of the United States is a relatively small body. Some think that if a measure is opposed with real spirit by even a limited minority, it had better be abandoned. Such a view is difficult to accept as regards the Senate's power in foreign affairs; it seems to lead to inaction. It is also questionable in matters where social reform is urgent, yet can be prevented by an interested minority. These issues were highlighted by the controversy over civil-rights legislation in 1949 and later. It was striking how jealously the Senate guarded its right of debate. The anarchic potentialities of the *liberum veto* lurk in the background of such unlimited debate.

Closure, when applied with proper discretion, is to be viewed as a safeguard of, rather than a hindrance to, the deliberative functions of parliaments. When deliberation is allowed to deteriorate into a circus by reading purely extraneous literary productions, like *Childe Harold* or the *Pilgrim's Progress*, into the record, it damages the deliberative as well as the representative function of parliaments.

Parliamentary committees: England · Since the pressure is undeniably great in the English Parliament as in others, critics of the system of closure have been looking for relief in other directions. As a consequence, they have advocated an expansion of the standing-committee system in the House of Commons. This system is of rather recent origin, though it possesses historical roots. It grew out of the procedural reforms in the eighties. The arrangements have been fluctuating considerably as to both number and size of committees. The late appearance and the still rather limited scope of these committees is a peculiarity of the English House of Commons. Redlich has pointed out that the Commons could so long avoid a practice which had become very widely accepted elsewhere because of the procedural device of turning from the formal proceedings to what is known as the Committee of the Whole House. This committee is simply the House with relaxed rules of procedure; members may, for example, speak several times on the same matter. The Committee of the Whole has its greatest utility in the field of financial and budgetary functions. These functions, when referred to smaller permanent committees as in Congress, the Chamber of Deputies, or other parliaments, constitute the real strength of the committee structure. In England, where the whole House deliberates upon these matters in Committee of the Whole House, the demand for permanent committees arose in connection with the increase in all kinds of legislation in the second half of the nineteenth century and the growing complexity and technicality of this legislation. However, these committees are not specialized, as in the United States; they consider every kind of legislation as it comes up. In explaining the persistence of this system, it has been said: "To the party in power it is obvious that the more able and expert the committee, the greater its power to make life difficult for the minister and the civil service. . . ."[17] At present there are seven such committees, with an eighth committee devoted to Scottish affairs. The other committees are not specialized as to subject matter. Each committee has thirty to fifty members, with the possibility of adding from ten to thirty-five specially interested members. The members of these committees are nominated by a Committee of Selection. This Committee of Selection consists of eleven members nominated by the House. In nominating members, "regard to the composition of the House" is interpreted as meaning that the parties should be proportionally represented. The chairmen of these committees have been appointed by the Speaker since 1934. The chairmen are not necessarily members of the majority supporting the government, but the business of the committees is definitely and decisively directed by the government. It is a striking contrast to Congressional practice that M. P.'s are so little interested in committee membership that the fourth committee is often not set up at all.

Also, M. P.'s get on and off committees with great ease, depending on their interest in particular bills. This, of course, is due to the relatively small power of the committees. While committees are formally allowed considerable scope in amending bills referred to them, they are in fact quite restricted. The government may, however, make "concessions." Such concessions are in matters of technical detail; for the broad scope of the bill has been settled before it is referred to the committee. English parliamentary committees are supposed to aid and do aid Parliament in these matters of detail; very important bills are often reserved for consideration by the Committee of the Whole House. The committee's work is scrutinized by the whole House in what is known as the report stage; the tendency of the House to employ this discussion for doing over the work of the committee led to a rule that the discussion must stay within the ground staked out by the committee's recommendations.

The conception, and to a large extent the practice, of the English standing-committee system is perhaps most succinctly summarized by a quotation from Sir Courtenay Ilbert, at one time Clerk of the House. "It proceeds on the view that when the general principle of a bill has been affirmed, a reasonable chance ought to be afforded of having its provisions discussed, that this chance is improved by sending a bill to a Standing Committee, that, as a general rule, discussion in a Standing Committee is more business-like and effective than discussion in a Committee of the Whole House, and that the time of the House is saved by dividing the House into compartments for discussing the details of legislative measures."[18] Going well beyond these traditionalist arguments, various writers have advocated an extension of the committee system to improve the opportunities of members of the House to participate in the deliberative function of the House. A system of six standing committees, each concerned with the activities of one of the great "spending departments," would have most salutary effects. Such committees, it is felt, could not only aid in considering bills, but they could also maintain a continuous review of the work of the departments with which they are concerned (equipped as they would be with full powers of investigation), and secondly, they could receive the estimates of these departments as soon as they were ready, go through them, and draw up a report for the House when it came to consider these estimates. Another significant function, namely, the scrutinizing of all the orders and regulations issued by departments under statutory delegation, is now almost exclusively attended to by the House of Lords and forms a really significant function of that body. Whether the House of Commons could find the time for it seems doubtful. It would have to develop specialized committees. In opposing such a development, many Englishmen have insisted that they do not wish to see their Parliament go the way of the American and French assemblies. The different relation between Parliament and the executive seems to them to forbid it. In recent years, however, sentiment in support of reform has been gaining ground. There is a growing literature on the subject. As one of the writers on the subject has said: "All this points, and out of every consideration, to the need for a reformed committee system." At least the nineteenth-century system of select committees should be revived; better it would be to allow the Standing Committee on Legislation to become specialized. "The kind of new committee that is needed should be set up for the whole life of a Parliament to give its members time to specialize . . ."[19]

Committees in the United States · The extensive development of committees in American legislatures, though connected by a thin thread with early English beginnings, which "waned under the deadening influence of the cabinet system," commenced after 1800. There were committees in Virginia and elsewhere, and the experience of the former undoubtedly influenced the Constitutional Convention. Only in that colony had the committees started the modern American practice of framing and amending bills. Special (select) committees were, to be sure, common in England and in all the colonies for the work on particular bills, but in Virginia, as throughout the United States today, there were standing committees. In spite of considerable arguments to the contrary, it seems best to follow the view that "this process has been a matter of convenience, a natural development of orderly system, not begun with any deliberate purpose. . . ."[20] Congress, constitutionally separated from and therefore not subject to executive leadership, was soon confronted with the executive function of drafting new legislation, of supervising the administration of such legislation, and of considering the expenditures involved in all such legislation. For these functions another method of procedure had to be adopted than the general debate, increasingly cumbrous in an ever-more-numerous assembly. Whenever a large group of men find themselves in such a situation, they are likely to resort to some form of committee for the preparation of decisions requiring attention to detail. This procedure is so obvious that it would hardly require comment if the committee system in American representative assemblies were not constantly subjected to a barrage of criticism. It is true that such committees are at variance with the representative function of parliaments. But, as was pointed out before, it greatly enhances the capacity of parliaments for deliberation.

Those who cry out against the secrecy of committee proceedings forget what every experienced parliamentarian would tell them: "No man is the same in private and in public. The more numerous the observers and auditors, the less the frankness, sincerity, confidence. Universal experience tells us that in all manner of conference and deliberation, we reach results more speedily and satisfactorily if those persons directly involved are alone." It has been shown that the English Parliament, at the time when it was a deliberative body, closely guarded the privacy of its proceedings. Thus the baneful effect of "talking to the galleries" was eliminated. There is little room in a committee meeting for oratory. Businesslike procedure became essential in connection with the legislative and fiscal autonomy of Congress. While at first the committees "were looked upon as merely organs to investigate some fact, and to digest and arrange the detail of a complicated subject," in the course of time they have become the active, directing centers of congressional life. Bills originate with members occupying a powerful position on the committee to which the bill is bound to be referred; the advice of committeemen is sought by administrators, who thus anticipate the discussion of increased budgets; representatives of various interest groups are in constant contact with the members of the Congressional committee charged with supervising the governmental activity which most closely touches their daily affairs—railroad representatives trail members of committees on interstate commerce; labor representatives pursue those concerned with labor; educators, patriots, farmers, women, all join in the fray.

In the United States Congress, where bills are at once referred to some committee without any previous discussion by the whole House or Senate (and the same is true of many state legislatures), many bills are killed in committee. This pigeonholing of measures has naturally and persistently aroused the ire of some part or other of the public (whoever happened to favor the bill); in contrasting the situation with that prevailing in England, these critics forget that many of these bills could not even get introduced into the House of Commons. During the five Congresses preceding 1965, 90,916 bills and joint resolutions were introduced, of which 4388 public and 3274 private measures were enacted. This is 4.8 per cent of the public and 3.6 per cent of the private bills.[21] By contrast, every writer on English parliamentary practices remarks upon the difficulty of getting any bill discussed which is not a "government bill." In the United States, the majority party will, if it is the party of the President, push "administration measures," whether advocated by a presidential "Message to Congress" or introduced by a Senator or Congressman favorable to the administration. But in either case, immediate reference to a committee merely insures it attention and possibly retention of its major "policy," but innumerable changes of real importance are bound to be made. There is hardly a piece of major legislation, even if introduced with the full support of the President, which will not thus be cast and recast in the process of Congressional work upon it. Take so important and permanent a statute as the Social Security Act: its legislative history is a tortuously winding road from the President through experts and the Department of Labor to the Congress and its committees, checked and pushed by the interests, popular clamor, and the administration forces. The same kind of process may be observed again and again.*

In their effort to crystallize the policy which they are to recommend to Congress, Congressional committees hold hearings. These hearings, being sometimes public and sometimes private, have also been subjected to a considerable amount of criticism. The length to which committees have gone in their efforts to compel witnesses to appear and testify has been denounced as autocracy, and the extent of the power of Congress in this respect is highly controversial. Since the investigation of past performance and the determination of possible lines of change and reform are closely interwoven, this usual distinction is more significant legally than politically. Closed hearings before Congressional committees have been defended on the ground that witnesses can then more readily be induced to communicate confidential information. Certain it is that this is true at times. Yet Massachusetts, with her tradition of uniformly public hearings, has not been greatly handicapped. Whichever practice is better, hearings either public or private are an integral part of committee work.

Considering the active leadership which emanates from the committees in American legislatures, naturally the question as to who selects them is of vital significance. Underlying the three formal alternatives of selection (1) by the Speaker, (2) by a committee appointed for this purpose, or (3) by the whole House, selection by the parties prevails today in practically all legislatures. Speaker Reed, in the heyday of power of that office, remarked that if he was a czar, the power he had was held on sufferance of the majority of his party. Committee appointments entrusted to him reflected necessarily the preferences of his party colleagues. The questionable effects of the Speaker's power were mostly observable in his appointments of members of the minority party. It was here that tyrannical, unrestrained power could be exercised, and not in the appointment of his own party colleagues. He might, and he often did, appoint strong minority members to committees overcharged with routine business in order to keep them away from an important policy-determining committee. Since 1910 the party caucus, directly or indirectly, controls the membership of committees, as it long had in the Senate. From this it follows that what the change really did was to extend party control to the minority-party members of the several com-

* As a staff member of the special committee (Herter Committee) set up in 1947 to study the background of the European Recovery legislation, the author was impressed with the range of uncertainty surrounding key provisions of the legislation to the end.

mittees. Although the new arrangement has at times produced considerable difficulties, and there are those who would suggest going back to the old plan, party control of both minority and majority members of the committees seems more in keeping with effective deliberation. In this respect, then, American and English practice are today much more nearly alike, for the Committee of Selection in the House of Commons, to which the naming of members for committees is entrusted, is subject to party control both as to majority and minority.

It remains to say a few words concerning the number of such committees. Apart from select committees, there were forty-four committees in the House at the beginning of the seventy-third Congress, and thirty-three committees in the Senate at the same time (1933). A number of these committees were abolished in 1946 when the reorganization was enacted. There are now twenty committees in the House and sixteen in the Senate. Committees range in membership from nine to fifty in the House and from seven to twenty-seven in the Senate.[22] The average important House committee has around thirty. Contrasting these figures with those in England, we find Congressional committees to be more numerous, but smaller in size. The different nature of their work readily explains this difference. Accepting the complexity of modern legislation as inherent in the industrial society in which we live, we have only one remedy for the multiplication of committees in our legislatures, and that is to permit administrative bodies and officials to extend the range of delegated legislation, as has been done in England, to allow them unrestrained and uncontrolled power in administering this trust within the limits imposed by intermittent appeals to the electorate, and to forego any effective scrutiny of expenditures by others than the leading members of the majority party. This English method of handling the problem has found so many well-informed detractors where it is practiced today that its desirability may be seriously doubted. The strength of the English Parliament lies in the broad integrating value of its debates upon issues of general policy; the strength of the American legislature, in its deliberations upon specific legislative proposals and administrative activities. Whether a combination of the two could be effected, as some reformers on both sides of the water seem to hope, it is difficult to say. The two tasks of debating general policy and supervising the details of legislation and administration seem to take a large part of the time of any one set of men. Which will be given preference depends upon the political structure as a whole.

Committees in France • The French parliament under the Third Republic came nearer combining English and American practices than many students of these problems appreciate.[23] French parliamentary government under the Third Republic was almost government *by* parliament, not merely government under the more or less effective supervision of parliament. It took the French parliament just about the same twenty-odd years that it had taken the American Congress to evolve its system of committees. To be sure, permanent committees had been appointed in the revolutionary assemblies, notably the "convention." The experience with these committees, among which the Committee of Public Safety was the most notorious, brought on a violent reaction. The fusion of power which they effected and the resulting dictatorship led the Directory to forbid the formation of such committees by express constitutional prohibition. Reflecting the horror felt for the Terror, such committees remained taboo until almost the end of the nineteenth century. Since that time they have emerged as perhaps the most distinctive feature of French parliamentarianism.

The French committee system, like the American, was based upon the parties in the Chamber. Since 1909 the several parties were represented on the committees according to their numerical strength in the House. The parties, or groups, as they were called, made up their own panel, and through their leaders these panels were combined and presented to the Chamber for formal approval. Ordinarily, therefore, the coalition supporting the cabinet had a majority in the committees when it had a majority in the Chamber (for important exceptions see below, p. 356 f.). In view of the decisive role the committees played in all matters requiring the action of the Chamber or touching the relation of the Chamber to the ministries, this arrangement was highly desirable, of course, and even indispensable for effective work. As in the United States, so in France, bills, whether coming from the government (called *projets de loi*), or from a particular deputy (called *propositions de loi*), as well as other matters coming before the house, were at once referred to the appropriate committees. The Chamber considered the bill as reported out of committee. The government often reintroduced provisions which had been changed in committee. But the committee, through its reporter, provided the leadership in seeing the bills or the budgets of the various ministries through the Chamber. Accordingly, these committees were placed in front of the house right next to the ministerial bench. This seating arrangement, characteristic of the French representative system, strikingly illustrated the difference between English and French parliamentarism. Parliamentary work was directed not so much by the government as by the committees. Nevertheless, the committees were, at least in matters concerning legislation, supposed to confine themselves to preparing the decision of the Chamber. Yet, many bills were simply buried by the committee. What is more, outside the field of legislation, for example in the realm of administrative supervision, the committees handled many matters without ever referring them to the Chamber. The powerful Foreign Affairs Committee attended to many issues which never came before the Chamber. In these fields, the committees were acting for the Chamber rather than preparing its work. The Chamber tended so much to be guided by the advice received from its committees that ministries often kowtowed to the views of committee members in drafting legislation. In the jargon of French politics, this art was called "to play the committees" (*jouer les commissions*), an expression supposedly invented by Briand.

The intimate collaboration between administrative officials and deputies was further facilitated by the French practice of having the committees appoint reporters so that the committees did not necessarily communicate with the Chamber through their chairmen. Rather, the committee members divided this reporting among themselves. It was customary to request one of the members to report on a matter before the committee, and then to appoint that member reporter (*rapporteur*) of the bill to the Chamber, if his report was, on the whole, acceptable to the committee majority. The reporter of a government bill was assumed to be collaborating with the government. The written reports, often very elaborate, were printed and distributed to members after having been introduced into the Chamber, and were published as *Parliamentary Documents*, of which they constituted the bulk. On the whole, the reporter was pretty free, as was the committee, to decide when to bring in his report, and efforts to impel deputies to come forth with their reports within a given time remained a dead letter. In fact, a deputy at times held out the report as bait to the government in order to exact a concession.

As the committee system more and more deeply entrenched itself in French parliamentary politics, the committees developed a formidable initiative in matters of general policy. When, in December 1932, M. Herriot wished to secure the Chamber's consent to a token debt payment to the United States, he found himself blocked by the two hostile committees on finance and foreign affairs; they listened to M. Herriot, adopted a joint resolution opposed to payments which the Chamber passed, 357 against 37, and thus forced the resignation of Herriot's cabinet. Such a role would have been unimaginable for the committees to play thirty years earlier. As a number of critics have pointed out, the fact that the chairmen of some of the key committees belonged to the opposition rendered the system incapable of action, since every major policy became a football of party politics, particularly as the interpellation discussed above provided the well-informed committee chairman with a powerful instrument for bringing his complaints before the house. The joint leadership of committee and cabinet in the

French parliament was recognized in many rules of procedure; the chairman of the committee and the reporter of the particular bill were heard at any time, irrespective of the list of speakers; when the previous question was moved, the right to speak was limited to the mover, one member opposed, a speaker for the government, and a speaker for the committee in charge, and so forth. Only by moving the question of confidence could the government reassert its authority in a clash with such a committee. In a debate in the Chamber, discussion flew back and forth between the government bench and the committee bench a good part of the time. The committee as well as the government could demand additional meetings. Merely on the strength of the committee's work, many minor propositions were accepted by the Chamber without any discussion, or very little of it. As a result, there developed a procedural device known as "vote without debate." Matters which some committee or the government considered urgent were put upon the calendar with the provision that "there be no debate." If thirty deputies demanded a debate, it automatically went off the calendar. If one deputy wished to comment, he could do so in writing and the committee then submitted a supplementary report in which it attempted to answer the particular member. He could repeat this process twice more; but after that only thirty members could prevent a vote without debate. This technique substituted written discourse for public debate. Such a procedure manifestly lent itself to abuse, since many deputies did not take the trouble to read the order of the day with care. The institution of the "vote without debate" illustrated perfectly what a learned observer pertly put thus: "To the Chamber, the votes, to the committee, all the discussion." The deliberative function of the French parliament had to a considerable extent been transferred to the permanent committees. But since the French committees were strictly confidential, even the proportional composition of these committees, representing as they did all groups in the Chamber, could not silence the fierce opposition which such frank recognition of the dwindling deliberative function of the whole house caused.

There can be little doubt that the French parliamentary committee system, combining the strength of American committees with the lack of any government and party control, was an important factor in the failure of French parliamentarianism. Military defeat does not necessarily prove anything about the value of political institutions, but the lack of effective leadership, the absence of integrated national policy prior to the emergency measures of 1938–1939, can be traced to this committee system, which was so intimately linked up with the French conception of parliamentary supremacy. For parliament's true functions of representation and deliberation, there were thus substituted executive and administrative responsibilities which committees composed of a motley assortment of partisans were ill-adapted to discharge satisfactorily.

It is curious, in the light of this record, that the French should have returned to this system after the liberation. But although the Fourth Republic revived the government by parliament in which committees remained dominant, the constitution of 1958 has tried to redress the balance. This constitution limits the number of permanent committees to six, in hopes that within large committees pressure groups will have less influence. (These interests seem again to have entrenched themselves in "working groups" of the committees, but their recommendations are reviewed by the entire committee before being passed on to the Assembly.) The cabinet minister in charge of a bill may now remove it at will from the committee, introduce it himself to the Assembly, propose amendments to the committee's form, block amendments from the floor, and insist on a vote regarding all the changes made in committee which he finds objectionable.[24]

Fiscal and budgetary control in Britain · There is one field of parliamentary activity in which the value of the committee system has been quite generally recognized, and that is the field of financial, and more particularly of budgetary, control.[25] The committees dealing with these matters are generally looked upon as the most important ones in the system. In the United States the chairmen of the committees on Ways and Means and on Appropriations have traditionally been considered second in importance only to the Speaker of the House. In Britain, on the other hand, expenditures (estimates) and revenues (ways and means) are traditionally handled by the whole house, sitting as Committee of the Whole. Since it is a fixed custom that the Commons must not increase items of expenditure, and since the cabinet would (and at times does) make any reduction in such expenditures a question of confidence, the nature of the discussions in the Commons has completely changed. No detailed deliberation is devoted to the expenditures of the government; formal motions, for example, to reduce the salary of the Secretary of Foreign Affairs are made the occasion for a discussion of general policy. This procedure produces deliberation upon issues of public policy, rather than fiscal control. "It is with no disrespect to this House that I say that it is not an efficient body for checking expenditure," was the verdict of one chancellor of the exchequer. W. I. Jennings has wisely commented that "expenditure depends primarily on policy, and the most efficient form of financial control can do no more than secure that due economy is observed in the execution of policy."[26] With great concern it was noted that twenty days in the parliamentary year were devoted to the estimates of a score of departments, some of which spent tens of millions of pounds and had enormous staffs performing very varied functions. In order to remedy this situation, a parliamentary committee in 1918 recommended the setting up of several Standing Committees on Estimates, and other authorities have followed it in urging such a change. The actual Select Committee on Estimates which was organized afterwards did not have the necessary powers, namely, to recommend the reduction or elimination of items which did not affect policy, to hear evidence of the administrative departments, and to secure the advice of accountancy experts. Nor was their work, backed by the power of the Commons when sitting as a Committee on Supply, extended to the point of enabling them to disallow minor budget items contrary to the wishes of the cabinet without such action becoming a question of confidence. It must be borne in mind that Treasury control, combined with the work of the Comptroller and Auditor-General, has succeeded in eliminating corruption almost entirely.[27] A Select Committee on Public Accounts, together with these administrative officials, sees to it that no major expenditure unauthorized by Parliament is incurred. But this type of control does not affect the authorizing of expenditure in the first instance. It is at this point that the English Parliament has abdicated its deliberative function, except for the broad lines of policy, as previously stated.

A number of select committees have studied and restudied these problems, most recently the Select Committees on Procedure of 1956–1957, 1958–1959, 1962–1963, and 1964–1965.[28] Since financial control "via a prior parliamentary sanction of all expenditure proposals is a thing of the past," new methods are needed that "will facilitate systematic discussion." This systematic discussion should be focused on broad policy issues, for "a representative assembly in an advanced industrial society ought to be able to provide more than an innocuous and desultory discussion over two or three days." But if the general debates cannot accomplish this, then what of the financial select committees? None other than Harold Wilson, as a result of his experience as the chairman of one of them, has stated that "these committees cannot do much . . . to control the general volume of public expenditure."

What then is the actual function of these select committees? It is their effort to secure an economic use of resources in the pursuit of policies, plans, and programs of a general nature. It is therefore the trend to "widen the scope and improve the opportunities for planned inquiry." Sir Gilbert Campion, then Clerk of the House, did in fact propose a functionally structured subdivision of these committees, combined into one over-all committee. So far, this has not happened. It is therefore still in terms of the four "rules" formulated by Campion in his revision of Erskine May's classic *Parliamentary Practice:* (1) financial initiative of the Crown; (2) preliminary consideration of financial charges in a Committee of the Whole House; (3) legislative authorization and appropriation of charges; (4) no more than one stage of appropriation per day.[29]

Congressional control over expenditures · The American Congress, in keeping with the general concept of Congressional control over the executive, has always insisted upon debating the details of budgetary appropriations. However, American experience with committee control was rather deplorable as long as authority for making the appropriations was widely scattered among different committees and numerous appropriation bills. But these difficulties were in some measure remedied by the Budget and Accounting Act (1921). Since that important enactment, the federal government has a comprehensive budget prepared by the Bureau of the Budget and presented to Congress by the President; this budget is then considered in conformity to its great divisions, corresponding to the organization of the government, and embodied in a series of related appropriation acts.[30] Under the procedure which prevailed in the American Congress until the Second World War, all appropriations had to be reported by the Committee on Appropriations, which deliberated upon them after a preliminary survey by its subcommittees corresponding to the various administrative departments. Since the war, under the Legislative Reorganization Act, the Committees on Expenditures of the Executive Departments are "authorized and directed" to study "the operation of Government activities at all levels with a view to determining its economy and efficiency." This implies a further complication of existing machinery.

Whenever legislation is enacted which entails appropriations, such appropriations have to be passed upon by the Committee on Appropriations as well as by the committee concerned with that particular type of legislation. The reason is that such appropriations must be considered in relation to all other appropriations. Such a procedure naturally causes many delays, and by contrast English procedure is praised for its dispatch. There is nothing startling about this contrast; it is merely a special example of the technical efficiency of power when it is fully concentrated. It has been rightly pointed out that such concentration of power is at variance with the American governmental system. Moreover, the evils which were associated with legislative determination of appropriations in the past have been largely due, not so much to the possession by the legislature of such power over appropriations, as to the lack of any definite and comprehensive program such as the annual budget message of the President has since provided. It was, in other words, a question of redressing the distribution of power over appropriations so as to produce a clear division between the function of formulating a comprehensive program, which properly belongs to the chief executive of the government, and the function of deliberating upon this program and readjusting it in terms of an emerging compromise over major policies of the major party, a function which properly belongs to a representative assembly. It is significant that even countries with executive establishments dependent upon parliamentary support, such as that of France, have developed committees specially charged with the supervision and control of governmental finances. In fact, these countries have been inclined to look upon such committees as the very core of parliamentary prerogative.

The French finance committee · The French committee on finances (*Commission des Finances*) in both the Chamber and Senate occupied a very central position in the Third and Fourth Republics. A great deal of the criticism of the parliamentary system was focused on these all-powerful committees and on the role they played in connection with France's budgetary and financial difficulties.[31] These committees often were the center of parliamentary opposition to the government, in spite of the system of proportional representation. The leading position of the chairmen and reporters (as discussed above, p. 351 ff.) frequently gave opposition leaders their chance. It could, of course, be provided, that such presidencies and reports be given to members of the majority, as is in fact the case in the United States, but in France the chairmen (presidents) of committees often acquired a quasi-permanent position. What is more, the fluidity of French parliamentary groups often brought it about that a member delegated to a committee by such a group, but belonging to one of its wings, did not follow the majority of this group in relation to the government. Barthélemy went so far as to comment, "Under the French system the best of the majority are in the government, while the best of the opposition are in the Finance Committee." Yet it would be fallacious to assume, as was sometimes done, that the chairman and the reporter necessarily exceeded the finance minister in power; but they could be his powerful rivals.

Unfortunately, the discussion of the procedural issues involved in the finance committee's powers was carried on in a partisan spirit. Rarely were these questions detached from the writer's preferences in matters of policy. In keeping with the general practice of the French parliament, the budget used to come before the whole house in the form which the finance committee had given it. Finally, the finance committee attempted to substitute its own budget for that proposed by the ministry, and to report a compromise between the two. Such a situation was almost suicidal under the difficult financial conditions that prevailed in France.

In the Third and Fourth Republics, the French always retained a single budget law, the *loi des finances*, which was reported by the general reporter. In addition, there were a series of separate budgets for important services, each reported by a separate *rapporteur*, thirty-four such separate budgets being reported for 1933. The general report on the finance bill undertook to coordinate these separate budgets. While originally undertaken with the sound purpose of more effective scrutiny of the government's budget proposals, this division of labor gradually led to a deplorable lack of unity. The separate reports were not the result of any discussion and deliberation of the committee, but were the work of the particular reporter. Since such reports came to be looked upon as rungs in the ladder toward a ministerial post, they gradually grew in bulk, until some of the later reports were huge quarto volumes. It is obvious that such reports had no practical relation to the work of the committee. The general budget received thorough discussion, but the special reports constituted rather a mine of detailed information on the conduct of French administration, than a method of fiscal control. Cases were quite frequent when administrative abuses, after having been attacked in such reports, were later remedied. Such practices were naturally furthered by a member's reporting the same budget year after year; they led to a *camaraderie* of the specialists in the administration and in parliament, both maintaining a certain solidarity against the minister, the parliament at large, and the public.

Although, strictly speaking, the committee should not have concerned itself with anything but fiscal matters, it was inevitably drawn into a consideration of the relative merits of divergent policies. Consequently, the burden of work was enormous, with the result that discussion in the committee was cut short by tactical considerations, and considerable delays were occasioned. (In light of French experience, the above-noted innovation of further responsibilities along these lines in the Congress appears more than questionable.) These delays had a disastrous effect as the emergency deepened. Contrary to the rules which provided for distribution of the budget report well in advance, the committee often asked the Chamber to consider matters on which no report had become available. Toward the end of the Third Republic, the finance committee had also commenced to unseat ministries by refusing consent to important measures (see above, p. 351). When taken together with the committee's substituting of its own budget for that of the government, France finally may be said to have had a dual government which produced anarchy, when effective action was required. Facing this situation, Barthélemy exlaimed: "The leftist group [in the committee] deliberates, the committee decides, the government follows." The lack of really effective leadership on the part of the government gave a great impetus to the finance committee's strength.

The problems of the finance committee cannot be separated from those of parliamentary, and, one might add, of constitutional government. It is a question of devising a procedure which will insure a competent decision after a sufficiently mature deliberation. Under the Fifth Republic the stranglehold that the finance committee used to have on the Assembly and on the cabinet has been loosened, but no effective solution has yet been found. Rejection of the budget by the finance committee no longer prevents the cabinet from bringing it before the Assembly, and when there, the minister in charge can stop all proposals to cut taxes or increase expenditure. Moreover, if the final vote is not taken within seventy days, the government can impose the budget by decree. These measures are in keeping with the present authoritarian trend and the tendency of some administrators to identify speed and efficiency with competence, even at the price of constitutionality.[32]

Administrative control · The discussion of the last two paragraphs has shown how intimately the problem of administrative control and supervision is bound up with the fiscal problem. It is nevertheless distinct. Both in the United States and in France (as well as in many other countries), the committee system, particularly when coupled with the interpellation, is an essential tool of parliament in controlling the administration.[33] It is natural, therefore, that voices should have arisen in England demanding a similar system of standing committees to restrain the "bureaucracy." Later it will be shown that many techniques exist for making officials responsible for their conduct. Under modern conditions, parliamentary supervision has had a very strong appeal. Here were persons well acquainted with the particular matter in hand through their legislative activity; why should not they see to it that the laws were faithfully executed? It is hard to deny the good sense of such a plan, and particularly in the earlier phases of the movement for constitutional government such control seemed wholly beneficial. The deep-seated suspicion with which the average man in France and the United State viewed the "bureaucracy" served as a powerful incentive toward the establishment of such control mechanisms.

As the century wore on, and as parties began to appear, it was discovered that such control by parliament and parliamentary committees was, in effect, control by parliamentarians. Such a system of control offered to these individuals and the party groups behind them opportunities of pressure which could be turned to quite different account than the protection of the public's interest against administrators. The evils of patronage, corruption in connection with governmental contracts, nepotism, and so forth, made their appearance. Parliamentary control soon began to look like parliamentary tyranny. Factionalism was introduced into the administrative services, with many an influential parliamentarian having a group of henchmen in various ministries who looked to him for promotion in return for assistance offered him in the promotion of various more or less legitimate interests. The difficulty lies in part in the intangible quality of such control. Unlike the preparation of a bill or a budget, we have conversations, questions, a certain atmosphere of either hostile criticism or collegial collaboration — all matters which are subject to a good deal of manipulation and diplomacy. This setting is in many cases further emphasized by the lack of publicity, which raises additional problems (see p. 363 ff.). In spite of all these troublesome complications, detailed parliamentary control seems essential if the administrative services are to be held in check. Reliance cannot safely be placed upon control by the cabinet at the top alone. There are many minor abuses and irregularities which certainly do not justify the ousting of a cabinet. Such developments can readily be reported to the plenary session, and thus be given some publicity. What is more, the existence of such a watchdog keeps the officials on their toes. They will seek to anticipate the reaction of a parliamentary committee. It might be argued, of course, that an entirely separate body of quasi-judicial persons should be entrusted with this task, so as to forestall the development of the various forms of collusion of which mention has been made. But such a procedure would further complicate an already top-heavy structure, and it would deprive the members of legislatures of a most valuable school in which to learn about the difficulties of administering a certain body of laws. Nor is it apparent why such a group should not be likewise subject to the temptations which as present beguile legislators.

Recently, Scandinavian constitutionalism has produced another idea which is interesting an ever-widening circle, and that is the *ombudsman* or guardian. His introduction into the British system has been discussed widely as a means of checking the abuse of administrative power by a rapidly growing bureaucracy. Such an official has been giving satisfaction especially in Denmark; in a way it is an adaptation of the ancient Chinese institution of the censors who traveled about the country and heard complaints against government officials. However, the ombudsman does not have wide discretionary power, as had the Chinese censor, but is primarily called upon to hear complaints and bring them to the attention of officials, Parliament, and the public.

In commenting on the use of a parliamentary commissioner, the official report said in 1965: "In Britain, Parliament is the place for ventilating the grievances of the citizen. . . . It is one of the functions of the elected MP to try to secure that his constituents do not suffer injustice at the hand of the

Government. The procedure of Parliamentary Questions, Adjournment Debates and Debates on Supply have developed for this purpose . . . We do not want to create any new institution which would erode the functions of MP's in this respect, nor to replace remedies which the British Constitution already provides. Our proposal is to develop those remedies still further. We shall give MP's a better instrument which they can use to protect the citizen, namely, the services of a Parliamentary Commissioner for Administration."[34] In spite of a certain amount of opposition, this plan was realized since. The commissioner is, however, excluded from local self-government, government corporations, and the police; what is more, no private person can present a complaint, as the commissioner is strictly "parliamentary" and therefore quite different from the ombudsman — a half-ombudsman, it has been said.[35]

The investigatory function of representative assemblies · Since the Cabinet does not require the confidence of Congress, as do European cabinets, investigating committees look into and in due course make public whatever abuses they may believe to exist.[36] The impending threat of such an investigating committee fulfills somewhat the same role as the threat of a scandal involving parliamentary support in England. Such an investigation brings to the attention of the public, frequently preceding an election, matters which will discredit the "ins." Such committees are naturally most likely to be appointed when the President has lost his majority in one of the houses of Congress. The Legislative Reorganization Act of 1946 considerably broadened the scope of such Congressional activity by authorizing substantially larger staffs for Congressional committees, which are intended to enable such committees to develop their own sources of information, because the Congress cannot depend upon the executive departments to supply all the information they need. In England, royal commissions of inquiry are looked upon in a somewhat similar light, but since they are appointed by the Crown, that is, the government in power, they are more likely to explore and report upon areas where changes in basic policy are impending than into the administrative services themselves. Still, as Redlich observed, "a royal commission has many advantages over a parliamentary committee; it can, while a parliamentary committee cannot, prolong its work beyond the limits of a session, if necessary even for years; and it is possible to appoint scientific experts as members so as to secure a completely impartial treatment of the subject."[37] There are, according to the leading study, several motives to be distinguished: (1) to prepare the way for a predetermined policy; (2) to ascertain the most feasible solution of a problem; (3) to have a non-parliamentary representative body resolve a major controversy, and in this connection to forestall public criticism and anticipated pressure; and (4) to gain time. Hence members may be chosen because they are representative of a major interest, or because they are expert, or because they are impartial, and possess integrity and authority. Royal commissions have declined in importance, because of the growth of administrative and other expertise available to the government and its bureaucracy through other channels. It seems that the royal commissions were functionally related to an open, liberal society, with a not-yet highly developed bureaucracy, whenever problems of reform called for the expert assessment of complex political or social problems. When it is considered desirable for interested groups to have access to policy making in a society yet strongly elitist in its governmental tradition, but challenged by a powerful public opinion, an instrumentality like the royal commission seems favored and suitable as a procedural device.[38]

Investigatory committees have been considerably abused in the United States in recent years. Especially the Senate's Internal Security Committee and the House Un-American Activities Committee have aroused a good deal of adverse political and legal comment. They constitute a perversion, since they do not carry on their activities with any clear objective to exercise legislative and policy-making functions or to exercise administrative control. Rather they operate as star-chamber type pseudo-criminal courts. Their abolition has been demanded by a rising tide of professional criticism, based upon scientific analysis of their operations.[39]

Such perversions apart, the investigatory function of parliamentary and Congressional committees is bound to grow as the complexities of public policymaking increase. In the words of a leading expert: "The most spectacular method of congressional review is the investigating committee, the requirements for which are an intrepid sponsor, at least a rumor of dissatisfaction, adequate financing, the authority to subpoena witnesses and papers, proper publicity, and a diligent staff." And he adds that "their most pronounced weakness is that they operate after the fact . . . Moreover, the investigations may be conducted to prove a point, not to supply facts objectively . . ."[40]

Control of foreign affairs · A distinct set of problems is found in the realm of foreign affairs.[41] The English Parliament has been very slow to enter into this field, which was for a long time looked upon as a "prerogative" of the Crown. To be sure, the clash over the Bulgarian atrocities, between the humanitarian principles of Gladstonian liberalism and Disraeli's skillful diplomacy, afforded Gladstone the major plank for his famous Midlothian Campaign, though the policy of collaboration with the Turk was blandly continued after he entered office. The shock of thus seeing problems of imperial concern carried before the multitude in order to build popular appeal served as a considerable lesson to the British Foreign Office; henceforth it carefully guarded its secrets against Parliament. This system culminated in the complex situation preceding the First World War, when fear of the parliamentary reaction induced Sir Edward Grey to pursue a more secret policy than had been followed for a century. France also carefully avoided parliamentary control of foreign affairs; the two parliamentary committees on the subject, which were beginning to build up a measure of surveillance, remained highly secretive themselves. Since the United States did not at that time carry on a very active foreign policy, but merely drifted along with the aid of a few "policies," such as were supposedly contained in the Monroe Doctrine and the principle of the Open Door in China, sporadic attempts by Presidents and Secretaries of State did not invite any measure of effective control. Hence not until after the First World War do we find anywhere a vigorous parliamentary participation in foreign affairs.

The general disaster of the First World War, the establishment of the League of Nations, the outburst of democratic and pacific enthusiasm, all aided in lending color to various efforts to realize the promise which had been held out by Wilson's "point" about the abolition of secret diplomacy and the substitution of "open covenants openly arrived at." As a technical device, the French and American system of a special committee made a strong appeal. In England it was ardently advocated; in Germany a special article of the constitution was devoted to the establishment of a standing committee on foreign affairs; in Holland, in Sweden, in Norway, in Czechoslovakia, everywhere standing committees on foreign affairs were set up. The French committees in both the Senate and the Chamber became more vocal. But if the idea had at first been that parliamentary control would aid in making international relations smoother, the activities of the Foreign Relations Committee of the United States Senate in connection with the Peace Treaty and the League Covenant should have given a warning. It was soon discovered that everywhere parliaments and their committees were inclined to outdo their ministers in insisting upon national "interest" and national "honor." The nationalist reaction first entrenched itself in Germany in the foreign affairs committee of the *Reichstag*, membership of which gave to the deputies the air of "being in the know." In the French parliament, nationalist elements likewise managed to dominate the scene in the plenary sessions as well as in the committees, and the more conciliatory policy of Briand met its first as well as its last serious defeat in these committees.[42] Even in the small and pacific Netherlands an able foreign minister was forced out by parliament because he had made a conciliatory treaty with the Belgian government concerning the Scheldt River which supposedly violated national "interests."[43] Another almost insuperable difficulty appeared as a result of large Communist parties in many of these parliaments which, on the basis of the proportional principle, had a right to seats on these committees. The Communists recurrently raised suspicions of collaborating with the government of the Soviet Union, often through the Third International, and were therefore felt not to be entitled to any confidential information. Sometimes this difficulty was met by forming a more informal group of members of the committee who received the really confidential information.

After Hitler's entry into power in Germany, parliamentary influence took yet another, and perhaps more disastrous, turn. In curious contrast to the preceding nationalist inclination, the parliaments of France, Britain, and the United States now became the decisive factor in fashioning a policy of appeasement. The sad record may be gleaned from a rather doleful document issued by the State Department, purporting to show that they did all that the Congress and the people would let them do. At the crucial turning point of Hitler's reoccupation of the Rhineland, e.g., when the French government, or at least some members, wanted to act forcibly, the parliamentary committees forbade such action unless it were supported by the British and Americans. The British conservative majority preferred to conclude a naval agreement with Hitler. The indecisiveness, the confused and meandering course of foreign affairs, as conducted by the major democratic powers, while no doubt due in part to the novelty of the situation and the as yet "unknown" potentialities and dangers, nonetheless is traceable at least in part to the ineptitude of parliamentary committees of foreign affairs.[44]

That situation seems to be somewhat changed since the Second World War. Whether as the result of experience, or of the more evident threat of Communist totalitarianism and imperialism, the parliaments of England, France, and the United States have shown a greater readiness to support a policy of containment of the aggressive tendencies, while at the same time the governments have displayed considerably greater vigor in shaping policies appropriate to this end.

The problem of publicity · The parliamentary control of foreign affairs squarely raises the issue of publicity. It is a question which has much bearing upon the whole system of parliamentary committees. Committee meetings are secret, either wholly or in part, and many of the most serious attacks are levelled at this feature of the system. No one has stated more forcefully the arguments in favor of making all deliberative transactions public than did Jeremy Bentham. He opens his classical *Essays on Political Tactics* with a discussion of publicity. "Before entering into the detail of the operations of the assembly, let us place at the head of its regulation the fittest law for securing the public confidence, and causing it constantly to advance towards the end of its institution. This law is that of publicity."[45] It should be noted that Bentham made an exception to his rule of publicity where "it would favor the projects of an enemy."

Bentham offers a number of reasons for his insistence on publicity: (1) to constrain the members of the assembly to perform their duty; (2) to secure the confidence of the people, and their assent to the measures of the assembly; (3) to enable the governors to know the wishes of the governed; (4) to enable the electors to act intelligently in elections; (5) to provide the assembly with the means of profiting by the information of the public; (6) to give amusement. The objections seemed to Bentham to resolve themselves into one, namely, that "the public is incompetent to judge of the proceedings of a political assembly." This objection he will not allow, because the public will judge, whether informed or not, because it desires to do so. If they were willing to forego judging because incompetent, they would be not common men, but philosophers. Omitting reference to those who do not judge at all, he argues further that those who judge anyway will judge ill upon incomplete information; they will, according to Bentham, judge better when fully informed. To deny them such information is to say: "You are incapable of judging, because you are ignorant; and you shall remain ignorant, that you may be incapable of judging." This argument would be conclusive if men were wholly rational. Though overstating a good case, Bentham's arguments prevailed. Publicity of parliamentary proceedings was instituted everywhere in the course of the nineteenth century, in England as well as on the Continent. But this could be done for two reasons: (1) many of the more crucial issues were and are discussed in secret party conclaves; and (2) others were and are handled in equally secret committee sessions. It is quite natural that the committee system should have been attacked on this score. Many prominent students of politics, including Woodrow Wilson, have bitterly condemned the secrecy of committee deliberations. An experienced Congressman like Robert Luce, after citing Wilson's writings, on the contrary asserts that "the complete justification of privacy is that its absence would enure to the injury of the public business." He stresses the privacy of cabinet meetings in England and America, and calls attention to the analogy with the relations between doctor and patient, clergyman and parishioner, lawyer and client. It may be doubted whether such arguments meet the core of Wilson's objections to secrecy. He put the matter thus: "Legislation, as we nowadays conduct it, is not conducted in the open. It is not thrashed out in open debate upon the floors of our assemblies. It is, on the contrary, framed, digested, and concluded in committee rooms. It is in committee rooms that legislation not desired by the interests dies. . . . There is not enough debate of it in the open house, in most cases, to disclose the real meaning of the proposals made. . . . There is not any legitimate privacy about matters of government. Government must, if it is to be pure and correct in its processes, be absolutely public in everything that affects it." The last phrases are evidently an over-statement, but the objections to the secrecy of the deliberative process of legislation are not met by merely pointing out such exaggerations. Other things being equal, secrecy should be avoided as being undemocratic. Would Bentham have taken the same view had he known our modern "yellow journalism" with its sensationalism and its irresponsibility? As has been mentioned before, at the time Bentham considered the subject the English Parliament was just emerging from its previous practice of carefully guard-ing the secrecy of parliamentary proceedings. Bentham himself, in surveying "the state of things in England," noted the contrast between the as yet unaltered rules designed to insure strict secrecy and the actual practice: "It is to these fortunate crimes that England is indebted for her escape from an aristocratic government resembling that of Venice."

The experience of many conscientious representatives may be put thus: "When a man thinks his words are to be repeated, he has an eye to the ultimate consumer. Instead of talking solely to those who are to make the immediate decision, he frequently talks with remote effects in mind. This would turn a public committee conference into a sparring spectacle for personal or party advantage." But elected assemblies *should* have an eye to the ultimate consumer, Bentham would reply. The conflict of values, therefore, cannot be resolved except in terms of an explicit recognition of the double function of elected assemblies and the consequent need for differen-tiating their techniques accordingly. A measure of privacy for deliberations should be provided, and the committee system provides that opportunity. But the value of publicity should likewise be recognized, and public debates, of either the whole house or some of its committees, be provided for.

What is detrimental to the prestige of parliamentary institutions is the tendency of parliamentarians nonchalantly to allow the committees to take complete direction. The pressure of the mass of modern activity is the main explanation of that tendency. Each member of the assembly is so busy as the member of one or more of its committees that he would just as soon forget about the plenary sessions. All over the world committee work has been crowding out general debate in open session. And what time committee work does not take, the ever-increasing electorate with ever-more efficient means of communication absorbs. The thousands of letters, telegrams, and telephone calls which many popular representatives get at certain crucial moments are merely the peaks of this ever-rising curve of public business.

Is it a fever curve? When the substance of our activities is mounting, we become indifferent to procedure; a very busy man is apt to be less polite than a man of leisure. All this is widely admitted; reports on parliamentary procedure in the United States, in England, and elsewhere are full of such observations. Impatient men are ready to pronounce the breakdown of the system. In order to get efficiency, they would scrap all publicity and revert to the complete secrecy of bureaucratic direction.

As in the period after the First World War, so at present the tendency toward, and the willingness to condone, secrecy has been greatly increased by the fear that information will be transmitted to Communist powers and their agents. Nor can this fear and suspicion be treated lightly by any reasonable man. All governments, but more especially totalitarian governments, are committed to secret service and espionage work. "Intelligence" functions have been growing by leaps and bounds in the United States.[46] When a government is frankly committed to the espousal of world revolution, all other governments, especially constitutional governments, are faced with the problem of how to avert their overthrow by these revolutionary forces. How far can one go in permitting advocacy of such views? How much of one's own policy can one permit the agents and accomplices of such a world-revolutionary organization to know about? These are two of the elementary, and yet also the most persistent, questions that face the student of constitutionalism. Especially when one is concerned with constitutionalism's inherent requirement of maximizing publicity on all aspects of public policy and the discussion and deliberation upon such policy in the representative assemblies, do such questions become insistent.

Ultimately, this is one aspect of the "reason of state." For the problem of security and survival faces the constitutional order just as much as it does an autocratic government. But can you justify the violation of the constitution when the survival of the constitution is at stake? Constitutional theorists often answered "yes," but with an uneasy conscience. Modern constitutional democracies have been granting ever-wider discretion to those who are supposedly handling "security" and "intelligence" matters.[47] In all such arrangements, the problem of how to provide for suitable supervision by a representative assembly has been difficult to solve. Instances like the recent (1967) issue over secret manipulations by the CIA in the field of international education are indicative of the unresolved complexities. No simple, dogmatic answers are feasible in this field. It all becomes a matter of judgment upon such elusive matters of "fact" as whether the danger is "clear" and is "present." Yet some such standard is the nearest criterion we have for coping with these complexities.

We noted above that the French parliament of the Fourth Republic provided for greater publicity of its committee meetings. The same trend is observable in the postwar German constitutions. But while publicity is acknowledged as desirable, the opportunity for excluding the public is generally believed to be essential. The American Congress, the English Parliament, the French parliament, all provide for public debates as well as secret committee deliberations. In England, parliamentary procedure proper recognizes such privacy most sparingly, but all descriptive accounts of the English system point to one conclusion: the compactness of English party organization permits all essential deliberations to be carried on among party leaders outside of Parliament proper, the "ins" in the clubs and the cabinet, the "outs" in the clubs alone. Elsewhere, party organization being less authoritarian and the leadership less effective, much deliberation and the compromise which results from it are carried on in the committees.

A glimpse at the caucus · The origin of the caucus may be traced as far back as the reign of Elizabeth I, when the Puritans would confer in advance of sessions. This practice aroused the wrath of the queen, who had Peter Wentworth and his friends put into the Tower. It has been rightly surmised that "these gatherings of Puritan members in advance of the session marked the beginning of caucuses." And it would seem that Queen Elizabeth and her council did not like such caucuses. Yet they were to become an established instrument of political warfare.[48] In the United States the problem of the "secret" party conclave is not unknown, of course. In fact, a great deal of controversy has surrounded the development of the caucus in the American Congress. It is significant, and in keeping with British experience, that the caucus should have made its appearance in conjunction with strong presidential leadership, such as that of Jefferson and Wilson. But the caucus is rather insignificant in American state legislatures, and more particularly in Massachusetts was not employed until recently. In the United States Senate it does not play a significant role either. Perhaps this weakness of the caucus in the Senate is directly related to the weakness of presidential leadership in the Senate. The caucus was somewhat strengthened in the House through the revolt against the Speaker in 1909–1910, but on the whole the privacy of committee proceedings in Congress has made the caucus a preliminary rather than a decisive stage. If genuine deliberation could no longer take place in these committees, the caucus might conceivably become increasingly the forum where actual deliberation would take place. Deliberation, with its need for privacy, will retreat to party conclaves if the regular legislatures do not provide suitable opportunities for the thrashing out of questions involving a frank facing of difficulties. The Senate has several times debated this subject, and in the course of these debates it has been stated that caucuses have rarely, if ever, undertaken to bind members to any particular action; their main power lies in the part they play in filling committee memberships and other such personnel questions, and in their ironing out dissensions over policy matters bearing upon party fortunes, particularly as they are related to presidential elections. These are matters of great political importance which do not come before committees, nor could they be considered in the presence of the opposition party. It is not readily apparent how national party organizations could be held together without some effort at concerted action of their national representatives.

Nor would it seem possible to steer a party group in a representative assembly without it. The Germans call these parliamentary groups *Fraktion,* while in England their importance is expressed in their recognition as "parliamentary party." In America, the caucus "may be considered to be the constituent body of the party in each chamber," for it ratifies committee assignments and selects party leaders, but it does not often act on policy and seldom meets as a corporate group. Its disciplinary force is weak, and Republicans do not even try to commit their members. For policy guidance, steering committees, policy committees, and legislative committees have sprung up. "The main function of the caucus (or conference) is . . . to assign personnel to the various positions essential to the legislative process."[49] In this operation, committees on committees chosen by the caucus have a decisive role. British and Continental practice goes considerably further in imposing party discipline by way of caucuslike groupings. Generally the trend is toward greater and greater discipline. This means, of course, that the deliberative function of representative assemblies is declining. What deliberation and discussion there is occurs in more or less secret party gatherings; to the extent that party congresses are gaining in stature, they constitute a trend for public deliberation and discussion of broad policy issues to take place in such contacts. The trend is world-wide.

The problem of consent and constraint · The problems of procedure are closely related to the general functioning of a constitutional government. Rules of parliamentary procedure appear as restraints upon the exercise of power which the majority accepts as readily as the minority. Intrinsically, the majority could change the rules to give it complete ascendancy, as happened in the days of the Stuart kings and Cromwell. Actually, such a change is out of the question as long as the other party is accepted as a partner in a contest requiring the participation of both — in the long run. In the United States, the constitutionally fixed recurrence of elections at stated intervals obliges the contestants to look beyond temporary advantage. In

England, the periodic "appeal to the country" seems practically as inevitable, though a parliamentary majority could presumably change that as well as anything else in the constitution. But, of course, the protection of the minority does not extend to the point where it uses procedural means for the purpose of destroying the possibility of parliamentary work. Filibustering and various other devices resembling the boycott, when carried beyond a certain point, become attacks against the constitutional order as such. The power of the minority, as well as the power of the majority, can be abused and needs to be restrained. This limitation was exceeded by the policy of obstruction of the Irish Nationalists in the seventies of the last century in England, of the various subject nationalities in Austria before the First World War, and of the Communists and Fascists in Continental parliaments after the First World War. The Irish as well as their Continental brethren denied the constitutional order under which they lived, and therefore the right to exist of the parliament to which they belonged. In France's Third and Fourth Republics, the manipulation of procedure for destructive ends by individual politicians and by parties which had no stake in the constitutional system resulted in occasional paralysis of the government. The present constitution, therefore, dictates certain rules of procedure and provides that the standing orders of parliament may not be changed without review by the Constitutional Council.

One cannot, however, solve the problems of abuse of procedure by constitutional prescription. The parliamentary system of modern constitutional government must ultimately rest to some extent on certain tacitly accepted conventions. Josef Redlich's treatise was devoted to unfolding this aspect in great detail.[50] From the vantage point of English (and Austrian) experience before the war, he emphasized that the acceptance of such conventions depends upon a measure of general agreement amongst the people concerning their political order. But he went beyond that when he claimed: "Parties of such intransigeance that they reject the political order (*Staatsverband*) as such, which demand the subjection of this order to the Church, or which want to destroy the whole social order, parties, finally, which are rooted in a principle as deep as religious conscience, namely the principle of nationalism, such parties are in irreconcilable conflict with these conventions upon which parliamentarism rests. . . ." And Redlich continued: "Where political antagonisms of such force appear, that they destroy the political allegiance of the individual, because his political philosophy is rooted in still deeper and firmer political convictions, like his religious feelings, his national consciousness, or (in the future) his desire for social and economic equality, there the primary foundation of parliamentary government, the convention back of the majority principle, loses its moral force.

With it the principle of the protection of the minority also loses its support." These prophetic words, written in 1905, foreshadowed the doom of the Hapsburg Empire; while not tenable in this pointed form, they yet indicate the point at which government by consent faces its most severe test. Without a certain amount of constraint, even the most skillfully structured pattern of consent cannot operate with success.

Conclusion · The role of parliaments as deliberative assemblies has declined in the twentieth century. Not only the increasing complexity of advanced industrial societies, but also the development of highly organized parties and interest groups, of planning agencies and bureaucracies, has jeopardized the parliaments of the world. Gone are the days when a Bentham could project his model of a highly rational assembly of ultility-minded representatives who never had to shun the glare of publicity, manipulated as it increasingly is by powerful mass-communication media. And yet representative assemblies continue to play a central role in constitutional systems. Successive reforms have sought to adapt their procedures, where antiquated, to the new conditions. Presiding officers, speech and debate, questions, interpellations, and closure have all been slowly transformed to meet the changed situation. Everywhere committees of every variety are forging ahead as the means for adapting the work of parliaments to the tasks confronting them. Fiscal and budgetary control have been revamped in America, Britain, and on the Continent. Administrative control has been expanded and the investigatory function of deliberative assemblies extended to the point where it threatens the basic human rights of the citizen with deviant views displeasing to the authorities. The control of foreign affairs has proved a particularly difficult problem in light of the rise of totalitarian powers practicing secret diplomacy in the service of expansionist, if not world-revolutionary, goals. These is no easy answer, it was shown, to the problem of publicity, anyhow. The simplest views of the liberal age, of men like Kant and Bentham, have had to yield to more differentiated views, based on a great deal of practical experience. A glance at caucuses and other extraparliamentary devices raises the general problem of consent and constraint in representative assemblies.

At the same time, some of the more mature parliamentary bodies are evolving toward a fairly equilibrated balance between their representative and their deliberative functions and the techniques required for the realization of both. The failure of French democracy naturally suggests that the exaggeration of debate characteristic of the French chambers was unwholesome. Bentham's unique endeavour at constructing a theory of parliamentary tactics is of significance primarily because of his emphasis upon the importance of a working *opposition*. But it must not be dogmatically taken as complete or final. Where it was so taken, it materially contributed to the failure of various parliamentary regimes. England and the Dominions, as well as the United States, were not swayed by the logical brilliance of Bentham's deductions. While the development followed his demands as far as the English speakership was concerned, it did so for different reasons and in a different way. The Speaker in the House of Commons did not combine leadership with impartiality, as Bentham had required, but abandoned leadership in favor of neutrality, while the leadership in legislation was assumed by the cabinet. In the United States, under the constitutionally safeguarded separation of powers, the Speaker of the House of Representatives abandoned neutrality in favor of leadership, and even though he today divides such leadership with several others, he still plays a decisive partisan role. Similar conditions exist in most of the American state legislatures. In the British Dominions which have adopted parliamentary cabinet systems of government, the Speakers have assumed the neutral position of their English colleague. The English cabinet's legislative leadership has been cemented by the development of the office of the whip, and even the opposition has found it expedient to coordinate its activities through such whips. While the party system, broadly speaking, has decisive effects upon parliamentary procedure, the latter often reacts back upon the parties. To the extent to which procedural rules become fixed, they can and do mold party development. They can thus become powerful tools in the hands of a majority. Ultimately rules of parliamentary procedure appear, therefore, as self-restraints upon the exercise of power by a "sovereign" body of representatives.

The analysis of experience has, it is hoped, shown that the representative and the deliberative functions of elected assemblies are both important, but that they are fairly distinct. Elected assemblies are responding to real needs when they differentiate their techniques to fulfill both functions. If men could deliberate without thinking of the reactions of those who are to elect, or rather re-elect, them, such differentiation would be unnecessary.

Chief Executives and Cabinet Systems
XVIII

Introduction · Political leadership: mystique and reality · National emergencies and personal insecurity · Growth of social problems and planning · Policy making and policy execution · Chief executives versus cabinet · Model cabinet government: Great Britain · The cabinet subservient to parliament: France · An ill-fated experiment: Germany · The collegial council: Switzerland · One-man rule: the American President · Cabinet and presidential secretariat and the problem of informal advisers · Conclusion

Introduction · Of the American President, Harold Laski has said that he is "both more and less than a king; both more and less than a prime minister." The issue of executive leadership is dramatically projected in such a comparison. The American President was conceived by the makers of the American constitution as a republican equivalent to the hereditary monarch of British constitutionalism. Hamilton, in the *Federalist*, went to great length comparing the two offices, insisting that "there is no pretence for the parallel which has been attempted between him and the king of Great Britain."[1] He felt that anyone who thought that the President had anywhere near the power of the British king was absurd. Since that comparison was made, kings have vanished or become shadows of their former selves, while the American President has assumed the central position in the American scheme. This, we saw in a preceding chapter, was at least in part the result of his becoming the leader of the majority party. In the meantime, in Britain the prime minister has emerged as the keystone of the arch of what is today a cabinet rather than a parliamentary government. The same is true of the British Dominions and Eire. Countries with less sound political traditions have struggled in vain to produce a similar integration, and when they failed have reverted to autocratic schemes of executive leadership.

Along with the chief executives, their cabinets or councils have undergone considerable change. Their relationship both to the chief executive and to the elected representative assemblies has evolved in accordance with the increasing emphasis upon executive leadership. Cabinets are older than parliaments. Princes surrounded themselves with councils or cabinets for the direction of their bureaucracies as soon as central administrative systems arose. In fact, these bodies, composed of leading administrative officials, are the very core of such centralized systems. It is therefore no wonder that the cabinet tends to occupy a somewhat independent position and is not ordinarily, as the phrase used to go, "an executive committee of Parliament." Cabinets today depend once again upon the chief executive, as they always have in the United States. What is more, the old formulas about policymaking and policy execution require extensive revision.

Political leadership: mystique and reality • The crux of executive power is political leadership. The doings of the Fascists have brought to the fore a conception which was dear to the hearts of romantic critics of constitutionalism and rationalism throughout the nineteenth century. Englishmen, Frenchmen, and Germans vie with each other in glorifying the hero, the Caesar, the superman. Carlyle, Maurras, Nietzsche, they all and many more vented their artistic spleen by contrasting the creative force of the leader with the equalitarian mediocrity of the majority and the mass. Nietzsche was inspired by Burckhardt, as Maurras was inspired by Taine, both great historians with a pessimistic bent of mind. Leopold von Ranke, greatest of German historians in the nineteenth century, while desirous of describing things "as they had actually been," nevertheless saw history essentially as the product of the great state builders, the Cromwells, Richelieus, and Fredericks.[2] Looking at events primarily through the eyes of contemporary observers, like the Venetian ambassadors whose reports he so thoroughly explored, he too absorbed the Renaissance view of man and history.

Sociology and political science, psychology and economics, have more recently exploded a good part of these cherished historical premises. Indeed, economic determinism proceeded to interpret the political leader as nothing but the product of favorable economic circumstance. "He thinks he pushes while he's being pushed"; this snarl of Mephistopheles would best describe the "leader" in a treatment of history preoccupied with price movements, inventions, discoveries, and trade. Meanwhile, Freudian hypotheses about sex as the ultimate propeller of human activity provided new hunches for an interpretation of history, not to mention the school of debunkers who delighted the reader by offering him the intimate view a butler takes of his hero, which proverbially destroys the illusion of greatness. Napoleon scolding Josephine for having mislaid his overcoat is a spectacle which suits the equalitarian impulse of democratic man. Increasing insight into the psychological processes associated with leadership, suggestion, egocentricity, and the whole range of propaganda, also contributed toward the eclipse of the view of leadership as the decisive determinant of social development. But these mounting doubts of the intellectuals could not quell the psychic impulses which are generated in men by a feeling of insecurity: the demand for the leader increased as international and class conflicts undermined the confidence of the masses in the future.

Many attempts have been made to discover the traits of *the* leader, to discover an abstract, general pattern of qualities or characteristics which constitute "leadership."[3] Indeed, many take it for granted that these qualities are known. Yet, actually, the greatest diversity of opinion prevails as to what constitutes even "executive ability," let alone leadership ability. A survey of the various inquiries, as well as our general knowledge, leads to the conclusion that these qualities depend very largely upon the conditions under which leadership operates. The nature of the group and of the task will make much difference. This also holds true, in a more limited way, concerning political leadership. An American President needs different qualities from a British Prime Minister, and his qualities today need to be different from what they were a hundred years ago. Take only the single instance of radio and television appeal; the indications are that elections are being vitally affected by that intangible quality. Although it is quite difficult to secure adequately conclusive data, it seems fairly clear from a number of studies that the "Great Debates" between Kennedy and Nixon in the presidential elections of 1960 provided Kennedy with a distinct advantage on account of his greater appeal over the air. If true, this factor decided the election in his favor, since the margin was extremely small. Another striking instance was provided by the French presidential elections in November 1965. Although de Gaulle has a powerful appeal over the air, he did not fully exploit it, and thereby gave a relative newcomer, Lecanuet, a chance to cut into De Gaulle's following sufficiently to reduce the General's vote to a little over 45 per cent.[4] Evidence is also accumulating in American Congressional and local elections in support of the proposition that television appeal has become a vital factor.[5]

The situation in Britain seems to be similar. Such television appeal tends to enhance the demagogic and plebiscitary aspect of representative bodies and authorities. It is still true, however, that no man can hope to be a success as Prime Minister in Britain who lacks the capacity of handling himself effectively in the give and take of parliamentary debate; the American President does not need that ability, but he needs instead the capacity to deal with Congress in indirect ways. For upon this ability depends his success as a policy maker and legislative leader. He can hope neither to put through major policy nor to effectuate supporting legislation, if he does not know how to cooperate effectively with the leaders of the majority in Congress (or to counterbalance a loss of support in his own party by gaining the support of the opposition, as did Eisenhower with the help of Johnson).[6] This functional approach to the problem of political leadership becomes even more essential when we go farther afield. A religious leader differs markedly from a business leader, and both contrast sharply with a military leader.

We are not at present in a position to "explain" political leadership, and we may never be. When we consider a great religious or spiritual leader, like Luther or Jean Jacques Rousseau, we are apt to admit that we are facing the ultimate creative force in human society working through such a leader. The same would be true of the scientific or artistic leader. When we come to political and social leaders, to the shapers of organizations and governments, we are obliged to be more skeptical. Many students of history would see a clear analogy between a work of art and a "state"; indeed to Machiavelli the state appeared the greatest of all works of art. But recent history has shown or at least suggested that many, if not all, men can participate in the building and maintaining of a government; that a constitutional system is never the work of one great leader. Once law is placed in the center of attention, it is evident that many minds and many, many hands have gathered and are gathering the detailed insights, devising the particular solutions to particular problems, and that no one can know enough to devise a "state." As we have pointed out before, the "state" concept as such was an outgrowth of a view constructed to justify and rationalize the despotic powers of monarchical rulers in the seventeenth century.

It is possible, however, to spell out, so to speak, certain functional aspects of a political leader.[7] One such functional aspect is the leader's representativeness. We all know that an Irishman is more likely to get Irish votes than a Yankee. Likewise a man wanting to reform a church would have to be a member of that church. Again, no one who was not a member of a given profession or craft would be apt to succeed in "reforming" such a profession, no matter how sound his views might be. Representativeness is, as we have shown, compounded of likeness of behavior, of outlook, and of general qualities. Another functional aspect of political leadership is a capacity to find solutions to commonly recognized problems. Here the creative aspect is more apparent. The solution of problems presupposes intelligence; without intelligence there cannot be leadership — that much is certain. But intelligence unrelated to problems recognized by the group is unproductive of leadership. Intelligence is a matter of degree. Leadership, therefore, is likely to be a matter of degree also. A governmental system always presents many concrete problems; some are very small and specific, others vast and comprehensive. The man who suggests a convincing solution acquires political leadership as others follow his lead.

A third functional aspect, related to the preceding, but distinct, is the capacity to foresee problems that are not generally recognized, to bring them into clear view and to dramatize their urgency. Again it is a matter of intelligence, but of analytical insight rather than inventiveness, plus the ability to generate and radiate emotion. All the progressive movements, particularly of recent time, contained leaders of this type. They show, at the same time, how easily this capacity is stultified by unexpected developments. Thus, Marx's analysis, while a brilliant anticipation of the rising labor-class problem, overlooked the importance of the managerial class in an expanding industrialism by indiscriminately lumping it together with capital owners as the capitalist class. His expectation of an inevitable labor majority has therefore remained unfulfilled, and the policies of socialist parties built upon that expectation have foundered. If the leader functions well as an anticipator and solver of group problems, he will naturally seem superior to his fellows.

Whether physical prowess distinguishes the leader, as it did Achilles, or whether a keen wit enables him to succeed where others fail, prestige will invariably be associated with his position. Prestige is not a separate result of leadership; it is part and parcel of it. Napoleon, the winner of battles, can afford to be a ruffian; a successful leader commands a margin of freedom from communal restraints. This fact is universally recognized. It is not limited to despotic regimes; everyone knows that there is such a margin in the most democratic constitutionalism, and when the British constitution to this day maintains that "the king can do no wrong," it gives symbolic recognition to that fact. Here we can see once again the root of constitutional restraints: they are designed to prevent the erstwhile leader from becoming a despot, which he might otherwise become by utilizing this margin of freedom for the systematic destruction of his opponents.

National emergencies and personal insecurity · We have alluded, in the previous section, to the psychic impulse which a sense of insecurity generates in man, the impulse, namely, of either becoming a leader or following one. There is nothing mysterious or novel about this; it is a most natural way to try to cope with pressing difficulties. Few are the people who, when seeing their house on fire, will calmly go their way as if nothing had happened. Most men will either run in and get everybody to leave the house, form a bucket line, and send for help — in short, *become* a leader; or they will call the fire department, that is, *seek* a leader. What an intelligent person will do depends a good deal upon whether the fire department is within easy, quick reach, whether the fire is far advanced, who is in the house — in short, upon all the conditions surrounding the concrete situation. This case, therefore, illustrates well the fact that the same person may elect to be a leader in one situation and a follower in another. The essential question always must be: What course of action offers the greatest probability of getting me results? If one sees no solution, he is likely to follow any man who asserts with a show of reason that he has a solution. It is an undeniable fact that at present a great many people have a sense of personal insecurity, well supported by incontrovertible evidence, such as the death of a close relative in war, bankruptcy, unemployment, etc.[8] These anxieties have lately been reinforced by the terror of nuclear and biologic weapons.

The heightening sense of personal insecurity has made electorates more volatile than they were in the liberal age, when democratic constitutionalism became predominant. This sense of personal insecurity is in part, at least, the outgrowth of very widespread dissatisfaction with government. Where that dissatisfaction becomes critical, not only revolutionary movements, but also demagogic appeals multiply. The "gusts of popular passion," which Hamilton and other men among the founders of the American republic feared so much and declaimed against, are easily aroused under such conditions of anxiety. The hope for a "savior" or hero who can straighten out the general disorder and re-establish an effective body politic spreads, and only he who is bold or deluded enough to be prepared to assert that he knows the answers can satisfy the ardent longing of the many for an "escape from freedom," in the telling phrase of Erich Fromm.[9]

Can constitutionalism, can democracy, guard against the demagogue? Within limits, yes. Like the thoughtful parent, it can provide for cooling-off periods. Institutional restraints, such as have been surveyed in earlier chapters, can be provided. Even the constitutional emergency powers can be surrounded with safeguards. But when the sense of insecurity becomes too extreme, when people in their search for some remedy become frantic, all these institutional devices will prove of no avail. That is the reason why the capacity of self-control, of facing emergencies calmly, of enduring an abiding sense of insecurity without losing one's head, is an essential condition of a lasting constitutional order. Those qualities, in short, which makes a man a political leader himself, which make him seek solutions to his problems, must be widely dispersed amongst a people to enable it to govern itself. Potentially a large part of a democratic nation is possessed of the capacity for political leadership. That is the crux of the matter.

Growth of social problems and planning · The issues which give rise to the sense of personal insecurity just discussed are all more or less definitely rooted in the growing complexity of our industrial system. The steady forward march of technological change, the rapid succession of inventions, and the deepening awareness of class conflict have generated social tensions much more rapidly than the social inventiveness of man could cope with them. Some acute thinkers, like the late Lord Stamp, have gone so far as to suggest that there should be a general moratorium on all inventions.[10] Leaders in the most advanced nations, unable to cope with the total situation, have attempted to treat now one aspect, now another, always finding their specific solutions defeated by unexpected secondary and tertiary effects in other spheres of social life. Take, for example, the field of agricultural policy in the United States. No one could deny that after the First World War the farmer's plight in America was serious. There was a rapid succession of remedial policies, trying to solve the problem first by stimulating exports, then by storing surpluses, then by restricting production; but in each instance the farmer was not materially helped, while other groups, foreign nations, taxpayers, consumers, raised a sharp protest against the consequences of the policy adopted. The same experience can be observed in the field of unemployment. Outright doles, insurance schemes, public works, they all have been tried in turn by all the industrialized nations and have been found impracticable in the end. The labor market became disturbed, insurance reserves could not be safely invested, the taxpayer objected to unnecessary public improvements while his property deteriorated.

From a Communist viewpoint all this is inevitable; only an economy totally controlled by the government can cope comprehensively with this situation. But a thorough analysis of experience in the Soviet Union reveals that over-all plans suffer from the same difficulty that a less comprehensively controlled economy encountered: unanticipated secondary and tertiary effects vitiate and upset the neatly balanced blueprint as much as natural catastrophes such as droughts. The early and simple objective of industrializing Russia being accomplished, the Soviet Union is left confronting the same uncertainties with which planning is confronted in the United States. Planning is discussed in further detail below, so all we might add here is the summary statement that no modern state can escape responsibility for planning on an increasing scale.

Policy making and policy execution · In the last section we spoke of an agricultural policy. Earlier in the volume reference was made to the modern shift in emphasis from legislation to policy making. When, in Bentham's time, attention was focused upon legislation, men thought of it in terms of making rules. But Bentham dramatically insisted upon its embodying social "inventions." He saw it as what has become known as "public policy." Public policy is a course of government action, indicted by the need for overcoming a difficulty. Profoundly convinced of the possibility of "solving" problems in terms of increasing the sum total of human happiness, Bentham was forever at work to find such solutions. His enormous direct and indirect influence upon English and American social reformers has helped to make his outlook an integral part of modern democracy.

It has long been customary to distinguish between policy making and policy execution. Frank J. Goodnow undertook to built an almost absolute distinction upon this functional difference. "There are, then, in all governmental systems two primary or ultimate functions of government, *viz.* the expression of the will of the state and the execution of that will. There are also in all states separate organs, each of which is mainly busied with the discharge of one of these functions. These functions are, respectively, Politics and Administration."[11] But while the distinction has a certain value as a matter of relative emphasis, it cannot any longer be accepted in absolute form. The problem of how a public policy is adopted and carried out is bogged down by an ideological superstructure which contributes little or nothing to its solution. Take a case like the Agricultural Adjustment Act. In simple terms, it contained a policy adopted with a view to helping the farmer to weather the storm of the depression. To accomplish this purpose, crop reduction, price fixing, and a number of lesser devices were adopted. Crop reduction in turn led to processing taxes. Processing taxes required reports by the processors, inspection of their plants. Crop reduction itself necessitated reports by the farmers, so-called work sheets, and agreements between them and the government as to what was to be done, and so forth and so on. What here is politics, and what administration? The concrete patterns of public-policy formation and execution reveal that politics and administration are not two mutually exclusive boxes, or absolute distinctions, but that they are two closely linked aspects of the same process. Public policy, to put it flatly, is a continuous process, the formation of which is inseparable from its execution. Public policy is being formed as it is being executed, and it is likewise being executed as it is being formed. Politics and administration play a continuous role in both formation and execution, though there is probably more politics in the formation of policy, more administration in the execution of it. Insofar as particular individuals or groups are gaining or losing power or control in a given area, there is politics; insofar as officials act or propose action in the name of public interest, there is administration.[12]

The same problem may be considered from another angle. Policies, in the common meaning of the term, are decisions about what to do or not to do in given situations. It was pointed out that today most legislation is looked upon as deciding policy. Hence, policy making in the broad sense is not supposed to be part of administration. While these propositions are true in a general way, they tend to obscure two important facts, namely, (1) that many policies are not ordained with a stroke of the legislative or dictatorial pen, but evolve slowly over long periods of time, and (2) that administrative officials participate continuously and significantly in this process of evolving policy. To commence with the latter fact, it is evident that in the process of doing something the administrator may discover another and better way of accomplishing the same result, or he discovers that the thing cannot be done at all, or that something else has to be done first, before the desired step can be taken. In our recent agricultural policy, examples of all these "administrative" policy determinations can be cited, as likewise in our social security policy. What is more, such administrative participation alone renders policy making a continuous process. This process is so much in a state of flux that it is difficult, if not impossible, to state with precision what the policy in any given field is at any particular time. But, if this is true, it follows as a corollary that public policy will often be contradictory and conflicting in its effects upon society. Seeing that policies are in fact contradictory and conflicting, the question is raised: who is responsible for what, and to whom? To what extent does such responsibility affect the actual conduct of affairs? No consideration of executives or cabinets can be undertaken without bearing the role of the administrator in mind.

It is no longer true that the mere dependence of a cabinet upon the "confidence" of an elected assembly ensures responsible conduct on the part of the officials in charge of the initiation and execution of public policy. It is objectionable to consider responsibility secure by this simple device, not merely because of interstitial violations but because there is a fundamental flaw in the view of politics and policy it assumes. The range of present-day public policy is so far-flung that the "rights" of the parliamentary majority to oust a cabinet from power is largely inoperative. The majority supporting the cabinet may violently disagree with a certain policy advocated and adopted by the cabinet, but considerations of party politics, in the broadest sense, will throttle their objections because the particular issue is "not worth a general election" and the chance of the M. P.'s losing his seat.[13] This is what gives the British cabinet its key political function, often described as that of "formulating policy." It is more correct to say that it is that of "making the major decisions." And yet, sometimes the most important decisions are made by the Prime Minister as leader of the party, and presented to the cabinet as a *fait accompli*.

Thus, when the executive depends upon parliamentary support, the pattern of executive leadership is related to that of the representative assembly. But cabinets may possess a very high degree of independence from such a representative assembly, like that of England before the time of Walpole, or of the United States at present, or of other governments molded upon the American federal pattern, as are most of the American states. This interrelationship is, of course, important. On the whole, systems with a measure of independence seem to be more stable. As contrasted with the dependence of French cabinets, the English pattern seems to strike a happy medium.

Here the Prime Minister's leadership of the dominant party gives the cabinet very comfortable independence without freeing it altogether from considerations of parliamentary support. Still different is the situation in Switzerland, where the cabinet, as in the United States, is constitutionally independent but at the same time preoccupied with administrative problems, accepting in the realm of legislation the verdict of the representative body. From this quick survey it can be seen that the pattern of executive leadership shows numerous variations.

Chief executives versus cabinet   •   The relative strength and power of the single executive as contrasted with some collegial body, like the cabinet, is today at least as important as the relation of either to a body of elected representatives. There is need for a broad comparative analysis of executive leadership in such terms.[14] Generally speaking, executive leadership may be vested largely in a single individual, as it is in the United States, where the Cabinet consists essentially of helpers of the chief executive. Or executive leadership may be exercised by a group of equals, as it is in Switzerland. Or it may fit somewhere in between — England, the Dominions, or France show intermediary patterns. Moreover, these national patterns have been changing gradually from the collegial toward monocratic control, owing to the development of large parties and the prime minister's increasing importance as party leader. The tendency toward the monocratic (presidential) pattern seems almost universal. Frequently it has been perverted into dictatorship; the slower evolution of the positions of *Il Duce* merely foreshadowed the rapid rise of the *Führer*. The collegial pattern is more nearly compatible with parliamentary control, but it fails to produce the integration and symbolic representation of unity which the mass electorate seems to demand. In France under the Third Republic, each of the several members of the cabinet figured as the leader of one of the groups which together constituted the parliamentary support of the cabinet. In Switzerland, the members of the Federal Council are not even necessarily leaders of groups or parties, but are merely representatives of such groups with high administrative qualifications. We find approximations to the collegial pattern in pre-Fascist Italy as well as in a number of the smaller countries of Europe. In many of these countries the pattern was subject to considerable variation, in response to different personalities — a fact which is of some importance even in more nearly monocratic systems. The instability of the pattern was particularly marked in Weimar Germany. For a time, an effective leader such as Stresemann or Brüning would create a situation approximating the English arrangement. But the many parties would at other times, in the absence of such a leader, force a strictly collegial cabinet.

Model cabinet government: Great Britain · Combining strong executive leadership with parliamentary and popular influence, the British system of cabinet government is probably the most extraordinary masterpiece of constitutionalism. Both simple and subtle, it is the achievement of generations of people developing one of the soundest political traditions ever possessed by man. So remarkable has been its appeal that time and again admirers have sought to adopt and adapt it, never realizing its ever-evolving operational secrets sufficiently to understand its peculiar conditions of operation, its limitations as well as its strength. As has been well said, to pretend to a knowledge of its up-to-date functioning would presuppose knowledge which is only quite fragmentary. The firm tradition of cabinet secrecy, which used to be carried to the point of not permitting any notes to be taken, has been largely observed. In commenting on it, Herbert Morrison, who had much experience to back up his opinion, stressed that "Cabinet Ministers have one duty above all others: it is to speak the truth as they see it without fear . . . Thus a Minister . . . would perhaps be less likely to speak his mind, if secrecy were not observed . . . the public interest requires secrecy."[15] This justified conviction carries with it a certain ineluctable elitism which even the most democratic politician will have to accept. Even so, the British cabinet is a responsible agent of the majority party.

Historically speaking, the English cabinet developed as a committee of the Privy Council.[16] It does not, as is sometimes assumed, comprise all the officials responsible to Parliament, but only the more important among them, including the heads of the principal departments. There are the First Lord of the Treasury, the Chancellor of the Exchequer, and the First Lord of the Admiralty, as well as the Lord President of the Council and the Lord Privy Seal. In recent decades the cabinet has usually had around twenty members, more or less. They are selected by the Prime Minister according to a variety of considerations. Among them, political expediency plays a predominant role. The man or woman who commands a substantial following in Parliament is likely to be the party choice. Various factions within the party must be taken account of; personal considerations and administrative necessities enter in. In view of this fact it is hardly appropriate today to call the Prime Minister *primus inter pares,* though it was true in the past. In fact he has been described as the central sun of a planetary system. While it would be misleading to call his cabinet colleagues his subordinates, it is clear that no individual could remain in the cabinet contrary to the Prime Minister's desire. Perhaps the most adequate statement would be that the Prime Minister is the superior of each individual member of the cabinet, but not of the whole cabinet taken together. The actual relationships are necessarily fluid, since they rest upon the extent and effectiveness of the Prime Minister's party leadership, his personality, personal ability, and industry.[17] But in recent years, the Prime Minister's party leadership undoubtedly counts most heavily. It is through this party leadership that his position has gradually been enhanced.

Leadership in the House of Commons is less important, for both the government and the majority party in the house are working under the same "mandate" of the people. Nevertheless, the party leader is chosen by a caucus composed of the members of Parliament in the respective parties supplemented by a few outstanding leaders from the outside. For this reason as well as for others, it is not practicable to make too rigid a distinction between the cabinet's parliamentary majority and its following outside Parliament. As Lowell has put it, "the governmental machinery is one of wheels within wheels; the outside ring consisting of the party that has a majority in the House of Commons; the next ring being the ministry, which contains the men who are most active within that party; and the smallest of all being the cabinet, containing the real leaders or chiefs. By this means is secured that unity of party action which depends upon placing the direct power in the hands of a body small enough to agree, and influential enough to control."[18] To be sure, even as late as 1954 Herbert Morrison reasserted the old formula "as the head of the Government he [the Prime Minister] is *primus inter pares.*" But he quickly added: "He is the leader of his party." And that is the crucial point. He is no longer merely *primus inter pares.* He may still not be stronger than the cabinet as a whole, but he is decidedly no longer on a par with his colleagues, but their directing superior who can and does threaten them with dismissal if they do not follow his lead. Morrison himself put it rather well when he said: "He is the leader of the Government, but (except on occasions of emergency) he ought not to, and usually does not, presume to give directions or decisions which are proper to the Cabinet . . . even though his position is rightly one of special authority . . ."[19] In any case, our position is supported by more recent scholarship. Thus a younger scholar wrote recently that it is inadequate to speak of the Prime Minister as *primus inter pares.* He added: "He is not merely the keystone, but the foundation stone and coment for other stones as well. He appoints his colleagues, he holds them together, and his reputation must carry the Cabinet and the Party forward to victory at the next election. He controls the party machinery as well."[20]

Indeed, as was said at the beginning of this chapter, the British Prime Minister's position resembles more and more that of the American President in that the people go to the polls to vote for him and "his" government. Even in the days of Disraeli and Gladstone, this was beginning to be true, and in vain did Queen Victoria protest against the trend of the times when she requested that Mr. Gladstone abstain from speaking at railway stations. The Midlothian Campaign of 1880 marks the turning point; characteristically, Mr. Gladstone's great oratorical efforts in that campaign were referred to as "pilgrimages of passion." The Prime Minister's pre-eminence among his colleagues is formally recognized in the fact that he attends to most of the dealings with the "sovereign"; it is upon his advice that the titular head of the government could in the past request the resignation of individual ministers. The most striking recent illustration of the Prime Minister's powers in this respect was Mr. MacDonald's conduct in 1931. Having resigned with the king's consent as head of the Labour government which had been in power, he proceeded to form a National Union government with which he soon afterward "went to the country," as the British saying goes, that is, called for a general election.

The further extension of the Prime Minister's leadership is in part due to the development of broadcasting. Like the American President, the Prime Minister can effectively appeal to the electorate at large; the cabinet as a group cannot. This trend became especially manifest under war conditions. In fact, the emergency powers discussed later made the Prime Minister a constitutional dictator. But even before the war, the Prime Minister had incomparable opportunities for shaping the political views of the people. There is every indication that Mr. Chamberlain forced major decisions upon his cabinet. The circumstances surrounding the resignation of a number of cabinet members, like Mr. Eden, gives clear evidence that the "appeasement" policy was Mr. Chamberlain's rather than the cabinet's. Until the spring of 1939 it was also that of the majority of the British people, as led by Mr. Chamberlain.

Formally speaking, of course, the cabinet is in charge; it is the cabinet which is responsible to Parliament. Apart from the legal responsibility of the entire ministry, this means that the members of the cabinet, both collectively and individually, are affected by certain actions of Parliament, which by convention oblige them either to resign or to dissolve Parliament and to call a general election. If none of these actions occur, new elections have to be called at the end of five years, except in wartime, thus preventing indefinite self-perpetuation. In the past, the more usual was parliamentary action. These actions of Parliament were three. Parliament could pass a vote of "want of confidence." Such a vote would indicate disapproval of the general policy of the cabinet and was therefore unsual. This is also true of the vote of censure, by which the Parliament could criticize the cabinet or one of its members; the last government to be overthrown was the Labour government of 1924. More usual was the defeat of a measure which the cabinet had sponsored and refused to abandon. Substantially identical with this is the case in which Parliament insists upon a measure along lines which the cabinet opposes. Any one of these steps could be taken by Parliament only if a certain number of the supporters of the government had become sufficiently dissatisfied to vote with the opposition party. A development of this sort presupposes a considerable freedom of the M. P.'s and a measure of confusion concerning a certain issue. This was the case with the Irish question, which frequently provided the occasion for cabinet changes in the later nineteenth century. But in the twentieth century cabinet changes have come about rather by the initiative of the cabinet itself, when it is decided to appeal to the people in a general election, as happened in 1910, 1918, 1923, 1931, 1935, and again in 1945 and in 1965. At other times a reconstruction of the cabinet has been undertaken in order to anticipate an adverse electoral decision, as in 1905, 1915, and 1931. In 1940, when Mr. Churchill was called upon to form a national coalition, it was the problem of dealing with the unprecedented emergency caused by the collapse of France and the danger of imminent invasion that caused the need of cabinet reconstruction on a national basis. A similar case is presented by the Suez crisis in 1956, which necessitated a comprehensive reconstruction of the cabinet upon the resignation of the then Prime Minister Anthony Eden. More like the earlier reconstructions was the change occasioned by the Profumo scandal, as well as the reconstruction which Labour Prime Minister Harold Wilson effectuated in 1966 in connection with the election which gave him the substantial majority he had lacked after first coming into office.[21]

What do these trends mean? They clearly indicate that the cabinet, and more particularly the Prime Minister, look toward popular party support for the maintenance of power. The compactness of party organizations, in other words, has brought about a gradual transition from a parliamentary to an electoral responsibility. To put it another way, the cabinet governs Great Britain today with the advice and consent of Parliament.

Serious difficulties have arisen through the rather considerable size of the cabinet. Twenty or more persons form a somewhat unwieldy body for the purposes of collective action. The recurrent demand before the war for a much smaller directing body led to the emergence of a small, informal group of five during the First World War. Under Lloyd George's active and energetic leadership, this group took upon itself the making of the most important decisions, but the large amount of criticism which this arrangement engendered led to its abandonment after the war. Lloyd George's memoirs show, however, the great value which this instrumentality possessed in his eyes during the emergency. Accordingly, a war cabinet was again organized during the Second World War.[22]

First, Mr. Chamberlain formed a war cabinet of nine men. Mr. Churchill, following him, reduced it to five, only to enlarge it later to eight members. But even these small cabinets by no means shaped war policy. Both Chamberlain and Churchill determined basic policy with the aid of more intimate advisers, as Churchill has described it in his memoirs. Churchill's war cabinet grew because of the need for maintaining an equitable balance in the war coalition between Conservatives and Labourites. He started with the leaders of the two parties (Chamberlain, it must be remembered, remained leader of the Conservative party for a while), whom he made Lord President of the Council and Lord Privy Seal; to these he added the Foreign Secretary, a Conservative, and a minister without portfolio representing Labour. Later, when Chamberlain left, another Conservative became Lord President, while there was added the Lord Chancellor of the Exchequer and the Minister of Aircraft Production, both Conservatives, as well as the Minister of Labour, who was Aneurin Bevin of the Labour party.

The functions of the cabinet are partly governmental, in the legal sense, and partly political. The governmental functions were characterized in the *Report of the Machinery of Government Committee* of 1918 as threefold: (1) the final determination of the policy to be submitted to Parliament; (2) the supreme control of the national executive in accordance with the policy prescribed by Parliament; (3) the continuous coordination and delimitation of the authorities of the several departments of the government. In commenting upon this description, W. I. Jennings remarks that the report "rightly makes no distinction between legislation and administration." In accordance with what will be said in the next chapter, Jennings states that "most legislation is directed toward the creation or modification of administrative powers," and furthermore that "the main function of government is the provision of services . . . for the welfare of the people." Jennings himself gives many examples showing that the relative importance of the decisions determines whether a matter belongs before the cabinet. To say that the cabinet decides on the policy obscures its function, which is to decide those issues that the individual ministers, including the Prime Minister, feel unable to decide by themselves. To this governmental function corresponds their political function of holding party support in Parliament and in the electorate together; for if the government makes too many unpopular decisions, the party will disintegrate and the government's popular support will be lost. However, pardons, personnel of the cabinet itself, and other appointments are usually not discussed in the cabinet, and the budget, while discussed, is taken up quite informally and orally, and not referred to a committee.

Regularly, in recent years, a matter is taken up in general form, is then referred to a committee, and is finally decided on the basis of a report circulated in writing. The cabinet has worked more and more through these committees. The committees, of course, have no authority to make final decisions, but only to report and recommend. The committee sittings ordinarily may be, and often are, attended by ministers who are not in the cabinet. Apart from these committees, the whole cabinet meets regularly once a week while Parliament is in session. In critical times, however, meetings may multiply. These meetings are quite informal and frequently of a rather conversational order.[23]

Such, to sum up, is the nature of the British cabinet, which has been described as the "pivot around which the whole political machinery revolves." Led by the Prime Minister, it directs the affairs of the country until its party support disintegrates. It does not merely execute and administer, as people who think in American terms are prone to assume. Except when the Prime Minister forces its hand, it makes all major decisions. It also decides upon, drafts, sponsors, and puts through Parliament new legislation, and takes full initiative in all fiscal and budgetary matters.

The British Dominions have, by and large, followed this pattern. Even where federalism was adopted, as in Canada and Australia, cabinet government under the leadership of a parliamentary prime minister has been evolved.[24] Dominion experience shows, and *a fortiori* the case of Eire shows also, that this form of constitutionalism does not depend upon the existence of a hereditary aristocracy, nor upon the existence of an exploitable colonial empire, nor upon an advanced industrialism — all arguments which have been set forth at one time or another. British cabinet government does, however, seem to depend upon (1) a capacity, so deeply rooted in British traditions, to accept as well as to provide leadership, (2) the existence of some kind of final arbiter such as the hereditary monarchy provides, and (3) a general acceptance of self-restraint and moderation as a virture of all men when confronted with political responsibility. It is only with great peril that these moral conditions of political liberty are gainsaid.

The cabinet subservient to parliament: France · Unlike Britain, France under the Third Republic failed to develop effective executive leadership. Twice France had succumbed to dictatorial perversion of its constitutionalism; no wonder that French republicans were unduly fearful of all extension of executive power. What is worse, the French cabinet, or council of ministers, was not even cohesive as a collective group; it was a loose gathering of individual parliamentary leaders. The French cabinet, therefore, remained subservient to parliamentary groups and factions.[25] It could not possibly be described as the core of the government. Some thought that it too tended to become the center of gravity in the parliamentary system, but as such it certainly did not radiate energy and activity. It is quite significant that writers spoke of it as "the ministries," thus emphasizing the ministers' separate and individual roles. So realistic and perspicacious a commentator as Robert de Jouvenel in *La République des Camarades* discusses *"ministres et ministères"* without referring to a collective cabinet at all. He merely describes how an individual parliamentarian is put into a ministerial position and how this minister copes with the permanent administrative services, how he is surrounded by his personal and private secretarial staff (called in French *le cabinet*), and how he tries to get through his administrative functions without either previous knowledge or opportunity to acquire it while he is in office. "To administer," says this witty commentator, "is to appoint officials whom one does not know to positions of which one is ignorant, in other words to distribute promotions and decorations in the midst of solicitations, recriminations, and threats." But the all-engrossing task was that of keeping on good terms with parliament, and, more particularly, with one's own parliamentary group. The French cabinet was a group of individuals whose task it was to act as liaison between the dominant parliamentary groups and the permanent administrative staffs in the various ministries. Of course there were considerable differences due to personality in France as in England; for example, Delcassé managed to occupy a position of very great independence as minister of foreign affairs between 1897 and 1905, and to conduct a policy which was largely unknown to the parliamentary groups supporting the ministries to which he belonged. Similarly, ministers of war have been able to maintain a position of some independence. But on the whole, French cabinet ministers were the helpmeets of the parliamentary committees (see ch. XVII, p. 352) in supervising the permanent administration.

It has just been said that the amount of changes to which French cabinets were subject was more apparent than real. The statistical picture in the fifty-four cabinets between August 31, 1871, and March 22, 1913, is twenty-eight ministers of foreign affairs, thirty-two of the navy, thirty-three of war, thirty-seven of justice, and thirty-nine of the interior. The same was true after the First World War. In the period from November 16, 1917, to July 23, 1926, we find that in fifteen cabinets there were seven ministers of foreign affairs, eight of war, nine of the navy, ten of the interior, ten of finance, and eleven of justice. Correspondingly, we find some individuals holding cabinet positions a great many times (one, in fact, twenty times). To put it another way, by taking all the cabinets from 1871 to 1930, we find that of a total of 1026 cabinet positions, 482, or almost half, were held by sixty individuals serving from five to twenty times. "The French democracy," M. Joseph-Barthélemy has written, "has been heavily blamed for its extreme fickleness and the reckless way in which its chambers have consumed one ministry after another. It has been described as a frenzied rush of cabinets across the political stage from one wing to the other. These criticisms, though perhaps justified to a certain extent by certain periods in the history of the Third Republic, are for the most partly greatly exaggerated and the conclusions drawn from certain well-established facts are not always well-founded." He then gives a good many illustrations of the fact that ministers often outlasted several ministries, continuing as ministers without interruption. This was quite natural in a situation where the cabinet was a loose collegial body and where the position of each minister was to some extent dependent upon his individual support in parliament. Certain groups could only be held in line by including the man whom they were willing to follow. These *ministrables,* parliamentarians with enough of a following to make them desirable members of a coalition, tended, of course, to return to office time and again.

In spite of the dependence of the ministry upon constant parliamentary support, French constitutional writers throughout the Third Republic were much more inclined to emphasize the separation of powers than are Englishmen. They continued to take seriously to some extent the classical doctrine according to which the parliamentary system as established by the constitution of 1875 depended upon a balance of power with parliament on one side and the president on the other. This doctrine, according to which the cabinet was the link between the representative body and the chief executive, did not correspond to the French reality at all. For, elected by parliament and without the power of dissolution, the French president possessed no independent authority to match the power of parliament. Hence, neither he nor the chairman of the council of ministers, the *President du Conseil des Ministres,* as the French prime minister was called, was in a position to establish effective leadership. To be sure, in the darkest hour of the First World War, after French armies had mutinied, Clemenceau was accorded genuine leadership. But the Tiger lost it as soon as the war was over. In the crisis of inflation, Poincaré also achieved a measure of genuine leadership; but both are really instances of constitutional dictatorship. Even in the terrible months before the outbreak of the Second World War, the French Republic struggled in vain to solve the problem. Though repeated grants of emergency powers enabled Daladier and Reynaud to undertake some of the most urgent tasks for the defense of the country, the authority remained divided; neither man achieved supremacy; both were at the mercy of certain parliamentary factions.

All these difficulties were further aggravated by the fact that the French executive depended not only on the Chamber of Deputies, but on the Senate as well. Inasmuch as the composition of the Senate and the Chamber were often at variance, the forming of a cabinet was greatly complicated, at times producing well-night insuperable difficulties. The situation was endurable only because of the looseness and fluidity of the groups in both Houses. Once strongly organized parties or blocs came into existence, complete stalemates threatened. At the breaking point, the situation was often saved by the very disjointedness of the cabinet, since it facilitated the dropping of individual ministers who had lost the confidence of either house.

The whole French executive system was really incomprehensible, unless one remembered that the paramount concern of the men who developed this system was to control the permanent administrative staff. Just as the dislike of the French public for this staff found expression in the epithet "bureaucracy," so the long-established dominance of this centralized bureaucracy has been the main target of attack for popular movements throughout the nineteenth century. M. Barthélemy voiced this French viewpoint when he wrote that a change of ministers is very desirable because the minister is actually the controller of the bureaucracy. The minister must, therefore, not have the spirit of a bureaucrat, which he undoubtedly would have if he remained in office for extended periods. His vigilance must constantly be kept on the alert for parliamentary control and the threat of removal. He is not a technical expert, but rather the political superintendent of a stable and specialized bureaucracy. This view, which was typical for French liberalism, prevented the emergence of well-integrated executive leadership under the Third French Republic.

In 1948 an attempt was made to mitigate the undirected parliamentarism of the prewar period by giving the cabinet a partial power of dissolution. However, the fundamental balance of power remained the same, the cabinet's position continued to depend on coalitions, and the deputies of the Fourth Republic, being often the same men as those of the Third, tended to act much as they did before the war.[26]

The constitution of the Fifth Republic, according to the man most directly responsible for its formulation, Michel Debré, was intended to institute neither a presidential nor a pure parliamentary system, but simply to re- create the classic balance and separation between executive and legislative. Since the 1962 referendum authorizing direct election of the president, power has shifted toward the executive. Nevertheless, De Gaulle himself conceives of the president as a mediator, above politics. The actual powers granted by the constitution, such as the ability to dissolve parliament, appoint a prime minister, hold a referendum (when asked by the cabinet or by parliament), and assume emergency powers in certain situations, do not in themselves guarantee a great deal of influence to the executive. De Gaulle's successors may find themselves as unable to prevent ministerial instability as the presidents of the Fourth Republic.

In Debré's mind, the chief governing organ of the executive would have been the cabinet. Its head is now a prime minister, and not simply a chairman of the council of ministers (*President du Conseil*). He is appointed by the president of the republic and not by the National Assembly. His ministers must resign their seats in parliament to serve in the cabinet. The constitution further strengthens the cabinet by distinguishing between the law-making and the rule-making powers, and, in a revolutionary reversal of tradition, by restricting parliament's competence to certain matters defined as within the domain of law (Article 34). Moreover, the parliament now meets for less than six months in the year, and its agenda is decided by the cabinet, which must now take full responsibility for its bills. The ministers have greater control over their bills in committee (see above, p. 353) and in the Assembly. The old, often overused vote of confidence has been replaced by a difficult, complicated motion of censure.

To date these reforms have helped cabinets avoid the *immobilisme* that characterized the Third and Fourth Republics. However, this progress has been made under exceptional circumstances, with an immensely popular and imposing chief executive and close to a one-party majority in both houses. Whether the system can continue to function effectively after De Gaulle remains a speculative question.[27]

An ill-fated experiment: Germany • A study of executive leadership under the Weimar Republic would seem quite out-of-date were it not for the undeniable fact that we learn as much or more from failures as from successes. It may be unfortunate but it is not surprising that the makers of the Weimar constitution looked with a certain measure of sympathy upon the French cabinet system. Having just freed themselves from the clutches of a powerful bureaucratic tradition, they, too, felt that their ministry was to be primarily the political supervisor of a permanent bureaucracy.[28] The French system, with its polyarchic diversity in the cabinet, corresponded, they thought, more nearly to the needs of Germany with her many parties. Like France and unlike England, she faced the task of building up a parliamentary tradition in terms of the free professions, particularly those of law and journalism, since a republican order could not hope to command the allegiance of the aristocracy, which had at one time formed the backbone of the English parliamentary and cabinet personnel. On the other hand, the instability of French politics appeared in such an unfavorable light that arguments like the one set forth in the famous essay of Redslob, *Parliamentary Government, True and False*, made a deep impression. Consequently, the German Republican (Weimar) constitution provided for popular election of the president, thus giving the head of state an independent basis apart from the chief executive, known as *Reich* chancellor. The resulting balance did not work, and in the end the popularly elected president became a mighty factor in the destruction of the whole parliamentary system. Owing to the double dependence of the cabinet upon the president on the one hand and upon the *Reichstag* on the other, both popularly elected representatives of the entire German people, it oscillated between the two masters. Unlike the unstable groups in the French parliament, the several German parties were highly organized. Unlike the English, none of these German parties ever commanded a majority. Since the constitution explicitly demanded (Article 54) that the chancellor and his ministers needed the confidence of *Reichstag* (diet), and that they must resign individually as well as collectively if the *Reichstag* withdrew its confidence, the president adopted the method of asking a certain parliamentary leader to form a cabinet and to appoint him chancellor only after he had succeeded. This practice, which is also found in France, had the unfortunate consequence of calling to the attention of the public the bickering which is involved in forming a cabinet.

At first this method centered in negotiations between the parties for the formation of a coalition. Until 1923 cabinets were formed by the parties whenever they could get together, and when they could not, the initiative of the president sufficed to bring about a coalition with sufficient support to carry. After 1923 cabinets were regularly supported by a minority in the center, in spite of constant efforts to broaden the base of support. After 1926 an increasing inclination developed to have the cabinet organized by presidential initiative and then have it seek the support of parliament as it went along. Through this development the central idea of parliamentary government, namely, majority support, fell into discard. It was an endeavor to return to the German monarchic tradition of an independent government of administrators in terms of three slogans: "government of the middle way," "cabinet of personalities," and "government above parties." The most serious difficulty resulting from such an arrangement was the ever-present danger that the two radical wings of the house which were thus excluded from the cabinet would combine in a vote of nonconfidence without having any intention of combining to form a new government. The parliamentary maneuvering of Brüning, chancellor from 1930 to 1932, sought to escape from this dilemma. He always retained the idea that the cabinet must command the support of a parliamentary majority. How right he was is apparent from the hopeless impasse which resulted when the ministries of von Papen and von Schleicher, which followed his, attempted to conduct business without such a majority. It has often been said that such a presidential cabinet system was bound to arise in Germany on account of the multiplicity of parties, but it has been cogently argued that this is not really true. Not the number of parties but their relationship to the electorate matters. Fundamentally, the German parties were so definitely linked with economic groups in the community that their leaders, when united in a cabinet, could not command a sufficiently representative position as long as they were believed to be the creatures of these parties. Only the president, as the representative of the entire people, could give them this broader appeal.

It has been persuasively argued by a man who had an opportunity to observe the developments from inside that the real source of the trouble was, however, the lack of a prodemocratic majority in the *Reichstag* after 1920. "The really astonishing thing is not that thirteen years later the German democratic constitution collapsed in Germany, but rather that this did not happen much sooner."[29] This lack of a prodemocratic majority was the "deadly worm" which destroyed the Weimar Republic. By contrast, the Federal Republic of Germany has had more than 90 per cent of its electorate favoring constitutional democracy, though without enthusiasm.

The complexities of the dependence of German cabinets in the Weimar Republic were reflected in their internal patterns. While parties were themselves taking the initiative and bringing about ministerial coalitions, their delegates in the cabinet tended to occupy relatively independent positions in spite of the express recognition in the constitution that the chancellor is the head of the cabinet. Later on, when the president became decisive in forming cabinets, executive leadership by the chancellor closely resembling the situation in England seemed in prospect. Undoubtedly the innate centrifugal tendency of postwar coalition ministries was greatly aided by a traditional lack of cooperation among ministers. The fierce struggle between the permanent civil servants, proverbially a source of considerable difficulty, commenced to feed upon party conflicts. The permanent officials learned how to manipulate the party dissensions in the *Reichstag*.

As in so many other matters, so in its cabinet system also, the Weimar constitution combined too many discordant elements and was drafted with too little realistic consideration for the traditions of German politics and administration. If, instead of the popularly elected president, who, in spite of his national majority, was looked upon as a partisan, the system had been built around a hereditary monarch, it is possible that it would have worked as well as the constitutional parliamentary monarchies of Holland and the Scandinavian countries are working; for in all of them the party system is rather similar to that in Germany. There are many parties and they are fairly well organized and clearly connected with economic interest groups. On the whole, it is probably true that a cabinet system directly dependent upon parliamentary support is very hard to combine with a republican chief of state. France, though making a success of this combination for a while, encountered profound difficulties in the later years of the Third Republic, and her defeat in World War II suggests caution in placing too much confidence in the precedent it established. Moreover, France did not have to battle with the complications arising from a federal setup. For a federal system, the Swiss and American types would appear to be much more suitable. The attempt of German democracy to combine American, English, and French elements resulted in a complete failure.

The provisions embodied in the Basic Law of 1949 have so far proved more satisfactory. The position of the president was reduced; he was deprived of his independent popular base, being elected by a special convention consisting of the federal parliament (*Bundestag* and *Bundesrat*) and of specially elected representatives of the state parliaments (Article 54). At the same time, the chancellor's office has been strengthened. The evolution of the chancellor's position, under the impact of the same forces that have transformed the British Prime Minister's position, has been in the direction of giving him ever-greater power, at least as long as Adenauer occupied the office, even though his parliamentary and popular support was that of coalition leader. Hence Germans eventually spoke of their system as a "chancellor's democracy." The chancellor became "the pivot in the political system." The term "chancellor's democracy," intended as a term of derogation, was to suggest that Adenauer's rule was undemocratic, authoritarian, plebiscitarian. But when cleared of its propagandistic overtones, it focuses appropriate attention upon the fact that responsibility became concentrated upon the chancellor, in spite of a highly pluralistic system in which several parties, powerful interest groups, and last but not least a traditional federal system, tended to disperse and thereby to weaken government responsibility. Such a concentration of responsibility was the more striking since the extent of effective responsibility had been notoriously unimpressive in Germany's past. A novel provision (though to some extent anticipated by provisions in the constitutions of Bavaria and Württemberg) was to insure that the chancellor could not be overthrown by a vote of nonconfidence composed of a diffuse negative vote; it stated that "the federal assembly can only express its lack of confidence (*Misstrauen*) by the majority electing his successor. . ." (Article 67, entitled "constructive nonconfidence vote"). Since the chancellor has the further weapon of dissolving the assembly if they refuse to express their confidence in him (Article 68), Adenauer was able to serve out his term (four years) three times. The "constructive nonconfidence" provision seemed, in this perspective, to have achieved the assimilation of the British system, and to have enforced a broad popular and parliamentary responsibility along the guide lines of policy.[30]

The strong leadership of Konrad Adenauer deceived many into thinking that these provisions meant that no government could be overthrown. They forgot that only the skillful political maneuvering of an experienced party politician could succeed in holding so large and disparate a grouping as the Christian Democrats together. Once his successor, lacking such skill, lost the party's support, the overthrow of his (Erhard's) cabinet could be brought about by the threat of such a constructive nonconfidence vote. All that was needed was to negotiate the support for a new coalition (or the old one on a reconstructed basis). Opinion is very divided on whether the gain of having a government until a successor is chosen outweighs the disadvantages connected with so protracted a confidence crisis (*Vertrauenskrise*) as preceded the eventual resolution of the conflict. It is interesting in this connection that the German chancellor did not use the right of dissolving the *Bundestag* (diet) and calling for new elections. Presumably he did not because the very cause of the crisis, namely, his loss of support in his own party, made such a step appear suicidal both for himself and his party. Anyhow, the *Bundestag* could have prevented such an election by electing a new chancellor, which they were preparing to do in any case, so that a decision to dissolve would probably only have speeded the chancellor's downfall.[31]

Yet, after all is said about this recent crisis, it is still fair to say that this is decidedly a more stable system than the Weimar Republic. Whey did the Germans not adopt either the American presidential or the Swiss council system — both highly successful and stable forms of constitutional democracy? They rejected the American system because they feared that so powerful an executive might easily become a dictator under German conditions. They rejected the Swiss system as not sufficiently responsive to changing situations to be suitable for a large country with weak democratic traditions. But the recent crisis has, as a matter of fact, called forth demands in the press for the establishment of a presidential system.

The collegial council: Switzerland · The organization of executive leadership in Switzerland is different from that of any other independent government. Although there is a president, he is merely the chairman of the Council, usually elected for one year. He is a concession to the un-Swiss idea of a "head of government." Indeed, it is only by analogy that we can call the Swiss Federal (Executive) Council a cabinet; because there is no fictitious or real person whose cabinet it could be.[32] In other words, the Swiss setup is so strongly antimonarchical (much more so than that of the United States) that the nomenclature of Europe's monarchical past does not fit at all.

The Swiss collegial cabinet shares with the French system the tradition of polyarchic independence of the several ministers as department heads. But in spite of the fact that they are elected by the legislative assembly, they constitute a permanent and powerful executive, because the chief executives do not resign when defeated on any policy in the representative assembly. The ministers simply work out a new legislative proposal more in keeping with parliamentary views, or they abandon the particular policy altogether. Professor Brooks has called this type of cabinet system "government by commission," and there is indeed some similarity between the relationship of, let us say, the Interstate Commerce Commission to Congress and the Swiss Federal Council to the Swiss legislature. The origin of this unique system must be sought in the Swiss cantons, which are organized on this pattern. But the adoption of this traditional cantonal organization by the federal government was greatly aided by the profound suspicion with which the constitution makers of 1848 looked upon anything resembling monarchy. It was a conscious decision by which they rejected the American plan of a popularly elected president.

Although this Federal Executive Council is elected by a joint session of both houses of the legislature after a new election, and although the terms of the councilors are four years, it has become the recognized custom, to which there are very few exceptions, to re-elect members as long as they are willing to serve. Consequently, members of the council usually serve many terms. Professor Brooks cites cases where members have served continuously for thirty-two, twenty-seven, and twenty-five years. When one considers that it is now usual to elect to the Federal Executive Council only men who have served for a considerable period in the representative assemblies, and that many councilors have previously served either in the cantonal representative bodies or in administrative or judicial posts, it is clear that the Swiss Executive Council is composed of men thoroughly seasoned in the art of politics and administration. The Federal Executive Council is presided over by the president, who is, as was said, elected by the federal assembly each year. He has no powers over the Council. His bureau acts as a secretariat for the Council as a whole; in other words, unlike the English Prime Minister, he is a real *primus inter pares*. His office is an honor and his functions are "representative," that is, ceremonial. He is quite often in charge of the department of foreign affairs, though he may be head of any other. The several members of the Federal Council, while on an equal footing with each other and the president, act collectively on certain issues of general importance.

In the words of the Swiss constitution, the Federal Council is the "supreme directive and executive authority of the union." This general provision is implemented by another which gives a detailed list of particular functions. Related to the federal distribution of power, it indicates clearly that the

Council has the same functions in the administrative field which the assembly has in the legislative field. Besides, the Council has to supervise whatever administration of federal legislation is entrusted to the cantonal authorities. The Council has to make detailed reports to the federal assembly. These reports are the subject of extended discussion, and as a result the assembly may address specific demands, known as postulates, to the federal councilors. A resolution to back such a postulate is unconditionally binding upon the Council.

It is clear that the Swiss constitution wishes to make the executive a genuine administrative executor of the decisions of the representative assembly. It would, however, be very unrealistic to allow oneself to be blinded by these constitutional provisions. The members of the Federal Executive Council are leading politicians, often actually party leaders. When this party leadership is supplemented by the special knowledge which they possess as heads of the administrative departments, their word must necessarily carry a great deal of weight. Although the range within which patronage pressure can be brought to bear in Switzerland is very narrow, people have often claimed that it helps to consolidate the Council's leadership. Professor Fleiner has said that the continuous expansion of federal functions and of federal administrative authority has given the members of the Federal Council such a secure position tha the Council has become more and more independent of the assembly and has extended its influence upon it. This is perhaps more significantly expressed in the fact that the Executive Council is not based upon a party majority in the representative bodies. Naturally, since councilors are continually re-elected, the party composition of the Council must vary considerably from that of the legislature. At the same time, members of the Council are elected from parties radically opposed to each other. Consequently, the Swiss Council is not like a coalition ministry in France or Germany. On the contrary, it traditionally includes representatives of all the important parties, even those which are in general opposition to the government's policies. From the point of view of those who are accustomed to think in terms either of single-party support or of an effective coalition, it may seem difficult to imagine such a plan. The deliberate emphasis on the administrative aspects of its work may save the Council from some of the pitfalls of such an arrangement. Nevertheless, very sharp differences of opinion are bound to develop from time to time, and occasionally a member of the Council will arise to oppose the proposal of a colleague before the legislature. Since ultimately the legislature can and will decide the issue, the necessary unity is imposed upon the Council from without.

Under these circumstances the Council will in a great many matters follow the decision of the member who has the particular matter in charge. Since

Switzerland has developed an admirable civil service, many decisions are thus effectively neutralized and judicialized. This tendency has been enhanced since 1919, when it was decided to refer certain matters directly to the permanent administrative staff. (See next chapter.) Significantly, in all such matters appeal is allowed to an administrative court, thus further emphasizing the judicial controls. After much hesitation this administrative court was organized in 1928 as part of the federal court. It may be well, in conclusion, to quote an estimate of the Swiss executive which, written many years ago, would still seem to be correct: "Apart from all criticism and suggestions for reform, however, it is generally conceded that the Swiss executive has developed high efficiency within the limits of its powers and opportunities. In the opinion of two well-known English students 'the members of the Federal Council yield to no other government in Europe in devotion to their country, in incessant hard work for a poor salary, and in thorough honesty and incorruptibility. A diplomatist who knew them well and appreciated their good qualities aptly remarked that they reminded him of a characteristic industry of their own country, that of watchmaking. For, having to deal with very minute and intricate affairs, their attention is unremittingly engaged by the most delicate mechanism of government, by the wheels within wheels of federal and cantonal attributes, by the most careful balancing of relations between contending sects and churches and by endeavors to preserve the proper counterpoise between two (French and German), not to say three (the third being Italian) nationalities.' "

One-man rule: the American President · Swiss and American democracy have much in common. But their executive leadership is totally different, even though both countries separate legislative and executive establishments and therein contrast with the British system of "parliamentarism." Whereas in Switzerland, as we have just seen, the executive leadership is assimilated to the permanent administrative services, the American President has become the pivotal point of the American political system.[33] If his personality is powerful and his political support solid, he is today the most impressive type of democratic leader. Though restrained by Congress, the states, and the courts, he provides the dynamic direction of national policy, but always with an eye toward public opinion. The fact that the elections come at stated intervals, so that their timing cannot be manoeuvred to suit the party in power, helps to keep this great power under popular control. Not only the President's own desire either to be re-elected or to determine his successor after four years of service, but also the Congressional elections every two years, have this effect; for the President must seek to keep his Congressional support unimpaired. Insofar as this desire to anticipate popular reaction works as an influence upon the President's policy, the *Federalist's* contention that the President's position could not be compared with that of the British king still has merit. But as the successful leader of the majority, the President has more power at his disposal than any constitutional monarch could ever dream of.

The makers of the constitution were much concerned to secure for the President a position removed from politics and the "gusts of popular passion." The *Federalist*, inspired by the monarchical leanings of Hamilton, is almost lyrical in its enthusiasm for the electoral college as a device for insuring that independence. When the constitution was drafted, the party had not yet emerged as the mainstay of popular government which it is today. All that remains of the electoral college is a mode of electing the President by majorities in the states, rather than by a majority of the nation as a whole. A number of proposals have been made to alter or abolish this system. It usually creates the impression that the President has received a much larger majority than he actually had in percentage of all voters. Thus Roosevelt in the 1944 election had only 53 per cent of the voters, but carried all but ten states — many with very slight majorities. In view of the fact that only one President has ever been elected by a minority (President Hayes in 1876), a change does not seem very urgent, particularly as the present system has the value of maintaining federalism by giving strength to state party organizations. This latter fact, it must be admitted, has the counterbalancing disadvantage of obliging a presidential candidate to seek and make compromises with state leaders prior to the election, and hence has been urged as a primary argument for change. But since the President-to-be would still have to get the votes, it may be doubted whether pre-election deals would be eliminated.

Much has been made of the fact that over the years the election has usually been won by the candidate who had the largest campaign fund. It has been an arrow in the quiver of those who maintain that America has become a plutocracy. This interpretation of the facts is too strained. Since those who contribute money to campaign funds are a widely scattered cross section of the electorate, it is only natural that their verdict before the election should roughly resemble the verdict of the election itself. Claims by the Socialist and similar parties that they are being defeated by the money power fail to take into account the fact that in a democracy appeals to the masses for small contributions are as productive of funds as the large donations of a few rich individuals. Socialist parties in Europe have always been maintained by such contributions, and on the whole their financial position, more particularly that of the British Labour party, has been quite strong as a result. Even so, the ever greater expense incurred in elections has created real problems. The financing of parties by the government has not only been advocated, but experimented with. We shall return to these developments when dealing with the parties.[34]

Is it proper, then, to say that Franklin D. Roosevelt was more powerful than Thomas Jefferson, or Andrew Jackson, or Abraham Lincoln? Only in the sense that the power of the United States has greatly increased. As one of the world powers, America has made her President a personage of extraordinary prestige and influence in international affairs. But in terms of the internal balance of forces, it would seem that the earlier President had relatively as much power. The vastly increased service functions of modern government have enhanced the position of all governmental authority, but, along with the President, Congress, the courts, and the state and municipal authorities, all share in this expansion of power. Indeed, two modern developments have brought with them something of a curb to presidential power as contrasted with Jackson's days: one is the professional expert and administrator, and the other is the technique of mass communication and of polls which has brought the citizen's view into the limelight.

It is obvious, then, that the position of the Cabinet in the United States is very different from that in Switzerland. The American Cabinet consists of the heads of departments.[35] Since Washington's administration, they have been his "secretaries." The President appoints the Cabinet without any interference; the Cabinet is his. And yet the exigencies of party support give certain secretaries a position of their own. Often the choice falls upon men to whom the President owes his election — indeed, pre-election deals are not infrequent in order to build up the necessary support for the nomination or to secure the funds with which to carry on the campaign. If the party following of the President is rent by factions, it will often be necessary for him to include leaders of the several contending groups so that their support may be gained and maintained. Lincoln's appointment of Seward and Chase in 1860 would be a historical example, to which Wilson's appointment of Bryan, or the second Roosevelt's choice of Farley, might furnish parallels. Similar cases could be cited for more recent Presidents. Men appointed under such conditions are difficult to dislodge. It is unrealistic to look upon them as merely the administrative subordinates of the President. Today, at any rate, they are of vital importance to him in his national representative function. It is only through them that he can associate with himself a number of representatives of the different social forces which make up the support of his political party. One may "represent" the business man, another the farmer, a third labor, and so forth. Similarly, allowance will be made for regional interests and claims. All in all, the President must take into account personalities which have become associated with broad groupings in the electorate, if he is to be a representative of the nation.

While the difference between a collegial cabinet, such as the Swiss, and our own is very great, the distinction should not be made absolute. Through both systems the decisive social forces will secure a share of the government's power, through opposition as well as participation, of course. The share may vary as the balance of social forces shifts, but no considerable group can be excluded for any length of time without the government's losing its representative position, and thereby its power through consent.

It is inescapable that under such conditions, where the President and his Cabinet are viewed as the representatives of the common national interest and the representatives of various social groups, respectively, a good many important policies will be determined by discussions *not* of the Cabinet collectively, but of the President with individual Cabinet members. Sometimes, of course, an important piece of legislation, particularly when it touches several departments, will be discussed in the Cabinet. But votes are seldom taken on such matters, and they are considered mere expressions of opinion. There is a well-known story told about President Lincoln who concluded a discussion in the Cabinet during which everyone had taken sides against him by remarking: "Seven nays, one aye, the ayes have it." And yet, it is true only in a limited sense that "the cabinet is merely the kind of organization which the President wishes to make of it and is his own council in a very peculiar sense," as Charles A. Beard claims. Lord Bryce once observed that "There is in the government of the United States no such thing as a cabinet in the English sense of the term."[36] While this statement may be less true today, due to the changes in the English pattern, the difference still vitiates suggestions for changes in American practice based upon the English example. The most thorough recent descriptive analysis of the presidency states that "the president does not necessarily feel obligated to accept the majority judgment of his Cabinet on a given point." Then citing the Lincoln story, it continues: "Rather than functioning as a collegial 'directory' today the Cabinet discharges its primary function in serving as a sounding board for the testing of ideas on such matters as the President may wish to refer to it, as an interdepartmental news exchange, and as a point of personal contact for the President with his top subordinates. . ."[37] The author of this study as well as other students entertain serious doubts about President Eisenhower's attempt to revive the Cabinet, and one of the most brilliant of them comments: "The Cabinet has been a problem for at least a generation. Only tough custom and past glory have kept it from sliding noiselessly into oblivion."[38] A President who is likely to be successful must have about him men who are capable of taking a line of their own. But the extent to which this will be true is likely to be a measure of the President's intrinsic ability, not the result of institutional devices. In short, the American President and his Cabinet are a working group of political leaders and administrators, dependent upon popular support through a party which may, and often will, also control the Congress. There have been recurrent "kitchen cabinets," small, ephemeral, informal groups of advisers whom various Presidents have employed; more recently, the President has been provided with a regular Executive Office. "No visible feature (of the government) more clearly demonstrates the tremendous accretion of presidential powers, influence and responsibility than does the spectacular growth in recent years of staff personnel and agencies attached to the President's office."[39] This Executive Office of the President consisted in 1965 of seven major units, (1) the White House office, (2) the Bureau of the Budget, (3) the National Security Council, (4) the Council of Economic Advisers, (5) the Office of Emergency Planning, (6) the National Aeronautics and Space Council, and (7) the Office of Science and Technology. These seven powerful units constitute a large administrative apparatus. Let us briefly look at the first four. The White House office is composed of a number of special assistants and other staff immediately serving the President. It has been called the "nerve center" of American federal administration. The Bureau of the Budget, with hundreds of officials, attends to many of the tasks handled by the ministry of finance and the ministry of justice in other countries. It became part of the presidential office under F.D.R., and since that time has enabled Presidents to coordinate and integrate the vast, sprawling bureaucracy of the great service departments. Its five subdivisions deal with budget review, financial management, legislative reference, management and organization (planning), and statistical standards. The National Security Council is in a sense an "inner" cabinet committee, created for the purpose of coordinating security and military policy. The Council of Economic Advisers studies economic trends and makes recommendations which the President once a year submits to Congress in an elaborate report. It is the closest to over-all planning and programming that the United States federal government has allowed itself to go. Its work contrasts with the emergency planning carried forward by the fifth unit.[40]

But with all this growth of presidentially directed and institutionalized policy control, it still remains true that informal advisers are so essential that no institutional arrangement will take their place. Having once been invested with his monocratic powers, no President is likely to distribute this power to others, and if a particular President should, out of indolence or altruism, move in that direction, his successor is likely to redress the balance on assuming office. The concentrated powers of the American President are a part of the pattern of constitutional relationships established by the separation of powers; they are endurable only because the pattern provides other restraints through limiting the concentrated powers themselves. It is another method of coping with the problem which in the opinion of Bryce (and many another liberal thinker) is the greatest which confronts free peoples: how to enable the citizens at large to conduct or control the executive business of the government.

Executive leadership in the United States is not limited to the federal government, of course. As several times noted in the preceding discussion, the states play a vital part, as do some of the great cities, notably New York. There has been a natural tendency for the chief executives of the states, the governors, to be looked upon as roughly parallel to the President. In the course of the nineteenth century, the governors became more independent of the legislatures as direct popular election was adopted for them. But unlike the Cabinet of the President, some of the chief officers of the state governments were made elective in turn, and this made them largely independent of the governor altogether. Thus a plural executive resulted which had the effect of dissipating executive leadership in the states. The only way a measure of integration could be recaptured was through effective party control, and hence the bosses became supreme. However, the expansion of governmental activities has created, since the turn of the century, an increasing demand for reforms and they have been making slow headway in recent years. Especially the budget has been seized upon as a promising mechanism for enlarging the governor's power of control and integration. But in a serious emergency, the existing confusion may lead to great strains and the adoption of rather radical measures for overcoming them. The current racial strife in a number of states, leading to the calling out of the state militia, and even federal troops, is an ill omen.

Cabinet and presidential secretariat and the problem of informal advisers • The increasing scope of governmental activity has seriously impeded efficient direction in all major industrialized countries. We therefore find a general trend toward strengthening the administrative effectiveness of the chief executive as a coordinator. Both in Britain and in the United States, there have recently been created special secretariats whose function it is to deal with these over-all questions. The cabinet secretariat owes its origin to the First World War. Until that time, British cabinets had been conducted in the most informal way, with matters coming up and being decided without any clear record. Since there were no minutes of the meeting, it was difficult, later on, to ascertain what the decision had been. Although it was proposed to abolish this secretariat after the war, the *Machinery of Government* Report recommended its retention. It operates essentially as a coordinating office by circulating memoranda and other documents, preparing the agenda for the cabinet and its committees, as well as the minutes and reports, and, finally, keeping the records unless instructed otherwise.

The American President's secretariat is similarly designed. It is, however, concerned with strengthening and making more effective the President's relations with the public, Congress, and the numerous governmental agencies which should somehow be coordinated and made to contribute toward the President's national policy. The *Report on Administrative Management* (1937), which first suggested explicitly the organization of such a secretariat, spoke of ". . . men with a passion for anonymity." This phrase elicited a good deal of laughter at the time, and yet there can be little doubt that these men, if they are to be effective as spokesmen for the President, must possess the capacity of keeping themselves personally in the background. On the whole they have been remarkably successful in doing so.[41]

Do these secretariats provide that opportunity for critical advice? Hardly. Strong executives who perceive the need for such independent judgments will always seek it more informally, and preferably from persons who do not officially depend upon them. Such men have undoubtedly wielded a great influence upon public policy precisely because they brought to the problems of the chief executive detachment and a nondepartmental, nonbureaucratic viewpoint. It is an ever-present need of men in positions of leadership to find some such persons of discretion, judgment, and insight. In a constitutional democratic system this is always possible, and famous instances can be readily cited, such as that of Colonel House's work for Wilson. It is one of the incurable weaknesses of a despot that he encounters insuperable obstacles in the way of securing such advice, because he lacks all effective means for checking upon the dubious or sycophantic advisers. Napoleon and Frederick the Great, the Czars of Russia and Oliver Cromwell, all struggled in vain with the same difficulty. There is no more telling symbol of the isolation of the absolute ruler than Harun-al-Rashid prowling about the city in disguise to learn what the people think of this rule.

Conclusion · Executive leadership has at all times been essential to the success of government. Constitutionalism, and more especially constitutional democracy, have been confronted with a most delicate task: how to discover institutional patterns which would provide vigorous and effective action, without allowing those who were called upon to take such action to turn into irresponsible despots. Two countries have evolved outstandingly successful executive leadership: Great Britain and the United States.[42] Very different in conception and practice, each subtly fitted into a distinctive tradition, they each possess peculiar elements of strength and weakness. But so organically have both the British cabinet system and the American presidency evolved in relation to the governmental pattern as a whole that the numerous proposals which have been advanced for overcoming the weakness of one by altering it to be more nearly like the other have rarely met with more than literary and academic approval. There are operative behind and underneath them both, however, responsible administrative services which are becoming continually more alike and which infuse into them both the continuity and competence without which no lasting work can be done in our technological age.

Responsible Public Administration

XIX

Introduction · "For forms of government let fools contest; Whate'er is best administer'd is best" — wrote Alexander Pope in 1733. This sentiment has been gaining ground again in recent decades. It is not sound constitutional doctrine, but it rightly focuses attention upon the importance of effective administration as a test of government, whether constitutional or not. For a government that is badly administered can never be expected to last long. Allusions in the preceding chapter were necessarily made to administrators and administrative systems. Indeed, patterns of administration have a way of persisting through diverse regimes, and many of the basic approaches and techniques are hundreds of years old. In France, the land of restless constitutional change throughout the nineteenth century, the officials, *les fonctionnaires,* remained essentially the same. An official of the French Foreign Office in 1930 would have been at his ease in conversing with an official of the same office a hundred years earlier.

The core of government in modern times has been a rationalized administrative service, a bureaucracy. We have sketched its rise and general nature earlier in this book. We have pointed out that the failure to perceive its central position has led many writers to place bureaucracy in juxtaposition to democracy — as if a democracy could get along without an effective administrative service. There are those who would try to construct a contrast between England and the Continent on this score. Actually, England developed a rationalized central administration at an even earlier time than Continental countries simply because such a development went hand in hand with national unification; this unification the English kings succeeded in achieving at an earlier date than most other rulers for a variety of reasons.

Tout, in exhaustive studies, has unraveled the growth of this central administration. He has shown the impact of ecclesiastics at a time when few others could read or write. It was only *after* the establishment of that central core of administrative government that the constitutionalizing could make real headway. We have shown how this constitutionalizing process was aimed at placing restraints upon the administrators, at making them responsive to popular preferences, by subjecting them to elected representatives. The constituent group in nation after nation arose to demand that the administrators be subjected to a constitution giving the ultimate power of direction to the people ever-more comprehensively defined. It is, therefore, not a question of *either* democracy *or* bureaucracy, of *either* constitutionalism *or* efficient administration; the task of our industrial age has been and remains the achievement of a combination of the two, of a working balance between them — in short, of a responsible bureaucracy.

Growth of the professional administrative service • "All the states in the contemporary world," Hans Rosenberg wrote in his incisive study of the Prussian experience, "despite enormous differences in the moral, legal, and material basis of their authority and in the function, efficiency, control, and responsibility of governmental action, form part of a single political order."[1] This single political order is the professional administrative service, based upon "merit." And although what has sometimes been referred to as "meritocracy," as contrasted with "bureaucracy," is generally speaking a relatively recent achievement, there can be little question that the abler monarchs, in search of administrative talent, went beyond the nobility who traditionally composed the ruling class. Indeed, as we have shown earlier, the monarchical governments succeeded in direct proportion to their readiness to be coldly rational about their personnel. England, France, Prussia, and Hapsburg were all equally ready to grab talent wherever they could find it. England was in many ways the most practical; the titles of nobility remained continuously at the disposal of the Crown and were liberally handed out in recognition of new talent. In the course of the nineteenth century all the more highly industrialized countries developed administrative services based upon tested qualifications. This rationalization went forward in inverse ratio to the strength of constitutionalism, however, owing to the simple fact that fully developed constitutional governments, like those of Britain, the United States, and Switzerland, had to overcome the vested interest of entrenched political-party organizations. The pressure of need was everywhere great enough to bring about a fully developed bureaucracy sooner or later.

What was this need? Besides the task of centralization and integration of ever-larger dominions, it was the need of attending to the many service requirements of rapidly progressing industrial and technical civilization. To quote Rosenberg once more, "everywhere government has developed into a big business because of the growing complexity of social life and the multiplying effect of the extension of the state's regulative function." It would perhaps be more accurate to say, though, that the growth of the government's administrative services parallels that of business; the best governmental services have right along been the equals of the very best business concerns in the mastery of the art of large-scale organization. The answer to the question lies in the very nature of government and its function in society. One of its outstanding objectives is to regulate the relations between individuals and groups in a society, to keep them at peace and enforce their mutual obligations, to maintain the general as against particular interests, and to restrain the abuse of power by individuals or groups. These tasks, which have always been recognized, are bound to multiply as a society increases in size and complexity. Take as an example modern traffic. There was no need for many traffic policemen at a time, only a little more than a hundred years ago, when the streets were primarily occupied by a leisurely assortment of pedestrians and horse-drawn vehicles. But as cities became more and more populous and mechanical means of locomotion greatly increased the speed of vehicles, traffic police became ever-more numerous. The regulatory or police function of government necessarily increased the number of government servants. Nor was it a matter only of the police. As more vehicles became more numerous, the government found itself obliged to develop a licensing system which required quite a few officials for its administration; hospital services had to be increased to handle the numerous accidents; courts had to be stepped up to render judgment in controversial cases. If we have a "wonderland of bureaucracy," it is the natural accompaniment of our wonderland of industrial progress.

Various attempts have been made to gauge the increase in the number of government officials and employees. Finer, in an interesting compilation, presented approximate figures for comparing England, France, and Germany. These figures reveal that there has been a markedly greater increase in officials than in population. In France the population increased about 20 per cent between 1841 and 1928, while the government services numbered about ten times greater at the end than at the beginning of the same period. In England the population grew to about two-and-a-half times its size in the same period, the service to about sixty times its size; while in Prussia the population grew about as rapidly as in England, but there was only a twenty-fold increase in officials.[2] Clearly, then, the ratio of growth of population to officialdom is, in geometrical proportion, roughly similar in all these countries. The comparison of France, England, and Prussia suggests that the *complexity* of our industrial society, its machines and other modern features, is more likely to be responsible for the growth in administrative services than the increase in the size of the population. But is it not rather a result of socialistic theories, many ask? While such theorizing has played its part, a realistic view of society demands the counterquestion: why did such theories arise? Are they not themselves expressions of the need of an industrial society? In Chapter XXII, where we discuss at some length the relation between government and the economy, these problems are more fully explored.

Problems of recruitment and training • It has been said before, but must be said again, that all effective administrative work depends upon successful training and recruitment of personnel. European kings developed educational systems in large part for the purpose of providing themselves with trained personnel. In doing so, they followed the example of the churches, which had always been intensely interested in education for precisely that reason. Many of the great European universities owe their beginnings to this desire of church and government for trained personnel. In modern times the increasing specialization of the services has raised the issues of scientific training in a more pointed form. A thorough discussion of recruitment and training problems falls outside the scope of the present volume. There are, however, certain general aspects, vitally affecting the securing of responsible conduct, which we should consider here. In an earlier chapter it was shown how the educational system and the recruitment of government officials depend on each other in a general way. The nations, however, have developed marked differences in the training for the public service; these differences are bound up with the entire pattern of folkways and national tradtions. On the Continent a government-supported system of schools and universities forms part of the bureaucracy itself; democratic Switzerland does not differ in this respect from authoritarian Prussia. In England and the United States nonpublic schools and colleges and universities are found alongside the public institutions of learning, which more nearly correspond to the concept of democracy. But even today the endowed schools play a vital role; their relative independence from communal restraints often allows them to take the lead and thereby to enrich and to hasten educational progress. In times of stress the private institutions of higher learning also seem to be better capable and more inclined to offer resistance to inroads made by public agitation and leading to interference with academic freedom.

A comparison of England, France, and Germany reveals an interesting contrast in educational objectives for the higher grades of governmental service. These contrasts are gradually being blurred as the impact for common economic and industrial conditions makes itself felt. But they are still important as persistent influences and deserve a brief sketch. In England social and cultural values have been given the central place. The idea that a higher servant of the Crown should be a cultured gentleman seemed a matter of course in the Victorian age. It was embodied in the rules and regulations of the famous reform of the Indian service, and was later applied to the home services as well. This "imperial" origin has affected the British civil service to this day, though less and less strongly. Originally it was a question of securing representatives of a "governing class"; through school and college the selective process was at work, even while a strenuous effort was being made to find those young men who showed marked intellectual ability. The ancient traditions of literary and classical scholarship at Oxford and Cambridge, when combined with the pride and *esprit de corps* of their highly selective student body, were, it was felt, likely to secure the kind of man who would with "equanimity" shoulder the "white man's burden" in India. As Robert Moses summarized the situation: "Like the English Cabinet and the English aristocracy, the Indian civil service was to be opened to gentlemen who had inherited breeding and culture, and to those of the middle class who had made themselves gentlemen by acquiring the same breeding and culture."[3] In the decades since that was written, India has become independent, though she has retained Dominion status, and the situation at home has changed much. A vast system of scholarships has brought the opportunity of advanced study to all able students, no matter what their family background. Under the impact of the greatly increased demand for higher education, not only have the newer universities of Birmingham, Manchester, and other city centers forged ahead, but they have been joined in recent years by a considerable number of new universities which are training an ever-increasing number of highly qualified civil servants. Comprehensive assessments, such as Lord Robbins' Report, have stressed this key aspect of contemporary university education. In keeping with this trend toward rapid democratization, the rigid distinction between the upper grade, the administrative class, and the lower grades is weakening as exceptionally able men are given an opportunity to rise from the bottom in the bureaucracy. But this forward march of democrcy must not blind us to the persistence of the traditional outlook; an American is likely to be amazed by the fact that even ardent Labour party folks do not send their children to the public school, and when queried reply that "they would not learn to speak properly." In short, both recruitment and training for the public service remain strongly affected by the country's aristocratic past.

The British civil service has been increasingly under attack for these "elitist" or aristocratic aspects. H. R. G. Greaves has stressed, as we have done, "the preoccupation with the social background and antecedents of those who were to be recruited for the reformed service" which characterized the original conception of the civil service. He has likewise emphasized the failure of these reforms to demand certain essential qualities of the recruit: initiative and enterprise, originality and constructiveness of mind, human understanding and contact, scientific and social studies and training. These points and other related ones were even more sharply attacked by an American analysis. Recognizing that there has occurred an enormous increase in the power of the permanent officials, one might say that "administrative discretion is the essence of the modern state." In light of what has already been said above on this score, one can understand that such a view comes naturally to partisans of such objectives as full employment. Certain it is that socialization and planning mean a great expansion of the bureaucracy. The problem is how to make this bureaucracy "representative," that is, responsible. It has been noted that the civil service, during the first three years of the last war, increased 72 per cent, and, without the Post Office, 137 per cent. As a result, the composition of the civil service changed; there was the usual influx of outsiders, and technicalities went by the board when recruiting went from the civil service to the Ministry of Labor and National Service. In view of a parliamentary select committee's judgment that the Treasury had failed to bring expert judgment to these administrative and management problems between 1919 and 1939, this is hardly surprising. The "complete revamping of the entire system," envisaged as part of the arrival of the "planning state," has not been undertaken by either of the Labour governments; in fact, its failure to do so has been alleged by some to be the cause of its not becoming a socialist state. The changes are occurring gradually, as is the habitual British way. It may well be right that the new situation requires more men of action, rather than political philosophers who are Latin scholars; it is certainly true that more technical expertize will be required. But the prediction that a Labour government would "reform the civil service from top to bottom" has so far proved premature.[4] The age is certainly "collectivist," and a recent analysis of British politics rightly stresses this point. If it is true that in contrast to both liberalism and socialism "the reigning Collectivist politics" produced "a new and distinctive conception of public policy" — and I am inclined to agree — then surely this new conception is that "the state" is responsible for the whole economy and thereby for the welfare of all the people.[5] This basic trend manifests itself in increasing emphasis on technical, as contrasted with humanist, education as a preparation for the public service.

In France, which combines a strong bureaucratic tradition with great emphasis upon the humanistic, linguistic element in education, logical and literary brilliance used to be given great weight in the training and selection of future officials. The famous *École Normale Supérieure* and the equally famous *École Polytechnique* were veritable hothouses for budding literary genius, and a large percentage of the future holders of France's most prized honor — membership in the *Académie française* — found themselves in the same classroom at one of these *écoles*, which were open only on the basis of competitive scholarship. In the preparation of future civil servants, Romanist legal training, in spirit so closely related to humanistic studies, also played a vital part. That training covered both private and public law, but it was primarily a study and inculcation of principles, rather than an analysis of cases. This literary-legal conception of French training for public service dates back to the French revolution, with its battle cries of *raison* and *nation*. The cult of the French language, seen as the most logical product of this heritage of revolutionary ideals, was the natural one. To be a great Frenchman, a man had to be a near-genius in the use of the French language, and it is extraordinary how many notable French politicians, known to the outside world for their political achievements, men like Poincaré and Herriot, were writers of note and real artists in the use of the mother tongue. What is even more startling to the outsider is that men who hated and detested each other politically, like the Royalist Charles Maurras and the Republican Raymond Poincaré and the Socialist Léon Blum, found themselves united in this cult of the French language. It is only natural, therefore, that logical and literary achievements should have been given a decisive place in the training and recruitment of French officials. The French revolutionary tradition of strong central control has aided the imposition of rigid standards through a government-controlled school and university system. The same methods of teaching and the same subjects taught throughout France created a common intellectual atmosphere among all strata of educated people in France, which of course permeated the governmental services. But again developments in recent decades tended toward a change in the direction of recognizing technical efficiency and ability in engineering and other scientific specialties. These technicians, however, did not gain ascendancy over the brilliant lawyers and orators whom the literary tradition favored.[6]

An extensive reform of the French civil service was one of most generally agreed-upon policies advocated by the resistance movement. It was in measure achieved. The central aspect of this reform was the establishment of institutes of public administration at the universities, and at the *École Nationale d'Administration* in Paris. Here the higher civil servants, the *hauts fonctionnaires*, are trained in the social sciences and certain tool courses, such as statistics and management. The reforms have only partially achieved their goals, but there is a trend toward more social and economic studies and toward a greater participation of lower- and lower-middle-class students in the training programs.

Germany, much influenced by French traditions, nevertheless developed an emphasis of her own. Without a national cultural capital, her cultural life remained divided between Vienna and Berlin, Munich and Dresden, Frankfurt, Hamburg, Cologne, and the many other regional centers of distinctive speech, architecture, and folkways. The training of potential civil servants focused upon legal and social studies. While these legal studies were carried on dogmatically and logically, as in France, nevertheless there was considerable stress placed upon the historical and practical aspects of the law, and periods of apprenticeship were interwoven with theoretical studies. What is more, the cameralist tradition of economic training led to the inclusion of economics and of political and administrative science,[5] with a good many variations in emphasis in different states and universities. With schools and universities under state control, legal training always retained an element of localism; even though the great national legal codes, enacted after the establishment of the Empire, provided an impulse toward unification, it was not until the coming of the Weimar Republic that effective moves were initiated for the unification of training requirements. Among the genuine achievements of the several monarchies was the development of standards of severe probity for their officials — standards which freer governments often envied, but eventually succeeded in emulating (especially England and several of the small countries, like Sweden, Norway, Denmark, Holland, and Switzerland). The emphasis upon legal training had its share in developing high standards of probity; rightly conducted, education in the law has that effect. But although Germany clung to the idea that a man whose logical faculties had been highly developed would be able to turn his hand to any concrete task, the increasing complexity of our technological civilization brought about a gradual increase in technical personnel. Undertakings like the governmental railroad administration called, of course, for large staffs of engineers and other experts.

After the profound unsettling of this bureaucratic tradition by the Hitler regime, it reasserted itself within the context of the new constitutional democracy.[8] The civil-service tradition proved to be one of the more stable factors upon which to rebuild the German political order. Indeed, complaints continue that the "bureaucracy" is thwarting the full democratization of Germany.[9] One of the most controversial issues, raised by the occupation authorities, was the need for separating the civil service from politics, especially by eliminating the civil servant from parliamentary bodies. Even more important, though, was the need for democratizing the service by converting it into a career service open to talent, rather than maintaining it as a preserve of the privileged classes. As part of this latter objective, a great effort was made to introduce the system of competitive examinations for entry and promotion. These efforts encountered stubborn resistance on the part of German politicians and officialdom in spite of a considerable amount of support for it in public opinion. When, in the winter of 1948, after protracted delays, military government decreed a "reformed" law for the officials of the bizonal administrative services, it received much popular acclaim. This reform, imposed by occupying foreigners, did not, of course, remain in force. But it helped those who wanted to reform the German civil service. Still, the much-criticized "monopoly of the jurists" has been largely maintained, though under continuing pressure from the public and social-scientific analysis, it is slowly yielding to a broader conception.[10]

Many of the smaller countries developed along lines similar to those of Weimar Germany. Among the smaller countries, Switzerland is of particular interest to America because of the similarity of her governmental pattern. Besides, Switzerland was a full-fledged democracy when she began to enlarge and rationalize her governmental service. Except to the extent to which she was helped by the example of France and Germany, she is full proof of the contention that a democracy is able to do a better job, in fact, than other systems. For there can be little question that upon close scrutiny by an unbiased investigator, the Swiss appear to have a more effective, democratically responsive officialdom than any other country except Sweden — and Sweden also is very democratically governed. The probity, industry, and general ability of the Swiss official are striking to all but the Swiss, who are inclined toward a hypercritical, almost carping attitude toward their government. The Swiss railways, for example, demonstrate the efficiency of Swiss officialdom; facing an extremely difficult operational task because of the mountainous terrain of most of Switzerland, they are about as well run as any railroads in the world; the service is punctual and suprisingly reasonable. Another task of especial difficulty which the Swiss government has been handling with exceptional ability is the administration of the forests. Owing to the many avalanches, all forest land in Switzerland is operated under close governmental supervision, if not actual control, and the results are outstanding. The Swiss have given continuous recognition to technical expertise. Their nonparliamentary system has permitted the several members of the council-cabinet to become successful administrators as the heads of departments and thus to help integrate the service as a whole.

Recent American developments and problems · The rapid survey of four European countries has shown that, in spite of marked differences in tradition, they resemble each other in the conviction that very thorough training is necessary for a permanent government service which is to cope successfully with rapidly expanding governmental functions in an industrial age. America has been slow in recognizing this task. Until very recently, the specter of bureaucracy has stood in the way of clear thinking on the subject, in spite of almost unanimous protestations from students of government and administration. Certain powerful economic interests were inclined to the view that a weak governmental service was less apt to bother them. Such a view is correct only as long as these interests themselves do not need the assistance of the government. The catastrophe of the great depression opened the eyes of the more intelligent leaders of industry and commerce to the advantages to be derived from an effective administration of statutory regulations, which the popular majorities insisted upon putting on the statute book in any case. As a consequence, the great univerities have all undertaken the job of "training for the government service." However, down to the present much of this training is carried on without detailed integration with the requirements of the services themselves. Only recently has the Civil Service Commission become interested in cooperating with the universities and helping the great administrative services in setting "examinations" which take account of what is relevant. Before that, even a casual study of the examinations given to establish a panel or "register," as it was called, revealed a lack of constructive cooperation between the universities and the public service.[11] Even now, the instructors in charge of training future government officials are ordinarily denied access to the examinations, which are treated as closely guarded official secrets. Fortunately, the former unsatisfactory state of affairs has led to gradual improvements. Men like L. D. White, Arthur Fleming, and a determined group of experts in personnel administration, have been making progress; the example of the independent personnel administration of the TVA demonstrated how much can be accomplished once outworn concepts of training and recruitment are scrapped and the issue of technical competence is squarely faced. Since the Second World War the rapid expansion of the military services and their concern with technical competence have reinforced these trends; training programs and research grants have led to more and more intensive cooperation which could not help but affect the civilian services.

There lurks in this general approach, however, a very serious danger. Federal as well as state agencies in the United States have hitherto seen improvement largely in terms of acquiring people on the basis of their technical achievement — engineers, chemists, geologists, and so on. Even the lawyer is found in these agencies as a technician: as solicitor, band-law or oil-law expert, and so on. No general conception, such as the cultural, literary, or legal education of European countries, has given a common framework to the entire bureaucracy. On the whole this has left the coordinating, strictly administrative jobs unprovided for. Whenever an expert or technician had an aptitude or knack for it, he would take on the job, or he would drift into it, as it were. There is much that is healthy in such a haphazard development, and yet there is today such a vast body of special expertise in the art of administration as such that the administrator has come to be recognized as a specialist himself. The Bureau of the Budget, especially through its management experts, has stimulated much constructive thought and some action. So did the Hoover Commission. The special problems which arise in connection with operating larger and larger organizations has brought into existence a special field of training and study, just as the growing complexities of business organization have led to the establishment of graduate schools of business administration. The recognition of such specialists has the added advantage of fitting right in with the American constitutional pattern. An attempt to formulate and implement a general government-guided system of training and education would probably run afoul of established traditions of constitutionalism in America. Such a scientifically trained specialist may in time satisfy the requirements without which a functional responsibility, such as will be sketched presently, would be difficult to achieve.[12]

Responsibility and dismissal · We have seen that the constitution is essentially an instrument through which the government is not only organized, but its powers are regulated and restrained. The generations which fought for a constitution primarily in order to restrain the concentrated power of monarchical governments, and to subject it to legal rules, tended, therefore, to identify such restraints with responsibility. It thus became customary to consider government according to a constitution "responsible government." People remained perfectly aware in practice of the decisive importance of *impelling* action as well as of *restraining* it. But formulas such as "that government is best which governs least" show an inclination to minimize the errors of omission. The Victorian age was likely to be more exercised over mistakes a government had made by acting, than over the failures resulting from a government's not acting. In a rapidly expanding economy there was enough of a margin to take care of such failures. It is, however, significant that in countries where that margin was less sizable, public opinion remained more favorable to governmental efforts. No issue is more typical as an indicator for this than social insurance. Germany, though the least democratic, had done the most by 1900, while the United States had done the least. The situation is, of course, greatly altered today.

Governmental activity has been on the increase everywhere; governmental services have been multiplying in response to recognized welfare needs; that government is responsible which *responds* to the demands for *action*. Even in England and the United States, the classic homelands of "let-well-enough-alone liberalism," the growing complexity of modern government and administration has brought about the organization of a permanent civil service whose responsibility cannot be enforced through changes in cabinets except on lines of broad general policy.[13]

As we have said, the key problem of constitutionalism in an industrial society is how to make sure that the activities of these governmental services remain responsible. Generally speaking, this problem has at times been obscured by "liberal" demands that we return to nineteenth-century methods of parliamentary and electoral debates. But since the electorate can do no more than either re-elect or defeat a Congressman or an M. P., this means that the discussion has been arbitrarily limited to the question of "hiring and firing" Congressmen who cannot possibly undertake the creative direction of the public services of what Marshall Dimock has engagingly called the "Creative State."

It is in keeping with this general preoccupation with dismissal as a technique for enforcing responsible conduct that the Supreme Court of the United States, in its celebrated decision of the Myers Case, proceeded essentially on the assumption, embodied in an *obiter dictum,* that the power of removal was a necessary part of making officials responsible to the President.[14] For that reason, the Court held, the President must have unlimited power of removal in order to retain responsibility for the administration of his office. This view is questionable, to say the least. The learned judges might have taken a different view if they had examined administrative experience elsewhere; in several constitutional democratic countries of Europe with not only efficient but responsible administrative services, practically all the officials are appointed on life tenure. The power of dismissal is, in other words, only one of many techniques for making official conduct responsible. In fact, dismissal is not even a particularly effective method for producing responsible conduct, but has many disadvantages and shortcomings, which ought to be considered for purposes of comparing the removal power with other means or techniques for producing responsibility. Again, the problem of how to produce reponsible conduct cannot be considered without reference to the nature of the activities which are being carried on. Evidently the Supreme Court would be prepared to grant that its own conduct is "responsible" without anyone having an unchecked power of removal. Recently the Supreme Court itself seems to have partially recognized its mistake in the Myers Case when it ruled in the Humphreys Case that Congress could lay down for officers possessing quasi-legislative or judicial functions such qualifications as it saw fit. In case of controversy, such qualifications would be interpreted by the courts, which further extends the judicial power into the administrative field. This, however, raises other difficulties in connection with administrative justice.

Five ways of enforcing administrative responsibility · Whenever the need for action is paramount, the technique of dismissal is decidedly crude as a method for securing conduct responsible and responsive to the wishes of the principal. Hence modern governments have had to rely to an increasing extent upon other methods to induce their officials to act in accordance with the wishes of the people. Dismissal remains, of course, as the ultimate sanction, but immeasurable damage can have been done before it occurs. Where the official acts in collusion with private interests, he may even do so in anticipation of being hired by these interests, so that dismissal holds very little punishment for him. On account of the preoccupation with electoral forms of representation and responsibility there used to be, especially in Anglo-Saxon countries, an overemphasis on the power of hiring and firing, appointment and removal. We just criticized the view that the President would have to have the power to fire any and all administrative officials of the federal government, if he were to be held responsible for the administration. What is the experience in other countries and what does it suggest? It seems that one can distinguish five types of measures which contribute to the actual realization of such administrative responsibility as one would want to secure in a functioning administrative setup. First, there are the disciplinary measures, which are based on the psychology of discouragement. Second, there are the promotional measures. These are based on the psychology of encouragement. Third, there are financial measures of control and audit of expenditure, based on the rule of anticipated reactions. Fourth, there are the judicial measures based upon civil and criminal law. Such judicial measures are necessary concomitants of a legalized order or a constitutionalized government; they, among all administrative methods, have been most emphasized in English-speaking countries. Fifth, there is the spirit of craftsmanship, of a thing well done. This spirit embodies critical standards in terms of objective achievement. This fifth method of enforcing responsible conduct is becoming increasingly important at present. It has for a long time played a very important role in all the professions and therefore it has profoundly influenced the judicial branch of the government (except where judges are elective). It is in some respects akin to religious responsibility; for the standards of science are taken as relatively settled absolutes.

Disciplinary measures • Partly as a result of this religious element, disciplinary measures based on the psychology of fear have always loomed large in the efforts to enforce responsibility in administrative setups. In fact, many persons would try to persuade us that only the harshest disciplinary measure, dismissal, affords an effective technique for enforcing responsible conduct of officials. That this view is erroneous we have already shown. That disciplinary measures are, nevertheless, an important weapon in the armory of the enforcer of responsibility must be admitted.[15] But before the extreme penalty of dismissal or removal is applied, five other measures are available, each of them a valuable tool and effective within limits. They are reprimand, fine, temporary suspension, reduction of salary, and transfer to another, presumably less attractive, post. To neglect all these and to focus exclusive attention upon removal is like trying to set up a criminal law with capital punishment as the sole penalty. According to administrative experience elsewhere, removal should only be used when all the other disciplinary measures have failed; it should, in other words, be recognized as the extreme penalty for the worst offenses, and it should never be used except on the basis of an established judicial procedure. Here, in fact, lies the core of the administrative law which we have discussed above. Preferably, all these disciplinary measures should be imposed only after a hearing.

It seems desirable to consider one further problem of especial significance in this area, and that is the role and the importance of contacts with the public. Private employers are becoming increasingly aware of the decisive role which all their employees must play in the public relations of business concerns. Competition through service is becoming an ever more important factor, and the contact of the general public with particular businesses is through their employees. It is evident that the government through its expanding services is placed in a similar position.[16] The Postal Service has long recognized this, and has evolved careful regulations concerning the dealings of its employees with the public. By contrast, the arbitrary official of autocratic regimes abroad has been acknowledged as the antithesis of democracy. Although such conduct was often condoned as part of administrative efficiency, we know today that this view is mistaken. Just as morale within the service is of decisive importance in bringing about responsible administration, so likewise morale should extend beyond the confines of the service itself.

The most serious disciplinary issue revolves around the problem of the employees' right to organize, to bargain collectively, and to strike if their demands are rejected. It is difficult to see how popular government can recognize a right to strike, though it seems equally questionable to deny it.

Whatever the abstract arguments, the right of public official to strike is not recognized by many democratic governments. In the United States, most public employees recognize that such strikes really are not in their true interest. But it is obvious that in lieu of the possibility of bringing their complaints and grievances forcibly to the attention of their employer (the government), public officials must be provided with carefully devised institutional safeguards for mediation and arbitration. Such mechanisms have a fairly long tradition in some countries; they are rapidly developing in the United States. The American Federation of Government Employees has always staunchly defended this right of government employees to organize and present their views collectively. The United Federal Workers of America took an even more militant attitude, including a demand for the recognition of the right to strike. Here, again, it is evident that a democracy has to face the issues which are being raised by the ever-expanding size of its administrative activities. It cannot possibly hope to develop and maintain responsible conduct unless it accords its employees a status at least equal in dignity and self-respect to the status its labor laws impose upon and demand from private employers. The problem is one of considerable scope and concern for the Labour government in Great Britain. Here the rapid expansion of the public services, due to nationalization of basic industries, has brought into governmental employment many workers formerly in private business and accustomed to the right to strike. Unlike the Communists, who simply ruled that any worker striking against the workers' republic was a saboteur, the Labour government has had to deal with recurrent and at times crippling strikes. Its trade-union element is naturally very adverse to any curtailment of its right to strike. The situation represents one of the toughest issues of democratic socialism. In sum, even though the government does not feel justified in conceding the right to strike, it hesitates to discriminate against employees who join an organization which advances this claim. For merely to demand this right is not a crime, since reasonable men may differ as to the right answer. Employees who are denied the rights of ordinary citizens cannot possibly be expected to remain loyal and responsible public servants.

The right policy is to be sure that all necessary disciplinary rules are loyally accepted by the entire staff, irrespective of the organization to which they belong. This formula works reasonably well as long as those responsible for the rules respect the rights of the persons working under them. It must be kept in mind, however, that there are quite a few difficult borderline cases, where the infraction of a given rule has been due to faulty behavior or hostile attitudes on the part of the higher-up. Possible frictions of this type are endless; it is evident that adequate representative organizations of the employees is the only possible way of coping with the situations as they arise.

Promotional measures • Promotional measures are based upon the psychology of encouragement. They consist essentially of promotions themselves, salary increases, titles, orders, and decorations. A considerable amount of responsibility can be secured from officials by a judicious employment of all of these; but most of these possibilities have been badly neglected in the United States. In the thirties the Commission of Inquiry on Public Service Personnel Problems, in a notable report, insisted upon the decisive importance of promotion when it wrote:

There can be no career service in government, or anywhere else, without promotion. The creation of promotion opportunities, however, is not easy to bring about, especially in large organizations, because the top officials with the power to appoint and promote may not know the younger subordinates or have any contact with their work. . . . A regularly organized system of promotion, maintained by the chief executives through a properly established personnel office, thus performs three indispensable services: first, it makes the service attractive to promising young men who will not enter an employment which is known not to give the opportunity of advancement based on proved merit; second, it results in an energetic staff by displacing the stagnant atmosphere of a stationary service; and, third, it brings to the top positions men who combine energy with knowledge of public administration, rather than partisans, amateurs, or men, with or without energy, who do not know the public service. From the standpoint, therefore, of the establishment and maintenance of a career service, the promotion system is indispensable.[17]

The educated young man of ambition who enters the civil service of England, France, or other European countries is driven by competition with his equals to exert himself to the utmost in discharging his duties. To strengthen further the impetus toward self-exertion, the British have developed a system of annually certifying that service has been satisfactory as a condition for promotion as well as for salary increases. In the United States the situation is not nearly so satisfactory. Until recently it was difficult to get young people of ambition and ability to enter the government service, except as a stopgap, because there was no clear road to promotion. While there has been considerable improvement in recent years, there are still many uncertainties, and the person who exerts himself to conduct his office responsibly often finds himself unrewarded by promotion. A very serious setback to the maintenance of a sound career service was caused by the methods of Senator McCarthy in the early fifties. By highly irresponsible use of the power of investigation, he proceeded to jeopardize, and in not a few cases to destroy, the reputations and hence the careers of devoted public servants by means of reckless accusations amounting to public slander. It was natural that young Americans should have sharply reacted against a life career that would be unexpectedly exposed to such wanton risks. Fortunately, an aroused public and Congressional opinion put an end to this kind of proceeding so flagrantly contrary to the spirit of a constitution which explicitly outlawed bills of attainder — the comparable method of waging partisan warfare against public servants.[18]

It is a curious thing that in a country in which the lure of promotion is generally recognized by business leaders as of decisive importance in managing a large-scale organization efficiently, the need of a career in governmen has been overlooked. To be sure, one should avoid making a fetish out of the career element in enforcing responsibility. The overstimulation of ambition may lead to very undesirable practices. Students of the problem of promotion have sometimes tended to neglect its dangers and to make it a panacea of all ills. What must particularly be guarded against are schemes which seek to provide for a certainty of promotion. If a career in government service is taken to mean that, a good part of the value of promotional opportunities in stimulating responsibility is lost. The possibility of promotion, not the certainty of it, is necessary in order to be assured of responsible work. Those who are unwilling to gamble with themselves are not safe as a gamble for anyone else.

Closely related to promotion are titles. If the greater responsibility of a higher office is to be publicly recognized and honored, an appropriate title has to be provided for such an office. Since much valuable ambition is generated by the desire for honor, it is almost absurd to fail to make use of the opportunities which human nature offers in this respect. Generally speaking, America's tradition is opposed to the use of titles. However, courts, churches, universities, and the defense forces, four very important branches of national life, employ them extensively. Titles such as "colonel" are even used as a form of address in strictly private business relationships. The steady increase in the use of titles in American life testifies to a growing consciousness of rank and status. It could be correlated to rapid stratification in some sectors. It is, however, not easy to prove this contention. It is quite possible to argue that these titles, associated as they are with churches, universities, the military service, and certain honorific positions in the government, and devoid as they are of any hereditary element, constitute survivals resulting from the autonomous traditions of these nonmodern segments of the society.

Certain offices are generally conceived as honorific in their very names.

A powerful impetus for responsible government service may thereby be secured. Yet much that is most valuable in this sphere is beyond human control. Titles seem to follow something which corresponds to Greshan's law in economics — their value seems to decrease with the increase of the numbers acquiring them. The history of titles shows that you can never recoup a deteriorated title. The only possible method is to impose a still higher rank. The history of both the M.A. and the Ph.D. in the United States provides a significant illustration. When the Ph.D. first appeared, it was usually the degree of a foreign university and was supposed to confer the distinction of foreign study. Gradually, as American universities developed their graduate research work, they offered the Ph.D. degree, with very stiff requirements, patterned upon the tradition of the European universities, notably Oxford and Cambridge. But in the decades past, it became more and more common to demand a Ph.D. in academic life and in the public services. Hence the institutions conferring it multiplied, until it seems to some necessary to develop a new and still higher title. Needless to say, any effort to create titles must be guided by what people desire as an honor.

Orders and decorations, on the other hand, can be and have been created. Therefore, if the growth of titles does not proceed fast enough, honors can be established through orders and decorations. However, there are in this field other considerable limitations. For the honor which is attached to such orders and decorations is great only if there is a general belief in the traditional significance of the person who establishes the order. If a king sets it up in a monarchical country, the decoration has that quality, but if the President of the United States does it, it does not necessarily have the same effect. For the President is a party man. This point is well illustrated by the history of Congressional decorations. Honorary degrees by American universities also have only a limited appeal, particularly because of the abuse made by them by various institutions in search of funds. This is quite natural, for orders and decorations are likewise subject to the general proposition that the value of a thing is enhanced by its rarity.

There has always been a tendency to associate orders and decorations with aristocratic and therefore exclusive tendencies, and they are instinctively felt to be undemocratic. Consciously democratic constitutions are inclined to forbid the accepting or the wearing of foreign orders and decorations. In the United States, only the military have developed an elaborate system of orders and decorations, but the trend is toward decorations in the civilian sector of public life. For one thing, decorations, like titles, provide a very inexpensive reward for public service. Nevertheless the Swiss, in 1931, extended to all citizens the prohibition of foreign decorations, titles, presents, and pensions, formerly limited to government officials. While electoral participation was limited, the debate was highlighted by the conflict in principle between such decorations and democracy.

Fiscal measures · Time-honored and yet often not sufficiently appreciated are the fiscal techniques for securing responsible conduct of administrative business. They are essentially three: forecasting the expenditures through an appropriate budget, controlling the payments when they are being made in order to insure their consonance with the budget, and auditing the accounts afterward.[19] In relation to the administrative organization itself, these controls are partly internal and partly external. Budgeting is both internal and external. The drawing up of the budget (with which the President with the assistance of the Bureau of the Budget is charged in the United States, while in England it is the Treasury, and in other countries the ministry of finance) is internally done by administrative officials. The approving of this budget, on the other hand, is external and entrusted to parliaments as we have seen. The controlling of the payments as made is internal in Europe, where the treasuries or ministries of finance have ultimate control, though in England the Comptroller and Auditor-General has some share in the control. In the United States, on the other hand, the Comptroller-General as an independent "legislative" officer has complete control (short of court review), an arrangement which has led at times to serious friction. Auditing, finally, is external everywhere. Highly judicialized techniques are preferred on the Continent (*Cour des Comptes* in France, *Bundesrechnungshof* in Germany),[20] executive work in England (Comptroller and Auditor-General) and in the United States (Comptroller-General). But everywhere parliamentary supervision, by some sort of committee on accounts, implements this machinery wherever there is parliamentary government. Probably the preference of Continental countries for a judicial setup in the audit field is due to traditions derived from their monarchical past. Some sort of independent body, like the *Cour des Comptes,* established by Napoleon, is essential for the maintenance of financial integrity. These bodies continued to develop into courts, because under the separation of powers as practiced by monarchical constitutional governments, judicial safegaurds of administrative integrity were compatible with monarchical traditions; these monarchies looked upon them as acceptable alternatives to parliamentary supervision. When, later on, parliaments were able to extend their jurisdiction, they found these independent bodies quite acceptable as aides in discharging their supervisory function. From these circumstances, as well as from the general theory of the separation of powers, it might be argued that the United States would be well advised to follow the pattern of a judicialized procedure for auditing, and such a change has indeed been advocated. The present fusion of controlling and auditing functions in one "independent officer" certainly has not produced results which argue for the continuance of such an arrangement. Hence if a court of accounts were set up, the controlling function could then be put back under the administrative direction of the Treasury Department, where it belongs. The Hoover Commission, taking a line similar to the one here stated, proposed to divest the Comptroller-General of his accounting responsibilities (even now not well worked out and integrated) and to set up an Accountant-General in the Treasury Department. He would have had authority to prescribe general accounting methods and enforce accounting procedures. He would be charged with "combining agency accounts into the summary account of the government, and produce financial reports for the information of the Chief Executive, the Congress and the public." The report pointed out that "there are serious weaknesses in the internal operations . . . in the fiscal field. These weaknesses penetrate into the heart of every governmental transaction. . . . Some of the fiscal concepts of the Federal Government come down from Alexander Hamilton. They were archaic when the total expenditures of the Government were $4,000,000,000 per annum. Now . . . they are totally inadequate."[21]

Whatever the general framework of government, these several techniques have been found invaluable aids in securing financial responsibility. Politically speaking, they operate largely in accordance with the rule of anticipated reactions. It is, as in all such cases, futile to offer elaborate statistics as to what items have been disallowed, or what misdemeanors have been detected. They are, taken individually, important enough. But a much larger result is due to the fact that administrative officials who know that their expenditures must first be approved, and later audited, are much more careful in their financial conduct.

Judicial measures • The preceding discussion of disciplinary, promotional, and fiscal measures has sketched a wide variety of techniques for making the conduct of governmental officials more responsible. But most of these measures presuppose a willingness at the top to employ them when necessary. They are largely administrative in nature. Suspicion, first of the king and later of party bosses, has inclined the majority of people in England, America, and the British Dominions to look for outside controls. The judiciary provides the most obvious and ancient technique for this purpose. Judicial methods for dendering official conduct more responsible are, therefore, of considerable importance. The modern conception of the rule of law demands that all officials be subject to civil and criminal law. Whatever exceptions may be necessary regarding certain actions taken in the course of official duties, it goes without saying that no civilized community will suffer its government personnel to steal, cheat, or rape with impunity. But such checks upon personal misconduct of officials can only take care of a minor part of the task of enforcing responsibility.[22]

Even if it be admitted that such judicial methods make an official responsible for doing something which should not have been done, they certainly do not provide any safeguards against the failure to do what should be done. The common law has developed certain special writs like *quo warranto* and *mandamus* to prevent or enforce official action. By these writs the courts may, in the name of the "sovereign," compel an inferior official to comply with the law. Yet, since administrative action is largely positive and an administrative agency must primarily be interested in "getting things done," judicial measures are narrowly limited in their effectiveness in securing governmental responsibility. What is more, many things which officials should not do are beyond the reach of the judiciary. Take, for example, offensive and overbearing conduct toward the public. This is certainly a bureaucratic vice of widest occurrence. Yet courts cannot deal with it at all; rarely will the offense reach the point of extremity where the offended citizen could sue for tort. Again consider the case of slothful red tape or even deliberate lying. The damage to individuals may be very great, but nothing can be accomplished through the courts. Take the following case: a subaltern clerk in an American consulate rejected an invitation from an American citizen to a foreign relative (which is required as evidence of a *bona fide* visit), claiming it was not executed according to the "rule," and requested a duly sworn invitation instead. The clerk added that the visa could not be issued unless the duly executed form were in the hands of the consul four weeks before the intended departure. But there were only five weeks left, and consequently it was impossible for the alien to secure such an invitation within the time limit stipulated by the official. However, inquiry at the State Department revealed that no such rule existed; was there, could there be, any judicial remedy for the improper and irresponsible conduct of the clerk concerned?

Governmental versus personal liability · Not only are courts largely unable to bring about official action, and partly unable to prevent irresponsible conduct, but they are furthermore hampered, in the United States, by the ancient rule that "the king can do no wrong." This rule means that the government cannot be held liable for acts committed by an official in the discharge of his duty. Damage suits against officials must, therefore, always establish that the official acted *ultra vires*. If the court finds that he acted *ultra vires*, the claim has to be enforced against the individual officer. It is evident that in many cases the individual officer is totally unable to pay the claim. If, on the other hand, the court finds that the official did not act *ultra vires*, then the damaged party is dependent upon the grace of a "sovereign legislature" for adequate compensation. The disadvantages of this situation are, however, by no means limited to the "public" which may sustain damages. Inasmuch as it exposes the official to constant danger of a ruinous suit for personal damages, it makes him overly cautious and thus irresponsible from the point of view of a vigorous pursuit of his duties. The recognition of this exceedingly unsatisfactory state of affairs has led legislative bodies to provide specifically for the responsibility of certain large-scale government enterprises in the case of torts committed by any of its officials. Certain municipalities have recognized their obligation for damage done by their fire departments, and the federal government has provided similarly in the case of the TVA. It is indeed as evident as anything can be that the government should take the same responsibility for any large-scale service enterprise it manages as would be provided for if that enterprise were privately owned and operated. If it is to the community's benefit to undertake such tasks, the community and not the damaged individual should bear the losses involved in its operation. Actual experience in local government bodies where a certain amount of that type of corporate liability is allowed tends to show that objectively responsible conduct in terms of the particular service can be secured by internal measures such as those we have sketched earlier in this chapter.

To put the matter positively, it appears that relieving the officer of the government from this type of personal liability has the great advantage of placing the responsibility where it belongs. If, let us say, a man lying asleep on his porch is accidentally shot by a policeman, the important point is not whether the policeman acted according to his legally defined duties. Even if he did not, it might be a gross injustice to burden him with the liability as long as he believed that shooting was the only effective means of handling the situation. If an American citizen is seriously damaged without due process of law by an officer of the government trying to maintain law and order, he is entitled to just compensation. This compensation should come from the party responsible for the damage, namely, the American government and the American people as a whole. It is then up to the government to determine whether its officials acted responsibly or not, and to collect, in the latter case, what they can from the official, or to punish him according to established disciplinary procedure. All the facts point toward the conclusion that responsibility is more effectively enforced by such a provision. In fact, only such a plan will insure that a government service wielding vast powers of control, supervision, and regulation in every phase of the public's

activities will not deteriorate into an irresponsible bureaucracy, either irre-
mediably damaging private individuals in executing "laws" however bad, or
timorously shirking responsible action because of the absence of unequivocal
"legal" authority. The problem of how to "judicialize" such a responsibility,
how to organize courts which would specialize in adjudicating controversies
arising out of administrative action, is a grave one. We have treated it in
broad outline when dealing with the judiciary as a governmental technique.

Measures based upon an objective standard · It remains to inquire
into what we called methods based upon an objective standard of performance as a possible technique for insuring responsible conduct. It is a question of craftsmanship, of sound professionalism, and hence very important
as a basis for "sound" action. Perhaps the most ancient instance of the
application of such an objective standard is found in the judiciary. As we
pointed out when discussing the judiciary in relation to the bar, judicial
decisions are relatively responsible, because judges have to account for their
action in terms of a rationalized and previously established set of rules. Any
deviation from these rules on the part of a judge will be subjected to extensive scrutiny by his colleagues and by what is known as the legal profession.
The judges' sensitivity to criticism of their brethren off the bench, their
feeling of responsibility toward that wide fraternal community, is a typical
illustration of the kind of objective standard of performance with which we
are here concerned.

Administrative officials seeking to apply scientific standards similarly have
to account for their action in terms of a rationalized and previously established set of *hypotheses* or *rules*. Any deviation from these hypotheses will
be subjected to thorough scrutiny by their colleagues in what is known as
"the fellowship of science." If an official in the Bureau of Standards, for
example, should make regulations which would show lack of acquaintance
with the essential knowledge in his field, he would be criticized so strenuously by fellow engineers that his authority would presently vanish. There
are, of course, here as well as in the judicial field, wide areas where doubt
and controversy prevail. With regard to those activities, indecision or arbitrary selection among possible alternative solutions remains unavoidable.
But it should be evident that even in these cases the necessity for justifying
the choice will impose enough responsibility upon the official to make him
wary of changing his conduct in a similar matter without weighty evidence.
Thus a certain amount of regularity and predictability is secured.[23]

Conclusion · The ways, then, by which a measure of genuine responsibility can be secured under modern conditions appear to be manifold,

and they must all be utilized for achieving the best effect. No mere reliance upon some traditional device, like cabinet dependence upon majority support in parliament, or popular election of the chief executive, important as they are, can be counted upon to render the vast public services of a modern government responsible. Traditionalists have continued to take it for granted that in England, at least, such cabinet responsibility effectively ensures responsible conduct of public affairs by officials high and low. Some of these men have gone so far as to suggest that the United States will never have a healthy political system until the British scheme is adopted. Actually, the task of making the administrative services responsible leads much farther afield. At best, responsibility in a democracy will remain fragmentary because of the indistinct voice of the principal whose agents the officials are supposed to be: the heterogeneous masses composing the electorate. But it can be approximated. Appropriate training, reasonable care in selection at recruitment time, a well-ordered system of disciplinary procedure, a sound system of promotion, tight fiscal controls, and a strong sense of professional pride and craftsmanship, are all necessary parts of a democratic administration that is truly responsible. If all these devices are kept operative while the leaders, the executive and legislative representatives, respond to the majority's preference in matters of general policy, democratic government, by pooling many different interests and points of view, continues to provide the nearest approximation to a policy-making process which will give the "right" results. For right policies are policies which seem right to the community at large and at the same time do not violate "objective" scientific standards.[24]

Responsibility to the people does not require partisans of a particular general outlook, whether Republican or Democrat, conservative, progressive, or socialist, but it does require specialists who know their job and will, therefore, effectively execute the general rules decided upon by executive or legislative leadership in accordance with popular preferences. Fortunately, people aware of such "objective" standards and sensitive therefore to objective responsibility within a given function are often glad to be relieved of the obligation of making decisions where no objective standards are available. The very passion for objectivity and impartiality which renders them judicially or scientifically minded makes them shrink from any rash and arbitrary decision. They are delighted to leave that task to the "people" or to their elected representatives. For such specialists often do not realize that *some* decision has to be made. To these representatives, both executive and legislative, then falls the difficult task of working toward such decisions by bringing together the judgment of the expert and the "will of the people."

Political Parties:

Outline of a General Theory

XX

Introduction · Party origins and the cabinet system · A two-party system grows out of one party. The policy of the government as a factor in the development of parties · Ideological and material objectives · Material interests and integration · Parties secure power for their leaders · Party organization and finance · A general theory of party? · Parties and factions · Some recent theories of political parties · Parties in relation to social structure · The over-all pattern of European parties · Conclusion

Introduction · Parties are, it is now generally agreed, indispensable features of democracy. Yet, one hundred and fifty years ago, their place and function were generally unknown.[1] At the founding of the United States, the "people" were looked upon as capable of acting as a unit. Washington, as everyone knows, warned in his farewell address against "factions." Later historians have mockingly remarked that Washington was inclined to look upon efforts to disturb Federalist rule as "factionalism." This is true, except that Washington did not think of the "Federalists" as a party; what came to be the platform of the Federalists was to him still the one sound, patriotic, American policy to which there did not exist any well-defined alternative. To be sure, in England in the course of the eighteenth century the idea of parties as a part of the governmental scheme had been dawning on the minds of the most acute observers. There is more than a hint of that in Hume's essay on parties. And Bolingbroke, while persuasively arguing against Walpole's system, which he readily identified with "corruption," and while extolling the ideal of a patriot king, still himself realized the importance of party. Curiously enough, the American colonists were revolting at the same time against this corruption in Parliament and against the tyranny of the king who tried to cope with it. To understand this paradox, one should recall that George III and his Tory ministers had been emulating the technique of Walpole and the Whigs by building up a faction of royalist henchmen in Parliament. He was, in other words, tarred with the same brush of "factionalism," although his underlying ambition had been to become such a patriot king as Bolingbroke had depicted. He was going to rule as an independent chief executive according to the original scheme of the constitution of 1688. But by organizing a party, he acknowledged the place and function of parties in the constitutional order; it is no wonder that the party outlived him and his personal ambitions.

In the theorizing about parties, we find the four typical concerns of theoretical analysis: origins, objectives, patterns (structure) and functions (operations). They cannot be sharply separated, but in a general way the following analysis will seek to deal with them in turn.

Party origins and the cabinet system • Historically speaking, the English cabinet's parliamentary responsibility arose out of the party struggle; it is generally agreed that the evolution of the party and of parliamentarism is inseparably intertwined. It is therefore rather difficult to discuss the development of one without the other.[2] But since the Whigs and Tories of the last years of Charles II's reign are admittedly the prototype of the modern English two-party system, it must be conceded that the parties antedate the cabinet system. We may say, as we did in Chapter XV, that the single-member constituency with plurality elections is peculiarly adapted to the two-party system under responsible parliamntary government. But we must remember that the plurality vote and the resulting sharpness of party division preceded the cabinet system. The reason why the responsibility of the cabinet to Parliament, the parliamentary cabinet system, that is, was engendered by the party strife is that each party in its effort to buttress its position, but more particularly the Whig party under Walpole and Pelham (1715–1760), sought to secure for itself a solid majority in Parliament. Such a majority greatly facilitated the realization of all policies for which the cooperation of Parliament was necessary. Walpole proceeded to secure such a parliamentary majority for himself and his cabinet by a carefully worked out system which to his contemporaries and to moderns alike can appear only as a system of corruption. Wraxall tells us in his memoirs that the government under Pelham handed each of their partisans in Parliament from five hundred to eight hundred pounds at the end of a session, the amount varying according to the services rendered. These payments were official enough to be entered on a record kept in the Treasury. More recent investigations have shown that the Whigs at that time had worked out a very elaborate system of governmental favors, ranging from direct payments to voters and members of Parliament, to patronage and the various favors available in foreign trade and the privileged trading companies. All this is well enough known, and was intimately bound up with the struggle for independence waged by the American colonies a few years later. What is less readily seen is that the English two-party system was rooted in a traditional struggle for spoils between two distinctly aristocratic factions or divisions of the (aristocratically controlled) electorate. In fact, Walpole once remarked that he and Lord Townshend constituted the "firm" to which the king had entrusted the country's government.

A two-party system grows out of one party · It would, however, not be generally conceded today that the long Whig rule under Walpole was the true origin of the English parties. Historians have for a long time argued about this problem, and while some, with Sir Erskine May, have dated party growth back to the Puritans under Elizabeth, others, like Lord Macaulay, have refused to admit anything worthy of the name prior to the Roundheads and the Cavaliers of the Long Parliament.[3] The truth lies in between. Some of these differences in opinion are traceable to different conceptions as to what constitutes a party. Obviously, the more one stresses organizational features, the later one will have to put "party origin." When "party" is taken to mean something akin to faction, the partisans of the Red and the White Roses in the fourteenth and fifteenth centuries were members of a "party." But since these factions of nobles were simply striving to seat their head on the throne, no question of principle entered in. On the other hand, the Puritans under Queen Elizabeth lacked all effective organization, and they hardly attempted to control Parliament (without parliamentary responsibility, such control was not particularly important). They had deep-seated convictions, to be sure; but many of these beliefs transcended the strictly political sphere. Under James I, however, the Puritans took on something of the quality of a party which developed into the Roundheads of the Long Parliament. While the Puritans did not explicitly claim it, they really sought the control of the government. Or, to put it another way, they sought to escape from the control which the king had hitherto exercised over the government. The Tudor kings had developed a system of patronage and corruption for the purpose of keeping Parliament in line. What matters to us is that the Puritan party developed as an opposition to the government as such, and more particularly to so-called royal prerogative. This remained so down to the Long Parliament period, when the Puritans themselves gained ascendancy. Then they in turn claimed an exclusive control, which eventually called forth the Cromwellian dictatorship. This Puritan party was not recognized as a legitimate undertaking; the government belabored them by calling them rebels, and they returned the compliment by denouncing the Crown as tyrannical. It was only after these violent revolutionary experiments with one-party rule had proved abortive that the English people settled down to a mutual acceptance of each other's political viewpoint. Thus we find that a two-party system develops out of a one-party predominance. Only after the resulting civil war had shown a people the danger of party violence, did the two-party system with its dependence upon a certain amount of tolerance become acceptable to the group at large.

The policy of the government as a factor in the development of parties • Why should the two-party system have taken hold in England and nowhere else? What conditions favoring its development in England were absent in all other countries? The development of a cabinet system was an important contributing factor. Another very important condition is the *early* development of the parties.[4] England escaped the religious division (and the consequent development of a Catholic party) on account of the overwhelmingly Protestant nature of the country. England buttressed this religious uniformity by depriving Catholics and other religious dissenters (nonconformists) of political privileges until well into the nineteenth century. As a result, England could evolve the fundamental and simple division of conservatives and liberals (with some reactionaries and radicals thrown in on each side) during the course of two centuries of more or less undisturbed domestic peace. She could therefore enter into the era of the industrial revolution with that pattern firmly established. What is more, the radical tendencies engendered by this industrial revolution for a long time found an acceptable voice in the traditional Liberal party. A distinct Labour party arose only in the twentieth century. This party, after six decades of growth, seems now definitely to have superseded the Liberal party as the party of progress.

On the Continent conditions were vastly different.[5] After the restoration in France, a major cleavage existed between republicans, in favor of the principles of 1789, and those opposed to these principles on various grounds. But the French restoration ministers, unlike those of the Stuarts, never attempted to organize a party of the Crown, for they knew that such a party was liable to call forth an opposition which would eventually establish parliamentary supremacy. So the tactics of Louis XVIII and Louis Philippe followed the maxim of divide and rule so as to avoid the consolidation of parties. Thus a multiple-party system established itself in France, but the situation remained unstable, as the revolutions of 1830 and 1848, the Second Empire, and its overthrow in 1870 clearly show. By the time the Third Republic had firmly established itself, the Socialists had got under way as a factor to be reckoned with. Since socialism assumes a fundamental cleavage in the electorate, class antagonism between capitalists and workers, the party divisions of the electorate assumed the proportions of a permanent disruption of the people into mutually exclusive and lastingly hostile interests.

In Germany the development took a different course, but the result was the same.[6] Here the Socialists could consolidate their position even more definitely before a cabinet system supported by parliamentary majorities was set up by the constitution of 1919. The Prussian development before 1871 was indicative of the future. Bismarck, instead of seeking majority support for the government's policies, openly flouted the parliamentary opposition. After his internal and external victories, he made no serious attempt to collaborate with the party most ready to support him — the National Liberals — but sought to secure his majorities as he needed them. When the Socialists, as a result, were forging ahead rapidly as the party of progress, he attempted to suppress them by force; toward the end of Bismarck's career the failure of these efforts brought the Socialists back into parliament as a firmly entrenched party proclaiming the Marxist doctrine of inexorable class warfare. Disunity thereafter became the earmark of German representative bodies.

Party development appears, therefore, greatly affected by the policy of the government in the period of the beginnings of parliamentary, representative government. Does this mean that we are confronted by situations totally at variance with one another in the several countries? Evidently not. In spite of a number of variations, there remains much similarity in the party formations of all the European nations. And while the two-party system, so called, has its distinct advantages from the standpoint of parliamentary responsibility, we should not deceive ourselves into overestimating either its importance or its permanence. After all, the two large English parties have frequently been divided into warring groups; such groups have often caused the downfall of the government. Besides, even in England since the Reform of 1832, two parties have been the exception rather than the rule. The Peelites, the Radicals, the Liberal Unionists, the Irish Nationalists, and the Labour party have followed each other as third parties, and it would, in the light of all the facts, be more appropriate to describe the English as a two-and-one-half-party system.

Ideological and material objectives · The English evolution suggests another hypothesis to the student of politics: Parties in order to live and function must be compounded of ideological and material purposes or objectives.[7] A party, to achieve any degree of permanency, must and will have both an interest in certain ideas concerning law and government and the possibilities of their reform, i.e., an ideology and a program; also a party must have an interest in securing the power of government and all that goes with it in the form of patronage and the rest. In other words, the distinction between patronage parties and parties of principle, which used to be popular with writers on politics in Europe, is untenable. There is no such thing as a party which lacks either of these elements. Moreover, this is a distinction of which one should be particularly wary from a practical viewpoint; it is one of the most common errors made in dealing with politics to contrast the ideal aspirations of one's own group with the actual performance of one's opponents. Politicians continually build appeals on this presumption. A measure of sophistication concerning such claims is an indication of political education in an electorate. In countries with limited experience in democracy, many people are readily beguiled by such claims.

But a realistic recognition of the material advantages which parties seek must not become the ground for undiscriminating denunciations of parties as such. "Parties are inevitable," Bryce justly said, "no free large country has been without them." Conceding this claim, quite a few insist that for that reason popular government must go. There is, we are told, always much corruption and patronage connected with party government. This cannot be denied by anyone who studies the historical records attentively. But what can be denied is that this tendency toward corruption and patronage is in any way peculiar to party government. Autocratic regimes do not differ in that respect; they, too, are never free from corruption and nepotism, and in periods of decay are notoriously honeycombed with both. The records of the Hitler regime published since 1945 show that it was no exception. The real difference is that the dirty laundry of popular regimes is washed in public, whereas under autocratic rule it is washed behind the scenes or not at all. In our time autocracies are usually single-party regimes. This means that control which comes from alternation with another party is lacking. It is difficult to see why the absence of all criticism should make for greater purity in the conduct of the government. The autocratic regime which strives for the good of the country all of its own free will is to be found only in the utopian ideologies of Marxism and Fascism.

A realistic political science can state with some confidence that all parties strive for a combination of ideological and material objectives. What is more, observation of the actual working of government points toward the conclusion that the ideological objectives are developed by parties as a weapon in their struggle for gaining control of the government. It is a platitude of practical politics that the outs are invariably more emphatic in their advocacy of principles than the ins. Therefore autocratic one-party regimes are apt to be more corrupt and venal than two-or-more-party setups. So-called "historical" instances pointing supposedly in the opposite direction, like the Prussian monarchy under Frederick William I and Frederick the Great, turn out upon closer investigation to have been subject to very special conditions which account for the relatively small amount of corruption *in spite* of the autocratic nature of the regime. Frederick William I was fired with a passionate ambition to clean up the vast corruption which had prevailed under his spendthrift father, and at the same time to overcome the large remnants of feudal dispersion and corruption which disunited and weakened his scattered domains. Frederick the Great was engaged in very extensive foreign warfare, which necessitated as high an efficiency as was attainable in his administrative staff, and the later phases of his reign were filled with an unceasing effort to rebuild and consolidate his exhausted kingdom. But as soon as he was dead, a process of large-scale corruption set in and brought this autocratic government to the brink of complete disaster during the Napoleonic wars. All this suggests the conclusion that corruption is even more common in autocratic than in popular government.

Material interests and integration · Although it is true that all organized parties strive for material as well as for ideological objectives, and that their programs contain both, considerable differences exist between parties regarding the balance between the two. Continental Europe observers have often commented upon the relatively large role which material objectives seem to play in the history of English and American parties. This is undoubtedly in part due to the fact that the parties in these countries have had a real prize for which to fight, namely, the actual control of the government, whereas in many of the Continental countries, but particularly in Germany, the limited power of the representative body has tended to keep a considerable section of the public and the parties speaking for them on the outside of actual government, and consequently emphatic in their advocacy of ideology. Both Liberal and Socialist parties were deeply affected by this; they developed, on the Continent, a programmatic dogmatism which goes ill with practical politics. Furthermore, all evidence seems to point toward the conclusion that the larger the party, the more pronounced are its material interests. This has been shown quite convincingly for American parties, which throughout their history have been sensitive to the broad economic interests of various sections of the country.[8] It is evident that a party in order to hold together a rather heterogeneous following (and any party aspiring to an actual majority must do that) will shun a decided stand on questions of principle, while at the same time making concessions to a variety of theoretically perhaps incompatible interests. By such a policy a party manager may gain the adherence of sufficiently large groups to lead his banner to victory. The attitude of many an American politician toward some of the demands of labor and socialism illustrates this point. Theoretically, socialism is based upon the idea that the interests of employers and employees are incompatible, and that capitalism must eventually be destroyed and supplanted by state or government control. Practically, the interests of working-men are in higher wages, lower hours, better working conditions generally, in unemployment and old-age insurance, and so forth. These material interests are precisely those which an American politician will quite readily support, if workingmen's support is essential for his being re-elected, whereas he probably would contemplate with horror the possibility of becoming a "Socialist." Of course, in the United States both Republicans and Democrats expound a long series of "principles" in their official platforms, but many of these principles are so vague as to turn out on closer inspection to be similar for both parties. As a result, the material interests, including patronage, are the cement of parties wherever the system of election by plurality prevails and as we have seen in Chapter XV, this is made one of the points of attack upon this system by the proportionalists. There is, to be sure, a considerable difference between the several kinds of material interests. Patronage is one thing, concession another. An act prohibiting child labor, while a material interest to some, is very much fraught with ideological issues for others. Parties have the function of integrating the multitude of interests, values, and beliefs of a political community by developing programs of action for reform (or conservation), often elaborated into comprehensive ideologies. An ideology and a program are as vital to the life of parties as is an effective organization, and the recurrent arguments over their relative importance are rather futile; it changes with the over-all political situation. In the course of realizing this function, parties develop a succession of leaders after the original founder-leaders have passed away. Parties thereby help solve the problem of succession which is one of the most serious issues confronting any government.[9]

These general propositions hold for all parties. Political science cannot accept such historico-legal assertions as that American or British parties are *sui generis* and cannot be compared with any others. It is not idle, but very important, whether they are claimed to be "parties of the honored few" (*Honoratioren parteien*)[10] or patronage parties; they are neither, but like all parties pursue *both* ideological and material objectives. The fact that American party programs are overlapping and to some extent devoid of content does not disprove this point; far from it. No one who attentively studies the record of the administrations of F. D. Roosevelt or John F. Kennedy, and who appreciates the deep ideological cleavages involved in American party divisions on such matters as social security and race relations, to mention only two major issues, can reasonably assert that American parties are "merely" patronage parties, or that ideology (*Weltanschauung*) plays no role. Every party formation, like other historical phenomena, is of course in one sense unique, but that does not exclude generalization. Bryce's much-cited saying that American parties resemble differently labeled bottles which are empty is very misleading; they do in fact resemble big boxes with a general label containing many small bottles with different labels and content — and some of these are found in both boxes.

Nor is this situation as unique as it appeared to nineteenth-century analysts. The progress of democratization had produced similar developments in England, France, Germany, and other countries. As parties strive to secure a majority of a pluralistically diversified electorate, they find themselves forced to dilute ideological purity by concessions to all sorts of material interests as well as shades of conviction on their general ideological line. In the United States, issues of foreign policy (internationalism vs. isolationism) and of domestic orientation (conservatism vs. progressivism) divide both major parties; similar trends, though not yet quite as pronounced, are to be observed in the divisions of parties in European countries over such issues as European unification, social insurance, nationalization, and the like.

There seems to be a certain natural sequence, a kind of rhythm, in the way material objectives intrude themselves and attentuate the ideological orientation. David Hume already noted this in the eighteenth century, when he wrote: "Nothing is more usual than to see parties which have begun upon a real difference continue even after that difference is lost."[11] The difference he is talking about is that in programmatic conviction, i.e., ideology. One might even construct a kind of developmental model. First, a party with a distinct and coherent program comes into power. This program gradually loses its appeal in the course of the party's efforts to realize it. Some parts turn out to be impossible of achievement. Others arouse the antagonism of some of the party's own following when the practical implications become apparent. The party then breaks up into divisions. This disintegration offers to another party, irrespective of whether it has evolved a distinct and realizable program or not, the chance of concentrating and unifying its forces; then that party gains ascendancy. After a while, this party is subject to the same process of disintegration. This means that once party organizations have come into existence, the existence of a realizable program is no longer necessary. A party can not only continue to live, but may be able to displace the other party in the government, merely because its organization under a powerful leader is more effective than is that of the other party. The party lives by the strength of its organization, and therefore the organization is the main thing, the program a side issue.[12]

The problem of party organization has in recent years come more and more into the foreground of attention, not only because of the radical difference between single parties in totalitarian regimes and the competitive parties in constitutional systems, but also because of the so-called "iron law of oligarchy" which Robert Michels formulated. It is no "iron law," but it strikingly highlights the role of leadership in political parties.[13]

Parties secure power for their leaders • We have now found that parties live independently of their programs, although programs are vital at their inception. We also have seen that parties pursue material as well as ideological objectives. A third general rule or law is that parties strive to secure power for their leader or leaders, rather than for themselves. For only through such leaders can the body of the party membership hope to secure the material and ideological gains which they seek. The leaders may, of course, cheat them. This inevitable preponderance of the leader is the result of the same forces which produce monocratic leadership in government; for the party is almost constantly in the position of a nation at war. The unceasing struggle either to maintain or to gain ascendancy in the government provides that pressure from which we saw monocratic, or at least strictly hierarchical, leadership to result. It has been argued that this dominance of the leaders is something peculiarly English. But this is not true; wherever a party is seeking actual control of the government, such hierarchical structure is bound to develop and to maintain itself. Starting from a large body of careful observations, Robert Michels showed that in keeping with the general rule just stated, parties advocating democracy and equality are just as prone to be authoritarian and boss-controlled as other parties.[14] Michels' particular interest centered upon the German Socialist party, which showed this hierarchical, bureaucratic trend in a very marked degree. It was with acute insight that the leader of German Social Democracy was often jokingly referred to in international Socialist congresses as "Kaiser Bebel." There is nothing particularly shameful about the existence of such leadership, as the innocent reader of Michels' study might be led to infer. Nor yet can this trend be explained by the bureaucratic tradition of Germany. The Socialists were violently opposed to this tradition. It was the difficulty of their position and the resulting intensity of party warfare which necessitated such strictly hierarchical organization. That many of the contemporary lamentations about the decline of Parliament lose much of their force when considered in the light of such statements (and they could be many times multiplied) was shown more specifically above. What matters here is that monocratic, or at least oligarchic, leadership is inherent in party organization, because parties are fighting groups.

Party organization and finance • All that has so far been said suggests that stable organization is a central feature of political parties. Such organization has, generally speaking, undergone an evolution from more autocratic to more cooperative and democratic forms. Even so, it has become increasingly bureaucratic and elaborate. There is a considerable range and variety, as parties adapt themselves to different constitutions and political regimes. In federal systems, more especially, the parties will exhibit varying degrees of decentralization and localism, depending upon the balance between central and local power in each particular federal regime.[15] As a regime becomes more democratic, party organization tends to do the same. Intraparty institutions making for cooperation and participation of the membership will be devised, such as primaries, large-scale conferences of elected delegates, and even referendums. Two quite distinct processes, namely, that of organizing consent and that of organizing action, interact. The resulting democratic and hierarchical propensities constitute the core conflict — the dialectic — of party organization.

Internal party democracy has been a subject of much reforming activity as the process of democratization has progressed. Especially in the United States, such institutions as the primaries and party conventions have been promoted and developed in the name of party democracy. The plans and projects for extending the process are quite numerous. The existing institutional structures possess considerable range. The party conventions have been actively concerned with nominating candidates and detailed research has in recent years developed massive evidence for an understanding of their workings.[16] Not only top leadership recruitment, but program and policy determination have through such instrumentalities come more and more under enough control to render the party leadership responsible to their members. While these processes started earlier in the United States and have been carried farther, the national conventions with all their drama and gaudy tam-tam are not in point of sober fact so unique as it is some time claimed. Particularly the parties of the Left in Europe, the British Labor Party, the German Social Democratic Party in Germany and other Socialist parties in the smaller countries of Europe select their leadership and determine questions of program and policy in fairly open contests. The struggle over the nationalization of industry in Britain's Labor ranks, the corresponding struggle over the program of the German Social Democrats are only particularly striking instances of this democratic process. By no means has it remained restricted, however, to the parties of the Left. At present, the Conservative Party in Britain, while not quite as open as Labour, has nonetheless seen open leadership contests in party meetings, and the struggle between Adenauer and Erhard for the leadership of the German Christian Democrats mobilized all the resources of consensual politics. In the Federal Republic, the Basic Law actually requires legal fixation of such internal party democracy; characteristically, the needed legislation is still "in the making."[17] In the meantime, actual practice has shaped a variety of devices. These European parties have actually gone beyond American precedents in many ways. National party conventions are not only held in national election years, but have become annual events, attended by thousands of delegates.

We cannot here go into the many fascinating and very hotly debated issues, such as the direct primary, which have divided students and practitioners of party politics in the leading democracies. Suffice it to point out that apart from conventions the decentralisation of party activity, the vigorous participation of local units in both programmatic and personnel issues all testify to the vitality of this area of politics.[18] In many ways, its acid test is the way in which parties are financed. For the organizational and control problems of parties are highlighted in the controversies over party finance. As soon as parties organize, the financing of personnel and operations becomes a pressing task.[19] Until fairly recently, such financing came from two primary sources: membership dues and voluntary contributions. As expenditures mounted, contributions were apt to cause a serious amount of dependence upon the preferences of such givers, if not outright corruption. A rising clamor for controlling this sort of distortion of the electoral will has taken two forms, one negative, the other positive. Negatively, laws have been instituted, such as the pioneering British Corrupt and Illegal Practices Prevention Act of 1883,[20] to control the expenditures of the candidates for public office, or at least to secure full publicity for them, as in many American states.[21] Positively, the financing of parties out of the public treasury has been spreading, for example, in the United States and the Federal Republic. Such financing is subject to serious objections, especially as concerns the divisions between rival parties. A number of schemes have been proposed for dealing with these difficulties. The most ingenious is one which would give the taxpayer a direct control over which party should be benefited by his contribution. There can be little doubt that in a modern industrial society, where governmental policy affects practically all economic activity, the financing of parties needs to be publicly controlled. Since it is generally recognized that parties have become public institutions with important public functions, among which the political education of the public is of vital concern to the functioning of the constitutional order, there is no particular reason why such organizations should not be publicly supported.[22]

Most recently, the American Congress has adopted a taxlike contribution to presidential elections.[23] At the same time, the German constitutional court has held that the general financing of parties is incompatible with what the majority of its judges believe to be the spirit of the Basic Law (it contains no explicit provisions against it), pointing out however that a financing by the

442 · The Functioning Processes of Constitutional Government

government of general elections would be compatible, provided it is given to all parties for their actual expenses.[24]

Financing aside, a number of newer constitutions stipulate, and legal provisions elsewhere oblige, parties to be "democratically organized." There has as yet not crystallized any general opinion as to what such inner party democracy requires, but it is fairly generally believed that it forbids the kind of autocratic direction which Lenin first boldly outlined in his famous pamphlet *What is to be Done?* and which has served to shape the inner structure of the Soviet Communist and other totalitarian parties. Broadly speaking, such democratic organization would seem to presuppose the opportunity for intraparty opposition to be heard, and hence for a party's acceptance of those basic civil liberties of which freedom of speech may serve as the paradigmatic illustration.

A general theory of party? · We are now, I believe, able to pull together the several rules or hypotheses into a tentative general theory of a party. This is of course also a statement of its general nature, i.e., a characterization or "definition." A political party as a group of human beings is stably organized. It has the objective of securing or maintaining for its leaders the (control of the) government or the rule over a political community; linked with this is another objective, namely that of giving to the members of such a party ideological and material satisfactions, benefits, and advantages. Within the body politic it has four major functions: (1) selecting future leaders; (2) maintaining contact between the government (including the opposition) and the people at large; (3) representing the various groupings in the community; and (4) integrating as many of these groups as possible. It has its origin in the need of cooperatively organized political communities to gather parts of the membership into organizations which will "spell out" alternative courses of decision, policy, and action. In order to make such a description general enough to cover other than political communities and their government, e.g., churches, trade unions, universities, and so forth, it would be necessary to substitute "community" for "political community." In the past, such elements have rarely become stably organized.

This theory, while developed from earlier ones and taking recent theorizing into account, differs from them in several respects. For one, we speak of government or rule of an organization, rather than of power within it. The reason is that "power" is too broad a term; it would make a newspaper a party, since it surely secures and maintains power for its publisher and top editorial personnel.

Parties, because they seek to control the government, are structured in accordance with the governmental structure. More particularly will they be decentralized or federally structured if the government is; and hierarchically, and indeed autocratically, run, if that is the pattern of the government. This is the fatal flaw in proposals which claim that what is needed in one kind of government is the reconstitution and reconstruction of party government along lines prevalent in another. Such a view alleges that those who would seek to reform the governmental structure are attempting the impossible.[25] That may be true enough; but the alternative remedy is equally unattainable, namely, to structure the party differently from the government. Such proposals overlook a crucial fact, namely, that a party system, precisely because it is directed toward the control of the government, will closely resemble the government's pattern. While I am prepared to agree that the parties are hardly "associations" in the usual sense, nevertheless the members of the party still demand both ideological satisfactions and material benefits and advantages. These advantages, in the United States, are as scattered as the government authorities which dispense them.

Max Weber used to emphasize the fact that parties rested upon "formally free recruiting," that is, that they allowed anyone to join up. Weber introduced this criterion to differentiate parties from aristocratic factions and the like. But since many parties do not permit "free recruiting"; since political science ought not to deviate markedly from common usage, and we are accustomed to applying the term to the Communist party and others, free admission is not a criterion of all, but only of parties under constitutional democracy. The distinction, however, is quite important. Parties either will allow free recruiting, and then may be called constitutional parties, or they will not, and then they are autocratic. Constitutional parties are part of the functioning process of constitutionalism as a system of effective restraints. In England, the two-party system has been particularly important in this way. But what if there should be only one party, as in many American states? The expression "one party" here is very deceptive. Actually, there are in effect two parties in such states. In Wisconsin, for example, there were the progressive and conservative Republicans. As long as there is a constitution, and hence free recruiting of membership, this could not be otherwise.

Autocratic parties, on the other hand, constitute the organized following of a group which has gained complete control of a government but which feels the need for large-scale popular support. If differences of opinion and clashes of loyalty occur in such a following, they cannot under such a government lead to the formation of new parties, and they therefore result in factional strife. Such factionalism is, of course, violently denounced by the preponderant group, and may be forcefully suppressed.

The problem is particularly characteristic of single-party regimes, and it has become more insistent in recent years.[26] Where the integration of the electorate becomes of primary concern, movements have arisen, often called parties, which propose to "reassemble" the people, or whatever the rhetoric might be. In many newly established states, the existence of a homogeneous nation is a hope rather than an established fact. After liberation, the organizing of the national community is the primary task. In the mind of leaders of such movements, the two-party or multiparty system is not the only kind of democracy. Where classes are weak or nonexistent, as in many new states, the building of consensus may be possible by movement of an inclusive sort, and as long as there is free discussion and the citizen has a chance freely to share in the choosing of his rulers, the regime is not necessarily autocratic.[27]

Parties and factions · Madison, in the *Federalist* (No. 10) wrote many years ago that he understood by faction "a number of citizens, whether amounting to a majority or a minority of the whole, who are united and actuated by some common impulse of passion, or of interest, adverse to the rights of other citizens, or to the permanent and aggregate interests of the community."[28] It is obvious in light of the foregoing that such a definition fits political parties, and make a distinction between party and faction impossible. It is very common among political writers, after defining a political party, to remark that their definition historically fits many contending groups, such as the patricians and plebeians of Ancient Rome, the Guelfs and Ghibellines of the Middle Ages, and so forth, but to add that such groups had perhaps better be called factions.[29] Such vagueness is quite undesirable. If a definition does not distinguish a party from a faction, we must either hold the two to be identical in fact, or alter the definition so as to distinguish them.

Our definition of a party contains elements which suggest a clear-cut distinction between party and faction. In the first place, the requirement of stable organization is a distinguishing feature of a party. In the second place, the ideological satisfactions of which our definition speaks are, as we know from previous discussion, related to principles or ideals believed in and pursued as desirable objectives for the political community as a whole. It may often be difficult in actuality to determine whether a stably organized group pursues such objectives if there is no recognition of free speech by the group in power. But eventually, after a certain lapse of time, it will almost always be possible to answer this question one way or the other. Thus, both of the historical examples cited above must be admitted to have pursued such objectives. What gives them the character of factions is rather the absence of stable organization; for a group with scattered leadership, such as the Ghibellines, cannot be said to possess a stable organization.

Some recent theories of political parties • Parties have continued to be a focal point of theoretical analysis in recent years. Some writers, notably Gerhard Leibholz, have argued that the existence and operation of parties at the center of the political system is the distinguishing feature of contemporary politics, and that we should therefore speak of a "Parties' State" or *Parteienstaat* in contradistinction to earlier forms of political order. While the theory here presented enables one to make full allowance for the role of political parties, it does not favor making it the primary criterion of present-day constitutional government; for such a terminology overstresses their position as contrasted with other elements in contemporary pluralistic systems.[30]

Another widely discussed theory addresses itself to the problem of both origin and structure. It holds that there were essentially two different processes by which parties came into being. In one, parties originated from the coalescing of parliamentary groups and electoral committees. In the other, parties were started by separate and distinct groups such as trade unions, churches, and ideological movements. The former, he holds, exhibit a pronounced parliamentary leadership and a decentralized pattern of organization. The latter subject the parliamentarians to more or less rigid control of the party regulars and their bureaucracy; they also subject the local groupings to centralized direction and control. He believes that these divergent origins continue to mold and help to explain much in the behavior of parties.[31] This typology is clearly derived from French politics; it has little application to the British and American development of parties, or to the present behavior of parties in these countries, or indeed in Germany and elsewhere. Such divergencies may play a certain role, but it does not seem that they are important as compared with the basic characteristics of parties as organizations of voters under specific electoral systems as shown above. The "theory" has not even remained uncriticized in the country of its origin.[32]

Another significant contribution was made by Sigmund Neumann, when he undertook to analyze parties on a broad comparative basis.[33] Focusing his attention upon the functional aspect of party theory, he proposed to make a dichotomic distinction between two types of parties with sharply contrasting major functions: parties of representation and parties of integration. That these were certainly important functions of political parties had been stated by others as well as myself. Neumann, however, in going beyond this recognition of both these functions, claimed that parties have moved from being parties of representation to being parties of integration. "Instead of a party of individual representation, the contemporary society has increasingly produced a party of social integration."[34] There can be no question that a shift has occurred in this direction, that parties are more concerned with integration than with the representation of individuals; but not only have they continued to be concerned with both, but in light of a broader conception of representation such as was presented above, this integrative function is intended to provide representation of the nation at large, and as such is, in fact, older than individual representation. In other words, the shift, as exhibited by the history of various party systems, is on the one hand a shift from total to partial to individual representation and back again, and on the other it is a shift from partial to total integration. This latter shift is manifested in the old democracies by the close resemblance of the parties and the consequent tendency to win or lose on the basis of very narrow majorities — when a party deviates from this practice, as did the Republicans in 1964, it invites disaster. The trend is also manifest in those regimes which are based on an ideologically motivated mass movement, whether totalitarian or not. These mass parties have, as noted above, become increasingly important. In short, the two functions of representation and integration, while distinguishable, are not separable.[35] For only because the party represents the voters, whether individually or in groups, and at the same time integrates them, can it operate as it does. But whether a party integrates only those voters who share a certain ideology, or whether it integrates a party of the people large enough to approximate a majority, or whether it finally seeks to integrate the entire people and achieve a predominant status and corresponding permanence, that is really the significant question in this respect of the representative and integrative function. It allows us to speak of phases in the development of parties, but not necessarily in a one-directional sense, if we remember that party systems have in the past at times originated in one party which then subdivided and split. This may well happen in connection with a differentiating social structure attendant upon a process of industrialization.

Parties in relation to social structure · Racial and religious as well as social-class groupings of one sort or another suggest that it is not possible to analyze party systems with reference to psychological dispositions and attitudes alone.[36] Party cleavages built exclusively upon such dispositions are the exception rather than the rule. They presuppose a very homogeneous social substratum so that the electorate is on the whole "fundamentally at one," as Balfour once put it, and therefore "can safely afford to bicker." It follows that an understanding of party systems really presupposes a thorough knowledge of the various layers of the social substratum, the class structure of society, if you please. The student of politics must go to school here with the sociologist and the social anthropologist, and perhaps the geographer. In his justly celebrated *Political Panorama of the West of France,* André Siegfried, originally a geographer, studied the problem in a limited region, district by district, seeking to discover interrelations between social and political party change.[37] But a clear correlation does not exist. The area which Professor Siegfried investigated was relatively static and conservative, yet Siegfried could not discover any definite correlation between changes in social structure and party development. Under conditions of highly dynamic flux, such as those of many postwar states, the lack of correlation is even more marked.

Integration under such conditions becomes an urgent political task; it always is of some importance, as pointed out above. Interest groups integrate, too, as do all groups, but they do so within the context of groupings of related interests sharing some common concerns. Thus there are interests of different industries in a national manufacturers association, of different trade unions in a federation of such unions, of different churches in a federation of them. Even in a multiparty system, parties may effectively integrate sections of the social structure for political action and enable them to participate in the process of decision making. The great problem here is how to secure effective over-all integration of the political community. It may be secured by a traditional (monarchical) or by a popularly elected chief executive, or stabilized coalitions of parties may achieve this when the social structure is relatively stable.

In any case, political parties will, we have seen, appeal to men in terms of their ideal and material interests. Naturally, therefore, they will respond to the groupings among them. Churches, classes, and cultural (racial) and occupational groups are indubitably the most important such divisions amongst the electorate. Fortunately for the analyst, the nations with which we are here concerned show many similarities — enough, in fact, to enable us to treat them as if they had the same social structure. They all are industrialized. Hence they all have the division between capitalist, management, and labor. They have a technical intelligentsia, a middle class of engineers, lawyers, doctors, teachers, scientists, and officials. They have a farmer class which is divided into big farmer-landowners, and peasants and farm workers. Their traditional religion is Christianity, as divided into Catholics, Protestants, and various shades of agnostics. Besides these, they posses a certain number of Jews. The only grouping with regard to which they differ markedly from each other is national-cultural (racial) divisions, and these are static and hence more or less continuous in their impact.

The overall-pattern of European parties · Recent historical researches have provided much material and some brilliant analyses.[39] Conservatism shows very diverse forms in different countries and at different times, for it is by definition concerned with maintaining the existing order. It is primarily compounded of the groups and interests who happen to be "in possession," the "haves," the *beati pessodentes*. Conservatives are content with things as they are, and inclined to believe that change will come gradually and the less done about it the better. A conservative in the United States is a constitutionalist; a conservative in prewar Britain was an imperialist and a believer in parliamentary government under the Crown; a conservative in pre-1914 Germany was a monarchist. Sometimes, then, there will be no conservative party; only a very few people want to keep things as they are. But in most countries and at most times there are enough such people to constitute a sizable group in the community. Hence the programmatic viewpoint, the ideal objectives of conservatives are variable in the extreme. By reversing the positions taken by the leading advocates of change, whether they be called Liberals, New Dealers, or Socialists, it is always possible to derive the position and the interests back of the respective conservative parties or groups.

The first comprehensive challenge to things as they were, by an orderly constitutional party, comes in the form of the Liberal party in England. This challenge presents phases which constitute the evolution of Liberal parties. In its first phase, the Liberal party forms an aggressive opposition to the traditional monarchical government; in England this occurred from 1680 down into the nineteenth century, and on the Continent since the French revolution, or more explicitly, since the Napoleonic Wars. In its second phase, the Liberal party attempts to cope with the social problems raised by industrialization, but, inasmuch as the more radical Socialist elements are becoming the effective opposition, the Liberal party begins to adopt a defensive attitude, and insofar as it does, it becomes conservative. In its third phase, the Liberal party gets embroiled in the conflicts engendered by the rising nationalism everywhere without being able to offer a clear-cut answer in terms of its own tenets, and therefore it breaks up into nationalist and internationalist factions. The acute crisis of the second phase is reached when socialism triumphs or at least supersedes liberalism as the main opposition, while the acute crisis of the third phase culminates in the Fascist dictatorship exterminating the Liberal along with all other parties.

If the story of Liberal parties begins with England and ends with Germany, the situation is reversed when we come to socialism. The reasons for this situation are implicit in the history of Liberal parties.[40] It seems at first sight as if the strength of the Liberal party in each country between 1848 and 1914 stood in inverse proportion to the growth of an organized Socialist party. Where the Liberal party did not fulfill the function of an effective opposition, the Socialists pushed forward to take their place. But of course the Liberals also were not an effective opposition where they more or less dominated the government, as in Italy. This destroys the validity of the impression first gained; if the Liberal party is very strong, the Socialists also grow rapidly. This seems to suggest that the growth of the Socialist parties is dependent upon whether they represent the most clear-cut alternative to the party in power.[41] Whether this party is Conservative or Liberal does not seem to matter. This fact is explainable in terms of our second hypothesis, according to which a party requires for its growth a valid idealogy as well as material objectives. What were these ideals of the Socialist parties? They addressed themselves to the solution of the social problems raised by industrialism, proclaiming them more important than any other matter within the purview of politics. Religion, foreign policy, constitutional government, all these can wait until the pressing needs of industrial society have been successfully met.[42] The great dogmatic thinkers of this new creed, like Karl Marx, theoretically justified this subordination of all other issues to the social problem by insisting that the problems of religion, foreign policy, or government were all rooted in the social problem, were in reality an outgrowth of the conflict of social classes. The state was proclaimed to be an instrument for the exploitation of one class by another. Such a position would naturally find its most ardent supporters among the groups who suffered most under the industrial system, the factory workers.

The First World War acted as the instructor of Communism as we speak of it today; not a theory, but a stern reality of a new managerial bureaucracy where the managers of great industrial and agricultural production units direct masses of workers in accordance with what the bureaucrats at the top consider best. The new "International" became permanently located in Moscow, the capital of one of the world's great empires. The Third International carried on a militant policy of stirring up revolutionary unrest wherever it suited Stalin's diplomacy. In this work it was backed by the vast physical power of the Soviet Union, although the Soviet government recurrently washed its hands of the business and finally dissolved the International when, as one of the "democracies" fighting for the Four Freedoms and the Atlantic Charter (signed by the Soviet Union in 1944), it no longer fitted the Soviet Union's role. Since the revival of the world-revolutionary policy of the Soviet Union, the International has reappeared in a new guise, the *Cominform,* or Communist Information Bureau. This situation contrasts profoundly with the internationalism of Socialist parties before the First World War, which consisted largely of periodic conventions meeting in different cities of Europe (Brussells, Amsterdam, Copenhagen, Stuttgart) and discussing resolutions which might express the sentiment of Socialists throughout the world. After 1919, most of their practical work was taken over by the International Labor Office in Geneva.[43]

Electoral support for Communist parties varies considerably from country to country. While very weak in the United States, Britain, and the Dominions, they commanded almost a third of the votes in France and Italy after the Second World War and continue to receive about a quarter of the votes. In Germany and Austria, Communist strength has waned, after reaching almost 20 per cent before 1933, and after 1945. In the elections of August 1949, the Communists only received about 8 per cent of the votes in Western Germany, and prevailing estimates suggest that their true strength in Eastern Germany is not much greater. In Austria, in October 1949, the Communists polled 41 per cent of the votes.

The formation of parties upon the foundation of the Catholic faith is conceivable in two ways, ideally speaking. Since the Catholic faith espouses an active ethic, it maintains a very definite belief about the end of all government as an aid toward man's ultimate end: the salvation of his soul. But there is also the more practical proposition of fighting for greater freedom and independence of the church whenever the government attempts to interfere. In either case, the Catholic parties appear as the mainstay of a comprehensive program of opposition to Marxist materialism, at least to their own followers. From this point of view it is no longer a question of independence of the church from the government, but of protection for the government by the church. To these ideological objectives are joined, as in all parties, the concrete advantages to be derived from securing adequate or favored treatment for faithful members of the church. But the historical origins of Catholic parties in Europe are sometimes more clearly related to one or another of these objectives.[44]

Throughout Europe, the Catholic, or Christian, opposition to socialism could not be effective wherever the underlying religious faith had been shattered, even though the opposition itself was firmly rooted in property and other interests. If the tradition of self-reliance, of self-government, of self-restraint is weak in these masses, and if they therefore demand, or rather yearn for, authoritative leadership, the "nation" or the *Volk* offers itself as another goddess. Around this golden calf the Fascist masses of Europe danced for twenty years.[45] Bonapartisan, Fascism, National Socialism, were three forms of the same national religion, each born of the terror of the middle classes at seeing their security threatened by the masses.[46] In the ancient world the challenge of Christianity was directed against the tribal multiplicity of gods, each protecting his or her particular city. In contemporary civilization, the challenge of Fascism is directed against the catholicity of a Christian faith transcending all national loyalties. Communism, cherishing the ideal of a mankind composed of workers and united by an international bureaucracy of supermen, attempts to substitute a millennial hope of all-round material prosperity for the transcendental faith in eternal salvation of the soul which the Christian churches espouse. The terrified small property owners, farmers, peasants, shopkeepers, craftsmen, white-collar employees, professional men, and their like, unwilling to become mere "workers" under an international bureacracy, yet unable to maintain a faith in Christian views, return to the tribal fetishes which once dominated the minds of men. The parties dedicated to these views proved themselves as intransigent as the Communists.

Since 1945 and the defeat of Fascism, the political parties of pre-Fascist days have experienced a rebirth. While Britain voted the Labour party into full power for the first time in history, Continental European party development has seen several new factors; the situation is highly unstable, but must not be interpreted in terms of analogies to the twenties when the meaning of Fascist dictatorship and its deleterious effects were not known and appreciated by the middle classes. These elements of the population, never too enthusiastic about democracy, even in France, are now definitely antidictatorial. There is, as a matter of fact, a general negativism about European political attitudes which resembles the outlook of other restoration periods as discussed before. Among the new aspects of the party line-up, the more important are the definite crystallization of the Christian Democrats as a major party of the middle class in France, Italy, and Germany, with the corresponding disappearance of nineteenth-century liberalism, and the effective collaboration of these Christian Democrats with the moderate Social Democrats and Socialists. A majority of both Christian Democrats and Social Democrats favor planning and socialization; they are definitely middle of the road. In France they have lost much of their status as a middle ground between right and left to the Gaullist party, which also claims that position. The Gaullist party, however, is weakened by its dependence for a program on a leader who deprecates all parties, even his own. The new presidential system in France may lead to an eventual coalescence of right and left into two or three distinct, cohesive groups, but it is difficult to predict the extensive realignment that will undoubtedly take place after De Gaulle.[47] As contrasted with the tenuous situation in France, the Christian and the Social Democrats between them have a solid majority in both Italy and Germany. It is one of the most striking developments of the post-1945 period that, after an initial burst of pro-Communist sentiment, the Communist parties have been losing all three countries. This decline in Communist support is especially striking in Germany, where it has fallen to below 10 per cent of the total vote, but it is also quite marked in Italy and in France, where the voting strength of the Communist party is down to around 25 per cent of the total vote. The development has been accelerated and reinforced by economic assistance and military and political support from the United States, but that is not the only factor; the sense of the apprehension of (and in Germany the experience with) Soviet totalitarianism is of at least equal importance.[48]

The Socialists, although the straight-line descendants of the prewar parties, have become more staid and ready to work with the established order. Both in leadership and in program they follow the old line of a moderate "Marxism," and their voting support is largely that of organized labor, with some intellectuals in the leadership from the middle class. These parties, in short, along with their electorates, have come to accept a defined role.

Conclusion · The general problems of the political parties, then, are threefold: the party's relation to the pattern of the government whose control the party seeks to secure; the relation between leader and followers; and the relation of the party to the social structure of the society in which it seeks to appeal for support. Through their leadership the parties establish and maintain the contact between the government and the people. The general problems of a theory of political parties can be better understood and adequate answers provided if the genetic (origins), morphological (pattern and structure), teleological (objectives, purposes) and the operational (functions) questions are distinguished. Much futile argument can be avoided if general theory is explicitly fashioned in such a way as to cover these four aspects. Political parties originated and developed in response to democratization; they continue to do so. Both representation and integration are functions of parties. They may be structured strictly hierarchically or on a participatory basis; it depends upon how difficult their position is. Political parties have the objectives of securing and maintaining control of the government or the rule over a political community, and thereby serve the further function of selecting the top leaders in democratic societies.

Party development is more highly dynamic than any other sphere of political life; there is no final rest, no ultimate pattern; for party development responds to the evolving social structure, and to the community's evolving values, interests, and beliefs. No harmonious "swing of the pendulum" characterizes it, as has at times been alleged, even when it is described as a "law of politics." Rather, there is constant change in one direction or another, with never a return to the starting point. The panorama of the history of modern parties is a reflection of the secular evolution of modern society in the mirror provided by the elected assemblies of constitutional democracies.

This similarity of social structure has resulted in comparable party systems, at least in most European countries. This comparability is obscured by different party labels. The panorama of party development all over Europe, the comparative analysis of Liberal, Socialist, Catholic, and finally Communist and Fascist parties, amply documents the generalizations that have already been set forth. A full-length portrait would of course only be possible within the scope of a general history of Europe and its social movements during the last hundred and fifty years. But for purposes of comparative political science, a rapid thumbnail sketch of the major features of European party systems may still be useful.

Interest Groups and Economic Councils

Introduction: the deterioration of political representation in terms of the general interest • General interest and special interests • American lobbies • Chambers of commerce and similar semiofficial bodies in France, Germany, and other countries • Central banks • Trade unions • The Russian revolution and the trade unions, particularly in Germany • The German National Economic Council • The Fascist "corporative state" • Interest groups in the United States today • Conclusion

Introduction: the deterioration of political representation in terms of the general interest • Interest and pressure groups are the living "public" behind the parties. Such groups were viewed with moral indignation and alarm by the last generation. They were held up to scorn both by muckrakers and by sane students of politics. They were believed to be the sinister force gnawing at the foundations of modern democracy, of representative government; the word "lobby" supposedly comprehended a whole congeries of abuse, corruption, fraud, and the like. There was and is a kernel of truth in these assertions. The activity of these "interests" has manifestly weakened the belief in *popular* government by undermining the faith in a united *people*. Wilson's attack upon Congressional government and its committee system (discussed above) was built around allegations concerning the power which interest groups had arrogated unto themselves. "It is in committee rooms that legislation not desired by the interests dies. It is in committee rooms that legislation desired by the interests is framed and brought forth."[1] Even earlier, a searching appendix to Bryce's *American Commonwealth* was devoted to the "lobbies." While in the United States and in the British Dominions, as well as in England, the "interests" worked and pressed upon each party, in countries with a multiple-party system the interests often associated themselves to a greater or lesser degree with particular parties. The rise of socialism and of Socialist parties identified with the industrial workers' interest provided an ideological framework for special parties of workers. As the workers united, other special interests, too, sought effective political organization. As parties thus became identified with special interests, or members of representative assemblies yielded to special interests and thus appeared as their tools, the representative quality of these assemblies changed.

This development has a long history. For more than a century Marxists of various shades have been indoctrinating the masses throughout Europe with the theory of "the economic determination" of human activity, and reactionaries have been preaching with wit and passion that democracies are honeycombed with the corruption of big business. The United States, too, reverberated from time to time with the revelations of the dark machinations of interest groups, and the high protective tariffs stand as a lasting memorial to the logrolling proclivities of Congress, a reminder to anyone who has eyes to see or ears to hear. It is natural that plans should have made their appearance for legalizing these pressures and influences, for coordinating them with and fitting them into the regular framework of government. In France, economic advisory councils representing the "interests" had come down from the days of the "estate" and the mercantilist efforts of Henry IV. In Germany, Bismarck had tried to bring together the representatives of management and labor through an economic council, but had failed, since parliamentarians feared that he wished to balance the popular forces as represented in the *Reichstag*.[2] After the First World War, such councils appeared everywhere as part of the new constitutions. Fascism and National Socialism seized upon these trends and developed comprehensive "corporative" setups. These corporative structures were supposed to replace the traditional representative scheme, whereas the economic councils are intended to function as a complement rather than a substitute. The trend has reappeared now: the 1958 French constitution in its Article 69 provides for the establishment of a national economic and social council; in Italy, corresponding efforts of the Christian Democrats after the war to have interests represented in the senate were defeated. Apart from the Bavarian senate, which is partially based upon such interest representation, the idea seems buried in Germany. It also appeared in the draft constitution for a European political community, which provided for an economic and social council. Nor is interest representation lacking in the European communities. In the Common Market organization, an Economic and Social Committee has been playing a rather considerable role; the absence of an effective representative body has of course aided this development.[3]

The problems such occupational representation raises are certainly difficult. Are these movements expressing a rapid stratification of our modern industrial society? Are these organs capable of effective operation, of fulfilling the deliberative function which once fell to elected assemblies?

General interest and special interests · We must now go back to some of the general points made in the course of our analysis of representation. In discussing representation, it was shown that Burke formulated the classical norm of a representative's task: to consider issues and to decide them in terms of the general interest. A reminder of how far from a description of reality such a view was at the time of Burke may be had in an autobiographical remark of his contemporary, "One-Speech" Hamilton. Before retiring from parliamentary life he wrote his patron, who had requested his continuance, that he might consider the request were he permitted to vote according to his own convictions. The permission was not granted.[4] The difficulty with Burke's view is that most people are quite positive that they are considering the general or public interest, even when they are concerned with very special interests; for it is usually possible to rationalize the special interest as an essential part of the general interest. Thus the welfare of, let us say, the shipping industry is of paramount importance to the English people, and therefore its continued existence a matter of public interest. The same can and will be said of the workers, the farmers, the doctors, either in whole or in part, and always with some show of truth. It was given radical expression in the statement of one of Eisenhower's department chiefs: "What is in the interest of General Motors, is in the public interest," or words to that effect. It seems, therefore, that the "general interest" is similar to Rousseau's "general will": obscure and undefinable. And yet some interests are more general than others. The interest of farmer Jones is more remote from the public interest than the interest of the farmers of Windham County or the American dairy farmers. Again, the interest of the groups of farmers is less general than the interest of all American farmers. A true and ideal "American" representation would therefore consider the interests to be most important which all Americans have in common and which are therefore most "general." It is obvious that no man is likely to be able to "represent" the American people in such abstract, ideal terms. The nearest approximation is oftentimes the man who owes his seat in parliament or his place in Congress to a particular, powerful patron. One of the shrewdest observers of Congress once told the writer that a certain Senator, now dead, although well-known for his subserviency to one big corporation, was nevertheless one of the most useful members of Congress, because once the interests of that corporation were taken care of, he was free to consider the general public interest. This is a strange approximation to an ideal, and yet Mr. Burke made much the same point when he defended the "rotten boroughs" in England: "You have an equal representation, because you have been equally interested in the prosperity of the whole, who are involved in the general interest and the general sympathy; and perhaps these places furnishing a superfluity of public agents and administrators . . . will stand clearer of local interests, passions, prejudices, and cabals than the others, and therefore preserve the balance of the parts, and with a more general view and a more steady hand than the rest. . . ." This is a far cry from the norm of an "ideal" representative, and yet it shows the extent to which representativeness is a matter of more or less. This is equally true of the representativeness of particular parts of the government. The American President would seem to me "more representative" than any individual member of the House or the Senate, but the Senate and the House, when acting with large bipartisan majorities, would be "more representative" than the President (who is necessarily of one party). In relation to certain functions, the Supreme Court, as we have seen, is "more representative" than either Congress or the President because it is "nonpartisan."

The narrower the special interest is, the lower is the representative quality of those whose actions are directed toward its realization. And an interest is narrow or broad depending upon the number of human beings whose interest is identified with it.[5] The most general interest is the interest of widest application, conceivably comprising all humanity. The great appeal of the Marxist view lies partly in its claim to universality, at least as far as all workers of the world are concerned. The same is true of peace and pacific endeavors. At the same time, interests of very general application are frequently lacking in intensity of appeal to the interested party.* They are for that reason of rather remote concern to the man seeking re-election to Congress. He must, necessarily, be more concerned with the fortune of the local soap factory, the needs of the farmers in his district, or whatever may be indicated by the particular social pattern of the community in which he is being elected. Such a state of affairs is less perturbing from the viewpoint of modern political science than from that of the standpat democratic doctrinaire. The more general interest is recognized as a compound of many less general interests, and by bringing spokesmen for these various interests together, such a compound may emerge if the working conditions are right. Faulty electoral methods, outworn procedures for deliberation and action, and unrestrained license of the press may, however, bring about conditions under which the less general interests become so hardened and so violently pitched against each other that no working compromise can result. Then the complex mechanism of representative government will stall and eventually break down. Such breakdown is not, however, the result of special

---

* The fervor of the advocate of such interests cannot be argued to invalidate this proposition; for such fervor is engendered by other impulses than the "interest" of the advocate himself — except insofar as he may sense the immense potential power to be derived from the effective realization of a universal interest.

interests dividing the community, or of the advocacy of such views by elected representatives; it is rather the result of the particular maladjustments which prevented compromise between these interests.

American lobbies · Whatever the reasons, it is a fact that the pressure of special interest groups manifested itself in an organized form quite early in the United States. The large size of the country, the legislative initiative assumed by Congress, the comprehensive vagueness of party programs, all contributed to a development which brought interested citizens together in support of or in opposition to legislation which was of special interest to them. The number of such organizations and the interests they represent have become so impressive that they are in the process of becoming institutionalized. Broad surveys of the whole range of activities, as well as searching and detailed studies of particular activities, have multiplied, analyzing the rise of this "assistant government,' as it has aptly been called. Since the administrative departments have been taking a greater part in legislation, and since they have been vested with ever-more discretion in administering them, they also have become the target of the pressure of these interest groups. The following are of outstanding importance: the Chamber of Commerce of the United States, the National Association of Manufacturers, the American Farm Bureau Federation, the National Grange, the National Education Association, the AFL-CIO, the American Legion, the American Railway Association, the Committee of Utility Executives, the Federal Council of Churches, the American Medical Association, and a dozen strong trade associations, such as those of the woolgrowers, and coal, oil, lumber, meat packing, and sugar interests. It is a far cry from the activities of these large, publicly conducted organizations to the scheming and usually corrupt methods of the early lobbyist, looking for land grants and similar concessions. Every one of the modern organizations more or less persuasively identifies itself with the public or the national interest. "The American Federation of Labor talks of working for 'labor and the people.' 'Its accomplishments have benefited all the people, for the trade union movement is as deep and wide as human life.' The Chamber of Commerce of the United States takes the position that 'what is good for business is good for the country.' The Farm Bureau Federation states that 'in reviving and invigorating American farm life, we are regenerating and preserving the nation.' Similar statements may be encountered in the literature of others of these associations."[6] These statements are not untrue, but they hardly describe adequately the purpose for which these organizations were created. The nature of interest is such, however, that in the long run the subjective purpose pales into insignificance beside the objective reality in which various less general interests merge into the more general interests of the more comprehensive community. There are today hundreds of such organizations voicing the "will of the people" in one field or another. To the older institutions, more particularly Congress, falls the difficult task of weighing these pressures and effecting the necessary compromise.

In his magistral treatment of American pressure groups, the late V. O. Key has shown how complex the activities of interest groups in America have become, as they seek to manipulate public opinion, legislatures, administrators, courts, and even each other. "Implicit in the importunities of a lobbyist may be the threat that his organization will at the next primary or election throw its strength against the legislator who does not vote right." Such lobbying before legislatures has drawn the greatest amount of attention, but their more quiet work with administrators and courts is often equally, if not more, effective; here again the representatives may be mobilized. Even more effective is often the pressure exerted to have men favorable to the particular interest appointed to the administrative or regulatory post, according to the old adage, "if you can't lick them, join them." As for the courts, here the work of the large organizations of colored people have perhaps scored their most striking successes. Intergroup lobbying is most conspicuous where legislation or administration calls for the balancing of group interests.

Chambers of commerce and similar semiofficial bodies in France, Germany, and other countries · In Europe the development of pressure groups has been influenced more extensively by the government. In England certain reform movements played an altogether decisive part in the parliamentary history of the nineteenth century. Such great names as Bentham, Cobden, and John Stuart Mill are definitely associated with these activities. All these movements played their game *in* Parliament, rather than *upon* it, and associated themselves with parties or founded them, rather than standing aloof, distributing praise and blame as the modern American organizations do. On the Continent, organizations constituting the counterpart of the American private associations have flourished with bureaucratic sanction. Some of these organizations have for a long time been officially recognized. In France and other countries, the chambers of commerce constitute semipublic authorities. The personnel of these chambers acquired semiofficial status and the government delegated important functions to them. The nearest American analogy is the American Farm Bureau Federation, which, through the county agent, shares with the government the task of local agricultural extension work. In Europe, analogous activity was developed through the chambers of agriculture, organized in direct parallel to the chambers of commerce. While these two sets of organizations concerned themselves with the promotion of agriculture and commerce, chambers of handicraft were organized to protect traditional craftsmanship against the inroads of either.

After the First World War, the Social Democrats promoted the corresponding chambers of labor to look out for the interests of the industrial worker.[8] In a sense, the multiplication of these organizations amounted to a *reductio ad absurdum* of the original idea of promoting trade and commerce, and yet in a democratic society, such competition was bound to result. But owing to the link with the government which was in keeping with European bureaucratic traditions, they tended to become popular extensions of the particular national ministry. There are other organizations which have played a conspicuous role in politics, notably the trade unions and central banks. Still others, particularly in the field of reform, have lacked the financial backing for effective organizational activity. There was, however, a tendency for the government to assist financially organizations which made it their business to promote ideas which the government officials approved, and to resist those which they frowned upon. Thus, organizations fostering patriotism and similar purposes were promoted by the government in France. The same tendency was even more markedly observable in Germany. Under the Weimar Republic, by contrast, the government sought to counteract the nationalist tendencies by supporting the League of Nations Association, as well as international student exchanges. The French government likewise helped the International Student Center in Paris. Oftentimes, conflicts in outlook between the ministries and their officials led to their supporting competing organizations here, as in the economic field. This intermingling of governmental and civic activities was inimical to the long-run interests of both. It decreased genuine civic participation in these organizations. It also involved the government in conflicts which it should have been in a position to mediate.

The efforts of American Military Government to have German chambers of commerce and similar bodies dissociated from the government and deprived of the monopolistic position which they occupied have been only partially successful. But the basic trend has been for these organizations to become more and more powerful. The derogatory term *Verbändestaat* has been coined; Professor Eschenburg among others has made himself the voice of protest against the role of these bodies.[9]

Central banks · Differing from each other in structure and function, central banks have nevertheless been of decisive importance in influencing the policy of popular governments. Although a good part of their influence has been clandestine, it has nevertheless been powerful. There is general agreement that in times of financial stringency the paramount need of the government to have adequate credit resources may bring about a questionable degree of political dependency upon those who hold the strings to the credit resources of the country. Since it is the primary function of central banks to maintain the liquid banking reserve of the country, the central bank in turn finds itself obliged to insist upon conservative methods of governmental conduct which may ill accord with the popular majority. Andrew Jackson's famous fight with the Second Bank of the United States provides a striking illustration of the political issues involved. But owing to its abundant tax and credit resources, the American government has not been seriously troubled with the issue since. As in so many cases, the issue was seen most candidly, and fought over most bitterly, in France, where the *Banque de France* had become the stronghold of conservatism. Through Empire, Restoration, Monarchy, another Empire, and Republic, the Bank remained in the hands of the "two hundred families."[10] Under the Napoleonic Law of 1806, which remained essentially unaltered down to 1936, "the powers of the shareholders were vested in the general assembly composed of the 200 French citizens who held the largest number of shares for six months before an election." Since the minimum thus established was eighty-five shares and the shares were quoted in 1935 at 10,000 francs, it took 850,000 francs to qualify. "Small wonder that membership came to be regarded as a sign of financial importance and that a list of members read something like a social register with counts, dukes, and representatives of the *haute finance*." The French party system and the ascendancy of parliament over the cabinet underlaid the political powers of the Bank.

The great parliamentary debate preceding the basic changes in the position of the Bank in 1936 reviewed once more all the argument brought forth from time to time by the long-drawn tug-of-war between the Bank and successive governments throughout more than a century. The Socialists and their friends proceeded under the slogan "Let's make the Bank of France France's Bank" (*Faire de la Banque de France la Banque de la France*). These were sharpened, however, by the economic problems of the depression and the role which government spending should play in dealing with these problems. There had been bitter clashes between the Bank and the government during the inflation ten years earlier, but the Bank's position had on the whole been the popular one, since it tried to resist inflation. Now it was a question of credit expansion which the Bank opposed, and the voters, restless and impatient to see something done, turned toward those who proposed to break the stranglehold of the Bank's anti-inflationary position. Here we face the crux of the whole issue: Governments today are so intimately connected with the whole economy that the control of spending by the government is almost the key to controlling governmental policy in the economic realm. The government's credit, in other words, can no longer be equated with that of a small commercial enterprise and its right to borrow established on the basis of a simple balance sheet. What is this balance sheet, anyway? What, specifically, is investment and what is current expense? Is the government justified in considering as investment all expenditures made for the purpose of conserving natural resources? If not, how much of it? The answer to these questions strikes at the very core of public policy; it is evident that the answer cannot safely remain lodged in a bank whose directors are chosen by a small group selected on the basis of their wealth, such as the general assembly of the Bank of France constituted. For even granting that these groups of people possessed special qualifications which enabled them to form a more "expert" judgment, the fact remains that their activity did not maintain the credit of France. Denying the *government* credit may indeed, by causing a complete stall, bring about the collapse of the credit structure. Like a steam boiler without a safety valve, a democracy without an outlet for popular policies is liable to explode when tension rises. The French system fortunately had such a safety valve. The Bank's position rested upon a statute which could be changed, once the situation got serious enough.

Politically, the basic charge was that the Bank consistently favored governments of the right and repeatedly made it clear that the credit of the government would be better if the government would be a more conservative one. Since credit means confidence, there can be no doubt that the conservative big-business representatives would have more confidence in a government controlled by their own group. But such dependence evidently was intolerable to many. The defenders of the Bank's "independence" contended that great instability would result from the Bank's transformation into a political weapon of the dominant party; by such claims they obscured the undeniable fact that great instability also resulted from the Bank's remaining a political weapon of one class, regardless of the will of the majority. Attempts were made to cope with the problem by distinguishing between control of the Bank by the "state" and control of the Bank by the "party." But of course no one could suggest how under democracy the party and the state could be separated — a striking instance of the tyranny of the word "state," which is meaningless under democratic conditions, as we have seen.

The act as finally passed, while democratizing the Bank and placing it under government control to some extent, did not achieve nationalization. Representation on the Board of Directors (*Conseil de Regence*) was divided between the government, the banking interest, and the users of credit.

Twelve of the twenty-three directors were to be appointed by the government, thus giving the government clear control. The same was true of the executive committee, and to insure that no inside group could entrench itself, elections were staggered and self-succession barred. Broader control was vested in the stockholders, who each received one vote, regardless of holdings, as in the elections to the boards of Federal Reserve Banks. Thus the Bank was allowed to operate for private profit, but its policies were under government control. This meant that the Bank was no longer able to dictate the government's spending policy, but it also meant that all bars to uncontrolled government spending were removed. This cannot be helped. If democracies cannot learn to control spending, they cannot hope to exist for long. The experience in Sweden, Switzerland, and other highly democratic, yet industrialized, countries with relatively sound practices in this field holds out hope that there may yet be majorities for sound fiscal policies. In 1946, as we shall see, the Bank of France was nationalized and, although maintaining some independence, is now part of the planned and directed economy (see next chapter).

In England the same issue of central banking control came to a dramatic head in the summer of 1931. Conservative investors both in Britain and abroad were seriously aroused over the fiscal policy of the second Labour government. They wanted to see drastic cuts made in the various social benefits, particularly in the unemployment benefits. The cabinet of Ramsay MacDonald was deeply split; MacDonald himself and his Chancellor of the Exchequer, Snowden, desired to make the cuts and rehabilitate the government's credit; but the larger part of the Cabinet, including Henderson and other conservative trade-union leaders, were not prepared to make such concessions. The powerful Trades Union Congress was adamantly opposed. MacDonald, caught between these two irreconcilable powers, resigned and formed a new cabinet consisting of a coalition of Conservatives, Liberals, and National Labourites (as he called them). In the ensuing election, the issue of the currency was made a central point, and the small investor was terrified by the assertion that the Labour party was committeed to a policy of currency inflation. Interestingly enough, after winning an overwhelming victory to "save the pound," the cabinet of National Union proceeded to devalue the pound. Hence, in England, the conservative forces allied with the Bank triumphed over the progressive elements. Indeed, the Bank of England and its governor, Sir Montagu Norman, played an important part in driving Labour from power. It is not surprising, therefore, that one of the central planks of the Labour party should have been the nationalization of the Bank of England, which has since been achieved.

In the United States, where the entire Federal Reserve Board is appointed by the President with the advice and consent of the Senate, and where three out of nine directors of the several Reserve Banks are appointed by the Board in turn, the problem is not likely to arise in the form in which it has plagued European politics; control is already securely lodged in the government as supported by the majority of the voters. Characteristically, the chairman of the Federal Reserve Board under the New Deal was one of the outstanding defenders of the government's spending policy.

Trade unions · If central banks have provided the most effectively organized rampart of business and general capital interests, trade unions have been the defenders of workers and general labor interests. And just as central banks have at times tried to thwart the decisions of the majority by refusing to grant credit to the government, so trade unions have made analogous attempts through general strikes. The analogy between the two operations was brought out by the slogan about the "strike of capital"; a general strike of either capital or labor is indicative of a clash between the majority and a minority which is powerful enough to risk a challenge, through a test of strength, to the constitutional authority. As was pointed out earlier, such conflicts cannot and need not be outlawed; they *need not* be outlawed, because they are not sanctioned by the law to start with, and they *cannot* be outlawed, since they are essentially appeals to force "to right a wrong" caused by the breakdown of law and the constitution.

The trade-union movement is more than a hundred years old.[11] In its origins it goes back to the craft guilds of the Middle Ages. The craftsmen, dislodged by the factory system in the industrial revolution, found themselves at the mercy of employers and hence proceeded to organize for collective bargaining. Numerous obstacles were placed in their way. Through use of all the resources of the law, as well as through extralegal and even illegal methods, employers sought to weaken the trade unions in virtually all industrial countries. But the organization of the workers went relentlessly forward, born of inherent necessity. While imaginative thinkers and writers spun out elaborate systems of socialism and constructed utopias of Communist havens — men like Saint Simon, Fourier and Proudhon, Marx, Engels, and Bakunin, Owen, Emerson, and many others — the hard-headed secretaries of trade unions hammered into shape first one union and then another, then federations of unions covering entire industries, countries, continents, reducing working hours, improving working conditions, raising wages, until in retrospect the projected goals of the Communist utopia which Marx and Engels suggested in the Manifesto look like the mild liberalism of a friendly college professor. Today, the International Labor Office stands at the apex of this vast network of workingmen's organizations. It could be pointing the way toward the democratic world order which peoples and governments have not yet managed to achieve, were it not for the dissensions which the Communists have injected into the movement by trying to convert it into an instrument for furthering the political aims of the Soviet Union.

The forward march of the trade-union movement has been beset with internal as well as external difficulties, of course. As we noted in the discussion of party development, unions have been deeply divided in their general outlook. While the majority of trade-union officials have been conservatively progressive, slow to accept Marxism on the Continent, slow to accept the Labour party in England, slow to go into party policies in the United States, there have always been more radical elements. The Communists have, in fact, precipitated a split in the unions in France and Italy. In both countries a very important segment of the trade-union movement is controlled by the Communist party. There have also been powerful Christian trade unions wherever Catholics had organized a party of their own. These unions, while rejecting Marxist and other forms of a secularist and atheist outlook, strove determinedly to accomplish the practical objectives of the trade unionist everywhere.

It is only with the coming of totalitarianism that trade-union power and progress have been halted. To be sure, there are organizations formally called trade union in Russia, as there were in Germany and in Italy in the thirties. But these organizations, far from being trade unions in the old sense of being free associations of workingmen, freely organized and open, are closed regiments whose leadership is controlled by the government. From being instruments for pressing the workingmen's interests against the employer and the government, they have become organizations for regimenting the workers and pressing the interests of the government and the party against the workers.[12]

A peculiar break has occurred in the United States. Here the trade-union movement has until very recently been relatively weak as compared to Europe. Among the many causes two stand out: the individual worker's opportunity for personal betterment and the generally high standard of living for skilled workers. But its very weakness obliged the trade-union movement to remain united; the American Federation of Labor followed persistently for many years the policy of the most skillful pressure groups in giving and withdrawing support from politicians in the light of their "labor record." Under a plurality system of elections, organized labor could thus be the balancer and decide the election in many a closely contested district.

But the system of craft unions upon which the American Federation of Labor was reared tended to be dominated by the most highly skilled workers, the steamfitters, the precision mechanics, and dozens of other highly paid technicians; it tended to neglect the interests of the vast army of the semi-skilled and unskilled. These workers had come to play an increasing role in the mass-production industries. For some years there had been murmurings of revolt against this system, and a demand for organization by industries had been heard to an increasing extent. After all, such organizations had been the basis of trade unionism in Europe for many years; no reason existed why it should be barred in the United States. When the open break came, in 1935, it led to the establishment of the Congress of Industrial Organization, the CIO, under the aggressive leadership of John L. Lewis. The movement scored striking successes in the mass-production field, such as automobile, electrical-equipment manufacture, and transport. Of course, the United Mine Workers were, in a sense, an industrial union right along. This split in labor's ranks, while probably difficult to avoid, had very unfortunate immediate effects upon labor's dealings with the government. Regulatory mechanisms, set up for the benefit of labor, such as the National Labor Relations Board, were torn between the rival claims of the two great organizations. As a result a merger of the two great trade-union federations was effected. The need for effective cooperation among trade unions is so great that differences in point of view can only temporarily interfere with their cooperation.[13]

The Russian revolution and the trade unions, particularly in Germany · It is undeniable that Communism, since the establishment of the Soviet Union, has had a disruptive effect upon the trade-union movement. In imperial Russia the trade unions were outlawed. They afforded no outlet for the activity of even the mildest social reformers.[14] Sporadic and clandestine attempts were made to organize the workers, but usually the initiators ended up in Siberia, if they were not shot. The daily contact of factory workers nevertheless afforded an opportunity for skeleton organization. Councils or soviets composed of these more progressive elements in the factories (and in the army) offered themselves, therefore, as the most readily available means of organized support after the revolution. The Communist party, politically speaking, was an organization bringing these elements together in a pan-Russian and comprehensive group. Therefore, if later all the councils were found in the hands of the Communists, there is nothing startling about that. The soviets are the natural arena of Communist party activity.

As is so often the case, what was an inherent necessity in one political arena is carried by doctrinaires into another where it has no such place. Thus we find that the revolutionaries in Germany and other parts of Central Europe who were partisans of the Russian revolution set up councils of workers and soldiers. But here they ran afoul of the well-established and highly disciplined Socialist trade unions and the bureaucracy of the Social Democratic party securely backed by its following. The workers' and soldiers' council consequently did not have any specific function. The great congress of such councils, which convened at Berlin in December 1918, was readily dominated by men connected with the old trade-union hierarchy, and refused to foster the erection of a soviet or conciliar republic. When, thereupon, the radical followers of Liebknecht, calling themselves Spartacists and Communists, went into the streets and began to barricade themselves, civil war broke loose. The radicals were bloodily suppressed, since the soldiers' council were unable to prevent the support of the moderates by the remnants of the imperial army. Since Social Democracy had been effectively organized for years, there was no real value in the councils. Very soon after their first appearance, Hugo Preuss had formulated the fundamental objections to this sort of hidden dictatorship in a famous article. "In the old bureaucratic state," he wrote, "the citizen had little to say; in the present state he has no say at all; at this moment more than ever before the people as a whole are nothing but the object of a government which is set above them by inscrutable council. The only difference is that it rests its authority not upon God's grace, but upon the equally obscure people's grace. . . . Not classes and groups, not parties and estates in isolated opposition, but only the entire German people represented by a democratically elected National Constitutional Convention can create a truly popular government."[15] Such thoughts made a great appeal to the more moderate elements (which did not cherish the thought of a fate similar to that of the Mensheviks in Russia), backed as they were at this time by a large number of the bourgeoisie who were prepared to give support to whoever seemed ready to prevent real revolutionary violence. For the highly educated German middle classes did not only think of Russian development; they also had before their minds the course of the French revolution, which they had learned to detest from their childhood. This revolution, as well as the Commune of 1871,[16] had shown what absolute power concentrated in the hands of self-appointed councils meant. Theoretically, of course, these councils had been subject to recall at any time, as was in keeping with Rousseau's ideas of direct democracy. But how could such recall be effected when anyone advocating it was immediately carted off to the guillotine as an enemy of the people? The masses of German workers as well as the middle class (insofar as they actively participated in political life at this time) would have none of such concentrated power in anybody's hands. In fact, the general attitude toward workers' councils became so hostile that the efforts of radical elements to work such a structure into the proposed constitution met with defeat. A compromise provision was appended to the document as its last article to bring to an end a new armed uprising which had been raging in Berlin in March 1919.

The German National Economic Council · The National Economic Council[17] with its never completed substructure of regional, district, and factory councils was a confused compromise substitute for the national workers' council which the radicals had demanded. It placed all groups in the economic life of the country on an equal footing, or attempted to do so, thus realizing a highly conservative set of ideas for functional or occupational representation. Catholic parties had long advocated such a return to medieval, static forms of representation. As mentioned before, even Bismarck had evolved such a plan after the adoption of his tariff system in 1879. As a first step, he organized a Prussian Economic Council in 1880 which, however, met only three times. A bill for a similar council for the nation failed of acceptance because the *Reichstag* remained suspicious of the project. But the idea never died. These undemocratic ideas of conservatives and reactionaries were merged with the equally undemocratic ideas of the social revolutionaries. It was perhaps the first time that the totalitarian alliance of right and left against the democratic middle found active expression. As far as Germany is concerned, it fitted well, of course, into the pattern we have just described of interrelated interest groups and government departments. This realistic basis assured the National Economic Council of a measure of success, even though the first exaggerated expectations were sadly disappointed.

The German National Economic Council as organized under Article 165 of the constitution was not wholly unique. Similar organizations with similar powers were found in France, Japan, Czechoslovakia, Poland, Spain, Mexico, and Yugoslavia. It is characteristic that most of these countries had leanings toward dictatorship and strong remnants of feudalism in their social structure. France, under Vichy, experimented with such a corporative system with little success. But the economic council under the Third Republic was rather a technical advisory body than part of the constitutional order. This was different under the constitution of 1946, which provided for such a council as we have noted. In the Fifth Republic an economic and social council is also part of the constitutional order. (Article 71) The government was given a much larger share of appointees, namely, one third of its 205 members; the rest are elected by various interest groups and professional associations, including labor unions. Its purpose is to aid the government, rather than the parliament, in the performance of its planning and policy-making tasks. In view of the decline of the position of the French parliament, its role has been enhanced.[18]

In the period between the two world wars, the German council best illustrated the possibilities and the limitations of such councils as parts of a constitutional order. As an experiment, a provisional council was organized in 1920. This provisional council was never replaced by a permanent one, although a bill for its establishment was under consideration when the Hitler forces came into power. But even this provisional council was an independent part of the German constitutional order, and its relative success is indicated by the fact that the bill pending in 1933 for the establishment of the permanent council measurably increased the powers of this body; it proposed to give it the right to initiate legislation.

What were the functions of the provisional council, how was it composed, and how did it work? The functions of the council were concentrated in the fields of business regulation, social welfare, and finance. It played a part in both the legislative and the administrative work in these fields. The government was obliged to submit to the council all legislation dealing with such matters, and it submitted the reports of the council to the other two legislative bodies together with its own memoranda. In the administrative field, the council was called upon in many laws to nominate representatives on various technical boards in the field of economic regulation, labor, and so forth. On the whole it is believed that the council made substantial contributions in these activities. It goes without saying that it slowed up the process of such legislation, and consequently voices were heard in parliament and among permanent administrators which denounced the council as an unnecessary encumbrance. It was claimed that the various interest groups organized in the council proceeded to press their claims again when the bill came up in the parliament for decision, after having tried to exert their influence when the bill was being drafted by the administrators. But on the whole, the body could be made to work within the parliamentary system.

More serious problems arise when one turns to the question of its composition. It was generally agreed that the provisional council was too large, and this was due to the fact that every pressure group tried to secure as many seats as possible. What indeed is the relative importance of various activities within the whole economic life of the nation? It is clear that a certain measure of arbitrariness is unavoidable. The provisional council was composed as follows: there were six groups, so called, Agriculture and Forestry with sixty-eight representatives, Gardening and Fisheries with six, Industry with sixty-eight, Commerce, Banking, and Insurance with forty-four, Transportation, Communication, and Public Enterprises with thirty-four, and Handicrafts with thirty-six. To these were added thirty representatives of the consumers (for example, German Association of Housewives, with four representatives), sixteen representatives of the officials and the free professions, and twenty-four members appointed by the government. This makes a total of three hundred and forty-six members. In the first six groups employers and employees were jointly represented, each nominating half of the members. In practice, this hitching together of management and labor did not work. The labor members of the various groups all collaborated, being directed by the united German trade-union organization, and thus established what became known as a division (*Abteilung*) to which the division of the employeers corresponded, supplemented by the others as a third division. We thus find eventually three divisions, management, labor, and groups not identified with either. The pending bill had recognized this development and proposed to assign membership in the council on the basis of these divisions. Thus in Division I, the various great organizations of industry, commerce, agriculture, and so on, were each to name their representatives, while all the members of Division II were to be nominated by the General German Union of Trade Unions (*Allgemeiner Deutscher Gewerkschaftsbund*). Actually this had been the situation even in the provisional council. The original pretense of effectively integrating employers and employees had not materialized. The government in order to break the deadlock which resulted at times from the opposition of these two groups, particularly in social questions, fell back upon the third division, composed of consumers, officials, free professions, and appointees of the federal governmen and the state governments.

The gradual ascendancy of the division over the groups brings us to the inner working of the council. After a first outburst of enthusiasm when the great captains of industry participated in the deliberations of the council, the plenary sessions atrophied. After 1924 no more plenary sessions were held at all. All the work of the council shifted to the committees. Three of these committees were of leading importance, corresponding to the three main fields of council activity, one dealing with business regulation (*wirtschaftspolitisch*), another with social reform (*sozialpolitisch*), and the third with financial matters (*finanzpolitisch*). The government voluntarily granted them an advisory supervision of ordinances and decrees as well as participation in legislation. The members of these committees were designated by three divisions of the council, each naming an equal number. Under the provisional council, the chairmanship of these committees was entrusted to members of the permanent civil service designated by the respective ministries (Economic Affairs, Labor, Finance), but the draft changed this and had the committes elect their own chairmen. As the business of the council had developed, the major committees were really to all intents and purposes the council. Working through numerous subcommittees and temporary committees, they received the drafts of the bills directly from the government, with the steering committee, composed equally of members from the three divisions, acting merely as an intermediary.

It is obvious from what has been said that the German Provisional National Economic Council, as it functioned under the Weimar Republic, served essentially to coordinate the manifold organizations which modern economic life has brought into existence, and to legalize or constitutionalize, their participation in legislation and administration. In Czechoslovakia, where a similar council was at work, the experience with it was very much like that in Germany. Such councils can undoubtedly fulfill a useful function under modern conditions, but it seems arguable whether the amount of additional work involved is worth the result. In truly democratic countries, where the interest groups are largely independent of the government, considerable objection arises to such "coordination." Perhaps if they are kept advisory, councils have a permanent role to play. It is as yet difficult to say whether such more restricted bodies, attached to the cabinet itself, are preferable. In the United States, with its highly developed pressure group politics, novel problems would undoubtedly arise. It seems highly improbable that a body composed of the representatives of interest groups could resolve the conflicts which the Congressman struggles continually to compromise in his efforts to retain the support of his constituency.

The Fascist "corporative state" • As noted before, the idea of representation by interest groups has roots in antidemocratic traditions, sentiments, and viewpoints. It is therefore hardly surprising that bodies built upon this principle should have been features of totalitarian systems. Indeed, these bodies are at times represented as alternatives to popular representation by districts or territorial subdivisions of the electorate. They are an extension of the Government's long arm into the economy; the coordination of all organizations, the aboliton of all freedom and independence of association, make the managers of economic interest groups part of the governmental and party hierarchy and bureaucracy. Following the pattern of the Provisional German Economic Council, there was, in the Fascist Grand Council of Corporations, a threefold division of economic activities, as well as several groups such as agriculture and industry. The threefold division was that of employers, employees, and others (consumers, professional people, and the like). These divisions and groupings were composed of various organizations. Each activity was recognized by the government through *one* organization only. Though the officers of some of these organizations were "elected," they practically all owed their offices to the government which either directly appointed them, or maneuvered their election through effective pressure. A measure of autonomy was, perhaps, preserved by some of the organizations of large business interests, banks, and so forth. But essentially the government and the party behind the government used the "corporate" or rather associational structure of modern economic life for the purpose of coordination and control. Associations which before the advent of the Fascists maintained a vigorous life of their own, particularly in the labor field, were all fascistized. In the conflicts between Fascist trade unions and Fascist employers' associations the government rendered the final decisions. It inclined now to the one side and now to the other, as the exigencies of general policy seemed to suggest, but on the whole the workers, being the weaker party of the two, came out at the short end. Fascist myth-makers looked upon this setup of bureaucratized associations as a first step in the direction of complete pacification in the industrial realm, when workers, employers, and consumers would be united in real "corporations"; but there were no signs, except in official speeches and writings, to indicate that any such trend was materializing. As H. Finer, in his able analysis of the Fascist system, remarked: "the term 'corporative' has been used, if not invented, to rouse a sense of wonder in the people, to keep them guessing, to provoke inquiry, and to contrive, out of the sheer mystification of an unusual word, at once to hide the compulsion on which the Dictatorship finally depends and to suggest that a miraculous work of universal benevolence is in the course of performance. . . . The 'corporative state' is a tool of propaganda." To this G. Salvemini, an Italian scholar of high repute and an avowed enemy of Fascism, rightly added: "From 1926 to 1935 the sole reality in Italian political life was the dictatorship of a man and his party. But side by side with this reality a new myth had grown to gigantic proportions — the myth of the 'corporative state.' "[19] Hence, apart from Mussolini's propaganda, the discussion of his governmentalization of all associational life leads back to the ordinary problems of bureaucracy previously discussed.

Interest groups in the United States today · Ever since Pendleton Herring's *Group Representation before Congress* was published in 1929, there has been developing a more constructive attitude toward these organized interest groups. This attitude is helpful, if it is not carried to the point of cynical disregard for the key aspects of constitutional democracy.[20] Such an outlook is becoming more general; it tends to look upon the voter with an independent mind of his own as a weird or undesirable citizen. These pressure groups fit in better with the idea that it is all a matter of trends and forces. "The" farmer and "the" workers displace in this view the citizen who as a common man participates in the common concern of the community. No doubt this concept of a common man, that is to say, of a man as free citizen, has a distinctly normative flavor. Even so, the discarding of this norm spells considerable dangers for constitutional democracy. Happily, these associations are democratically organized.[21] Control over them is, at least according to the bylaws, exercised by the rank and file in the various organizations. This democratic pattern is recognized by the Chamber of Commerce just as much as by the AFL-CIO. But none of the labor unions, and only a few of the professional associations, like the American Medical Association and American Bar Association, are actually in control of their trades. Others, like the American Association of University Professors, occupy an intermediary position with their members exercising a varying, but rarely decisive, influence in the colleges and universities of the country. Still others, like the associations of schoolteachers, have as a rule even less control. All these occupational and professional groups have as one of their primary functions the representing of the interest of the particular group for which they speak. As pressure groups before legislatures and administrative bureaus, they watch over whatever government policies would affect their members. The extent of such activity is, of course, affected by the measure to which the government has adopted any policies, and it therefore varies greatly; on the whole, it has been increasing in the last few decades.

Perhaps the most startling extension of pressure group activity occurred when the National Recovery Administration undertook to coordinate the American economy on a vast scale with the help of these organizations. This experiment, even though it failed, signalized the rise of organized interest groups and their potential claim to participate in the government in an active and legal way. During the Second World War, trade associations again exercised governmental functions in various ways. Even in peacetime, numerous advisory bodies in various fields of governmental endeavor are staffed by the representatives of organized interest groups. Indeed, successful participation in such groups is one effective road toward participation in government today.[22] Another striking instance of the close collaboration between occupational interest groups and governmental agencies is presented by the county agents. These are officials who are connected in an administrative-executive way with all three levels of the American government, federal, state, and local, as well as with the Farm Bureau Federation, one of the three great farmers' organizations. The United States Department of Agriculture, the extension services of the schools of agriculture in the state universities, the counties, and the farmers individually through affiliation with the local Farm Bureau, all contribute toward the maintenance of the administrative work which this official and his staff carry on.[23] In the labor field, similar developments are in the making through the National Labor Relations Board of the federal government and cognate agencies in the states. In Massachusetts, for example, definite coordination has been worked out through administrative measures. All this goes to show that occupational groups are beginning to play a role in the American governmental process, just as they have been doing in other highly industrialized countries. Perhaps this approach is more promising than the one comprised under the formula of "legalizing the lobby." It is not so much a question of giving a legal status to these pressure groups as it is a matter of transforming them from mere pressure groups in their relation to the government and the general public into groups taking an active part and a measure of responsibility in the conduct of modern administration.

Conclusion · In conclusion, it may be said that the genuine representative significance of all organizations arising in connection with men's activities within the total context of modern industrial life has become sufficiently apparent to make it necessary to reckon with them as pretenders to the throne of government. Where the interests are sharply divided, certain of these groups have proceeded to take over the government and to revolutionize it in such a way as to suit their particular needs and conceptions. Such efforts have been accompanied by dictatorial methods — relapses into crude techniques of government which violate the fundamental premises of constitutional limitations. In order to overcome the onesidedness of their representative basis, they have sought to extirpate the groups which they did not represent. Constitutional governments of the established kind have seen a widespread movement for the participation of all kinds of occupational and professional groups in the administration of that part of national life in which they happen to be particularly concerned. Such participation saddles the administration internally with all those conflicts which it is supposed to mediate. Functional representative devices must be considered with great care; they tend to have a divisive, rather than an integrating, effect. The task remains of distilling the general, public interest out of the often-conflicting special interests which constitute part of the whole. But it looks as if functional representative devices are here to stay as elements in any pattern of constitutionalism under modern industrial conditions.

PART 4

TENSIONS

BREAKDOWNS

ADJUSTMENTS

Socialization and Planning

XXII

Introduction · The nature of planning · The nature of socialization ·
Bureaucratization · Socialization and planning in Great Britain · Socialization and planning in Continental Western Europe: (1) France. (2) Italy.
(3) Germany · International planning · Conclusion

Introduction · Since the emergence of modern constitutionalism in the
seventeenth and eighteen centuries, some unforeseen tensions have developed throughout Western society. Of these, some are of a spiritual and
moral nature and are associated with the decline of Christianity as a living
and vital force; as such they lie beyond the scope of this book.[1] Others are
of a more earthy and pragmatic sort and have themselves been nurtured to
some extent at least by constitutionalism and democracy. Among them planning, propaganda, and plebiscitary mass action (direct democracy) are of
major importance; they in turn have occasioned the ever more frequent
employment of emergency powers. Such "constitutional dictatorship" was
superseded in a number of countries by totalitarian dictatorship, both of the
right and of the left. The aggressive propensities of the latter, whether under
the banner of world revolution or world conquest, have precipitated wars,
both hot and cold, which have further extended the employment of emergency powers, and have called for planning, propaganda, and plebiscitary
mass action on an unprecedented scale. No study of constitutional democracy in the second half of the twentieth century could overlook these tensions, breakdowns, and resulting readjustments. If there has been a reaffirmation of constitutionalist principles and practices in France, Italy, Austria,
Germany, and India, it is counterbalanced by the disappearance of constitutional democracy from Czechoslovakia, Yugoslavia, Poland, and China, to
mention only the most important countries.

Each one of the tension areas raises a problem of readjustment. Can the
particular practice be combined with constitutional democracy? Can it, in
other words, be constitutionalized? This is the anxious question. Nowhere
is this questioning more persistent than in the field of "planning" and socialization. There are many who would maintain that planning of a central kind

means the end of constitutional democracy.[2] Others have on the contrary insisted that planning is simply an extension of constitutionalism into broader fields, that a constitution is itself a plan.[3] The same range of arguments has been urged with regard to socialization and socialism. A sizable group of writers link constitutional democracy with a free-market economy, including free enterprise.[4] The traditional view of moderate socialists, from Lassalle to the Labour party and the Social Democratic parties throughout Europe, insists on the contrary that socialism is the fulfillment of democracy, that "political" democracy without "economic" or "industrial" democracy is incomplete or worse.[5] It seems desirable to explore this vital issue in some detail and in concrete rather than in ideological terms. It is worth noting, moreover, that the negative view which insists upon the ideological and practical incompatibility of planning and socialization with constitutional democracy is shared by conservatives and by the totalitarian opponents of constitutionalism. Here lies the key to the strange and often disastrous combinations in electoral and parliamentary politics that seem so illogical from a rational standpoint.

One other introductory remark is in order. It is customary to speak of planning and of socialism in virtually the same breath. This is in part due to the fact that socialist ideology has always stressed its interest in a rationalized, planned economy. The assumption of a necessary link between the two is reinforced by the fact that the Soviet Union, believed and represented to be a "socialist state," has engaged in large-scale planning and is by some economists credited with having achieved "the highest state of development" in planning. But the fact that socialism and planning have been thus linked in theory and practice does not mean that planning is necessarily so linked. Nor indeed does it mean that socialization, as distinguished from socialism (for instance, a country may "socialize" its railroads without embracing socialism as a system for all or most economic activity), need necessarily imply planning. To illustrate the latter argument, one may point to the socialized utilities in many European countries completely devoid of economic planning twenty-five years ago; to illustrate the former, one only has to think of the considerable planning for war mobilization of the economy in the United States and other countries[6] involving no socialization at all. One may even plan oneself out of socialism, as the neoliberals seek to do. It is clear, then, or should be, that while planning and socialization are closely related tendencies or approaches to the economy, they should be clearly distinguished and treated accordingly in their relation to constitutional democracy. They are two distinct attempts to "rationalize" economic life by eliminating those aspects of economic activity in a free-market economy believed to be contrary to rationality: in the case of planning, the anarchy of uncontrolled competition and the attendant waste of resources and concentration of economic power. The related costs of advertising and of distribution are to be eliminated; while in the case of socialization, it is profit and the divergencies in the distribution of wealth which are to be done away with.

The nature of planning · Like any descriptive concept, planning can be given a very wide or a very narrow connotation, often qualified by such adjectives as "national," "regional," "international," or "economic." Planning may in broad terms almost merge with any predetermined policy for the execution of which a "plan" is made. Thus Alexander Hamilton's *Report on Manufactures* (1795) is often considered as planning of an early sort. Narrowly speaking, planning is restricted to the activities involved in setting up an over-all plan covering an entire economy in most of its ramifications and, according to some writers, in being worked out in quantitative statistical terms. Thus conceived, "planning can be defined as guidance of economic activities by a communal organ through a scheme which describes, in quantitative as well as qualitative terms, the productive processes that ought to be undertaken during a designated future period" (Landauer).[7] The trouble with this definition and with similar ones given by economists is that it fails to take account of a basic distinction arising for the student of constitutional democracy from the fact that the ends or purposes of such a planning process may be determined in radically different ways. For if the end or purpose of the planning is authoritatively determined by a body such as the Politburo, the plan is reinforced by the compulsive force which can and will be marshalled for the execution of the decisions of such a "totalitarian" body. Planning under democratic conditions has to treat its end as variable in terms of popular approval or disapproval. The resulting difficulties of enforcement raise in many people's minds the question as to whether planning can be carried on under such conditions at all. The seriousness of this issue cannot be denied.

It is, nevertheless, our contention that a certain kind of planning is not only compatible with constitutional democracy, but is its natural extension in a mature industrial society. But this planning is not the same as the "blueprint planning" of an autocratic system. In fact, it is its diametric opposite in the very same sense in which legislation, government information, parties, unions, and a host of other public activities are opposites of entities or activities by the same name in an autocratic system. In fact, as mentioned, a constitution may itself be considered an ambitious "plan." It is well known that the primary task of the men who projected the constitutional plan at Philadelphia was an economic one: interstate commerce, tariffs, currency, and debts were among the problems for which the Constitutional Convention sought a solution. As Mr. Walton Hamilton has shown in his brilliant study on the commerce clause, the makers of the constitution had a definite ideal society in mind, economically as well as politically — and it was not simply a free-market economy, either, but to some extent at least a mercantilist, directed economy.[8] What was true at Philadelphia was equally true of later constituent assemblies. In India, in Weimar Germany, in Czechoslovakia, in Mexico, a socializing commonwealth was envisaged, and an attempt made to order and plan a "social democracy." The new constitutions of Europe, more especially the constitutions of France, Italy, and Germany, are likewise "plans," and much of the discussion in the postwar constitutional conventions was concerned with such crucial issues of the modern economy as what was to be the extent of socialization. These plans were evolved in public debates, and often were accepted or rejected by the electorate in mass referendum. The provisions for constitutional amendment provide machinery for the periodic revising and recasting of these plans. It is questionable to insist that because these constitutions are not stated in quantitative terms they are not plans. As a matter of fact, ends or purposes which are universally admitted to be key aspects of any plan can rarely be stated in quantitative terms. A constitution outlawing forced labor (Constitution of the United States, Article XIII) is providing a very important ingredient to a particular society, as is the corresponding guarantee of freedom of choice in one's occupation. It is part of a definite plan — an open society — which that constitution seeks to organize.[9]

It is, from this standpoint, unfortunate that economists, who necessarily emphasize the economic aspect in planning and whose technical services are of decisive importance, should have pre-empted the discussion in the field of planning to the extent to which they have in fact done so. For economic values, while of great, even paramount, importance for the general outlook of the mass of humanity, are not by any means the only ones. Freedom of speech, to give only one example, may not seem important to those who have it, and security in one's person even less so — but the statement often heard that people cease to care about freedom when they have no bread may well be true in countries which have enjoyed freedom over a long period or which have never known it. People who have enjoyed the blessings of a system of planned economy in which unemployment was eliminated by regimentation and forced labor show only limited enthusiasm for that "solution." In short, a planning process which involves coercion on any considerable scale will be unenforceable in a democratic society.

We cannot escape from the difficulties which this situation presents by interpreting "planning" to mean any rational effort to utilize social intelligence in the determination of public policies (Merriam); for it obscures the distinction between the autocratic approach, which insists that "an economy is planned when one central authority adopts and carries out a program designed to realize a single and unquestioned end to the whole of the community over which it has jurisdiction," and the approach of a constitutional democracy, which knows no "unquestioned end." It is the very essence of the democratic process to permit the questioning of any end at any time.[10] But to assume that this questioning will necessarily proceed according to rational methods is basically unrealistic. Planners proceeding on such assumptions will fail to meet popular needs and demands. In short, since interests and values are not wholly rational, any deliberate rational co-ordination of values and assignment of priorities in accordance with such coordination is inhibited.

Democratic planning, dedicated as it must be to achieving the greatest satisfaction for as many as possible, cannot afford to neglect the reactions of those whom a given policy affects. Based upon the basic decision of the electorate which the constitution embodies, the broad pattern of such a plan will be submitted to and periodically reviewed by representative bodies. Where the referendum is an established institution, it may be employed for clarifying some basic aspects. But generally speaking, the procedures applicable to sound budgeting (itself a plan for government operations) are *ceteris paribus* the procedures applicable to democratic planning. It is, however, characteristic of the as yet primitive state of affairs in this field that none of the new constitutions, let alone the old ones, deal with planning as they do with budgeting, even though the practice of exempting "extraordinary expenditures" from regular budgetary controls points toward planning, as does any proposed budgeting over several years. Some interesting "experimenting" is going on in this line. Thus in the Commonwealth of Puerto Rico, a planning board prepares annually a six-year financial program to project trends. In this case, the need for rapid economic development provided the general agreed consensus on a planning goal."

It is in the nature of things no easy matter to state the objectives of planning in a developed democratic society, except in such platitudinous generalities as "general welfare" or "the greatest happiness of the greatest number." An underdeveloped society can fix such a goal, the more so if it is autocratically ruled. Industrialization became such a goal in the case of the Soviet Union, preparation for war in the case of Hitler's *Reich*. But the democratic process, as we have seen, consists in compromises on concrete and specific policies, with different groups and individuals going along, although with different purposes in mind.

In short, cooperative, democratic planning under a constitution may be defined as guidance and coordination of the community's economic activities through an over-all program, especially in the use of economic resources, in accordance with the community's preferences, as expressed through the constitution and through representative bodies. This over-all program describes, in quantitative terms where possible, the various measures required in guiding production and distribution over a definite planning period of, say four years.

The nature of socialization · The term "socialization" is often used interchangeably with "nationalization." This is unfortunate, as there are several ways of socializing property which do not transfer title to the "nation," but to other entities. It is more precise to speak of nationalization as a particular kind of socialization. Thus, a city may socialize its street railways, or a state under a federal system may provide for socializing banks within its jurisdiction.

As everyone knows, socialization has for many generations been associated with the political, social, and economic philosophy known as socialism. It was an old story when the *Communist Manifesto,* in 1847, demanded the "centralization of control in the hands of the state" of such key enterprises as banking and transport. But in spite of this fact, it is necessary today to dissociate the two concepts, for socialization is a recurrent event in contemporary society, often accepted and even promoted by nonsocialists, while socialism is an ideology, a system of ideas concerning desirable social changes. The many publicly controlled and publicly operated utilities may be a source of satisfaction to socialists, but they are accepted by nonsocialists for purely pragmatic reasons unrelated to any ideological preconceptions.[12]

The preceding remarks imply a conception or definition of socialization as the process of transforming private into public property, ordinarily followed by governmental operation and management of such enterprises. However, besides such government operation, other forms have been recognized, such as semiautonomous government corporation and even union-managed enterprises. Socialization is recognized in the constitutions of France, Italy, Germany,[13] Mexico, and India. In all these constitutions it is associated with the statement of basic rights as a limitation upon the right of private property. In the French constitution, the provision is, like all basic rights, found in the preamble of 1946, reaffirmed in 1958; socialization is made dependent upon either of two criteria: (1) that an enterprise have the character of a national public service; or (2) that an enterprise be a monopoly in fact. The German Federal Republic's Basic Law is quite detailed and specific, and the constitutions of the states even more; the provisions are broad, and not only monopoly but any kind of "abuse of economic power" are reasons for socializing property. The Italian constitution follows the same line, but speaks of "public interest" and "social utility" as grounds for socializing, as is monopoly; it also seeks to restrict private initiative where it damages "security, liberty, or human dignity." India's constitution contains a similar commitment to the "welfare state." It provides that "the ownership and control of the material resources of the community are so distributed as best to subserve the common good," and that "the operation of the economic system does not result in the concentration of wealth and means of production to the common detriment." (Articles 39,b,c).[14] We shall discuss presently what has happened under these constitutional provisions of the several countries.

Even where the constitution does not now provide for socialization "in the public interest," socializations seems to be going forward in many places, although there is also some "privatization." Marx and Engels would indeed be surprised if they could see how much of their original program is now realized in "capitalist" states. Socialist governments, though constitutionalist, have gone further. In Britain, under the first Labour government, socialization was adopted for the central bank, inland transport, and the basic source of industrial production (coal, electricity, and gas), while steel was reprivatized under the subsequent Conservative government, but has since been socialized once more.[15] Without a written constitution, Britain was able to accept the basic decision of her electorate in lieu of the more elaborate process which would be required in the United States.

In view of the role of government in all socialization, it has become customary in France to describe as "*étatisme*" this general tendency toward socialization, that is to say, toward increasing the role of the "state." It has been translated as "governmentalism." To call this trend "governmentalist" is in keeping with the general meaning of socialization, since a municipal, as well as a state or national, government can readily be envisaged as engaged in "governmentalizing."

Some measure of socialization is clearly compatible with constitutional democracy. The opinion often heard in the United States that socialization subverts constitutionalism is palpably contrary not only to the experience of many European countries, where socialization of, say, railroads, has for a long time been accomplished without any destruction of the constitution. But even in the United States, socialization has gone forward, especially on the local level. As a matter of fact, close government control of a given industry, such as the railroads, communications, and air transport, constitutes a kind of "cold socialization." If property is seen as a bundle of legal relationships or "an accepted medley of duties, privileges and mutualities,"[16] that is, of rights and obligations, then any legislative (authoritative) act by which some of these rights or privileges are transferred from private persons to the community should, broadly speaking, be included under socialization. Even though the transfer of such a right or privilege may only prevent an owner of cattle from selling milk if the animals have not been tested for T.B. — a step obviously desirable from the standpoint of health — it would still be part of the broad socializing tendencies of our time. It is a denial of the harshly individualistic doctrine of "buyer beware" and substitutes governmental for private action. But it is also possible to continue to speak of such cattle as "private property" simply by defining property as consisting of a different bundle of relationships or "miscellany of equities." When seen in this perspective, it becomes clear that private and socialized property are not simple, absolute antitheses, but are a whole series of gradations. What property "means" depends in any case upon definition by law and sanction by public authority. It is in this sense that the new constitutions are justified in stating that "private property" is protected. It is a bitter lesson, but an inescapable one, for the property owner to learn that the meaning of property is itself subject to constitutional determination.

Bureaucratization · The early advocates of socialism were curiously naïve regarding the remedial potentialities of the "state." Having seen with their own or their fathers' eyes the realities of the police state, of the despotic governments of "enlightened absolutism," it would seem that they might well have been as cautious concerning the wielders of power and authority as were the political leaders who founded the United States and wrote the Declaration of Independence. But they evidently believed that a state, once it was controlled by the right kind of people, that is to say, Socialists, would be a "creative" and wholly beneficial agent. Later, as the nineteenth century wore on and the blessings of liberty turned out to be somewhat less unmitigated than had at first been hoped, many Socialists pinned their hope on some kind of disappearance of the state, in short, on anarchism. Of course, they themselves (and more specially Marx) would have strenuously objected to any such suggestion in spite of their explicitly stated expectation that "the state will wither away," and that there will ensue a spontaneous cooperation without any coercive organization. The anarchist implications of such socialist doctrines as those of Fourier and Proudhon are more generally admitted, especially since Marx castigated them as "utopians" for this very reason, among others. It is important to recall this excessive hopefulness of the older socialist doctrines because it focuses attention upon a striking blind spot in their social analysis. This blind spot is the inability to visualize clearly that a socialized society would be a bureaucratized society and, what is even more important, that a *socializing* society is a society considerably advanced on the road toward bureaucratization.[17] For as Marx himself pointed out, the increasing concentration of economic power in a relatively small number of large-scale enterprises with the consequent rise of monopolies is the stepping-stone for socialization. Marx's analysis was too crude and simple; but it nevertheless contained a very important insight into the degree of ripeness of a given economy.

The factor to which Marx and many of his followers paid slight attention was the extent to which such large-scale enterprises themselves become bureaucratized until a point is reached where the transfer of top control to public authorities calls for hardly any changes in organizational pattern or in relations to the general public. Whether it is then desirable to centralize control administratively in the government, rather than to provide the government with the supervisory and inspectoral authority for which monopoly power calls, is a matter of expediency rather than ideology. Bureaucratization is a general trend in contemporary society; it is as noticeable in American universities with their tens of thousands of students as it is in industry and government. The key problem from a democratic and constitutionalist viewpoint is how to render and keep these bureaucracies responsible, as shown earlier (see ch. XIX). If the problem of responsibility can within reason be taken care of, then a "commonwealth of mutual servants" may in course of time be inclined to treat the question of socializing a given economic activity purely in terms of administrative rationality; the criteria would presumably be linked to such issues as the nature of effective incentives and the like. It may be either profit or power, or it may be a combination of these and other incentives.[18]

Probably the most difficult issue confronting such a commonwealth of mutual servants is the ability of the workers in any one of its sectors to stall the entire economy, or a large part of it, through the strike weapon. Traditionally, democratic constitutionalism has been very hostile to strikes in the government service. In the United States, where even unionism in the government service has always been sharply criticized, such strikes are subject to severe restraints, as they are elsewhere. But as important and highly unionized segments of the economy become part of the public service, that is, bureaucratized, the strong pre-existing union organizations, accustomed to collective bargaining, are loath to and in fact refuse to surrender the strike weapon. Since the rationale of unionization is the overcoming of the weakness of the individual worker as he faces the larger and larger corporate organizations in industry, the government, being the largest and most anonymous employer, certainly confronts organized labor as perhaps the most difficult and powerful employer of them all. It is often said that the government under constitutional democracy is after all subject to the influence of popular control. While this corrective may be of some value, especially in the long run, it will hardly satisfy a unionized labor force which finds itself confronted with declining real wages, as is often the case under socialization. The constitution of Puerto Rico deals with the problem (as does the Italian) by decreeing the right to strike, including businesslike public activities.[19] This is a development which earlier socialist theory tended to neglect almost entirely. In the Soviet Union, strikes are completely outlawed since it is part of the Communist position to "coordinate" all independent organizations. Therefore, the labor unions become subordinate to government control there, as they do in Fascist states. This policy is rationalized in terms of the over-all ideological position which claims that the Soviet Union is the people's government, the "perfect democracy," and therefore entiled to the loyal support of all. No challenge to public authority can be permitted. But a constitutional democracy, especially one whose constitution guarantees the right to strike as part of the freedom of association, cannot adopt such a method. Whether there are any other workable methods must at present be considered an open question. Neither the denial of the right to strike, nor the crippling of all plans and programs decided upon by the government representing the majority and occupying a strategic monopoly position, can be accepted as a true solution. The road toward a solution would seem to lie in the direction of developing adequate criteria for and against the calling of particular strikes in the public services, but the experiences to date are not clear in their implications.

Socialization and planning in Great Britain · Under Britain's first Labour government, committed to a planned socialist economy as a long-range policy objective, planning and socialization were closely linked. They have remained so under the most recent ones. However, it is desirable even so to keep the two processes apart, since the policy of planning may be a relatively greater success than socialization, or vice versa. This might mean that under democratic conditions, the more successful policy may gain greater majority support than the other. On the other hand, either policy may prove the more insistently necessary, even though no more successful; or again, socialization may prove more difficult to abandon as a policy. It is a fact that few industries that have been socialized anywhere have been afterwards privatized again, American railroads after the First World War being one major exception, British steel another, and various German industries, including the Volkswagen firm, being even originally a government enterprise.

The objectives of the Labour government's planning have been described very differently by different authors, as our general analysis would lead us to expect. Among the major objectives more or less generally recognized must certainly be included the following: reconstruction and more especially increased industrialization to replace foreign assets consumed during the war, relocation of industry to provide a more rational distribution of the population and greater security, stabilization of prices and wages and the maintenance of a high level of employment such as resulted temporarily from war and postwar exigencies, and finally the maintenance and possible extension of a free democratic society.

Apart from controls which owe their continued existence not to any plan, but rather to continued scarcities and other difficulties resulting from the last war, British planning must be considered on two levels: national economic planning and town and country planning. National economic planning proceeds along two main lines. There is much effort at joint consultation with both management and labor, and a great part of the economy is therefore "surveyed" rather than "planned." The result is a "program" which is being urged by "discussion and persuasion," reinforced by the "indirect influence" exercised by price controls, import and export licensing, raw-material allocations, and the like, in shaping the decisions of business management.[20]

There is first of all, then, a central planning set up which in its various branches is trying to estimate the national income and the division of expenditure between capital and consumption, as well as manpower and raw-material resources in their relation to the foregoing, and, finally, export and defense needs. There is secondly a long-range development planning which divides into three main sectors: (1) the sector of socialized (nationalized) basic industries; (2) the sector of agriculture; and (3) the sector of relatively free private industry and trade (about 80 per cent of the economy). The first, socialized sector is by many believed to be the real nub of the NEP setup; for seemingly the government can more readily direct through and in accordance with its plans those industries which are owned and controlled by the government. Due, however, to international competition and new inventions, this idea may prove to be of limited application. Certainly some of the greatest difficulties in the planning of the Labour government have been encountered in this very field (for instance, in coal).

Before we describe the scope of these nationalized industries, however, it may be well to point out that the early period of labor peace has more recently given way to protracted strikes in nationalized industries, with promise of more to come. This problem of strikes against the government, as we have already pointed out, is perhaps the most touchy issue of a partially socialized economy. The British Labour government, as long as it upholds the tradition of constitutional democracy, cannot travel the road of a totalitarian dictatorship which, like the Soviet Union, outlaws the strike. Hence, consultations with autonomous unions controlled by their membership rather than by the government must be held regarding wage policy, relating this policy to other aspects of the planning program. Unfortunately, like other rights, the right to strike is a weapon in the hands of enemies of the constitutional democratic system. The same difficulties present themselves when an approach to a solution of this problem is sought through work councils, which are intended to enable the workers to participate in management. The British tradition of councils of officials in service should be of some help, but the problem remains a serious one. It imposes limits upon the scope of socialization in a democratic society which parallel the limits imposed by excessive bureaucratization.

The scope of nationalization in Britain largely coincides with the Labour party's program. Through the Bank of England Act and the Borrowing Control and Guarantees Act, banking is largely nationalized and the flow of credit controlled. We have already mentioned that the basic power sources of industrial production, coal, electricity, and gas, are nationalized. Steel followed, and inland transport was taken over. It should be remembered that telephone and telegraph services, as well as radio broadcasting, have been governmental services almost from their beginning, in accordance with the European tradition of governmental control of communications as discussed in the next chapter. Accordingly, cable and wireless services were nationalized, as well as civil aviation. But whereas in the railroad field public ownership is usually justified on the ground that it is a "mature" industry, aviation was believed to need public ownership because it could not be developed without government subsidies. In point of fact, the governmentally controlled airlines in Europe are very costly compared to the United States lines, and government control has been exercising a deleterious effect upon transoceanic air traffic development.

While the aforementioned industrial sector is a decisive part of the economy, it is still a minor one. According to the Labour party program and concept, it will remain so. As one writer, speaking for the government, put it: "What is aimed at is a partnership involving public ownership of basic common service industries on the one hand and private ownership in a numerically much larger group embracing the vast majority of manufacturing industries, commercial enterprises, and distributive trades on the other."[21]

In order to effectuate such a partnership, a considerable framework of organization and instruments of control is required. Wherever the task can be accomplished by general rules (laws) it should, in keeping with the requirements of constitutionalism, be done. Thus administrative controls and discretion can be kept within limits. Nevertheless, there are possible areas of incompatibility between administrative rationality and constitutional processes which may be serious since administrative initiative and direction remain of decisive importance. They are concentrated in three boards or councils subject to over-all cabinet control. The final authority of the cabinet in the British setup is paramount from the standpoint of constitutional democracy. The clear-cut support upon which the British cabinet system is built, and which its electoral system favors, gives the cabinet enough stability to carry out a broad plan once it is approved by the electorate in a general election. The high integration of the British system encourages the testing of a plan, especially since the opposition is able to criticize and query at every turn . As one observer has put it: "The Cabinet is the formal, authoritative embodiment of the will to plan of the majority party; it decides the main objectives, and from it the main orders descend; the figures, facts, and the advanced stages of all plans are prepared by its subordinate agencies." My only quarrel with this summary is the contention that the cabinet "decides the main objectives"; it seems to me that these are decided by the electorate, and more specifically by the agents of its majority, the cabinet.[22]

From the cabinet stemmed a number of committees, boards, and offices which reflect the complexity of a modern government in all its ramifications. These are interdepartmental committees, essentially, dealing both with general and more limited aspects of planning. In addition, there is a planning staff, a statistical office, and an economic section, all of the cabinet secretariat, as well as different advisory bodies. These boards are used to cooperate with representatives of labor, management, and the general public on proposals of the staffs and offices, as well as to consider general information.

One tool or device deserves special attention, the Industrial Working Party. Composed of representatives of employers, labor, and the government, these Parties were set up for a particular industry to study and report on its possible improvement, its efficiency, capital requirements, labor conditions, and so forth. These Working Parties were to draw up a plan for a whole industry on which the government might act.

It has been claimed in retrospect, and with good reason, that Labour's approach to economic affairs was radically transformed in the course of their effort at developing a planned and managed economy. At the heart of this transformation was on the one hand a disenchantment with "nationalization," and on the other a "shift from the manpower budget to the financial budget."[23] It could also be called a shift to economic management. For in the course of Labour's postwar attempt to set up a "socialist commonwealth," they came to realize what has been noted already, namely, that the larger the government's share in the economy, the more vigorous the insistence of various interest groups to share in the government's work and activity. As one key analyst put it: "Insofar as government has committed itself to intervention in the economy, it must have access to or control over instrumentalities that lie in the command of producers," that is to say, ". . . it must . . . so act as to win a substantial degree of consent and cooperation from the groups being regulated."[24] All this has led to what has rightly been called "the new group politics," or, in German, *Verbändestaat*. Among these groups, trade associations and trade unions are probably the most important.[25] Interestingly enough, the same development has also taken place within the European Community, where, as in Britain and elsewhere, the comprehensive planning and developmental activities have been accompanied by a rapid growth of European interest groups.[26]

Finally, for town and country planning — the second level, as we called it — there operated the Ministry of Town and Country Planning (now called Ministry for Housing and Local Government), established in 1943 following the Barlow Report. Under the Town and Country Planning Act, this department is charged with securing a more rational distribution of the population and a corresponding rationalization in the location of industry. It works with the Board of Trade and the various NEP planning outfits and has published a number of very useful studies. Central in its attention is the problem of planning Greater London.[27]

Socialization and planning in Continental Western Europe · As already mentioned, the postwar constitutions of France, Italy, and Germany all contain provisions for the socialization of monopolies, basic public services, and industries. Besides, socialization has always been more common in Continental Europe, with municipalities producing their own gas and electric power, and the like, and with the national government operating telephones, telegraph, and radio broadcasting as well as railroads. This is as true of democratic Switzerland and Sweden as it was of autocratic Germany. The constitution of the Weimar Republic, adopted in the wake of the Communist revolution, contained very broad and explicit provision (Articles 7, 13), for the socialization of natural resources, as well as any businesses, whether engaged in production or distribution. A Socialization Commission busied itself for some time after 1919 with plans for the carrying out of these enabling provisions of the constitution, but the political reaction as well as the divisions in their own rank cut down the strength of the Socialist parties, and no comprehensive plan materialized. In Switzerland, while the free market and free trade are still recognized, the exigencies of war and the pressure of socialism, especially since 1945, have produced constitutional provisions in support of social security, regulation of monopolies and cartels, and of banking and the like; however, no broad provisions of this kind which have been accepted in France, Italy, and Germany are as yet supported by the majority; the right to work was rejected as a constitutional principle by an overwhelming majority (525,000 against 125,000 roughly). In Sweden, planning as well as socialization have been pushed vigorously. Sweden under a Socialist government has adopted the "double budget," which is in effect a plan to level out the business cycle by making annual budgets show either deficits (in depression years), or surplus (in boom years).[28]

In contrast to Sweden, the three major European countries here under review have until recently been long on socialization but short on planning. Until the advent of the Marshall Plan in 1947, comprehensive planning was a matter of blueprints and general debate in France, Italy, and Germany; even the famed Monnet Plan was a nice blueprint rather than a working program.

(1) *France.* At the time of the Liberation, French public opinion inclined to look upon socialization as a panacea for all the ills and weaknesses of the country's economic and industrial life. The shock of France's collapse had convinced most Frenchmen that there was something radically wrong with their society and their economy. The collaboration of a number of top-ranking industrialists with the Fascists, from whom they expected the same crushing of progressive and labor forces that had occurred in the Fascist regimes, had discredited big business and made them appear ripe for liquidation and nationalization. Few realized the kernel of truth in Herriot's bon mot: "Nationalization is like a drum: it makes a lot of noise, but there is nothing inside." To nationalize without a detailed plan for the economy of which these nationalized industries would form a part made little sense. Yet even the details of the execution of these nationalizations were not at all clearly worked out. As a matter of fact, when the Socialist-Communist predominance in the constituent assembly became dubious in the spring of 1946, there developed a rush to put nationalizations through at all costs. An observer could not help but feel that the Communists, at least, were to some extent motivated by an indifference to the chaos these measures might create, if, as has frequently been alleged, they did not actually wish to promote such chaos.

In the course of 1945–1946 a string of industrial and mining enterprises were nationalized, including coal, gas, and electricity; the Renault automobile works; some airplane manufacture; central banking and a large share of deposit and credit banking; as well as insurance in considerable part. All these enterprises were put under boards of a mixed composition, with the government, labor, and management represented, but the undertaking is perhaps best characterized by one observer of coal nationalization, who wrote that it was "jammed through on the eve of adjournment after a ludicrous debate of an hour and a half on the floor."[29] It is hardly surprising that the gravest difficulties should have developed in industries and businesses socialized in so casual a fashion. In fact, each sector of the economy remained largely independent, without coordination by the national government. And since the French "right to strike," guaranteed in the constitution, was not abrogated or even more closely defined for these socialized enterprises, a series of disastrous strikes rocked the French economy and made it a prey to Communist disturbances of the gravest sort. In other words, the reality was far different from the ideals enunciated at the time of the Liberation: the setting up of a true economic and social democracy entailing the eviction of the great economic and financial feudalities and the return to the nation of the monopolies, the sources of mineral wealth, of power, and so forth.

Since 1946 the nature of French economic planning has undergone considerable transformation. These first crude and rather disruptive measures, which aimed at drastically increasing production in basic industry, have given way to less coercive, more flexible methods and more diverse goals. In the process, the French have created a model for a new type of "indicative but active" planning. Under this system, government economists predict the trends in the economy for the following several years, then indicate the most favorable growth rates and methods for the country and for specific industries, leaving it to private industry and individuals to adjust their sights accordingly. The government also actively encourages industry to move in appropriate directions by manipulating public investment (which forms from 25 to 35 per cent of total national investment), loans, and credit. It can fix certain prices, as it did in 1963, freeze all prices temporarily, or apply direct controls such as those on setting up a business in the Paris area, opening a gas refinery, and building. Investment and production in the major nationalized industries are also subject to control, but the planners have come to prefer leaving them almost as unhampered as private industry. Much of the government's influence, in fact, especially among smaller groups and firms, is primarily hortative and psychological. In this respect it may be compared to the presidential guide lines on wages and prices in the United States.

The machinery for drawing up the successive four- or five-year plans reflects the traditional French reliance on administrative expertise. Since 1946, when the first Planning Commissariat was established, most of the decisions regarding both ends and means have been made by this small group of civil servants (about one hundred and fifty, of whom only about forty are in the professional staff), working under the nominal supervision of an Interministerial Committee for the Plan, a Planning Council, and the Economic and Social Council. The planning commissioner, M. Ortoli, is responsible directly to the prime minister, and his office therefore functions with considerable independence and autonomy, although it is not formally a separate ministry. The technicians of the commissariat decide on the main lines of the plan, then present it to the cabinet, the Economic and Social Council, and, most recently, the parliament, for a final decision on priorities. They then work it out with the help of about thirty "modernization commissions," one for each sector of the economy. A few commissions are organized "horizontally" for single problems, like finance or manpower, common to many sectors.

The modernization commissions represent the most original and perhaps the most controversial aspect of the French planning system. Each is composed of from thirty to fifty members selected by the planning commissioner from various groups in the economy, but selected for their special knowledge of a particular economic area rather than for their status as representatives of different interests. Votes are rarely taken in the commissions so as to promote a cooperative, nonpolitical approach. The modernization commissions have had attributed to them by their admirers the double function of advising the commissariat and providing democratic participation in the earliest stages of economic planning. However, they cannot meet the requirements of this second role. Those concerned with democratic control of planning have pointed out that the commissions do not decide the over-all objectives of the plan or even the methods by which it will be implemented. Their job is simply to apply to each sector the decisions made in the Planning Commissariat. Moreover, representation on the modernization commissions bears little relation to the importance of the different groups in the economy or in proportion to the population as a whole. Trade-union members, for example, are even now strikingly under-represented.

If the commissions continue as simple advisory bodies, democratic control of the planning process must be vested in the French parliament. Yet the assemblies have never been given a chance to influence significantly any of the basic planning decisions. The first plan (1947–1953) was ordered by decree; the second (1954–1957), presented to the National Assembly more than a year after it came into force; the third (1956–1961), promulgated by decree, again after it had already started. The fourth plan (1962–1965) was the first to be submitted to parliament before it came into force, and even then was not voted into law until after it had been in effect eight months. Because a plan, in its final stages, is worked out as a whole, the government has insisted that it be voted as a whole, unsusceptible to amendment. This necessity, however, reduces parliamentary control to a plebiscitarian registering of approval or disapproval. Parliament, on passing the fourth plan, inserted a clause requiring that it be consulted on the principle options of the fifth plan (1966–1970) before the entire scheme had been worked out. But when this was done in 1964, the options presented to them amounted to little more than a choice of three growth rates, only one of which was elaborated in any detail. The assemblies, having no alternative of their own except a weak counterproposal by a left-wing socialist group for a higher growth rate and more government intervention in the economy, had to approve the option favored by the Planning Commissariat.

Parliament's desire to attain some measure of control over planning stems in part from the increased importance of these decisions in recent years. Immediately after the war, the ends to be pursued — recovery and the reestablishment of basic industry — were obvious, and dispute focused only on the means. Now, in a fully developed economy, the ends themselves demand political choices. In such a situation, in fact, the very efficacy of extended control planning comes into doubt. The widespread enthusiasm of the early 1960's for the French system of planning, an enthusiasm based on their 70 per cent increase in gross national product in twelve years, has now been severely dampened by the experience of the 1960 and 1963 inflations, both of which demanded drastic revisions in the original plan. Much of the present growth rate, it has been pointed out, represents normal recovery from an extreme postwar low, and is only slightly above the average for all Common Market countries. Nor can the improvement in the economy be directly attributed to the effects of economic planning. Where the government has limited itself to forecasting and providing information, the benefits have almost certainly been small. Where it has used its influence to promote certain industries and rationalize the competitive structure, the results are questionable. The obvious benefits of consolidation and directed development may have somewhat obscured the nearly invisible disadvantages of weakened competition and misallocation of investment funds.[30]

At the moment the right is preaching a return to an uncontrolled market economy, the left demands greatly increased government intervention, and the government is trying to defend the present flexible setup. But even the Gaullists are divided between those who would gamble on increased production and a higher growth rate, and those who emphasize stabilization to prevent inflation. The time has come when these decisions on the goals of the plan, on its methods and on its very existence, cannot be made adequately by technicians. Some means must be found to base the planning choices on the preferences of the public, expressed through its elected representatives.

(2) *Italy*. Italy's planning has been carried out more nearly in keeping with democratic and constitutional procedure. This is at least in part due

to Italy's experience with Fascism. Indeed, this experience has caused Italy to approach socialization and planning with a more cautious, not to say suspicious, attitude. For since both nationalization and planning were initiated by the Fascist government, most Italians are anxious to avoid anything that might mean the reappearance of Fascist practices. Yet there can be no question that measures adopted by the Fascists continue in force in these fields. The Institution for Industrial Reconstruction (*IRI* or *Istituzione per la Ricostruzione Industriale*), which was established by Mussolini in 1933 to ward off a collapse of the banks by taking over their industrial holdings, continues to exercise the functions assigned to it at that time and later. Likewise, the right to strike in publicly owned enterprises, abrogated by Mussolini in 1923, was also denied in 1948 by De Gasperi, the Italian premier, at which time the government reaffirmed the Fascist decree.

Socialization in Italy has taken three major forms, all envisaged by the constitution. First, there is outright government ownership and operation, as in posts, telegraphs, and telephones. Second, there is partnership between government and management, as in many of the enterprises under the Institution for Reconstruction, which holds varying amounts of stock. Finally, there is socialization of the kind which vests operational control in corporate entities below the national government, like municipalities or even trade unions. The latter program is an outgrowth of the syndicalist tradition in Italy. The constitutional provisions are contained in Article 43, which reads as follows: "To the end that general utility may be attained, the law may from the outset reserve or may transfer, by means of expropriation and with indemnity, to the state, to public bodies, or to groups of workers or of users, specified enterprises or categories of enterprises which relate to essential public services or to sources of energy or to situations of monopoly when the foregoing are characterized by outstanding public interest."[31] These constitutional provisions rest upon the general conception of property outlined in the previous article. This latter divides property into public and private property, recognizes and guarantees private property, but only within the framework of statutory law which determines how it may be acquired, enjoyed, and limited. The purpose of such statutory determination must be to assure "social needs" and to render property accessible to all. It is obvious that such a social conception of property would lead straight to the proposition that it may be expropriated by law in the general interest, with due compensation. The one important safeguard is that such expropriations must be *by law;* as long as law making remains democratically controlled, the essential condition of constitutionalism or *Rechtsstaat* appears to be preserved, provided minority rights are adequately protected by the constitution.

In spite of the broad sweep of a socialized conception of property, Italian practice in this field has socialized risks and profits rather than property itself in the broad sector covered by the *IRI*. Contrary to impressions one might derive from the text of the constitution, the situation is largely what it was under the Fascists. Their very simple solution had been to transfer blocks of shares from the banks to the government's *IRI*. No effort was made to direct existing management until the exigencies of war preparations necessitated it.[32] In other words, the *IRI* is still the old holding company of Fascist days, which operates as a sort of government insurance against risk; it elminates the sanction of failure through bankruptcy, upon which capitalism depends, without substituting the governmental sanctions upon which socialism or governmentalism must be able to count. Thus Italy's intrinsic advantage in possessing a concentrated control mechanism for effectuating a unified policy is not being employed for the one purpose which might have justified such socialization.

Italy is the one country in which planning is in a sense institutionalized by the constitution. After stating that private initiative, though free, must not conflict with social utility, security, liberty, or human dignity, Article 41 of the constitution announces that "the law determines the suitable programs and controls so that public and private economic activity may be directed and coordinated toward social ends." In spite of this broad grant of power, the Italian government has done little real planning. The Italian government's long-term program was called "a very tentative expression of views rather than a firm program of goals and of the means to achieve them."[33] It recommended "vigorous public action" in the form of more effective planning and public investment. Independent observers had come to the conclusion that the political and social climate of Italy actually rules out the possibility of effective planning.[34] Even the "opening to the left," *appertura alla sinistra*, which brought more radical socialists back into the government, has not materially altered the situation. Very limited socialization remains unmatched by any comprehensive planning.

(3) *Germany.* Socialization has been provided for in a number of state constitutions, notably Hesse and Bremen. However, little has been done to implement these provisions. The Basic Law, as far as property and socialization are concerned, follows a philosophy very similar to that of Italy. In Articles 14 and 15 of the Basic Law a social conception of property is outlined, stressing the obligations which property entails as much as the rights, and permitting expropriation with compensation when the public welfare requires it. Land, natural resources, and means of production may be socialized, and under Article 74 such actions may be taken by either the federal or the *Land* governments. There is, however, no explicit recognition of planning or programming for the economy as a whole, although the broad grant

of concurrent legislation to make laws for the economy could presumably be used as a valid base for claiming such jurisdiction. In fact, the architect of Germany's "economic miracle," Dr. Ludwig Erhard, was and is a bitter foe of all planning. As a convinced "neoliberal" he espoused the concept of a "social market economy" in which a radically liberalized market would be restricted only where urgent social requirements imperiously demanded it.[35] As a consequence, the German economy was not only left to develop in classical competitive ways, but was even stimulated artificially in this direction by facilitating foreign imports through currency manipulation, lowering of tariffs, and other means. It is of course possible to argue that this policy too involved a kind of planning, as did the encouragement to workers to become "capitalists" by owning shares, especially of privatized enterprises such as the Volkswagen works. "In West Germany," it has competently been said, "rationalizing economic policy is the concept which occupies the place taken in other Western countries by national economic planning."[36]

A kind of partial socialization, reminiscent of the theories of the guild socialists, has been developed in Germany by providing for the participation of workers' representatives in the management of industrial plants. The most radical of these schemes is the one employed in the coal and steel industry, where it was introduced during the occupation by the British. It provides for a labor-elected "labor director" who is attached to the executive board. German corporations markedly differ from American ones: a typical shareholders' corporation has an executive board (*Vorstand*) consisting of a number of active directors, one of them their chairman; and of a supervisory board (*Aufsichtsrat*) concerned with general policy and supervision. Half of the members of this supervisory board are also labor-elected and cooperate closely with the labor-elected shop council. The most thorough political-science study of the codetermination has summed up the effect of this scheme by saying that "drastic changes have occurred in the distribution of responsibility for making these [management] decisions."[37] Not only are they made by different people; not only can other groups contribute to these decisions; not only are business and production managers appointed by and accountable to the supervisory board and the general stockholders' meeting; but also trade unions and shop councils, as well as their members, are vitally involved. This means greater knowledge on the one hand, delay and indecision on the other. It has also meant a reduction in class antagonism in quite a few cases, and a broader understanding of the problems of a business enterprise in a competitive market economy.

For other German businesses, a less far-reaching system of workers participation in management is provided in the law regulating the constitution of an enterprise above a certain size (*Betriebsverfassungsgesetz*). Under this law, labor is represented by one in three members of the supervisory board, besides having its shop councils. This system has been a marked success, according to progressive managers. Like the codetermination law, it has secured an increasing understanding of managerial problems by the workers, has facilitated communication between managers (owners) and the employees, and has contributed important knowledge to the making of sound supervisory judgments. However, criticism is widespread among trade unions and in the Social Democratic party, and an extension of the more radical scheme is strongly advocated. Whether this is a sound proposal may well be doubted. But some degree of "socializing" by granting representatives of labor a real voice, even if not a determining one, in the management of industrial and other business enterprises offers a real contribution to "industrial democracy." It means an extension of the basic ideas of constitutional democracy to the governing of the great organisms of an advanced industrial society.

In view of the federal structure of the German Republic, it is especially unfortunate that no attempt was made to project into the field of planning the compromise arrived at in the fiscal field (taxation and budgeting). With legislative and administrative responsibilities, that is, policy-making functions, in a number of vital fields such as agriculture assigned to the *Länder*, effective planning will be well-nigh impossible without elaborating integrated procedures which would tie in the federal council (*Bundesrat*) as well as the parliament (*Bundestag*) — not inherently impossible under the constitution. The gravest difficulties are to be expected otherwise, since the party composition of the federal authorities is bound to differ from that of some of the states, and smooth cooperation is going to be hard to achieve when the one favors a free-market economy while the others want a socialized and directed economy.[38]

India developed a comprehensive planning program. Its desperate economic plight made such a development well-nigh inescapable. The constitution is silent on the subject; but no sooner had India become independent than a Planning Commission and a National Development Council were set up in 1950 and 1952 respectively. These crucially important bodies are vigorously centralizing in their effect. They have evolved a series of plans which even though defective have played a decisive role in the development of India, primarily in terms of a decision to industrialize the country rapidly. More than a hundred public bodies have been created under the central government, as companies, boards, commissions, etc. As one scholar comments: "planning, which has been done in the context of a federal state and a parliamentary democracy, has been modified both in the interests of a rapid economic and social development." He adds that this planning machinery has "grafted new institutions which have affected the functioning of political institutions. . ."[39]

International planning • Probably the most ambitious undertaking in the field of international planning now operating is the European Common Market — the European Economic Community. Initiated in 1958 by a comprehensive international treaty, the Treaty of Rome,[40] it has been engaged in evolving a variety of policies for merging the economies of Belgium, France, Germany, Italy, Luxembourg, and the Netherlands into one which presumably could be joined by others on their application — an assumption that was shattered when De Gaulle refused the British entry in 1963. All customs duties are to disappear in this area by 1969, and common policies in various sectors of the economy are in the making.

This Common Market is in a way an outcome of an earlier ambitious international planning effort which the United States inaugurated with the proposal that the European nations get together for the purpose of planning their reconstruction so as to qualify for large-scale American aid. It was an unheard-of challenge to the European nations, accustomed as they were to think of planning entirely in terms of national advantage and international competition. This proposal did not produce a well-integrated plan for reconstruction and development, but rather a "shopping list," as critics called it.[41] As a result, requirements were overestimated and had to be pared down rather mechanically after American protests. The greatest difficulty, however, resulted from the fact that the several European nations were not, as we have seen, really ready for planning such as this United States proposal implied. There resulted, as a consequence, the rather paradoxical situation in which the United States, while unofficially and sometimes (in Congress) officially voicing protest against Europe's liking for socialism and a directed economy, was at the same time urging the European governments to engage in over-all planning on an unprecedented scale. There was a notable lack of stress found in American official observations on the need of securing widespread popular support for these plans, nor was there adequate analysis of the extent to which European governments had informed the public and its representatives of the basic policies involved in these plans. However, both the British and French governments developed fairly elaborate plans. The leader in the French planning was Jean Monnet, who became the key figure in the setting up of the European Coal and Steel Community, which prepared the ground for the Common Market by developing a joint pattern of activity in the two fields within its jurisdiction.[42] Until recently, the key body in the Common Market setup was the High Commission established at Brussels.

Its work has been highly successful, and the integration of the six economies has proceeded even faster than according to schedule, in spite of a series of crises. Unfortunately, the French government has recently been engaged in strengthening the hand of the Ministerial Council, in which each government is represented separately.

Besides the Coal and Steel Community and the Economic Community, the Six have also formed a European Atomic Community (Euratom), which has been coordinating work in the field of peaceful use of nuclear energy, but reaching beyond it into the general problems of planning energy development. All three bodies have unquestionably shown that international planning is possible, when really needed and backed by determination to achieve it.

Conclusion · In the field of socialization and planning, it is difficult to form conclusions. The adherents of constitutional government are confronted with two equally uninviting alternatives. Discussion of the problems of socialization and planning is largely carried on in terms of negatives. The friends of planning demonstrate with cold facts and inexorable logic that an unplanned economy produces very undesirable results, economically and otherwise. The adversaries of planning proceed to describe the "road to serfdom" which a planned economy has involved and will involve. The trouble with the two contending parties is that they are both close to being right. Both the free-market economy (or approaches to it) and the planned economy give us much to complain about; there is either lack of security or lack of freedom. To those who are willing to face the facts, there can be little question that the starry-eyed expectations of earlier generations concerning socialism are doomed to disappointment. But this recognition of the shortcomings of socialism does not oblige us to resume an attitude of smug acceptance of the existing state of things. Planning may not of necessity be the road to serfdom. But if it is not, the supporters of planning will have to give a great deal more constructive thought to how planning may be fitted into the processes of constitutional government.[43]

At this stage in the development, there is great lack of clear thinking on this subject by both friend and foe of planning. As our all-too-brief sketch of developments has shown, European governments have pushed socialization without any clear plans as to how such socialization may be integrated with, or could form an essential part of, an over-all plan. Such planning as has taken place has been overtaken time and again by so-called unpredictable factors, the recurrence of which is perfectly well known: bad crops, strikes, inefficiency, and so forth.

Very fine achievements have been recorded in more limited fields; some of them, like the TVA,[44] we have not been able to review here, because of their specialized character. But while the TVA has been supposed to be a planning agency for the region in which it operates, former-Chairman Lilienthal's suggestion that the life principle of democratic planning is "an awakening in the whole people of a sense of common moral purpose" is too broad and vague, and his related suggestion that "the TVA idea of planning sees action and planning not as things separate and apart, but as one single and continuous process," while sound as far as it goes, forgets that the TVA had its basic plan handed to it in the form of enabling legislation. Its fundamental objectives were settled for it, and therefore TVA did not have to grapple with the most difficult task confronting democratic planning, that is, the task of correlating conflicting purposes involved in any over-all plan. The TVA was like a war, and all democracies have proved their ability to handle the planning task under such conditions of *simplified* purpose. This is not said to belittle the efforts of the TVA in keeping democratic processes at work; far from it. But the issue posited by planning and socialization is deeper and more perplexing.

Some time ago I wrote that "the road to serfdom lies through the timid disbelief in the capacity of the people to rule themselves." And in the last analysis, this is the nub of the problem, as it is in the other tension areas we shall have to consider. There *is* a democratic way. Whether it lies through assimilation of the planning process to well-tried budgetary and fiscal techniques, as I am inclined to believe, or whether it can be accomplished through syndicalist methods, as guild socialists argue, or whether planning can be made part of responsible administration, it is in any case clear that democratic nations are not going to surrender to chaos and despair, because they may have to restrict one freedom in order to make another freedom secure. Freedom, like property, is a bundle of rights and privileges, changeable in its composition, yet basically needed and wanted. If too much of the bundle is lost by the failure to make a plan, free men may find some way of planning the way out. There is enough concrete experience at hand to show that it may be done.

Propaganda and the
Control of Communications

XXIII

Introduction · When we speak of "the people," we may think of a
vague mass of unassorted individuals. This public is largely represented by
three identifiable and institutionalized elements, namely, the modern means
of mass communication, especially the press and broadcasting on one hand
and the interest groups on the other. Of these, the press, in all its shades,
represents opinion to such an extent that as a forum for the discussion of
public questions it still holds the foremost place. Hence freedom of the press
is considered a cornerstone of constitutional democracy (see above, ch. IX).
At the same time, press, radio, and television, and to some extent interest
groups, are of great importance as channels of communication from such
representative bodies (as well as the government's executives) to the public
at large. In view of this fact, it is significant that parliamentary debates do
not find their way into the press as they used to. In the United States
speeches of individual Senators and Representatives, and in Britain, France,
and other countries the discourses of ministers, are fully reported. But the
debates as such do not mold public opinion. Presidential appeals appear on
the first page of the newspapers, but arguments made in the Senate against

presidential demands, even speeches of the highest quality and understanding based upon careful study of the circumstances receive relatively little consideration. Due partly to the increasingly representative position of the President, it is also in part traceable to the much greater "news value" which the President has as compared to Congress. There is only one President, whereas there are many Senators and Representatives. Consequently, from the news reporter's point of view, any slight move on the part of the President is worthy of attention.

In spite of the profound impact of the press in general upon government and politics, political science has tended to neglect the press. Many years ago Walter Lippmann called attention to the fact that political science, as expounded to future businessmen, lawyers, public officials, and citizens at large, paid little or no attention to the sources of popular information. The will of the people was treated as if unrelated to the information available; news gathering was not considered a part of the political process. Actually the emergence of constitutional government, and in particular the crystallization of the systems of popular representation as we know them, are inextricably interwoven with the growth of the modern press. Without it constitutional government is unimaginable. Thomas Jefferson dramatized this view by saying that if he were confronted with the choice of having a government and no newspapers, or newspapers and no government, he would have no hesitation in preferring the newspapers; as an ardent believer in minimizing the role of government, he felt that the government could not be restrained without independent newspapers ready to criticize.[1]

The press in all countries remains, of course, subject to governmental regulations. Such regulations may help to fit the papers into the institutional pattern as well as into the economic organization and physical environment of the community. The most striking instance was provided in occupied countries after the Second World War, where licensing and strict control of the press were imposed by the Western democracies in the avowed interest of "freedom of the press," because it was felt that only thus could the enemies of democracy be kept out of positions of influence. For similar reasons, the press in many emergent nations has been severely limited in its freedom.

But there are many problems, political and governmental, concerning the press in a modern democracy. The size of the United States, for example, produces a press markedly different from that of England. The literary preoccupations of the Continental European press are an outgrowth not only of cultural preoccupations, but also of the governmental censorship to which that press has been subjected for long periods of time. In spite of these contrasts, there is a considerable measure of uniformity in the modern press.

This similarity has been enhanced in recent decades by the leveling impact of technical processes, such as the linotype machine, the telegraph, and the general effect of modern economic forces implied in large-scale production. In considering the press as a political instrument, we are dealing, of course, only with one aspect. A modern newspaper or magazine is many things to many people: business, books, sports, fashions, and so forth.

The mass-communication media have produced one of the most dangerous tensions in contemporary constitutional democracies. Walter Millis has described the frightening effect of the jingo press in the United States in bringing on the Spanish-American War.[2] This early case has been since repeated in so many versions, the sensationalism of the tabloids has become so familiar to all, that it is almost tedious to mention the deleterious effects which the activities of men like Hearst, Beaverbrook, Northcliffe, Coty, Hugenberg, and many others have had upon the workings of mass democracy. The electorate has, however, in course of time, developed a very healthy skepticism concerning all this distorted information. Increasingly, as careful researches have been able to show, people vote and form their political opinion regardless of, and often contrary to, the newspapers they read. The elections of Truman and Kennedy, not to speak of Harold Wilson and other Social Democrats, have been won in the face of sharp, and often vicious, press campaigns against them.

Propaganda[3] · Any student of constitutional democracy today must face the issue raised by propaganda. But what is propaganda? It seems to many to have arisen as an "inescapable trend" from the very workings of a free industrial society, with its market mechnisms developing monopoly situations. To others it appears an evil machination of willful and wicked men which may be eliminated by an appeal to man's rational faculties or by some kind of regulation. Still others would trust the spontaneous working of competetive drives; so they exclaim that "the cure for propaganda is more propaganda." The difficulty with much of this discussion is the failure to describe with sufficient precision what is meant by propaganda. From the popular notion that propaganda is simply lies, or, perhaps, the other fellow's opinions, to the often highly sophisticated views of social psychologists, there is a plethora of "definitions." These definitions are often useful within their context, but they do not necessarily bring out the aspect which is of primary importance to the student of constitutional democracy. From the governmental standpoint, the crucial aspect is that of power, control, and organization. Hence the description of propaganda should be approached in terms of those originating it; in short, we should look at it from the vantage point of the propagandist.

Even a casual inspection of the propagandist and his purposes yields a definite distinction between several communication processes. If all propaganda presupposes a propagandist, such a person (or group) may be descriptively defined as one who hands out information in order to gain ideal or material advantages for himself or the group for which he is acting. The tie-in between propaganda and parties as defined earlier is very close; indeed, modern parties are large propaganda organizations. Like every propagandist, they seek to get people to take or not to take particular actions; and yet these activities are accepted as part of the democratic process, in spite of the widespread unpopularity of parties which is related to their propagandistic way of presenting the issues. Party life illustrates an important generalization about propaganda activities, namely, that propaganda is frequently directed toward one or two objectives: to persuade people to join an organization, or to persuade them financially to support an organization. This, from a political standpoint, is the hard core of the work of a propagandist, while around it cluster the more genteel activities which are concerned with attitudes, propensities, and states of mind which dispose people toward joining or supporting an organization (these psychic dispositions constituting the focal interest of the psychologist).

With this general description in mind, it is possible to relate propaganda to constitutional democracy. For such propaganda may obviously be available on a broadly competitive basis to all comers, including, of course, the government, or it may be the monopoly of the government or nearly so. The latter situation is, broadly speaking, characteristic of autocratic and more especially of totalitarian, governments. In such closed societies, one group, often referred to as the "elite" or "ruling class," will control all major channels of communication. The classic doctrine of such a society was developed by Plato in his *Republic, Laws,* and *Statesman,* but it has had numerous adherents throughout history, and more especially recommends itself to all fundamentalists with a firm and unshakable faith in the righteousness and truth of their own doctrine. It has therefore always been a favorite of dogmatic religious organizations and organized churches. Constitutional democracy, on the other hand, seeks to ensure a "free market of ideas"; it undertakes, through appropriate legal safeguards, to ensure to every citizen and group of citizens the opportunity to counter a particular propagandist and his campaign by counterpropaganda to the limit of his resources. These resources may well be of a nonmaterial sort: enthusiasm, devotion, superior knowledge, may count for more than money. This has often been overlooked by critics of democratic society; observing the undeniable effect of financial support given by vested interests to propaganda campaigns and organizations favorable to their interests, they have argued that the "free" society is not free at all. But the cases are numerous in which even a single individual has in course of time defeated such entrenched interests, provided the legal system is protecting the citizen's right to carry on a campaign. This protection is, of course, particularly important for permanent minorities, such as the Negroes in the United States. Thus, whatever the particular campaign may be concerned with, under the competetive conditions of constitutionalism there are usually opposing groups on hand to point out the fact that propaganda is being made. War, antiwar, isolationist, interventionist, socialist, capitalist — these are typical of competing campaigns. In the process, a good deal of propaganda is neutralized. Thus the partisanship of a good part of the American press in some of the presidential campaigns failed to sway the electorate sufficiently to bring about the defeat of the candidate the press was opposing. Other propagandists were at work to counteract what the press was saying.

Opinion polls and propaganda analysis · Opinion polls, while often claimed to be neutral "factual" data, can have a powerful propagandistic effect. They are, even if one discards the so-called "bandwagon effect," apt to influence those who are inclined to "run with the crowd." I am more particularly referring to those polls in which the public is being asked to express its views on complicated issues of public policy, especially when they have not as yet been extensively discussed in parliament or the press. Such polls are based on the highly questionable assumption that the mass public ought to guide legislators and others who possess a real understanding of the issue at hand. But what ought to be done "in the public interest" may be a very difficult matter presupposing a good deal of knowledge.[4] The same criticism that applies to referendums, namely, that they promote demagogy and irresponsibility (see next chapter), also applies to such polls and with even greater force. They constitute, in their present unguided form, a serious abuse and have at times had a pernicious effect upon public policy. It is different with polls on impending votes, or testing personal reactions to policies already instituted and experienced by the public. Here, where the question is "what have you *done*," or "what will you *do*," the polls are more reliable guides.

Public opinion polls raise the issue of propaganda analysis. There was a time when it was felt that the distorting effects of propaganda could be minimized by what was called "propaganda analysis." Based upon a self-righteous belief in one's own "rationality," this "analysis" assumed that its addressees would themselves discern the "irrationality" of revealed propaganda. The difficulty in propaganda analysis arises from the fact that there are endless differences as to what are goals deserving of approval. Most people have little trouble in discerning the propaganda of their political adversaries. It is one of the most important features of a sophisticated democratic society that it takes propaganda in its stride. All information has a potential propagandistic effect, and public opinion polls are no exception to it. In the early days of the press and pamphleteering, this basic aspect of mass communications was often more clearly understood than it is nowadays.[5]

The beginnings of the press as an instrument of opposition, particularly in England down to the end of the eighteenth century · The medieval constitutional order passed away before the powers divided under it could avail themselves of the new opportunities which the press offered. The tremendous outburst of pamphlet literature in the sixteenth century, of which the writings of Martin Luther stand as the most lasting monument, heralded the coming of the press. Even more important were the regular "newsletters" which had made their appearance still earlier. In the course of the sixteenth century these became more and more elaborate. Wealthy merchants particularly, like the Fuggers of Augsburg, organized a regular service. Printed periodical publications containing news reports and opinions did not get under way until the seventeenth century. In 1609 two printed weeklies made their appearance, one in Augsburg and another in Strasbourg, probably the oldest regular periodicals. Soon after, another one appeared in Leipzig. While these were independent commercial enterprises, in England and later in France the governments, which at that time maintained a strict control over all printed matter, usually had a hand in it. The *Weekly News* started in England, and in 1622 was devoted to what purported to be foreign news. "The transition from the spasmodic series of reports from abroad published before 1622 . . . to the not altogether regular issues of the newspaper is easy and natural. At the start it had nothing in common with what we understand by a newspaper today except the fact that it was a continuous enterprise." Thus Shaaber summarizes the beginnings of the newspaper.[6] Nine years later, in 1631, the first French newspaper, called the *Gazette*, was started at the instigation of Richelieu, who granted it a monopoly in the distribution of news. Since Richelieu was able to control the paper, he was subjecting to governmental supervision the entire process of distributing news.[7] In a sense, this system has continued in some European countries down to the present day. The great news agencies such as the old Agence Havas in France, Wolff's Telegraphenbüreau in Germany, and Stefani in Italy, unlike the Associated Press in the United States and the Reuter Agency in England, were always subject to governmental supervision, rather than under the influence of the commercial groups controlling the enterprise.

The first genuine challenge to the system of governmental direction occurred in the course of the English civil war. It is natural that during that period when Parliament and the Crown were fighting for supremacy, the parliamentary party should demand freedom of the press along with other instruments of popular opposition. Yet when the Puritans came into power, their Parliament repeatedly enacted measures for the suppression of what seemed to it objectionable publications. Still, John Milton's ardent appeal for liberty in his celebrated *Areopagitica* (1644), and the unsatisfactory experience which the official licenser reported at the end of one year (1694), led to a certain lenciency. Cromwell, to be sure, could not suffer an independent press, but his natural tendency was in that direction. After the restoration, suppression once more became the order of the day.[8] Charles II adopted the policy of Richelieu, and licensed the publishing of an official newspaper by L'Estrange, the *London Gazette*. This same gentleman also acted as censor and prosecutor of unlicensed publications. Nevertheless the Whigs continued to publish, particularly after 1679 when the licensing law was repealed. James II, on his accession, attempted a revival of rigid censorship, but the development overtook him. After the Glorious Revolution the publishing of newspapers became more general. A series of intelligencers made their appearance. Partisanship availed itself to an ever-increasing degree of the opportunity the press offered, particularly as the public acquired the taste for constant news. The literary talents of Addison, Swift, Bolingbroke, and Steele were all placed at the disposal of this rising tide of journalistic effort. The opposition party in particular derived considerable benefit from the constant agitation in the daily press. Yet all these intelligencers, journals, and the like lacked the institutionalized security which the modern press commands. The lack of power of the press during the entire eighteenth century is indicated by its not being allowed to report parliamentary debates. Privacy of debate was still considered the privilege of the aristocracy which was directing public affairs.

Toward an "independent" press: England · The press in England during the eighteenth and the first half of the nineteenth century was essentially partisan. There can be little doubt that it helped materially in holding a parliamentary opposition together. It was in this period that the reporting of news was merged in one paper with interpretation and opinion, and to these were added literary and other items.[9] It was natural that this should have been so, for it helped to secure readers who might be indifferent to the political controversies. During this entire period, however, and down to 1855, the so-called stamp tax handicapped those who might want to start new papers. It made it easier for the governing classes to regulate the contents of the press. Since the party controversies in England flowed in more or less established channels, this handicap was not seriously objected to until the time of the French revolution. But after English radicalism got under way, a movement, it will be remembered, which was directed against the aristocratic nature of English politics in general, the restrictions imposed by the stamp tax as well as by the libel law and the import duties on paper (abolished in 1861) were bitterly attacked. In spite of these restrictions, radicalism was able to carry forward its struggle for the reform of Parliament, that is, the electoral system, considerably aided by the press. After all, the financial restrictions could be overcome by sufficient zeal. The libel law, which formerly had been interpreted to mean that to criticize the ills of the electoral system was "to utter seditious words against the matchless constitution,"[10] could not well be used against the revelations of outright scandal and corruption, nor could the libel law cope with the fervent pen of a writer like Charles Dickens (after 1836), who was a trained journalist. It is therefore not surprising to find that Cobden's famous struggle against the tariff on grain (1838–1846) was already largely fought out in the press. Nor is it any cause for wonder that in the decades which followed, the restrictions on the press were removed one after the other. After 1860 the press entered upon its new career and commenced to rival Parliament as a platform of political discussion.

France: the press as an agent of revolution • In France, where governmental restrictions persisted up to the revolution and were revived by Napoleon, the opposition nevertheless availed itself of the press. It was largely clandestine. The periodic upheavals in France during the nineteenth century were accompanied by constant changes in the position of the press. The press itself, of course, was instrumental in bringing these changes about. The revolution of 1830, for example, was maneuvered by a group of newspaper editors. At the critical moment in July 1830, the journalists met first.[41] This is not surprising, since the first of the oppressive ordinances that the government had decided upon outlawed any publication without governmental authorization. The opposition journalists asked their leader to draw up a protest. In it he announced: "The legal regime has ended, that of force has begun. Obedience ceases to be a duty. We shall try to publish our journals without asking for the authoriziation which is imposed upon us. It is for France to judge how far resistance should go." The statement was signed by forty-three journalists and appeared in *Le Temps* and in the *National* on July 26. This is perhaps the most dramatic occasion when journalism opposed a government. Here the press took over the function which was exercised by Parliament in England during the Commonwealth. It was the first time that the "fourth estate" emerged as political decisive. In the course of the latter half of the nineteenth century, the vital role of the press became a generally accepted fact. It seems unimaginable nowadays for a political opposition to operate without developing an effective press of its own.

The problems of the American law of libel: no restraint · The development of the press, of course, could not have taken place without considerable changes in the legal framework which prevailed earlier. Freedom of the press has been looked upon as perhaps one of the most essential features of political bills of rights, and there is no democratic constitution which does not expressly provide for it. American politics has been carried on without any material restrictions upon the conduct of the press, except the common law of libel. There is no statutory inhibition. As a result, when the British Foreign Office made its survey of press laws throughout the world, it reported that it could find none in the United States.[12] Actually there are some state laws dealing with particular matters affecting moral standards, and the federal government enforces some standards through its control of the postal service. But by and large the legal restraints under which the press of the United States operates are covered by the common law of libel.[13] This holds the press responsible civilly and criminally for defamation of character. How very limited that restraint is may be gauged from a report that one of the most sensational of the tabloid newspapers paid $5000 in all for libel suits totaling $7,000,000 in claims. Nevertheless the liability for libel does make the press wary in dealing with private citizens and corporations. This is not the case when they report governmental or other public affairs. The protection of the press from prosecution for libel in reporting and commenting on governmental performance is connected with the peculiar nature of the common law of libel. It demands that the party bringing suit show that damage has been done to it. Moreover, a suit for libel requires of the plaintiff that proof be brought to show that the alleged statements are untrue, proof which it is often impractical for government agencies to furnish. This general rule has prevailed since a famous case in the eighteenth century, involving one Zenger, had settled it.[14] In Zenger's case the issue was clear, for he was put in jail for printing reports about the government the truth of which nobody denied. Paradoxically, on the strength of this precedent papers nowadays frequently print news the falsehood of which nobody doubts. It is a question, in part at least, of where the burden of proof shall fall. In the eighteenth century all that the government had to do was to allege that the statements were libelous, and all that it had to prove was that they had been printed by the person being prosecuted. The interest of the government was the sole consideration. It was unhesitatingly identified with the public interest. Such an arrangement is manifestly unacceptable in a democratic setting, but whether the exactly opposite arrangement of leaving the determination of what is in the public interest to privately controlled business enterprises is the solution to the problem may be seriously doubted. Perhaps some of those who led the struggle for freedom of the press might have lost much of their enthusiasm if they could have foreseen this outcome. Recently, constitution makers have concerned themselves with the problems resulting from the abuse of freedom of the press, as well as of other freedoms by antidemocratic elements and movements. Since the rise of these movements to power was often associated with an unprecedented campaign of antigovernmental propaganda, the tendency is now to deny the protection of these rights to such anticonstitutional propagandists. The dangers inherent in such attempts are great, since they undermine the basic principle of "free competition" in the market of ideas. Much detailed inquiry is needed for developing more precise and specific criteria than "subverting the constitution" and the like (see above, ch. IX).

The political effects of a commercialized press • The question of irresponsible comment on and slanting of the news has raised a general problem of economic versus partisan and political control. It is a problem which is confronting democracy in all the more highly industrialized nations. The tendency for advertising to go to the papers with the largest circulation, combined with the mechanical developments in this century, has converted the great metropolitan press into a few huge corporations linking already powerful and highly organized papers in extensive chains.[15] Such is the case in the United States with the Hearst, Scripps-Howard, Time Inc., and other organizations. Such is likewise the story of the Northcliffe, Rothermore, Inveresk, and other trusts in England, of Hugenberg and Springer in Germany. Only France of the large countries, retained a more divided press. It is perhaps no accident that these great corporate enterprises tend to deteriorate the quality of the news and to throw their weight in the support of jingoistic nationalism. At any rate, even if one concedes that the masters of these undertakings are not the scheming and undemocratic plotters that they are sometimes depicted to be, the problem remains as to how to cope with organizations that look upon the process of opinion formation, so essential to the conduct of democratic government, as secondary to that of making money. The accepted American doctrine of the difference between facts presented in the news and opinions expressed on the editorial page is too superficial to serve as an adequate basis. It is obviously a situation arising from very powerful underlying trends which may be quite indirect and unrelated. In England, the rapid decline in independent papers, due to a variety of factors, has become the subject of public concern. A widely discussed royal commission report has taken a very pessimistic view of the future.

The forces behind the mass press · What are some of these phenomena to be considered here which seem definitely related to the rise of the mass press suggested by the names of Hearst, Beaverbrook, and Springer? Certain technical developments since the American Civil War, such as the conversion of wood pulp into newsprint, the invention of the linotype machine, and many others, cheapened the cost of production. At the same time the spread of popular education constantly expanded the available reading public, and the rapid increase in population did the rest. We find that between 1850 and 1900 the number of daily-newspaper publishing establishments, as classified by the United States Census Bureau, increased in America from 254 to more than 2000. At the same time the circulation of their publications increased from 750,000 to 15,000,000 per day. Between 1900 and 1910 both figures continued to rise, but the increase in establishments was much less than that in circulation, namely, from 2226 to 2600 and from 15,000,000 to 24,000,000 per day. After this the number of papers actually began to decline, and by 1920 had fallen to 2441. This decline continued, and in 1965, there were 1751 such papers in the United States. In the same period circulation rose to 60,358,000. These figures suggest something of the enormous transition that was taking place.[16] Pulitzer, Hearst, and Harmsworth, afterward Lord Northcliffe, are simply individuals who rode the crest of the wave. They were essentially skillful businessmen who perceived the possibilities of cheapening the wares which journalism had to offer, from both a material and cultural point of view, and in making a profit from the broad market. Sensationalism gained an ever-more extended hold upon the press in this period. Scandal and corruption in the government were as acceptable as any other untoward developments. The implications of the profound cynicism thus engendered in the masses did not worry these master showmen of the press. They did, however, markedly alter the configuration of modern politics. Of course these popularizers of journalistic goods did not completely displace the older and more established papers. Their inventions and discoveries were bound to spread as they were being imitated by competitors. Eventually, after the First World War, so-called tabloids actually outdid Hearst and his brethren. In order fully to appreciate this mass press one must compare it to the older and more traditional patterns of the press of the leading countries.[17]

A comparative survey of the nature of the modern press in certain leading countries · In any comparison of the press in relation to the government in the various leading industrial nations one must keep in mind the differences between these countries as far as the place occupied by the government in the whole political process is concerned. But it would be misleading to cast the analysis into a rigid pattern of "national" types. The comparison of governmental systems should not obscure other similarities and differences. Thus the labor press in all these countries bears a marked resemblance in its tendency to focus interest upon trade-union activities. As was said before, there are also marked differences which have only an indirect relation to the government structure, such as the geography of the country.

A brief survey of the press in terms of governmental structure reveals some interesting correlations. In America, where the government is federally divided and where a major political interest is focused on the contest between two large political parties of somewhat similar outlook, the press tends to be restrained on strict party politics. In any case, much of its interest is centered upon local matters. England's centralized government is contested for by parties which are divided by their ideology. Hence the press is vigorously partisan. Besides, Britain's imperial tradition causes the British press to be much concerned with affairs in distant lands. (This tendency has been sharply on the increase in the United States.) Moreover, the possibility of distributing a paper overnight throughout the country makes it possible to serve certain groups, such as finance or labor, by a paper distributed from a single center, like *The Times* or the *Daily Herald.* In the United States this phenomenon is restricted to a few papers, especially to *The New York Times.* In France, where parliament is divided into many contending groups, the editorship of a moderately successful paper is one of the safest careers leading into politics, and many prominent politicians have been editors. It is not likely that such men will give up their independent control. Consequently the French press is divided into many individual enterprises. At the same time, the dominant position of Paris in the country's politics offers the same opportunity for distribution of a paper from a single center and gives the Parisian press national scope. Federally divided Germany used to have many ideologically conflicting organized parties. Hence the press tended to be partisan, but with many different organs, to serve the different parties, available to the reader seeking a cross section of the opinion of various groups. There were also significant papers in different parts of the country. Under the Federal Republic and with the decline of ideological controversy, Germany has fewer papers, but the Social Democrats and trade unions control many of them. We see, then, that there is a certain correlation of pattern between government and press. It testifies to the vital role the press plays in political life under constitutionalism.

The English press · English politics today revolve around two primary poles, the leader of the majority party, who is Prime Minister and who directs the government, and public opinion, which criticizes and in a measure controls this government (see above, ch. XVIII, p. 384 f.). Such public opinion develops influence and maintains it through many different channels, but the strongest position here is occupied by the press. In spite of the vast extension of the sphere of personal contact through radio broadcasting and television, the printed word remains a widely scattered influence.[18] Particularly since the eighties of the last century, when the curtailment of parliamentary debates began, the press has become the most effective critic of the government. In spite of all the emphasis upon mere reporting of the news, the selection of items is of such importance that it is, from a political viewpoint, decisive. So-called slanting of the news, which may take the form of continued emphasis or merely passing notice, as well as many other forms, makes the newspaper a "views"-paper. Perhaps the most important technique of slanting the news is the tactics of appropriate headlines. What is particularly interesting in England is the dovetailing of this general newspaper technique with the work of Parliament. The method of questions (see above, ch. XVII, p. 340 f.) would be ineffective today if it were not for the potential interest that the press might take. Parliament itself can hold a debate, of course, but a newspaper can work up a question by giving it appropriate attention through editorials, related news items, letters to the editor, and so on. In spite of the vigorously partisan nature of most of the English press, a tradition of fairness toward the party adversary has been maintained. Speeches of opposition leaders are faithfully reported. Deliberate lying is frowned upon. In return the government is inclined to treat the papers with respect, even to take them into its confidence. Since the First World War, however, the rise of the mass press has weakened this tradition. Situations like that which arose between the Northcliffe press and Lloyd George in 1921, the attitude of the *Daily Mail* and others in connection with Zinoviev letter incident in 1924, and the atmosphere which developed at the time of the forming of the National Coalition in the late summer and fall of 1931, showed a degree of bitterness and unfairness such as had not been witnessed in England since the agitation over the Reform Bill. These events focussed attention upon the fact that the newspapers are, after all, privately owned and capitalized enterprises. When confronted with the policies of the Labour party, it is difficult for them to maintain the degree of neutrality which they could maintain formerly.

As long as the country's electorate was divided between Conservatives and Liberals, there was some positive advantage, from the point of view of party management, in not having the papers too closely tied with the parties.

Thus, while *The Times* might be Conservative, the *Daily News* Liberal, and the *Manchester Guardian* radical, their editorial staffs developed personalities of their own which gave to each paper a more distinctive flavor than the broadly conceived party platforms under a two-party system would indicate. This situation was helped, of course, by the fact that in England, as elsewhere in the nineteenth century, these and many other leading newspapers were owned by families injecting a personal element and tradition into the policy of the paper. Through the papers, these families were permanent factors in the politics of the land. The family of John Walter, who had founded *The Times* in 1785, the Taylor Scotts, who owned the *Manchester Guardian* since 1821, the Rowntrees and Cadburys with their *Daily News*, all possessed a directing influence in their respective party councils. Under such conditions it is quite natural that England should not possess a governmentally controlled press. It does not need and could not have such a press, since whichever party was in power would have the necessary publicity channels. The British are masters at informal techniques of securing cooperation. The aristocratic tradition of England, with its orders, decorations, and titles, is one of these techniques which is in many ways more effective than any official press organ of the government could be. This informal cooperation has been particularly remarkable in the conduct of foreign affairs. *The Times* especially has been a leader in this field. Yet, ever since the days of its great editor, John Delane, *The Times* has been a factor of independent importance. While usually collaborating with the Foreign Office, it has often profoundly influenced its policy. In every important capital of the world *The Times* has correspondents of its own, very well paid, sometimes rivaling the position of the ambassador as a representative of British policy. As in foreign policy so in many other matters, *The Times* would have the leading specialists as contributors. One very striking instance of great political importance was the position occupied by *The Times'* military correspondent, Colonel Repington, who acted as a highly confidential go-between for the Foreign Office, the army, and the French embassy in the difficult negotiations concerning the military collaboration between England and France in 1906 and later. After the First World War the *Manchester Guardian* now *The Guardian* made considerable strides toward fulfilling a role somewhat similar to that of *The Times* for the more radical elements in the country. Yet as far as foreign affairs are concerned, the lack of effective support in the press had a good deal to do with the early difficulty the Labour party experienced when in office, particularly since the mass press did not hesitate to carry on rather violent campaigns.

The gradual conquest of newspapers by profit-seeking, large-scale business enterprises has led to an increasing emphasis upon magazines and reviews as the true focal point of opinion, at least among the educated classes.[19] The Liberal *Edinburgh Review*, started in 1802, and the Conservative *Quarterly Review*, founded in 1809, set a tradition of high achievement and represent the most effective efforts at long-range influence in politics. Although most of these magazines are again identified with some political party or group, they are not in any sense dependent upon them. On the Conservative side, there have been the *Spectator*, the *Saturday Review*, the *Outlook*, and the *Observer*. On the Liberal side the *Nation* used to be of great significance. It afterward merged with a Socialist publication, the *New Statesman*. Somewhat more remote from party politics and therefore perhaps even more influential were the Conservative *Fortnightly Review* and *Nineteenth Century*, the *Liberal Edinburgh* and *Contemporary Review* and the *Review of Reviews*. Besides these, the strictly economic journals, especially the *Economist* must also be considered of great influence in politics.

The American press · In America — to summarize well-known material for purposes of contrast — the press used to be far removed from the government.[20] The ideological conflicts engendered by the New Deal policies somewhat changed that. Though some journalists have from time to time been prominent in party councils, the American press does not have the same intimate personal relations with the parties which we find in England. Until fairly recently the American press was largely guided by the business considerations of securing large circulation. Since many readers were not very vitally interested in party politics, and only quadrennially in connection with presidential elections cared to hear much about it, the adoption of a partisan viewpoint would deprive a newspaper of a good deal of its circulation. This was not always so: in the early days of the republic, the conflict between Federalists and Republicans was highlighted in conflicting newspapers. The same thing may be said of the Civil War period. But the coming of the mass press changed all that. It is natural, therefore, that the American press should be independent of party politics. Papers like *The New York Times* will come out for a Republican candidate, even though traditionally Democratic. The American press exchanged dependence upon parties for dependence upon business influences which might be exerted either through ownership or through advertising. However, since advertising depends upon circulation and circulation depends upon reader interest, it is obviously not possible for a newspaper to heed the wishes of advertisers beyond the point where reader interest would be lost or reader antagonism aroused. On the other hand, reader interest is a somewhat intangible matter, leaving a fairly wide margin of discretion to the editorial office. Adolph S. Ochs, the long-time owner of *The New York Times*, once remarked that the more readers a paper has, the more independent it is of any advertiser. But this consideration does not apply to problems where all advertisers feel more or less the same way about an issue. Even so, a commission of inquiry at the time questioned "whether law can impose more than a low minimum of fairness and decency upon the instrumentalities and frame of reasonable regulation for the flow of their output through the channels of communications to citizens."[21] The dependence upon professional ethics, while a potent factor in shaping the behavior of the superior newspapers, is not a dependable insurance against misrepresentation in the mass press. Its very dependence upon sensationalism conflicts with it. Nevertheless, there has been some improvement in this field in recent years. In any case, newspapers often give very complete accounts of developments which the owners of the papers do not like at all. Newspapers as business enterprises are torn between the desire to utilize fully the sensational quality of some struggle, especially in the labor field, and the owners' and advertisers' desire to have it settled in favor of the business interests. The outcome of this conflict of motives is naturally uncertain. One avenue of escape has been the use of "columnists" of not only divergent but of antithetical views, giving the reader both the titillation of disagreement and the satisfaction of being reassured. It is part of the striving for political neutrality. In relation to deeper political issues, the role of the American press has not been, as in Britain, one of leadership and guidance. Rather it has been that of voicing the reactions of particular interest groups or of the readers at large.

What has been said of the newspapers is equally true of magazines, except that small group of weekly and monthly journals which are devoted to voicing the opinions of those who are opposed to the present order of things. Unlike the English magazines, a great many American journals used to be quite indifferent to government and politics. The challenges of the New Deal, the Second World War, the Fair Deal, and the New Frontier, however, caused the large-circulation magazines to show an increasing interest in politics and international affairs. This is an important development in view of the wide distribution of these journals. While most of their contents are in the form of stories and similarly neutral material, it is possible to inject a good deal of partisanship. This has become a more noticeable trend under the impact of the Cold War because of the constant attacks upon the capitalist order by the Soviet propaganda machine and its avowed as well as its unsuspecting partisans. There can be little question that if the American party structure corresponded to the division between Conservatives and Progressives, as it does at present only to a limited extent, American magazine journalism and perhaps even newspaper journalism would take on a much more vital relationship to politics, and, to the extent to which the division between Progressives and Conservatives is the true political division of the country, that is already the case. Whatever the outcome of the present developments, there can be do doubt that such magazines as the *New Republic,* the *Nation,* the *Reporter,* and *Commonweal* represent a vital body of political opinion in the United States whose influence and significance seem to be in inverse proportion to the number of its readers. To these magazines of longer standing may be added a whole flock of journals of more recent origin representing various shades of radicalism, such as the *Partisan Review,* which is leftist but anti-Soviet, or *The New Leader,* which speaks for anti-Communist trade-union intellectuals. These are, of course, only illustrations of the host, kaleidoscopically changing, of magazines of many hues.

Extending corporate control has been a factor of importance in the American magazine field no less than in newspapers. Among these trusts, the most remarkable is Time Inc. Although developed originally as the publishing company of the magazine *Time,* it controls today a whole group of communication media. *Time* itself, presenting the week's news from its own viewpoint, has a circulation of 3,429,592. The pictorial magazine *Life* actually reaches more than fifteen million readers today, while *Fortune* makes its appeal to the rich and the would-be rich through an ingenious technique of combining costly research and skillful writing. The power which, through the control of this trust, has been concentrated in the hands of the managers of Time Inc. was assuming questionable proportions, but the vigorous competition of magazines like *Newsweek, The Saturday Evening Post,* and *Look* has helped to check it.[22]

Perhaps even more remarkable was the rise of the *Reader's Digest.* It has achieved the largest circulation of any magazine at any time in history: in 1967 it claimed over 28 million in fourteen languages, more than half in the United States. Based upon articles in other magazines which it condenses, Reader's Digest has at times been sharply criticized for its editorial policy and for the influence it exerts by "suggesting" articles and the like, but its growth continues unabated.

The news agencies · In European countries, the governments have sought to influence the press through controlling the news channels. Governmental ownership and operation of the telephone and telegraph facilities made it possible to develop the news agency as a monopoly under government control. Thus after the war the French Agence Havas controlled not only the ordinary channels of news communication, but also possessed a virtual monopoly in many sectors of the advertising-agency field. In 1957 its successor, l'Agence France-Presse, became an autonomous organ with civil status and the stated goal of disseminating "complete and objective information." This new role, which it almost lost again in 1960, has considerably raised the prestige of the Agence throughout Europe.[23] The situation in Germany used to be virtually the same. American military government made a determined effort to break down this tradition, and the DENA agency, while centralized, was supposedly free from German government control (though not from military government control). Since the end of occupation, the German Press Agency (DPA) has resumed the older tradition, but with greater independence. In any case, the large papers like *Die Welt*, do not depend on it, but largely have their own news services and correspondents. Reuters, the British agency, while occupying a formally independent position, nevertheless has always cooperated closely with the Foreign Office in handling its news so as not to interfere seriously with the interests of Britain's international concerns.

America, in keeping with the general commercial and unpolitical spirit of its press, has developed a markedly different system. Since the government does not own or control, but merely regulates, the telephone and telegraph wires (as well as broadcasting), it does not have the same hold over the facilities needed by news agencies. The weakness of imperial and class interests in determining governmental policy (as compared with other countries) combined with the democratic traditions of a free press to foster the development of news services as competitive private enterprises. The Associated Press, United Press International, and the other smaller agencies are so definitely private that governmental subsidies would seem quite unthinkable. Systematic news gathering developed naturally as a part of the competition of newspapers for sale. From the rowboat and the Boston Exchange Coffee House to the almost instantaneous transmission of news today, American methods have been commercial, competitive, nongovernmental.

The oldest and largest of these agencies, the Associated Press, came into existence in 1848 as a cooperative enterprise of six New York publishers.[24] It has remained on that basis through the years, with all members paying toward the cost in accordance with their circulation. But it is not open to anyone who wishes to join: hence, membership in the AP is a valued asset of any paper. There has been a good deal of criticism of this exclusive feature, and some changes have been made, in any case, to counteract any monopolistic tendencies. The United Press and the International News Service (Hearst) were organized as purveyors of news on a simple profit basis. Between them, they served just about as many papers as the Associated Press. They have since been merged. Besides these general agencies, supplementary newsbureaus have sprung up in considerable number to gather particular kinds of news. Radical groups in the United States have tried to cope with the inadequacy of the general agencies, but for obvious financial reasons they have never been very successful.

Though it is undeniable that certain conflicts, such as strikes, raise problems in the news services similar to those we noted in connection with newspapers, the problem of political limitations upon news became really serious only with the rise of totalitarian dictatorship. These dictatorships forced the big news gatherers to toe the line by the threat of excluding them from their territory altogether. Only complete cooperation and a united front quite at variance with the intensely competitive spirit in this field could have been successful in combating such intimidation by ministries of propaganda in the totalitarian states.

In recent years, there has been more and more sharp competition between the news agencies of the press and the broacasting industry. A pattern of cooperation has been worked out whereby AP and other press news is presented over the radio, the listener being referred to the papers for further details. But the broadcasting industry has scored remarkable successes in direct word-of-mouth reporting from Europe. In times of crisis, reports direct from the crisis centers supplanted the traditional news agencies: for reasons not fully known, the average American has more confidence in these broadcast news reports than in the press news, even though they often originated from identical sources.

The emphasis has in recent years shifted from radio to television. In 1965, 688 television stations were reaching into 52.6 million American homes. In 1965, the impact of these stations was revealed in a series of studies made by a leading research organization. They showed that by 1964 "television [had] replaced newspapers as the public's primary news source." Of those interviewed, 41 per cent considered television most believable, while only 28 per cent did so for newspapers, with radio and magazines a poor third. Curiously enough, these findings did not hold for local government information, where newspapers were still considered the most valuable source; they also had a lead in matters concerning state government. For national elections, television was way ahead of all other media.[25]

Broadcasting: new medium of political influence · The possibility of broadcasting the spoken word and projecting visual materials to the four corners of globe has profoundly altered the realities of modern politics. Whether political leadership is contested, as in the democracies, or imposed, as in the dictatorships, the opportunity of reaching millions in the direct, personal way which only the spoken word and the actual view of the speaker offer has turned the modern community into a market place.[26] The conditions under which Athenian democracy flourished in the days of Pericles have once again been provided by these newest means of mass communication. Their potentialities have been further reinforced by the development of communication satellites. Inevitably, therefore, the issue of who shall control this channel of communication presents political problems of decisive importance, at least in a constitutional democracy. Autocratic governments see only one obvious answer: the government must control. Under democratic conditions government control is controversial. Great Britain, as well as France, has adopted such a system, as contrasted with the American system of governmentally regulated commercial enterprise. This divergence is quite in keeping with the differences between Europe and America in the field of news dissemination, which has just been described.

The British, after a period of experimentation in the early twenties, organized the British Broadcasting Corporation (BBC) by act of Parliament[27] in 1926. It was set up as a government corporation under a charter which gave it considerable independence from partisan influence, provided the governors, originally five in number, desired to exercise such independence. Actually, their predominantly conservative outlook inclined them toward an unprogressive program policy. During the early years this took the form of frowning upon political and controversial broadcasts altogether — always a safe policy for conservatives, as any reformer will testify. The charter ran for ten years, when, after an extensive discussion in Parliament, it was renewed in 1936. It was debated at great length in 1946, when the Conservatives put forward a proposal for increasing the independence of the BBC, but these proposals were defeated. No significant alterations were introduced in 1956.

Under the charter, the director-general is responsible to the postmaster-general, thus emphasizing the parallel with other channels, such as telephones. While the British postmaster-general is not the patronage chief of the government, as in the United States, his is a party outlook like that of any cabinet officer. In spite of this, the BBC has, on the whole, been free from the grosser forms of party politics. But there have been instances when the BBC has been the vehicle for effective political moves. For the rest, the corporation's executives have conceived of their task in terms expressive of the aristocratic conception of political leadership which gives Britain's democracy its peculiar flavor. In the words of the BBC's autocratic, yet able, first director-general, it must "carry into the greatest possible number of homes everything that is best in every department of human endeavour and achievement." An American scholar has rightly commented: "A constant attempt has been made to intermix culture and entertainment, in order progressively to raise the public taste and enable general enjoyment to be afforded by that higher quality of artistic accomplishment appreciation of which was formerly limited to a select few." Though this conception is very different from that prevailing in America, very effective arguments can be advanced in its favor.

But this is not the place to enter upon a general consideration of the cultural significance of such an educational conception of radio. As far as the immediate issues of politics and government are concerned, we find that the BBC has evolved policies which make the airwaves available to the major political groupings in a spirit of remarkable fairness. This spirit is essentially an application of the traditions of parliamentory debate discussed in an earlier chapter. Although talks are unimportant as compared with music and other entertainment so far as amount of time is concerned, they are the crux of the problem of control. It has been pointed out repeatedly by non-British observers that definite preconceptions have largely been taken for granted: the monarchy, the constitution, and Christian morals. But the belief in these institutions is not peculiar to the BBC; a large percentage of the listeners feel the same way about them. American radio, though subject to "private" control, has developed very similar taboos.

The issue involved in the expression of controversial opinion by a news commentator is one which has raised considerable difficulty in America as well as in Britain. But since any selection of facts is actually an expression of opinion, it is obviously impossible for any commentator to remain neutral, and hence, under a government monopoly, news broadcasts by a single commentator present an insoluble problem. During the early years, the BBC banned controversial matter completely. It was only after 1928, and after extensive agitation, that the BBC, upon cabinet action, could announce: "Controversy, political and economic, will be admitted on clearly defined occasions with adequate safeguards for impartiality and equality of treatment. . . . Debates and discussions will be the normal procedure." Such standards are more easily enunciated than executed. If a broad view of political controversy is taken, practically any topic of a socio-political nature is controversial, if controversial is defined (as it has been by the BBC) as "any speech regarded as controversial by any reasonable section of the public." Consequently, successive difficulties have been encountered, and the material offered has often been insipid and lacking in "punch."

When one turns to party politics proper, one finds that the BBC has taken the view that broadcasting "can exercise a greater influence over public opinion in matters of politics than can the press. . . ." But in spite of this programmatic declaration, the BBC has not provided nearly the amount or intensity of party controversy over the air which American broadcasters have conceded. This is, in part at least, due to much more limited facilities, but on the other hand, the taxpayer and listener are paying for the BBC facilities, whereas the advertiser pays for them in the United States. With minor exceptions, this field of party politics is limited to the parties represented in Parliament. Through an advisory committee the BBC has kept in touch with the parties, a fact which in turn raises the question of the danger of limiting such broadcasts to party regulars. The division of time between them has been made in proportion to their parliamentary representation, but without rigidity. The party in power gets the lion's share, however, through the rule that the government is entitled to explain major policies. "There are frequent addresses by ministers explanatory of their policy. This growing practice undoubtedly gives an advantage to the party in power," a leading scholar has summed up the situation. But he also thought that this was probably desirable.[28]

The great advantages of a governmentally controlled and operated system of broadcasting became apparent during the Second World War. The BBC could and did become the mainstay of British overseas propaganda. Post-war investigations have shown that the BBC was far more effective than American facilities in reaching the Continental listener, whether it be a resister in France or a disaffected enemy national. Similar advantages were afterwards accruing to the British in the Cold War. Far from having to fight from appropriation to appropriation for its program, as is the fate of the "Voice of America," the BBC is in a position to execute government policy without any uninformed interference from Parliament or the public. "Close relations are maintained," we are told, "especially with the Foreign Office." Parliament, of course, could challenge the government in a major issue as always, but until it does, the BBC remains an effective tool of British policy in international affairs.[29]

The French, like the British, developed a governmental broadcasting monopoly from the outset. However, this monopoly was placed directly under the minister of the interior, rather than set up as an "independent" corporate entity. As a consequence, French broadcasting has been more and more monopolized by the government under De Gaule. The president himself has made continuous and skillful use of the facilities of the *Office de Radiodiffusion et Télévision Française* (*ORFT*), at times abusing his position as head of state for party-political purposes.

French opposition politicians, hampered by government influence in the *ORTF* look longingly at the BBC's relative independence of both political and commercial control. A 1964 reform removed the administration of the French radio and television system from the minister of the interior and placed it under a government-appointed general director and an administrative council. However, this slight liberalization was not considered a sufficient guarantee of objective and adequate coverage in the 1965 elections, when formal equal time allotments only partly compensated for the government's constant opportunity to assert its point of view. In the postelection furor, many called for an enlarging of government broadcasting to include several semi-independent stations on the German pattern. They saw a multiplicity of competing sources as the best way to promote different degrees of opinion. To some extent France is served by independent radio networks, such as Europe I and Radio Luxembourg, stationed outside France. In 1964 only 22 per cent of Frenchmen interviewed listened "most often" to one of the three French government stations. Forty-eight per cent listened to the independents. But as television comes to play a more and more crucial role in elections and daily news reporting, the influence of these outside organs may be diminished.[30] Certainly in the Assembly elections of 1965, television played a highly significant role, the full extent of which may not be known for some time.

In contrast to the unitary pattern of British and French broadcasting, the federal states of Switzerland and Germany have developed decentralized systems. Germany, to be sure, under the Weimar Republic and Hitler's regime had adopted the unitary pattern. But after the Second World War, and partly in response to the division into occupation zones, as well as American pressure, the Federal Republic developed a number of separate *Land*-financed radio stations which in the fifties were implemented by two television stations (a third, which the federal government under Adenauer sought to establish, was prevented by the opposition of the *Länder*). Located in the main population centers, such as Hamburg, Cologne, Stuttgart, Munich and so forth, these outfits, known as Southwest *Rundfunk,* West German *Rundfunk,* etc., have enjoyed a great deal of autonomy and have served partisan purposes only occasionally. Several of the leading directors (*Intendants*) have belonged to the opposition parties, and the competition among them is very pronounced.[31]

In Switzerland a rather complicated pattern has been evolved. Programming responsibilities in broadcasting have been since 1931 centered in the Swiss Broadcasting Corporation (*Société Suisse de Radiodiffusion* – SSR). This body depends, however, upon the operational cooperation of nine regional bodies, which have their own studios. There is one main program in each of Switzerland's languages: French, German and Italian. The technical services of three transmitters are handled by the postal administration, and there is a real effort made to maintain a reasonable equality of service, in spite of the fact that the German-speaking population is by far the largest (75 per cent). On the whole, educational broadcasting and television is most developed on the German programs, but political issues are handled discreetly and on a nonpartisan basis.[32]

The American system of broadcasting • The American system reflects the peculiarities in the general political pattern of the community, just as does the press. Indeed, the study of the control pattern of radio derives part of its fascination from the fact that it so strikingly mirrors the distribution of power in the community. The government was not, in America, in a position to assume outright control or operation of radio broadcasting; such governmentalism was quite unacceptable to the majority of the people in the twenties. As a consequence, since the wave lengths and hence the available facilities were limited, creating a natural monopoly, the government assumed the role of umpire in granting licenses for the use of these facilities, and in imposing certain conditions of financial responsibility and technical competence upon prospective licensees, but amplified these by the vague general standard that the facilities should be used "in the public convenience, interest, or necessity." Before the issues raised by this formula of regulation are explored more fully, the general pattern of control needs to be broadly outlined.

Radio broadcasting has remained essentially a business enterprise in the United States. Although the statute dealing with the licensing system enunciates the people's general claim to the "air,"[33] it vindicates that claim only in times of national emergency, when the President is given power to "suspend or amend, for such times as he may see fit, the rules and regulations . . . and cause the closing of any station for radio communication . . . or he may authorize the use or control of any such station . . . by any department of the Government." The radio broadcasters, the advertisers, the public, and the regulatory agency all share in the "control" of radio. Their control is divided in a complex way. The control is ultimately control of programs, that is, of the content of the broadcasts. An error frequently made by people is to assume that the control of facilities necessarily gives control over program content. Documentary evidence is quite scare, but the following general formula will give some indication of the distribution of control over programs. A large part of the programs are commercial; that is, they are sold to advertisers and hence are not political, since the big broadcasters do not sell time for "controversial" subjects. The latter are broadcast on "sustaining time"; that is, time not paid for, but contributed by the broadcasting company. It is on the latter programs that the interest of the student of politics must center. It is here that the broadcasters exercise their most definite control. Since the broadcasters' primary interest is the profitable use of their facilities, they exercise their control primarily where program content either increases or decreases listening. They are indifferent to programs which have little listener appeal, unless the programs arouse listener antagonism; the broadcasters prevent the appearance of such programs if they can. Advertisers, though not primarily concerned with sustaining programs, take a vivid interest in excluding from the air any programs that might be said to question the so-called "capitalist" system. Advertisers also interest themselves in moral issues. But the general impression that one can buy air time for popularizing particular minority views is erroneous, especially as far as the big networks are concerned. It is much more nearly possible on small stations. A striking illustration was provided by pro-Nazi and pro-Fascist broadcasts which came over quite a few local stations before the Second World War — broadcasts which could never have been offered over the big networks. Italian olive oil thus could become the vehicle for extolling the "grandeur that was Rome." The public participates in the control in two ways: as it is the general listening public, and as it participates in pressure groups that secure time for the airing of particular views. A good measure of the attitude of the public toward radio is owing to the fact that none of these pressure groups is satisfied with the amount of time nor with the latitude for the programs which they are able to secure. And yet the total amount of programming provided for by such groups in America is quite considerable. The general public's control, which broadcasters like to stress, is largely powerful in a negative way, in direct contrast to the interest groups. The latter succeed in getting on the air what would otherwise not be there; the general public keeps things off the air which might otherwise be present. It is the same kind of control that all customers exercise over the wares they buy. Their control canot be much more than the rejection of what they do not like, since they are not sufficiently informed about the medium or its potentialities to become aggressively and positively interested. Hence their judgment never can be taken to settle the positive merits of program content.

Federal regulation · Federal regulation of the broadcasting industry is built on the concept that "the air belongs to the people." The right to use a certain frequency is acquired under a license, and can be revoked for due cause. AM stations must submit to review and receive renewal of their license every three years, FM stations approximately every two. As a matter of fact, such revocations have been exceedingly rare for all but very small stations, but the government's power to revoke nevertheless continuously influences the broadcasters. Anticipating the reactions of the regulatory agency, station owners and managers stay within what they believe to be the government's concept of "public convenience, interest, and necessity." The regulatory power was exercised by the Federal Radio Commission between 1927 and 1934, and it has been in the hands of the Federal Communications Commission since that time. The Federal Communications Act charges the commission with a contradictory objective by imposing upon it the duty to see that broadcasters operate "in the public interest," etc., while at the same time outlawing "censorship." The act nowhere indicates how the commission is to determine whether a station has been operated in the public interest without considering the nature of the programs offered by the station. The explicit rule against censorship may have had a good effect, however, in that it has kept the commission from laying down positive rules for broadcasters. Any such good effect must be weighed against the disadvantage of encouraging, nay almost forcing, the broadcasters to do some tall guessing about the commission's views, and hence leaving everything to guesswork.

The act places enormous powers in the hands of the commissioners when it enables them to destroy the profitable and flourishing business of a good station management. The sparse use of the power has not prevented the regulatory agency from being the target of recurring charges of corrupt practices. Congressional debates are full of such charges, alleging that commissioners can be bought to license stations — in fact, that each commissioner has "his price." There have been perennial demands for investigation in Congress, but it is difficult to secure any adequate evidence either to prove or to disprove such charges.

What role, then, does the Federal Communications Commission play in determining program content? Since almost all its influence comes through what the broadcasters themselves anticipate to be its reactions, the role of the commission varies greatly. At times, as in the case of the wartime agitation over foreign-language broadcasting, the commission's anticipated views were practically decisive. At other times, broadcasters will feel so completely within the range of established broadcasting practices that they will not give the commission's views a single thought.

In 1946 the FCC created a considerable stir by the publication of a special report dealing with the public-service responsibility of broadcasters. While recognizing the primary responsibility of the broadcaster, the commission pointed out that it was "by statute required to review periodically the station's operation, in order to determine whether the station has in fact operated in the public interest." This was certainly an unassailable position; but when the commission went on to claim that "the establishment of sound station policy with respect to news, information, and the discussion of public issues is a major factor in operation in the public interest," it stepped into the hornet's nest of "censorship." Loud outcries were raised by the trade journals, even though the report showed clearly that the commission was primarily concerned with such matters as time distribution. "The carrying of any particular public discussion, of course, is a problem for the individual broadcaster. But the public interest clearly requires that an *adequate amount of time* be made available for the discussion of public issues." Yet investigations had shown that "few stations are staffed adequately to meet their responsibilities in serving the community . . . particularly at the local station level." In its summary and conclusions, the report appealed to the industry for more effective self-regulation, but also emphasized the responsibility of individual licensees. The commission in addition called for the development of radio critics, the establishment of radio-listener councils, and the participation by colleges and universities through workshops and research. But above all, the commission reasserted its own responsibility in determining whether licenses should be renewed, and indicated four factors which would be of especial concern to it in this task: (1) the carrying of sustaining programs so as to balance progam structure; (2) the carrying of local live programs; (3) discussion of public issues; and (4) advertising excesses.[34]

There is also, of course, the problem of monopoly. In 1940, the FCC embarked upon an ambitious program of counteracting what it described as "monopolistic practices" in the broadcasting field. In June of that year it released a preliminary committee report, which it followed by a formal "Report on Chain Broadcasting" in May 1941.[35] In these reports the commission ordered discontinued certain practices which were mainstays of the great national networks, such as the exclusive contractual relationships between a network and its affiliates. It threatened that it would refuse to grant licenses to stations which did not obey its orders. The objective of the commission in making this attack appeared to be to insure "competition." It is an understandable, and yet a curious, objective. Certainly the broadcasting industry combines monopolist practices with the fiercest competition. In fact, this competition, whatever its results, has been the outstanding feature of the American system of broadcasting, and most of this competition is network competition. The situation is not unlike that in the newspaper field, with its multiplication of columnists and other features. The reason one local paper after another finds itself obliged to go in for these syndicated materials is "reader demand." The local stuff rarely can compete.

The development of radio commentators is generally speaking of great importance. Owing to the responsiveness of press and radio to "public appeal," these commentators are "popularly elected" almost as definitely as are the political leaders of the country. They represent a most interesting extension of democracy into the field of thought. Being in continuous contact with the masses, they act as popular tribunes in our contemporary society, and thus restrain those who in government and politics are clothed with the more traditional symbols of authority.

For years after its "Mayflower" decision in 1941, the FCC held to the view that radio broadcasters must, especially in news broadcasts, avoid the expression of political views. That case had arisen over the highly colored broadcasts of a crusading-editor type, attacking local politicians in Boston, over the local Yankee Network. The politicians organized a company to seek the radio license of the network's Boston station on the ground that its broadcasts were not "in the public interest, convenience and necessity." The FCC, while turning down the "Mayflower" group, enunciated the principle that broacasters must abstain from this sort of pronounced partisanship. In 1947 the FCC reversed itself on this issue and "permitted" a certain amount of such partisanship. While hailed by the industry as a contribution to "freedom of the air," it has not radically changed the actual content of American broadcasting.

Educational broadcasting • Educational broadcasting has been a real problem under the American system. It has been called its "stepchild." Ever since radio broadcasting began, educators in schools, colleges, and universities, in adult education centers and in civic groups, have sought to make effective use of the new medium. Their efforts have been crowned by only a moderate degree of success, but very recently, and in light of the tremendous influence of television, plans have appeared for a much more comprehensive and tax-supported educational broadcasting. Foundations and Congressional committees have added their weighty voices. For the broadcasters themselves, this field has from the beginning been a difficult one. They have admitted that a well-balanced program should include education. A number of universities have operated stations of their own; so-called schools of the air have been organized; regional councils have been active in the field. But the largest part of such broadcasting has remained the uneasy task of commercial broadcasters. In order to promote greater attention, the Federal Communications Commission has organized various undertakings, such as the early Federal Radio Education Committee of 1935. It has encouraged stations and networks to give sustained attention to the problem. But the disinclination of broadcasters to touch any "political" issues has left educational broadcasting and television without any serious focus in matters of primary civic concern. The National Association of Educational Broadcasters, which has sought since the early days to strengthen educational broadcasting, has been inclined to avoid the proverbial "hot potato" which would be at the core of civic education.

By the sixties, there were 104 educational stations in the field which "have produced Ionesco for every man, revolutionized the teaching of high school and college physics, and . . . made French cooking an American pastime."[36] But such worthy activities contribute little to American government and politics. It is different with so-called "public affairs broadcasting" — a field which the commercial broadcasters have, of course, also cultivated, especially in the newscast. But the question is whether there could not be analysis of real academic depth and competence to explore current history. There has been a certain amount of such analysis on many an educational station for years. Educational Television (ETV), if placed on a really large-scale footing, as recent developments seem to suggest,[37] might have a profound long-range impact on the caliber of American politics. One of its main spokesmen has claimed that "it is a force that is going to do things to the community." Obviously, if this were to happen, ETV would help reshape the future of American political behavior and thought. Such a prospect is not welcomed by all academics. But its implications could be very great.

Political television and the Great Debates · During the fifties, television emerged as the great new factor in democratic politics; it came into its own in the sixties. The presidential elections in the United States and France, the parliamentary elections in Great Britain and Germany, as well as the conduct of the government in these leading Western countries, have been increasingly influenced by political television.[38] While no definitive proof has been given, it is generally agreed that the poor showing of President de Gaulle in the first tour of his bid for re-election in 1965 may have been at least in part accounted for by the sudden emergence on the television screen of rival personalities with a definite electoral appeal. A recent study of American experience comments in conclusion that "we are on the verge of a television environment that will lead future observers to comment that we conducted politics in a rather primitive fashion." Maybe so, but in any case television has brought politics into the parlor of practically every home in the United States in a way never possible before. Nothing showed this more dramatically than the "Great Debates" between two untried rivals for the presidency in 1960.

These "debates" took place at short intervals on September 26, October 7, October 13, and October 21, 1960. According to one renowned American commentator, they were neither great nor debates. They were staged as a kind of joint press conference with the two candidates, John F. Kennedy and Richard M. Nixon, and thus gave the audience — between 55 and 75 million in the United States alone — an opportunity to assess the personalities of the two candidates "under fire." Even so, it is probably true that they advanced the level of public political education. Yet Theodore White has remarked that "the TV debates did little to advance the reasonable discussion of issues . . ."[39]

An appraisal of the various problems raised by these television debates on the part of a commission of the American Political Science Association in 1963 came to conclusions that might be summed up as follows: (1) debates are desirable, but when one of the candidates is President, they may not be. (2) There should be weekly debates, and they should include others of the candidates' teams. (3) Besides debates, there should be discussions. (4) There should be called into being a supervisory council of professionals in law, political science, economics, etc. (5) This board should determine format and participants in consultation with the candidates. (6) There should be representation of minor parties on at least one program. (7) Radio rebroadcasting should be provided. (8) Visual aids might be introduced. (9) Saturday evenings would be best. (10) The encounters should be in a studio. (11) There should be research to test the effectiveness. (12) Congress should remove legal obstacles. In questioning members of Congress, the commission had found that there was widespread doubt about the wisdom of having an incumbent President participate in such a program. Finally, they said that "Television debates are not likely to become the sole method of campaigning for the presidency. Nor should they." It remains to be seen whether the Kennedy-Nixon debates will remain as unique an instance as were the Lincoln-Douglas debates a century earlier.[40]

Press and propaganda in wartime • The division between constitutional and nonconstitutional systems of government in the field of propaganda and communication, while of great importance in differentiating these two types of government, tends to become blurred in wartime. In both the First and the Second World War, democratic governments found themselves compelled to institute official propaganda on a large scale, to operate official censorship, and to exercise a substantial amount of control over all means of communication. The old Latin dictum, *inter arma leges silent,* applies with peculiar force to the constitutional law of freedom of expression. Mr. Justice Holme's famous criterion of "clear and present danger" is broadly applicable to wartime situations (see above, ch. IX). This, however, holds only when the war involves a country's survival, i.e., becomes "total." During the Korean and Vietnam wars public criticism has been rife in the United States, and the same holds true for the Algerian war in France, and the Suez "war" in both France and England. While the general problems raised by such emergencies will be dealt with below, some special aspects relating to the press and other means of mass communication may well be remarked upon here.

Basically, all problems revolve around the central wartime objective of how to defeat the enemy. Opposition to this objective will not be tolerated by a democratic community, even as a minority right, to any considerable extent, when the danger is real. The more desperate the struggle becomes, the more disinclined will be the majority to allow any serious dissent. Hence, competition will be replaced by monopolistic control wherever these vital wartime issues are involved. This raises the central problem of informational strategy: how can information be made a part of the grand strategy of a total war?[41]

During the Second World War, the information services in the United States, especially the Office of War Information, took the line that the problem could be resolved in terms of the "strategy of the truth" or "the propaganda of truth." It was claimed that this was democracy's answer to the incessant barrage of totalitarian phrases, slogans, and word-symbols. Truth, it was said, will fight our battles for us in the great struggle for the mind of mankind. Insofar as the propaganda of truth is merely a rejection of the propaganda of lies, it has much to recommend it. Every propagandist worth his mettle will use the truth in preference to lies whenever he can — even a Dr. Goebbels. And a determination to avoid saying anything when you would have to lie is admittedly the better part of wisdom in a democracy, where public, especially parliamentary, discussion even in wartime is relatively free and hence apt to uncover lies rather quickly. "Lies have short legs," a German proverb says.

But the decision to avoid telling lies does not give us a positive standard as to what to say. What information to give out relative to the many happenings in any war calls for more selective principles than the proposition that we shall tell the truth. Also, in important situations there remains Pilate's old query: "What is truth?" Demagogues may orate: "Give us the facts, all the facts, and nothing but the facts," but the student of the contemporary social scene knows that it is impossible to live up to any such directive.

In short, the slogan about the strategy of the truth does not offer us an answer to our need for a strategy that would make the best use of all available information for the winning of the war. Indeed, no simple formula will do the trick. Informational strategy, like all strategy, calls for a clear analysis of the functional relation between such information and the task in hand. Like all weapons, information has a task to perform in a comprehensive undertaking such as "victory."

Victory, in the democratic perspective, means (1) the defeat of the enemy, and (2) the making of a better peace, that is to say, the establishment of a social order sounder and more workable than the one which issued in war. Informational strategy which neglects the second part in pursing the first part of this total objective is false and will lead to disaster, as did the propaganda carried on by the Committee on Public Information in the First World War.

Unfortunately, no such counsels were followed by those responsible for government propaganda during the Second World War. Who is willing to assert today that the American people were told "the truth" about the Soviet Union, about China, about democracy? Or that it was wise, or necessary, to broadcast misrepresentations in the face of conclusive evidence to the contrary? If one ask oneself what are the ingredients of an informational strategy that might have avoided such grave errors, the following criteria suggest themselves: war requires the considerable backing of a majority of a nation, and any public policy calling for action on the part of a number of people should be considered a battle which can be won only if advance preparations are made to prepare the people involved for the actions to be taken by them. This calls for :(1) research to determine whether prejudices, ignorance, or other grounds obstruct the likelihood of such action being taken when requested; (2) the channeling out of information in such amounts as will overcome these obstructions; (3) further research to determine whether the information is being absorbed and is having the desired effect; (4) announcing the policy in such a manner as to anticipate the major obstructions by highlighting the information previously broadcast.

Any program of channeling out information to prepare for a proposed policy of the government is bound to encounter a variety of difficulties resulting from counterpropaganda unloosed by hostile special-interest groups. It is one of the most important tasks of effective informational strategy to determine what these groups are and to anticipate their campaigns by appropriate information which would be designed to "blanket" their slanted statements, rumors, and the like. Rigid rules for such strategy cannot be formulated, because the strategy needs to be shaped in the light of the total situation.

It is generally agreed that political warfare seeks to accomplish two things, (1) to undermine the enemy's will to fight and (2) to undermine the will of allies of the enemy to support him. A special case of the latter is the task of diverting neutrals from the enemy and turning them into more or less active supporters of one's own cause. It is evident that these tasks call for a concrete and realistic understanding of *who is the enemy* and *who are his allies*. A great deal depends upon doing this with the necessary precision and accuracy, especially in a revolutionary age. No effective informational strategy can be devised unless the addresses of such information are known.

On the whole, it is fair to say that the United States and her allies were more successful with the second than with the first objective. The United States Bombing Survey's Morale Division was able to show afterwards how limited were the achievements in undermining the enemy's will to fight. In part the difficulty resulted from the failure to define the enemy clearly. Fascists and anti-Fascists were often treated alike. Informational strategy could conceivably become the way of going about propaganda objectives in a democracy. It could be made compatible with the basic limitations of governmental propaganda in a free country, even when at war. But this result is not likely to be achieved if the direction of such efforts is in the hands of men who do not understand the issues involved. The deleterious effect of both world wars upon the functioning of constitutional democracy is in no small degree traceable to the unrestrained, and at times totalist, handling of the necessary propaganda machinery, both in facing one's own people and when adddressing the enemy.

Governmental control and censorship · All governments have had recourse to censorship in wartime. Where the immediate danger was small and popular fervor considerable, as in the United States during the First World War, such censorship did not have to be carried very far. In England and France, where opposition to the war developed almost immediately after the outbreak of hostilities and gradually became more and more insistent, censorship was applied with considerable rigidity, and more so in France than in England. Long white columns in many French papers attested to the effectiveness of the working of this machine. Clemenceau, who chafed under these restrictions, published his paper *L'Homme Libre* under the significant new title *L'Homme Enchaîné* after the censor had deleted one of his editorials. During the Algerian war, editions of newspapers containing accounts of torture or other news damaging to the government were seized, but essential facts circulated anyway. The censorship imposed on themselves by most newspapers in order to avoid such seizure did, however, seriously limit popular understanding of the war.[42] Since this time, much of French censorship has been conducted under a nineteenth-century statute barring attacks on the president. It is hoped that these prosecutions will diminish, for while censorship may be used for a brief period, it is highly unsatisfactory as a control mechanism.

In a sense the war merely highlighted issues of longer standing. The capitalist basis of the press in free societies has been a source of contention which recent American elections have merely emphasized. There can be little doubt that a press largely hostile to the present popular trend in favor of the welfare state, and consequently oblivious to what is believed by many to be the public interest, raises very serious difficulties in a democratic age. The present state of affairs cannot be looked upon with indifference. The public at large is increasingly dissatisfied with the newspapers. In towns where a single individual controls the one or more papers, intolerable conditions can easily develop. But a constructive solution is difficult. Few would advocate a licensing system, such as was instituted in conquered

Austria, Germany, and Japan. Recent emergencies have intensified the issue.

The new constitutions in Europe vary in their approach to the problem. The French constitution is silent in the matter. The Italian constitution, in Article 21, after outlawing censorship, admits nevertheless that publications as well as shows and demonstrations that are 'contrary to good morals" are forbidden. Even more pioneering are the provisions of the German Basic Law. While outlawing censorship in Article 5 and guaranteeing freedom of the press, of radio and motion picture reporting, Article 18 declares that anyone abusing freedom of expression in order to attack the free democratic basis and order shall forfeit his basic rights (see above, ch. IX) by judgment of the constitutional court. It is difficult to see how the court is to carry out this difficult and dangerous duty without inquiring into the content of publications and other communications with a view to determining whether they do attack the free democratic order; in other words, they are called upon to institute *ex post facto* censorship. This attempt at judicial determination of what is admissible in the field of press and communication resembles the common-law tradition in the matter of libel discussed above. It constitutes an interesting attempt to avoid administrative control. For outright administrative control, particularly in matters of public policy, defeats itself because it undermines the confidence of the public. In course of time it would be inevitable that the same results would follow such administrative interference on the part of a constitutional government as have followed in dictatorial regimes. These problems of the control of channels of communication, and particularly those of the news, are, for technical reasons, inescapable in the sphere of radio broadcasting, but they present themselves for all mass-communication media. Everywhere the public is aware of the fact that we are not settling the political problems which are involved in these situations merely by insisting that the government not interfere. In fact, those groups which oppose the present order of things are emphatic in their demand for precisely such governmental interference. From the standpoint of the scientific analyst, both arguments are misleading, one because it treats private capital as a neutral control, the other because it treats the government as a neutral control. Whether we think of the newsreel, broadcasting, or the press, in every instance we are facing the same set of problems in contemporary constitutional systems.[43] How can we prevent the exclusive control of these channels of communication, and therefore of public opinion, by any one of the contending groups?

It deserves note that mass communications have a great role to play in integrating emergent political communities. In such undertakings the propaganda is taken for granted, as it is vitally related to the function of these media and their control. But there is frequently a lack of understanding of the very grave dangers which such a monolithic and governmentally manipulated system of mass communications constitutes for the development of a constitutional democracy such as is usually considered the goal of these developing countries.[44]

Conclusion · Grave difficulties threaten constitutional democracy from a commercialized press that lacks responsibility, and from other mass-communication channels, especially broadcasting and the movies.[45] Equally great dangers must be faced from an extension of governmental controls in these fields. The democratizing efforts of the United States and Britain have further emphasized the issues and difficulties. But an attentive perusal of the growing literature does not produce the impression that a simple solution to these growing difficulties is very likely. The Commission on the Freedom of the Press, actually concerned as it was with freedom of all mass-communication channels, struck a surprisingly hopeful note when it announced that the problems have been pretty well worked out as far as the restrictive activities of the government are concerned. The crux of the problem of the control of mass communications in contemporary society is their deleterious effect upon the beliefs which are vital to the life of free societies. To trace the vicious circle by which every new technique begets a new servitude is the primary task; the commission miserably failed in this vital task. In reading these reports, one had the impression of being in some fairyland. It seemed as if the problems of constitutional democracy were not confronting us at all.

Constitutional government rests upon the provision of effective restraints on the exercise of institutionalized power. The press of today is thoroughly institutionalized in its corporate structure, and yet we talk about it simply in terms of individual liberty. We realize its representative position, particularly in such cases as *The Times* (London) or *Le Monde*, yet we have not evolved any effective technique for coping with the problems involved. To be sure, an attempt has been made in England to nationalize *The Times* by making it a trust akin to the great universities. But this solution does not face the most pressing problem of all: class control versus governmental control. It is not the task of the present volume to suggest concrete practical measures in this any more than in any other field of political activity. It may be permissible, however, to indicate certain contemporary trends and to comment upon them in conclusion. Various methods which have been suggested for constitutionally restraining the press all amount to administrative censorship. Constitutionally apart, censorship raises the problem of standards, which is insoluble in a constitutional democracy. There is no group which is recognized as knowing what is good for the rest. The Second World

War brought a temporary censorship, but the experiences during that war as well as during the First World War and under dictatorial regimes since that time do not encourage further experimentation along that line. Censorship in particular fields, as it is practiced in many American states, is almost as unqualified a failure. How, then, shall we ensure that the press is really free, that it is not the instrument for propagandizing the views of one class as against that of others? This question has been asked time and again by thoughtful students of modern journalism. It is not easy to suggest answers. One suggested remedy would be the breaking up of trusts and monopolies. You could perhaps try to withdraw the legal foundation of the large-scale newspaper chain by appropriate changes in corporation law.

The exigencies of modern news gathering and the costs of a modern plant would still render the press subject to some of its owner's "inarticulate major premise." The radio, of course, has provided important competition and has thus in recent years contributed to the progress of the press. But, as has been shown, the broadcasting industry, in turn, is influenced by the same major premises. Indeed, advertisers have an even more complete hold, and the "editorial judgment" of the broadcaster is exercised under conditions varying widely from those prevailing in the press.[46]

In spite of these differences, there is a broad similarity. This similarity results from two common, unproved major premises, (1) that news is purely factual and hence not influenced by the general political outlook of the owners of communication media, and (2) that such communication media depend for their success primarily upon their users, readers, listeners. These make-believes, though certainly possessing a kernel of reality, are even in their more fanciful forms important factors in rendering the owners and operators of such media responsive to public criticism, preferences, and tastes. This general view is, as has been pointed out, peculiarly an American conception. It is a symbol of democratic virtue. No study of the realities of communication control can afford to neglect it, even when it makes allowances for the element of pure myth which it contains.

Direct Popular Action

XXIV

Introduction · Rousseau's objections to elected representatives · The Napoleonic plebiscites · The referendum and initiative: Switzerland · The referendum in the United States · Direct popular action and the general problem of representation · Plebiscites before the First World War · Plebiscites after 1918 · Postwar constitutional referendums in Europe · Conclusion

Introduction · Propaganda and the effects of the mass-communication media are, as we have seen, of great importance as factors causing stresses and strains within the fabric of modern constitutionalism. Apart from re-adjustments peculiar to their field of operation, such as constitutional limitations upon the rights of anticonstitutional forces, a more direct participation of the electorate in the major decisions of policy has suggested itself as a remedy. Indeed, the ever-recurring problem of "legitimacy," that is, the question of how authority can be made to appear legitimate to those over whom it is wielded, seemed to many ardent democrats at the beginning of the twentieth century to call for an ever-greater extension of personal participation of as many citizens as possible in as many decisions as possible. Basic constitutional questions and crucial issues of foreign policy, especially going to war, are, it was thought, particularly suitable for direct submission to the people. The activating of the citizen seemed further to suggest that any substantial group of them should be in a position to put a law before the electorate at large.[1]

The dictators of this century, following the example of Napoleon, have in turn relied upon such referendums or plebiscites for legitimizing their unconstitutional and anticonstitutional regimes. Such direct popular approval provides an impressive facade for the dictatorial *coup d'état* and can be used against democratic opposition at home and abroad on the pretense that "the will of the people" has been consulted.[2] That true freedom for this will of the people presupposes available alternatives is an aspect usually obscured in the shuffle of claims and counterclaims, though it should be obvious to all.

Securing popular acclaim by plebiscitary appeal has become a distinct trend in stabilized constitutional systems. The general elections in Britain and the presidential elections in the United States have exhibited an increasing plebiscitary character, as noted earlier. In Continental Europe, the reconstruction of constitutionalism has brought new incentives for such direct popular action. Where the basis of traditional legitimacy has disappeared, an appeal to the people sounds like a solution. Thus the sharp disagreements among members of the French Resistance, and between them and De Gaulle as well as the older leadership of the Third Republic, was resolved by a referendum on October 21, 1945. In this case, the electorate was asked to decide between three alternatives: revival of the old constitution, establishment of an all-powerful constituent assembly, or formation of a more restricted assembly with limited powers of provisional government. Since the war, increasing antiparliamentarism in France has resulted in a markedly greater use of referendums. Two instances for its use are provided for in the present French constitution. In marked contrast, the Germans, discouraged by the abuse of such appeals under the Weimar Republic and Hitler, have avoided them in their Basic Law. Efforts to revive them on hotly contested issues were rejected by the constitutional court.[3]

All this is in sharp conflict with the early hopes and aspirations associated with referendum and initiative which first manifested itself when provisions for a popular referendum (incorporated in the Swiss constitution of 1874) spread rapidly through the United States after the turn of the century. In Switzerland, direct popular action had remained the traditional form of political activity in some of the small rural cantons, and the modern referendum was an adaptation of these methods to more numerous electoral bodies.

Rousseau's objections to elected representatives • The great apostle of democracy, Jean Jacques Rousseau, had strenuously objected to the employment of representative assemblies for the purpose of enacting legislation;[4] the argument that Rousseau accepts magistrates does not go to the heart of the issue. For laws, he felt, were so important that they must be a genuine expression of the general will, of sovereignty, and he felt that representatives pervert the "general will" (see above, ch. XV). The complexities of Rousseau's doctrine of the general will are great. The general will seems to refer to an objective given, like the general interest, rather than to the subjective element of will. There are many passages in Rousseau which carry the implication that the general will is the voice of reason, others which suggest that it expresses the choices of a concrete, living superentity, an organism which is acting and deciding for itself. The vote of a majority of the individuals composing it is merely an indication of what this will might be. The good citizen, when participating in such a vote, should not ask himself what *he* wants, but what is good for the community. That voters do not actually do this is apparent enough. Hence Rousseau on one hand would restrict democracy to small units, such as the Swiss cantons; he would also leave room for the constitutional dictator and the great legislator of Greek antiquity.[5] On one hand, then, the general will is not merely the dictates of right reason in the traditional sense of rationalism and natural law; on the other, it is not the will of the majority. Even so, Rousseau believed that a majority of the citizens were the most promising source for discovering this general will.

Rousseau's animosity to representative assemblies may perhaps be explained by his observations in Switzerland, where the aristocratic government of Geneva contrasted strongly with the simple democracy of the rural cantons. Indeed, his attempt to resuscitate the older democratic forms in his essay on the government of Geneva (for which he was exiled) stands as a vivid reminder of his intense interest in these contrasts. The general idea of radical and direct democracy and the gradual spread of the referendum as an instrument of practical democracy in the second half of the nineteenth century are parallel developments mutually intensifying each other.

The Napoleonic plebiscites · Rousseau's views were applied in the course of the French revolution, or so it seemed to the actors on the revolutionary stage. The Committee on Public Safety claimed to act on behalf of the general public because the members were supposed to be subject to recall by the public at large. Unhappily, it remained quite obscure how this public was supposed to swing into action, since every opponent of the committee promptly landed on the guillotine. Such a condition could not long be endured; but the efforts toward returning to a constitutional order ended in the ascendancy of Napoleon Bonaparte, who in turn claimed to be the executor of the general will on behalf of the people, thus fulfilling the role of the (divine) legislator whom Rousseau had envisaged as a necessary corrective of human frailty in large political bodies. Napoleon, however, who in his youth had been deeply attached to the doctrines of Rousseau and had rendered a measure of lip service to them all his life, went further than the Committee on Public Safety had done.[6] At certain crucial moments in his career, such as his election to remain first consul for life and his assumption of the position of emperor, he called for popular plebiscites which would indicate what the public thought about these changes. Such was the theory. In practice, open registers produced a large measure of coercion, and the percentage of favorable votes was correspondingly high. In the first of these plebiscites it was found, on August 2, 1802, that 3,568,885 Frenchmen had voted "yes," and only 8374 "no," on the proposal of making Napoleon consul for life. In spite of local frauds, these figures are generally believed to be accurate. Undoubtedly the prefects and military officials exerted extensive pressure, but on the whole the vote was due to Napoleon's victories and the re-establishment of the church. The second plebiscite produced similar results. Assent to the establishment of an hereditary empire was given by 3,372,329 voters, while only 2569 objected. In this case we know Napoleon himself corrected the result, and the number of abstaining objectors may have been appreciably larger. There was also a great deal of local fraud. Voters who could not write were summarily reported by the authorities, and no real vote ever took place. A good many cases of actual intimidation are known. To proclaim such a popular vote an expression of the general will was a sordid sham, or a bad joke.

When the third Napoleon executed his *coup d'état* in 1851, he at once revived the practice of his illustrious uncle and ordered a plebiscite to be held on the question of whether the French people approved of his action. They did. On December 31, 1851, an electoral commission could report to the new dictator that 7,439,216 people had voted in the affirmative, and 640,737 in the negative. This dissent of about 7 per cent of the voting citizens considerably exceeds the opposition under the first Napoleon. The technique of open registers was discarded when loud protests were raised against it, but almost the same results were achieved by supplying only an insufficient number of ballots with "no" printed on them so that those who wished to object were obliged to write out their votes, which made them readily recognizable. It is now generally believed that the vote as reported is fairly accurate; nor is the difference between it and the vote given to Napoleon at the time of his election to the presidency (1848) so large as to imply the extensive use of force. A later plebiscite instituted to legitimize the elevation of Napoleon to emperor yielded similar results, though the actual percentage of negative votes was smaller. There were 7,824,189 votes for and 253,145 against the empire, or only about 3 per cent negative. But the abstentions are reported as amounting to 2,062,789. In certain parts of France, like the Vendée and the Rhone valley, they ran to 40 per cent and over. Just the same, Napoleon seems to have gained further adherents and could claim solid popular support. When, in the course of the evolution of the empire toward a measure of liberalism, a limited parliamentary regime was to be instituted in 1870, the proposed constitutional change was again submitted to a plebiscite. This time the outcome was more equivocal, which is important since the electorate had come to look upon the vote in terms rather of endorsing the government of Napoleon than in terms of the proposed liberalization. Particularly in the cities this plebiscite revealed massive opposition. To a considerable extent, this opposition came also, of course, from those followers of Napoleon who believed in the thoroughly authoritarian and dictatorial conduct of the government. Indeed, on the night of the plebiscite, when the first returns were coming in, things looked very black; for in Paris and the Seine department there were 138,000 "yes" votes, 184,000 "no" votes, 83,000 abstentions, and about 10,000 invalid votes. But the rural population solidly supported the Napoleonic dictatorship. For the whole of France there were 7,358,786 affirmative votes, and 1,571,939 negative ones, with about 2,000,000 abstentions and invalid votes. It will be seen that the latter remained about the same, but that about 20 per cent of the voters at this juncture turned out against the empire. The government did not attach too much importance to this trend. Yet within a year the empire had collapsed and its inner hollowness had been revealed.

The referendum and initiative: Switzerland · In Switzerland, direct popular action was put to a very different use.[7] The radically democratic elements fostered it as a curb on the ruling Liberals. After a rapid spread of the movement in the cantons during the sixties, the referendum (and the initiative) were embodied in the constitution in 1874. They were organized according to ancient traditions as a restraint upon the governmental agencies established under the constituoin. To consult the majority of the people at large as well as the majority of the people as divided into cantons was made obligatory in all matters affecting the constitution itself. Moreover, with sufficient backing any matter could be embodied in the constitution through a popular initiative followed by a referendum. Both methods have been extensively used since that time and a considerate judgment is possible today. According to a leading authority on Swiss constitutional development, Professor Marcel Bridel, direct democracy's most important decisions after 1874 were the initiative of 1891 for a partial constitutional revision, the referendum of 1921 on international treaties, and a proposal in 1939 to revise the provisions which the emergency clause contained.[8]

There can be little question that the methods of direct popular action as used in Switzerland are working fairly satisfactorily. It has been rightly remarked that in Switzerland the popular votes have tended to be on the conservative side, but in certain matters of social reform they have tended to favor progressive measures, such as the referendum on compulsory insurance for workingmen (1891), or the law for the purchase of railroads by the government (1900). When such measures tended unduly to enhance the power of the central government, they were, before the First World War, rejected, as happened to the constitutional amendment to extend the power of the federal government to uniform legislation on trades (1894), or the constitutional amendment for direct federal taxation (1918).

Since that time, the trend has been toward increasing governmentalism. This is especially true of the referendum of 1947 on "economic questions." By this comprehensive referendum, the growing governmentalism (*étatisme*) of Switzerland was sanctioned. This constitutional revision eliminated a great many inherent contradictions between the constitution and legislation of an "interventionist" sort. Many of the fields of activity associated with the progressive and New Deal legislation in the United States as well as with those of national (military) security were sanctioned by the Swiss people (556,803 for, 494,414 against) and the road cleared for a closely regulated market economy.

Since 1848 there have been fifty-five proposals for partial revision originating as federal legislation. Of these proposals, thirty-eight have been accepted by subsequent referendums and seventeen have been rejected. The percentage of rejections steadily declined; perhaps this was due to an increasing willingness on the part of the federal assembly not to introduce constitutional-amendment proposals unless there was a reasonable chance of success.

The obligatory referendum procedure is implemented, as noted above, by a constitutional initiative according to which 50,000 voters can demand a constitutional amendment. It has been said that this method acts as a spur in the flanks of the legislative steed, while the obligatory referendum is a bit in the mouth. The constitutional initiative finds favor with the voters less often than does the obligatory referendum, even though the percentage of voting is somewhat higher. The fact of the matter is that the initiative proceedings are employed for highly controversial subjects such as the right to work and the duty of the government to provide work (1894), or the estate tax (1922). With the present method, dating from 1891, there had been thirty-nine such initiative proposals, and of these thirty had been rejected, down to 1951. Economic and social measures have been the most frequent subjects of initiative and obligatory referendums. After an initial period of extreme proposals, the measures put forward under the initiative procedure have on the whole been moderately progressive. They have helped in the process of democratic popular education; they have given the Swiss people a feeling that the constitution is theirs for the making and unmaking. This means that not infrequently an initiative which was rejected has given rise to a counterproposal by the legislature which may then be submitted to the people, like the question of private manufacture of armaments in 1938. A proposal for the total revision of the constitution was made by initiative in 1935, but decisively rejected by the electorate. Nevertheless, in the opinion of Swiss students of their constitution, there are increasing signs of "old age"; the constitution of 1874 is proving more and more inadequate for the age of government participation in the economy, for it was conceived in the heyday of liberalism. The broad revision obtained through the amendment of 1947 would seem to prove the viability of the constitutional system, however. Similar methods prevail throughout the majority of the cantons. The federal constitution requires cantonal constitutions to be submitted to popular referendum. Initiative also is found in many of them. Thus the problem of constitutional amendment, always a thorny question in connection with constitutions (see above, ch. VIII, p. 142 ff.), has found a significant solution.

Direct popular action, however, is not limited to constitutional amendments. The constitution also provides for a referendum on important legislative proposals if eight cantons or 30,000 voters demand it. It is reported that of three hundred and thirty laws and resolutions which might have been subjected to such a referendum, thirty-five were actually so tested down to 1922, and of them nineteen failed of acceptance. Between 1922 and 1940, thirteen statutes were subjected to referendum, and ten of these were rejected by the voters. These were not necessarily the most important measures, but rather the ones which had aroused popular interest. While the federal constitution does not recognize a corresponding right to initiate legislation, this is provided for in many of the cantonal constitutions and is extensively used. The percentage of the voters whose signatures are required varies between 3.09 per cent in the canton of Basel Stadt to 12.77 per cent in the canton of Schwyz. In the federal realm, where the actual numbers are fixed at 30,000 and 50,000, the percentage has varied from about 12.5 per cent in 1848 to 6.1 per cent in 1910 (for iniative petitions). During the same period, the participation in these forms of direct popular action has been changing downward in the case of compulsory referendums, upward in the case of initiative and optional referendums. Optional referendums and initiative proceedings are extensively propagandized beforehand in connection with the collection of the necessary signatures for the petition, while the obligatory referendums come from the legislature with the official approval which tends to insure them success at the hands of the electorate. Swiss experience has been well summarized in the following phrases: "Direct legislation in Switzerland has not realized all the extravagant anticipations of its friends. But on the other hand it has completely falsified the dismal prophecies of chaos and revolution uttered by the conservatives of an earlier period. It has become a vital and freely functioning part of the Swiss political organism."[9] The recurrent refusal of the general electorate to sanction constitutional and legislative measures designed to benefit particular groups suggests that the referendum is an integrating mechanism, where the representative bodies may be inclined to yield to the pressure of particular interest groups. This, however, does not always work.

We cannot close this discussion without brief mention of a further extension of the referendum system in Switzerland — that is, the addition, in 1921, of a constitutional provision to the effect that treaties with foreign powers must, when requested, be submitted to a referendum if they are concluded for more than fifteen years. There can be little question that this provision is a logical consequence of the idea that the popular referendum is the truest expression of the popular will and should therefore be applied to all really important matters. Even before the enactment of this provision the referendum had been used in connection with the entry of Switzerland into the League of Nations (1920). Indeed, this entry was accepted by a very narrow majority of 56.3 per cent of those voting, with 77.5 per cent of those entitled to vote participating in this decision which involved Switzerland's venerable "neutrality. A later treaty, which was to settle the long-drawn-out controversy between France and Switzerland concerning their boundary, was rejected by the electorate. Whether this decision was a wise one and augurs well for the application of direct popular action in the field of international affairs is very questionable. The percentages against the proposed treaty were very high in many cantons, but they were significantly lowest in the cantons most immediately affected, Fribourg and Vaud actually having a majority in favor, and Geneva almost so (48.9 per cent).

In recent years, the marked conservatism of the Swiss electorate has manifested itself in such matters as women's vote and entry into the European Council and Common Market. In both these cases, however, slow but steady progress is to be noted.

The referendum in the United States · The constitutional referendum was first employed in Massachusetts in 1788 and again in connection with the ratification of the federal constitution, through the intermediary of conventions popularly elected for this purpose, and hence providing a kind of referendum. But while it disappeared in the United States for almost a hundred years, it was developed and extended in Switzerland, as we have seen. To it was added the initiative in both constitutional and ordinary legislation, and toward the end of the century these various methods for direct popular action were reintroduced into the United States, there to sweep through the several states, beginning with Oregon in 1904.[10] On the whole, the experience has been the same as in Switzerland; neither the ardent hopes of its first expounders nor the dire apprehensions of its opponents have materialized. Both referendum and initiative have become recognized parts of the American political machinery. But whereas in Switzerland referendum and initiative have been employed extensively in national affairs, in the United States they have so far been used only in the states. To be sure, at least one of the methods for constitutional amendment is a form of indirect popular referendum, for special conventions, as provided for in Article V, would presumably act in accordance with a popular mandate.

We find, in the several states and in many different forms and combinations, referendum, both compulsory and optional, and initiative, the latter two applicable to legislation as well as to constitutional amendment. Compulsory referenda are the most frequently used of these methods. It is said that during the ten years from 1899 to 1908, 472 constitutional questions were submitted to the electorates of forty-three states, and from 1919 to 1925 more than 600 such measures were thus voted upon. The optional referendum (also called popular referendum) was put to the test, between 1906 and 1925, 173 times in sixteen states. Finally, the initiative was brought into play 440 times during the same period, but of these, 120 times in Oregon. A few states with a highly developed interest in direct popular action, such as Oregon and California, contribute a considerable part of the total. As in Switzerland' we find that the optional referendum and the initiative elicit a higher percentage of voter interest than the compulsory referendum. Regarding the latter, the figures are very discouraging, rising only in a few localities above 50 per cent of the vote for governor, for example. Voter interest in Switzerland is higher than that. This is undoubtedly in large measure attributable to the peculiar nature of American state constitutions. The mass of legislative detail included in many of them, when combined with the compulsory referendum, necessitates the submission of a large number of trivial and uninteresting matters to the electorate. Optional referendums and initiated votes usually reach as respectable a percentage as 75 per cent of the vote cast for governor; even this percentage is materially below the Swiss figures. These procedures seem to arouse a larger amount of public interest; the measures brought before the electorate are, on the whole, neither foolish nor extreme, nor does the action of the electorate itself seem irrational. As in Switzerland, there is a higher mortality amongst optional referendum and initiated proposals, more than half being rejected, but it is rare that measures are either proposed or passed which have not also been proposed or passed by some state legislature. One difficulty with ordinary legislative referendums is that they might be employed by special-interest groups for the purpose of delaying the enactment of necessary, and sometimes even of urgent, legislation. States have tried to cope with this situation by accepting emergency legislation from the operation of the optional referendum. The difficulty is that no agreement exists as to what constitutes an emergency (see below, ch. XXV). Another difficulty troubling many states occurs in connection with constitutional amendments; they are often subject to referendum, and have had rough sledding in many states in recent years. The inertia and lack of understanding of how government functions is particularly noticeable in this field.

Upon investigation it has been found that signatures of voters subscribing to a list under petition often do not indicate any real urge on the part of the signers. Yet it is hard to see how the popular demand should otherwise be indicated. The trouble is that it favors petitions supported by financially potent groups. It may be pointed out, however, that other groups, like trade unions, command a sufficiently numerous following to secure signatures without any appreciable outlay of money. Social-reform initiatives in this country as well as in Switzerland have been brought forward by these groups. Inasmuch as one of the greatest advantages of direct popular action flows from the educational stimulus which results from the attendant agitation, official literature on the subject of referendums has in certain states been provided by the government, giving, in the case of California, the arguments pro and con. It seems that such arrangements materially increase the voters' interest. These instrumentalities for direct popular action are not perfect mechanisms. Only an inveterate Rousseauist could survey the experience to date and still maintain that they provide a panacea for the difficulties of popular government. The electorate is quite liable to remain inert. The same inertia afflicts the town meetings in New England whenever the community grows beyond 5000 or 6000 voters (see above, ch. XII). Even so, there can be no doubt that the referendum is now permanently established among the political institutions of the states. There is little question of abandoning it.

Direct popular action and the general problem of representation • The political problems created by the spread of the several methods of direct popular action, their tendency to corrupt the people and to weaken the representative assemblies, have been urged time and again.[11] The low percentage of voters participating in many of these decisions has raised the problem of the trustworthiness of the result. In the United States it has been widely questioned. In quite a few cases the electorate reversed itself in short order. The possible delays involved in referendum procedure serve as another point of attack. Besides these specific difficulties, there is the broader issue of just how direct popular action fits into the general pattern of democratic representation. It has generally been assumed that there is a conflict between representation and direct popular action, and those who stress the representative features of constitutional government tend to question direct popular action. But does not direct popular action itself possess representative quality? In the first place, it is exercised by the electorate on behalf of the people. Furthermore, the electorate itself is represented by those who are participating in the vote. We have seen above that the voting in these referendums is rather limited. Our analysis of representation showed that representation is the process through which the influence which the entire citizenry or a part of them have upon governmental action is exercised on their behalf by a smaller number among them, with binding effect on those represented as well as on those participating in the decision. It is evident that the voters participating in a referendum stand in precisely such a relationship to the total electorate and to the people at large. The real difference between direct popular action and the action of legislatures and other "representatives" lies in the field of deliberation. The voters cannot assemble and discuss matters. But under modern conditions it may be said that this difference is more apparent than real. A constant meeting of minds is made possible through newspapers and other communication media. All questions of general public interest stir up discussion and argument. The leader makes speeches which are reported in full columns, the average citizen writes a "letter to the editor," but both participate in the deliberation. What is more, many vital issues are thrashed out within the organized interest groups. The referendum within the United States Chamber of Commerce is a striking illustration. The representatives of these interest groups in turn participate in the public discussions through speeches, articles, and other communications. The day-to-day history of any referendum reveals the wide extent of actual discussion which goes into such a decision. And after all, the discussion in deliberative assemblies is not as unrelated to these forces as earlier views tended to imply. We have seen how party, press, and interest groups are influencing what is being said in the halls of legislatures, if they do not actually dictate it. In other words, our modern means of communication have set up a context within which representative action by a much larger part of the electorate than formerly has become practicable. It remains to remark in this connection that the contrast between England, the classical country of representative government, and countries like the United States and Switzerland must not be overstressed. After all, whenever an English election turns upon a hotly debated issue, it amounts almost to a popular referendum. This has often been pointed out as a primary aspect of the decline of Parliament (see above, p. 384). Whether it is actually caused by these developments may well be doubted, however; the two go hand-in-hand as parallel changes in connection with the changes in the underlying social and industrial pattern of life. If constitutionalism is to continue, direct popular action will continue to find effective constitutional channels. It will, in a sense, be self-restrained. In the United States, the most important check results from the fact that direct popular action is limited to the states. In Switzerland, the constitutional initiative might lead to the exercise of unlimited power, but so far the Swiss voters have shown great restraint in extending their own influence. It may be different, however, in countries with a less firmly rooted tradition of political democracy, particularly if rent more violently by the controversies of contemporary social conflict. Even in Switzerland, the introduction of direct action into the field of foreign affairs is a matter of some concern; in a larger country with a real foreign policy such a step might be disastrous.

It proved itself so in the Weimar Republic. Although an attempt was made to guard against the demagogic abuse of the referendum, the relevant constitutional provisions proved wholly ineffectual. Since the referendum was difficult to put into motion, practical politicians of the more moderate parties did not employ it for such purposes as are giving life and meaning to the referendum in Switzerland and the United States. No such scruples handicapped the Communists and National Socialists. Thus, the referendum became a vehicle for the expression of irresponsible mass nationalism and contributed its share to the disintegration of the constitutional order.

While in Germany these experiences have led to a marked hostility to all direct popular consultations, precisely the opposite has happened in France. Here the 1958 constitution provides for referendum not only as an alternate means for amending the constitution (see below, p. 553 f.), but also as a way for the president, on the request of the cabinet during parliamentary sessions, or of both houses of parliament, to present bills dealing with "the organization of the governmental authorities" before the people (Article 11). This second method has been used three times since the beginning of the Republic to bring about fundamental changes in the constitution, and at least two of these times jurists have had strong doubts about the constitutionality of the proceedings. The first method has never been used.[12]

Plebiscites before the First World War · Ever since the French revolution, direct popular action has also played a role in international affairs. referendums concerning the territorial status of controversial areas have been held from time to time.[13] The doctrine of popular sovereignty, as expounded by the French revolutionaries logically following Rousseau, led to the idea of national self-determination. At the same time, it proved a potent instrument in furthering the expansive aims of the revolution in its later phases. In Avignon, in Savoy, in Nice, as well as in Belgium and the Palatinate, Mulhouse, and in Geneva, plebiscites were held to determine whether the voters favored the attachment of their territory to France. The methods were fairly constitutional at first, but they gradually became more arbitrary. Military occupations preceded and accompanied the popular votes, and pressure was exerted everywhere. As may be surmised, the monarchical reaction had very little use for this method of consulting the people, and consequently no plebiscites were held until after 1848. Cavour extensively relied upon them in his effort to unify Italy, declaring that "the dukes, the archdukes, and the grand dukes will be found buried under the pile of ballots deposited in the electoral urns." And so they were. In all the Italian principalities the popular referendums went strongly in favor of unification. With the emergence of Bismarck's empire the plebiscite suffered another eclipse. The consolidation of national states throughout Europe did not offer promising opportunities, except in areas where the existing powers would not even contemplate such a method. Obviously, the plebiscite might well have exploded the Hapsburg Empire by the end of the nineteenth century if it had been offered to the subject nationalities. Its potentialities in the colonial sphere were even more portentous. The nascent "nationalism" in India and elsewhere might well have adopted the plebiscite as a promising weapon of combat had it been allowed to do so. After all, had not the American colonies broken away by precisely this method? What was the Declaration of Independence but the harbinger of just such a plebiscite? It is not to be wondered at that the age of imperialism would have none of so dangerous a technique. Nevertheless, isolated instances occurred. After the forcible separation of Norway from Sweden, in 1905, the latter insisted upon holding a plebiscite, despite the overwhelming sentiment expressed in favor of such a separation. All these instances suggest that the technique of direct popular voting seems relatively well adapted to the settlement of territorial controversies. Two major difficulties arise in connection with plebiscites. First, the policing of the voting is burdensome, but necessary in order to prevent intimidation of the voters. Also, appropriate methods for interpreting the results of the plebiscite are hard to agree on beforehnd, and yet without such agreement the controversy is likely to be more troublesome after the plebiscite than before. In the next section some historical experiences will be examind.

Plebiscites after 1918 · The principle of the self-determination of nations which Wilson had made a part of his peace program led to the most extensive application of the method of plebiscites, although Wilson himself did not entirely favor this particular technique for settling boundary problems. While he enunciated the general idea that "national aspirations must be respected," and furthermore that "peoples and provinces are not to be bartered about from sovereignty to sovereignty as if they were mere chattels and pawns in a game . . ." (February 11, 1918), he apparently became convinced, by the time the peace was to be made, that plebiscites were unsatisfactory. Did they sanction secession? After all, what would have happened if such a doctrine had been preached and accepted before the outbreak of the Civil War? The anarchistic potentialities of radical democracy made Wilson and his advisers recoil. But there were so many points in the territorial settlement of Europe which seemed beyond the scope of any rational compromise that the exigencies of practical politics resulted in the provision for a number of such plebiscites. At the very outset, the Danes came forward with the demand for a plebiscite in Northern Schleswig, such as was supposed to have been held in 1867 but which had been discarded by Bismark.[14] This plebiscite led to a division of the territory between Denmark and Germany. Held under the supervision of Allied troops, it was attacked by Germans as unfair; yet it was probably the most acceptable plebiscite held under the peace treaty. Other important plebiscites were written into the treaty as a compromise between the Allies themselves. Thus the plebiscites in East Prussia and in Upper Silesia resulted from the insistence of the English that the cultural composition of these territories should be ascertained. Again, the plebiscite in the Saar valley was the compromise secured by France when she was forced to relinquish her claims upon the left bank of the Rhine, which were being resolutely opposed by the English and Americans. In all these plebiscites the voting was supposed to be supervised by police forces controlled by governments other than those involved in the decision of the plebiscite. The troops and the higher officials of both contesting parties were removed. It is, perhaps, unfortunate that such policing could not have been undertaken by neutrals as the Germans repeatedly demanded. Particularly in the case of the Upper Silesian plebiscite, this failure of really neutral police supervision had the result of discrediting the outcome of the plebiscite. But it was not only the voting which caused trouble in that case, but also the interpretation of the vote. Adequate arrangements for the interpretation of the vote would seem as important as the neutralization of the contested territory. Undoubtedly the most acceptable plan is one whereby it is definitely agreed beforehand just how the outcome of the vote is going to be applied. For obviously a great difference may result from treating the territory as a whole, or from dividing it into several parts. The latter method lends itself to extensive gerrymandering. It was undoubtedly one of the best features of the Schleswig plebiscite that here the division of the territory was made beforehand. The map illustrates well what can thus be accomplished. By dividing the Schleswig area, a Danish majority appeared in the upper zone (I), whereas if the territory had been taken as a whole, the majority of the votes being for Germany, it would all have gone to Germany. Fortunately, this method of division had previously beein agreed to by Germany, so that no controversy could afterwards result from it.

For a while the plebiscite as a technique for settling boundary disputes seemed to hold distinct possibilities in a democratic age. The leading American authority on the subject rightly observed that the plebiscite is not to be considered a perfect tool, but that since there is no perfect method

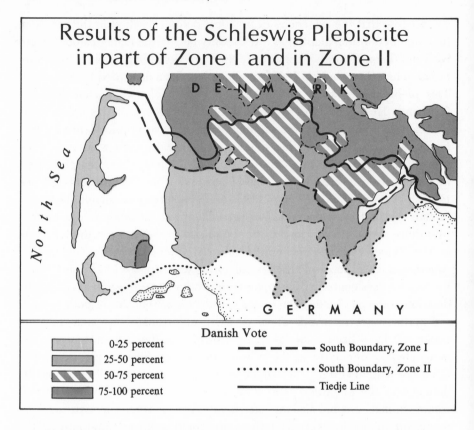

Results of the Schleswig Plebiscite in part of Zone I and in Zone II

	Danish Vote	
0-25 percent	– – – – –	South Boundary, Zone I
25-50 percent		
50-75 percent	············	South Boundary, Zone II
75-100 percent	———————	Tiedje Line

of establishing national boundaries, "the problem is one of alternatives, a choice between methods varying in imperfection." In the context of the present discussion we can push this view a bit farther and say that only such popular votes seem to possess the representative quality which is necessary for any permanent settlement. Only this method seems to correspond to the ideas prevalent today as to what constitutes a legitimate basic decision concerning cultural autonomy and the inescapable consequences of national attachment. While it is intrinsically possible to let representatives elected in the controversial district speak for their commuunity, as was done repeatedly in the nineteenth century, the possibilities of misrepresentation in an act as final as inclusion within the territory of a certain country makes such a method inconclusive, since people would have no way of reversing the decision by recalling their representatives if they disagreed.

An interesting plebiscite was held in the Saar in 1957. Soon after the war, the French sought to incorporate this western German territory into their own state. Eventually, and in line with growing Franco-German cooperation, a statute was adopted, in October 1954, which provided for a plebiscite of the Saar population, offering them the alternative of internationalization under the supervision of the Western European Union. At the time, it was assumed that the vote would be in favor, but the voters rejected the plan in 1955 by 67.7 per cent, and opted thereby for return to Germany; this was negotiated in 1956 and the Saar became an additional *Land* under the Basic Law in 1957.[15] This result is the more striking in view of the fact that in 1947 the Saarlanders had by referendum approved a constitution which attached the Saar to France, by 97.7 per cent.[16]

Postwar constitutional referendums in Europe • Despite the abuse of plebiscites by the totalitarians and contrary to prevailing European tradition, constitutions have been the subject of referendum procedure in many cases. But unlike the totalitarian plebiscites, these referendums presented genuine alternatives between which the majority could and did choose without fear of reprisals. The preconstitutional referendum in France (October 21, 1945) by which the method of arriving at a constitution was determined has already been mentioned. The constitution resulting from the deliberations of this elected constituent assembly was submitted to the French people on May 6, 1946, and was rejected, perhaps because it had "turned into a plebiscite for or against the Communist party . . . in the minds of many citizens." However, although the vote may be considered to some extent the result of a battle of slogans, the overwhelming rejection of this draft, even among the Socialists who officially supported it, may be interpreted as a rejection of the parliamentary supremacy of the Third Republic.[17] The next constitution, written by the same assembly and submitted to the people on October 21, 1946, was adopted by the French electorate under conditions which left its legitimacy in considerable doubt. About nine million voters voted for it, eight million against it, and another nine million abstained. "All Gaul is still divided into three parts," it was said with Gallic sarcasm, "those who say reluctantly yes, those who say unconditionally no, and those who simply don't give a damn." In a very dangerous sense, General de Gaulle's sharp opposition had gained its objectives; for the General, realizing that he could not defeat the constitution, had set about to discredit it by securing a two-thirds majority of voters who did not vote for it.

In 1958, De Gaulle's new constitution was approved by more than 80 per cent of the voters, with 15 per cent abstaining in France proper. However, in the midst of the Algerian crisis, this landslide may have been more a vote of confidence in De Gaulle than the result of deliberation on the merits of the constitution. As in 1946, the parties in favor of the constitution tried to give the impression that an affirmative vote was a vote for France, and one against a vote for Russia. They were aided by being able to present the constitution to the voters as the one alternative to chaos.[18] The referendum was put to rather dubious and unconstitutional use by the president of the republic in 1964, when he forced through a constitutional amendment for the popular election of the president. The constitution of 1958 had provided a cumbersome electoral college of over seventy thousand persons "comprising the members of parliament, of the general councils . . . as well as the elected representatives of the municipal councils." (Article 6) Such an electoral college would not, or course, provide the same degree of democratic, plebiscitary legitimation as would a popular election. Hence De Gaulle proceeded to set aside the clear constitutional provisions for amendment by the two houses of parliament, and submitted the amendment directly to referendum, as provided in Article 89, against the strong advice of his then-prime minister, Michel Debré, who thereupon resigned. The referendum, really felt to be a popular vote for De Gaulle's Algerian surrender, went overwhelmingly in his favor.[19]

In Italy the referendum was employed first of all for the basic decision regarding the monarchy. On June 10, 1946, the Italian people adopted the republican form of government by a substantial majority. Having settled this problem, the Italian constitution was drafted in an elaborate process but not submitted to the people.[20] The referendum is retained for the purpose of constitutional amendment, but only if demanded by one fifth of the membership of either house, or by 500,000 voters, or by five regional councils, and then only if the amendment was adopted by less than two thirds of the two houses of parliament.

In Germany the referendum had had a rather stormy career under the Weimar constitution. Hitler's plebiscites had raised substantial doubts in many minds as to the soundness of this device of "radical" democracy. Constitutional referendums were nevertheless held on the state constitutions in the American and French zones as a result of Allied insistence. These referendums produced very large majorities, upward of 70 per cent, largely because the constitutions were the product of genuine compromises between the two major parties, the Christian Democrats and the Social Democrats. Consequently, the two parties, commanding over 70 per cent of electoral support, could go to the people together.

A very difficult situation arose in connection with the Basic Law. It had originally been agreed between the three Western Allies to submit the draft constitution to popular referendum, largely on American insistence. German political leaders rejected this plan on two grounds, one a matter of prudence, the other a matter of principle. As to the latter, they argued that no true constitution could be made except by a "sovereign" people, and that the German voter should not be duped into thinking that such was the situation.

The Basic Law, a provisional charter, concludes with an article decreeing its disappearance as soon as the German people can freely decide upon their constitution. The prudential objection was that a referendum would oblige the two great parties to go before the electorate together, a task which would make compromises in the constituent assembly more difficult. Reluctantly, the Allies yielded to these views. Whether the lack of such a referendum really lessened the legitimacy of constitutional democracy may in retrospect be doubted. Since strong party organizations control the electorate their assent would have made any such referendum a foregone conclusion anyhow, once the Christian Democrats and the Social Democrats had decided to support it.[21]

Conclusion · In theory and in practice modern democracy has been developing direct popular action as an alternative to representative schemes. But such direct action has also been employed in rival dictatorial regimes as they sought to legitimize themselves by securing popular support. Napoleon I, Napoleon III, Mussolini, and Hitler, were alike in their search for such popular acclaim. The suddenness with which these dictatorial regimes collapsed suggest the unrepresentative quality of this primitive substitute for effective representation. Even so, direct popular participation handled within the framework of constitutional government, has worked with a reasonable degree of smoothness; in both Switzerland and the United States these methods serve a useful purpose in offering yet another technique for the handling of divided power by increasing the legitmacy of its use. But the difficulty of placing effective restraints upon its exercise makes it a questionable device in communities not thoroughly seasoned in popular politics and thoroughly attached to their constitutional morale.

All political power is subject to abuse, no matter what the legal form of its exercise. But concentrated power is very much more easily abused than divided power. Direct popular action, while it is not concentrated power under a constitutional system, is close to it. At any rate, it may well be doubted whether Jean Jacques Rousseau, after watching the operation of modern plebiscites nationally or internationally, would be inclined to consider them very useful tools for discovering the "general will." But then, it is only fair to add that he concluded his famous discussion of democracy by the apodictic remark: "If there were somewhere a people of gods, it would govern itself democratically. So perfect a government does not suit human beings." Considering that Rousseau meant direct democracy, this observation is borne out by political experience. Contemporary American democracy is not an argument against Rousseau's conclusion. For as commonly used in America, the word "democracy" means constitutional democracy. It means divided powers. It means civil liberties. It means that there is a moderator as well as a town meeting. It means concern for minorities, as well as decision by the majority. It means that the people are living in time as well as in space; that their good life will not be jeopardized by inexorable decisions of a temporary majority. In the last analysis free government depends upon the decisive group of common citizens which we have called the constituent group. It depends upon their determination to remain free, they themselves and their fellow men. As John Stuart Mill put it: "A people may prefer a free government, but if, from indolence, or carelessness, or cowardice, or want of public spirit, they are unequal to the exertions necessary for presering it; if they will not fight for it when it is directly attacked; if they can be deluded by the artifices used to cheat them out of it; if by momentary discouragement, or temporary panic, or a fit of enthusiasm for an individual they can be induced to lay their liberties at the feet even of a great man, or trust him with powers which enable him to subvert their institutions; in all these cases they are more or less unfit for liberty: and though it may be for their good to have had it even for a short time, they are unlikely long to enjoy it."[22]

Direct popular action in its several forms can serve to strengthen the democratic element. But if the dose is too strong, it will seriously strain the system. In spite of these handicaps and shortcomings, the methods of direct popular action, if guarded and circumscribed by constitutional provisions guaranteeing a free choice to the electorate, provide a modern constitution with an integrating device by which the dissensions of parties, pressure groups, and propagandas can from time to time be overcome. The "will of the people" has lost some of its luster as a basis of legitimacy and as a ground for securing universal acceptance. But there is still no better one in sight in this age of secular outlook and pragmatic doubt. Direct popular action thus provides a genuine instrument for modern constitutional democracy.

Constitutional Dictatorship

and Emergency Powers

XXV

Introduction · The commissioner · The (Roman) constitutional dictatorship contrasted with the commissioner · Martial rule · State of siege ·
Legislative emergency powers · Executive emergency powers · Modern
constitutional limitations inadequate: (1) The appointment of a dictator ·
(2) The determination of an emergency · (3) The precise time limit ·
The legitimate objective: the defense of the constitution itself · Explanation of inadequacy · The pattern of transition from constitutional to unconstitutional dictatorship · Military government and democratization · Military government and the rule of law · Military government as constitutional
dictatorship · Conclusion

Introduction · In the three preceding chapters, three major areas of
tension, breakdown, and adjustment of modern constitutionalism have been
discussed. But the most dangerous and serious of these situations is caused
by war, both foreign and civil. Modern technological warfare is all-engulfing
and calls for the participation of everyone. It causes casualties on a huge
scale among the noncombatant population whose productive and morale
potential is being made the target of enemy action. This type of warfare
has rightly been called "total." It is truly a marvel of the vigor and resilience
of constitutionalism in Britain and the United States that the system continued to function, and that in the United States even a presidential election,
not to speak of minor elections, could be carried through without endanger-
ing the conduct of the war. Few would have been willing to predict beforehand that this could prove possible.

In the late Middle Ages, the concentration of powers was brought on by
the exigencies of religious upheavals, of increasing and technically more
formidable warfare, and of the economic revolution accompanying them.[1]
The violence and the constant recurrence of these emergencies during the
latter half of the sixteenth and throughout the seventeenth century made it
possible for certain monarchical leaders to break down the medieval division

557

of powers to a very large extent and to concentrate these powers in their own hands. Owing to the military and administrative requirements of the emergencies, the princes who had been charged with military and administrative powers in medieval society were rather advantageously placed for a successful usurpation of this kind. In the twentieth century the demand for such concentration has arisen once again from the emergencies with which we are confronted: the conflict between classes in our industrial society and the exigencies of modern mass warfare. Is constitutional government likely to be able to cope with these situations of unprecedented magnitude and gravity? Many answer "no," and turn toward dictatorship as their solution. Every modern constitution has recognized the problem of temporary emergencies and has sought to provide for a temporary concentration of powers to be used in overcoming such emergencies. In Britain and in the United States, emergency power and martial law are the legal institutions which have been developed; in civil-law countries these problems are dealt with on the basis of the "state of siege" and the "exceptional state" (*Ausnahmezustand*). "Constitutional dictatorship" is the general term we shall use to designate all such methods for the temporary concentration of powers.

The commissioner · Similar methods were recognized by the medieval constitutional order, but the princes ultimately succeeded in transforming them into instruments for the destruction of medieval constitutionalism. How was this result accomplished? Essentially through the institution of extraordinary commissioners or *commissarii* whom the princes, following the papal precedent, appointed out of the fullness of their authority (*plenitudo potestatis*).[2] For it was held to be part of the royal prerogative to determine when an exceptional situation required exceptional measures. Thus in place of the regular officials with legally, if not constitutionally, defined spheres of jurisdiction, there appear specially appointed delegates of the king who, on the basis of a special instruction, are called upon to handle particular situations. We find commissioners authorized to inspect markets, to requisition food and other support for the army, to carry on negotiations, and so forth. Perhaps the most celebrated historical form of such commissioners are the intendants whom Henry IV of France employed to such a remarkable degree. These commissioners aided him materially in securing the revenue which enabled him to dispense with the Estates. But even before Henry IV the institution of commissioners had been developed by the French crown. A striking chapter in Bodin's treatise on the state is devoted to a discussion of the legal and practical aspects of such commissioners, which he himself knew through practical experience. Bodin clearly distinguished the commissioner from the regular official. Since the latter's activities were created by express and public law, his office was more or less permanent, and the official had a sort of right to his office. On the other hand, the commissioner, relying on a royal ordinance for his right to act, exercised only a temporary function; he had no right to his office, but was completely dependent upon his master. Therefore the commissioner's activities were determined by his instructions, while the regular official could practice a certain amount of discretion. If the tenor of the instructions was narrow, the commissioner's powers were correspondingly limited. But if the prince saw fit to make the instructions very comprehensive — for example, by requesting a commissioner to employ all necessary means for quelling a rebellion — then such a commissioner, unlimited as to the means he might use, was very likely to suspend existing laws and rights on a considerable scale. It is at this point that the analogy between these commissioners and the office of the dictator becomes apparent.

The Roman constitutional dictatorship contrasted with the commissioner • The Roman dictator was appointed for a given task, like that of concluding a war or suppressing a rebellion, and as soon as his commission was carried out his office similarly came to an end. Therefore, a Roman dictator could only be compared to a commissioner with very extensive powers; for he became the chief executive of the Roman Republic for the period of his appointment, whereas the commissioners in the sixteenth century and later were usually agents of a king who remained the chief executive and who employed them for more or less limited tasks.[3] In the Roman Republic for several centuries, dictatorship remained a bulwark for the Republican government and did not lead to a usurpation of powers. It afterwards became obsolete, until revived by Sulla during the civil wars. The constitutional bases of the earlier dictatorship essentially seem to have been four. In the first place, the appointment of the dictator took place according to precise constitutional forms. Secondly, the dictatorship was instituted by others than the dictator himself. A third condition of great importance was a strict time limit imposed upon the dictator for the fulfillment of his task, never to exceed six months. Finally, the dictatorship always was instituted in defense of the existing constitutional order, never with a view to destroying it. Obviously, all these conditions are themselves dependent upon the constitutional order, and can therefore properly be called constitutional limitations. When Sulla revived the dictatorship for the novel purpose of making a constitution, he violated these constitutional limitations in essential respects. He caused himself to be appointed by an *interrex* especially named by the Senate for that purpose, and he continued in the dictatorial position for three years, finally withdrawing from it on his own volition. The same restraint was not shown by Caesar. He mocked at Sulla for having resigned, and eventually, in 44 B.C., assumed a permanent dictatorship. This step was nothing else than a disguised assumption of monarchical power.

The commissioners of the royal governments were, on the contrary, personal servants of the king in whose hands power was being concentrated. Their object, therefore, was not so much the maintenance of a constitutional order, but of order as such. Their purpose was conceived in technical terms, and evaluated in terms of pure expediency, the so-called reason of state. It is thus quite apparent that from a political, as compared to the legal, standpoint, constitutional dictatorship is the very antithesis of such commissionerships (or commissioned dictatorships, as they have been called). Nothing shows this more clearly than the fact that when these commisioners became permanent, they formed the core of the monarchical bureaucracy. When the constitutional dictatorship becomes permanent, it becomes unconstitutional and leads to the perversion and eventual overthrow of the constitutional order. A concentration has replaced the division of powers.

Modern constitutional provisions for martial law and the state of siege cannot, therefore, be placed in a parallel with the commissioners of old, as has sometimes been done. As so often in the history of political institutions, a legal continuity hides a fundamental transition in political function. For it is undeniable that both martial rule in common-law lands and the state of siege on the continent of Europe are derived in part from institutions similar to the commissionership. Yet, like the Roman Republican dictatorship, martial rule, emergency powers, and the state of siege are all conceived in terms of maintaining a constitutional system rather than destroying it (until they are perverted into a usurpation of concentrated powers). To be sure, the apologist of absolutism would insist that the kinship of the two institutions lay precisely in the fact that both were extraordinary means for maintaining "the state." But the word "state" is itself a propaganda tool of the absolutist. It hides the fact that order for its own sake is being substituted for constitutional, legal order as the primary objective of the exceptional concentration of powers. Political science must keep the two methods quite distinct. This distinction, therefore, is not one of formalities, such as might be suggested by the terms "commissioned" and "noncommissioned" (sovereign) dictatorship, but one of objectives, properly designated by the terms "constitutional" and "unconstitutional" (unrestrained) dictatorship. The modern forms of constitutional dictatorship are martial rule, the state of siege, and constitutional emergency powers. The first is found for example, in England, in the Dominions, and in the United States; the second in France, in Germany before 1918, and in many other Continental countries; and the third is characteristic of the American federal government and the present French government, among others.

Martial rule • As we have already mentioned, the differentiation between martial rule and the state of siege is essentially related to the difference between a common-law and a civil-law system. The concept of martial rule is understandable only in terms of the rule of law which it replaces. Where this rule of law is taken to be the core of the legal system, because it alone guarantees a calculable stability of legal relationships, an emergency is essentially a condition of things which threatens the continued maintenance of this rule of law. The most decisive evidence of such a disturbance would be the fact that the courts are closed and can no longer perform their function. This the American Supreme Court held to be the condition for the application of martial law.[4] Similarly, Judge Mackintosh once said that when it is impossible for courts of law to sit or for the executive to enforce the execution of their judgments, then it becomes necessary to find some rude substitute for them and to employ for that purpose the military, which is the only remaining force in the community. But on the whole, the English courts have not been quite so strict. The important point is that ultimately the judiciary are the arbiters who determine whether or not the actions taken by executive organs are in fact necessary. On the other hand, there is no limit beyond which the authorities exercising such constitutional dictatorship may not go if they can afterward convince the court of the necessity of their action. It is hard to say much more about it, for the law of martial rule is very vague and is obscured by a maze of conflicting precedents. Nor is there any clearly defined measure by which the initiation of such a system of martial rule is definitely indicated. Although it is customary for the executive "to declare martial law" before initiating extraordinary measures, this declaration does not entail any very definite consequences. It may be a mere threat. It may presage the most extreme measures, violating all the customary constitutional limitations upon governmental powers. Sir James Fitzjames Stephen described it thus: "The common law right of the crown and its representative to repel force with force in the case of invasion and insurrection, and to act against rebels as it might against invaders." Whatever measures are taken, they must be defensible in terms of the nature of the emergency, which arose from the onslaught of hostile forces against the customary rule of law.

State of siege • Rather different is the state of siege. Here a specific declaration by the legislature or by the head of the government or by both is required by law, or even by the constitution. Thus, the French constitution of 1815 (*Acte additionnel*) required that the declaration of the state of siege take the form of a law. What is perhaps more important, the state of siege is defined in terms of a suspension of certain enumerated individual rights, more particularly the right to be tried in an ordinary court, the right to free speech, and the right to free assembly. It is at this point that the contrast with common-law practice can be most clearly seen, and it is indeed of decisive importance in civil-war situations. Whereas the executive and/or the legislature have the final word as to whether an emergency situation has arisen, the courts have this function under the common law. Politically speaking, this means that a political body, an admittedly partisan organ, has the ultimate authority in Continental jurisdictions, whereas a nonpolitical authority, which presumably tries to be nonpartisan, has the last word in Anglo-American jurisdictions. Continental countries seem to see the emergency in an effective threat against public safety and order, whereas in common-law countries emphasis is placed upon the suspension of the rule of law. In practice the two states of fact may largely coincide; but the concept of public safety and order focuses attention upon the political system, or "the state." On the other hand, the rule of law seems preoccupied with the safety of the private individual. This difference is undoubtedly responsible for the inclination of common lawyers to look upon the state of siege as an objectionable institution, traceable to the heritage of the Continent's monarchical past. Under the present French constitution the state of siege, to be decreed by the Council of Ministers and lasting no longer than twelve days without the consent of parliament (Article 36), is implicitly restricted to use only in very grave situations such as civil and foreign war. For lesser emergencies the constitution provides expanded executive powers on a temporary basis.

The Basic Law of the Federal Republic contains to date only very cautious and inadequate provisions for emergency powers; although the issue has been under discussion for many years now, it is still an open one. The experience with Article 48 and the determination of the Allies to retain such powers at the time the Basic Law was drafted have caused a serious lacuna in this constitution. It would lead too far afield to review in detail all the arguing that has been carried on over emergency powers since the then-minister of the interior, Gerhard Schroeder, put forward the first proposal. It was a proposal only remarkable for its complete lack of appreciation of the problems of "constitutional dictatorship." Naturally, it encountered immediate and vigorous criticism from the Social Democratic opposition, and more particularly the trade unions; the latter feared that emergency provisions might be used against them in strike situations. There have been three successive plans for dealing with the main objections during the last ten years, until finally some consensus is emerging. Recent drafts of the needed constitutional amendments have recognized that the opposition must be a participant in decisions concerning emergencies, that adequate safeguards must be provided against its abuse, more especially by setting up a reasonably workable system of parliamentary supervision, and finally that the constitutional court must be able to reinforce such parliamentary control.[5]

As a matter of fact, the ill-famed Article 48 of the Weimar constitution was not nearly as noxious as legend has made it. One tends to forget that without it the first president of that republic might not have been able to master the emergencies of the first few years, more especially those of 1923. What was bad about Article 48 lay really beyond that article, in the misconstrued dualism of presidential and chancellorian power which led to the second presidential term of the aged Hindenburg.[6]

Legislative emergncy powers • Basically and ordinarily, constitutional dictatorship applies to executive action. But under modern conditions, where a complex industrial society is conducted in accordance with correspondingly complex statutes, emergencies are likely to require adequate powers for legislative change as well as for administrative action. Most modern constitutions are silent on the subject. But since the need is paramount, emergency powers have come into existence, sometimes by usurpation, at other times by express delegation. When Lincoln, after the start of hostilities, found himself without an adequate army, but also without a Congress to authorize one, he proceeded by measures not authorized by either the constitution or Congress to achieve his apparently necessary purpose. Congress *afterwards* authorized what he had done and passed an act of indemnity. As long as such action as Lincoln's is taken for the manifest purpose of maintaining constitutionalism, as interpreted by the majority, this method "works"; it is subject, however, to the objection that all breaches of the law are destructive of the general belief in law upon which constitutionalism rests.

Actually, the Constitution of the United States is distinguished by its broad grant of war powers to the President of the country as commander in chief of the army, the navy, and the national guard (militia), when called into actual national service. The broad legislative powers of the Congress notwithstanding, these war powers, when taken in conjunction with the President's duty to see to it that the laws are faithfully executed, give him extensive emergency powers, especially since the Congress has been inclined to back the President in dealing with insurection and civil war. The courts, for instance in *Luther v. Borden* (7 How. 42), have also been prone to interpret the President's authority broadly. Subsequent history has thus borne out Alexander Hamilton's brief but emphatic statement in the *Federalist* that "the direction of war most peculiarly demands those qualities which distinguish the exercise of power by a single hand," and that "the direction of war implies the direction of the common strength; and the power of directing and employing the common strength, forms a usual and essential part in the definition of the executive authority." On this basis, the President is likely to be led to assume all the powers which the emergency requires, as Bryce noted, and the Congress can make him "almost a dictator," as it did in the Civil War* and the two world wars. It has been the acid test of American constitutionalism that such temporary grants of dictatorial powers have not brought the constitutional system to an end; after each such trial it has re-emerged virtually unchanged in its basic pattern.

Emergency powers of legislation were extensively granted during the First World War. None of these grants of power went farther than the British Defense of the Realm Act, which authorized the king in Council for the duration of the war "to issue regulations . . . for securing the public welfare and defense of the realm."[7] The power hereby conferred was used for matters rather far removed from the defense of the realm, but as long as the war lasted, few minded. A similar statute (the Emergency Powers [Defense] Act) was passed in England at the beginning of the Second World War and considerably broadened after the invasion of the Low Countries. Under it, the king in Council was empowered "to make such regulations as appear to him to be necessary or expedient for securing the public safety, the defense of the Realm, the maintenance of public order, and the efficient prosecution of any war in which His Majesty may be engaged. . . ." He could also require "persons to place themselves, their services and their property at the disposal of His Majesty. . . ." In the United States, similar powers were granted the President by a series of acts such as the Lever Act, Selective Service Act, Espionage Act, Priority Shipment Act, Trading with the Enemy Act, Overman Act, and others. But whereas the delegation of such legislative authority was part of the accepted pattern of British constitutionalism, the issue had never been fully faced in the United States. The delegation of powers during the First World War was, to be sure, never effectively challenged in court. But a similar delegation in a number of statutes during the great depression (NRA, AAA, etc.) was held unconstitutional by the courts (see ch. XII), notwithstanding the fact that the courts had allowed the concept of quasi-legislative power to develop under the Interstate Commerce and other regulatory acts for some time. Such a judicial rejection of Congressional readiness to delegate power is, of course, unthinkable in England, where the courts accept acts of Parliament as definitive. Yet insofar as the common-law tradition and its martial rule provide for judicial rather than legislative checks upon the exercise of emergency powers, the American practice is more nearly

---

* I prefer the neutral term "Civil War" to the too-partisan terms often used (especially in public places) by the North and the South respectively: War of the Southern Rebellion, and War between the States.

in keeping with it. Does that suffice to justify it? The formal argument is, of course, that only the amending power is available for changing the distribution of power, but we have seen how unrealistic that contention is in fact. Had Congress retained the right to revoke executive orders that seemed manifestly unreasonable, it might have been argued that the powers conferred were only quasi-legislative and hence unconstitutional. But was such a provision really necessary? Did it not go without saying that Congress, by changing the statute, could revoke the executive regulations that had been issued under it? The real issue would appear to lie hidden behind the fact that the solid New Deal majority in Congress had full confidence in the executive's general policy and hence was disinclined to be jealous of its authority. For the Supreme Court to substitute its judgment for that of Congress was a usurpation of emergency powers by the Court.

The distinction between legislative and executive or administrative powers in an emergency is as such questionable. For these emergency powers are being exercised to accomplish a definite result; they involve decisions large and small which together constitute the policy to be pursued in the accomplshment of this end: to overcome the emergency and to maintain constitutional government intact. There must be a broad grant of powers, subject to equally strong limitations as to who shall exercise such powers, when, for how long, and to what end.

Executive emergency powers · The new French constitution, in an attempt to prevent the kind of crisis of leadership which led to the fall of the Third Republic before the German military forces in 1939, provides that the president of the republic may, on his own initiative, at times when "the institutions of the Republic, the independence of the nation, the integrity of its territory or the fulfillment of its international commitments are threatened in a grave and immediate manner and when the regular functioning of the constitutional governmental authorities is interrupted," take whatever measures are required by these circumstances after consultation with the prime minister, presidents of the two assemblies, and the constitutional council (Article 16). The second condition, that the functioning of the government be interrupted, imposes a much greater limitation on the times this power can be exercised than does the first, which, referring only to a "threat" of danger, might cover any number of situations. Even this first condition, however, is less vague and easily expandable than Article 14 of the French charter of 1814, which gave the king the right to make any laws "necessary . . . for the safety of the state," or Article 48 of the Weimar constitution, which came into force "if security and public order are gravely disturbed or threatened."

Beyond these conditions on the determination of an emergency, there are practically no restrictions on the power of the executive under Article 16. The requirement that the president must consult with various officials does not entail any obligation to follow their advice. Nor does the requirement that parliament meet automatically and continue without dissolution throughout the emergency mean that it has any constitutional power at that time, except, one presumes, the power of impeachment in extreme cases. The only limitation on the measures themselves is a purely subjective and unenforceable one, that they "must be prompted by the desire" to bring back constitutional government "in the shortest possible time."[8]

The emergency powers of Article 16 have been used once, following the military coup in Algeria in April 1961. In view of the fact that one minister was in the hands of the insurgents, parts of the army had rebelled, and Paris was expecting an invasion of parachutists, it could be said both that the institutions of the republic were threatened and that the regular functioning of government had been interrupted. However, the president retained the emergency powers until September of the same year, although many jurists claimed that after the Algerian coup had failed in April, governmental functions had returned to normal. They also contested the president's right to forbid parliament during this period to vote a motion of censure or to legislate. Both the *Conseil d'État* and the constitutional council ruled themselves incompetent to pronounce on these questions.[9]

Modern constitutional limitations inadequate: (1) *the appointment of a dictator* · If we now ask ourselves to what extent the four criteria of a constitutional dictatorship outlined above are realized in the various provisions for martial rule, for the state of siege, and for constitutional emergency powers, we have a test by which to evaluate these arrangements. This test may afford us some clue as to the relative value of these several arrangements. At the same time, such testing will reveal a considerable amount of similarity between the three forms of constitutional dictatorship. As to the first criterion, it must be admitted that only constitutional emergency powers regularly fulfill the condition laid down by it, to wit, that the appointment of the dictator take place according to precise constitutional forms. In England, where the application of martial rule occurs at the discretion of a cabinet supported by a legally and constitutionally unlimited majority in the House of Commons, the appointment of the dictator may be said to be thus defined, but it is a pretty vague definition at that. The United States measures up to the first criterion with precise constitutional provisions concerning the appointment of a dictator when it provides, in Article I, Section 8: "Congress shall have power ... (15) to provide for calling forth the militia, to execute the Laws of the Union, suppress Insurrections, and repel Invasions." But the constitutional provisions omit the naming of a distinct dictator. This brings us to the second point.

(2) *The determination of an emergency* · Martial rule in England, the state of siege in nineteenth-century France, and the constitutional emergency powers in the United States all seem to square with the second criterion, according to which the dictator himself must not be vested with discretionary powers for declaring or calling off the state of emergency. This implies that someone must determine it. Who should that be? The American Congress and the English Parliament do indeed appoint someone else, and therefore these constitutions seem to be in accord with the second criterion of a sound constitutional arrangement for the exercise of these extraordinary powers. But this seeming accord is rather formalistic. For these legislatures, the English always, the American a large part of the time, are led by the executive leaders whom their majority supports. Their position of party leadership weakens the constitutional restraints. Too much depends not only upon the leaders' own good will, but also upon that of their party following. Hitler gained his first opportunity by securing broad emergency power under Article 48 of the Weimar constitution, which enabled him to distort the election results in March 1933 through the unsubstantiated claim that the Reichstag fire necessitated the outlawing of Communists and others. His own supporters in the *Reichstag* did not, of course, question his allegation. But even where the political purpose is not clearly anticonstitutional, as it was here, but merely a partisan view of what is needed for the maintenance of constitutionalism, that difficulty must be faced. The danger from recurrent "emergencies" to the constitutional system is intensified by the presence of sizable Communist parties because of the contact these parties maintain with a foreign power.

Where no constitutionally fixed time limit is provided, the issue is even more serious at the end than at the beginning of an emergency. In contemporary social conflicts it is possible to prolong and deepen the "emergency." This difficulty arose in both France and Germany before the war. Needless to say, Hitler never bothered with the account which he at one time promised after four years of his rule; nor was anyone in a position to question his use of the emergency powers he had illegally acquired. The succession of emergencies in France before the outbreak of the Second World War, as well as in Germany before the advent of Hitlerism, shows that parliamentary majorities bound up in their fate with the constitutional dictator, become more and more emergency-conscious as the day of reckoning approaches. This is no empty hallucination. As one authority puts it: "In view of the fact that all stand to gain by a common party victory there is no reason to suppose that the rank and file will be any less complacent than their leaders toward abuses . . . Where common party interests are at stake, therefore, it is clearly unrealistic to rely on a government-controlled majority in the legislature. . . . "[10] We must conclude, therefore, that the present arrangements for emergency powers in a number of countries do not accord with our second criterion. Whether their constitutional orders will therefore be perverted into governments with concentrated powers, as happened in Germany, France, and Italy, would seem to depend upon the extent to which recurrent crises will entail the employment of presumably temporary emergency powers brought into play for lengthening periods of "emergency." The Cold War provided a comparable frame of reference, and in the loose employment of the term "Cold War," there lurked very real dangers for the future of constitutionalism. It is not without significance that the Cold War was "declared" without the Congress in spite of the fact that the constitution requires declarations of war to be made by the Congress. The retort that the Cold War is simply a state of fact is not convincing, since the same can be said of all war. Its formal "declaration" is vested in the Congress precisely because from this state of fact are supposed to flow legal results which require legislative authorization.

(3) *The precise time limit* · The third criterion, namely, the imposition of a strict time limit during which concentrated powers can be exercised, is not rigidly fulfilled by any modern constitutional order. To be sure, there is supposed to be an implication of such a time limit in the provision of a legislative check upon the exercise of these powers. The constitutional limit of four years for a presidential term may also be said to constitute at least some time limit. Various constitutions and laws provide for the immediate reporting of any measures taken by the dictatorial executive and for their revocation if the legislature should demand it. By such provisions this restraint is merged with the second one, which would withdraw from the dictator the discretion of determining the end as well as the beginning of the emergency. It was shown with regard to these provisions that in view of parliamentary dependence upon executive leadership under the cabinet system, no real check is provided against the arbitrary abuse of this discretionary power. At any rate, such a procedural rule cannot be said to take the place of a fixed limitation of time as that which was imposed by the Roman Republican constitution. It may be true that the six months which the Roman constitution provided is not a suitable period in which to deal with the emergencies which are likely to arise in an industrial society. But whatever the particular period of time, a constitutionally fixed time limit is a

vastly different thing from any check which with proper manipulation is capable of indefinite extension. It is a curious thing that modern constitutional systems have never faced this problem squarely, in spite of the fact that with the vagueness of so-called social crises and emergencies it would be most important. Even a constitution so deeply permeated by a distrust of power and the fear of its abuse as the American constitution fails to insist upon some such limit.

The legitimate objective: the defense of the constitution itself • The final condition for the exercise of constitutional emergency powers is that the objective be legitimate, that is to say, that the concentration of powers be employed for defending the constitutional order, and not for destroying it. Changes may be required, but they must not touch the basis of the constitution itself. It is very disquieting that no explicit provisions safeguard the employment of martial rule and the state of siege in this regard. The purely military background of both institutions, and the consequent preoccupation with the technical problem of producing a certain effect, are inimical to adequate consideration of this problem. On the battlefield victory is an ascertainable technical goal, and the emergency evidently has passed once victory has been achieved. But in social and economic crises the matter is not so obvious and the tendency of partisans to identify their particular solution with the only solution is strong. Hence measures of extreme violence, like, let us say, the forcible destruction of all labor unions, may appear to be a necessary condition of social pacification to one group, while the forcible expropriation of all private industries may seem equally unavoidable to the other. Some would say that at such a point a constitutional order becomes impossible. It is undeniable that neither martial rule nor the state of siege under a parliamentary regime offers any safeguards against the abuse of power by violent partisans in a civil-war situation. Hence these arrangements for constitutional dictatorship are liable to be the first step in the destruction of an existing constitutional order. Constitutional emergency powers need not be exposed to this objection. The arbitral position of the courts in determining the *constitutional* exercise of all governmental powers can to some extent be brought into play in order to insure that the dictatorial powers be confined to defending the existing constitution. The United States Supreme Court gave striking illustrations of that fact in interfering with the atrocities of the Reconstruction period. But unless the judiciary or some other magistrate can thus be brought into play, the situation is likely to get out of hand. Moreover, the judicial power is also subject to abuse, and courts are likely to prove helpless in the face of a real emergency. As Robert H. Jackson reminded us, in vain did Chief Justice Taney cry out against Lincoln in *Ex parte Merryman.* Convinced that he was protesting at great peril to himself, "the weary and weatherbeaten old Chief Justice thundered forth the fundamental principles of civilian freedom," but had to admit in the end: "I have exercised all the power which the Constitution and laws confer upon me, but that power has been resisted by a force too strong for me to overcome."[11] While the judiciary, therefore, may act as a sort of keeper of the President's and the people's conscience, there are no ultimate institutional safeguards available for insuring that emergency powers be used for the purpose of preserving the constitution. Only the people's own determination to see them so used can make sure of that, provided the constitution has placed the limitations upon the exercise of dictatorial emergency powers which have been discussed. Unhappily, all modern constitutions are defective in this respect. Yet, how are the people to exercise their restraint, when the constitution does not contain effective working limitations? Therefore, emergency powers intended to save a constitution may grow into concentrated powers directed toward the destruction of the constitution.

Explanation of inadequacy · All in all the quasi-dictatorial provisions of modern constitutional systems, be they martial rule, state of siege, or constitutional emergency powers, fail to conform to any exacting standard of effective limitations upon a temporary concentration of powers. Consequently, all these systems are liable to be transformed into dictatorial schemes if conditions become at all favorable to it. The failure to deal with this issue altogether, which we noted in the recent constitution of Germany, is an ostrich policy which leaves the government without the constitutional resources which an emergency is likely sooner or later to present. One hesitates to contemplate what might have happened in the United States at the start of the Civil War, if the President had not been able to act decisively. But as we saw, even the provisions of the American constitution, though much the best, are too loose. Unless changes are made to tighten constitutional provisions for the exercise of emergency powers along the lines here indicated, the kind of civil war emergency which the rise of the Soviet's world revolutionary policy and power presages may well destroy constitutional systems from within and/or from without. To repeat: even such provisions are merely technical improvements, and no constitutional order can maintain itself which is not supported loyally by its citizens.

Why then do modern constitutions so uniformly neglect this problem of constitutional limitations? It may well be that the emphasis upon legislation as the real core of governmental action accounts for this. From Rousseau to the present time, martial rule, the state of siege, and constitutional emergency powers have been taken to be largely limited to executive action.

Indeed, they have been looked upon as extensions of this "power." At the same time, the doctrine of the central importance of rule making was retained, and all such emergency powers as were wielded by executives could only be used to suspend the laws but not to alter them. When extensive delegation of legislative powers occurred in France, Germany, and elsewhere, it was thought such delegation could be permitted because the elected assembly, the "legislature," remained as the guardian of legislation; it could revoke any rules it did not like. Thus the legislative body appeared as the guardian of the constitution. The more strictly executive or administrative phases of the process did not seem to matter in comparison. The notorious power of the Roman dictator over life and death might not be equalled on account of *habeas corpus,* but a boundless extension of administrative competence would be accepted, although it might endanger the lives of thousands or even millions. Such a doctrinaire approach to the problem overlooks the potential crystallization of such practices into a fixed pattern. Orthodox tradition looked upon the whole process as one of merely temporarily enlarging executive power. But in terms of the actual distribution of power, the process appears as a rapid concentration of power in the hands of a ruling oligarchy, represented by an individual capable of effectively dramatizing its position. The traditional view is too legalistic. To be sure, an emergency such as war or insurrection is an undesirable state of fact. For this undesirable state of affairs it seemed sufficient to find a specific technical solution. The phrase "state of siege" is indicative of this attitude. The siege must be lifted; that is all. An executive officer is seen in analogy to a military commander; he must take command and accomplish the desirable end. This done, nothing really fundamental has happened; things have returned to their normal state. The rule of law having been re-established, everything is precisely where it was before. Such a view now appears shortsighted. The temporarily concentrated powers cannot be separated and distributed again unless residuary power is left somewhere for that purpose. Recurrent measures crystallize into rules, and under crisis conditions a continuous state of emergency arises. Rigid constitutional limitations such as the one suggested by the present analysis will not save a constitutional regime which prevents the realization of what is considered right by the community. But they will add a most powerful brake which in the day of crisis may be decisive in bringing the skidding constitutional order back into its groove, while the necessary adjustments are made in the distribution of power according to the believed-in standard of justice.

The pattern of transition from constitutional to unconstitutional dictator • The details of the transition from a constitutional government to an unconstitutional one are not yet known. But the broad outlines of the process are distinctly discernible.[12] The following sketch may give an idea of the kind of situation that is typical. The constitutional government is weak. It lacks the support of tradition. The division of power under the constitution is faulty, resulting in too much friction or in too much power for small groups in the community. The constitution provides channels for the manifestation of mass emotions, however. Typical tools of radical democracy, such as general elections or referendum machinery (plebiscitary apparatus), are available under it. The dissatisfied groups throw their strength in this direction. They thrust forward one or more leaders who are able under the constitution to secure positions of power, and thus legitimate authority. They buttress intransigeant demands for broader channels of mass emotionalism by appeals to the tenets of radical democracy. In the meantime their mass supporters carry on guerilla warfare against all opponents, thus creating a civil-war situation. The attendant disorder and the eventual anarchy stir the indifferent elements in the community into action. The tension rises. More disorder, clashes between groups of citizens, murders, burnings, follow. Dictatorial methods for the maintenance of the constitutional order, indeed any order, appear inevitable. The resulting constitutional dictatorship lacks drive, because of the weakness of constitutional morale. It consequently tends to succumb to anticonstitutional elements, working either from within or from without. At the decisive point, these elements will seize the initiative, with the mass of the citizens unable to counteract such an initiative or to seize it in their turn. This, roughly speaking, has been the pattern of "transition," regardless of whether the particular totalitarians were coming from the right or from the left. Italy, Spain, Germany, France, Czechoslovakia, Hungary, Eastern Germany; it is a similar story again and again.

If one asks what measure might be suitable means for preventing this development, the answer seems at first to be: more radical measures for dealing with the emergency. But such measures usually will violate the constitutional tradition, and hence must be justified. This problem of "justification" is politically of crucial importance, because as the latent civil war develops, the decisive question is which side the army will take. In Russia the army was revolutionized through the war; the decision of the Kerenski government to continue the war was its fatal error. In Italy the army remained neutral, which was enough to give Mussolini the upper hand. In Germany the army refused to march against Hitler, as it looked upon the nationalism of the masses as the most effective support for the rearmament and remilitarization it desired. In Poland the army always supported Pilsudski, their own general. Likewise in Yugoslavia, the army supported *their* supreme commander, the king. It appears, in other words, that the concentration of powers cannot be forestalled if the armed forces remain indifferent. They must be positively attached to the constitutional order. It is here that the problem of constitutional morale meets its crucial test; the failure to perceive this problem spells eventual disaster. The Communists have learned this lesson and have seen to it that their partisans either infiltrated the army (Czechoslovakia) or developed a revolutionary army of their own (China). Neither Locke nor Rousseau saw this problem clearly, and much constitutional doctrine was equivocal about this matter. But the Swiss people have always been keenly aware of it, and their views have had a measure of resonance in the United States. Curiously enough, the keenest exposition of the problem in theory is offered by none other than Machiavelli. In his *Discourses on Livy*, as well as in his other works, he always returns to the *militia* as the central theme. In doing so, he rationalized the historical conceptions of Livy. By this token, the democratization policy of the Western Allies was crucially handicapped because it was prevented by its demilitarization objective from permitting the German democrats to organize a "militia" with which to maintain themselves. Continued occupation was, under these conditions, the only possible way out; but it meant that constitutional government would have existed only by grace of the occupying powers. The full measure of the gap implied here may be seen when one recalls that the American revolutionaries proudly claimed the "right to bear arms" as one of the basic rights of all free men. It looked at first as if the same error would be repeated after 1945. But it has since been corrected. To be sure, the German Basic Law contains a provision among its declaration of rights that "no one may be forced against his conscience into military service." This provision has since become attenuated in connection with the Basic Law's amendments to enable the Federal Republic to establish armed forces. The reluctance of the opposition and the widespread desire to avoid a relapse into militarism led to the establishment of a parliamentary commissioner who, being directly responsible to the *Bundestag*, would hear complaints about militaristic abuses and that sort of thing. The history of this institution has been a stormy one, but need not be retold here in detail. The commissioner has, on the whole, served as a gadfly and fulfilled his major function.

Military government • All writers on comparative government neglected the questions of military government until the course of the Second World War forced its problems upon their attention. This in spite of the fact that military government was a recurrent phenomenon throughout the nineteenth century and played a significant role during and after the American Civil War. Its normative aspects formed part of international law, but they received scant treatment since its practice did not appeal to a liberal age.

Military government needs to be distinguished clearly from martial rule, military law, and civil affairs. For military government is the government by the military of the civil population of occupied enemy territory, whereas the term "civil affairs," properly speaking, is used to designate functions of liaison and supervisory direction in occupied territory belonging to friendly powers. Military law is the law applying to persons in the military forces, and, as has been shown, martial rule consists in rule by the military of domestic territory and citizens.

Military government may be of two kinds when considered in relation to constitutionalism. It may be wielded on behalf of a constitutional government or on behalf of an autocratic (totalitarian) regime. In the latter case, it is an extension of the autocratic methods to an enemy population. This in the case of contemporary totalitarian dictatorship means the application of its particular techniques, especially the characteristic total disregard for the basic human rights of all who are subject to its control. There is obviously no reason why an occupied enemy territory should receive more lenient treatment than the government's own subjects. On the other hand, the military government established by a constitutional regime is an "exceptional state" resulting from an "emergency," and hence it has the characteristic features of a "constitutional dictatorship." Such military government is not bound by the constitutional limitations, of course, but it will partake of the "constitutional morality" of the home government. Indeed, the American army's *Field Manual on Military Government* which was in use at the beginning of the Second World War laid it down as an objective of military government to "protect the welfare of the governed." In other words, within the scope and limits of military necessity, military government was and is inspired by humanitarian considerations for the subject population. This intrinsic tendency of military government when carried out on behalf of a constitutional democracy is enhanced if it is the objective of the occupation to seek the establishment of a constitutional democracy in the occupied area. For in the latter case, military government becomes a "constitutional dictatorship" in the more specific sense in which such a dictatorship is directed toward the maintenance of constitutional government. In other words, a "democratizing" military government is in a particularly close sense committed to the constitutional traditions of the people for whom it acts and speaks. The failure to grasp this fundamental fact has caused some of the most embarrassing situations arising out of the Second World War.[13]

Experience prior to the Second World War · Experience with military government in modern times has been quite varied. Ranging from the merciless burning and pillage of the religious wars, as exemplified by the politics of a Wallenstein, a Richelieu, or a Cromwell, to the highly civilized occupation of the Rhineland by American armies after 1918, military government has tended to reflect the spirit of the times and of the government responsible for its execution. Francis Lieber in 1863 formulated this liberal conception when he wrote: "As civilization has advanced, during the last centuries, so has likewise steadily advanced, especially in war on land, the distinction between the private individual belonging to a hostile country and the hostile country itself, with its men in arms. The principle has been more and more acknowledged that the unarmed citizen is to be spared in person, property and honor as much as the exigencies of war will permit." This philosophy was codified in the Hague Convention of 1907, which provided in its Article 32 that ". . . the occupant . . . shall take all measures in his power to restore, and ensure, as far as possible, public order and safety, while respecting, unless absolutely prevented, the laws in force in the country." In view of what happened during and after the Second World War, this article sounds like an echo from another world. Perhaps even more idyllic is the sound of Article 46: "Family honour and rights, the lives of persons, and private property, as well as religious convictions and practices, must be respected. Private property cannot be confiscated."[14] These ideas had dominated the *Basic Field Manual on Military Government* of the United States War Department, published in June 1940. They hardly dominated American military government practice. They were part of that "civilized warfare" which had originated with Hugo Grotius' *Law of War and Peace* (1625), inspired as it had been by the revulsion humane men had come to feel over the barbarities of the religious wars. But there were many exceptions in American practice, for example, during the Civil War, and most European countries have not either lived up to these humane conceptions, especially in their colonial warfare.

The practice of military government after the end of the religious wars rarely was based upon the notion that it was the task, let alone the moral duty, of the occupying power to reform or make over the occupied country or its people. The idea played a role in the conduct of military government by the first Napoleon and during and after the American Civil War, the latter being a special case precisely because it was a civil war. Napoleon I, considering himself the "son of the revolution," had encouraged revolutionary changes in many of the countries he conquered, such as the establishment of the Helvetic Republic and the dissolution of the Holy Roman Empire and the creation of the Federation of the Rhine. The United States similarly has acted as a revolutionizing force. The idea of encouraging self-government has been a feature of American military government for a long time.

This idea, in cases like the Philippines, has served as a moral justification for ruling a foreign people. It gradually spread to other colonizing peoples and was dramatized in the slogan of "the white man's burden." Yet, while connoting a greater moral concern on the part of the occupant with the assumed welfare of the occupied people, it heightened the intrinsic offensiveness of foreign rule for the latter by implying that the conqueror was superior. In the case of the Rhineland occupation, the situation was further complicated by the conflict between the liberal-conservative outlook of the American and British governments as contrasted with the liberal-socialist revolution which had occured in Germany at the time of the surrender. Experience in most of these cases might have served to caution one against this kind of reformist military government, but the lesson of history was, as usual, largely lost.[15]

In 1947 a thoughtful student of the development of military government policy sized up the situation thus: "The paradox which American military government confronted at the termination of hostilities both in Germany and Japan, was that it sought to build the peace with policy weapons forged in the heat of war. Clarity there was on what was to be destroyed or eliminated. But much more difficult was the realization that political reconstruction carries with it other imperatives — encouragement to groups that have repudiated Nazism or militarism, and the creation of conditions that make it possible for such groups to provide constructive leadership in new directions."[16]

Military government and democratization · After some preliminary hesitations, democratization was in the Second World War made the major positive objective of American military government after the combat phase. This constituted a marked deviation from earlier ideas which had clustered around the twofold objective of (1) military needs, and (2) restoring law and order. Restoring law and order is not unrelated to military needs, but it is intended to serve and implement it. After the end of fighting, it would assume primary significance, however, and may be said to have been expanded into the task of establishing constitutional democracy. For such a democracy is readily conceived by its adepts as the only sound basis of "law and order." Such a view was encouraged by the obvious absence of law, if not of order in the Fascist and militarist regimes which the victorious Allies proposed to displace. That a comparable lack of law and order characterized at least one of the major Allies was glossed over in such elusive phrases as "peace-loving nations."

Unfortunately for all concerned, the term "democratization" had completely divergent connotations for the Western Allies and the Soviet Union. Agreements, such as the Potsdam Agreement, embodying this phrase were therefore in reality no more than compromises in terms of a formula. As events were to prove, these divergent conceptions of democracy were in a number of vital respects antithetical. The historian finds it difficult to accept the now often-heard excuse that Western Allied policy makers had to learn by experience that this was so. Actually, the contrasting and mutually exclusive conceptions of democracy were a matter of full and well-established record, and even the most casual inquiry would have revealed the clash of views. In what follows we shall use the term "democratization" exclusively in the Western sense; the policies and practices of the totalitarian people's democracies are not properly a part of a study of constitutional democracy.

Democratization, however, is not a controversy only between the West and the Soviet Union. It is also a bone of contention between the Western powers and among their citizens. In spite of the comparative evaluations of such writers as Bryce, each democratic nation inclines to identify the concept of democracy with its particular institutions, and each party is similarly inclined to identify its outlook with "truly" democratic views. Therefore, such issues as the importance of a free-market economy, the compatibility of socialism with a free society, and the like are bound to inject themselves into a policy which merely speaks of democratization without spelling out what is to be understood by the term "democracy." The experience with military government after the Second World War is replete with difficult situations and breakdowns resulting from disagreements over what democratization calls for. Whether we consider denazification, decartelization, re-education, or any other of the vital areas of military-government activity, the same basic issue appears.

In an effort to clarify the resulting situation and to guide the Germans who were approaching the task of formulating constitutions in three states of the American zone, American military government issued a statement of policy which defined "democratization" in terms of eight criteria which may be summed up thus: basic political power stems from the people, and those who exercise power must submit their program and policies to frequent popular elections; such elections must be competitive between at least two parties; such parties must be democratic, voluntary associations of citizens; basic rights of these citizens must be firmly guaranteed; public-opinion channels must be kept free of governmental domination; the "rule of law" must be recognized; and the exercise of governmental authority must be decentralized.[17] By this statement, the line was clearly and deliberately drawn which separates constitutional democracy from the "people's democracy" of the Soviet Union and its satellites, including the Soviet zone of Germany. Had such a basic definition been developed prior to Potsdam, and submitted to the Soviet representatives, the presumably hidden conflicts over democratization might have been brought to light. This might have greatly reduced the area of potential friction.

Military government and the rule of law · It was the contention of the writer, since borne out by events, that it would be wiser to restrict military government objectives to the establishment of government according to law in the conquered countries. Historically speaking, such government according to law has been the basic condition for the growth of constitutional democracy. This government according to law, comparable to the German concept of *Rechtsstaat,* is characterized by the general respect for and observance of law on the part of the governing authorities. It is frequently rather inaccurately referred to as the "rule of law."[18] Such an approach would have provided a common core for the different views on democracy, and it would have encouraged the Germans to shoulder the responsibility for democratization. It would also have enabled the Allies to avoid making "democracy" appear responsible for the painful tasks involved in liquidating Fascism.

The almost complete destruction of government according to law under the Fascists called for two interrelated steps: (1) to purge the law of those accretions which embody Fascist and National Socialist policy and prejudice; (2) to do everything possible to strengthen the authority of the regular courts after eliminating judicial personnel with markedly Fascist records. Of these two steps, the first proved easier of execution than the second, largely because the judiciary had become Fascist and Nazi to a much greater degree than had been thought probable. Indeed, one of the most difficult aspects of denazification resulted from the fact that so many judges were suspect that it seemed inexpedient to assign the task to the courts. The suspension of all specifically Fascist and Nazi laws was decreed at the outset, and more detailed "purging" was carried out by the joint effort of military government and the Italian, Austrian, and German authorities.[19] It was, in fact, Law Number 1 of the Allied Control Council which repealed the laws of the Hitler regime on September 20, 1945. It listed specifically twenty-five laws, but implemented the list by outlawing any injustice or inequality which might be caused by discriminating against any person by reason of his race, nationality, religious beliefs, or opposition to the National Socialist German Workers' Party or its doctrines. Considering the actualities of government in the Soviet Union and the United States, this provision was indeed a counsel of perfection well calculated to suffer in concrete application. In spite of it, Control Council Law Number 1 constituted the basic step in the reestablishment of government according to law which the adoption of the Basic Law of the German Federal Republic on May 8, 1949, completed.

For in this Basic Law the principles of the *Rechtsstaat* were unqualifiedly reaffirmed and reinforced by the Allied Occupation statute which subjected the occupying authorities to comparable restraints. In Italy the same result was achieved by the constitution of 1947; in Austria by the revival of the constitution of 1929. The occupation came officially to an end on May 5, 1955.

Military government as constitutional dictatorship · The complex and in many ways unfortunate record of Allied military government must be seen in the perspective of the establishment of constitutionalism in Italy, Austria, Germany, and Japan. Ever since the policy of democratization was first formulated, American criticism has been directed at it in some such general terms as "You cannot impose democracy by force." Much of the best liberal and democratic tradition in the United States has been cited in support of the contention that democracy cannot develop as a healthy and lasting form of government unless the people want democracy and have fought for it. From the viewpoint of those who, without deeper knowledge or insight, proceed on the assumption that democracy is something wholly new in the several countries subjected to Fascist and militarist rule in Europe in recent years, and that therefore it is to be bestowed upon them by outsiders, the objection is fatal indeed. But fortunately the situation was not as desperate as all that. Allied policy was directed in each case not toward "imposing democracy," but toward imposing restraints upon those elements of the population — demonstrably minorities — which would prevent democracy from becoming established or, if established, would undermine and eventually destroy it. Force can be used, and has been used, for suppressing the Fascists, the Nazis, and militarists. Force can be used, and has been used, for reducing the power of the big landowners and of those industrialists who supported the Fascist movements. Anyone who is even casually acquainted with the history of the first German republic and of its institutions as depicted in other pages of this study will realize that a substantial reduction in the power of these anticonstitutional elements would have substantially assisted those Germans who desired to establish a constitutional democracy. The situation in Japan is similar. This assistance to indigenous democratic elements by the forcible removal of obstructionist groups proved rather effective after the Second World War.[20]

When seen in this perspective, the policy of democratization as carried forward by the Western Allies was a policy of employing emergency powers of a dictatorial kind to re-establish constitutionalism. It therefore differed only in degree from the broad policy implied in the "hot war" against the Axis powers and in the Cold War against the Soviet Union. In Asia and in Europe, the policy of democratization is the spearhead of a general policy of supporting constitutional and democratic forces. Force is being employed for "containing" the antidemocratic force throughout the world. These antidemocratic forces, whether Communist or Fascist, have created in the past and continue to create a state of universal emergency throughout the world community by their appeal to force. As the *Communist Manifesto* made clear, and as the masters of the Soviet Union and Communist China have repeatedly reaffirmed, their appeal is to revolutionary force. We have seen at the outset of this chapter that war and insurrection create the states of emergency which call for the establishment of constitutional dictatorship. Thus, an evaluation of military government operations on the part of the constitutional powers of the West cannot penetrate to the full significance of many detailed items without comprehending the world-revolutionary situation of our time.

It is noteworthy in this connection that military government corresponds more nearly to the four criteria for organizing a constitutional dictatorship that were outlined at the beginning of this chapter. The constitutional dictator who is military governor is in fact appointed by a constitutional government he does not control, the exercise of his powers is expressly defined, and since he is subject to recall, his term may be said to be subject to a clear time limit. Full, and at times sharp and even unjust, criticism by the representative bodies and the public both in Britain and in the United States ensured the employment of these dictatorial powers for "constitutional" purposes.

Conclusion · In light of the foregoing, it seems clear that the military government instituted by a constitutional regime in the postcombat phase was directed toward the establishment of government according to law. The formation of groups of persons in the occupied areas ready and willing to initiate and promote democratic movements and constitutional efforts "at the grass roots" was encouraged. Such groups were presumably led by democratically minded men and women who had escaped from the totalitarian terror. This presupposed that military government policies were formulated and executed by men thoroughly familiar with the culture and the past traditions of the countries to be occupied. What is perhaps even more important, however, is that such policies and their execution should be in the hands of persons who would understand the nature of the world-revolutionary situation and would appreciate the limits of force in dealing with a conflict of this type.[21] Constitutional dictatorship, on the surface a contradiction in terms, is the final test of constitutionalism. For a government which cannot meet emergencies is bound to fall sooner or later. There is no object in arguing against such emergency powers on the ground that they endanger the constitutional morale, and hence the maintenance of the constitutional order. Of course they do. Any suspension of legal norms, no matter how temporary, raises doubts concerning their validity. But after all, what does an emergency mean if not that the constitutional order is threatened? Imminent invasion and civil war are only the most blatant and final stages of such a danger. No one in his right mind can argue that their emergence should not be forestalled. Unfortunately, no man can fortell the future. Hence, it will always be a matter of judgment, a matter of weighing risks as to which is more dangerous: the threatening emergency or the powers for combating it. Humanly enough, the more uncertain the choice, the more emphatic become the partisans. Nothing shows that more clearly than America's dilemma in the face of the world revolutionary situation. It is similar to the dilemma confronted in the rise of Hitler. Few would question in retrospect that even rather far-reaching measures designed to forestall that rise would have been in America's interest; yet at the time, in 1936, 1937, 1938, few were prepared to adopt such measures because they miscalculated the danger ahead.

Although modern industrialism forbids the employment of the Roman pattern of constitutional dictatorship, its underlying conceptions are still valid. Emergency powers should be very broad in scope, but the conditions for their exercise should be rigidly defined. The constitutional dictator should be appointed by a body which he does not in fact control, he should not be in a position to declare the emergency himself, and a fixed time limit should be attached to the grant of powers. But behind all these procedural devices there must stand an alert people, a real constituent power, determined to see to it that these limitations are effectively utilized to insure the legitimate employment of these emergency powers: to strengthen the constitution, if necessary, by timely changes. What can never be timely is a change in the basic constitutionalism itself. The problem of constitutional dictatorship, therefore, presents a more acute case of the general problem of constitutionalism. How are we to get effective, vigorous governmental action, and yet limit the power of governmental bodies so as to forestall the rise of a despotic concentration of power? Logically it is a paradox, but practically it has been done. The task requires all the wisdom man can muster. The prize is his greatest achievement: freedom.

Constitutionalism in Emergent Nations
XXVI

Introduction · Legitimacy · Suitability of constitutional democracy · Legitimate succession · Military force · The case of Puerto Rico · Development politics · A model sketched · A glimpse of the future

Introduction · Constitutionalism has become world-wide in its appeal, and democracy the universal goal. Yet neither appears to have gained vitality or strength in the process. Quite the contrary, doubt and confusion multiply. Constitutionalism and democracy are generally seen as the lesser evil, as the kind of political order left after other forms, including totalitarian dictatorship and traditional autocracies, have been discredited. The earlier nineteenth-century notion, implied in the slogan of "the white man's burden," that the problem is that of guiding the development of every country toward the adoption of constitutionalism and democracy, is being undermined by experience. In country after country serious difficulties have been encountered in making Western democracy, especially its parliamentary version, work. Is this really surprising, when one considers that Western constitutional democracy is rooted in and to some extent dependent upon basic religious and philosophical convictions which are not to be found in many of these new countries?[1]

Legitimacy · The difficulties arising from these convictional contrasts and divergencies have led many observers to the opposite extreme of believing that the political theory developed in the West is completely inapplicable to this new world. Such complete relativism, to some extent derived from the misunderstood relativism of cultural anthropology,[2] is incompatible with the spirit of science and the fundamental premise of all genuine theory. For such theory presupposes that there is one truth, and that the appearance of relativity is due to failure to observe and properly account for differentiating factors.

The numerous striking propositions which political theory offers concerning power, rule, and influence are, of course, applicable to developing countries; if they were not, they would not be true generalizations. Indeed, they help to make evident that in many basic aspects the politics of developing countries are not at all different from the politics, the drama of leadership and followership, in highly developed communities.

To illustrate, surely Max Weber's celebrated threefold division of legitimacy into a traditional, a rational-legal, and a charismatic one is meant to be applicable and is in fact quite meaningful in dealing with the political orders of emergent countries.[3] The basis of legitimacy of the present governments of Ethiopia, Israel, and Egypt, to take three examples at random, may be distinguished according to the Weberian triad, though numerous difficulties present themselves as to detail. These Weber would seek to minimize by claiming that the three categories were "ideal types" and hence could not be tested by concrete examples except in an approximate way.[4] But whether ideal-typical or not, and whether exhaustive or not, these concepts provide meaningful analytical tools for the study of non-Western political orders, because tradition, law, and rationality are pan-human categories, that is, they apply to all men.

To continue the argument about legitimacy a step further, surely the universal trend to make constitutions is the manifestation of the need and an expression of a search for some kind of democratic legitimacy.[5] Max Weber would perhaps have argued that it was the result of a widely felt need of rational-legal legitimation, because of the breakdown of tradition and the absence of charismatic leadership. "Legitimacy" is the proper term for designating the political constellation in which a ruler is believed by those he rules to have a right to do so (and this includes in the present world also to some extent the belief of those not ruled by him, but participants in the international order, such as it is). Hence a "constitution," no matter how unrealistic, in the sense of nondescriptive of who actually governs, has a certain value.[6] Indeed, even a constitution which is least satisfactory from the point of view of guaranteeing the observance of its rules, especially those meant to protect the private individual, is apt to contain numerous provisions which do describe the actual governmental practice; thus even the constitution of the Soviet Union, while certainly a facade in many ways, contains a rational-legal pattern and therefore legitimizes the rulers to a certain extent, in the eyes of both Soviet citizens and the world at large.

Besides providing a measure of legitimacy for the ruler(s) of a new state, a constitution also constitutes a symbol of national unity. Like the flag, it is a unifying and hence integrating symbol, often implying, or indeed explicating, a foundation myth. The symbolism and the implied myth are suggesting that a new person has come into being, a collective entity has been born. How otherwise could a constituent power have been operating to create the constitution? The constituent power, we have seen (ch. VIII), is closely related to the cataclysmic advent of a revolution, in this case a colonial revolution. After such a revolution, the constituent power is wielded by a constituent group which, no matter how small or large, sets up a government. If the ideology which inspired the revolution was democratic, there is a compelling need of organizing the community under a democratic constitution. This compulsion worked even in the case of the Soviet Union, it will be remembered, although there is nothing to be found in Marx about the need or desirability of a constitution. For him, "justice is a bourgeois prejudice," and so is law. But the new nations, inspired by Rousseau's passionate teachings — not always directly, of course — deeply felt the need of manifesting their nationhood in a constituent act. Hence the constitution is made to form both symbol and myth.[7] As Edward Shils has commented: "Ever since the American Revolution, the act of creating a state has tended to entail the declaration of the fundamental law of the new country in the form of a constitution. The process of constitution-making has been regarded as a major *symbol* of the formation of the new state."[8]

The task of integrating often very disparate elements resulting from colonial conquest and held together by colonial rule is perhaps the most pressing need of all the new states. When one speaks in these cases of "emergent nations," he gainsays the large amount of human effort that has to be expended in order to bring this "emergence" of a new nation about. And the attempts at constitution making are part of that gigantic effort.

Suitability of constitutional democracy · Is it reasonable to expect that the developing countries in one great leap forward not only "adopt" constitutions, but also make them work? Can they hope, without firm anchorage in the Judaeo-Christian religious heritage, to operate a developing economy in so complex a fashion? Are not the European nations themselves finding the machinery of constitutionalism increasingly difficult to manipulate as they face an ever more highly developed industrial economy and the rising expectations of its urban masses? Are emergent countries not bound to abandon the distinctively Western kind of constitutionalism in favor of a more integrated and more communally directed order? The constitution of the Soviet Union and of its former satellites, while surely no embodiment of Western constitutionalism, seem to many to provide a more suitable framework for the tasks of development and national integration. The Soviet Union and Red China, certainly, constitute regimes which operate with power concentrated in the hands of the lead group who are, or at any rate were, fired by a missionary zeal for and an abiding faith in themselves as the true providers of a better future. Especially in all those communities where there is little suspicion of power and scant demand for personal rights and liberties — their past religions having no particular concern with either — concentrated power seems to many the answer to the pressing problems of development.[9]

It has always seemed a bit curious that the fate which has overtaken the constitutions in quite a few emergent states should have come as a surprise to so many of their architects. After all, extended experience had been had with comparable situations in Latin America. There constitutions, usually modeled on the American *Vorbild,* or paradigm, have regularly been flouted and set aside by military juntas, practically without exception. But of course this history had been treated as nonexemplary and hence irrelevant. This may be due in part to the fact that the constitutions of the new states were largely of the parliamentary type. They were modeled on the paradigm of Britain as well as Ireland, the Netherlands, France, and other parliamentary systems. This was no doubt the consequence of the education and training of the leaders of the independence movements, who, in spite of their hostility to their colonial masters, tended to look to them for guidance in matters of political practice. Since they were powerful, so the argument runs, they must know how to run governments. In addition, the expert advisers of new regimes were quite often strong believers in parliamentary democracy — men like Sir Ivor Jennings, for example — as were of course the officials in the colonial offices who usually guided the preliminary steps taken before independence. Even in countries with a long constitutional tradition of their own, such as Germany, this factor played a role.

The notion of a constitutional democracy was in the minds of leaders and their constituents alike somewhat vague and often confused with that of a radical democracy in the Continental tradition of Rousseau.[10] While there was a general readiness to recognize the importance of limiting the exercise of governmental power, and of permitting free expression of opinion in regard to politics, there was an equally strong conviction that the majority's preferences should prevail. As a result, these systems tended to evolve rather rapidly toward a crisis, a critical conflict over which was more important, the constitution or the will of the people. In most countries, the constitution once adopted has been left as it was adopted, even though actual practice has tended to depart ever-more markedly from the original form and intent. And although there was at first a tendency to avoid its abrogation, the readiness to do so has recently increased. Not only in Pakistan and Indonesia, but in Nigeria, Tanganyika, and other African states, the constitution has not only been violated but in fact suspended. Even when the un- and anticonstitutional practices have not been carried quite that far, there has been a fairly widespread disregard for some of the most significant constitutional (basic) rights, and little if any respect for the necessary enforcement machinery, especially the existence of an organized opposition. Such an opposition is, under more recent party systems, the crucial equivalent of the older separation of powers. As already mentioned, it constitutes in a sense a new separation of powers in sequence (time) replacing the conventional separation in function (space). Something more will be said on this score presently. But let us first note here that the constitutional violations have included censoring of the press and imprisoning of journalists and writers, persecution and even suppression of racial, religious, and linguistic (cultural) minorities, and of course elimination and forcible amalgamation of opposition parties. There exists always and in any constitutional regime a certain spread between norm and actual performance; indeed, what has been called the living constitution (see above, ch. I) has always differed from what is written in constitutional charters and statute books. But it would obviously be improper to speak of a living constitution when in fact the very basic characteristic of a constitutional order is no longer operative, that is to say, when its regularized restraint of governmental power in the interest of protecting a personal sphere of the individual citizen and of his voluntary associations is destroyed. This tendency is unfortunately encouraged by the fact that the so-called constitutions which have been put forth in the Soviet Union and other totalitarian regimes have obscured the basic issue. If the constitution is seen as an instrument of class warfare, it obviously is something different from the democratic and personalist constitution defined above. "The basic task of the Constitution is the establishment of the dictatorship of the city and village proletariat . . . ." one reads in the Soviet constitution of 1918. As such it cannot be simply discarded as "mere facade"; for every constitution contains strong ideological elements. Not only any bill of rights it may contain, but also the organizational features it fixes, are ideologically determined.[11] But if the term "constitution" is employed in such a generalized sense (customary since Aristotle's discussion of the *politeia,* a term which is usually rendered as "constitution"), then a prefix such as "liberal," "democratic," or "personalist" ought to indicate that one is speaking of this specifically Western constitution. And since Western constitutionalism in the tradition of British political theorists from Fortescue to Locke provides the archetype of this notion, it may even be sensible to speak of a "constitutionalist constitution."

Legitimate succession · It has been a key feature of "constitutionalist" constitutions to provide for succession on a regularly recurrent basis, this recurrency having an important restraining influence. It is lacking in the totalitarian constitutions. It has also been the Achilles' heel of many of the new constitutions. Assassination has, of course, no particular institutional significance; else we would have to question the constitutionalist character of the American order. Yet, when such assassination is the precursor of revolutionary and counterrevolutionary transformations in the political order, it attains symptomatic significance for the weakness of constitutionalism. In Pakistan, Iraq, Syria, and South Vietnam, as in Nigeria and in many Latin American countries, such assassination has been the harbinger of a breakdown of the constitutional system.

In light of what has been said about legitimacy, it is obvious that such outbreaks of violence lack the kind of ambiance which would provide their perpetrators with any convincing claim to legitimacy. They must therefore strive to achieve it. Ideological movements have frequently served this goal with more or less success. Genuine or pseudo charisma of the leader of the coup may add to the belief of the masses that he and the movement he leads have a right to rule.

But sooner or later, all successions in the democratic age will call for the sanctioning of rule by elections. The development of modern mass parties has in stabilized constitutional democratic regimes provided for a certainty of succession far superior to that of alternative methods. To this certainty must be added the great advantage of thereby making it possible to change rulers rather frequently. A community is never long committed to an unsuccessful ruler or group. Practically all systems based on competitive elections have provided for rather brief intervals, two to seven years. Such a period, of say five years, is a bearable risk on a poor choice and certainly better than an entire generation. Generally speaking, of course, no mode of succession can *insure* a competent ruler, but the competition of two parties in rivalry for public support gives apparently the best chance of providing him, and this for two reasons. There is on the one hand their strong organizational self-interest in doing so, and on the other the fact that the party's own internal politics has usually provided a testing ground for the potential ruler's capacity for government. The party has, therefore, a crucial function in constitutional democracies and should be seen in this perspective. When one speaks of the function of "ensuring the government" and similar phrases which are conventionally used in defending a majoritarian system of elections (see above, chs. XIV, and XV), this succession problem is at issue. Indeed, the British system has on this score been traditionally contrasted with Continental and European systems in such terms as a "true" or "genuine" system of parliamentary government.[12]

Military force • Where such a system is lacking, or fails to function, military coups have often taken its place. Latin America apart, there have been such coups in Algeria, Burma, Egypt, Indonesia, Iraq, Laos, Nigeria,

Pakistan, South Korea, Sudan, Syria, Togoland, Turkey, and elsewhere. Attempted coups would lengthen the list; every few months a new country is added to it. As was remarked earlier, such military coups seem the characteristic alternative to a constitutionalist regime, when traditional orders have broken down beyond revival and totalitarian, especially Communist alternatives are rejected by military and related elites. The ensuing regimes are at times more "liberal" than the preceding regime; liberal, that is, in the sense of allowing a somewhat broader spectrum of opinion to be expressed. At the same time, "the military are, in fact, much like the civilian politicians they displace." The writer adds: "The fact is that government by the military in some respects brings to a more open expression certain of the political aspirations of those they displace and of those over whom they exercise power."[13]

Besides certain other motivations (and conditions) of military takeover, the breakdown of the constitutionalist regime as manifested in civil war, (e.g. Spain), plays a vital role, and not only in new emergent countries. Civil war is endemic in constitutionalism, especially where a rampant pluralism is reinforced and given institutional escapes through federalism. Unless, therefore, societies possess a certain homogeneity, the risks involved in its adoption are very great. A number of emergent countries, notably the Congo, Indonesia, Iraq, Korea, and Vietnam, have been involved in civil war; others like India are threatened by it, with flareups here and there highlighting the danger. Military takeovers have been motivated and rationalized as anticipating such developments. It was a crucial factor in the return of General de Gaulle to power in 1958 — who, however, in turn stopped the further expansion of military power. Usually pragmatic in outlook, military men cannot cope with the civil-war situation without seeking some kind of legitimation, but the legitimizing force of constitutionalism is becoming weaker. Even so, regimes like that of General Ky have once again like Latin American dictatorship sought to exploit the democratic and popular implications of constitutionalism.

The difficulty is, however, that military and related elites do not in any substantive sense constitute a constituent group. The constituent power mentioned before is another ill-understood dimension of the constitutionalist tradition. Restating an original Lockean normative proposition in descriptive terms, based on much constitutionalist experience, I described the constituent group some years ago as one which consists of a considerable number of the more vital and intelligent men who, animated by a desire for freedom, are determined to organize a constitutionalist regime. Unless this purpose is dominant, no constituent group exists. Therefore one might say that in most emergent countries, these groups were feeble and have since disappeared; for an elite group which seeks merely power or the establishment of a totalitarian system is not a constituent group.[14]

The disappearance of constituent groups is not surprising in view of the successive breakdowns and performance failures of constitutionalist orders. It has at times been rather impressively argued both inside and outside the developing countries that the reason constitutionalism has no application to them is that they are living in a state of permanent emergency. They plead that, after all, developed constitutional systems recognize that under the stress of crisis the regular procedures are suspended and the country lives under a system of constitutional dictatorship. It is very true that the United States, Great Britain, and other constitutional democracies have developed fairly elaborate institutions under the general heading of "emergency powers" and related terms, such as "state of siege," "martial law," and so forth (see above, ch. XXV). It is risky to argue, as is sometimes done in light of the European experience, that since constitutional government in Europe arose out of a background of absolutist and tyrannical regimes, the same might happen in Asia and Africa. Not only is the history of European constitutionalism by no means that simple, but such a statement largely neglects the positive forces that went into the making of constitutional government in Europe.[15]

The case of Puerto Rico · It is interesting at this point to ponder the fact that constitutional development in Puerto Rico has traversed a very divergent course from that of most ex-colonial countries. After a period of considerable violence, this once "desperate isle" has emerged as an autonomous state within the confines of the United States constitution. It was able to construct and maintain a constitutionalist regime of considerable vitality and apparent durability, because within the framework of a broadly planned economic prosperity and rapidly rising standard of living, Puerto Rico could build on the spiritual heritage presupposed by Western constitutionalism. Its homogeneous Spanish-speaking and Catholic-Christian population readily responded to the implicit values and beliefs of constitutional democracy. After all, medieval Spanish constitutionalism, embodied in the battle cry of Spain's free cities, the *fuero fundamental,* was their own heritage.[16] It was the "middle road to freedom."

This middle road to freedom was opened up by an exceptional colonial administrator who, animated by fervent democratic convictions, came to realize that only responsible self-government would provide the kind of inspiration and leadership which, when adequately supported, might improve the condition of the desperate isle[17] The political instrumentality of this transformation became the Popular Democratic party (PPD), led by an outstanding inspirational leader, Luis Múñoz Marín. The PPD has dominated the political life of Puerto Rico to such an extent that the minority parties had to be protected by special constitutional devices. These devices, which give them greater representation than their votes justify, are the obverse of what can usually be observed in Latin American, African, and Asian politics, where, as already noted, opposition is very generally hampered, if not altogether suppressed. Múñoz Marín has always remained alert to the danger of *personalismo*, and has successfully advocated various means of strengthening the opposition, especially in the matter of party finance. Yet, the enthusiasm of his following was such that he had the greatest difficulty in extricating himself from the governorship. In a dramatic meeting he insisted against a shouting crowd demonstrating against his decision that he must not run again. He wanted the Puerto Rican electorate to become "mature." Only very recently had the party taken formal steps to institutionalize and depersonalize its authority. Rightly, its best informed student commented that this was "a momentous step," adding that "while Múñoz remains as the party's fountainhead and symbol of authority, it is highly doubtful whether any real movement to institutionalize the party is possible."[18] Múñoz Marín has now stepped down, and the transformation is under way. It is to some extent a matter of generations; as young voters come of age who have been born under the new order of the Free and Associated Commonwealth, the electorate is increasingly apt to take things for granted which formerly were "ideological" and disputed.[19] Even the cherished *hispanidad* of the earlier days is somewhat fading. But what remains is the sediment of convictions derived from a Christian past which is manifest in the nearly universal background of Catholicism.

Development politics · If one reviews the reflections presented in the preceding pages in the light of the sketched data and brief hunches as to trends, he cannot help but feel somewhat bewildered. A similar impression is gained from the many and often brilliant efforts at comprehension of a very maelstrom of more or less chaotic changes. Is not the very term "development" a euphemism, a Western gloss upon a world in utter turmoil? Before concluding, it may be well to take up once more this basic consideration. At the outset the term "development" was primarily and perhaps even basically a term related to the economy, its planning and administration. As one very broad definition puts it: "Development in general takes place when an index of that which is deemed desirable and relatively preferable increases in magnitude."[20] It is usually related to "modernization," which has been spoken of as entailing "the replacements of sacred revelation and revealed codes by secular enlightenment in respect of guidance in human affairs."[21] These characterizations leave a wide margin of uncertainty even in economic and technical matters; when it comes to politics, who is to say what is "desirable" and what "relatively preferable"? Is not the entire "great game of politics" played with a view to determining what is the answer to such questions as these? An interesting illustration is provided by the sub-field of administration.[22] It is often noted that "economic development has been blocked to a large extent precisely because its implementation depends on a structure and disposition of bureaucracy, neither of which can be jarred out of the larger societal whole." Since that is very true, it is implied that the entire society's change is to be directed in terms of economic goals, the relative weight of which in the total scale of the given society's value system is precisely the issue. The recommendations which are offered as clearly rational, if administrative efficiency is desired, are taken from the Western experience in which the modern bureaucratic organization and its twin, the capitalistic economy, are embedded.[23]

Development, then, is not merely something "economic," nor are "econo-mists" (specialists in the broadly defined sphere of economic factors) neces-sarily the only experts to be consulted on development. There exists a tendency to speak of all factors other than the economic as "noneconomic" factors. Such a way of discussing developmental problems implies that these problems are essentially "economic," with cultural and political factors operating as "interferences." The political dimension is, however, *sui generis* and constitutes a distinct variable which the political leadership of develop-ing countries is particularly sensitive to. Aware of the distinctive nature of the political community which they rule, its characteristic values, interests, and beliefs, these leaders often underestimate the contribution that a truly general political science has to make to the solution of their problems. Even so, in matters of culture and politics, underdevelopment is a questionable proposition at best; some of the countries standing in most pressing need of economic development, like India and Latin America, are the homes of highly advanced cultures, with an advanced and complex tradition of poli-tics. While it may be very true that there should be a greater attention given to the "development of politics" in these emergent countries, as contrasted with the "politics of development," it is necessary to bear in mind that "politics" is an ancient craft in India and elsewhere. Anyone who has some-time studied the *Arthashastra* — misnamed the Indian Machiavelli — will agree that sophistication in matters political had advanced as far in India at the time of Aristotle as it had in the West.[24] The art and science of politics was, however — in contrast to Aristotle's science of the polis — understood as the science of kingship (rulership). Such a science can become very elabo-rate and sophisticated, as the development of mercantilism and cameralism in the age of absolutism clearly showed. So it remains an open question just what the "development of politics" in the sense of political development means.

The case of the Soviet Union shows — as did the absolute monarchs of the seventeenth and eighteenth century — that the needs of economic and industrial development can be met with considerable success by autocratic regimes. Sociological theories about rationality as a standard and its development in the West, and related notions about the legality of procedures in strictly Western terms, have obscured this obvious fact and have given rise to hopes that the progress of industrialization would bring with it, if not democratization, then at least constitutionalism. The actual progress of development in the Soviet Union and elsewhere has so far belied these expectations. Unfortunately, the difficulties which confront an emergent nation in adopting the Soviet model are as great, if not greater, than are those of following the Western example.[25] Communism too presupposes the Western heritage, in some ways more completely even than Western modes of political conduct. Its extremes of rationalism and rule-begotten legalism are inconceivable without the context of Marx's radical acceptance and elaboration of the technology of industrial advance, and its ethical antecedents.

If then neither the Soviet Union nor the West have any ready-made model to fit the needs of developing countries, is there no ground upon which to propose a rational model? Does the experience of mankind in politics fail to provide worthwhile insights by which to be guided in organizing the newly emergent nations? Many say "yes." But I believe that a more hopeful answer ought to be attempted. Such an answer comprises merely a paradigmatic design, but like a good map, it helps in basic orientation. In any case, the term "political development," when used in either the sense of the "politics of development" or of the "development of politics," and perhaps in both senses when we say "Development Politics," presupposes a "vision" of the goal or goals, a fairly definite sense of what would be the "desirable" or the "relatively preferable." American go-getters once were proud "not to know where we're going, but merely that we're on the way." They sensed it very well; their notions of "progress" were in their very instincts. Such naive and unproblematic sense is no longer ours. In the present world, the precipitating factor of "development politics" is foreign aid, that is, the willingness of the United States, the U.S.S.R., and other "developed" systems to provide capital and other resources, partly stimulated by the competition between them. The question presents itself, therefore, in rather different terms politically: Which system will make the best use of such aid, that is to say — in the jargon now in vogue — of the input of capital, know-how, and other resources needed for economic development?

A model sketched[26] • On the basis of the theoretical position outlined earlier, as well as numerous others, it is possible to sketch such a model.[27] A political order is an operational whole which enables a group of human beings to arrive at decisions and to evolve policies by way of institutions which provide them with the means of effective cooperation. At the same time, such an order requires internal balances which enable it to maintain itself, which means continuous reintegration of the diversities and divergencies which develop. If such institutions and processes as the order consists of operate to the satisfaction of a substantial majority of those subject to it, the order will be accepted. The power which is exercised in connection with the operation of institutions and processes, whether directly or indirectly, will be felt as beneficial, even though it constrains and compels, if those actions which the community feels to be necessary are taken and none or few are engaged in which appear unnecessary. Under such conditions, the rulers are believed to have a right to their power; they are legitimate. When such rulers have the capacity for reasoned elaboration of the grounds of their activities, that is, when they possess authority, their effectiveness and that of the order they constitute will be much enhanced. The actions of such rulers will appear *just*, in the sense of being believed to be adequate, by comparative evaluation in light of the community's values and beliefs. Law, then, is apt to be the system of rulers expressing the regularities of behavior, actual, potential and/or normative. These propositions provide, it would seem, the frame of reference of over-all requirements of a satisfactory political order.[28]

While what follows applies to all levels of community, it may be best to focus attention upon the national communities, since it is the prevailing form of the political order of emergent nations. What, then, is a good political order for a national community for the present and foreseeable future? It is not possible to answer this question by reference to any existing political orders, though the oratory of both sides would suggest that the issue is between parliamentary and presidential democracy on one side, and sovietism on the other. None of the existing political systems can be said to be "good" according to the standard just laid down. Everywhere on earth men are at present more dissatisfied with their government than they were only a short two generations ago. Why? Much misgovernment apart, technological and organizational developments have precipitated a situation which governments are unable to cope with. Popular demands in terms of high expectations of peace and security have at the same time been rising. The result has been widespread dissatisfaction on the part of the subjects, increasing propaganda and demagogy on the part of the rulers. Neither parliamentary government in its various forms of democratic constitutionalism nor the various forms of dictatorship have been able to break out of the vicious circle. None of them provide a satisfactory political order. All these tradition-based systems lack authority and legitimacy, that is to say, they fail to provide justice, equality, and freedom to an adequate extent. Defense is illusory against an impending nuclear holocaust; disputes, and indeed dangerous clashes, especially between management and labor (strikes) and between racial groups, remain unsettled; rules (laws) are inadequate and frequently remain unenforced, due to their number and complexity, and many measures are unnecessary while needed ones are not taken. Parties either fail to integrate or they become oppressive and oligarchical (boss rule). Finally, education on all levels is proving increasingly unsatisfactory in the face of a disintegrating and rapidly transforming value and belief system. All these difficulties and problems plague newly emergent communities even more than the so-called "developed" countries.

In the face of this mounting chaos, we cannot fall back upon formerly satisfactory ways of governing. Three undertakings appear centrally important in light of past experience: (1) how to fashion the political structure in such a way that it can continually be renovated and reformed; (2) how to plan the various actions which the emergent needs call for; and (3) how to carry through the plans and policies. No existing system is able to fulfill these requirements partly because it ideologically claims to embody an optimum solution. The kind of model we are asking for is one that is intended to circumscribe the minimal requirements of a good (satisfactory) order for the present and near-future, and not one that is best for all times and places (though such a claim may endear it to many persons). The following features appear to be necessary. First, an executive that can act effectively, that is, can take all measures necessary to cope with, the technical requirements of survival, both economically and militarily; a crucial part of such an executive is a responsible bureaucracy and a comprehensive *planning* agency. Second, enforceable *restraints* upon the government's operations which will protect the ruled "citizens" sufficiently to enable them to become and remain political *persons*. Third, some operative *participation* of all adult and sane members of the political community in the making of rules. In all national communities, on account of their size, this calls for an *elected assembly* which has a decisive share in fiscal matters. Fourth, there must be operative *general rules* expressing the more permanent shared values and beliefs as well as common interests; these rules must above all regulate the powers implied in the first, second, and third features (constitutional order). Furthermore, and fifth, a reasonably independent *judiciary* is needed which will interpret the rules and particularly define the terms of settlement for disputes arising between members and powers. The sixth feature is, in a sense, a derivative of the third; for the effective participation of the citizen presupposes decentralization to the greatest possible extent compatible with effective government. *Local self-government* and *federalism* usually appear in combination and are part of an ongoing process of adapting community structure and power to each other. Finally, and seventh, there ought to exist several voluntary organizations (*parties*) which will provide the organizational framework for developing alternatives of policy and personnel for the government, of protection for the participant members, of implementation for their operative participation, and which will engage in continuous re-examinaton and criticism, as well as support, of the rules. It is not necessary that more than one of these parties has definite prospects of conducting the government, as long as the positions of the others can be made effective through the representative assembly. This presupposes the existence of a free press and related communication media without which parties cannot effectively operate.[29]

Let me finally point out that existing political orders of every type and description exhibit one or more of these features, but none appears to include them all. Hence none of them can be considered good or satisfactory when this model is used as a matrix to assess them. The model is offered here as a basis for discussion, and in order to show that it is not impossible to delineate a model government suitable for the rising industrial world of the developing countries. Whether the future will actually bring them into being is another and open question.

A glimpse of the future · The sketch of a model such as has just been presented may have a utopian ring. Even so, it suggests that the future is neither hopeless nor rosy. Countries new and old need governments that will function effectively in solving the ever-more pressing problems of an advanced technological age. There seems little doubt that some of these governments will be constitutional democracies, quite a few others not. The rivalries between countries may remain rivalries between political systems and ideologies. In any case political change and adaptation will remain the order of the day. Whether the totalitarian dictatorships and the constitutional democracies gradually will come to resemble each other, as I predicted many years ago, they will certainly continue to evolve in response to their problems as they face new situations.[30] There is a global trend toward larger units. The forces behind this trend suggest the pattern of the future world order, if such an order can be achieved at all.[31] In this connection, it may be permissible to point out that in the constant discussion over the alternatives of constitutional democracy and totalitarian dictatorship, it is often forgotten that there is a third alternative which is becoming an increasing threat throughout the world, and that is anarchy. As at certain former periods in the history of mankind, notably the period of the declining Roman Empire, the forces and movements destructive of all political order are rising in various parts of the world. Even the mature and stable societies of the West, notably France and the United States, have experienced and are experiencing serious forms of anarchy, but within their confines they are still reasonably restricted and sporadic developments. They possess considerably greater and more dangerous potentialities in some other parts of the world, notably Africa and Latin America. To overcome these propensities toward the breakdown of all order, movements of national integration have come to play a decisive role.

Yet what is commonly spoken of as "national integration" really is rather far removed from the older European forms of nationalism. India, for example, is not a nation in the traditional Western sense, but a comprehensive culture of continental scope compounded of a very large number of linguistic and religious entities of highly complex and often strongly antagonistic local cultures. India is certainly as a political and social reality something very different from the European nations of the past.

Federalism appears the only way out of the difficulties. There is notable throughout the world a trend for such comprehensive cultures to consolidate into groupings of a more or less close-knit federal kind. This movement has become more pronounced in recent years; whether one considers Asia, Latin America, Indonesia, or the Arab countries, "pan-" movements have made their appearance and have spread. They usually employ the idea of federalism as offering a potential solution to their variety and heterogeneity. Unfortunately, in advocating such federal solutions it is often forgotten that successful modern federalism is closely linked with constitutionalism, and that without a firm constitution federalism is likely to remain a sham.

But in spite of great practical obstacles of this order, the emotional and ideological appeal of these "pan-" movements has been so strong in various parts of the world that most politicians have found it politic to render at least lip service to these efforts at consolidation. They have done so regardless of their belief or disbelief in the realizability of the aims of such "pan-" movements. Indeed, one might be tempted to say that this universal acclaim for the solution of serious political problems presupposes a full appreciation of the difficulties involved in such solutions. Be that as it may, there can be no question that very definite progress is being achieved in all the different areas. Not only pan-Africanism, but the ill-fated Southeast Asian Confederation of Maphilindo (Maylasia, the Philippines, and Indonesia) and the efforts of pan-Arabism, are part of this general trend. In spite of the many obstacles resulting from personal and group ambition, these consolidations are going forward from year to year. Any study of comparative federalism will show the continued growth of such groupings. It would be interesting to offer statistical evidence in support of these contentions, but it would lead too far afield and the general tendency is clear enough.

This universal world trend suggests an emergent world structure composed of a limited number of rather large units, running from 100 million to 700 million people each. They are essentially held together, each of them, by a common culture and tradition, reinforced by religious ties which in spite of plural components provide significant integrators — Christianity, Mohammedanism, Confucianism, Buddhism. It will be many decades before these large cultural entities are really effectively organized in a political and economic sense, yet there is reason to believe that in terms of modern technology and the world situation which mankind finds itself in, these large units will eventually become organized.

The sharp conflict which at present divides the world into three camps, one inclined toward the United States, the other toward the U.S.S.R., and a third trying to remain uncommitted, has tended to obscure the patent conclusion that missionary expansiveness is not simply another version of imperialism. Like the Christian missions of old, it may well be serving as pathfinder of imperial undertaking, but its hard core is of another, non-expedient sort. It is convictional.

The dramatic confrontation of these two convictional giants, 1945–1965, contained the danger of a most destructive cataclysm, with no balance-of-power system available to modify the impact. The advent of this confrontation had all the earmarks of a fortuitous historical coincidence. There was nothing in the past of these powers themselves which necessarily propelled them toward such a confrontation. It *was* in the nature of things political that once it should have occurred, and the threat made lethal by the invention of weapons of total destruction, the emergence of these two powers should elicit determined efforts to counterbalance their sway by effective consolidations in other areas. This is the occasion for European unification. The danger implicit in the confrontation has so far been avoided, because both convictional systems contained creedal commitments to "peace" and each was animated by a firm belief in the eventual prevalence of its own scheme of things.

Europe appears to be on the road to becoming an operating part of a world composed of Africa, all the Arab League States (Arabia), China, Great Britain and the Commonwealth, India, Latin America, Maphilindo, the United States of America, and the Union of Socialist Soviet Republics. Such a polycentric world is undoubtedly in the making. There are, of course, bound to be in such a system (if the present semianarchic conglomeration of emergent cultural wholes can be called a system) some odd elements which do not fit, any more than the "free" cities of Hamburg, Bremen, and Lübeck fitted into the imperial structure of Germany. There would be Turkey and Iran, Pakistan and Burma, as well as Cuba if she continues in her present course. Japan might, especially if reinforced by Korea, become a cultural whole by itself; for its teeming millions are approaching the hundred mark and are therefore already exceeding Arabia in size. There would also be Israel, creature of the new world of the United Nations and unique in its welding of cultural and convictional bonds.

The force of the trends which have been sketched should not be mistaken to produce automatism. Nothing human is predetermined in the rigid causal sequence of observed natural phenomena. All human enterprise calls for the conscious effort of goal-oriented actual persons. Serious obstacles may, therefore, result from human failings. The interference which may be the outcome of stupidity, ambition, and greed, ought never to be lost sight of. This is true, obviously, not only for Europe but for other emergent wholes. From India and Africa, from Latin America and Arabia, come the distress calls of voices which despair in the face of these all-too-human shortcomings. But the thrust is a mighty one, and the longing for cultural rebirth is universal. There is a growing insight into the interdependence of men everywhere, and a sense that diversity is part of community.

Ultimately, of course, these cultural communities are viable only within the context of a world community which embraces them all. The terror of the nuclear holocaust has mightily aided men everywhere in grasping this basic fact of universal interdependence. Foreign aid, so unthinkable a mere fifty years ago in the by-gone world of old-fashioned nationalism and power politics, is more and more appreciated as the expression of a pan-humanism which transcends and overarches all the divergencies, reinforces them in their self-reliance, and aids them toward equality.

NOTES

AND

BIBLIOGRAPHY

Bibliography

LIST OF ABBREVIATIONS

APSR = American Political Science Review

ASW und SP = Archiv für Sozialwissenschaft und Sozialpolitik

CD = Journal Officiel (Chambre des Députés)

CGD = Constitutional Government and Democracy

Cmd. = A paper issued by command of His Majesty (Britain)

ESS = Encyclopedia of the Social Sciences

HCD = Hansard, T. C. (ed.), *Parliamentary Debates*

HDSR = Handbuch des deutschen Staatsrechts

JöR = Jahrbuch des öffentlichen Rechts

MG = Man and His Government

PAR = Public Administration Review

POQ = Public Opinion Quarterly

PSQ = Political Science Quarterly

RGZ = Reichsgerichtsentscheidungen, Zivilsachen

SWPSSQ = Southwestern Political and Social Science Quarterly

TDA = Totalitarian Dictatorship and Autocracy

I. The Development of Modern Constitutional Government in Theory and Practice

Constitutional government and more especially constitutional democracy are terms which have a distinctly traditional flavor, in contrast to expressions like behavior, communications and culture. These more recent ways of approaching the problems of politics have helped to focus attention upon some aspects of government which had hitherto remained speculative; the insights that have been produced are considerable, but they do not affect the basic political experience which underlies the theory and practice of constitutional government, namely that power needs to be controlled and that means of course divided, in order to be satisfactorily employed for the political community. What the impatient have often been unwilling to acknowledge is that such division and control will help in the effective employment of the resources of the community which an unrestrained power tends to disemploy, even to squander. But it is not an easy system; the misconstructions are many and they can be fatal. For this reason, the Aristotelian notion that a constitution is "a system of fundamental political institutions" — that any kind of regime has some kind of "constitution" — continues to be repeated. The word may, of course, be used in this way, but then it does not serve to designate the very specific kind of order to which modern constitutionalism in the Western tradition has come to refer. It is a curious fact that the British, who have contributed more than any other people to the distilling of this modern concept, are most inclined to overlook its distinguishing features, like the healthy man who asks: what is health? A striking recent example is K. C. Wheare's in many other ways admirable *Modern Constitutions*, 1951, 1958. This problem was part of the issue that Giovanni Sartori, who had adversely commented on British views of constitutionalism, and W. H. Morris Jones, who sought to defend part of this tradition, debated in APSR under the titles of "Constitutionalism: A Preliminary Discussion." LVI, 853 ff., and "On Constitutionalism," LIX, 439 ff., with rejoinder ibid., pp. 441 ff. Sartori had suggested the term "garantiste" for the purpose of specifying a modern constitution; any other use of the term he thought was meaningless and "a duplicate of terms such as organization, structure, form, pattern, political system and the like." It is clear that in such expressions as "constitutional democracy" or "constitutional monarchy" the term is used in the modern sense; this conception has underlain the present work, and the distinction between it and various other possibilities is discussed in Ch. VII, more especially in the sections "Five concepts defined" and "The constitution as effectively regularized restraint." Karl Loewenstein, in his *Political Power and the Governmental Process*, 1957, has shown that the issue can also be viewed in terms of the threefold distinction between nominal, normative, and semantic. His discussion, incidentally, is a notable contribution toward overcoming a formal, juristic approach, such as characterizes the constitutional theories of writers like Hans Kelsen and Carl Schmitt whose works have been republished in recent years, but without any significant changes in their dogmatic approach. The same is true of the classic French tradition of Esmein, Duguit, Carré de Malberg, now represented by the works of Duverger, Prelot and others, or in Spain by M. J. Parga y Cabrera, *Los Regimenes Politicos Contemporaneos*, 1962. Rather different in approach is Georges Burdeau's vast work on Political Science in seven volumes of which the first and fifth are particularly germane to constitutional government and democracy. Enriched by the vivid sense of intellectual history, as French writing tends to be in our field, it is nonetheless much more attuned to political realities and concrete experience than was French writing in the past.

A new line was taken by Herbert Spiro in his *Government by Constitution*, 1959. Although nowhere very explicit about his conception of a constitution, he builds up to what he calls "guidelines for constitution-makers," which in his view represent the lessons of a comparative evaluation of the West's constitutional past. Spiro is thinking of the new nations and their problems of creating a workable political order. Plainly, his approach is developmental, in the sense of being willing to employ historical knowledge comparatively for model construction. That was and is, of course, also the approach of this book. It is not that of Gabriel A. Almond and G. Bingham Powell, Jr. in their *Comparative Politics — A Developmental Approach*, 1966. While they acknowledge that "one of the most important turning points in the development of political systems was the shift from traditional to constitutional restraints on political action," they nonetheless devote little space to this subject. And while they acknowledge their agreement with the view that bureaucracy is very important, they do not explore its functioning in any detail. Of course, their study is all-inclusive; like my *Man and His Government*, 1963, they take the political experience of mankind as the basis of their work. Yet the development of constitutionalism is in itself not only a matter of operational experience, but also of theoretical outlook. Here the study by John G. A. Pocock, *The Ancient Constitution and the Feudal Law*, 1957, is of very great value, because it shows just how the modern idea of constitutionalism crystallized in seventeenth century England. It raises the issue of how constitutionalism will fare in countries without many of the beliefs which supported the growth of constitutionalism in the West. This dependence is the theme of my *Transcendent Justice — The Religious Dimension of Constitutionalism*, 1964; it has increasingly occupied the attention of scholars concerned with the problems of developing countries (see for this the [new] last chapter and literature there). India and some of the lesser countries which have "made a go" of Western constitutionalism so far are confronted with a widespread sense of malaise. It has nonetheless seemed justifiable to include their experiences in this new edition, where its implications seemed reasonably clear and well-documented. I have been reluctant to do so in the case of Japan, because her present constitution was imposed by American occupation officials and efforts to revise the constitution in light of Japanese tradition have so far not been successful. Robert E. Ward's "The Origins of the Present Japanese Constitution," APSR, L, 980 ff., is quite clear on this point, as is the *Comments and Observations by Foreign Scholars on the Problems concerning the Constitution of Japan, 1964,* 1964, published by the Secretariat of the Commission on the Constitution. Many of these comments are trenchant, especially those of Karl Loewenstein in his lengthy memorandum which though highly critical nonetheless suggests that "there exists at this time no need . . . for a fundamental constitutional reform," because "the constitution has worked . . . with a considerable degree of success" (p. 202). It is a perplexing issue how much of this "working" is "constitutional," how much of it "extra-constitutional." It seems to me too soon to ascertain whether Japanese constitutional experience is relevant; I should not be surprised if it turned out to be. Similar comments apply to Israel.

Constitutionalism, and more particularly constitutional democracy, has acquired some of its perplexity in the course of this century, because challenges and failures have weakened its former appeal. No longer do believers in the preferability of some sort of constitutional order think of the "irresistible march of democracy." In *Totalitarian Dictatorship and Autocracy,* 2d ed., 1965, I have, together with Zbigniew Brzezinski, pointed out the contrast, as has the latter himself in collaboration with Sam Huntington in *US/USSR,* 1965. But the subtler challenges have arisen within constitutional orders themselves; they are partly at least due to the disintegration of the belief system upon which constitutionalism's development grew as upon its natural soil. A striking study of these trends in Europe during the inter-war years is Karl J. Newman, *Zerstörung und Selbstzerstörung der Demokratie — Europa 1918-1938,* 1965.

There have, of course, in recent years been quite a few general surveys of comparative politics — which this book is not. Among these surveys the most important is *Comparative Politics — A Reader,* 1963, by Harry Eckstein and David Apter. Since Eckstein, in his introduction, locates the present work in the perspective of the development of comparative politics at a certain stage, the conclusion might well be to leave well enough alone. For how could the past be lifted into the present? But then in his appraisal of comparative politics today, he observes that there is great variety and disagreement, and that "it should not be supposed that in describing the four main tendencies in present-day comparative politics — structural-functional analysis, the quest for scientific rigor, treatment of non-Western systems, and concern with the broader setting of politics — we have in fact described the whole field of comparative politics . . . Not at all; we have only described what is new and progressive in a field that is in fact to a large extent old-fashioned and conservative." Since Eckstein himself had noted that in some ways our approach was functional and that it had shown a considerable advance in taking the broader setting into account, it seemed promising to review and strengthen these aspects, while at the same time adding at least some treatment of non-Western systems. There remains then the question of "scientific rigor." It is impossible to argue with someone who disposes of the method he dislikes in name-calling terms such as "crude empiricism." This methodology Eckstein calls "an argument against social 'science'." But what is scientific about using the rigorous methods of Newtonian mechanics in dealing with problems of biology? It is perhaps tedious to recall Aristotle's well-known insistence that it is the sign of a scientific spirit not to seek greater accuracy than the data permit. Since Eckstein and Apter wrote, Klaus von Beyme has offered some searching observations on the problems of comparative politics in "Möglichkeiten und Grenzen der vergleichenden Regierungslehre," in *Politische Vierteljahrsschrift*, 7, 1966, pp. 63–96.

In writing about constitutional government, one raises the question of typology. Since I have dealt with it in *Man and His Government*, Ch. 10, I should like to note here only that typologies are quite numerous — from Plato and Aristotle through Marx and Weber to the present time — and they continue to be of considerable importance. As classifications, they reveal the focus of interest.

Since additional references are provided below, it seems sufficient to conclude these GENERAL NOTES with a brief methodological comment. Austin Ranney edited for the International Political Science Association *Essays on the Behavioral Study of Politics*, 1962, which serve as a broad introduction to the behavioral approach. This approach was subjected that same year to a pointed critique in a number of essays edited by Herbert J. Storing, *Essays on the Scientific Study of Politics*, 1962, which in turn drew a sharp answer from John H. Schaar and Sheldon S. Wolin in APSR, LVII, 125 ff., to which they replied in the same journal, ibid. pp. 151 ff. It seems to me that this discussion has materially contributed to the clarification of the issues; the student of comparative politics will be grateful for any contribution the newer methods can make. I have indicated here and there in this volume, as in *Man and His Government*, where such opportunities exist and demand further research. But there are many real problems of political science and political practice where more tried and traditional methods give greater promise of a satisfactory asnwer. The "quest for certainty" which John Dewey rightly questioned these many years ago is nowhere more likely to lead astray than in politics.

REFERENCES

1. TD, Ch. 10.

2. For the Aristotelian political philosophy, Ernest Barker's book, *The Political Thought of Plato and Aristotle*, 1906, is probably still the best, although its point of view is diametically opposed to that adopted here; it is inspired by the traditional acceptance of the Greek view of politics.

3. Charles H. McIlwain, *Constitutionalism and the Changing World*, 1939, and

Constitutionalism, Ancient and Modern, 1940, are learned restatements of the traditional doctrine.

4. The most challenging work treating the relation between capitalism and liberal constitutionalism is Harold Laski's *The Rise of Liberalism* (1936). It makes free use of concept of the bourgeois class, but, while the writers of constitutionalism are shown to have been members of the professional middle classes, little attempt is made to show in what way that class membership affected their writing. More light is shed upon this aspect of the matter by Bernard Groethuysen, *Origines de l'Esprit Bourgeois en France* (1927). The relationship between imperialism and constitutionalism is stressed by certain writers under Marxist influence who desired to explain the persistence of free institutions under capitalism, more especially Rosa Luxemburg, *Die Akkumulation des Kapitals; ein Beitrag zur ökonomischen Erklärung des Imperialismus* (1922).

5. See my *Transcendent Justice — The Religious Dimension of Constitutionalism,* 1964, for a fuller treatment, as well as the literature.

6. See William Cunningham, *The Progress of Capitalism in England,* 1916; Adam Smith, *Wealth of Nations,* Book IV, Ch. I, and Book V; Werner Sombart, *Der Moderne Kapitalismus,* 1916, Vol. I, 1, Chs. XXI–XVIII; and R. H. Tawney and E. Power, *Tudor Economic Documents,* 1924. See also below, notes to Ch. V. An interesting evaluation of these controversies was offered in F. A. Hayek, ed., *Capitalism and the Historians,* 1954.

7. The problem of how much weight to attach to the "nationalist" sentiment and appeal in Machiavelli is a difficult one. Ever since Fichte (whose views were brilliantly restated by Macaulay in one of his *Essays*), who, in his nationalist period, undertook to rehabilitate Machiavelli in his *Uber Machiavelli als Schriftsteller* (1807) it has been taken for granted by many that Machiavelli was a "nationalist." I rather incline to feel that national sentiment is too emotional a basis for Machiavelli's thought and that he was more truly interested in the state as a work of art. The doctrine of the reason of state derived from him is the outgrowth of Machiavelli's preoccupation with power as the essential resource of the state builder. I have analyzed this problem and reviewed the literature in *Constitutional Reason of State,* 1957, Ch. 2.

8. See Hans Delbrück, *Geschichte der Kriegskunst,* 1900; M. Oppenheim, *A History of the Administration of the Royal Navy,* 1896, Vol. I; Sombart, op. cit., Vol. I, 2, Ch. XLIX. See also below, notes to Ch. III.

9. See Derwent Whittlesey, *The Earth and the State,* 1939. He builds on the earlier work of R. Kjellen, *Grundriss zu einem System der Politik,* 1920, and *Die Grossmächte de Gegenwart,* 1916. See also Friedrich Ratzel, *Politische Geographie,* 1897.

10. See E. Troeltsch, *The Social Teachings of the Christian Churches,* 1923; tr. O. Wyon, 1931; Max Weber, *Protestant Ethic and the Spirit of Capitalism,* tr. T. Parsons, 1930; R. H. Tawney, *Religion and the Rise of Capitalism,* 1926; Otto Hintze, "Kalvinismus und Staatsräson in Brandenburg zur Aufang des 17. Jahrhunderts," in *Historische Zeitschrift,* Vol. CXLIII, 1931, 1931; C. J. Friedrich, *Intro-*

duction to *Johannes Althusius' Politica*, 1932, particularly Chs. II and IV. For a systematic treatment see Reinhold Niebuhr, *Christianity and Power Politics*, 1940.
11. Cf. my *The Age of the Baroque*, 1952, for more detailed discussion of these leaders.
12. Hans Kohn, *The Idea of Nationalism*, 1944, is the classic for this view. But see also C. J. H. Hayes, *Essays on Nationalism*, 1926; and E. H. Carr and Associates, *Nationalism*, 1940. Among more recent treatments, Karl W. Deutsch, *Nationalism and Social Communication*, 1954; and Rupert Emerson, *From Empire to Nation*, 1960, are outstanding.
13. Karl W. Deutsch and William J. Foltz, eds., *Nation-Building*, 1963, especially the introductory chapter by Deutsch himself on "some problems."
14. The standard works on the Roman law are: E. C. Clark, *History of Roman Private Law*, 1906–1919; R. von Ihering, *Der Geist des römischen Rechts*, 1866–71; P. F. Girard, *Short History of Roman Law*, 1906; Paul Krüeger, *Geschichte der Quellen und Literatur des römischen Rechts*, 1888; R. Sohm, *The Institutions of Roman Law*, 1892; James Muirhead, *Historical Introduction to the Private Law of Rome*, 1886; among more recent studies, mention might be made of E. F. Bruck, *Uber römisches Recht im Rahmen der Kulturgeschichte*, 1954; Max Radin, *Handbook of Roman Law*, 1927; Fritz Schulz, *History of Roman Legal Science*, 1946; Franz Wieacker, *Vom Römischen Recht*, 2d ed., 1965; Gerardo Broggini, *Coniectanea — Studi di Diritto Romano*, 1966.
15. Cf. my PL, Ch. IV.
16. The famous definition is found in Jean Bodin's *De Republica, Libri Sex* (Paris, 1576; Latin translation by its author, 1586), Bk. I, Ch. VIII, and reads: *Majestas est summa in cives ac subditos legisbusque soluta potestas.* Later on he adds the important stipulation that *summa* means that *majestas* recognizes no earthly superior, which shows that the definition was politically directed against the authority of Pope and Emperor. Bodin also insists that *majestas* is *potestas perpetua,* thereby excluding all temporary grants of power from the definition. Cf. also the introduction to fine edition of the English Bodin by Kenneth McRae, *Jean Bodin, The Six Books of a Commonweale*, 1962.
17. For the idea of the state as "sovereign association" see F. M. Watkins, *The State as a Concept of Political Science*, 1934. For a trenchant criticism of much jurisprudential claptrap see the article by Kenneth C. Cole, "The Theory of the State as a Sovereign Juristic Person," APSR, XLII, pp. 16 ff. Cf. also the trechant discussion by G. E. G. Catlin, *Systematic Politics*, 1962, Ch. 8. Professor Peter Badura rightly entitled an appreciative article on Catlin's work "The overcoming of the state by philosophy" in *Der Staat*, 1964.
18. Great stress was laid by Max Weber in his various writings upon "monopoly of force," for which see Talcott Parsons (with A. M. Henderson), *The Theory of Social and Economic Organization*, 1947; and H. H. Gerth and C. W. Mills, *Max Weber: Essays in Sociology*, 1946; as well as R. Bendix, *Max Weber — An Intellectual Portrait*, 1960.
19. For the historical background see Francis D. Wormuth, *The Origins of*

Modern Constitutionalism, 1949, especially Chs. IV and V. See also B. d Jouvenel, *Sovereignty*, 1957, French original, 1955: and MG, Ch. 30 "State and Nation: Sovereignty and its Limits."

20. The entire medieval literature on the prince is permeated by the idea of ecclesiastical sanctions for "just" conduct. See the essay by John Dickinson, "The medieval Idea of Kingship and Some of its Limitations, as Developed in the *Polykraticus* of John of Salisbury," in *Speculum*, Vol. I, 1926, pp. 308 ff; R. W. and A. J. Carlyle, *History of Medieval Political Theory in the West*, 1903–1916, passim; and (for an authoritative source) Thomas Aquinas, *De regimine principum*.

21. Friedrich Meinecke, *Machiavellism — The Doctrine of Raison d'Etat and its Place in Modern History*, 1965 (the German original, *Die Idee der Staatsraison . . .* 1925) and my review reprinted as an Appendix to *Constitutional Reason of State*, 1957. Concerning Protestantism, see Hintze's article cited above, note 10, as well as Max Weber's pointed essay, *The Protestant Ethic and the Spirit of Capitalism*, tr. T. Parsons, 1930.

22. Cf. Giovanni Botero, *Della Ragion di Stato*, 1589, and Meinecke's commentary, op. cit., Ch. III. Concerning the divine right of kings, see John N. Figgis's classical treatment of the subject *The Divine Right of Kings*, 2d ed., 1914. See also his *Churches in the Modern State*, 1913.

23. Cf. my *Constitutional Reason of State*, Ch. I. Also below, Ch. XXV.

24. See Eli F. Hekscher, *Mercantilism*, 1935, 2 vols.

25. The political doctrines of the Cameralists have been thoroughly explored by Hans Maier, *Die ältere deutsche Staats- und Verwaltungslehre (Polizeiwissenschaft)*, 1966.

26. S. N. Eisenstadt, *The Political Systems of Empires — The Rise and Fall of the Historical Bureaucratic Societies*, 1963.

27. The desire to fashion restraints for the rulers is, of course, quite ancient, and associated with the often religious sanctions for tradition; cf. Harry M. Orlinsky, *Ancient Israel*, 1954, Ch. VII; but many works of anthropologists, starting with the renowned Frazer, tell of such restraints.

28. Insofar as constitutionalism is related to liberalism, Guido de Ruggiero's *The History of Eureopean Liberalism* (1927) is excellent. Catholic political philosophy, of course, has always stressed the idea of governmental restraints in connection with the Church's efforts to prevent secular absolutism. From St. Thomas to contemporary writers such as Jacques Maritain the idea has found ever new expression. See John A. Ryan and F. J. Boland, *Catholic Principles of Politics* (1940), and Heinrich A. Rommen's magistral *The State in Catholic Thought* (1945). The stress, however, is upon natural law, and the role of institutional sanctions is minimized. The word "constitution" characteristically does not even figure in the index.

29. Cf. besides Wormuth, op. cit., Arthur E. Sutherland's *Constitutionalism in America — Origin and Evolution of its Fundamental Ideas*, 1965, especially Ch. 1. Cf. also my "Rights, Liberties, Freedoms — A Reappraisal" in APSR, LVII, 1963, pp. 841 ff.

30. See William Stubbs, *English Constitutional History*, and F. W. Maitland,

Constitutional History of England; in addition, G. P. Gooch, *English Democratic Ideas in the Seventeenth Century,* 2d ed., with notes by Harold Laski, 1927, is important.

31. The view here adopted of emphasizing the constitutional issues in the American War of Independence is that found in C. H. McIlwain, *The American Revolution,* 1924. See below, Ch. XIII, note 6. There is no good comparative constitutional history tracing the spread of English constitutional ideas on the continent. *The Impact of American Constitutionalism Abroad* is the subject of my Bacon Lectures, 1967.

32. Perhaps the most eminent exponent of the "living law" doctrine is Jerome Hall, whose *Living Law and Democratic Society,* 1949, and more recently *Comparative Law and Social Theory,* 1963, constitute landmarks in this discussion; cf. also Julius Stone, *Human Law and Human Justice,* 1965. The emphasis is involved in the entire discussion over the sociology of law since Ehrlich. Howard Lee McBain spoke of *The Living Constitution: A Consideration of the Realities and the Legends of our Fundamental Law,* 1927, in discussing the US basic law; Dolf Sternberger has discussed certain realities of German politics, namely the formation of coalitions and the operation of oppositions under the title *Die Lelendige Verfassung, Studien über Koalition und Opposition,* 1956.

33. Herbert Spiro, op. cit., pp. 210, 234 ff., 256 f., 273 ff., 295 ff., 333 ff., 357 ff., 382 ff., and 427; these guidelines form the hortative conclusion to Chs. 14 ff.

34. Spiro, op. cit., Ch. 26, and *World Politics: The Global System,* 1966. There is, of course, a vast literature on this subject; see for some of it, below, Ch. III and MG, Ch. 32; cf. also *Philosophy, Religion and the Coming World Civilization — Essays in Honor of William Ernest Hocking,* edited by Leroy S. Rouner, 1966, which includes a wide range of approaches.

35. An able analysis of these writers is given by Benjamin Lippincott, *Victorian Critics of Democracy,* 1938. Macaulay's famous letter to a congressman, as printed in *Harper's Magazine,* Vol. LIV, pp. 460 ff., Feb., 1877, should be consulted. We shall have occasion later in the book to refer to some of the many books on democracy. Here mention might be made, besides my own *The New Belief in the Common Man,* 1941, considerably altered and updated as *Die Demokratie als Herrschaft- und Lebensform,* 1959, 2d. ed., 1966, to A. D. Lindsay, *The Modern Democratic State,* of which unfortunately only the first volume appeared, 1943; Robert A. Dahl, *A Preface to Democratic Theory,* 1956; William Kornhauser, *The Politics of Mass Society,* 1959; Seymour Martin Lipset, *Political Man,* 1960; Gerhard Leibholz, *Strukturprobleme der modernen Demokratie,* 1958; Giovanni Sartori, *Democratic Theory,* 1962; Georges Burdeau, *Traité de la Science Politique,* Vol. V, 1950.

36. Karl Loewenstein, *Die Monarchie im Modernen Staat,* 1952, has given far and away the most intelligent interpretation in contemporary terms.

37. Arthur Rosenberg, *Democracy and Socialism,* 1939. See also Eduard Heimann, *Freedom and Order,* 1949, elaborating his earlier, *Communism, Fascism, or Democracy?,* 1938.

38. See especially Leslie Lipson, *The Politics of Equality; New Zealand's Adventures in Democracy*, 1948, skillfully weighing the impact of socialism upon the citizen's freedom. See Harold Laski, *Parliamentary Government in England*, 1938, especially Ch. I. H. R. C. Greaves, in *The Foundations of Political Theory*, 1958, 2d ed., 1967, is much concerned with these issues, but so was the entire Fabian Society. Cf. for an overview, Samuel H. Beer, *British Politics in the Collectivist Age*, 1966. A really searching analysis and interpretation of the Fabians remains to be written.

39. Among them Harold Laski, op. cit., 1938.

40. Rosenberg, op. cit., p. 216.

41. Benjamin Akzin has, in "The Place of the Constitution in the Modern State," *Israel Law Review*, Vol. 2, 1967, pp. 1–17, once more shown that a "formal constitution is a useful and in most countries an essential instrument for limiting and stabilizing political power." p. 11.

II. The Development Core: Bureaucracy

GENERAL NOTES

The writings on "bureaucracy" have become very numerous, even if one does not comprehend "administration" and "personnel" under it. In 1952, Robert K. Merton and associates published a *Reader in Bureaucracy* which provided a very valuable general introduction to this literature, from Max Weber and the theoretical conceptions to methodological problems, with numerous selections on growth, structure, recruitment and advancement, the bureaucrat as a human type, and pathological perversions. Five years later C. Northcote Parkinson amused professionals and laymen by his irreverent attack on excesses of bureaucracy in his *Parkinson's Law*, 1957 which deserves treatment, but in a style ill-suited to this treatise. Some of the works heralded in the previous edition have since become minor classics, while others have been forgotten. A valuable approach has been ventured recently by Michel Crozier, *The Bureaucratic Phenomenon*, 1964 which brings French animation and a sense of novelty to a staid subject.

To return to the earlier writings, outstanding contributions to the historical origins are: Thomas F. Tout, *Chapters in the Administrative History of Medieval England* (6 vols., 1920–1933); Fr. Olivier–Martin, *Histoire du Droit Français*, 1951, especially Book II, pp. 281–468; Leonard D. White, *The Federalists — A Study in Administrative History*, 1948; Gustav Schmoller, "Der Deutsche Beamtenstaat vom 16.–18. Jahrhundert," in *Jahrbuch für Gesetzgebung, Verwaltung und Volkswirtschaft*, Vol. XVIII, 1894, and "Über Behördenorganisation, Amtswesen und Beamtentum," introduction to *Acta Borussica*, Vol. 1, 1894, particularly Chs.

II and VII; Otto Hintze, "Die Entstehung der modernen Staatsministerien," in *Historische Zeitschrift,* Vol. C, 1907, pp. 53–111, now reprinted in *Gesammelte Abhandlungen,* 1962/64. The pathfinder for systematic study was Max Weber, *Wirtschaft und Gesellschaft (Grundriss der Sozialökonomik,* Vol. III), 1925, Ch. III, paras. 3, 4, 5, of the first part, and Ch. VI of the third part. Weber's attempt at systematic treatment makes an effort to avoid ideological distortions, but his bias in favor of power, rational efficiency, and the national state colors his treatment nonetheless. Other prejudices intrude themselves to some extent in Herman Finer, "The Civil Service," in *The Theory and Practice of Modern Government,* 1932, Vol. II, Part VII, and Leonard D. White, *Introduction to the Study of Public Administration,* 2d ed., 1939. An interesting challenge to these approaches is offered by Dwight Waldo, *The Administrative State,* 1948, stressing the importance of values. Excellent special studies on personnel devoted to American practice are: Lewis Merriam, *Public Personnel Problems,* 1938, and W. E. Mosher, *Public Personnel Administration,* 1941.

REFERENCES

1. See Tout, op. cit.; J. F. Baldwin, *The King's Council in England during the Middle Ages,* 1914.

2. Tout, op. cit. Vol. I, p. 181.

3. This subject has recently been greatly illuminated by Hans Rosenberg, *Bureaucracy, Aristocracy and Autocracy,* 1958. His researches support the general analysis here given, but concentrate on the class aspect.

4. W. Altmann, *Ausgewählte Urkunden zur Brandenburg–Preussischen Verfassungs- und Verwaltungsgeschichte,* Vol. I, pp. 55 ff.; Gustav Schmoller, "Über Behördenorganisation, Amtswesen und Beamtentum . . .," as cited, passim.

5. See E. B. Greene, *The Provincial Governor in the English Colonies of North America,* 1898.

6. Leonard D. White, *The Federalists — A Study in Administrative History,* 1948. See also Carl Russel Fish, *The Civil Service and Patronage,* 1904.

7. The importance of "rationalized" conduct was first stressed in broad cultural terms by Jacob Burckhardt in his justly celebrated *Die Kultur der Renaissance in Italien,* 1860, especially Ch. VII. The idea gained ground and was given very general sociological significance by Pareto and Max Weber.

8. These categories are developed in their application to modern administration by Leonard D. White, *Introduction to the Study of Public Administration,* Ch. III. See also C. J. Friedrich and Taylor Cole, *Responsible Bureaucracy,* 1932, pp. 29 ff.

9. Chester I. Barnard, *The Functions of the Executive,* 1940 as well as Ch. XVIII of this volume. Herbert A. Simon, *Administrative Behavior,* 1947; Otto Hintze, "Behördenorganisation und allgemeine Verwaltung in Preussen," the introduction

to Vol. VI of *Acta Borussica*, 1901; Walter L. Dorn, "The Prussian Bureaucracy in the Eighteenth Century," *Political Science Quarterly*, Vols. XLVI and XLVII, 1931, 1932; C. J. Friedrich, "The Continental Tradition of Training Administrators in Law and Jurisprudence," *Journal of Modern History*, Vol. XI, No. 2, 1939; René Hugot-Derville, `Le principe hiérarchique dans l'administration française,` 1913. The problem of the conditions under which monocratic leadership occurs has not as yet received the attention it deserves. Certain phases are considered below in Chs. XXII and XXV.

10. See for this rule MG, Ch. 11, "Influence."

11. See the works cited in Greer, *A Bibliography of Civil Service and Personnel Administration*, 1935, pp. 79 ff.

12. Morale was at one time the subject of extended discussion among philosophers, psychologists, political scientists, and administrators. For earlier studies we may mention H. D. Lasswell, *Propaganda Technique in the World War*, 1927; F. C. Bartlett, *Psychology and the Soldier*, 1927; William Ernest Hocking, *Morale and Its Enemies*, 1918; and Samuel Stouffer and associates, *The American Soldier*, 1949, especially Vol. I, Chs. I–VIII.

13. See H. R. G. Greaves, *The Civil Service in the Changing State*, 1947, especially Chs. III, IV, and VIII; William A. Robson, ed., *The Civil Service in Britain and France*, 1956; and Donald Kingsley, *Representative Bureaucracy*, 1944. Both books express Labour Party views not current in Britain.

14. The Presidential press conference is analyzed in several of the volumes dealing with the presidency, as cited below, Ch. XVIII.

15. James L. McCamy, *Government Publicity — Its Practice in Federal Administration*, 1939.

16. The problem of the expert is further developed below, Ch. XIX. Here we may note *The New Belief in the Common Man*, 1942, Ch. VI, "Responsibility and the Sense of Workmanship."

17. The clash between the idea of constitutionalism and secrecy was stated with greatest emphasis by Immanuel Kant in a number of works. See for a recent study, Edward A. Shils, *The Torment of Secrecy*, 1956. See also Francis Rourke, *Secrecy and Publicity — Dilemma of Democracy*, 1961.

18. See J. Donald Kingsley, op. cit. and L. D. White, *The Federalists*, cited above.

III. Territorial Expansion, Security and the Military Establishment

GENERAL NOTES

The literature on territorial expansion and more especially on modern imperialism is very large, while that on the interrelation between military and governmental development has been growing rapidly. An extraordinary study showing the universality of the urge toward territorial control was offered recently by Robert Ardrey, *The Territorial Imperative,* 1966. Neither the expansion of Rome nor that of modern Europe is conceivable without discovery of superior military techniques. The Second World War produced some interesting studies. Pendleton Herring's *The Impact of War,* 1941, explored the problems of the military in a free society from a fresh viewpoint. It contains a good annotated bibliography. Much of the most interesting material is found in the work of historians; see particularly Alfred Vagts, *The History of Militarism,* 1937; Alfred T. Mahan, *The Influence of Sea Power upon History,* 1890; and Hans Delbrück, *Geschichte der Kriegskunst im Rahmen der Politischen Geschichte,* 1900–1926, which unfortunately remains untranslated. A certain amount of work has recently been done in anthropology and comparative cultural sociology along these lines. See Gordon A. Craig's "Delbrück: The Military Historian" in *Makers of Modern Strategy.*

Before the Second World War, many a priori assertions were heard concerning the devastating effect which war was supposed to have on "democracy." Factual support was usually lacking. The many volumes of the Carnegie Endowment's *Economic and Social History of the World War,* 1924 and later, should have offered a welcome antidote, since they showed that democracy in fact *advanced* in the course of the First World War. Among the outstanding recent contributions to the study of relations between the government and the military, we note: Samuel P. Huntington, *The Soldier and the State, The Theory and Politics of Civil-Military Relations,* 1957; John Neef, *War and Human Progress,* 1950, pp. 93 ff.; Henry A. Kissinger, *Nuclear Weapons and Foreign Policy,* 1957; C. Wright Mills, *The Power Elite,* 1956, Chs. 8 and 9; Frederick M. Stern, *The Citizen Army,* 1957; Kenneth N. Waltz, *Man, The State, and War,* 1959; Raymond Aron, *Paix et Guerre,* 1962; Morton Halperin, *Contemporary Military Strategy,* 1966; and Thomas C. Schelling, *Arms and Influence,* 1966.

REFERENCES

1. Henry Sidgwick, *Principles of Political Economy,* Ch. XVIII, paras. 4 and 5.
2. Arnold von Luschin und Ebengreuth, *Osterreichische Reichs- und Rechtsgeschichte,* pp. 397, 411, 466–467 ff., 479.

3. Arnold J. Toynbee, in his *Study of History*, Vols. I and II, 1934, has gathered much significant material on this point.

4. M. Oppenheim, *A History of the Administration of the Royal Navy, 1509–1660*, 1896. See also Mahan, op. cit. For the American parallel, see Harold and Margaret Sprout, *The Rise of American Naval Power*, 1939; See also W. C. Abbott, *The Writings and Speeches of Oliver Cromwell*, 4 vols., 1937–1947 under "Navy"; G. M. Trevelyan, *English Social History*, 1942, especially pp. 194–195; and J. L. de Lolme, *The Constitution of England*, 1775, 1807 ed., pp. 453 ff.

5. See G. M. Trevelyan, *English Social History*, 1942, p. 194. For de Lolme see *The Constitution of England*, 1775, new ed. 1807, p. 453, for the quote. De Lolme, in the preceding pages, from 439 ff., takes Adam Smith to task for saying, in *The Wealth of Nations*, Book V, Ch. I, that "the English government derived the singular stability it manifests from the standing force it has at its disposal."

6. Delbrück, op. cit. pp. 255 ff. Also Sombart, *Kapitalismus*, Vol. I, 1, pp. 342 ff. The description of Prince Eugene is found in Ernest F. Henderson, *A Short History of Germany*, 2d ed., 1917, Vol. II, p. 51.

7. The generalization advanced in this paragraph is sometimes stated by historians in their special treatments of a specific history. Thus J. Beloch, in his *Griechische Geschichte*,1893–1904, explains the dispersion of political authority characteristic of the city-state in these terms.

8. See the Report of the Atomic Energy Commission, Dept. of State, No. 2498, 1946.

9. See Henry Guerlac, "Vauban: the Impact of Science on War," in *Makers of Modern Strategy*, 1943, pp. 26–48, and the literature cited there. See also the same author's unprinted dissertation, *Science and the War in the Old Regime. The Development of Science in an Armed Society*, 1941. Max Scheler, *Versuch zu einer Soziologie des Wissens*, 1924, pp. 99 ff.

10. Pitirim Sorokin, *Social and Cultural Dynamics*, 1937, Vol. III, Part II, Ch. XI.

11. E. P. Herring, *The Impact of War*, 1941, passim. Not exactly the point of the text, but related problems of the link between technology and science are touched upon in the following: Ch. XI of C. Bouglé's *Leçons de Sociologie sur l'Evolution des Valeurs* (tr. H. S. Sellars as *The Evolution of Values*, 1926); Max Scheler, *Soziologie des Wissens*, pp. 129 ff. See also Don K. Price, *Government and Science*, 1954.

12. Oppenheim, op. cit.; Sombart, *Krieg und Kapitalismus*, 1912, pp. 66 ff.; J. W. Fortescue, *A History of the British Army*, 1899; and similar works for France, Germany, etc., cited by Sombart. See also Albert T. Lauterbach's *Economics in Uniform: Military Economy and Social Structure*, 1943.

13. As in other parts of this chapter, considerable literature is provided by economic history, for example, regarding the debasing of the coins. Eli Heckscher's *Mercantilism*, 1935, gives the best general comparative treatment. Regarding trading companies, G. Cawston and A. H. Keane, *Early Chartered Companies*, 1896, and S. van Brakel, *De Hollandsche Handelscompagnieen der Sewentiende Eeuw*, 1908, are worth consulting, along with the standard economic histories. Regarding

the estimates on benefits derived from confiscation of ecclesiastical property, Thomas Tanner's *Notitia Monastica,* 1744 has been consulted; see also F. A. Gasquet, *Henry VIII and the English Monasteries,* 1888–1889. The figure regarding the price of the Ark Royal is found in E. Keble Chatterton, *Sailing Ships,* 1909.

14. Basic issues are the theme of J. M. Keynes' *How to Pay for the War,* 1940. A different approach is set forth by Robert Warren and others in *Financing the War,* 1942. On the historical side, see for a comparative study of feudalism in many cultures, Rushton Coulborn, ed. *Feudalism,* 1956. For Germany, see particularly Georg von Below, "System und Bedeutung der landständischen Verfassung," in *Territorium und Stadt,* 1900, pp. 163 ff., and the same author's *Landständische Verfassung von Jülich und Berg,* 1885. For France, see Georges Picot, *Histoire des Etats Généraux,* 2d. ed., 1888. For the battle on the White Hill see Julius Krebs, *Die Schlacht am Weissen Berge,* 1879, and the summary in Delbrück, op. cit. Vol. IV, pp. 233 ff.

15. For the doctrine of the prerogative see Francis D. Wormuth, *The Royal Prerogative, 1603–1649,* 1939. The French *intendants* are treated with discrimination by G. Hanotaux, *Origines de l'Institution des Intendants des Provinces,* 1884.

16. The problem of war in Marxist theory is discussed with insight by S. Neumann in "Engels and Marx: Military Concepts of the Social Revolutionaries," and by Edward M. Earle, in "Lenin, Trotsky, Stalin: Soviet Concepts of War," in *Makers of Modern Strategy,* Chs. VII and XIV. For an earlier theoretical analysis see Gerhart Lütkens, "Das Kriegsproblem und die marxistische Theorie," in *ASW und SP,* Vol. XLIX, 1922, pp. 467 ff. Acute specific comments are found in W. P. Maddox, *Foreign Relations in British Labour Politics,* 1934, pp. 53 f., and elsewhere; and in Merle Fainsod, *International Socialism and the World War,* 1935.

17. For the German events touched upon here, see Herbert Rosinsky, *The German Army,* 1940; and the detailed treatment, some of it biased, in Bénoist-Méchin, *Histoire de l'Armée Allemande 1919–1930,* two vols., 1938. See also Telford Taylor, *Sword and Swastika,* 1952, and Gordon A. Craig, *The Politics of the Prussian Army, 1640–1945,* 1955.

18. See for this problem (as far as the Soviet Union is concerned), Leon Trotsky, *My Life,* 1930; John Wheeler–Bennett, *Brest–Litovsk, The Forgotten Peace,* 1938; D. F. White, *The Growth of the Red Army,* 1943. The more common aspect of the army in the totalitarian scheme of things is analyzed in TD, Ch. 26 and the literature given there.

19. Karl Dietrich Bracher, Wolfgang Sauer and Gerhard Schulz, *Die Nationalsozialistische Machtergreifung,* 1960, offer an exhaustive treatment, supplementing the first author's *Die Auflösung der Weimarer Republik,* 1955.

20. In this connection, one might quote a sentence from Herring's book: "We can recognize the need of central controls and discipline without making these needs the central article of our faith. The point really is that a democracy to succeed must take for granted the social integration . . ." (p. 281). See also Stanley Hoffmann, *The State of War,* 1965. Mills, op. cit. Chas. 8 and 9 has advanced a highly questionable thesis concerning the role of the military in contemporary American society,

but that this role has been increasing there can be no doubt; cf. especially Schelling, as cited above.

21. The enormous literature on disarmament cannot be cited here. The close collaboration developing in this field between Western European nations, reinforced by the Atlantic Pact, may lead to some partial internationalization of the military establishments of these nations. Cf. Thomas C. Schelling and Morton H. Halperin, *Strategy and Arms Control,* 1961 and J. J. Stone, *Containing the Arms Race,* 1966.

22. Robert Ardrey, *The Territorial Imperative, A Personal Inquiry into the Animal Origins of Property and Nations,* 1966.

IV. Peace and Diplomacy

GENERAL NOTES

There has been a striking output of general treatments on foreign policy in recent years. Apart from the discussions in the leading texts on international relations and world politics, there are the studies of the foreign policy of particular nations and groups, surveyed in *Foreign Policies in a World of Change,* 1963, edited by Joseph E. Black and Kenneth W. Thompson. Among the general and comparative studies, mention might first be made of the more theoretical works, such as Raymond Aron, *Paix et Guerre,* rev. ed. 1962; Stanley Hoffmann edited a symposium *Contemporary Theory in International Relations,* 1960, whereas Richard N. Rosecrance, *Action and Reaction in World Politics,* 1963; Morton Kaplan, *System and Process in International Politics,* 1957, and G. Liska, *International Equilibrium,* 1957 attempted systematic analysis from different standpoints. The interaction of foreign and domestic politics is the theme of R. Barry Farrell, ed., *Approaches to Comparative and International Politics,* 1966, with contributions by Deutsch, Rosenau, Friedrich, Blanksten, Casanova, Long, Aspaturian, Young, Alger, Naroll, Benson, and the editor. In addition, there is the vast literature on international organizations and world government. See also the books on federation and related subjects cited below, Chapter XI. The ethical aspects are treated by Kenneth W. Thompson, *Christian Ethics and the Dilemmas of Foreign Policy,* 1959.

Among the many treatments of diplomacy in all modern languages, the political scientist will find three most suggestive. These are: Ernest Satow, *Guide to Diplomatic Practice,* 1917; Jules Cambon, *Le Diplomate,* 1922; and Fred Charles Iklé, *How Nations Negotiate,* 1964. Interesting recent works on the actual conduct of diplomacy are Dean Acheson, *Power and Diplomacy,* 1958; McGeorge Bundy and others, *The Dimensions of Diplomacy,* 1964; Don K. Price, ed., *The Secretary of State,* 1960; Charles W. Thayer, *The Diplomat,* 1959; and of course a great many biographies of diplomats, e.g. Harold Nicolson's biography of his father, *Sir Arthur Nicolson,* 1930 (published in the United States under the title *Portrait of a Diplo-*

matist). Regarding the general problem of democracy and diplomacy, there are also a considerable number of works; see the author's *Foreign Policy in the Making,* 1938. Since that time, a number of other works have appeared, all especially concerned with this problem in the United States, e.g. the fine study by H. Bradford Westerfield, *Foreign Policy and Party Politics,* 1958 and James A. Robinson, *Congress and Foreign Policy-Making,* 1962. See also *How Foreign Policy is Made,* 1949 by Kurt L. London; and Herbert J. Spiro, *World Politics — The Global System,* 1966. Responses on the local level were reported and analyzed by G. J. Mangone, *Foreign Policy and Onandaga County,* 1964.

REFERENCES

1. MG, Ch. 27, and Iklé, op. cit.
2. The importance of the distinction between policy determination and negotiation is emphasized by Harold Nicolson, *Curzon: The Last Phase, 1919–1925,* 1934, in a terminal essay containing "some remarks on the practice of diplomacy." It is an old distinction, but in constant need of re-emphasizing. D. J. Hill, *A History of Diplomacy in the International Development of Europe,* 1905, Vol. III, gives significant critical comments on the failure of Louis XIV (pp. 282 ff.) and Frederick the Great (pp. 537 ff.), but the judgments expressed in the text are *communis opinio doctorum.* For Louis XIV, see G. Pagès, *La Monarchie d'Ancien Régime en France,* 1928, pp. 134 ff. For Frederick the Great, see G. Küntzel, "Die Drei Grossen Hohenzollern," in *Meister der Politik,* ed E. Marcks and K. von Müller, 1923, Vol. II, pp. 391 ff. Re Napoleon, see J. H. Rose, *The Life of Napoleon I,* 1901–1924, Vol. II, pp. 213 ff.
3. See the general treatments cited above, and also Hans J. Morgenthau, *Politics among Nations: The Struggle for Power and Peace,* 1948. They all assume, more or less explicitly, that a coherent foreign policy is possible.
4. A brilliant example of the "art of negotiating" is offered in Crane Brinton's treatment of Talleyrand's diplomacy, *The Lives of Talleyrand,* 1936, pp. 166 ff. Cf. now Iklé, op. cit.
5. For the Franco-Russian alliance see W. L. Langer's study, *The Franco-Russian Alliance, 1890–1894,* 1929, p. 399. For the problem of Anglo-German relations see F. Meinecke, *Geschichte des deutsch-englischen Bündnisproblems, 1890–1901,* 1930.
6. For the problem of official language, see Satow, op. cit. Col. 1, pp. 58 ff. See *New York Times,* January 28, 1934, for the Soviet remark; for Curzon's breach, see Nicolson, op. cit. p. 358.
7. The relevant sections of Ch. XIX, "Responsible Government Service," should be consulted here. See D. J. Hill, *History of Diplomacy in the International Development of Europe,* 1905–1914, particularly Vol. I, pp. 359–360.
8. Besides the works by Nicolson, see Cecil Spring-Rice, *The Letters and Friendships of Sir Cecil Spring-Rice,* 1929; *The Life and Letters of Walter Hines Page,*

ed. B. J. Hendrick, 1923; the memoirs of Stimson and Byrnes, as well as of Robert Sherwood; *Roosevelt and Hopkins,* 1948, reproduces the atmosphere of the newer international politics from on high. The worm's view, if one can put it that way, of the lowly consular official is realistically and humorously presented by Donald Dunham, *Envoy Unextraordinary,* 1944. Another work of unusual interest, showing the frustrations of the professional diplomat under democratic traditions, is Ambassador Joseph C. Grew's *Ten Years in Japan: A Contemporary Record,* 1944.

9. For this problem see Cmd. 6420, 1943, "Proposals for the Reform of the Foreign Service."

10. This issue was at the core of the protracted controversy regarding the relation between the State Department and the organization to be set up for European Reconstruction. See Seymour Harris, *The European Recovery Program,* 1948.

11. Harold Nicolson, *Curzon: The Last Phase, 1919–1925.*

12. See J. Rives Childs, *The American Foreign Service,* 1948, which contains the text of the Foreign Service Act of 1946; and Price, ed. op. cit. A comparative study of why the foreign service in all democratic countries is so unpopular is urgently needed.

13. See Martin Hill, *Immunities and Privileges of International Officials,* 1947; the earlier study by Egon Ranshofen-Wertheimer, *The International Secretariat,* 1946; and Chester Purvis, *The Internal Administration of the International Secretariat,* 1946. The contrasting Soviet view is impressively argued in M. M. Boguslavski, *Staatliche Immunität,* 1965 (Russian original *Immunitet Gosudarstva,* 1962).

14. A fuller treatment of this point will be found in the author's *Foreign Policy in the Making,* 1938, particularly pp. 116-133. *Contra* Edward H. Carr, *The Twenty-Years' Crisis,* 1939. For the problem of the balance of power, see Nicholas J. Spykman's *American Strategy in World Politics,* especially pp. 20 ff. and the broad historical treatment in Charles Dupuis, *Le principe d'équilibre et le concert européen de la paix de Westphalie à l'acte d'Algeciras,* 1909; Dupuis stresses the use made of the concept of a balance of power as a tool of negotiation. See also Liska, op. cit.

15. The passages quoted from Lippmann are found in his *U.S. Foreign Policy,* 1943, on pp. 50 f., 149 ff., 164 ff., 169 f.

16. Hans J. Morgenthau, *In Defense of the National Interest,* 1951; George F. Kennan, *American Diplomacy, 1900–1950,* 1951; W. W. Rostow, *The United States in the World Arena,* 1960; Henry A. Kissinger, *The Necessity of Choice,* 1960; Gabriel Almond, *The American People and Foreign Policy,* 1960; Harold Jacobson, ed., *American Foreign Policy,* 1960; Kenneth W. Thompson, *Foreign Policy and Emergent Patterns,* 1962.

17. Raymond Aron, *Paix et Guerre entre les Nations,* 1962, p. 20.

18. Hans J. Morgenthau, *Politics among Nations: The Struggle for Power and Peace,* has taken the view that the struggle for power and peace go hand in hand.

V. Prosperity, the Police, and Legislation

GENERAL NOTES

Obviously, a general bibliography for this chapter would have to cover the entire field of modern economic history, manifestly an impossible task. Reference may be had to any one of the more recent and competent texts in the field. I like G. M. Trevelyan's *English Social History* (1942) for its attention to governmental and administrative aspects. In addition to this, attention may specially be called to Eli Heckscher's masterly all-European treatment of *Mercantilism* (1935). It is a veritable monument to the cosmopolitan scholarship of the smaller countries of Europe. To it may be added four somewhat controversial and yet very significant works: W. Cunningham, *The Progress of Capitalism in England* (1916), and his *The Growth of English Industry and Commerce* (5th ed., 1910–1912); W. J. Ashley, *Introduction to English Economic History* (1888–1925); and Werner Sombart, *Der Moderne Kapitalismus* (5th ed., 1922), particularly Vol. I, 1, pp. 334 ff. Besides these, Gustav Schmoller's Introduction to the first volume of *Acta Borussica* must be noted, as well as several of his essays reprinted in *Umrisse, Abhandlungen und Untersuchungen* (1898).

For general bibliography on legislation, see below, Chs. XIV, XVI, and XVII. On the police the literature is not very satisfactory from the standpoint of comparative government. It tends to be somewhat formalistic, following the older European tradition. Raymond B. Fosdick's *European Police Systems* (1915) and *American Police Systems* (1920) are still standard works. See also Rollin M. Perkins, *Elements of Police Science*, 1942, and O. W. Wilson, *Police Administration*, 1950; James Q. Wilson, "The Police and Their Problems: A Theory," PP XII, 1963, pp. 189 ff. In addition, Cmd. 3297 (1929), "Police Powers and Procedure," might be mentioned. The "police state" of the mercantilist-cameralist period is well represented, theoretically speaking, in A. W. Small's *The Cameralists* (1909). "The Challenge of Crime in a Free Society," a *Report by the President's Commission on Law Enforcement and Administration of Justice*, 1967, is an outstanding contribution.

REFERENCES

1. This is the view of Jacob Viner presented in his "Power versus Plenty . . . ," *World Politics* (1949), Vol. I, pp. 1 ff., but as my passages show (unaltered since 1937), it is not exactly novel. On the other hand, I sympathize with Viner's desire to make the point emphatically, in the light of such statements as that of Cunningham: "The mercantile system is concerned solely with man as a being who pursues

national power." See Section 136, *The Growth of English Industry and Commerce*, by William Cunningham. The entire controversy of the economic (materialistic) interpretation of history clearly is bound up with the few sentences of this paragraph. Suffice it, in lieu of references, to remind the reader that such an interpretation is not peculiar to Karl Marx, as is now often popularly assumed, but is found throughout the later eighteenth and the nineteenth century, and has become very common in the United States.

2. For an exposition of ideas of organic growth, see H. von Treitschke, *Politics* (1916), Vol. I, pp. 15 ff., 45 ff., or Seeley, *Introduction to Political Science* (1896), pp. 43–44 and 53–76, as illustrations of what nineteenth-century historians are full of. Friedrich Ratzel, in his *Politische Geographie* (3rd ed., 1923), has given an elaborate exposition of this doctrine, pp. 59 ff. Ratzel's ideas were elaborated by the school of "geopolitics," more especially by General Haushofer and provided a link with the vitalistic superstitions of the Nazis and Fascists. See, besides the works of General Haushofer and his school, analyzed by Andreas Dorpalen, *The World of General Haushofer* (1942), Derwent Whittlesey, *The Earth and the State* (1939) — much better on the earth than on the state. See also Johannes Mattern, *Geopolitik* (1942). Though not explicitly so stated, the conception of an "organic state" is equally present in Halford J. Mackinder's work. See *Democratic Ideals and Reality* (1919), Ch. II and V. His followers, such as E. M. Earle and Walter Lippmann, show this as clearly as the geopoliticians. The controversy concerning the organic nature of groups is very extended. See Francis W. Coker, *Organismic Theories of the State* (1910), and W. Y. Elliott, *The Pragmatic Revolt in Politics* (1928), particularly Parts IV and V. For John of Salisbury, see John Dickinson, *The Statesman's Book of John of Salisbury* (1927), Introduction, particularly pp. xx–xxi.

3. See for further elaboration MG, pp. 24 ff. David Easton has recently offered an interesting mechanical model, stressing input and output as the crucial features.

4. The observations contained in this paragraph have been a recurrent theme in the writings of monarchists. The French Royalists under Charles Maurras have been particularly emphatic. See his *Enquête sur la Monarchie* (1909). See also Bolingbroke's *The Patriot King* (1749), and Frederick the Great (of Prussia), *Anti-Machiavel* (1741). It should not be forgotten, however, that monarchical society has no monopoly upon furthering the development of culture. Witness Athens, Florence, or Nuremberg.

5. *The Age of the Baroque*, 1952, p. 13.

6. The earlier conceptions here alluded to are reflected in various features of the law of the "police power." Of this, Walton H. Hamilton has poignantly observed that "it is one of two balanced terms (the other being 'due process') which make up a formula for constitutionality." See Ernst Freund, *The Police Power, Public Policy, and Constitutional Rights* (1904), for a searching study of the classical doctrine. On the historical evolution, see for the general ideas of this paragraph G. Schmoller, "Der Deutsche Beamtenstaat vom 16. bis 18. Jahrhundert," *Jahrbuch für Gesetzgebung, Verwaltung und Volkswirtschaft*, Vol. XVIII; and Otto Hintze's article cited above, Ch. II, *Remarks*. See also the author's article, "Some Thoughts

on the Politics of Government Control," in *Journal of Social Philosophy*, Vol. I (1936), pp. 122 ff.

7. For the rise of the legislative function, see Charles H. McIlwain, *The High Court of Parliament and Its Supremacy* (1910), especially pp. 46 ff. For Bodin's views and their relation to economics, see R. Chauviré, *Jean Bodin* (1914), particularly Book IV, Ch. III.

8. For the *Ordonnances du Roi*, see Esmein's *Cours Elémentaire d'Histoire du Droit Français* (1903), pp. 774 ff., and the official publication of the *ordonnances* by the Imprimerie Royale. The "progressive" economic policy of Tudor absolutism is treated in all the general works cited at the outset. To these may be added, for documentation, R. H. Tawney and E. E. Power, *Tudor Economic Documents* (1924). It was the economic progressivism of absolutism which aroused the admiration of Schmoller and the historical school and led them to erroneous political inferences. See also G. M. Trevelyan, loc. cit., pp. 190 ff.

9. See Eli Heckscher, *Mercantilism*, Vol. I, Preface, for a lucid discussion of the different views taken and some of the literature. More specific is Philip W. Buck's *The Politics of Mercantilism* (1942), but the last chapter, "Mercantilism and Totalitarianism," is overdrawn. The quotations from Montchrétien and *The British Merchant* are found ibid. Vol. II, p. 187. Note also the interesting recent study by Lawrence A. Harper, *The English Navigation Laws: A 17th Century Experiment in Social Engineering* (1939), giving a good sketch of "The Mercantile Mind" in Ch. II. But why deny *all* connection between mercantilism and planning?

10. The commercial policy of the various countries, of course, has been treated in numerous monographs. Readily accessible sources of reference are Jacob Viner, "English Theories of Foreign Trade before Adam Smith," in *Journal of Political Economy*, Vol. XXXVIII (1930), pp. 249 ff. and 404 ff.; and Charles W. Cole, *French Mercantilist Doctrines before Colbert* (1931). For Colbert, see P. Clement, *Histoire de Colbert* (3d ed., 1892). To these should still be added Walton Hamilton's discussion of the impact of mercantilist thinking upon the makers of the American Constitution, in his and Douglas Adair's *The Power to Govern* (1937). Whether one must accept the mercantilist view because the Constitutional Convention held it depends upon one's readiness to emphasize the "intention of the framers" as a basis for constitutional interpretation. Hamilton's argument seems more nearly a *reductio ad absurdum*.

11. Among authorities who share the view here taken I note G. M. Trevelyan, who expresses the opinion that the influence of the chartered trading companies on English government and politics was great; op. cit. pp. 201, 215 ff. See E. Levasseur, *Histoire du Commerce de la France* (1911–1912), and the works cited in the *Remarks*. For special companies: William H. Price, *The English Patents of Monopoly* (1906), and Paul Kaeppelin, *La Compagnie des Indes Orientales* (1908).

12. See George L. Beer, *The Old Colonial System, 1660–1754* (1912), and Heckscher, op. cit., who rightly emphasized Adam Smith's position. See *Wealth of Nations*, particularly Book IV. See also Lipson, *Economic History of England*, Vol. II (1934).

13. These problems are the core of Edmund Burke's famous indictment of Warren Hastings in 1788, *Works* (Boston, 1839), Vols. VI–VIII, now skillfully selected from and provided with running commentary by Ross J. S. Hoffman and Paul Levack, *Burke's Politics* (1949), pp. 233–276.

14. For these problems of planning and socialization, see Ch. XXIII, below.

15. Arthur R. Burns, *Money and Monetary Policy in Early Times* (1927); also A. von Luschin und Ebengreuth, *Allgemeine Münzkunde und Geldgeschichte des Mittelalters und der neueren Zeit* (1904).

16. For the quotation, see William Cunningham, *The Growth of English Industry and Commerce* (5th ed., 1910–1912), Vol. II, p. 434.

17. See H. Brougham, *An Inquiry into the Colonial Policy of the European Powers* (1803), and Beer, op. cit.; S. L. Mims, *Colbert's West Indian Policy* (1912); C. G. Haring, *Trade and Navigation between Spain and the Indies in the Time of the Hapsburgs* (1918); Alfred Zimmermann, *Die Kolonialpolitik der Niederländer* (1903); A. Duchêne, *La Politique Coloniale de la France* (1928).

18. See Klaus E. Knorr, *British Colonial Theories, 1570–1850* (1944), especially Part I. The quotes are on p. 126.

19. See, besides Knorr, op. cit., J. S. Furnival, *Colonial Policy and Practice: A Comparative Study of Burma and Netherlands India* (1948), especially Ch. VIII, and the general sketch of imperialism above, Ch. III.

VI. Justice and the Judicial Function

GENERAL NOTES

The American literature on the political aspects of judicial methods was not very extensive until the Supreme Court fight in 1937. However, Charles Warren's justly famous *The Supreme Court in United States History*, rev. ed. 1937, described the many political issues in which the American high court has been involved. The standard legal histories give little aid in connection with this question, but W. S. Holdsworth, *A History of English Law*, 3d ed., 1922, Vol. I, and Frederick Pollock and F. W. Maitland, *History of English Law*, 2d ed., 1899, cannot be neglected, nor can the relevant sections in A. Esmein, *Histoire du Droit Français* (8th ed., revue par H. Nézard, 1927–1928), and other continental works, such as Heinrich Brunner, *Deutsche Rechtsgeschichte*, 2d ed., 1906 and 1928. To these may be added more recent works of special application: Roscoe Pound, *The Formative Era of American Law*, 1939, idem., *Organization of Courts*, 1940; R. M. Jackson, *The Machinery of Justice in England*, 1940; R. C. K. Ensor, *Courts and Judges in France, Germany and England*, 1933; Karl N. Llewellyn, *The Common Law Tradition — Deciding Appeals*, 1960; Julius Stone, *Legal System and Lawyers' Reasoning*, 1964; G. Leibholz, *Politics and Law*, 1965; Roland Young, *American Law and*

Politics, 1967. See also P. M. Viollet, *Droit Public: Histoire des Institutions Politiques et Administratives de la France,* 1890–1903. Literature on judicial methods has tended to explore the psychological and sociological implications of judicial techniques. Justice Cardozo's *The Nature of the Judicial Process,* 1921, is perhaps the classic, but Edward S. Robinson's *Law and the Lawyers,* 1935, particularly Chs. VIII–XII, gives a thorough analysis of judicial methods in the light of modern psychology. See also Henry J. Abraham, *The Judicial Process,* 1962, comparing England, France and the United States.

More recently Glendon A. Schubert and associates, *Judicial Decision-Making,* 1963, undertook to apply quantitative methods to judicial conduct; the results are considered rather controversial. A considerable literature has developed in connection with the constitutional role of courts; for this see Ch. XIII below. Among earlier treatments of justice, one might mention Roscoe Pound, *Law and Morals* 2d ed., 1926; Max Ascoli, *La Guistizia,* 1930; Georges Gurvitch, *L'idee du droit social,* 1932; and Gustav Radbruch, *Rechtsphilosophie,* 3d ed., 1932, though none agrees with the functionalist position taken here. Much closer is Julius Stone's *The Province and Function of Law: Law as Logic, Justice, and Social Control, A Study in Jurisprudence,* 1946, an outstanding contribution. Cf. also the volume on "Justice" of the yearbook *Nomos,* VI, 1963, and the writings of Chaim Perelman, especially *The Idea of Justice and the Problem of Argument,* 1963. Of course discussing "justice" means philosophizing about law, and that is a very long story for which see my *The Philosophy of Law in Historical Perspective,* 1958, new ed. 1963.

REFERENCES

1. Huntington Cairns, *Legal Philosophy from Plato to Hegel,* 1949, p. 123. See for a more lengthy analysis my op. cit., above, Notes.
2. Cf. my article in *Nomos,* VI, 1963, pp. 24 ff.
3. On primitive government, anthropology is producing an increasing literature which is confused in its terminology, unfortunately, because of the failure of political scientists and anthropologists to work together. However, efforts along such lines are being made. Standard sources of information remain: Sir J. G. Frazer, *The Golden Bough,* 1890; Robert H. Lowie, *Primitive Society,* 1920; A. M. Hocart, *Kingship,* 1927; and E. A. Hoebel, *The Law of Primitive Man,* 1954. Cf. also MG, Ch. 22. On the judicial functions of parliament, following the older literature (Thomas Smith, etc.), see Josef Redlich, *The Procedure of the House of Commons* (tr. A. E. Steinthal; 1908); and Charles H. McIlwain, *The High Court of Parliament and Its Supremacy,* 1910, where the problem is developed in its ramifications. For the relation of parliament to the courts see William Stubbs, *Constitutional History of England* (1874–1878). For the judicial functions of the French parliament see the study by Paul R. Doolin, *The Fronde,* 1935, particularly Chs. I and VI.

4. See Charles H. McIlwain, op. cit., particularly Ch. II. For literature on the Roman law phase, see above, Ch. I, note 14. On Bracton, see Holdsworth, op. cit. Vol. II, p. 230 ff., where the controversial questions of the extent of his "Romanism" are reviewed. See also Max Radin, *A Manual of Roman Law*, 1926. For Coke's claim, see Roscoe Pound's *The Spirit of the Common Law*, 1921, p. 61.

5. Charles Grove Haines, *The Revival of Natural Law Concepts*, 1930. For a radical criticism of this approach see Hans Kelsen, *General Theory of Law and State*, 1945. Much sociological jurisprudence is really looking for a naturalistic higher law. For Sir Thomas Smith, see *English Commonwealth*, II, ii, and II, v–vii.

6. Dr. Bonham's case found in *Famous State Trials*, or in *Reports*, Vol. VIII. See also the comments in McIlwain, op. cit. pp. 147–148. Regarding the statement of Bacon, see *The Works of Francis Bacon*, 1842, Vol. II, p. 235. See also Bacon's whole memorial on codification, ibid. pp. 229 ff. See also S. E. Thorne, "Dr. Bonham's Case," *Law Quarterly Review*, 1938, and T. F. T. Plucknett, "Bonham's Case and Judicial Review," *Harvard Law Review*, 1926.

7. On the judge's conflict with prerogative, see Francis D. Wormuth, *The Royal Prerogative, 1063–1649*, 1939. On Coke, see *Edward Coke, Oracle of the Law*, by Hastings Lyon and Herman Block, 1929, as well as Catherine Drinker Bowen's admirable biography, *The Lion and the Throne*, 1956. For the King's statements see *The Works of Francis Bacon*, Vol. II, pp. 493–494, as well as *Coke on Littleton*, para. 97b.

8. Bacon, *Works*, II, 394.

9. *Reports*, Vol. XII, pp. 64–65.

10. Rousseau, *Contrat Social*, Book II, Ch. VI.

11. Locke, *Of Civil Government*, Second Treatise, para. 132.

12. Richard Hooker, *Of the Laws of Ecclesiastical Polity*, end of Book I.

13. For further analysis of this basic process, cf. MG, Ch. 24.

14. See *International Conference on Military Trials*, London, 1945 (report by the United States representative, Robert H. Jackson). See also *History of the United Nations War Crimes Commission*, 1945.

15. On *stare decisis*, see the brilliant article by Herman Oliphant, "A Return to Stare Decisis," in *American Law School Review*, Vol. VI, pp. 215 ff; and K. N. Llewellyn, *Bramble Bush*, 1930, 1960, where the quotes are found, and the same, *Jurisprudence*, 1962, especially pp. 116 ff. Further interesting reflections in Edward S. Robinson, *Law and the Lawyers*, 1935, p. 257. Cardozo's remark is found in *The Growth of Law*, 1924, p. 62.

16. See Ensor, op. cit. For a rationalistic theory, see A. L. Goodhart, *Precedent in English and Continental Law*, 1934. See also Yvon Loussouarn, "The relative Importance of Legislation, Custom, Doctrine and Precedent in French Law," 18 *Louisiana Law Review* 235, 1958 and A. T. von Mehren, *The Civil Law System*, 1957.

17. For the French Superior Council see Maurice Duverger, *Droit Constitutionnel et Institutions Politiques*, 1955, 4th ed. 1959.

18. The basic issue was discussed with great learning by Charles H. McIlwain,

in *Foreign Affairs*, 1936, in an article entitled "Government by law." See also trial record of "The Justice Case," Vol. III, *Trials of War Criminals*, U. S. Printing Office, 1951.

19. For this see Albert P. Blaustein and Charles O. Porter, *The American Lawyer, A summary of the Survey of the Legal Profession*, 1954, especially Ch. VI. Special mention may be made of Frederick Pollock, *The Origins of the Inns of Court*, 1931, and T. F. T. Plucknett, "The Place of the Legal Profession in the History of English Law," in *Law Quarterly Review*, Vol. 48, pp. 328 ff. Concerning the relation of bench and bar, see Charles A. Warren, *A History of the American Bar*, 1911, and Thorstein Veblen, *The Theory of Business Enterprise*, 1919, Ch. VIII. For the Act of Settlement, see Holdsworth, op. cit. Vol. VI, pp. 230 ff.

20. Concerning the case of the miller, see Rudolf Stammler, *Deutsches Rechtsleben in Alter und Neuer Zeit*, 1932, para. XXXI, "Der Prozess des Müllers Arnold, 1779–1787," pp. 413 ff.

21. The reforms of Cocceji are treated in Max Springer, *Die Coccejische Justizreform*, 1914.

22. The problem of the relationship between courts and classes has been much emphasized by Marxist writers. See, for example, Ernst Fraenkel, *Zur Soziologie der Klassenjustiz*, 1927, and Martin Beradt, *Der Deutsche Richter*, 1930. In the United States this problem of special prejudice of the judges has been brought forward often in connection with the discussion of the Supreme Court's constitutional review (see below, Ch. XIII); attacks in the thirties focused renewed attention upon it. A forceful statement of this point of view was Edouard Lambert, *Le Gouvernement des Juges et la Lutte contre la Législation Sociale aux Etats-Unis*, 1921; Charles A. Beard, *The Supreme Court and the Constitution*, 1912, and John R. Commons, *The Legal Foundations of Capitalism*, 1924, have leaned to similar interpretations. Cf. also Otto Kirchheimer, *Political Justice*, 1961, especially Chs. V–VII.

23. The literature on administrative law is very extensive. See K. C. Davis, *Administrative Iaw*, 1951 for an authoritative statement. Among the classical statements for Britain, William A. Robson's *Justice and Administrative Law*, 1928, 1948, holds first place; he demolished A. V. Dicey's earlier view as expressed in *Law of the Constitution*, 8th ed., 1926. Cf. also James Hart, *An Introduction to Administrative Law, with Selected Cases*, 1940, and J. R. Pennock, *Administration and the Rule of Law*, 1941. For France, the leading studies are Georges Vedel, *Droit Administratif*, 9th ed., 1963. For Germany of the Federal Republic, consult Ernst Forsthoff, *Verwaltungsrecht*, 8th ed., 1961; for the Weimar Republic, the classic treatment is by Walter Jellinek, *Verwaltungsrecht*, 1928, 1950. The quotation is found in Harold Laski's "Administrative Tribunals" in the ESS.

24. For the Conseil d'Etat, see Charles E. Freedeman, *The Conseil d'Etat in Modern France*, 1961, and René David and Henry P. de Vries, *The French Legal System*, 1958.

25. Georges Langrod, *Some Current Problems of Administration in France Today*, 1961, p. 48.

26. The quotation is found in Robson, op. cit. pp. 324 f. See also James M. Landis, *The Administrative Process*, 1939, and more detailed, Joseph Chamberlain, Noel T. Dowing, and Paul R. Hays, *The Judicial Function in Federal Administrative Agencies*, 1942.

27. On this, see John Middleton and David Tait, *Tribes Without Rulers*, 1958.

VII. The Constitution as a Political Process

GENERAL NOTES

Besides the general literature on constitutionalism discussed in connection with Ch. I, the understanding of the *process* of constitution-making depends in the first place upon the increasing number of detailed historical studies. Two admirable such historical analyses of the American case have recently been published: Clinton Rossiter, *1787 — The Grand Convention*, 1966, and Catherine Drinker Bowen, *Miracle at Philadelphia*, 1966. Besides these, the documentary history which covers the background of the Confederation deserves mention: W. U. Solberg, *The Federal Convention and the Formation of the Union*, 1958; see also the lawyer's view in Arthur E. Sutherland, *Constitutionalism in America*, 1965, Ch. 9. By contrast, the process in Britain, slow and meandering, has in recent years been illuminated by such works as J. G. A. Pocock, *The Ancient Constitution and the Feudal Law*, 1957 which have added a new dimension to the classic treatment by William Stubbs, *The Constitutional History of England*, 1874 and others. The documentary collections by Stubbs, Prothero, Gardiner, Adams and Stevens, and Violette are, of course, of great value to the empirical student of these processes.

For France, there is much historical writing on the successive constitutions. For the First Republic, the great histories of the revolution should be consulted; I mention F. A. V. Aulard, *The French Revolution — a political history*, 1904 (in 4 vols.), as well as his *Etudes et Leçons*, 1901–1924; and Eric Thompson, *Popular Sovereignty and the French Constituent Assembly*, 1952; see also Georges Lefebure, *Etudes sur la Revolution Française*, 1954. For the Third Republic, besides Gabriel Hanotaux's magistral works, Maurice C. Deslandres' *Histoire Constitutionnelle de la France: l'avènement de la Troisieme république, la constitution de 1875*, 1937 should be consulted, along with F. H. Brabant's *The Beginning of the Third Republic in France*, 1940. The Fourth Republic's beginnings are competently analyzed by David Thompson, *Democracy in France*, 2d ed., 1952, and by Gordon Wright, *The Reshaping of French Democracy*, 1948. Cf. also the detailed documentary study by R. R. Kapferer, *Die Verfassung der IV. Französischen Republik*, 1963; André Siegfried's suggestive essay, *De la IIIe à la IVe République*, 2d ed., 1952; and Francois Goguel, *France under the Fourth Republic*, 1952 (in French, *Le Regime Politique Français*, 1955).

The Fifth Republic's constitutional genesis is still shrouded in secrecy, since no public convention, but experts and administrative units (Ministry of Justice, Counseil d'Etat, etc.) shaped it for plebiscitary acclamation. Cf. for this process my own "The New French Constitution in Political and Historical Perspective," *Harvard Law Review*, Vol. 72, 1959, pp. 801–837 and the study by Marcel Prelot, *La Nouvelle Constitution* (no date, but no doubt 1958–59) which is a Gaullist interpretation. For a similar view, sketching the transition from Fourth to Fifth Republic cf. R. Aron, *France, Steadfast and Changing*, 1960. For the criticism of the Fourth from a Gaullist position, the most telling books are by Michel Debré, the architect of the Fifth, who explained his views in three sharply worded attacks: *La République et son Pouvoir*, 1950, *La République et ses Problèmes*, 1952, and *Les princes qui nous gouvernent*, 1957. See also Michel Debré, "La Nouvelle Constitution," *Revue française de science politique*, Vol. 9, 1959 pp. 15 ff., translated in W. G. Andrews, *European Political Institutions*, 1962. For various aspects of the 1958 French constitution, see also the articles by Nicholas Wahl and Stanley Hoffmann in *The American Political Science Review*, Vol. 53, 1959.

No satisfactory history of the Weimar Assembly has ever been written, though W. Apelt's *Geschichte der Weimarer Verfassung*, 1946 is useful if somewhat too legalistic; compare the general histories by S. W. Halperin, *Germany tried democracy; a political history of the Reich from 1918–1933*, 1946; and Erich Eyck, *Geschichte der Weimarer Republik*, 2 vols. 1954–1956. Cf. also the general constitutional histories by Forsthoff, Huber and others. Swiss constitutional history is reviewed in William E. Rappard, *La Constitution Fédérale de la Suisse, 1848–1948*, 1948. Cf. also André Siegfried, *La Suisse — Démocratie-témoin*, 2d. ed., 1956 and Marcel Bridel, *Précis de Droit Constitutionnel et Publique Suisse*, 1959.

REFERENCES

1. Constitutional theory has been burdened by a wearisome discussion about written and unwritten constitutions, or rather of the distinction between constitutions embodied in one document and those in many documents. The most definitive discussion, perhaps, is found in James Bryce, *Constitutions*, 1905; a sane, but all too brief counterstatement is in H. R. G. Greaves, *The British Constitution*, 3rd ed., 1955, pp. 20–21. See also H. W. Horwill, *The Usages of the American Constitution*, 1925, and Howard Lee McBain's *The Living Constitution*, 1927.

2. For this constitution, cf. TD, Ch. 10.

3. Ideologically speaking, a further development of these issues may be found in the author's *The New Belief in the Common Man*, 1942, especially Chs. II and VI.

4. See Charles H. McIlwain, *The High Court of Parliament and Its Supremacy*, 1910, particularly pp. 75 ff., 82 ff., 286 ff. See also the surveys in D. L. Keir, *The Constitutional History of Modern Britain, 1485–1937*, 1938.

5. For the changing pattern of this "personal sphere," see the author's "Rights, Liberties, Freedoms: A Reappraisal," *Transcendent Justice*, 1964, Ch. 5; cf. also Roscoe Pound, *The Development of Constitutional Guarantees of Liberty*, 1957; Zachariah Chafee, Jr., *Three Human Rights in the Constitution*, 1956, and the same *How Human Rights got into the Constitution*, 1952, as well as his collection of *Documents on Fundamental Human Rights*, 1951–1952. In 1959, a report was published of the U.S. Commission on Civil Rights and an abbreviation, *With Liberty and Justice for All*, states the official American position. The more advanced views of some of the Supreme Court justices in E. Cahn, ed. *The Great Rights*, 1963; and a broad overview in B. Mirkine–Guetzevich and M. Prelot, "Chrestomathie des Droits de l'Homme" in *Politique*, 1960. Note also the contributions of Carl Becker, Max Lerner, and Robert E. Cushman to *Safeguarding Civil Liberty Today*, 1945.

6. In recent years a vast amount of historical research has produced a juster estimate of medieval politics and has brought to light the constitutional nature of much of it. Cf. J. G. A. Pocock, *The Ancient Constitution and the Feudal Law*, 1957. As for the earlier work, the list of works which may be cited is a long one; perhaps it will suffice to refer to William Stubbs, *English Constitutional History*, 1874–1878, which is, of course, outstanding. The general pattern is explored in Otto von Gierke, *Das deutsche Genossenschaftsrecht*, 1868, particularly Vols. I and II, which in part were translated and published with a learned introduction by Ernest Barker, *Natural Law and the Theory of Society*, 1934. To these should be added Charles H. McIlwain, *The Growth of Political Thought in the West*, 1932, particularly Chs. V, VI, and VII; R. W. and A. J. Carlyle, *A History of Medieval Political Theory in the West*, 1903, particularly Vols. I and III; and Henry O. Taylor, *The Medieval Mind*, 1911, passim.

7. The literature on Cromwell is rapidly increasing. This we may owe to the drift toward dictatorship. But Cromwell wanted a constitution. Cf. *Age of the Baroque*, Ch. 10. See Wilbur C. Abbot's monumental collection of documents, *Writings and Speeches of Oliver Cromwell*, 4 vols. 1937–1947, which contains much penetrating comment and an exhaustive bibliography. See also Wilbur K. Jordan, *The Development of Religious Toleration in England*, 1932–1940, especially, Vol. III, Ch. II. Very significant also is *Puritanism and Liberty: Being the Army Debates (1647–1649)* . . . (selected and edited by A. S. Woodhouse, 1939). A very able study is that by Michael Walzer, *The Revolution of the Saints*, 1966, though he does not stress the constitutionalist preoccupation; for this, Francis D. Wormuth, *The Origins of Modern Constitutionalism*, 1949, and Charles Blitzer, *An Immortal Commonwealth*, 1960 are very valuable.

8. See K. C. Wheare, *Modern Constitutions*, 1951, pp. 1 ff.

9. MG, Ch. 3, and the literature cited there. Cf. also *Nomos*, VII, "Rational Decision," 1964, for contrasting views.

10. Cf. *The Impact of American Constitutionalism Abroad*, 1967, for numerous illustrations, and literature.

VIII. The Constituent Power, the Amending Power, and Revolution

GENERAL NOTES

The general problem of constitutional and political change, and of revolution, has received increasing attention. Aristotle's classic doctrine, however, has not usually served as the point of departure. Nor has a really comprehensive inventory of historical experience, such as probably underlies Aristotle's theory, been attempted. But even partial comparisons have yielded some striking results, like Crane Brinton's *The Anatomy of Revolution*, 1938, and Eugen Rosenstock-Hüssy's *Out of Revolution*, 1938. R. B. Merriman's strictly historical *Six Contemporaneous Revolutions, 1640–1660*, 1938 also is interesting. G. S. Pettee's *The Process of Revolution*, 1938 is more specifically concerned with discovering verifiable generalizations. The work of Hegel, Comte, and Marx suggests that modern theories have been inclined to take it for granted that change is change in a certain direction rather than change in any cyclical sense. Besides these, a large body of material regarding revolutions was gathered by writers in the sixteenth and seventeenth centuries who were interested in the "right of revolution." But this material is of little value from the standpoint of modern critical historical scholarship. Nevertheless, it suggests some data not ordinarily covered by modern works. Another body of uncritical dogmatic writings is offered by Socialists and Marxists.

Harold Laski, in *Reflections on the Revolution of Our Time*, 1943, attempted a re-assessment of the Russian revolution in terms of the Russian, German, and Italian versions of its counter-revolution. Sigmund Neumann, in *Permanent Revolution*, 1942, did the same, but from the standpoint of traditional liberalism rather than of socialism. James Burnham, in *The Managerial Revolution*, 1941, from still another standpoint, sought to find a synthesis of Sovietism, Fascism, and Nazism, as well as of parallel trends elsewhere in terms of world-wide ascendancy of a new class, the managers whom Arthur Koestler, with poetic license, dramatized as the commissars in *The Yogi and the Commissar*, 1945. Lately the idea of a "multiple revolution" has come to the fore; we are in danger of broadening the concept of revolution to include every major change in society.

A general overview of the discussion in recent years is offered by *Nomos*, Vol. VIII, "Revolution," 1966, in which not only general theories are discussed by a number of authors, but the relations of revolution to ideology, international order and Marxism are explored. Chalmers Johnson's *Revolutionary Change*, 1966 attempts a systematic analysis which leads him to the conclusion that "they never occur as a result of forces beyond human control," p. 166; whereas Hannah Arendt in *On Revolution*, 1962, sees it as a "lost treasure." As contrasted with such general visions, the political and governmental revolution has to be seen as "more rapid" political change, involving a greater amount of violence. Cf. for this MG, Ch. 34.

REFERENCES

1. On betrayal see Rebecca West, *The Meaning of Treason*, 1947, and a later and more comprehensive edition, *The New Meaning of Treason*, 1964; Adam Yarmolinsky, *Case Studies in Personal Security*, 1955; M. Grodzins, *The Loyal and the Disloyal*, 1956; André Thérivé, *Essai sur les Trahisons*, 1951; Margret Boveri, *Der Verrat im Zwanzigsten Jahrhundert*, 4 vols. 1956 ff.

2. For the *Instrument*, see Samuel Rawson Gardiner, *Constitutional Documents*, 2d ed., 1899, pp. 405 ff. See also Gardiner's summary and comments in the Introduction, pp. liii ff. For Cromwell's speeches, see T. Carlyle, *Oliver Cromwell's Letters and Speeches*, 1849. The first quotation is found on pp. 423 f. of Vol. II, the second and third on pp. 424 and 425. The following sentences are from p. 433. Cf. Abbott, op. cit.

3. Karl Loewenstein, "Opposition and Public Opinion under the Dictatorship of Napoleon the First," *Social Research*, IV, 1937. A. Esmein, *Eléments de Droit Constitutionnel Français et Comparé* (8th ed., revue par H. Nézard, 1927–1928), Vol. I, pp. 449 ff.

4. It is very important to keep in mind that the "constituent power" as used here is not identical with the *pouvoir constituant* of French constitutional law, which corresponds to the amending power of American constitutional law. See Esmein, op. cit. Vol. I, pp. 612 ff. However, the legal doctrine is confused, and often includes part of what is here called the constituent power, mingled with the amending power. The expression "constituent power" turns up in the preamble of the official English translation of the German Basic Law of 1949; it is in this case more nearly used in the sense suggested here. That sense is also implicit in the last article of that constitution, which reads: "This Basic Law shall become invalid on the day when a constitution adopted in a free decision by the German people comes into force" (art. 146). Concerning the Swiss constitution, see above, Ch. VII, "General." The constitutional issue in the American revolution has been emphasized by Charles H. McIlwain, *The American Revolution, a Constitutional Interpretation*, 1923.

5. The problem of constitutional change through usage has occupied English and American students for a long time. An able recent review is given by Peter H. Merkl, *Political Continuity and Change*, 1967, especially Ch. 6. For earlier studies, cf. Herbert W. Horwill, *The Usages of the American Constitution*, 1925; Karl Loewenstein, *Erscheinungsformen der Verfassungsänderung*, 1931, and Oliver P. Field, *The Effect of an Unconstitutional Statute*, 1935. Some of the most fundamental aspects of this problem have been stated in the course of the controversy concerning the significance of a written constitution from Burke to Bryce. Cf. also Karl Loewenstein, *Political Power and the Governmental Process*, 1957, Ch. V. The figures are taken from A. L. Lowell, *Popular Government*, 1930, Ch. XII.

6. James Bryce, *Studies in History and Jurisprudence*, 1901, Vol. I, pp. 124 ff. The question as to whether an independent amending power existed in Germany was always considered in the extensive discussions on judicial review. See Fritz

Morstein Marx, *Variationen über richterliche Zuständigkeit zur Prüfung der Rechtmässigkeit des Gesetzes*, 1927, for a general survey.

7. For the background of the enabling act see Arnold Brecht, *Prelude to Silence*, 1944, pp. 97 ff., where Brecht coins the intriguing phrase "sliding revolution" for this kind of subversion from within.

8. For a bold program of constitutional reform, see W. Y. Elliott, *The Need for Constitutional Reform*, 1935. See also Henry Hazlitt, *A New Constitution Now*, 1942.

9. Jane P. Clark, *The Rise of a New Federalism*, 1938. See below, pp. 623, 625. For England, see H. R. G. Greaves, *The British Constitution*, 6th ed., 1960, Introduction; and Hiram Miller Stout, *British Government*, 1953, especially pp. 22 ff.; a broad survey of the history is offered by K. B. Smellie, *Great Britain since 1688*, especially Chs. V, IX and XII. For France see Esmein, *Droit Constitutionnel*, pp. 543 ff., and Gordon Wright, *The Reshaping of French Democracy*, 1948.

10. Michel Debré, "La Nouvelle Constitution," *Revue française de science politique*, Vol. 9, pp. 15 ff., 1959, translated in W. G. Andrews, *European Political Institutions*, 1962. For background, see the works cited under "General" Ch. VII.

11. The question of possible limitations on the amending power is very controversial. For France the matter is stated with acuteness by most writers on constitutional law. See, for example, Esmein, *Droit Constitutionnel*, Vol. II, pp. 543 ff. A more extended discussion is found in Charles Lefebure, *Etudes sur les Lois Constitutionelles de 1875* (1882), pp. 217 ff. The general problem is considered by Egon Zweig, *Die Lehre vom Pouvoir Constituant* (1909). The American situation is considered in an article by William Marbury, "The Limitations upon the Amending Power," *Harvard Law Review*, Vol. 33, pp. 323 ff. (1919), where it is argued that such limitations are valid. The opposite view is usually taken by political scientists; see Munro, op. cit. p. 192. Whatever may be the logic of the matter, it is improbable that an amendment to Article V of the Constitution would not be accepted. It is interesting that none other than Alexander Hamilton should have sounded the note of constitutional realism when he wrote: "Wise politicians will be cautious about fettering the government with restrictions that cannot be observed, because they know that every breach of the fundamental laws, though dictated by necessity, impairs that sacred reverence which ought to be maintained in the breast of rulers towards the constitution of a country, and forms a precedent for other breaches where the same plea of necessity does not exist at all, or is less urgent and palpable." (*The Federalist*, No. XXV.)

12. It was proposed to do so in the *Draft Treaty for a European Community*, arts. 112–114.

13. Leon Trotsky, *Mein Leben*, 1930, p. 320, ". . . Revolutions are the mad inspirations of history."

14. See Crane Brinton, *Anatomy of Revolution*, 1938, passim. Brinton perhaps overstresses thee similarities of the French and Russian Revolutions, and minimizes those aspects of the latter which are dealt with by Sigmund Neumann in *Permanent Revolution*, 1942. See also George Pettee, *The Process of Revolution*, 1938.

15. In MG Ch. 34 I have developed the comparative theory of revolution further. For the present purpose, these general observations are sufficient.

16. K. H. Silvert, *A Study in Government: Guatamala,* 1954, Part I; cf. also George I. Blanksten, *Ecuador: Constitutions and Caudillos,* 1951 and the latter's "The Politics of Latin America," in Gabriel A. Almond and James S. Coleman, eds., *The Politics of Developing Areas,* 1960, pp. 455 ff.

17. Walter Lippmann, *The Method of Freedom,* 1934.

18. Dietrich Bracher et al., *Die nationalsozialistische Machtergreifung,* 1960. See also Curzio Malaparte, *Coup d'Etat* (tr. Sylvia Saunders, 1932).

19. See my "The New French Constitution in Political and Historical Perspective," *Harvard Law Review,* Vol. 72, 1959, pp. 806 ff.

20. For the process of France's negative revolution, see Gordon Wright, *The Reshaping of French Democracy,* 1948, and the source book by André Siegfried, Roger Seydoux, and others, *L'Année Politique,* 1946. For the background of the Third Republic, see D. W. Brogan, *The Development of Modern France,* 1940.

21. On the Italian negative revolution see *The Government of Republican Italy,* 1961, by John Clarke Adams and Paolo Barile, especially Ch. 3; and Piero Calamandrei and Alessandro Levi, *Commentario Sistematico alla Costituzione Italiana,* 2 vols., 1950, Vol. I, especially pp. LXXX ff.

22. Among the many works on postwar Germany and the negative revolution of military occupation, mention should be made of my article in APSR, Vol. 43, June and August, 1949; Lucius D. Clay, *Decision in Germany,* 1950; Eugene Davidson, *The Death and Life of Germany — An Account of the American Occupation,* 1959; John D. Montgomery, *Forced to be Free,* 1957; Edward H. Litchfield, ed. *Governing Postwar Germany,* 1953; John Gimbel, *A German Community under Occupation,* 1961; Peter H. Merkl, *The Origin of the West German Republic,* 1963 and finally a searching study in the German perspective, Hans Peter Schwarz, *Vom Reich zur Bundesrepublik,* 1967.

IX. The Constitution as a Political Force

GENERAL NOTES

The central theme of this chapter is adumbrated and implied in constitutionalist writings since the English constitutionalists began merging the medieval idea of a fundamental law with the basic pattern of governmental organization. The second World War produced a great many books, mostly brief, dedicated to extolling the virtues of constitutional democracy as contrasted with Fascism. Poets, novelists and historians, too numerous to cite, vied with one another in this ideological celebration and thus testified to the constitution being a political force. Charles A.

Beard's *The Republic,* 1943, presented a running commentary on the key passages of *the* Constitution to *Life's* millions of readers. Any emphasis upon civil liberties or human rights in constitutionalism implies that the constitution be taken as more or less unalterable and fixed. Actually, every constitution does in fact contain elements that are very stable and fixed. Some of these are organizational features of the political order; others embody broadly held beliefs and widely cherished values. Since the fifties, the reaffirmation of certain basic rights and liberties has stimulated anew the discussion of the underlying issues, and more particularly the idea of a constitutional myth. Cf. W. Y. Elliott's *The Pragmatic Revolt in Politics,* 1928, and Gaetano Mosca, *The Ruling Class,* 1939 (Italian original, 1884), building on Rousseau's original notion of the *veritable constitution.* These notions are in turn linked to natural law thinking and to its revival in this century. Cf. PL, Ch. 19 and the literature cited there, as well as Julius Stone, *Human Law and Human Justice,* 1965, Ch. 7. The symbolic importance of a constitution and more especially a bill of rights is forcefully stated in Arthur E. Sutherland, *Constitutionalism in America,* 1965; it is implicit in such modern studies of constitutional history as Robert G. McCloskey, *The American Supreme Court,* 1960. Cf. for the basic issues my "Rights, Liberties, Freedoms: A Reappraisal" APSR, Vol. LVII, 1963, pp. 841 ff. of which a revised version appeared as Ch. 5 of *Transcendent Justice — The Religious Dimension of Constitutionalism,* 1964.

REFERENCES

1. The citation from Rousseau is found in *Social Contract,* Book II, Ch. XII. Holcombe' phrase is from *State Government in the United States,* 3d ed., 1931. The general idea of the bill of rights is discussed in its historical setting by Benjamin F. Wright, Jr., in his *American Interpretations of Natural Law,* 1931. Karl Loewenstein, *Political Power and the Governmental Process,* 1957, especially pp. 147–153, develops the distinction between a normative, a nominal and a semantic constitution. The constitution's norms, when it is normative, "govern the political process" and it is clear that only such a constitution can be a political force.
2. See my "Rights, Liberties, Freedoms: A Reappraisal," loc. cit.
3. Carl J. Friedrich and Robert G. McCloskey, *From the Declaration of Independence to the Constitution — The Roots of American Constitutionalism,* 1954; Carl J. Friedrich, "Rights, Liberties, Freedoms," *University of Pennsylvania Law Review,* Vol. 91, pp. 312 ff., 1942.
4. Carl L. Becker, *The Declaration of Independence,* 1922: Ursula M. von Eckhardt, *The Pursuit of Happiness,* 1959. It continues to be the concept of many; e.g. Mr. Justice Hugo L. Black, in his most recent contribution to a collective volume entitled *The Great Rights* (ed. Edmond Cahn, 1963), speaks of rights as provisions that "protect individual liberty by barring government from acting in a particular area or from acting except under certain prescribed procedures" (p. 43).

That was precisely the formula of the French *Declaration* of 1789; it animates the British and American tradition of the seventeenth and eighteenth centuries throughout.

5. From the vast literature on human rights, the following might be selected: H. Lauterpacht, *International Law and Human Rights*, 1951; B. Mirkine–Guetzevitch and M. Prelot, "Chrestomathie des Droits de l'Homme," *Politique*, 1960, containing a number of essays of historical and comparative outlook; Zechariah Chafee, Jr., *Three Human Rights in the Constitution*, 1956; the same: *How Human Rights got into the Constitution*, 1952; Chafee has also published a collection, *Documents on Fundamental Human Rights* (3 pamphlets, 1951–52); Roscoe Pound, *The Development of Constitutional Guarantees of Liberty*, 1957; in 1959, a report was published of the United States Commission on Civil Rights and an abbreviation of it under the title *With Liberty and Justice for All* — this report concentrates on voting, education and housing, i.e., in our terminology, one civil liberty and two social rights or freedoms.

6. John Stuart Mill, *On Liberty*, 1861, and volume V of *Nomos*, entitled "Liberty" and devoted to an exploration of Mill's thought; note also that the definition given is of course not meant to be an exhaustive one.

7. Maurice Cranston, *Human Rights*, 1963; cf. also Leonard Krieger, "Stages in the History of Freedom," in *Nomos*, IV, 1962, for perspective.

8. Cranston, op. cit., does not wish to admit this, and argues to the contrary. A similar position is adopted by Isaiah Berlin, *Two Concepts of Liberty*, 1958, pp. 44–45, who calls it a "hybrid form of freedom." Actually, it was already recognized during the French Revolution, following Rousseau.

9. Cranston, op. cit., pp. 66 ff.

10. Arts. 22–28.

11. The right to work is actually not new; it was explicitly urged even before the French Revolution by Turgot who in the *Edit sur l'abolition des jurandes*, 1776, wrote: "Dieu, en donnant à l'homme des besoins, en lui rendant nécessaire la ressource du travail, a fait du droit de travailler la proprieté de tout l'homme, et cette proprieté est la première, la plus sacrée et la plus imprescriptible de toutes." It appears in Robespierre's proposal of a restatement of the *Droits de l'homme et du Citoyen* of April 24, 1793. See for these texts "Chrestomathie des Droits de l'Homme," in *Politique — Revue Internationale des Doctrines et des Institutions*, 1960, Nrs. 10–13, pp. 179–180 and 248. The classic *Declaration* is reprinted there on pp. 246–249. In this collection is also found the next *Declaration* of 1793. Cf. also the discussion, op. cit. by McCloskey and myself, on the American rights.

12. In *The Great Rights*, ed. Edmond Cahn, 1963 the distinguished authors still largely operate with that notion, especially Justice Black.

13. Art. 24 of *Universal Declaration*.

14. Cf. Gerhard Anschütz, *Die Verfassung des Deutschen Reiches . . . ein Kommentar*, 14th ed., 1933, especially pp. 505 ff. and the literature there cited.

15. This right is related to the freedom of self-realization, of course. This freedom was found, in the history of philosophy, to be one of three, the other two

being the freedom of self-perfection and of self-determination; but we wish it to be understood to comprehend these other two to be included under it — for self-determination is involved in self-realization, looked at from the viewpoint of the acting self, and self-perfection is the special form which self-realization takes in those human beings who are capable of the convictional trust in a higher destiny. Cf. Mortimer J. Adler, *The Idea of Freedom*, Vol. I, 1958, pp. 606 ff., for the trichotomy. It has recently been interestingly commented upon by C. W. Cassinelli in an unpublished study entitled *Freedom, Control and Influence: An Analysis*, 1963, especially Ch. 1, III. Cassinelli retains, however, the trichotomy and does not develop the notion that self-realization comprehends the other two. Quite contrary to these prevailing views Isaiah Berlin, *Two Concepts of Liberty*, 1958, pp. 25 ff., would restrict "self-realization" to the concept of freedom of the idealist philosophers — it is really a form of the doctrine of self-perfection.

16. Zechariah Chafee, Jr., *Free Speech in the United States*, 1941.

17. See my "Rights, Liberties, Freedoms: A Reappraisal," op. cit. The problem of the abuse of constitutional liberties and what to do about it is highly controversial. Loewenstein, op. cit., pp. 329–336 adumbrates the problem; its theoretical dimensions are explored in my *Constitutional Reason of State*, 1957, Chs. I and VII.

18. Thomas Jefferson, *Writings*, 1859, Vol. viii.

19. See the *Report of the Commission*, cited above, fn. 5, passim, for a broad and persuasive statement.

20. The problem of conflicts in written constitutions has vexed lawyers, particularly when reflecting upon judicial review. Cf. Karl Loewenstein, op. cit., Ch. XI. Some historians contest the issue of the Civil War as stated in the text.

21. A suggestive discussion of the implications of a preamble, though from a predominantly legal point of view, occurs in Edward S. Corwin's "We, the People" in *The Doctrine of Judicial Review*, 1914, pp. 81 ff. The Weiwar preamble is ably discussed in Hugo Preuss, *Reich und Länder*, ed. Gerhard Anschütz, 1928. Duguit's position is stated in his *Traité de Droit Constitutionnel*, 2d ed., 1921–1925, Vol. III, Ch. VI, and expanded in Vol. V. The French constitution of 1875 had no preamble; its makers looked upon it as a very provisional charter. Later, however, a school of writers, ably led by M. Léon Duguit, maintained that the *Déclaration des Droits de l'Homme* of 1789 formed an integral part of the French constitution (see *Traité de Droit Constitutionnel*, 3d ed., 1928, Vol. II, pp. 182–185). The constitution of the Fifth Republic, in keeping with its authoritarian cast, does not provide for rights, though they are mentioned in the preamble, except the basic one, analogous to *habeas corpus*.

22. The Marxist–Communist doctrine of class struggle is not so much the cause as it is the manifestation of this cleavage in the community. The problem of conflicting loyalties was well put and investigated in Paul Kosok, *Modern Germany — A Study of Conflicting Loyalties*, 1933. For pre-1914 Austria, see Oscar Jaszi, *The Dissolution of the Hapsburg Monarchy*, 1929. For Poland, see Raymond L. Buell, *Poland*, 1939, and R. Machray, *Poland, 1914–1931*, 1932. For Czechoslovakia, see *Czecho-*

slovakia: Twenty Years of Independence, 1940, R. J. Kerner, ed. Most important is T. G. Masaryk, *The Making of a State,* 1926.

23. Arnold Brecht, *Aus nächster Nähe — Lebenserinnerungen eines beteiligten Beobachters, 1884–1927,* 1966, p. 312; the entire Ch. 30 is devoted to this problem. "A majority which said: yes, to both democracy and republic did not exist after 1920," he asserts ibid.

24. Sage remarks on the general problem of this paragraph are found in Charles E. Merriam, *The Making of Citizens,* 1931, Chs. II and III, and the same author's *Political Power,* 1934, passim.

25. See William E. Rappard, works cited above Ch. VII *General;* and Robert C. Brooks, *Civic Training in Switzerland,* 1930.

26. Burke, op. cit. Vol. III, p. 421.

27. For the debate, see *Verhandlungen der Verfassungsgebenden Deutschen Nationalversammlung,* 1105A, and *Bericht und Protokolle des Achten Ausschusses über den Entwurf einer Verfassung des Deutschen Reichs,* pp. 24–25. For the imperial constitution, see Burt Estes Howard, *The German Empire,* 1906, pp. 403 ff. For the controversy about "Reich," see also Gerhard Anschütz, *Die Verfassung des Deutschen Reichs,* 14th ed., 1933, Introduction and pp. 36 ff. Regarding the British Commonwealth cf. D. B. Miller, *The Commonwealth and the World,* 1958; K. C. Wheare, *The Constitutional Structure of the Commonwealth,* 1960; and Patrick Gordon–Walker, *The Commonwealth,* 1962.

28. The literature on symbols and symbolism is very large. Anthropology and psychology have combined to bring to light the importance of symbols by exploring subrational, emotional elements in human behavior. Thurman Arnold's *Symbols of Government,* 1935 popularized the issue, but the series on *The Making of Citizens* which Charles E. Merriam edited, documents the problem on a wide front. Consult MG, Ch. 5. For the specific issue of nationalism, see Carlton J. Hayes, *Essays on Nationalism,* 1926; Hans Kohn, *The Idea of Nationalism,* 1944; Karl Deutsch, *Nationalism and Social Communication,* 1953; and Rupert Emerson, *From Empire to Nation,* 1960, Chs. X–XIV and XIX. Cf. also Benjamin Akzin, *State and Nation,* 1964.

29. Suzanne K. Langer, *Philosophy in a New Key,* 1942.

30. For an influential definition of symbols, cf. Sapir's article in the ESS. Cf. also that given in the *Dictionary of Philosophy,* 1942. A very broad setatement of the role of symbols was offered by G. H. Mead, *Mind, Self, and Society,* 1934. See also Talcott Parsons, *The Social System,* 1951. But for political scientists the authoritative statement is found in H. D. Lasswell and A. Kaplan, *Power and Society,* 1953. Gabriel Almond has listed "symbolic capability" as one of the output potentials of a political system, *Comparative Politics — A Developmental Approach,* 1966, with G. B. Powell, Jr., pp. 199–201, while David Easton, *Systems Analysis of Poiltical Life,* 1966 neglects this factor.

31. Mexican War Speech, January 12, 1848, in *Complete Works,* ed. Nicolay and Hay; 2d ed., 1905, Vol. I, pp. 338 f.

X. The Separation of Powers

GENERAL NOTES

The separation of powers (and the concomitant checks and balances) have been a part of the stock-in-trade of so-called political theory ever since Locke and Montesquieu. Yet after they had served their purpose as platform planks of anti-monarchical agitation, they settled back into the dogmatic slumber of an "accepted principle of constitutional law." Hardly any attempt was made to explore the principle as a working hypothesis related to ascertainable matters of fact. Instead, it was treated as a more or less practicable norm in the particular form which the respective national constitutional law had given it. Practically all the "general" literature is either legal or doctrinal. Today the emergence of governments built upon an almost complete concentration of powers has once more set the stage of scientific reconsideration of the question: under what conditions and in what forms can a separation of powers occur and be maintained? This chapter develops the general position outlined in the introductory chapter. Virtually all the general works, discussed above under Ch. I, contain a discussion of the separation of powers.

REFERENCES

1. Polybius's famous discussion occurs in his *History*, Book VI, Chs. XI ff. An early application of the doctrine to English constitutional law occurs in Sir Thomas Smith *De Republica Anglorum*, 1583.

2. The quotations are from *Oceana*, ed. Morley, 1887, pp. 27–37. See also the interesting discussion in Francis D. Wormuth, *The Origins of Modern Constitutionalism*, 1949, Ch. XIV. Cf. Charles Blitzer, *An Immortal Commonwealth*, 1960.

3. See Locke, *An Essay Concerning the True Origin, Extent and End of Civil Government*, Chs. X–XII. Here Ch. X, dealing with the forms of government, is merely a brief preface to a statement of the doctrine of the separation of powers.

4. For the *Instrument*, see Gardiner, *Constitutional Documents*, pp. 405 ff. For Cromwell's speeches, see W. C. Abbott, *The Writings and Speeches of Oliver Cromwell*, 1939, Vol. II, Ch. XVI.

5. The citation from Blackstone is found in his *Commentaries*, 1765 (ed., T. Cooley, 1876), Vol. I, p. 146.

6. The point made in this paragraph has received insufficient attention in the extensive literature on Montesquieu. See Joseph Dedieu, *Montesquieu et la Tradition Politique Anglaise en France*, 1909. One difficulty has been the purely linguistic one that *power*, *pouvoir*, and *Gewalt* are only roughly comparable.

7. Kant's statement of this analogy occurs in *Anfangsgründe der Rechtslehre*, para. 45. The relevant passage is as follows: "Every state contains three powers, i.e. the general and united will in threefold personification (*trias politica*): the power to rule (sovereignty) in the person of the legislative, the executive power in the person of the governor (in accordance with law) and the law-interpreting power (attributing to each what is his according to law) in the person of the judge (*potestas legisla-*

toria, rectoria et judiciaria). [. . .] similar to the three propositions in a practical syllogism: the major premise which contains the law of a will, the minor premise which contains the command to proceed according to that law, i.e. the principle of subsuming [. . .] under the law, and the consequent which contains the sentence or judicial decision as to what is law in the particular case." Cf. also my "Le problème du pouvoir dans la théorie constitutionnaliste" in R. Polin, ed., *Le Pouvoir,* (*Annales de Philosophie Politique* T. 1) 1956, pp. 33–51.

8. See E. B. Greene, *The Provincial Governor in the English Colonies of North America,* 1898; Benjamin F. Wright, Jr., "The Origins of the Separation of Powers in America," in *Economica,* Vol. XIII, 1933; and William S. Carpenter, "The Separation of Powers in the Eighteenth Century," in *American Political Science Review,* Vol. XXII, 1928. The quotation is from Felix Frankfurter, *The Public and its Government,* 1930, p. 77. Perhaps the ablest and certainly one of the most influential attacks on the separation of powers doctrine is J. Allen Smith, *Growth and Decadence of Constitutional Government,* 1930.

9. See my *The Impact of American Constitutionalism Abroad,* 1967, Ch. II.

10. The importance of the two-party system as a constitutional restraint was first clearly stated by Walter Bagehot in his epochal *The English Constitution* (1867). 1928). The crucial importance of the conventions concerning the parties for restraining the power of the government was made the touchstone of true parliamentary government by Robert Redslob in a brilliant essay, *Die Parlamentarische Regierung in ihrer wahren und ihrer unechten Form,* 1918. See H. R. G. Greaves, *The British Constitution,* 6th ed., 1960; Robert A. Dahl, ed., *Political Oppositions,* 1966, especially Chs. I by Allan Potter and XI and XII by Robert Dahl.

11. See Benjamin Constant, *Cours de Droit Constitutionnel,* 1814; Robert von Mohl, *Staatsrecht, Völkerrecht und Politik,* 1860, Vol. I, pp. 3 ff., Vol. II, pp. 4 ff.; and Georges Burdeau, *Science Politique,* new ed., 1966, Vol. I.

12. "The Development of the Executive Power in Germany," in APSR, Vol. XXVII, 1933, by Carl J. Friedrich. The transition to parliamentary government in France is brilliantly portrayed by Joseph Barthélemy in his *L'Introduction du Régime parlementaire en France sous Louis XVIII et Charles X,* 1904. For the city of Strassburg, see Gustav Schmoller, *Deutsches Städtewesen in älterer Zeit,* 1922, pp. 214 ff.

13. Regarding Sweden, see "Legislative Assemblies — Scandinavian States and Finland," by Herbert Tingsten, in the ESS, Vol. IX; P. E. Fahlbeck, *Die Regierungsform Schwedens,* 1911; and Axel Brusewitz, "Maktfördelning och demokrati i den konstitutionella utvecklingen," in *Statsvenska Tidskrift,* 1923, as well as Nils Herlitz, *Grunddragen av det Svenska Statsskickets Historia,* 1928, particularly pp. 177 ff.; and Dankwart A. Rustow, *The Politics of Compromise — A Study of Cabinet Government in Sweden,* 1955.

14. See *Problems of the American Public Service* (ed. Commission of Inquiry into Public Personnel Problems), "Responsible Government Service under the American Constitution," by Carl J. Friedrich, pp. 48 ff.

15. MG, Chs. 23–25.

16. R. E. Cushman, *The Independent Regulatory Commissions,* 1941.

17. See Robert A. Dahl, *Pluralist Democracy in the United States: Conflict and Consent*, 1967, especially Chs. 10, 11 and 13.

18. See, for instance, Woodrow Wilson, *Congressional Government*, 1887, pp. 265 ff; Frank J. Goodnow, *The Principles of the Administrative Law of the United States*, 1905, p. 53 and passim; Elliott, *Need for Constitutional Reform*, 1935.

19. See John Adams, *A Defense of the Constitutions of Government of the United States of America*, 1787, pp. 308–309: "All nations, under all governments, must have parties; the great secret is to control them. There are but two ways, either by a monarchy and standing army, or by a balance in the constitution. Where the people have a voice, and there is no balance, there will be everlasting fluctuations, revolutions and horrors. . . ." For Constant, see *Cours de Politique Constitutionnelle*, 1872. For the prerogative, see the author's *Constitutional Reason of State*, 1957, passim; Francis D. Wormuth, *The Royal Prerogative, 1603–1649*, 1939, especially Ch. V; and Charles H. McIlwain, *The Political Thought of James I*, 1918. Dicey's statement is found in his *Law of the Constitution*, 8th ed., 1926, p. 420. Laski's view is stated in a pamphlet entitled *The Crisis and the Constitution*, 1932, Ch. VI.

XI. Federalism and the Territorial Division of Power

GENERAL NOTES

The writings on federalism were reviewed in their historical perspective in my essay "Origin and Development of the Concept of Federalism in the United States" (1959, as cited below). This should be read in conjunction with Otto von Gierke's chapter on federalism in his *The Development of Political Theory*, 1939; Sobei Mogi, *The Problem of Federalism*, 1931; R. Emerson, *State and Sovereignty in Modern Germany*, 1928, Ch. 3; and the classic, if wrongheaded, Edward A. Freeman's *History of Federal Government in Greece and Italy*, 1863. From the extensive literature of recent years, the following may be mentioned as generally valuable, though others are cited in the notes below: K. C. Wheare, *Federal Government*, 1946, 1953; Arthur W. MacMahon, ed., *Federalism — Mature and Emergent*, 1954; Robert Bowie and Carl J. Friedrich, eds., *Studies in Federalism*, 1954; William S. Livingston, *Federalism and Constitutional Change*, 1956; Edward McWhinney, *Federal Constitution-making for a multi-national World*, 1966; Peter Hay, *Federalism and Supranational Organizations*, 1966; Arthur Maass, ed., *Area and Power*, 1959; Gaston Berger, et. al., *Le Federalisme*, 1956; Dusan Sidjanski, *Federalisme Amphytionique*, 1956; Christopher Hughes, *Confederacies*, 1963; Konrad Hesse, *Der Unitarische Bundesstaat*, 1962. I should like to add my own comparative treatment soon to be published and based on my essay "Selected Trends and Issues in Contemporary Federal and Regional Relations" in *Status of Puerto Rico: Selected Background Studies prepared for the United States — Puerto Rico Commission on the Status of Puerto Rico*, 1966.

REFERENCES

1. The following discussion is taken from my paper, "Federalism, National and International in Theory and Practice," read before the Oxford Round Table Meeting of the International Political Science Association in 1963.

2. See for this my article "Origin and Development of the Concept of Federalism in the United States," in *Jahrbuch des öffentlichen Rechts der Gegenwart*, Neue Folge, Band 9, pp. 29 ff. See also Stanley Hoffmann, "The Areal Division of Powers in the Writings of French Political Thinkers," in *Area and Power*, ed. Arthur Maass, 1959. For a general, though in spite of its prolixity incomplete, history see Sobei Mogi, *The Problem of Federalism — a Study of the History of Political Theory*, 1931; for the best general analysis of nineteenth century juristic writings Rupert Emerson, *State and Sovereignty in Modern Germany*, 1928; for the earlier theory Otto von Gierke, *The Development of Political Theory* (tr. B. Freyd, 1939 — English edition of his well known study on Althusius, 1880).

3. For the complex problems of the Commonwealth, cf. Frank H. Underhill, *The British Commonwealth — An Experiment in Cooperation among Nations*, 1956; and Nicholas Mansergh, et. al., *Commonwealth Perspectives*, 1958.

4. Arts. 77–87 of the Constitution of the Fifth Republic. Cf. Gonidec, *Droit d'Outre-Mer*, 1959 for a commentary. Cf. also for a good summary, Roy Macridis and Bernard E. Brown, *The De Gaulle Republic — Quest for Unity*, 1960, Ch. XI.

5. A separate art. 88 provides for association in the Constitution of the Fifth Republic.

6. Ernst B. Haas, *The Uniting of Europe, Political, Social and Economic Forces, 1950–57*, 1958; Raymond Aron, *Paix et Guerre entre les Nations*, 1962, pp. 734 ff. also uses this contrast of empire and federation but his concept of federalism is old-fashioned and legalistic.

7. Arnold H. Heidenheimer, "Federalism and the Party System: The Case of West Germany," *American Political Science Review*, Vol. LII, 1958; Peter H. Merkl, "Executive-Legislative Federalism in West Germany," same review, LIII, 1959, pp. 732 ff.; Karlheinz Neunreither, *Der Bundestag zwischen Politik und Verwaltung*, 1959, summarized in the same review, LIII, pp. 713 ff.; Alfred Grosser, *La République de Weimar*, 1957.

8. Oskar Jaszi, *The Dissolution of the Hapsburg Monarchy*, 1920; Josef Redlich, *Das Oesterreichische Staats– und Reichsproblem*, 2 vols., 1920 and 1926; also Josef Redlich, *Kaiser Franz Josef von Oesterreich*, 1928; cf. also Adolf Fischhof, *Austria and the Guarantees of its Existence*, 1869 and Hans Kohn, *The Hapsburg Empire, 1804–1916*, 1961, pp. 53–54.

9. Cf. K. V. Rao, *Parliamentary Democracy in India*, 1961, especially Ch. IX, who

claims, however, that there exists no real federalism in India: "But strictly speaking and applying the tests more closely, we see that neither historical antecedents nor the socio-economic conditions nor even the essential federal principle in reality, exist in this constitution . . ." (p. 274). It is evident that the view of federalism as process would not support this conclusion. What could be more evidently conditions requiring a federal order than India's plurality of religions, languages and traditions?

10. Immanuel Kant, *Grundlegung zur Metaphysik der Sitten*, 1785, contains the most persuasive statement.

11. S. N. Eisenstadt, *The Political Systems of Empire*, 1963, especially Chs. 4–6.

12. A. Vyshinsky, *Soviet Constitutional Law*, 1948; on Soviet federalism, see Guy Lacharrière, *L'idée fédérale en Russie de Riourik à Staline*, 1945; R. Schlesinger, *Federalism in Central and Eastern Europe*, 1945; S. M. Ravin, *Das Prinzip des Föderalismus im sowjetischen Staatsrecht*, 1961.

13. Cf. MG, Ch. 30, as well as Bowie and Friedrich, *Studies in Federalism*, 1954, Introduction.

14. See above, Ch. VIII.

15. Arthur Maass, ed., *Area and Power*, 1959, while following the general theory here outlined, has pleaded for using the term "areal" rather than "territorial" or "spatial" division of powers; I remain unconvinced, because in the general theory of government and the state, one speaks of the importance of the territory within the boundaries of which it operates, and the demand for more land has been called the drive for "space" or "territory" nor for "area." The term "territory" has much more general significance in life, for which see Ardrey, *The Territorial Imperative*, 1966.

16. The one exception is Esthonia which after the first world war instituted a non-territorial system which proved very temporary. Here an attempt was made to put to test proposals which Karl Renner, *Der Kampf der Oesterreichischen Nationen um den Staat*, 1907, as well as *Das Selbstbestimmungsrecht der Nationen in besonderer Anwendung auf Oesterreich*, 1918 had advanced for solving the problems of the Hapsburg Monarchy, by incorporating each nationality as an electoral body and then federalizing the empire in terms of these ethnic groups, constituted by persons without reference to territory and on the basis of personal preference. For Esthonia, see Albert Pulleritz, ed., *Estland — Volk, Kultur, Wirtschaft*, Tallin, 1931, pp. 39 ff.; Evald Uustalu, *The History of the Estonian People*, 1952. This work gives the historical background.

17. E.g. Ch. 6 (A. E. Sutherland), Ch. 4 (Bowie), Ch. 9 (Brinser) and Ch. 10 (Friedrich and Mavrinac), concerned respectively with commerce and transportation, defense, agriculture and labor in Robert R. Bowie and Carl J. Friedrich, eds., *Studies in Federalism*, 1954, dealing with Australia, Canada, Germany, the United States and Switzerland on a comparative basis.

18. For a pointed statement of this view, representative of the outlook of many "radical" democrats found among European socialists, cf. Franz L. Neumann, "Federalism and Freedom: a Critique" in *Federalism, Mature and Emergent*, ed. Arthur W. MacMahon, 1955, pp. 44–55.

19. For the following discussion, see my "Selected Trends and Issues in Contemporary Federal and Regional Relations," in *Status of Puerto Rico: Selected Background Studies prepared for the United States–Puerto Rico Commission on the Status of Puerto Rico,* 1966.

20. Klaus von Beyme, "Federal Theory and Party Reality in the Soviet Union," *Public Policy,* Vol. XIII, 1964, pp. 395–412.

21. Ernst B. Haas, *The Uniting of Europe — Political, Social, and Economic Forces, 1950–1957,* 1958, especially Ch. 11.

22. Edgar Bonjour, *Histoire de la Neutralité Suisse,* 1946, 1949.

23. David B. Truman, "Federalism and the Party System," in Arthur W. MacMahon, ed., *Federalism Mature and Emergent,* 1955, pp. 115 ff. and William H. Riker, *Federalism,* 1964, p. 101.

24. J. D. B. Miller, *Australian Government and Politics,* 1954, 1959, pp. 145–146. For Labour's general attitude, see L. F. Crisp, *The Parliamentary Government of the Commonwealth of Australia,* 1949, pp. 79–82, especially p. 81.

25. See for this point George Liska, *International Equilibrium: A Theoretical Essay on the Politics and Organization of Security,* 1957, pp. 137 ff.

26. See for the *Reichsreform,* Arnold Brecht, *Federalism and Regionalism in Germany,* 1945, Part III, especially pp. 73–92.

27. That danger is further reduced by the conclusion of the Economic Union between the Benelux countries in 1960, the culmination of a slow evolution; cf. Albert Bleckmann, "Die Benelux Wirtschaftsunion" in *Zeitschrift für Ausländisches Oeffentliches Recht und Völkerrecht,* XXII, 1962, pp. 239 ff. with the documents pp. 296–352.

28. Cf. the valuable introduction by B. F. Wright in his fine new edition, as well as the commentary by Jacob Cook in his, both published in 1961.

29. Mention might be made here of Karl Deutsch, *Nationalism and Social Communication,* 1953 as well as Karl Deutsch, ed. and co-author, *Political Community and the North Atlantic Area — International Organization in the Light of Historical Experience,* where the early phases of a federalizing process within the framework of an international organization (NATO) are dealt with; note especially pp. 36 ff. and 46 ff. and the entire Ch. III which discusses integration as a process.

30. Robert O. Tilman and Taylor Cole, eds., *The Nigerian Political Scene,* 1962.

31. For greater detail, see my "Selected Trends and Issues in Contemporary Federal and Regional Relations" (above, GENERAL NOTES), Section I, and my essay, "Federalism and Nationalism," in *Orbis,* Vol. X, No. 4, 1967.

32. This pattern fits both the League of Nations and the United Nations, as well as the Achaean and Aetolian Leagues, the North Italian, the Hanseatic, Swabian and Belgian city leagues, the Swiss and Dutch Confederation, as well as their American and German counterparts.

33. See MG, Chs. 22–28.

34. For a comparative discussion of the amending process, see *Studies in Federalism, Ch. XVI.* For the most vivid portrayal of the transition from confederation to federal government in the United States, see *The Federalist,* Nos. 1–10. In Ger-

---

many the problem of the participation of the *Länder* as units in the amending power was not clearly faced by the Weimar constituent assembly, nor did it receive much attention afterward; it was occasionally adduced as proof that the German constitution did not recognize such a power. The Basic Law still leaves the matter to federal legislation (see art. 79).

35. See the general discussion of executive leadership in Ch. XVIII. The desire to secure effective leadership has, of course, always been recognized as a prime factor in establishing a federalism. For a comparative evaluation, cf. Bowie and Friedrich, *Studies in Federalism*, Ch. II.

36. See Jean Siotis, *Essai sur le Secrétariat International*, 1963, and Inis L. Claude, *Swords into Plowshares*, rev. ed., 1959, especially Ch. 10.

37. See my article "Federalism and Opposition" in *Government and Opposition*, No. 3, 1966, pp. 286–296 for a more detailed discussion.

38. It will be noted that this set of propositions follows with some rather significant variations, the statement in Robert A. Dahl, *Political Oppositions in Western Democracies*, 1966. It does not seem empirically sound to speak of "maximizing" the phenomena cited, since it is unknown what the "maximum" would be. On the subject of minimal and maximal solutions cf. MG, pp. 663 f. and passim.

39. Cf. for this vexed issue the several papers in *Nomos*, VII, "Rational Decision," 1964, including my own paper on the historical dimension.

40. A special feature was the chance it offered the Nazis to naturalize Hitler; without that he could not have become chancellor.

41. This problem is, of course, not peculiar to federal regimes, but is ubiquitous in contemporary society. For the underlying theoretical and philosophical issues, cf. my *Constitutional Reason of State*, 1957.

42. Felix Frankfurter and James M. Landis, *The Business of the Supreme Court — A Study in the Federal Judicial System*, 1928, fail to make this point explicit, through it is implicit in their account. Robert G. McCloskey, *The American Supreme Court*, 1960, Ch. VII, and others, describing the history of such courts have shown this general trend. Cf. Paul A. Freund, "Umpiring the Federal System," in MacMahon (as cited in GENERAL NOTES), Ch. 10.

43. See for all this Arthur E. Sutherland, *Constitutionalism in America — Origin and Evolution of its Fundamental Ideas*, 1965, Chs. 13–15.

44. See Burke Marshall, *Federalism and Civil Rights*, 1964, where Harlan is cited on p. 84.

45. Gerhard Braunthal, "Federalism in Germany: The Broadcasting Controversy," *Journal of Politics*, XXIV, 1962, pp. 559–561; Donald R. Reich, "Court, Comity, and Federalism in Western Germany," *Midwest Journal of Political Science*, VII, 1963.

46. Taylor Cole, "New Dimensions of West German Federalism," *Comparative Politics and Political Theory*, 1966, pp. 99–122, especially at p. 106 f. Edward McWhinney, *Comparative Federalism — States Rights and National Power*, 1962, Ch. 3.

47. Cf. Bowie and Friedrich (as cited in GENERAL NOTES) which contains

special sections on the various topics of Australian and Canadian federalism. Its bibliography should be supplemented from the excellent contribution by Alexander Brady to William S. Livingston, *Federalism in the Commonwealth*, 1963. Cf. also the admirable *Preliminary Report of the Royal Commission on Bilingualism and Biculturalism*, 1965.

48. Kenneth C. Wheare, *The Statute of Westminster and Dominion Status*, 3d ed., 1947; Arthur B. Keith, *The Dominions as Sovereign States: Their Constitutions and Governments*, 1938; Alexander Brady, *Democracy in the Dominions*, 1947; and the works cited in footnote 3 above. Regarding the Imperial Defense Committee, see the discussion by W. I. Jennings in *Cabinet Government*, 1938, Ch. X. See also the parliamentary debates (HCD) on the subject, March 27, 1928.

49. Cf., e.g., S. A. H. Haqqi, "Federalism, Single Dominant Party and The Problem of Linguistic Autonomy in India," a paper read before the Geneva Congress of IPSA, September, 1964, p. 2; but others are of the opposite opinion, e.g., N. Srinivasan, *Democratic Government in India*, 1954, p. 147: "The federal character of the Constitution is indisputable. . . . The new constitution of India has effected an adjustment of federal–state relations suited to the conditions of India that is *sui generis*. . . ." The latter position seems sounder in terms of our view of federalism.

50. Shri N. V. Gadgil, *Constituent Assembly Debates*, Vol. XI, p. 657 (as cited by Haqqi). For an admirable review of the extensive literature on Indian federalism and its background, cf. T. J. Leonard's essay in Livingston, op. cit.

51. S. V. Kogekar, "Federalism in India," a paper read before the *Oxford Roundtable* of IPSA, September, 1963, passim; the next quote is p. 6.

52. K. C. Rao, *Parliamentary Democracy in India*, 1961, p. 269.

53. Rao, op. cit., Ch. VIII, especially pp. 285–286. See also his penetrating discussion of emergency powers, especially in Ch. VIII.

54. Besides the constitutional text (given as an appendix in D. Pickles, *The Fifth Republic*, 1962, pp. 234 ff.), consult the section in that book on the Community, as well as relevant sections in David Thompson, *Democracy in France*, 1964; and R. Macridis, *Supplement to The De Gaulle Republic*, 1963.

55. The general literature on the unification movement in Europe has become very voluminous. A good general review of the politics up to the mid-fifties is provided by Ernst B. Haas, *The Uniting of Europe — Political, Social, and Economic Forces, 1950–1957*, 1958; for a more recent assessment see Arnold J. Zurcher, *The European Community — An approach to Federal Integration*, 1964, pp. 67–115 and for the preceding period the same author's *The Struggle to Unite Europe, 1940–1958*, 1958. The British view (favorable) is well stated in Uwe Kitzinger, *The Challenge of the Common Market*, 1961. Besides these, the *General Reports on the Activities of the Community*, Brussels, published by the EEC Commission, are an important source, as is the *European Yearbook*, The Hague, published since 1954 under the auspices of the Council of Europe. R. R. Bowie and the author's *Studies in Federalism*, prepared by a group of researchers for the *Ad Hoc Assembly* in 1953 contains an introduction by the author reviewing the background of the draft constitution and its shortcomings.

56. Bowie and Friedrich, op. cit. In the appendix, there is found the text of the draft treaty for a constitution, preceded by the *Resolutions* of the preparatory *Study Committee;* these latter are more far-reaching.

57. May 6, 1963, cf. *European Yearbook*, 1964.

58. Carl J. Friedrich, "Admission of New States, Territorial Adjustments and Secession," Study 15 in Bowie and Friedrich, *Studies in Federalism*, 1954.

59. See above, footnotes 4 and 5.

60. W. Phillips Davison, *The Berlin Blockade — a Study in Cold War Politics,* 1958; Hans Speier, *The Soviet Threat to Berlin*, 1960.

61. Royal Institute, *Britain in Western Europe*, 1956. Roland Young and James A. Robinson, *Parliamentary Decision-making in Great Britain, The Case of the Common Market,* (a paper delivered at the American Political Science Association meeting, 1962).

62. Jane P. Clark, *The Rise of a New Federalism*, 1938.

63. Morton Grodzins, "Centralization and Decentralization in the American Federal System," in *A Nation of States — Essays on the American Federal System*, ed. Robert A. Goldwin, 1963, pp. 1–23, especially pp. 21 ff. Cf. also his magistral *The American System: A New View of Government in the United States* (edited by Daniel J. Elazar), 1967; and the interesting study by M. J. C. Vile, *The Structure of American Federalism*, 1961.

64. 88th Congress, Report 84, entitled "Intergovernmental Relations" and issued as a "Report of the Committee on Government Operations — United States Senate" April 1, 1963.

65. William A. Robson, *Local Government Crisis*, 1966, pp. 145–150. The entire study is most illuminating.

66. Hiram Miller Stout, *British Government*, 1953, Ch. XVI; Stout gives a good overall view of the situation. For further detail, cf. the next chapter.

67. The quotation is from W. A. Robson, *The Development of Local Government,* (1931, 1947) p. 189.

68. The pros and cons of a federal system are ably summarized in Arthur MacMahon's Ch. I of *Federalism, Mature and Emergent*.

XII. Local Self-Government:
Basis of Constitutional Democracy

GENERAL NOTES

Among the more general works dealing with this important subject, I would recommend three as of broad importance: Lewis Mumford, *The City in History*, 1961; William A. Robson, ed., *Great Cities of the World, Their Government, Poli-*

tics and Planning, 1954, 1957; and Henri Pirenne, *Les Villes et les Institutions urbaines*, 1925 (English edition under the title *Medieval Cities*, 2d ed., 1939). Although local government is in modern times seen as a mainstay of constitutional government, the city and town are also the cradle of constitutional government; this is especially true in the Low Countries, Germany and Italy; for the latter cf. the classic study by J.C.L.S. de Sismondi, *Histoire des républiques italiennes au moyen age*, 10 vols., 1840–41. For the history of American local government, Ernest S. Griffith, *History of American City Government — The Colonial Period*, 1938, and the volume edited by Handlin and Burchard, *The City in History*, 1963, which is distinguished by a philosophical and sociological approach. The latter is also a special feature of Max Weber's remarkable essay on the city, included in his *Wirtschaft und Gesellschaft*, 2d ed., 1925, second part, Ch. VIII, pp. 504–601, not to my knowledge as yet translated into English. On Britain, William A. Robson's *The Development of Local Government*, 1931, 1947, is the best; Sidney and Beatrice Webb's *English Local Government from the Revolution to the Municipal Corporations Act*, 1906–1929 in 9 vols. is the most exhaustive. Others below in the notes. A broadly conceived recent study of American aspects is *City Politics*, 1963, by Edward C. Banfield and James Q. Wilson; philosophical in its thrust is Morton and Lucia White, *The Intellectual versus the City*, 1962. A broad survey of the problems of the local government's relations with the federal system is offered by the *Report of the Commission on Intergovernmental Relations*, 1955 with its supplemental *Report on State–Local Relations*, 1955. I should like to add two other general references: Anwar Syed, *The Political Theory of American Local Government*, 1966 which *inter alia* contains a discriminating discussion of Jefferson's and de Tocqueville's views, and Giovanni Sartori, *Democratic Theory*, 1962 which from the Italian perspective has an interesting chapter on the basic difference between Greek and modern democracy the non-recognition of which confuses so much general thought on local government as a basis of constitutional government.

GENERAL NOTES

1. The statement is from Granville Hicks' *Small Town*, 1946, p. 276, the sentence, from p. 117. Other local studies pointing in the same direction are Arthur E. Morgan, *The Small Community — Foundation of Democratic Life*, 1942, James West, *Plainville USA*, 1945, and W. Lloyd Warner et al., *Democracy in Jonesville*, 1949, p. 628.
2. In publications of *Conseil des Communes Européens* this speech has been extensively reproduced since 1951 when the Council was founded.
3. Edward C. Banfield, *Political Influence*, 1961, Ch. 12 and throughout.
4. James Bryce, *The American Commonwealth*, Ch. XLIX, especially at p. 626: "The town meeting has been not only the source, but the school of democracy."
5. See Plato, *Laws*, 738, d, 6–e, 8; also 737 e, 1. Aristotle, *Nicomachean Ethics*, 1170, b, 31; *Politics*, 1326, a, 5–b, 25.

6. Lewis Mumford, *The City in History*, 1961, p. 242.

7. For Botero see *Delle Cause della grandezza delle città*, 1588, English translation, 1606, in which he shows why cities grow and what prevents such growth from continuing indefinitely. For Bodin and Althusius, see their major works, indicating a declining interest in size of the community, since the sovereign territorial state is their recognized concern. Montesquieu's discussion of the intermediate powers is scattered throughout his work; see especially *De l'Esprit des Lois*, 1748, especially Books VIII and XI. Rousseau's discussion occurs in *Contract Social*, Book, I, Ch. X, Book II, Ch. IX, Book III, Ch. IV.

8. John Dewey, *The Public and Its Problems*, 1927.

9. Bryce, in his *American Commonwealth*, offers an interesting suggestion regarding the relation of corruption to size of cities which has since become commonplace. "City governments begin to be bad when the population begins to exceed 100,000 and includes a large proportion of immigrants." But the retrenchment of Tammany Hall and its eventual defeat by the Fusion group showed that remedial action may eventually be generated even in vast metropolitan communities. For a hopeful view see Guy Greer, *Your City Tomorrow*, 1947.

10. Edward C. Banfield, *Big City Politics*, 1965; cf. also Victor Jones, *Metropolitan Government*, 1942, pp. XIX–XX. See for these issues also Luther H. Gulick, *The Metropolitan Problem and American Ideas*, 1962; and on the special problems of New York, Robert C. Wood, *1400 Governments*, 1961.

11. For the quaint remark on "dictatorship" of the justice of the peace, see John Ranney and G. Carter, *The Major Foreign Powers*, 1949, p. 209.

12. The quotation is found in Rudolf Gneist, *Selfgovernment*, p. 69. The translation is mine.

13. For the statement by Sir E. D. Simon, see his admirable *The Smaller Democracies*, 1939, p. 89.

14. There are 90 departments (plus four overseas): 450 districts, 3000 cantons, and about 38000 communes, ranging from Paris to small hamlets (more than half have less than 500 inhabitants). See Brian Chapman, *Introduction to French Local Government*, 1953, *The Prefects and Provincial France*, 1955, as well as Hervé Detton, *L'Administration Locale en France, Notes et Etudes Documentaires*, 1965, and the chapter on local government in F. Ridley and J. Blondel, *Public Administration in France*, 1964. For Italian local government, see Robert C. Fried, *The Italian Prefects*, 1963.

15. But see A. Diamant for the description of a contrasting trend, "The Department, the Prefect and Dual Supervision in French Administration," *Journal of Politics*, XVI, 1954, pp. 472 ff.

16. The quotation is from Sir E. D. Simon, *The Smaller Democracies*, 1939, pp. 48 and 40. One may also note Lord Bryce's view given in *Modern Democracies*, Vol. II, p. 449, and quoted approvingly by Simon. Swiss attachment to canton and commune is discussed by Robert C. Brooks, in *Civic Training in Switzerland*, 1930, Ch. XV.

17. See article 28 of the Basic Law. The official German text is undated. For an

interesting account of the impact of American military government upon a local community, cf. John Gimbel, *A German Community under American Occupation,* 1961.

18. Rolf Richard Grauhan, "Zur politischen Theorie der Stadt," in *Archiv für Kommunalwissenschaften,* 1965, pp. 87 ff. Grauhan is soon to publish a volume on the subject of the mayors of German cities.

19. W. A. Robson, "Local Government" in ESS.

20. See works cited in footnote 10.

21. The issue is stated very effectively by William A. Robson in *The Government and Misgovernment of London,* 1939, pp. 344 ff., extensively revised in 1958, and now to be considered in light of the "Herbert" Report, *Report of the Royal Commission on Local Government in Greater London,* 1957–60, Cmnd. 1164–1960.

22. Robson, op. cit.

23. Ibid., p. 349.

24. Robert C. Wood, *Suburbia: its People and Their Politics,* 1959.

25. See Robert S. and Helen M. Lynd, *Middletown: A Study in Contemporary American Culture,* 1929, and *Middletown in Transition: A Study in Cultural Conflicts,* 1937, as well as W. Lloyd Warner and associates, *Yankee City,* 4 vols., 1941, 1942, 1945, 1948.

26. See the interesting experience referred to by David Riesman in his chapter "Criteria for Political Apathy" in *Leadership and Social Action,* 1949.

27. Robert A. Dahl, *Who Governs?,* 1961.

28. Adolf Gasser, *L'Autonomie Communale et la Réconstruction de l'Europe,* 1946.

XIII. The Guardianship of the Constitution: the Issue of Judicial Review

GENERAL NOTES

There is a great body of writings on the guardianship of the constitution, especially through judicial review. The great classics, like Locke and Montesquieu, tended to take it for granted that the people's representatives would guard the constitution which conferred on them the authority they wielded. But beginning with the *Federalist* the notion has spread that an independent high judicial authority would be more dependable as a protector of the basic law and the rights of the citizen. It was slow to gain ground in Europe and until now has not found favor in Britain. Writers like Benjamin Constant wished to have the monarch act as such a guardian; in the Weimar Republic the president was proclaimed the guardian by some writers; de Gaulle took over this notion and had it embodied in the Constitution of the Fifth Republic, where the president as guardian is reinforced by a Constitutional Committee. The continental dislike found its most vigorous expression in Edouard Lambert's *Le Gouvernement des Juges*, 1921. But the judiciary has remained the most typical constitutionalist guardian.

The literature on the subject is very extensive. In the United States in recent years two major conflicts have caused a far-flung discussion: the Supreme Court fight of Roosevelt in 1937, and the desegregationist decisions of the Court in 1954 and later. Robert G. McCloskey's *The American Supreme Court*, 1960, offers a sane historical perspective in light of the recent conflicts which Charles Hyneman has made the central issue of his *The Supreme Court on Trial*, 1963; it should be read along with Eugene Rostow's *The Sovereign Prerogative: The Supreme Court and the Quest for Law*, 1962; the collection of essays edited by Murphy and Pritchett, *Courts, Judges and Politics*, 1961 is also helpful. The more special question of the relation of Court and Congress has been treated in several recent works; among these I should like to mention Charles H. Pritchett's *Congress versus the Supreme Court*, 1961 and Walter Murphy *Congress and the Courts*, 1962. The Congressional concern with constitutional questions has been magistrally explored by Donald Morgan in his *Congress and the Constitution*, 1966. These issues have in turn revived interest in the background and behavior of judges and the newer techniques of quantitative behavioral methods have been brought to bear upon this by Glendon Schubert *Constitutional Politics: The Political Behavior of Supreme Court Justices and the Constitutional Policies they make*, 1960, but these findings have been rather severely criticized by the more conventional learning; John Schmidhauser's is another effort along similar lines in *The Supreme Court: Its Policies, Personalities and Procedures* (1960). During the earlier controversy Robert Jackson published his brilliantly partisan *The Struggle for Judicial Supremacy*, 1940, harkening back to Justice Chase's original cautious view. A similar position was taken by E. S. Corwin in *Court over Constitution*, 1938, and by Felix Frankfurter, *Mr. Justice Holmes and the Supreme Court*, 1938.

How broad a role judicial review has come to play in English-speaking countries, in spite of the British reluctance, has been shown by Edward McWhinney in his *Judicial Review in the English Speaking World*, 1956. A similar comparative view can be gathered from the collection of studies edited by Herman Mosler, *Verfassungsgerichtbarkeit in der Gegenwart*, 1962; see also the authoritative study of the German constitutional court, sponsored by the court itself, *Das Bundesverfassungsgericht*; these continental European developments have been analyzed by Taylor Cole, "The West German Federal Constitutional Court: An Evaluation after six years," *The Journal of Politics*, Vol. 20, 1958, pp. 278 ff.; Gottfried Dietze, "America and Europe — Decline and Emergence of Judicial Review," *Virginia Law Review*, Vol. 44, 1958, pp. 1233 ff.; and Edward McWhinney, *Constitutionalism in Germany and the Federal Constitutional Court*, 1962. For the impact of American doctrine and the writings concerned with it see the chapter in my *The Impact of American Constitutionalism Abroad*, 1967. Among the new nations, India has been most conspicuous in its adoption of the American doctrine of judicial review; for this see the work by Professor Rao cited above. All in all, it is an ongoing discussion and the fact that the recent constitutional revision in Jugoslavia has brought increased judicial guardianship with it suggests that the principle may gain ground even in rather adverse conditions.

REFERENCES

1. Dicey's statement is found in his *Law of the Constitution*, 8th ed., 1926, p. 420.
2. "The New French Constitution in Political and Historical Perspective," in *Harvard Law Review*, Vol. 72, No. 5, March 1959, p. 816.
3. The statements of Hamilton on behalf of judicial review (though the doctrine is not found in the Constitution) are given in the *Federalist*, Nos. 78–82.
4. Re literature on Coke, see above, Ch. VI, footnote 7.
5. Blackstone's statement is given by him in *Commentaries on the Laws of England*, 5th ed., 1773, Introduction, Sections 2 and 3.
6. Charles H. McIlwain, *The American Revolution*, 1924.
7. Adam's views are expounded in *Defense of the Constitutions of the Government of the United States of America*, 1787. *Marbury v. Madison* is 1 *Cranch* 137, 1903.
8. Felix Frankfurter, "The Supreme Court" in ESS. For Australia, cf. Alexander Brady, *Democracy in the Dominions*, 1948; and E. M. Hunt, *American Precedents in Australian Federation*, 1930.
9. William Rappard, *L'Individu et L'Etat*, 1936, pp. 448–453.
10. Both quotations are from H. F. Pringle, *The Life and Times of William Howard Taft*, 1939.
11. The quotation is from Robert Jackson, *The Struggle for Judicial Supremacy*, 1940, pp. 312–313.
12. Walton H. Hamilton, "The Path of Due Process of Law," in *The Constitution Reconsidered*, 1938. See also R. L. Mott, *Due Process of Law*, 1926, and Louis A. Warsoff, *Equality and the Law*, 1938, especially Ch. IV.
13. See Benjamin F. Wright, Jr., *The Growth of American Constitutional Law*, 1942, pp. 240–241.
14. Oliver Wendell Holmes, *The Common Law*, new ed., 1938.
15. Donald G. Morgan, *Congress and the Constitution*, 1966, p. 14.
16. For the commerce problem as seen in New Deal days, see E. S. Corwin, *The Commerce Power versus States' Rights*, 1936, where restrictive doctrines are attacked, and Felix Frankfurter, *The Commerce Clause under Marshall, Taney and Waite*, 1937.
17. Arthur E. Sutherland, *Constitutionalism in America — Origin and Evolution of its Fundamental Ideas*, 1965, p. 239.
18. Gottfried Dietze, *In Defense of Property*, 1963, p. 199.
19. On the subject of scientist and lawyer and the possibilities of a "naturalist" jurisprudence, see Edward S. Robinson, *Law and the Lawyers*, 1935, Ch. I; see more recently Jerome K. Hall, *Comparative Law and Social Theory*, 1963; Michael Polanyi, *Personal Knowledge*, 1958, pp. 277 ff., 308 ff. and throughout; and Ch.

Perelman and L. Olbrechts–Tytega, *Traité de l'Argumentation,* 1958, which rightly presents itself as a "new theory."

20. The Constitutional Council of the Fifth Republic is analyzed in Duverger, *Institutions Politiques et Droit Constitutionnel,* 1965. Salo Engel, in "Judicial Review and Political Preview of Legislation in Post-War France," 6 *Inter-American Law Review* 53, 1964, argues against Duverger's suggestion that the French courts are now free to advance a doctrine of judicial review.

21. For further detail, see my *The Impact of American Constitutionalism Abroad,* 1967, Ch. 4.

22. For this speech, still eminently worth reading, see *Réimpression de l'Ancien Moniteur,* Vol. XXV, pp. 293 ff. Concerning Siéyès' constitutional jury, see Esmein–Nézard, *Droit Constitutionnel,* 8th ed., 1928, Vol. I, pp. 638 ff., where Siéyès' great speech before the Convention is summarized.

23. The German Basic Law of 1949 does not clearly recognize the individual litigant, as earlier drafts did. However, the fact that the Basic Rights (arts. 1–19) are declared to be "binding as directly valid law on legislation, administration and judiciary," together with art. 19 (4), which gives any person the appeal to a court if his rights are infringed, has since established this right. Yet similar provisions in state constitutions led to protracted controversies over the implementing legislation. For Austria, see Ludwig Adamovitch, *Grundriss des österreichischen Verfassungsrechts,* 1947, pp. 96 ff. and 303 ff. and the same author's *Die Prüfung der Gesetze und Verordnungen,* 1924, for the general issues. See also Charles Eisenmann, *La Justice Constitutionnelle et la Haute Cour Constitutionnelle de l'Autriche,* 1928.

24. The entire literature bears upon this point. Special mention may be made of Edouard Lambert, *Le Gouvernement des Juges et la Lutte contre la Législation Sociale aux Etats-Unis,* 1921, and the same author's essay (jointly with Halfred C. Brown), *La Lutte Judiciaire du Capital et du Travail Organisé aux Etats-Unis,* 1923. See for a striking analysis John Peltason, *Fifty-eight Lonely Men,* 1961, who shows how the issue presents itself in the context of racial conflict.

25. See, for detailed discussion of the American history, Charles Warren, *The Supreme Court in United States History,* 1922.

XIV. The Problem of Representation

GENERAL NOTES

The literature of political science on representation was until recently rather unsatisfactory. On the one hand there was the philosophical literature ranging from Hobbes' *Leviathan* through Rousseau's *Contrat Social* to J. S. Mill, Green and Bosanquet, discoursing in normative and speculative terms which have elicited extensive commentaries. There were also legal studies, like Gerhard Leibholz' *Das Wesen der Repräsentation* . . . 1929, of which an overview is given in the chapter on parliamentary representation in his *Politics and Law*, 1965, pp. 64 ff. Much of this writing is concerned with the alleged dichotomy between representation and delegation.

The distinction between representatives bound by an imperative mandate, and representatives not so bound is historically important; the detailed workings of such a system were analyzed, e.g., in May McKisack, *Parliamentary Representation of the English Boroughs during the Middle Ages*, 1932. The comparative dimension is most ably treated by Otto von Hintze, in his essays "Weltgeschichtliche Bedingungen der Repräsentativverfassung" and "Typologie der ständischen Verfassung," both to be found now in his *Gesammelte Abhandlungen*, 2 vols., under the title *Staat und Verfassung*, 1962, 1964.

A number of American writers have in recent years re-examined the problem of representation. Among these Alfred de Grazia's *Public and Republic: Political Representation in America, 1951* and Ferdinand Hermens' *The Representative Republic*, 1958, are to be noted. For Britain, A. H. Birch's *Representative and Responsible Government*, 1962, re-examines the conventional wisdom, while in the German perspective, Dolf Sternberger's *Grund und Abgrund der Macht*, 1962, contains interesting observations.

Finally, the "representativeness" of representatives has, since Stuart Rice's early explorations (in *Quantitative Methods in Politics*, 1928, pp. 189 ff.) been a part of many studies on electoral behavior, e.g., E. Burdick and A. Brodbeck, eds., *American Voting Behavior*, 1959; B. Berelson and Associates, *Voting*, 1954; and A .Campbell and Associates, *The American Voter*, 1960, for the U.S.; for Great Britain, J. F. S. Ross, *Elections and Electors — Studies in Parliamentary Representation*, 1955; Robert E. Lane, *Political Life*, 1965; G. Almond and S. Verba, *The Civic Culture*, 1965; V. O. Key, *Public Opinion and American Democracy*, 1961; Symour Martin Lipset, *Political Man*, 1960, especially Chs. VIII and IX. See also Robert A. Dahl, *A Preface to Democratic Theory*, 1956, who although he does not highlight representation deals with it in several contexts, e.g. pp. 112 ff., pp. 144 ff.

REFERENCES

1. Otto von Gierke, *The Development of Political Theory*, 1939 (a translation of his *Johannes Althusius*, 1880), Ch. IV, at p. 241. See for this also MG, Ch. 17.

2. Cf. M. F. Powicke, *The Thirteenth Century — 1216–1307*, 1953, for general background; "Medieval Representation in Theory and Practice: essays . . ." *Speculum*, 29, pp. 347–476. For a comparative view cf. Heinrich Mitteis, *Der Staat des Hohen Mittelalters . . .* , 6th ed., 1959.

3. This aspect is discussed by Gierke, loc. cit.; cf. also for background John Dickinson, *Death of a Republic*, 1963.

4. Hobbes's view is expounded in *Leviathan*, Book I, Ch. XVI. See also Hanna

F. Pitkin, "Hobbes's Concept of Representation," APSR, June and December, 1964.

5. The discussion in J. J. Rousseau here referred to is found in *Contrat Social,* Book, III, Ch. XV.

6. Besides the works cited in footnote 2 above, see the works reviewed by Helen M. Cam and associates, "Recent works . . . on . . . : representative assemblies" in a report to the *Tenth International Historical Congress,* Florence, 1955, and the general studies noted in the GENERAL NOTES above. For the estates, see Georg von Below, "System und Bedeutung der landständischen Verfassung," in *Territorium und Stadt,* 1900, pp. 163 ff.; Otto von Gierke, *Das Deutsche Genossenschaftsrecht,* Vol. I, paragraph 51 and elsewhere. For the orthodox view, see William Stubbs, *English Constitutional History,* 3d ed., 1887, particularly Ch. XV. The related problem of "charisma" has been dealt with explicitly by Max Weber in *Wirtschaft und Gesellschaft,* 1922, Book III, Chs. IX and X. Much of the more recent literature on leadership gives some attention to it.

7. For Burke's views, see *Works,* Boston, 1839, Vol. II, pp. 12 ff. See also the significant comments by M. Einaudi, *Edmundo Burke e l'Indirizzo Storico Nelle Scienze Politiche,* 1930, particularly pp. 78 ff. Harvey C. Mansfield Jr.'s *Statesmanship and Party Government — A Study of Burke and Bolingbroke,* 1965, while in many ways illuminating fails to explore both representation and responsibility, though they seem central to his topic. Cf. also *Nomos* X, 1967, passim.

8. The definition by Robert von Mohl is found in his *Staatsrecht, Völkerrecht und Politik,* 1860, Vol. I, pp. 8–9.

9. Cf. for the problem of legitimacy and its literature MG, Ch. 13.

10. The literature on Economic Councils is given below, Ch. XXI.

11. Cf. Alfred de Grazia, *Public and Republic — Political Representation in America,* 1951, especially Ch. IX. The unsound aspects of the slogan "one man, one vote" have been explored by the same author in *Apportionment and Representative Government,* 1962; in this study the range of problems raised by *Baker v. Carr* is analyzed.

12. Besides the work cited in the previous note, cf. Ferdinand Hermens, *The Representative Republic;* see also for a fuller development the author's *The New Belief in the Common Man,* 1942, Ch. V.

13. Charles H. McIlwain has rightly insisted upon this emphasis on legislation in Bodin. See his *The Growth of Political Thought in the West,* 1932, pp. 286 ff. For the identification of parliamentary deliberation and conversation, see Carl Schmitt, *Politische Romantik,* 2d ed., 1925, passim, and *Die geistesgeschichtliche Lage des heutigen Parlamentarismus,* 1923, pp. 20 ff. For the remainder, see the bibliography below, Ch. XVII. For the problem of "agreement on fundamentals," see above, Ch. IX, and especially "Democracy and Dissent" in *Political Quarterly,* 1939, Vol. X, No. 4.

14. See concerning this difficult subject the able monograph by Gordon Reid, *The Politics of Financial Control — The Role of the House of Commons,* 1966.

15. For the theoretical background of this plan, see Ralph H. Bowen, *German Theories of the Corporative State,* 1947.

16. For a recent able reassessment of the relation of representation and responsibility see A. H. Birch, *Representative and Responsible Government,* 1964, especially, Ch. 1.

XV. Electoral Systems in Theory and Practice

GENERAL NOTES

Electoral systems have been the subject of controversy among theorists and practitioners for many years. Walter Bagehot's classical discussion of this question in his *English Constitution,* 2d ed., 1873, Ch. V. responding to John Stuart Mill's challenge in *Representative Government,* 1860, Ch. VII, raised the basic issues beyond the general theory of representation. It revolves around the problem of majority rule and minority rights. On the subject of minority rule, cf. Robert A. Dahl's *A Preface to Democratic Theory,* 1956 who after confronting the Madisonian and populist (radical majoritarian) positions developed his "polyarchal" conception which he further elaborated by a fuller exploration of conflict in *Pluralist Democracy,* 1967. Highly significant also is the re-assessment of constitutional democracy's stress on majority by Giovanni Sartori, *Democratic Theory,* 1962, especially Chs. V and XIV. See also Elias Berg, *Democracy and the Majority Principle,* 1965. On the history of the principle, cf. J. G. Heinberg, "History of the Majority Principle," in APSR, XX, 1926, pp. 52 ff. and the literature cited there, especially Gierke.

The new constitutions, as well as the court challenge to apportionment as practiced in the United States, have produced a considerable body of writings on electoral systems, enlarged by the methodologically motivated interest in the quantitative data which elections provide. Besides the works cited in the GENERAL NOTES for the previous chapter, the following deserve mention among others: the Institute of Electoral Research in London brought out a world survey, *Parliaments and Electoral Systems: A World Handbook* in 1962; Enid Lakeman and James Lambert, *Voting in Democracies: A Study of Majority and Proportional Electoral Systems,* 1955; J. M. Mackenzie, *Free Elections,* 1958; W. Birke, *European Elections by Direct Suffrage,* 1961; on particular countries, see the references below, especially notes 21–23; on reapportionment, notes 13–15. But special mention may be made of F. Hermens, *Europe between Democracy and Anarchy,* 1951. On presidential elections see below REFERENCES to Ch. XVIII.

REFERENCES

1. For the problem of qualifications, see the remarks of Bagehot, op. cit., 2d ed., 1873, pp. 209 ff.

2. V. O. Key, *The Responsible Electorate*, 1966.

3. For the British system, see W. I. Jennings, *Parliament*, 1940, Ch. II; and more recently Roland Young, *The British Parliament*, 1962, Ch. II; and Stout, op. cit., 1953, Ch. XII; see also specifically David Butler, *The Electoral System in Britain, 1918–1951*, 1953.

4. F. A. Ogg, *English Government and Politics*, 2d ed., 1936, pp. 298–299.

5. For Mill, see *Representative Government*, Ch. X.

6. Bagehot, op. cit., p. 214.

7. The pamphlet by Thomas Hare is entitled *The Machinery of Representation*, 2d ed., 1857. The theme is more fully developed in his *Treatise on the Election of Representatives, Parliamentary and Municipal*, 1859. Victor de Considérant's scheme is contained in *De la Sincérité du Gouvernement, Lettre à MM. les Membres du Grand Conseil . . . de Genève*, reprinted, 1892. The title of Thomas Gilpin's pamphlet is *On the Representation of Minorities of Electors to Act with the Majority in Elected Assemblies*, 1844.

8. The first edition of Bagehot's work, cited above, appeared in 1867 soon after John Stuart Mill's study. These studies were first published in the *Fortnightly Review* between 1865 and 1867. His discussion of P.R. is found in the sixth, entitled "The House of Commons" published March 15, 1866.

9. These figures are taken from Johannes Schauff, *Neues Wahlrecht*, 1929, p. 249.

10. John Stuart Mill, op. cit., Ch. VII. All the quotations which follow are found there. Italics added.

11. Alain, *Elements d'une doctrine radicale*, 1925, p. 207; but the actual article was dated 1907.

12. Regarding this statistical controversy cf. E. V. Huntington, "Methods of Apportionment in Congress," in APSR, Vol. XXV, 1931, pp. 961 ff. For an earlier study of the gerrymander, cf. E. C. Griffith, *Rise and Development of the Gerrymander*, 1911.

13. *Baker v. Carr;* cf. the study of the Twentieth Century Fund, *One Man, one vote — A Statement of the Basic Principles of Legislative Apportionment*, 1962; cf. also the balanced assessment of the pros and cons by Alfred de Grazia in his *Apportionment and Representative Government*, 1962, 1963; Andrew Hacker, *Congressional Districting — The Issue of Equal Representation*, 1963.

14. Robert E. Engle, *The Representation Amendment to the Illinois Constitution to weigh representative votes so as to equalize and vitalize representation*, Chicago, 1963.

15. National Municipal League, *Compendium on Legislative Apportionment*, 1960.

16. Figures are from an unpublished seminar paper by J. A. C. Grant, 1962.

17. Gordon E. Baker, *State Constitutions: Reapportionment*, 1960 (NML State Constitutional Studies, 2), p. 5. Cf. also M. Jewell, *The Politics of Reapportionment*, 1962.

18. de Grazia, op. cit., p. 176.

19. Ferdinand Hermens, *Europe between Democracy and Anarchy*, 1951 — a

revised edition of the author's well-known study of 1941.

20. Detailed illustrations of the working of this and other systems were given in the first edition, pp. 271 ff., and in the second, pp. 282 ff. They are implemented by Hermens' studies, as well as Robinson O. Everett, ed., "The Electoral Process," *Law and Contemporary Problems,* Vol. 27, 1962; and J. M. Mackenzie, *Free Elections,* 1958.

21. D. E. Butler, ed., *Elections Abroad,* 1959.

22. For the French system, cf. Peter Campbell, *French Electoral Systems and Elections, 1789–1957,* 1958; J. M. Cotteret and Associates, *Lois Electorales et Inègalités de Representation en France,* 1960; and F. Goguel and G. Dupeaux, *Sociologie Electorale: Esquisse d'un Bilan: Guide de Recherches,* 1951.

23. See Dolf Sternberger and associates, *Wahlen und Wähler in Westdeutschland,* 1960.

24. Newton D. Baker in the *Cleveland Plain Dealer,* July 25, 1935.

XVI. and XVII.   Parliaments

GENERAL NOTES

Parliaments or popularly elected assemblies have traditionally been thought of as legislatures, and generally are spoken of as such in conventional constitutions. But in Great Britain which produced the "mother of parliaments," legislation has always been as much the task of the government as of parliament, or as the ancient formula had it, of the "king in parliament." We have seen in discussing the separation of powers that John Locke considered that what was most needed was to divide the power of legislation between crown, lords and commons. On the continent of Europe, legislation has usually been shaped and proposed by the government, and in the twentieth century this has also become the prevailing practice in the United States. It is therefore appropriate to discuss the life and work of such popular assemblies rather in terms of their representative and deliberative function; for these are the two primary functions which such an assembly contributes to the modern political order. So much of the writing deals with such assemblies in general that it seems best to discuss the general literature for the two chapters conjointly; the references bring out the more specific aspects anyhow.

Among the general comparative studies, K. C. Wheare's *Legislatures,* 1963, provides a convenient overview in conventional terms. Two other broadly conceived volumes in the British perspective are by Lord Campion and D. W. S. Lidderdale, *European Parliamentary Procedure,* 1953 and *Parliaments,* 1962. Besides them, and in the American perspective, Robert Luce's *Legislative Assemblies,* 1924, and *Legislative Procedure,* 1922, are still very useful, written as they are out of much practical experience. There is an interesting comparative study of federal assemblies by Robert Bowie in R. R. Bowie and C. J. Friedrich, *Studies in Federalism,* 1954; Harvey Walker's *The Legislative Process,* 1948 is broadly comparative for America. Apart from these there are, of course, studies for individual parliaments, such as W. I. Jennings, *Parliament,* 1940, 3d ed., 1960, and Roland Young's *The American Congress,* 1958. See George Galloway, *The Legislative Process in Congress,* 1953; the same, *History of the House of Representatives,* 1962; James Burnham, *Congress and the American Tradition,* 1959; Roland Young, *The British Parliament,* 1962; Eric Taylor, *The House of Commons at Work,* 3d ed., 1958; W. F. Dawson, *Procedure in the Canadian House of Commons,* 1962; J. L. McCracken, *Representative Government in Ireland,* 1959; W. H. Morris–Jones, *Parliament in India,* 1957; D. W. S. Lidderdale, *The Parliament of France,* 1951; Gerhard Loewenberg, *Parliament in the German Political System,* 1966; S. King–Hall and R. K. Ullmann, *German Parliaments,* 1956; Elis Hastad, *The Parliament of Sweden,* 1957; Giovanni Sartori and Associates, *Il Parlamento Italiano 1946–1963,* 1963; E. van Raalte, *The Parliament of the Kingdom of the Netherlands,* 1959; and C. J. Hughes, *The Parliament of Switzerland,* 1962. It goes without saying that all the broader treatments of governmental institutions in the various countries, notably the British Dominions, contain chapters on their respective parliaments. A rising chorus of attacks upon popular assemblies has questioned the role and function of parliaments; Bernard Crick, *The Reform of Parliament: The Crisis of British Government,* 1965; G. W. Keeton, *The Passing of Parliament,* 1952; and Joseph Clark, *Congress: The Sapless Branch,* 1964, might be mentioned here, but there are many others. The works by Michel Debré mentioned below were harbingers of a revolutionary reduction in the French parliament's role and position.

A novel feature of writings on parliaments are the behavioral and quantitative studies of recent years. Cf. John Wahlke and Heinz Eulau, eds., *Legislative Behavior: A Reader in Theory and Research,* 1959; John Wahlke and Associates, *The Legislative System: Explorations in Legislative Behavior,* 1962; Donald Matthews, *U.S. Senators and their World,* 1960; David Truman, *The Congressional Party,* 1959; Duncan McRae and Fred Goldner, *Dimensions of Congressional Voting: A Statistical Survey of the House of Representatives in the 81st Congress,* 1958; S. E. Finer and Associates, *Backbench Opinion in the House of Commons,* 1961. In this connection, mention should be made of the fact that earlier studies in a lighter vein, such as R. de Jouvenel's at times produced as much insight as these more scientific labors.

Partly inspired by such explorations of the human side of elected assemblies, the process of negotiation, conflict and compromise — i.e. the political process — has been studied, especially in the U.S.; see H. H. Wilson, *Congress: Corruption and Compromise,* 1951; Stephen Bailey and Howard Samuel, *Congress at Work,* 1952; Bertram Gross, *The Congressional Struggle: A Study in Social Combat,* 1953; William S. White, *Citadel,* 1957; R. Peabody and N. Polsby, eds., *New Perspectives on the House of Representatives,* 1963; and Daniel Berman, *Congress Assembled — The Legislative Process in the National Government,* 1964.

Finally, there are the studies relating elected assemblies to parties, interest groups and public opinion. They will be considered in the chapters dealing with these topics below.

XVI. Parliaments as Representative Assemblies

REFERENCES

1. John Stuart Mill, *Considerations on Representative Government,* 1860, Ch. V. In the Liberal Arts edition of 1958, the following passages are found on pp. 72, 75, 76 and 81.
2. See W. I. Jennings, *Parliament,* 1940, especially Ch. X, and pp. 7, 109–110. For America's division before the second World War, see *The New Belief in the Common Man,* 1942, Ch. III and references; this situation deserves more detailed study. Robert H. Sherwood has some interesting hints in his *Roosevelt and Hopkins,* 1948, Chs. VI and VII.
3. The *schemas* of parliamentary seating arrangements are found in Joseph R. Starr, *Topical Analysis of Comparative European Government,* 1934, pp. 30 and 115. Regarding seating arrangements in Congress, see Robert Luce, *Legislative Procedure,* 1922, p. 241.
4. Cf. for a general discussion Bernard Crick, *The Reform of Parliament,* 1965.
5. For this paragraph, Josef Redlich's masterly analysis in *The Procedure of the House of Commons,* 1908, Vol. II, pp. 115 ff., is still important. A valuable recent contribution is J. A. Thomas, *The House of Commons, 1832–1901,* 1939. Figures are given by Redlich on p. 125.
6. Shaw's statement is quoted by Harold Laski, *Parliamentary Government in England,* 1938, p. 155. Laski comments, "The language is forceful; it is not more forceful than the facts."
7. Cf. on the German parliament, Loewenberg, op. cit.
8. Cf. Ridley and Blondel, *Public Administration in France,* 1964, p. 50 and Williams and Harrison, *De Gaulle's Republic,* 2d ed., 1961, p. 252.
9. Giovanni Sartori, "Les Parlementaires Italiens" in *Revue Internationale des Sciences Sociales,* Vol. IV, 1961, pp. 647–666. Cf. also the same author's *Il Parlamento Italiano, 1946–1963,* 1963, in which the material in all its fullness is offered together with the studies of four other collaborators.
10. Gaetano Mosca, Robert Michels, Max Weber and Vilfredo Pareto in their op. cit.
11. Cf. Sartori, in the article cited loc. cit., p. 661.
12. Bernard Crick, op. cit., Ch. V. Cf. also Sydney Bailey, eds., *The Future of the House of Lords,* 1954.

13. The wisecrack was made by Aug. Birrell, a liberal leader.

14. Bernard Crick, op. cit., Ch. VI. Even though one abstains from adopting the author's practical proposals for change, he can learn much from his pointed analysis.

15. Hiram Miller Stout, *British Government*, 1953, p. 119, Ch. VII. But is this anachronism so clear in a state the head of which is hereditary?

16. The text of the Bryce Committee is reprinted (with omissions) in Howard L. McBain and L. Rogers, *The New Constitutions of Europe*, 1922, p. 573 ff; its intellectual value is generally overrated; its proposals were weak and complicated.

17. The quotation from the *Labour Speakers' Handbook* is given in F. A. Ogg, *English Government and Politics*, 1929, p. 356. Bentham's views are set forth lucidly and convincingly by Lewis Rockow, "Bentham on the Theory of Second Chambers," APSR, Vol. XXII, 1928, pp. 576 ff. They are also succinctly stated in Bentham's *Essay on Political Tactics*, 1816–1817, Ch. I, para. 5 (followed by a statement of the advantages intended by Bentham, but actually supplied by his editor, Dumont; whether we should question the conclusions of Rockow on this account is doubtful).

18. Cmd., 9038/1918, p. 4.

19. For the Congress, cf. Roland Young, op. cit.; for the problem of foreign policy, H. Bradford Westerfield, *Foreign Policy and Party Politics*, 1955; and James A. Robinson, *Congress and Foreign Policy-making*, 1962; for Switzerland see C. J. Hughes, *The Parliament of Switzerland*, 1962.

20. The quotation from Elliott is found in his *The Need for Constitutional Reform*, p. 191. The statistical figures are taken from *Statistical Abstract of the United States*, 1966 and *Statistisches Jahrbuch der Schweiz*, 1933.

21. Karlheinz Neunreither, *Der Bundesrat zwischen Politik und Verwaltung*, 1959, also his summary "Politics and Bureaucracy in the West German Bundesrat," APSR, Vol. 53, 1959, pp. 713 ff. and "Federalism and Bureaucracy in West Germany," *Political Studies*, Vol. VII, 1959, pp. 233 ff. On the earlier situation, cf. Arnold Brecht, *Federalism and Regionalism in Germany*, 1945; Hugo Preuss, *Reich und Länder* (ed. Anschütz, 1928).

22. For Austria, the formal provisions are discussed by Ludwig Adamovich, *Grundriss des österreichischen Verfassungsrechts*, 4th ed., 1947; a realistic appraisal in terms of political science categories has been provided by Christa Altenstetter, *Der österreichische Föderalismus*, 1967, Heidelberg dissertation to be published.

23. Hughes, op. cit. See also G. Sartori and Associates, *Il Parlamento Italiano, 1946–1963*, 1963.

24. W. H. Morris–Jones, *The Parliament of India*, 1957.

25. See Stuart A. Rice, *Quantitative Methods in Politics*, 1928, Ch. XIV.

26. W. I. Jennings, *Parliament*, 1940, p. 508.

XVII. Parliaments as Deliberate Assemblies

REFERENCES

1. The secrecy of parliamentary proceedings is described by Edward Porritt, *The Unreformed House of Commons: Parliamentary Representation before 1832*, 1903, Vol. I, pp. 589–596, and by Th. E. May, *Constitutional History of England*, 7th ed., 1882, Vol. II, See also HCD, Vol. XI, 1808, cited by Redlich, op. cit., p. 291.
2. Redlich, op. cit., Chs. I and II, and Porritt, op. cit. for general background.
3. D. N. Chester and Nona Bowring, *Questions in Parliament*, 1962, pp. 91 ff.
4. W. I. Jennings, *Parliament*, 1940, p. xii.
5. The full title of Bentham's work is *An Essay on Political Tactics, or Inquiries Concerning the Discipline and Mode of Proceeding Proper to Be Observed in Political Assemblies: Principally Applied to the Practice of the British Parliament, and to the Constitution and Situation of the National Assembly of France.* This work was first published in French in 1816 by M. Dumont and translated into German, etc. from this edition. Bentham's ideas are further set forth in Bowring's edition, 1843 (hereafter referred to), Vol. II, pp. 302 ff. and 310 ff. Hamilton's book is entitled *Parliamentary Logic,* republished in 1927; its editor, Courtney S. Kenny, has offered some shrewd comments in an introduction and notes. Bentham's comments on Hamilton, quite vitriolic to be sure, are found in his *The Book of Fallacies* (ed. cit.), Vol. II, pp. 383 ff.
6. See Jennings, op. cit. Ch. III. The statement from Bentham is found in op. cit. Vol. II, p. 330. Regarding Speaker Onslow, see Porritt, op. cit., pp. 448 ff. See also generally ibid. Chs. XXI–XXII. The reference to Stubbs is found in his *Lectures,* 1906, p. 314. For Edward Coke, see Hastings Lyon and H. Block, *Edward Coke: Oracle of the Law,* 1929, pp. 60 ff. For the following quotations from Redlich, see op. cit., pp. 422 and 410 ff. The quotation is again from Redlich, op. cit. (in the author's own translation), p. 405. See his entire discussion in the English edition, Vol. II, pp. 131–168.
7. For the American Speakership, the important historical study is M. P. Follett, *The Speaker of the House of Representatives,* 1896. For a more recent study of the institution as it exists today, see Robert Luce's *Legislative Procedure,* 1922, Chs. XIX–XXII. The quotation from Bryce whose discussion of the problem is still worth pondering is found in *American Commonwealth,* Vol. I, p. 208. The next quotation is from an article by Elwood Mead in the *Independent,* January 8, 1917, which is cited by R. Luce, op. cit. p. 486. Speaker Carlisle's statement is found there, p. 466. This view was reasserted by Speaker Longworth in 1926: "I believe it to be the duty of the Speaker, standing squarely on the platform of his party, to assist in so far as he properly can the enactment of legislation in accordance with the declared principles and policies of his party, and by the same token to resist the enactment of legislation in violation thereof," *Congressional Record,* 69th Congress, 1st Sess., p. 382.

8.   C. A. Beard and William Beard, *The American Leviathan,* 1930, p. 302.

9.   For Bryce's discussion see *American Commonwealth,* Vol. I, pp. 203 ff., rev. ed., 1924. Viscount Gladstone's account is found in APSR, Vol. XXI, 1927, pp. 519 ff.

10.   The remarks of the Marquess of Hartington are to be found in HCD, Vol. CCLXVII, 1882, p. 1327.

11.   Zachariah Chafee, Jr., *Three Human Rights in the Constitution,* 1956, Ch. I. See also my further comments in *Tulane Law Review,* Oct./Nov., 1957.

23.   D. N. Chester and Nona Bowring, *Questions in Parliament,* 1962, passim.

13.   Closure is one of the most hotly contested issues of modern politics. For the "classical" doctrine of adjournment, see again Bentham, op. cit., Ch. XIII.

14.   Speaker Brand's statement is to be found in HCD, Vol. CCLVII, 1881, pp. 2032–2033.

15.   For Speaker Reed's remark, see *Congressional Record,* January 31, 1890, Vol. XXI, p. 999.

16.   Lindsay Rogers, *The American Senate,* 1926, pp. 248–250.

17.   John C. Ranney and Gwendolyn M. Carter, *The Major Foreign Powers,* 1948, p. 121. See also K. C. Wheare, *Government by Committee,* 1955.

18.   The remarks of Sir Courtenay Ilbert are found in his English edition of Redlich, Vol. III, pp. 215–216. See also Young, op. cit., p. 87 ff. the brevity of whose treatment shows how relatively unimportant committees are, politically; but see Wheare, op. cit.

19.   Bernard Crick, *The Reform of Parliament,* 1965, p. 207. Besides a trenchant general argument for reform the book contains some very valuable tables showing the decline of select committees and the like (in a number of appendices). Cf. also the historical review published by the Hansard Society, *Parliamentary Reform, 1933–1960,* 1961; see also "Present-Day Problems of Parliament" in *Inter-Parliamentary Bulletin,* 1966.

20.   The first quotation from Luce is found, op. cit., on p. 100, the second one on p. 151; Bertram Gross, op. cit.; Galloway, op. cit.; Bailey, op. cit.; cf. also George Galloway's *History* for background.

21.   *Statistical Abstract of the United States,* 1966.

22.   Figures from the *Congressional Directory,* 89th Congress, 2d Session, January, 1966.

23.   The history of committee procedure in the French Chamber is sketched by Joseph–Barthélemy, *Essai sur le Travail Parlementaire et le Système des Commissions,* 1934, Ch. I. For the party basis of committees, see ibid., pp. 82 ff. (we have omitted reference to the older system of *bureaux* because it is complicated and no longer significant). About committee leadership, see Barthélemy, op. cit. p. 9 and passim. About the reportorial stage, Barthélemy gives examples on pp. 180–181, and he discusses the advisory reports in ibid. p. 197. For the vote without debate, see ibid. pp. 207 ff. For the situation under the Fourth Republic, see Gordon Wright, *The Reshaping of French Democracy,* 1948; for the antecedent situation, see D. Thomson, *Democracy in France,* 1946.

24. For the new French situation, see Williams and Harrison, *De Gaulle's Republic*, 1961, and D. M. Pickles, *The Fifth French Republic*, 1962.

25. See for this difficult subject now Gordon Reid, *The Politics of Financial Control — The Role of the House of Commons*, 1966.

26. Jennings, op. cit., p. 334. See also A. H. Hanson and H. V. Wiseman, *Parliament at Work: A Case Book of Parliamentary Procedure*, 1962.

27. S. H. Beer, *Treasury Controls*, 1956.

28. Reid, op. cit., p. 168. I am following Professor Reid's able analysis here, especially his concluding chapter, "Is Parliamentary Financial Control a Myth?" pp. 146 ff. The quotes are to be found there. Cf. also Crick, op. cit., Appendix A, showing the decline of the Select Committees.

29. Erskine May, *Parliamentary Practice*, 17th ed. by Campion, 1964, p. 713 — analyzed in Reid, op. cit., Ch. 2.

30. Arthur Smithies, *The Budgetary Process in the United States*, 1955, has given us a thorough, authoritative analysis, especially Parts I and II; Robert A. Wallace, *Congressional Control of Federal Spending*, 1960; for an overview, Young, op. cit. Ch. 9.

31. The discussion in this paragraph follows Ch. IX of Joseph–Barthélemy, op. cit., Ch. IX, as far as the facts are concerned, though the interpretation varies at times. Specific reference may be made to p. 278, where he discusses the presidents and reporters; to p. 286, where the statement about government and opposition is made. That the *rapporteur* was actually controlling the government is alleged by A. Thibaudet, *La République des Professeurs*, 1927, p. 243, as well as by others. Barthélemy's remark about the leftist group is found on p. 354.

32. Pickles, op. cit., pp. 99 ff.

33. For this paragraph, see Barthélemy, op. cit. Ch. VI, "Le contrôle parlementaire par les commissions." He also emphasizes the suspicion of the bureaucracy as a central attitude behind the French public's and the parliament's interest in committees as a method of organizing effective control, for example, on pp. 24–25. For the U.S., cf. Young, op. cit. Ch. 7, and Joseph P. Harris, *Congressional Control of Administration*, 1964.

34. Cmd. 1767, Oct. 1965, para. 4; J. E. Kersell, *Parliamentary Supervision of Delegated Legislation*, 1960, which concentrates on how to handle constituency complaints — a problem central to the discussion of the pros and cons of the ombudsman.

35. Cf. for an overview the symposium edited by D. C. Rowat, *The Ombudsman*, 1965, as well as the study by T. E. Utley, *Occasion for Ombudsman*, 1961. Cf. also Stephan Hurwitz, *Der Ombudsman — Der Dänische Parlamentskommissar für die Zivil — und Militärverwaltung*, 1962 (Copenhagen); and the Whyatt Commission Report, entitled *The Citizen and the Administration*, which advocated the establishment of a parliamentary commissioner; it was widely criticized, especially in terms of the tradition of ministerial responsibility.

36. Young, op. cit. Ch. 10; Bailey and Samuels, op. cit. Ch. 11.

37. Josef Redlich, *The Procedure of the House of Commons*, 1908, Vol. 2, p. 193.

38. Cf. H. M. Clokie and J. W. Robinson, *Royal Commissions of Inquiry*, 1937; and Solomon Encel, *Cabinet Government in Australia*, 1962.

39. Erwin N. Griswold, *The Fifth Amendment Today*, 1955, gives a forceful statement; see also Henry Steele Commager, *Freedom, Loyalty, Dissent*, 1954; and Mr. Justice Douglas in his "The Bill of Rights is not enough" in Edmond Cahn, ed., *The Great Rights*, 1963, especially pp. 122 ff. Cf. also Irving Brant, ibid., p. 37, where it is suggested that such investigations resemble bill of attainder proceedings, although they are constitutionally prohibited.

40. Young, op. cit., pp. 187–188; cf. the entire ch. 7 on control.

41. See for a fuller treatment my *Foreign Policy in the Making*, 1938. Besides the works cited above, footnote 19, Ch. XVI, cf. Holbert Carroll, *The House of Representatives and Foreign Affairs*, 1958; Malcolm Jewell, *Senatorial Politics and Foreign Policy*, 1962. For the extended controversy in the twenties and thirties see my op. cit. and the literature cited there, as well as footnote 11, Ch. XVII of the 1950 edition.

42. See for this Joseph–Barthélemy, *La Conduite de la Politique Exterieure dans les Démocraties*, 1930 and Ch. VIII of his *Essai* cited above.

43. E. van Raalte, *The Parliament of the Kingdom of the Netherlands*, 1960, provides the background; extended interviewing in the late twenties enabled the author to give the analysis offered in op. cit., 1938.

44. Among the many writings on this score, mention may be made of Martin Gilbert and Richard Gott, *The Appeasers — The Decline of Democracy from Hitler's Rise to Chamberlain's Downfall*, 1963, which tells the story of Britain; cf. also the striking analysis of British failure to appreciate the dangers ahead in Brigitte Granzow, *Mirror of Nazism*, 1964, with a pointed introduction by Bernard Crick; for the U.S. see the discussion in John C. Donovan's *Congress and the Making of Neutrality Legislation, 1935–1939* (unprinted dissertation, Harvard, 1949); the several documents are found cited in *United States Foreign Policy*, U.S. Senate, 87th Congress, March 15, 1961.

45. Bentham's views on secrecy are set forth in his essay, Ch. II (*Works*, Vol. II, pp. 310 ff.) . The point had been made earlier and with broad implications for constitutional government by Immanuel Kant in a number of works; see the author's *Introduction to the Philosophy of Kant*, 1949. For Luce's views, see his *Legislative Procedure*, pp. 150–151. For Wilson, see *The New Freedom*, 1913, pp. 125–129. See also Edward A. Shils, *The Torments of Secrecy*, 1956.

46. Cf. the rather journalistic, but informative book by David Wise and Thomas B. Ross, *The Invisible Government*, 1964; see also Allen B. Dulles, *The Craft of Intelligence*, 1963. Cf. also below, Ch. XXIII.

47. See my *Constitutional Reason of State*, 1957, for further theoretical and historical background.

48. Zachariah Chafee, Jr., *Three Human Rights in the Constitution*, 1956, p. 41. See also J. E. Neale, *Elizabeth I and Her Parliaments, 1559–1581*, 1953.

49. Young, op. cit., p. 60. There also the next quote on p. 62.

50. This paragraph's point constitutes the central theme of Redlich's volume. The

quotations (in the author's own translation) are found in the original, p. 799. In the English edition this passage occurs in Vol. III, p. 197.

XVIII. Chief Executives and Cabinet Systems

GENERAL NOTES

The problems of leadership, and more especially those of executive leadership, have received an increasing amount of attention from political scientists, sociologists, and psychologists in recent years. The rise of one-man dictatorship has brought to light facets of the problem which had lain dormant. I have discussed these problems and some of the main writings in *Man and His Government,* Ch. 9, and in *Totalitarian Dictatorship and Autocracy,* 2d ed., 1965, Chs. 1 and 3. Parliamentary government has turned into cabinet government in Britain, into presidential government in France, into a chancellor's democracy in Germany, while the American president's dependence upon Congress has increased, as many major policy decisions of the welfare state involve large outlays of money. Hence executive-parliamentary relations have everywhere become a subject of intensive debate and extensive analysis, as manifest in such surveys as that edited by Jean Meynaud, *The Role of the Executive in the Modern State,* 1958. There are also comparative assessments such as Friedrich Glum, *Das parlamentarische Regierungssystem in Deutschland, Grossbritannien und Frankreich,* 1950, or Georges Burdeau, *Traité de la Science Politique,* 1949 ff., Vol. V, especially pp. 271–295. The issue is of long standing, as may be seen from such works of the thirties as Harold Laski's *Parliamentary Government in England,* 1938; Emile Giraud, *La Crise de la Democratie et le Renforcement du Pouvoir Executif,* 1939, or even earlier, Robert Redslob's *Le Regime Parlementaire,* 1924, which influenced the Weimar constitution makers in an earlier version, 1918, and in turn M. Michel Debré.

The American presidency and the British cabinet system have undergone rapid evolution as well as intense further scrutiny since the war. The Hoover Commission made its celebrated *Report on the Organization of the Executive Branch of the Government* in 1949. In the same year, Louis Brownlow, *The President and the Presidency* appeared. Since then, men of very contrasting personality and background have occupied the White House and have elicited sharply divergent comment. Edwin Corwin and Louis Koenig, *The Presidency Today,* 1956; Clinton Rossiter, *The American Presidency,* 1956; and finally Joseph E. Kallenbach, *The American Chief Executive — The Presidency and the Governorship,* 1966, added new depths to a field already provided with such well-known studies as E. P. Herring's *Presidential Leadership,* 1940; and Wilfred C. Brinkley's *President and Congress,* 1947, as well as that broad historical survey by George F. Milton, *The Use of Presidential Power, 1789–1943,* 1944. For Britain, W. I. Jennings *Cabinet Government* underwent two new editions, 1951, 1959. In a class by itself is Herbert Morrison, *Government and Parliament,* 1956, based as it is upon extensive experience. Alongside it, A. H. Birch, *Representative and Responsible Government,* 1964; John P. McIntosh, *The British Cabinet,* 1962; Byrum Carter, *The Office of the Prime Minister,* 1956, represent the newer realist approach as contrasted with A. B. Keith's standard, *The British Cabinet System,* 2d ed. by N. H. Gibbs, 1952. In a different vein, we have Kenneth Wheare's *Government by Committee,* 1955, and two studies comparing British and continental experience: E. van Raalte, *De Ontwikkeling von het ministerpresidentschap . . . ,* 1954; and Gerhard Ritter, *Deutscher und britischer Parlamentarismus,* 1962. W. L. Guttsman's *The British Political Elite,* 1963, is concerned with the changing social composition of the British Cabinet, thus carrying forward Harold Laski's well-known pioneering study, *The British Cabinet: A Study of its Personnel, 1801–1924,* 1928.

The contemporary interest in decision-making and policy has led to new approaches, especially in the field of foreign policy. Cf. William Y. Elliott and Associates, *U.S. Foreign Policy: Its Organization and Control,* 1952; Robert Ellsworth Elder, *The Foreign Policy Machine,* 1960, dealing chiefly with foreign affairs; J. Frankel, *The Making of Foreign Policy: An Analysis of Decision-Making,* 1963; for background see Don K. Price, ed., *The Secretary of State,* 1960. The British parallels were discussed by Donald Bishop, *The Administration of British Foreign Relations,* 1961.

REFERENCES

1. For the detailed comparison, see *The Federalist* (ed. H. C. Lodge), pp. 436–6.
2. The doctrines of these writers are found in their individual works. See Thomas Carlyle, *On Heroes, Hero-Worship, and the Heroic in History,* 1841, Lecture VI; Charles Maurras, *Enquête sur la Monarchie,* 1900; new ed., 1924, especially Book I and Appendix; Friedrich Nietzsche, *The Will to Power,* tr. A. M. Ludovici, 1910, especially Vol. II, Book IV; Jakob Burckhardt, *Weltgeschichtliche Betrachtungen,* 1918 ed., pp. 210 ff.; H.A. Taine, *L'Ancien Régime,* 1876, passim; Leopold von Ranke, *Die Grossen Mächte,* in *Meisterwerke,* 1914–15 ed., Vol. X.
3. Cf. on the general problems of leadership, MG, Ch. 9.
4. The elections to the Assembly in March, 1967 showed the same trend; in the first round, de Gaulle's party, calling itself the party of the Fifth Republic, received not quite 38% (*Le Monde,* March 7, 1967) and their parliamentary representation dropped from 282 to 244 (*Le Figaro,* March 14, 1967).
5. See for further detail below, Ch. XXIII, pp. 520 ff.
6. This is the bearing of much of the newer writing on the presidency, especially Richard Neustadt, *Presidential Power: The Politics of Leadership,* 1960 and Theo-

dore Sorenson, *Decision-Making in the White House*, 1963. Robert A. Dahl has rightly commented that "the President is more at the mercy of Congress than, for example, the British prime minister is at the mercy of parliament." (*Pluralist Democracy*, as cited, p. 105). Cf. also Clinton Rossiter, op. cit.

7. The three primary universal roles of leadership, namely initiating, maintaining and protecting, as discussed in MG, Ch. 9, are involved in the functions here discussed; some of the difficulties resulting from an excess of power have led presidents and other chief executives to lean on confidential advisers; cf. Louis Koenig, *The Invisible Presidency*, 1960, for interesting recent illustrations.

8. See Harold Lasswell, *World Politics and Personal Insecurity*, 1935, for a broad statement. See also Ch. XXV below and Malcolm Smith and Cornelius Cotter, *Powers of the President during Crisis*, 1960, as well as Nathan Grundstein, *Presidential Delegation of Authority in Wartime*, 1961.

9. Erich Fromm, *Escape from Freedom*, 1941.

10. See below, Ch. XXII. The problem of the interrelation of government and science involved here has received increasing attention in recent years; cf. Don K. Price, *The Scientific Estate*, 1965, Chs. 2, 7 and 8. Cf. also Michael Polanyi, *The Logic of Liberty*, 1951, Chs. 2–4 and 6.

11. F. J. Goodnow, *Politics and Administration*, 1900, p. 22.

12. For the general problem of "policy" cf. MG, Ch. 3, pp. 79 ff.

13. See for all this W. I. Jennings, *Cabinet Government in Great Britain*, 1936, new ed., 1959; and A. H. Birch, *Representative and Responsible Government*, 1964, especially Part IV. See also Hans Daalder, *Cabinet Reform in Britain, 1914–1963*, 1963.

14. Besides the works cited above, footnote 6, and in the GENERAL NOTES, the following are important: Richard Fenno, *The President's Cabinet*, 1959; Corinne Silverman, *The President's Economic Advisers*, 1959; and Stephen Horn, *The Cabinet and Congress*, 1960.

15. Herbert Morrison, *Government and Parliament*, 1954, p. 13. See also the same author's *British Parliamentary Democracy*, 1962.

16. A. H. Dodd, *The Growth of Responsible Government from James I to Victoria*, 1956, has provided fuller historical background. To this should be added the works cited in the GENERAL NOTES.

17. W. I. Jennings, *Cabinet Government*, 3d ed., 1959, pp. 173 ff., gives a number of interesting cases illustrating these differences. His analysis underlies the entire discussion.

18. The quotation from Lowell is found in *The Government of England*, Vol. I, p. 56.

19. Morrison, *Government and Parliament*, 1954, p. 38.

20. Bernard Crick, *The Reform of Parliament*, 1964, pp. 36–37.

21. Cf. Daalder, op. cit. for further detail. On the Profumo Scandal, the Report of the Lord Denning Commission is authoritative, cf. *The Times* of London, September 26, 1963.

22. Harold Zink and Taylor Cole, *Government in Wartime Europe*, 1941, Chs. 1

and 2; for background cf. John Ehrman, *Cabinet Government and War, 1890–1940*, 1958.

23. For Lloyd George's view, see his *War Memoirs*, particularly Vol. III, Ch. I, and passim. For Churchill's own view, see his *The Gathering Storm*, 1948.

24. Geoffrey Marshall, *Parliamentary Sovereignty and the Commonwealth*, 1957; S. Encel, *Cabinet Government in Australia*, 1962; for an overview cf. Alexander Brady, *Democracy in the Dominions*, 1947, Chs. IV, VIII, XII, and XVI.

25. Cf. Philip M. Williams, *Crisis and Compromise: Politics of the Fourth Republic*, 1964, Ch. 17; Dorothy M. Pickles, *France — The Fourth Republic*, 2d ed., 1958, and Roy Macridis, *Supplement to the de Gaulle Republic*, 1963. Robert de Jouvenel's comments are found in *La République des Camarades*, 1914, pp. 93 ff.; the quotation, on p. 115. For the figures, see *Annuaire du Parlement*, Vol. VII, pp. 795–826, Vol. X, pp. 912–923; *Europa Yearbook*, 1927, pp. 207–210; and John G. Heinberg, "The Personnel of French Cabinets, 1871–1930," APSR, Vol. XXV, 1931, pp. 389 ff. The quotation from Barthélemy is found in his *The Government of France* (authorized translation by J. Bayard Morris), pp. 105–106.

26. See for this R. R. Kapferer, *Die Verfassung der IV. Französischen Republik — Die Grundlagen ihrer Entstehung dargestellt an der politischen Situation Frankreichs in den Jahren 1940–1946*, Heidelberg, 1963.

27. See besides the general works on the Fifth Republic, cited above, especially Dorothy M. Pickles, *The Fifth French Republic*, 1960 and Roy Macridis, *The de Gaulle Republic*, 1962, the work edited by M. Martin at the moment of transition from the Fourth to the Fifth Republic, *Les Institutions Politiques de la France* (in two vols., no date, but presumably 1960) and the tenth volume of the Encyclopédie Française edited by Edgar Faure and Louis Trotabas and entitled *L'Etat*, 1964, Section B, Ch. II, with contributions by Maurice Duverger and J. Fauvet, containing a significant section entitled "Le Président Gouvernant," pp. 211 ff.

28. The Weimar system has been subjected to numerous analyses and criticisms. Among them Dietrich Bracher's *Die Auflösung der Weimarer Republik*, 1957, is outstanding. Other important studies are Erich Eyck, *Geschichte der Weimarer Republik*, in 2 vols., 1954–56, and *Gustav Stresemann: His Diaries, Letters and Papers*, condensed from *Gustav Stresemann: Vermächtnis*, 3 vols., 1932–33. Bracher's work has been translated.

29. Arnold Brecht, *Aus nächster Nähe — Lebenserinnerungen eines beteiligten Beobachters, 1884–1927*, 1966, Ch. 30.

30. Peter H. Merkl, *Germany: Yesterday and Tomorrow*, 1965; Alfred Grosser, *La Democratie de Bonn*, 1958; R. R. Allemann, *Bonn ist nicht Weimar*, 1956; Thomas Ellwein, *Die Bundesrepublik Deutschland*, 1963.

31. Cf. for this Konrad Adenauer's own memoirs which in spite of their bald style and discreet caution are revealing: *Erinnerungen*, 1965 and 1960 (so far in 2 vols. — extending to 1955).

32. Robert C. Brooks, *Government and Politics of Switzerland*, 1918, particularly when supplemented by his *Civic Training in Switzerland*, 1930; cf. also Fritz Fleiner's *Schweizerisches Bundesstaatsrecht*, 1922–1923, and W. E. Rappard's

significant *La Constitution Fédérale de la Suisse, 1884–1948,* 1948. The specific references are to pp. 187 and 222ff. of Fleiner's volume. The closing quotation is from Brooks, *Government and Politics of Switzerland,* pp. 132–133. For background see Denis de Rougemont, *La Suisse–Histoire d'un Peuple Heureux,* 1965.

33. Besides the works cited in the GENERAL NOTES, cf. Rexford Tugwell, *The Enlargement of the Presidency,* 1960; Wilfred Binkley, *The Man in the White House,* 1959; Ruth Silva, *Presidential Succession,* 1951; Eugene Roseboom, *A History of Presidential Elections,* 1957; B. Brown, *The People's Choice,* 1960; and Malcolm Moos, *Politics, Presidents and Coat Tails,* 1952. Two monographs trace specially the development of the American cabinet: H. B. Learned, *The President's Cabinet,* 1912, and M. L. Hinsdale, *History of the President's Cabinet,* 1911. Three major works dealing with the presidency of F. D. Roosevelt are: Robert Sherwood, *Roosevelt and Hopkins,* 1948, Henry L. Stimson and M. Bundy, *On Active Service in Peace and War,* 1948; and Cordell Hull, *The Memoirs of Cordell Hull,* 1948.

34. On campaign funds, see Louise Overacker, *Money in Elections,* 1932 and the literature on party finance, cited below, Ch. XX.

35. See for this the works cited above, footnote 14.

36. Lord Bryce's citation is from the *American Commonwealth,* 1924, Vol. I, p. 85. The quotation from Beard is found on p. 263 of his *The American Leviathan.*

37. Joseph E. Kallenbach, op. cit., p. 439.

38. Clinton Rossiter, op. cit., p. 148.

39. Kallenbach, op. cit., p. 440; Edwards Hobbs, *Behind the President: A study of Executive Office Agencies,* 1954; and the study by Silverman cited above note 14.

40. See Warren I. Cikins, "The Council of Economic Advisers: Political Economy at the Crossroads," in PP IV, 1953, pp. 94 ff.

41. For the Cabinet secretariat see W. I. Jennings, op. cit., Ch. IX. See also Fritz Morstein-Marx, *The President and His Staff Advisers,* 1947. See also work cited in note 7 above.

42. See my report to the IPSA Round Table at Jablonna, September, 1966, "The Concept of Governmental Responsibility . . ." published in *Politische Vierteljahrschrift,* 1967, where the implications of the recent plebiscitary tendency are stressed.

XIX. Responsible Public Administration

GENERAL NOTES

Problems of responsible administration have continued to occupy the attention of political scientists; and a separate branch of the discipline has become well established since the second world war. The leading works in the field all give major attention to these problems. Besides Leonard White's classic text *Introduction to the Study of Public Administration,* 4th ed., 1955, not only the newer methods as heralded in Herbert A. Simon, *Administrative Behavior,* 1947, which was a remarkable study of decision-making in administrative units, but also structural-functional studies have advanced the field. A milestone in the over-all merger of politological and sociological approaches was the *Reader in Bureaucracy,* edited by Robert Merton and Associates in 1951, which is built around a critical evaluation and full exploration of Max Weber's initial studies. A decade later, we find the volume edited by Duvaine Marveck, *Political Decision-makers: Recruitment and Performance,* 1961; programmatic in its thoughtful overview had been Dwight Waldo's *Perspectives on Administration,* 1956; and Emette Redford's *Ideals and Practice in Public Administration,* 1958. Broadly conceived also is Fritz Morstein-Marx's *The Administrative State,* 1957. The problem of responsibility occupies the center of John Millett, *Government and Public Administration: The Quest for Responsible Performance,* 1959; and George Graham, *America's Capacity to Govern,* 1960. Noteworthy general treatments are Herbert Simon and Associates, *Public Administration in a Democratic Society,* 1950; James Charlesworth, *Governmental Administration,* 1951; E. N. Gladden, *The Essentials of Public Administration,* 1955; and James Thompson and Associates, *Comparative Studies in Administration,* 1960. Personnel Administration is the focal point of the well-known treatise by W. Mosher and Associates, 3d ed., 1950; see also John Corson, *Executives for the Federal Service,* 1952; Paul David and Ross Pollock, *Executives for Government: Central Issues of Federal Personnel Administration,* 1958; Marver Bernstein, *The Job of the Federal Executive,* 1958; Franklin Kilpatrick and Associates, *The Image of the Federal Service,* 1964. Brian Chapman, *The Profession of Government,* 1959, adds the British perspective; and Paul Appleby in *Public Administration for the Welfare State,* 1961, applied his sound empirical knowledge to India. The bureaucratic aspect is made the center by Charles Hyneman, *Bureaucracy in a Democracy,* 1950; and Peter Moll, *American Bureaucracy,* 1963. For a French reassessment of this approach cf. Michel Crozier, *The Bureaucratic Phenomenon,* 1964. A strikingly original over-all approach was developed by Bertram Gross, *The Managing of Organizations: The Administrative Struggle,* 2 vols., 1964.

A very interesting new approach is the study of administration by the case method. Here the pathfinder is Harold Stein; he edited *Public Administration and Policy Development: A Case Book,* 1952. More recently Edwin A. Bock has edited *Essays on the Case Method,* 1962; *Case Studies in American Government,* 1962 (with Alan K. Campbell); and *State and Local Government: A Case Book,* 1963. Case studies are little histories of particular events; on the broader side, besides the histories mentioned earlier in Ch. II, Paul van Riper, *A History of US Civil Service,* 1958, provides the background for the type of challenge contained in William S. Carpenter's *The Unfinished Business of Civil Service Reform,* 1952.

REFERENCES

1. Hans Rosenberg, *Bureaucracy, Aristocracy and Autocracy*, 1958, p. 1, referring to Arnold Brecht, "How Bureaucracies Develop and Function," *The Annals*, 1954, CCXCII, 2; the next quote in Rosenberg, ibid.

2. Herman Finer, *The Theory and Practice of Modern Government*, 1932, Vol. II, p. 1167. Cf. also K. B. Smellie, *Hundred Years of English Government*, 1937, chapters on administration; and W. A. Robson, ed., *The British Civil Servant*, 3d ed., 1948.

3. Robert Moses, *The Civil Service of Great Britain*, 1914, Ch. II.

4. See J. Donald Kingsley, *Representative Bureaucracy*, 1944, and H. R. G. Greaves, *The Civil Service in the Changing State*, 1947.

5. S. H. Beer, *British Politics in the Collectivist Age*, 1965, pp. 388–389.

6. For the political aspect of the *Ecole Normale* see the interesting, if highly partisan, discussion by Hubert Bourgin, *De Jaurès à Léon Blum*, 1938.

7. See William Robson, *The Civil Service in Britain and France*, 1956; and the chapter on the civil service in F. Ridley and J. Blondel, *Public Administration in France*, 1964. Emil Strauss, *The Ruling Servants*, 1961, compares the Russian, British and French civil servants.

8. For this effort at perversion see TD, Ch. 16.

9. See the author's "The Continental Tradition of Training Administrators in Law and Jurisprudence," *The Journal of Modern History*, Vol. XI, No. 2. For a general survey, see Fritz Morstein–Marx, "Civil Service in Germany" in *Civil Service Abroad*, 1935.

10. Ralf Dahrendorf, *Gesellschaft und Demokratie in Deutschland*, 1965, Ch. 16. See also Franz Neumann's magistral *Behemoth*, 1944, where the learned author interprets the bureaucracy in terms of a "new ruling class," especially pp. 369 ff. and 378 ff. Here the ministerial bureaucracy is seen as a partner of "industrial capitalism," while in the lower civil service "the key positions are in the hands of the party" and the remainder are terrorized.

11. For this problem, see the splendid Princeton symposium *The Public Service and University Education*, ed., Joseph E. McLean, 1949, especially the papers by John M. Gaus and Donald C. Stone. Besides the work cited in the GENERAL NOTES, special mention should be made of Don K. Price, *Government and Science — Their Dynamic Relation in American Democracy*, 1954.

12. The value judgments in the text are supported by the *Hoover Commission Report*, especially *Section VI*. For a broad survey of postwar developments, see S. Sweeney and T. Davy, eds., *Education for Administrative Careers in Government Service*, 1958.

13. Ari Hoogenboom, *Outlawing the Spoils: History of the Civil Service Reform Movement, 1865–1883*, 1961; Leonard D. White (assisted by Jean Schneider), *The Republican Era 1869–1901: A Study in Administrative History*, 1958: R. K. Kelsall, *Higher Civil Servants in Britain: From 1870 to the Present Day*, 1955; W. A. Robson, *The Civil Service in Britain and France*, 1956; Peter G. Richards,

Patronage in British Government, 1963. The increasing sophistication in this field is manifest in the Bar Association Report, published in 1960 under the title *Conflict of Interest and the Federal Service.*

14. The *Myers Case* is found 272 U.S. 52, 1926; the *Humphreys Case,* correctly cited as Rathbun v. United States, 295 U.S. 602, 1935. See the able comment by Cushman, APSR, Vol. XXX, pp. 72 ff., concerning this case. The *Myers Case* has also been extensively commented upon; see, for example, James Hart, *Tenure of Office under the Constitution,* 1930; and E. S. Corwin, *The President's Removal Power under the Constitution,* 1927.

15. This subject is dealt with in a number of the general works on public administration cited above in the GENERAL NOTES. See also Section 6 in Merton's *Reader* as cited, pp. 353 ff.

16. McCamy, cited above, Ch. II, note 15.

17. The Commission of Inquiry on Public Personnel Problems published its report, *Better Government Personnel,* in 1935. The statement here quoted is founded on pp. 45 ff. See also Arthur K. MacMahon and John D. Millett, "The Selection of Bureau Heads," and Herbert A. Simon, "Inducements and Incentives in Bureaucracy," both in Merton's *Reader,* 1952, pp. 312 ff. and 327 ff.

18. On the bill of attainder, see McIlwain in ESS. The effect of McCarthy's and similar methods on the prestige and effectiveness of the civil service calls for more detailed study; cf. Edward A. Shils, *The Torments of Secrecy,* 1956, especially Ch. 5, pp. 105 ff.

19. For this, see George C. S. Benson, *Financial Control and Integration,* 1934, for a good classical statement. The British situation has recently been analyzed by Gordon Reid, *The Politics of Financial Control,* 1966; cf. also R. J. Swenson, *Federal Administrative Law: A Study of the Growth, Nature and Control of Administrative Activities,* 1952; and Henry Friendly, *The Federal Administrative Agencies: The Need for Better Definition of Standards,* 1961, passim.

20. On the *Cour des Comptes* and the *Rechnungshof* cf. the works on administrative law, cited above, Ch. VI, note 23.

21. For the United States Comptroller and related problems, see *Hoover Commission Report,* "Budgeting and Accounting," Part III.

22. See Ch. XIII above on the problems of judicial review and the literature cited. See also Ch. VI above.

23. The sense of craftsmanship was emphasized by J. M. Gaus, in his contribution, cited above, to *The Frontiers of Public Administration.* It also receives due attention in Barnard's study, p. 146. See the author's restatement of the problem in Ch. VI, "Responsibility and the Sense of Workmanship," in *The New Belief in the Common Man,* 1942.

24. Paul Appleby, *Morality and Administration in Democratic Government,* 1952.

XX.   Political Parties: Outline of a General Theory

The theoretical and practical problems of political parties have become one of the major concerns of political science and sociology since the publication of M. Y. Ostrogorski's challenging volumes, *La Democratie et l'organisation des partis politiques*, 1902, translated by F. Clarke. The history of parties in various countries has been studied; in recent years works on the role and functioning of political parties in general have multiplied. The titles are often not quite indicative. Thus Maurice Duverger's *Partis Politiques*, 1951, is as much oriented toward French experience as V. O. Key, Jr.'s *Politics, Parties and Pressure Groups*, 1942, 4th ed., 1958, is preoccupied with the US. James Bryce's *Modern Democracies*, new ed., 1924, revolves around the problem of parties, as does Robert A. Dahl, ed., *Political Oppositions in Western Democracies*, 1966. The general theory of political parties owes a great deal to Robert Michel's *Political Parties*, 1915, original German, 1911, although the work is primarily concerned with trends in the German Social Democratic Party; similarly Gaetano Mosca's *The Ruling Class*, 1939, original Italian version under the title *Elementi di Scienza Politica*, in 1895, consists of generalizations based upon Italian experience, as does V. Pareto's *Mind and Society*, 1935, in 4 vols; original Italian version under the title of *Trattato di Sociologia Generale*, 1916, in 2 vols. Their emphasis on elites, political classes and oligarchy has profoundly affected not only the view of parties, but of democracy. Max Weber, too, contributed in *Wirtschaft und Gesellschaft*, 1922, an embryonic theory of parties; see also his "Politik als Beruf," published in translation in Gerth and Mills, *From Max Weber — Essays in Sociology*, 1946.

Among the studies of recent years, the following might be mentioned as representing the several trends of inquiry: Austin Ranney, *The Doctrine of Responsible Party Government: Its Origins and Present State*, 1954, rev. ed., 1962; Austin Ranney and W. Kendall, *Democracy and the American Party System*, 1956; I. Hinderaker, *Party Politics*, 1956; W. Goodman, *The Two-Party System in the United States*, 1956; Clinton Rossiter, *Party Politics in America*, 1960; Fred Greenstein, *The American Party System and the American People*, 1963; Frank Sorauf, *Political Parties in the American System*, 1964; and the symposium by Robert Goldwin, ed., *Political Parties, USA*, 1964. The British party scene was given comprehensive treatment by W. I. Jennings, Party Politics, in 3 vols, 1961–62; the Dominions in A. Brady's *Democracy in the Dominions*, 1948; but see also Hugh Thorburn, ed., *Party Politics in Canada*, 1963; and James Jupp, *Australian Party Politics*, 1964; the French system is reflected in Duverger, op. cit.; the German ones in Ludwig Bergsträsser, *Geschichte der deutschen Parteien*, 7th ed., 1952; for contrast see Carola Stern's able *Porträt einer bolschewistischen Partei*, 1957; and Mario Einaudi and Associates, *Communism in Western*

Europe, 1951. For Sweden see Dankwart A. Rustow, *The Politics of Compromise — A Study of Cabinet Government in Sweden*, 1955; he is critical on pp. 257 f. of what I say on parties; on p. 227 he approves of my remarks on the British aristocracy, and claims a parallel for Sweden. Chapters in the symposium edited by Sigmund Neumann, *Modern Political Parties*, 1956, are devoted to the systems in these several countries as well as others.

A vigorous attack on the American system was put forward by James McG. Burns, *The Deadlock Democracy: Four-Party Politics in America*, 1963. The behavioral approach is given primary attention in Avery Leiserson, *Parties and Politics: An Institutional and Behavioral Approach*, 1958; and in Samuel Eldersveld, *Political Parties: A Behavioral Analysis*, 1964; both are concerned with the United States. Cf. also W. N. Chambers' interesting *Political Parties in a new nation: The American Experience*, 1963, which undertakes to explore the American experience from 1776–1809 with a view to the problems of developing countries. Most relevant here is also Robert W. Anderson's realistic appraisal of *Party Politics in Puerto Rico*, 1965.

A rather difficult dimension of party theory is presented by the development of single party regimes and more particularly the totalitarian parties. I have dealt with these problems in MG, Ch. 29 and TD, Ch. 4. In some developing countries, plural party systems are evolving, but they are the exception. Still, a general theory of parties has to be framed so as to allow for them.

REFERENCES

1. For the change in outlook concerning parties, see John Adams, *Defense of the Constitutions* (1787). For the remarks on Washington, see, for instance, S. E. Morison, *The Oxford History of the United States* (1927), Vol. I, p. 234. See also L. D. White, *The Federalists* (1948) for further detail. Bolingbroke's ideas are set forth in *The Patriot King* (1749). For the whole problem of corruption, see the penetrating study by L. B. Namier, *The Structure of Politics at the Accession of George III* (1929).

2. For the beginning of this paragraph, see the articles by W. C. Abbott, particularly "The Origin of English Political Parties," in the *American Historical Review*, Vol. XXIV (1918–1919), pp. 578 ff. Consult also M. T. Blauvelt, *The Development of Cabinet Government in England* (1902); G. M. Trevelyan, *The Two-party System in English Political History* (1926); and the work by Namier quoted in the previous paragraph. For the statement from N. Wraxall, see his *Memoirs* (1779), Vol. II, pp. 498 ff. See also the discussion of the cabinet system above, Ch. XVIII.

3. For Sir Erskine May, see *The Constitutional History of England since the Accession of George the Third* (3d ed., 1871), Ch. XVIII. Lord Macaulay's views are stated in his *The History of England* (ed. Firth, 1913), Ch. I. A very able analysis of the emergence of party organization in the course of the Long Parlia-

ment is given by J. H. Hexter in *The Reign of King Pym* (1941), especially Chs. III, VIII, and IX.

4. For Britain, see Jennings, op. cit., Vol. II, 1961, as well as R. T. McKenzie's *British Political Parties: The Distribution of Power within the Conservative and Labour Parties*, 1955, rev. ed., 1964.

5. For France, cf. Maurice Duverger, *Les Partis Politiques*, 1951 which in spite of its general title deals primarily with French parties; it has been vigorously criticized by G. E. Lavau, *Partis Politiques et Réalités Sociales*, 1954.

6. For Germany, Ludwig Bergsträsser's *Geschichte der politischen Parteien in Deutschland*, 7th ed., 1952, is the standard work, but somewhat dated, both in method and documentation. For such documentation, cf. Ossip Flechtheim, *Die deutschen Parteien seit 1945 — Quellen und Auszüge*, 1955.

7. The discussion in the paragragh is developed from the views of Max Weber and Robert Michels, but with important modifications. Michels has shown that the "ideal" objectives are often more closely related to power than are the material ones.

8. See for this Ranney, op. cit., Rossiter, op. cit., Sorauf, op. cit., and more specifically Heinz Eulau, *Class and Party Rule in the Eisenhower Years*, 1962. The point here made was badly distorted in C. Wright Mills, *The Power Elite*, 1956, especially Chs. 1, 10, and 12. Among the older studies, cf. H. F. Gosnell, *Machine Politics: Chicago Model*, 1937; A. M. Bingham, *Insurgent America: Revolt of the Middle Classes*, 1935; and P. H. Odegard and E. A. Helms, *American Politics: A Study in Political Dynamics*, 1938, new ed., 1947. For Holcombe's views, see his *Political Parties of Today*, 1924, and *The Middle Classes in American Politics*, 1940. On ideology, cf. MG, Ch. 4.

9. On the problem of succession, cf. MG, Ch. 29, where this particular function is made the overall feature of parties at all times, whether the system is democratic or not. Cf. that chapter also for some of the other generalizations and supporting evidence.

10. This was a widespread view in Europe around 1900; it helped shape the mistaken claim of Max Weber, e.g. *Wirtschaft und Gesellschaft*, 2d ed., 1925, pp. 768 ff. and elsewhere; cf. also pp. 407 ff. in Talcott Parsons' English selections, entitled *Max Weber: The Theory of Social and Political Organization*, 1947. The emphasis on charisma was critically examined by myself in MG, pp. 172 ff. and the article there referred to.

11. Hume's "Essay on Parties," contained in *Essays and Treatises*, 1760, Vol. I, pp. 93 ff., has the quotation on p. 97.

12. This model was first constructed on the basis of English party development by Julius Hatschek, but seems to be fairly generally valid. Cf. his *Englisches Staatsrecht*, Vol. II, 1905, pp. 8 ff. See also Key, op. cit. Ch. 7.

13. Neumann, ed. op. cit., introductory chapter. See also V. O. Key's magistral treatment, op. cit., Ch. 12. See for the totalitarian parties, TD, Ch. 4, and Stern, op. cit.

14. For Michel's views, see op. cit., pp. 400 ff. and passim; see for the SPD in

imperial Germany, Carl Schorske, *German Social Democracy, 1905–1917,* 1955.
15. My "Federalism and Opposition" in *Government and Opposition,* Vol. I, 1966, pp. 286 ff. argues the particular advantage of such division. For the general point, cf. Key, op. cit., Chs. 8, 9, 11, and 12, especially at pp. 362 ff. and his *Southern Politics,* 1950, especially pp. 392 ff.
16. Cf. the remarkably rich documentation and trenchant analysis in *The Politics of National Party Conventions,* by Paul T. David, Ralph M. Goldman, and Richard C. Bain. (1960) Based upon the five volume study of *Presidential Nominating Politics in 1952* which APSA sponsored and which David, Goldman and Malcolm Moos edited, this study, in the words of Peter H. Odegard, "offers a systematic analysis of the presidential nominating process. Leadership centers of both the party in power and the opposition are examined, and critically appraised; the main patterns by which presidential leadership is discovered, confirmed or rejected are described; demographic and political factors affecting the character and training of convention delegates and candidates are examined in detail; the technical aspects of apportionment, delegate selection organization and behavior, as well as the organization, procedure and voting structure of the convention are described at length; so too are the presidential primary and the influence of the mass media . . ." in *APSR,* LIV, p. 499. For a general analytical view prior to this documentation see Key, op. cit. ch. 15.
17. The matter has now become of great urgency, due to the constitutional court decision on party finance. For the wide-ranging discussion cf. Ulrich Duebber, *Parteifinanzierung in Deutschland* (1962) and Theodor Eschenburg, *Probleme der Modernen Parteifinanzierung* (1961). For an overview cf. Ellwein, op. cit.
18. The works, cited in the General Notes, by Key, Ranney, Hinderaker, Sorauf and others all deal with these problems, of course.
19. See Richard Rose and Arnold J. Heidenheimer, eds., "Comparative Political Finance — A Symposium" in *The Journal of Politics,* Vol. 25, No. 3, August, 1963; Herbert E. Alexander, *Financing the 1964 Election* and *Regulation of Political Finance,* both published by the Citizen's Research Foundation (the latter article in cooperation with the Institute of Governmental Studies of the University of California, Berkeley) in 1966; and Donald G. Balmer, *Financing State Senate Campaigns: Multnomah County Oregon, 1964* (Citizen's Research Foundation, 1966). For the general problems, cf. also Key, op. cit., Ch. 18.
20. Rose and Heidenheimer, op. cit., p. 680.
21. For an interesting study of how such acts work in practice, see Douglas Price, "Campaign Finance in Massachusetts in 1952" in PP VI, 1955.
22. For the interesting experimentation in Puerto Rico, see Henry Wells, *Government Financing of Political Parties in Puerto Rico,* Princeton, 1961 (Citizen's Research Foundation).
23. The matter remains controversial at this writing. The project would permit taxpayers to designate $1 of their income tax ($2 for joint returns) for expenses of the next presidential election campaign. Contributions would be divided evenly between the major parties, but not to exceed actual expenses or the total

number of votes above 10 million cast for major party candidates in the last election. There are also provisions for minor parties, supervision and so forth. In its defense Senator Long said on October 19, 1966 that the plan would assure that presidential candidates were obligated to "all citizens . . . not just to the big contributors. It will do more to improve government than anything we can do." In the debate, he added: "The candidates won't have to go around with hat in hand looking for fat cats." (*Congressional Quarterly, Weekly Report,* October 21, 1966, pp. 2565 and 2566.)

24. Heinz Laufer, "Zur staatlichen Finanzierung der politischen Parteien," *Aus Politik und Zeitgeschichte,* Beilage zu *Das Parlament,* Nov. 2, 1966; Ulrich Dübber, *Parteifinanzierung in Deutschland* . . . 1962; and Ulrich Lohmar, *Innerparteiliche Demokratie* . . . 1963.

25. The argument here refuted was put forward, inter alios, by Professor E. E. Schattschneider, *The Struggle for Party Government,* 1948; cf. also Ernst Fraenkel's penetrating analysis in *Das Amerikanische Regierungssystem,* 1962.

26. C. H. More, "Mass Party Regimes in Africa" in *Africa: The Primacy of Politics,* 1966, ed. H. J. Spiro.

27. Julius Nyerere, "One Party Rule"' *Atlas,* 3:185 ff., 1962.

28. On the subject of factions and more particularly Madison's concern with it see Robert A. Dahl, *A Preface to Democratic Theory,* 1966, Ch. 1 and more recently "The Dangers of Faction" in *Pluralist Democracy in the United States,* 1967, pp. 11 ff., and 204 ff.

29. For this paragraph see the famous historical discussion by Mr. Ostrogorski, op. cit., Vol. I, pp. 117 ff.

30. Cf. Gerhard Leibholz, *Der Strukturwandel der Modernen Demokratie,* 1952, and several of the distinguished author's papers in the volume *Politics and Law,* 1965.

31. Maurice Duverger, *Political Parties,* 1954 (French original published in 1951).

32. G. E. Lavau, *Partis Politiques et Réalités Sociales,* 1954.

33. This basis was provided by a number of contributors to the volume *Modern Political Parties,* 1956, to which Neumann himself contributed the general theory foreshadowed in an article in *World Politics,* 1954, "Toward a Theory of Political Parties."

34. op. cit. p. 560.

35. See Frank Sorauf, *Party and Representation,* 1963, and the forthcoming *Nomos* volume on representation. Cf. also above, Ch. XIV.

36. Cf. Robert Alford, *Party and Society,* 1963, for a recent treatment; also Seymour Martin Lipset, *Political Man,* 1960, Ch. IX. The relation of party to social structure raises, of course, the problems of interest groups; for this see the next chapter. Cf. M. Duverger, ed., *Partis Politiques et Classes Sociales,* 1955.

37. André Siegfried's study is contained in the well-known monograph, *Tableau Politique de la France de l'Ouest,* 1913. The French situation is well presented

in Lavau, op. cit. and the work of Francois Goguel, especially his *France under the Fourth Republic*, 1954.

38. Fine examples of such comprehensive studies for England are E. L. Woodward, *The Age of Reform, 1850–1870,* and E. K. Ensor, *England, 1870–1914.* For France cf. the study by Lavau cited above.

39. For a more detailed and highly competent elaboration the reader is referred to the work edited by S. Neumann, op. cit., and containing contributions by Beer (Britain), Carter (Commonwealth), Micaud (France), Rustow (Scandinavia) and others. Actually Samuel Beer, *British Politics in the Collectivist Age,* 1965, is primarily a broad panorama of British parties.

40. Cf. the symposium edited by A. Bullock and M. Shock, *The Liberal Tradition,* 1957; cf. also Francis de Tarr, *The French Radical Party from Herriot to Mendès-France,* 1961, and Daniel Bardonnet, *Evolution de la structure du parti radical,* 1960.

41. See Charles Trevelyan, *From Liberalism to Labor,* 1921, a revealing personal account; Arthur Rosenberg, *Democracy and Socialism,* 1939, Franz Mehring, *Geschichte der deutschen Sozialdemokratie,* 12th ed., 1922, Michels, op. cit., Werner Sombart, *Grundlagen und Kritik des Sozialismus,* 1919, 2 vols., and E. Matthias, *Sozialdemokratie und Nation,* 1952. Three studies have carried the story beyond Schorske, op. cit.: A. J. Berlau, *The German Social Democratic Party — 1914–1921,* 1949; Richard Hunt, *German Social Democracy — 1918–1933,* 1964; and Douglas Chalmers, *The Social Democratic party of Germany,* 1964.

42. Cf. Henry Pelling, *Origins of the Labour Party,* 1954; J. H. Reid, *The Origins of the British Labour Party,* 1955; Philip Poirier, *The Advent of the British Labour Party,* 1958; Henry Pelling, *A Short History of the British Labour Party,* 1961; for the philosophical background consult Adam Ulam, *Philosophical Foundations of English Socialism,* 1951.

43. Concerning this whole subject, see the excellent monograph by Merle Fainsod, *International Socialism and the World War,* 1935. For the German "revolution," see Arthur Rosenberg, *The Birth of the German Republic, 1871–1918,* 1931, tr. by Ian F. D. Morrow. See also Charles Picaud, *Communism and the French Left,* 1963.

44. For the problem of Catholic parties, there is a considerable amount of special literature. Cf. M. Einaudi and F. Goguel, *Christian Democracy in Italy and France,* 1952; William Bosworth, *Catholicism and Crisis in Modern France,* 1962; Arnold Heidenheimer, *Adenauer and the CDU,* 1960. For historical background see Karl Bachem, *Vorgeschichte, Geschichte und Politik der deutschen Zentrumspartei,* 1927–1932, as well as Ludwig Bergsträsser, *Der Politische Katholizismus,* 1921–1923.

45. Cf. TD, Ch. 4, and Theodor Abel, *Why Hitler Came to Power,* 1938, reprinted in 1965 under the title, *The Nazi Movement;* for Fascism, cf. Frederico Chabod, *A History of Italian Fascism,* 1963; and Dante Germino, *The Italian Fascist Party in Power,* 1959, Chs. 1 and 2. Robert C. Tucker has suggested that

the existence of such movements is the really crucial aspect of such regimes; cf. his "Towards a comparative politics of movement-regimes," APSR, 55: 281 ff., 1961.

46. An imaginative effort at developing the comparative aspects, from a predominantly ideological standpoint, is Ernst Nolte, *Three Faces of Fascism*, 1966, first published in German in 1963.

47. On the Gaullist Party, see Pierre Viansson–Ponté, *Les Gaullistes*, 1963, but one should consult works on France, such as Macridis, Wahl, Aron, etc.

48. On the comparative position of Communism in Italy and France, cf. Mario Einaudi, J. M. Domenach and A. Garosci, *Communism in Western Europe*, 1951.

XXI. Interest Groups and Economic Councils

GENERAL NOTES

The general topic of the relation of the various associations and groups to government is of rather recent interest. The connection of this subject with representation has been stressed by the writers noted above under Ch. XIV. The detailed examination of the actual behavior of different groups used to be more particularly an American preoccupation. E. P. Herring, in his two volumes, *Group Representation before Congress*, 1929, and *Public Administration and the Public Interest*, 1936, offered the broadest analysis. These studies were carried forward by V. O. Key, Jr., whose basic treatise, *Politics, Parties, and Pressure Groups*, 1942, 4th ed. 1958, has become the standard work for America. With it might be compared S. E. Finer's *Anonymous Empire: A Study of the Lobby in Great Britain*, 1958. More general, but widely hailed, is David Truman's *The Governmental Process: Political Interests and Public Opinion*, 1951; an outstanding case study was presented by Harry Eckstein, *Pressure Group Politics: The Case of the British Medical Association*, 1960; cf. also Harmon Zeigler, *Interest Groups in American Society*, 1964. A very challenging study is Grant McConnell, *Private Power and American Democracy*, 1966. A broad comparative approach provides the basis for the volume edited by Henry Ehrmann, *Interest Groups on Four Continents*, 1958, who had given a trenchant analysis of *Organized Business in France*, 1957, a subject which Jean Meynaud has made his own; see *Les Groupes de Pression en France*, 1958, and *Nouvelles Etudes sur les Groupes de Pression en France*, 1962. For Britain, besides the work by Finer just cited, see J. D. Stewart, *British Pressure Groups: Their Role in Relation to the House of Commons*, 1958; and Allan Potter, *Organized Groups in British National Politics*, 1961; and Ch. XII in Samuel H. Beer's *British Politics in the Collectivist Age,* 1965. The comparable phenomena in Germany were analyzed by Rupert Breitling, *Die Verbände in der Bundesrepublik*, 1955; Gerard Braunthal, *The Federation of German Industry*, 1965, is more specialized. The Italian interest groups have found their competent student in Joseph La Palombara, *Interest Groups in Italian Politics*, 1964. This entire world of Western pluralism also forms the subject of a critical assessment by Stanislav Ehrlich, *Grupi Nacisku — w Strukturze Politycznej Kapitalizmu*, 1962 (available in German, 1966). I cited quite a few of the earlier studies in the previous edition, works which are now dated, but still interesting, by Odegard, Childs, Schattschneider, and Zeller. The estates type of political representation has not been treated with much interest in the United States (and England), since it was regarded as "feudal." Actually, the estates period represents a phase in the evolution of modern constitutionalism, and deserves greater attention in view of the modern interest in functional representation. See the references given by Otto von Gierke in his *Deutsches Genossenschaftsrecht*, Vol. I, pp. 534 ff. and 819 ff., which offers a broad sketch of the legal and institutional characteristics. Gierke also perceived the intimate political and legal relation between these older forms and the modern associational concept and traced it through the study of the *Genossenschaft* concept. See also Gierke's *The Development of Political Theory* (1939) (tr. by Bernard Freyd). For a highly significant analysis of the importance of all groups intermediate between the individual and the "state," see Emil Lederer's *The State of the Masses* (1940), especially Chs. V and VI, where the delusion of a "classless" society in the usual Marxian sense is shown to be the basis for totalitarian despotism. For a dicussion and the general literature on "Government Control" see above, Chs. V and XIX, and below, Ch. XXII.

REFERENCES

1. The quotation is taken from Wilson's *The New Freedom*, 1913, p. 125. Bryce's discussion is given in *American Commonwealth*, Vol. 1, pp. 691 ff.

2. Regarding Bismarck's council, see Julius Curtius, *Bismarcks Plan eines deutschen Volkswirtschaftsrates*, 1919, and the same author's article, "Der preussische Volkswirtschaftsrat, seine Errichtung, seine Tätigkeit, die Ursachen seines Eingehens," in *Wirtschaftliche Nachrichten aus dem Ruhrbezirk*, 1921, pp. 593 ff.

3. See arts. 50 and 51 of the "draft Treaty embodying the statute of the European Community," in *Studies in Federalism*, eds. Bowie and Friedrich, 1954, Appendix II, pp. 838, and the Proceedings of the Ad Hoc Assembly concerning these provisions. The workings of the Committeee of the EEC are described in the official documents, especially in the *European Yearbook;* cf. also the *Bulletin of the EEC;* and Buiter, *Interest Groups and the European Community* (no date) and Gerda Zellentin, *Der Wirtschaft-und Sozialausschuss*, 1962.

4. The story about "One-Speech" Hamilton is told in C. S. Kenny's new edition of his *Parliamentary Logic*, 1927. The quotation from Burke is from his "Speech

on a motion for a committee to inquire into the State of the Representation of the Commons in Parliament," May 7, 1782, *Works,* 1866 ed., Vol. VII, p. 98.

5. On the subject of public interest cf. *Nomos V,* 1962, presenting a range of contrasting views; cf. also Glendon Schubert, *The Public Interest,* 1960, who stresses the ideological facade which the public interest concept provides for many private interests, and Richard E. Flathman, *The Public Interest,* 1966, who indicates his slant by calling his study "an essay concerning the normative discourse of politics," vindicating the concept and rightly arguing that "it performs a specific function" and helps to restrain policy-makers who might otherwise identify particular interests with the general one.

6. The "purposes" of the various organizations are quoted from E. P. Herring, *Public Administration and the Public Interest,* 1936, pp. 22–23. See also Ch. XXII.

7. See for this V. O. Key, op. cit., part one, Chs. 2–6, quote at p. 151; cf. Karl Schriftgiesser, *The Lobbyists,* 1963; and L. Milbrath, *The Washington Lobbyists,* 1963.

8. Cf. Ehrmann, op. cit.; and the symposium edited by Donald Blaisdell, *Unofficial Government: Pressure Groups and Lobbies,* 1958, cf. also the section on chambers of commerce in Henry W. Ehrmann, *Organized Business in France,* 1957.

9. Theodor Eschenburg, *Die Herrschaft der Verbände,* 1955, which is quite hostile to the pluralism of interest groups and hankers after the "state above the parties." Cf. for a more detached view Rupert Breitling, *Die Verbände in der Bundesrepublik,* 1955; their constitutional position is explored in *Das Grundgesetz und die Verbände,* 1963, by Gerhard W. Wittkämper.

10. The best study of "The Government and the Bank of France" is that by Karl R. Bopp in *Public Policy,* Vol. II, pp. 3–35. The quotations are from p. 29 of this study. See also Hans Joachim Arndt, *Politik und Sachverstand im Kreditwesen,* 1963; and H. Rittershausen, *Die Zentralnotenbank,* 1962.

11. The writings on the political role and functioning of trade unions is, of course, very large. The following might be suggested for America: Leo Wolman, *The Growth of American Trade Unions, 1880–1923,* 1924; Margaret R. Clark and S. Fanny Simon, *The Labor Movement in America,* 1938; Marc Akerson, *American Labor Unions, 1900–1918,* 1958; for Europe: Walter Galenson, *Trade Union Democracy in Western Europe,* 1961; for Britain: Eric Wigham, *Trade Unions,* 1956; B. C. Roberts, *Trade Union Government and Administration in Great Britain,* 1956; the same, *The Trades Union Congress — 1868–1921,* 1958; Henry Pelling, *History of British Trade Unionism,* 1963; H. A. Clegg and Asssociates, *A History of British Trade Unions since 1889,* 1964; for France: Val Lorwin, *The French Labor Movement,* 1954; André Tiano and Associates, *Expériences françaises d'action syndicale ouvrière,* 1956; Pierre Monat, *Trois scissions syndicales,* 1958; J.–D. Reynaud, *Les syndicats en France,* 1963; for Germany: Wolfgang Hirsch-Weber, *Gewerkschaften in der Politik,* 1959; for Italy: Joseph La Palombara, *The Italian Labor Movement: Problems and Prospects,* 1957, rev.

ed., 1964; Daniel Horowitz, *The Italian Labor Movement,* 1963; beyond such concrete studies, there is of course the extensive literature on syndicalism, epitomized by such names as Sidney and Beatrice Webb, Jules Guesde, Georges Sorel, A. Labriola, Werner Sombart, Robert Michels, Paul Louis.

12. Cf. TD, Ch. 19 and literature.

13. Cf. Arthur J. Goldberg, *AFL–CIO: Labor United,* 1956.

14. Regarding the situation in prewar Russsia see Leon Trotsky, *The History of the Russsian Revolution,* tr. Max Eastman, 1932. For Germany, cf. Arthur Rosenberg, *Democracy and Socialism,* 1939. See also for further literature C. Hauschild, *Der vorläufige Reichswirtschaftsrat, 1920–1926,* 1926, pp. 641 ff.

15. Hugo Preuss's article appeared in *Berliner Tageblatt,* November 14, 1918, and was republished in *Staat, Recht und Freiheit,* 1926, pp. 365 ff. Besides the National Economic Council, the bottom layer, the factory councils, were organized by the *Betriebsrätegesetz* of February 4, 1920. Concerning these factory councils, see C. Guillebaud, *The German Works Council,* 1928; cf. also Adolph Sturmthal, *Workers Councils,* 1964.

16. The Paris Commune has been adequately described and analyzed in Edward S. Mason, *The Paris Commune,* 1930, with literature. For the German situation, cf. Arthur Rosenberg, *The Birth of the German Republic, 1871–1918,* 1931. Very interesting for this period is Klaus Epstein, *Matthias Erzberger and the Dilemma of German Democracy,* 1959, Ch. XII.

17. For the German National Economic Council, see Dr. Hauschild's collection of materials just cited, and Friedrich Glum's *Der deutsche und der französische Reichswirtschaftsrat,* 1929.

18. For the workings of this council, cf. D. M. Pickles, *The Fifth French Republic,* 1962.

19. Gaetano Salvemini, *Under the Axe of Facism,* 1936, particularly Part I; cf. also TD, pp. 257 ff.

20. V. O. Key, Jr., who in his op. cit. Part I, had so detachedly described the main pressure groups operative in American politics, emphasized this point in his posthumous *The Responsible Electrorate,* 1966.

21. Cf. the works cited above in the GENERAL NOTES; among recent special studies, mention might be made of L. E. Ebersole, *Church Lobbying in the Nation's Capital,* 1951; Philip Foss, *Politics and Grass,* 1960; and the symposium edited by Milton Derker and Edwin Young, *Labor and the New Deal,* 1958. Remarkably insightful also Grant McConnell, *Steel and the Presidency,* 1962.

22. E. P. Herring, *The Impact of War upon American Government,* 1941.

23. See John Gaus, *Public Administration and the U. S. Department of Agriculture,* 1940. Agriculturalists have already become very active in the EEC; cf. e. g. A. A. Robinson, *Dutch Organized Agriculture in International Politics,* 1961.

XXII.   Socialization and Planning

GENERAL NOTES

The extensive literature on socialism and communism is involved in the general topic of this chapter. It is not practicable to review the writings of a primarily ideological slant, important though they are for a deeper understanding. I have dealt with them in many places, especially, of course, in MG, TD, and PL. Descriptive and analytical material on the relation of modern government to the economy is also quite voluminous; the historical dimension was briefly dealt with above in Ch. V. For the contemporary world and from the standpoint of the student of political science, Merle Fainsod, Lincoln Gordon, and Joseph Palamountain, *Government and the American Economy*, 1941, 3d ed., 1959, is authoritative. In the economic perspective, the names of Pigou and Keynes are highlights in what came to be known as welfare economics, no longer the focal point of economic theorizing, to be sure. Since no strictly economic view provides an adequate answer to the insistent political, governmental, behavioral, and institutional issues of a reasonably free and open society, some economists have made forays into politics. Their writings have challenged what John Kenneth Galbraith, perhaps the most persuasive of these laymen, has called the "conventional wisdom" of industrial societies. His felicitously chosen words, like the "countervailing power" which he proclaimed the secret of capitalist pluralism in *American Capitalism*, 1952, and the *Affluent Society*, 1958, have become common coin in discussions of the "welfare state" and hence of planning and socialization. These works have carried the discussion well beyond the controversy precipitated in the forties by Friedrich Hayek's *The Road to Serfdom*, 1944, and elaborated in *Individualism and the Economic Order*, 1948, and *The Counterrevolution of Science*, 1952. The interrelation of economic and political theory was focused by Robert Dahl and Charles Lindblom, *Politics, Economics and Welfare*, 1953; that the theory and practice of advanced industrialism was carrying both beyond the welfare state is the theme of Gunnar Myrdal's *Beyond the Welfare State: Economic Planning and its Implication*, 1960, who had already boldly struck out for *An International Economy*, 1956, as well as explored *The Political Element in the Development of Economic Theory*, 1955. These writings are the fruit, in part, of the Scandinavian experience with socialization and planning. That experience has become widespread since 1950. In Britain, France, and Europe as well as India, even in Germany and the United States (Puerto Rico!) planning on the national and local as well as enterprise level has become the order of the day, and has led to numerous symposia and conferences. William A. Robson edited *Problems of Nationalized Industry*, 1952; Sheldon Glueck, *The Welfare State and the National Welfare*, 1952; A. H. Hanson, *Public Enterprise*, 1955; and George Watson, *The Unservile State: Essays in Liberty and Welfare*, 1957. Governments initiated broad surveys amounting to prophesies with undefined implications for programming and planning, like the US President's Materials Policy Commission Report entitled *Resources for Freedom*, I, 1952. The fate of free enterprise in such a context occupied Marshall Dimock in *Free Enterprise and the Administrative State*, 1951; the increasing complexity of such a state inspired books like Emmette S. Redford's *Administration of National Economic Control*, 1952, and James Anderson, *The Emergence of the Modern Regulatory State*, 1962. As these realities came into view, socialization gradually lost the glamor which it had once possesssed as the cure-all for industrialism's ills; the *New Fabian Essays*, 1952, edited by R. H. S. Crossman; and A. H. Hanson, *Nationalization — A Book of Readings*, 1962; or a book like R. Kelf–Cohen's *Nationalization in Britain: The End of a Dogma*, 1959, as well as other works referred to below bear witness to this trend; William A. Robson has brought the mature judgment we come to expect of him to these issues in *Nationalized Industry and Public Ownership*, 1960; the corresponding re-assessment for France is offered in Mario Einaudi and Associates, *Nationalization in France and Italy*, 1955. Whether these developments really signalize a decline of pluralism may well be doubted, when one considers the rich variety of associational life as depicted e.g. in Samuel Beer's *British Politics in the Colllectivist Age*, 1965, though Henry Kariel has made food for argument out of it in *The Decline of American Pluralism*, 1961. Certainly, Karl Mannheim argued cogently in *Freedom, Power and Democratic Planning*, 1950, that socialization and planning mean more rather than less freedom, Hayek notwithstanding. A penetrating analysis of *The Corporate Planning Process* was offered by Melville C. Branch in 1962.

The writings have come to support the thesis advanced in this work many years ago that planning was likely to loom in the years ahead, in contrast to socialization. Lewis Ben explored the interrrelationship in *British Planning and Nationalization*, 1952; and so did M. Boiteux and Associates, *Le Fonctionnement des enterprises nationalisées en France*, 1956. The development of planning has more recently been assessed by J. W. Grove, *Government and Industry in Britain*, 1962; by John and Anne–Marie Hacket, *Economic Planning in France*, 1963; and by Hans-Joachim Arndt, *West Germany: Politics of Non-Planning*, 1966; this is Vol. VIII in a series of studies on planning, edited by Bertram Gross under the title of *National Planning Series*, and covering a number of developing countries, such as Mexico and Venezuela, as well as Israel (Benjamin Akzin and Y. Dror), Great Britain (E. H. Hagen), Italy (La Palombara). The general problems of planning in relation to constitutional democracy were a central concern of Charles Merriam; cf. e. g. his *On the Agenda of Democracy*, 1941, pp. 72 ff. and his *Systematic Politics*, 1945, pp. 104 ff., 157 ff., and 338 ff. A similar programmatic approach characterizes Lord (William A.) Beveridge's *Full Employment in a Free Society*, Am. ed., 1945.

REFERENCES

1. For these issues see the writings of R. Niebuhr, A. D. Lindsay, Harold Laski, Karl Mannheim, E. Rosenstock–Hüssy, and Karl Popper, among more recent writers, along with the author's.
2. Cf. Hayek, op. cit. and the recurrent studies in *Ordo*, a yearbook of the Neo-liberals, e. g. G. Thole, "Die französische Planifikation — ein Vorbild?" Vol. XV/XVI, 1965, pp. 167–274, a searching critique of French *dirigisme*.
3. Cf. Merriam, op. cit., and my *The New Image of the Common Man*, 1950, Epilogue "Looking Backward and Forward," pp. 318 ff. and Ch. VII.
4. See the discriminating discussion in Joseph A. Schumpeter, *Capitalism, Socialism, and Democracy*, 1942, especially Chs. XIX–XXIII.
5. Cf. Crossman, op. cit. passim. Cf. also C. A. R. Crossland, *The Future of Socialism*, 1957.
6. TD, Ch. 17 and literature; also Bertram Gross' *Planning Series* as cited.
7. Carl Landauer, *Theory of National Economic Planning*, rev. ed., 1947, p. 13.
8. Walton Hamilton and Douglas Adair, *The Power to Govern*, 1937. See also the many significant extracts included by Francis W. Coker in his *Democracy, Liberty and Property — Readings in the American Political Tradition*, 1942, especially Part III.
9. Critics of socialization believe that socialization necessarily narrows the choice of occupation. John Jewkes, *Ordeal by Planning*, 1948, p. 202, writes that the choice of occupation is "inevitably restricted with growing socialization." But he backs these remarks, as do others, by stating that "the big opportunities are to be found as administrators in the State organization." This is no real argument, but a semantic confusion: to lump all state administrators together as "bureaucracy" and call it a "narrow" choice, while not doing the same with "industry" or "business" in the free-market economy is misleading. The real problem is how to maintain freedom of choice between various jobs in this vital field without falling prey to the black-listing of a centralized police setup which builds up elaborate records on each employable person. The only feasible method seems to be much greater care to provide protection for the junior official against being so black-listed by throwing all pertinent records open to his inspection, and allowing him a hearing against unfair comments, as is done in some European countries. On the other hand, it has to be admitted that Labour party spokesmen have been admitting the posssibility of industrial conscription and related measures which would be unconstitutional under the provisions of the German Basic Law as quoted. For the British views see the Debate on the State of the Nation, on August 6 and 7, 1947, especially the remarks of Attlee and Cripps.
10. *Basic Law*, art. 12. See Merriam, first op. cit., pp. 72 ff. The authoritarian position is stated well (without Fascist or Communist encumbrances) by René de Visme Willliamson, *The Politics of Planning in the Oil Industry under the Code*, 1936; the quote is found on p. 18.
11. See the recurrent Reports of the Puerto Rico Planning Board, e. g., "Projec-

tions of Economic Development in Puerto Rico," 1957, "Economic Report to the Governor," 1959.

12. Ben, op. cit.; Boitieux, op. cit. See also the able study of the progress of collectivism in Switzerland, William E. Rappard's magistral *L'Individu et l'État dans l'evolution constitutionelle de la Suisse* (no date given), wherein the learned author traces what he believes to be the debilitating effect of these developments upon Swiss constitutional democracy.

13. Preamble of the 1946 French constitution, reaffirmed in 1958. In the German Basic Law, articles 14–15 and 74 (Nos. 14–17); in the Italian constitutions, articles 41–44.

14. See for an analysis, Ralph Braibanti and Joseph J. Spengler, eds., *Administration and Economic Development in India*, 1963, especially the contributions by S. P. Jagota and Braibanti. See also K. V. Rao, *Parliamentary Democracy of India*, 1961, pp. 310 ff.

15. Beer, op. cit., Chs. VII and VIII.

16. See article by Walton Hamilton, "Property" in ESS.

17. TD, Ch. 16; these trends were discernible much earlier. See for that Taylor Cole, and the author's study, *Responsible Bureaucracy*, 1932, for a detailed analysis of the trend toward bureaucratization, and one democracy's methods of dealing with it. Se also "Some Thoughts on the Politics of Government Control" in *Journal of Social Philosophy*, Vol. I, pp. 122 ff., 1936.

18. Cf. e. g. Taylor Cole, *The Canadian Bureaucracy*, 1949, especially p. 278. Cf. also Lloyd Musolf, *Public Ownership and Accountability: the Canadian Experience*, 1959.

19. Comité del Gobernador para el Estudio de los derechos Civiles en Puerto Rico, *Informe al Gobernador*, August, 1959, pp. 94 ff.

20. See the works cited in the GENERAL NOTES, especially Crossman, Robson, Beer and Crossland.

21. Francis William's *Socialist Britain*, 1948, p. 91.

22. Herman Finer, "Planning and Socialization in Great Britain" in *International Labour Review*, Vol. LVII (reprint, 1948), p. 13.

23. Beer, op. cit., pp. 194–195.

24. Beer, p. 321 and the entire Ch. XII. Cf. also Herring, *Public Administration*, p. 192.

25. See above, Ch. XXI, where I cite Eschenburg, in note 9; cf. also R. Dahrendorf, *Gesellschaft und Demokratie in Deutschland*, 1966.

26. My forthcoming *Europe — An Emergent Nation?*, 1967, Chs. 3–7. See for an earlier work, Ernst B. Haas, *The Uniting of Europe*, 1958, Chs. 5, 6, 9, and 10.

27. For an interesting recent critique, cf. W. A. Robson, *Local Government in Crisis*, 1966. See also M. P. Fogarty, *Town and Country Planning*, 1948; and J. Tyrwhitt, *Planning and the Countryside*, 1946. For the bibliography see F. J. Osborn, *A Reader's Guide to Town and Country Planning*, 1948. The Barlow Report (Cmd. 6153) is a Royal Commission report on the distribution of industry, rendered in 1940.

28. For Sweden, see Dankwart A. Rustow, *The Politics of Compromise — A Study of Cabinet Government in Sweden*, 1955.

29. See Gordon Wright, *The Reshaping of French Democracy*, 1948, p. 172. The main official sources for the French situation are the Debates and Documents of the *Assemblée Consultative*, 1944–45, of the *Assemblée Nationale Constituante*, 1945–46, those of the *Assemblée* and the *Conseil* since that time, and the semi-annual reports of the *Commissariat du Plan*. Cf. for this now R. R. Kapferer, *Die Verfassung der IV. Republik* . . 1963; and William A. Harbold, "The Formulation of Economic Policy in Postwar France," PP V, 1954, pp. 125–55.

30. See John Sheahan, *Promotion and Control of Industry in Postwar France*, 1963; and Vera Lutz, *French Planning*, 1965, for some criticisms of the French planning system; Pierre Bauchet, *Economic Planning: the French Experience*, 1964 (a translation of *La planification française*, 1962); and John and Anne Marie Hackett, *Economic Planning in France*, 1963, for a more favorable view. Pierre Delvolvé, "Le Parliament et la Preparation du Ve Plan," 71 *Revue du Droit Public* 661, 1965, reviews the problems of democratic control.

31. The constitutional texts are available in the official documents, of course, but students will find the running commentary, *La Costituzione della Repubblica Italiana*, 1948, by three members of the General Secretariat of the House of Deputies, V. Falzone, Filippo Palermo, and Francesco Cosentino, very helpful. The main official sources are the debates and documents of the Constituent Assembly and especially its Third Subcommission, dealing with economic aspects, and a report on a four-year development program by P. Saraceno, made as a report to the National Economic Council in 1947. For the developments since then, see Einaudi and Associates, op. cit.; Joseph La Palombara, *Italy: The Politics of Planning*, 1966.

32. Ernesto Rossi, *Il Malgoverno*, 1955.

33. ECA, *Country Study, Italy*, 1949, pp. 44–46.

34. John Clarke Adams and Paolo Barile, *The Government of Republican Italy*, 1961, pp. 190 ff. In commenting on a particular phase, these authors say: "It takes more than such obstacles to discourage a useless governmental agency, however, and the AMB (Azienda Monopolio Banane) is still flourishing at the expense of banana-eating Italians." Cf. also the forthcoming volume by Dante Germino and Stefano Passigli, to be published in 1968.

35. Ludwig Erhard, *Deutsche Wirtschaftspolitik, Der Weg der Sozialen Marktwirtschaft*, 1962, discusses his conception throughout, but especially pp. 138 ff., 201 ff. (against cartels), 267 ff. (defending law against restraint of trade), 337 ff. (well-being for all), 388 ff. (a ten-year retrospect in 1958), 419 ff., and 476 ff. Cf. also for a critical evaluation, Arndt, op. cit.

36. Arndt, op. cit., p. 121.

37. Herbert J. Spiro, *The Politics of German Co-determination*, 1958, p. 157.

38. See ECA, *Country Study, Germany*, 1949, as well as the highly informative *Long Term Program (1952–3) for the United States and United Kingdom Occupied Areas of Germany* (no date, issued in February, 1949, I believe).

No attempt is made here to live up to Lilienthal's injunction: "The people must be in on the planning; their existing institutions must be made part of it; self-education of the citizenry is more important than specific projects or physical changes." See *TVA — Democracy on the March*, 1944, p. 198.

39. Jagota, in Braibanti and Spengler,, op. cit., pp. 173 ff. at 175, and p. 200.

40. Besides the Treaty establishing the European Economic Community (1958) constituting the basic plan, the publications of the EEC should be consulted, especially *The European Yearbook*, published since 1955. The same holds for the ECSC for which also compare Henry L. Mason, *The European Coal and Steel Community — Experiment in Supranationalism*, 1955.

41. See Seymour Harris, *The European Recovery Program*, 1948.

42. See the Introduction to *Studies in Federalism* (ed. Bowie and Friedrich), 1954, for further background.

43. See John Gaus, "The Planning Process in Government," Ch. VII, in *Problems of the Post-War World* (Thomas C. McCormick, ed. 1945) and J. Millet, *The Process and Organization of Government Planning*, 1947.

44. Lilienthal, op. cit., Ch. XVIII; C. H. Pritchett, *The Tennessee Valley Authority*, 1943, Ch. V; and Philip Selznick, *TVA and the Grass Roots*, 1949.

XXIII. Propaganda and the Control of Communications

GENERAL NOTES

The topic of communication has acquired an entirely new and exciting dimension during the last twenty years, as a result of the application of cybernetics, the term proposed by Norbert Wiener for the systematic study of communications of all kinds in his pathfinding *Cybernetics*, 2d ed., 1961. Karl Deutsch, Ithiel de Sola Pool and others have sought to develop the implications for politics; cf. the former's *The Nerves of Government*, 1963, especially Ch. 5, seeking to systematize his pioneering *Nationalism and Social Communication*, 1953. The application of these new approaches is still in its beginnings, but progress has been steady; cf. Walter Schramm, ed., *Mass Communications*, 1960; Lucien Pye, *Communications and Political Development*, 1963; Joseph Klapper, *The Effects of Mass Communication*, 1960; Richard R. Fagen, *Politics and Communications*, 1966. In contributions like the last named, we are face to face once more with the problems of propaganda which occupied so prominent a place in the thirties, stimulated especially by the writings of Harold Lasswell and his pupils; besides his early *Propaganda Technique in the World War*, 1927, reference may be made to his study (with Dorothy Blumenstock) *World Revolutionary Propaganda*, 1939. Together with R. D. Casey and B. L. Smith he published a comprehensive bibliography *Propaganda and Promotional Activities,* 1935, an addition to which appeared in 1946. All this work was based, of course, on the earlier, more traditionally oriented work of Lowell, Lippman and Dewey: A. Lawrence Lowell, *Public Opinion and Popular Government,* 1913, and *Public Opinion in War and Peace,* 1923, Walter Lippmann, *Public Opinion,* 1922, and *The Phantom Public,* 1925; and John Dewey, *The Public and its Problems,* 1927. The considerable writings and researches on social psychology cannot be detailed here; suffice it to mention the names of Albig, Allport, Doob, and Bruner. A highly significant recent work is V. O. Key, Jr., *Public Opinion and American Democracy,* 1961. The special literature on the press, radio and television is cited in the references below.

On the government's public relations, naturally a topic of particular interest to political scientists, James C. McCamy's magistral study *Government Publicity,* 1939, has been implemented by J. A. R. Amlott, *Public Relations and American Democracy,* 1951; Dan Nimmo, *Newsgathering in Washington: A Study in Political Communication,* 1964, and others. The contrast in totalitarian regimes is detailed in TD, Ch. 11 (with literature). Cf. also on revolutionary propaganda some brilliant generalizations in Serge Chakotin, *The Rape of the Massses,* 1940. On the propaganda of the second world war which resembles totalitarian methods, cf. Daniel Lerner, ed., *Propaganda in War and Crisis: Materials for American Policy,* 1951; Charles A. H. Thomson's *Overseas Information Services of the U. S. Government,* 1948; and Paul A. M. Linebarger, *Psychological Warfare,* 1948. In addition to these one may still consult with profit the report of the Commission on the Freedom of the Press, published in 1947, especially the Commission's general study *A Free and Responsible Press: a General Report on Mass Communication: Newspapers, Radio, Motion Pictures, Magazines and Books,* and Zachariah Chafee's *Government and Mass Communications;* the viewpoint of both is conventional. By contrast George Alexander's *Propaganda Analysis: A Study of Inferences Made from Nazi Propaganda in World War II,* 1959, is a sophisticated effort to assess the degree of accuracy that content analysis achieved.

A very ancient dimension of propaganda is rhetorics. One might even venture the guess that Aristotle's *Rhetorics* has never been quite rivaled in all our more recent literature in philosophical breadth and depth, as well as political awareness. It is therefore rather important that Chaim Perelman has undertaken to modernize the ancient topic of rhetorics; his *La Nouvelle Rhetorique — Traité de l'Argumentation,* 1958, with L. Olbrechts-Tytega, represents a significant contribution (cf. my review in *The Natural Law Forum,* VII, 1962). It links our topic with the philosophical problems in logic and linguistics. Cf. also the *Festschrift* for Perelman, *La Théorie de l'Argumentation — Perspectives et Applications,* 1963.

REFERENCES

1. The view from Lippmann is found in his *Public Opinion*, p. 320. Jefferson's statement is cited by Dexter M. Keezer in his article "Press" for the ESS, 1934, p. 326, but without reference.

2. See Walter Millis, *The Martial Spirit*, 1931; Arnold Brecht, *Prelude to Silence*, 1944; and the author's *The New Belief in the Common Man*, 1942, especially Ch. III.

3. For the general literature on propaganda see the GENERAL NOTES above. To these may be added Lindley Fraser, *Propaganda*, 1950, and the psychologically oriented general treatment by Frederick Irion, *Public Opinion and Propaganda*, 1950.

4. Cf. W. Hennis, *Meinungsforschung und repräsentative Demokratie*, 1958, for an appraisal and critical evaluation.

5. Cf. my forthcoming *Political Pathology* for a more extended treatment of the disfunctional dimension of propaganda.

6. The quotation from Matthias A. Shaaber is from his *Some Forerunners of the Newspaper in England, 1476–1622*, 1929, p. 325.

7. For the *Gazette* see E. Hatin, *Histoire Politique et Littéraire de la Presse en France*, 1859–1861, Vol. I, pp. 28 ff.

8. See also F. K. Hunt, *The Fourth Estate*, 1850, Chs. IV and V.

9. The later English development is well discussed also by Alexander Andrews, *The History of British Journalism*, 1859; and by Stanley Morison, *The English Newspaper*, 1932. Cf. also Thomas Perry, *Public Opinion, Propaganda and Politics in 18th Century England*, 1962; and E. L. Woodward, *The Age of Reform*, 1938, pp. 28–30.

10. The quotation is from Frederick B. Artz, *Reaction and Revolution, 1814–1832*, 1934, p. 286.

11. Artz, op. cit., pp. 263 ff. for the several quotations; cf. also the literature cited there.

12. The publication of the British Foreign Office appeared in 1926 under the title, *The Press Laws of Foreign Countries*, edited by M. Shearman and O. T. Raynor. The figures are taken from Keezer, op. cit., p. 341.

13. Zachariah Chafee, Jr., *Free Speech in the United States*, 1941, and op. cit. (GENERAL NOTES); the difficult issues of irresponsible "freedom" are skillfully adumbrated by David Riesman in two articles "Democracy and Defamation: Control of Group Libel" and "Democracy and Defamation: Fair Game and Fair Comment," in *Columbia Law Review, May and November*, 1942.

14. Concerning the Zenger case, see G. J. Patterson, *Free Speech and a Free Press*, 1939.

15. The literature on these undertakings is considerable, but not very weighty. Walter Millis's *The Martial Spirit*, 1931, particularly Chs. I-IV, is valuable for the historical role of Hearst and Pulitzer in bringing about the Spanish–American War. For the Hugenberg concern, Ludwig Bernhard's peculiar and in many

respects candid study, *Der "Hugenberg Konzern"; Psychologie und Technik einer Grossorganisation der Presse*, 1928, is quite informative.

16. Consult Keezer, op. cit. for early figures; *U.S. Statistical Abstract*, 1966, for later ones. See J. Kayser, *Le Quotidien Français*, 1963, for an analysis of today's French press.

17. For France, Ch. VI of Carlton J. H. Hayes's *France: A Nation of Patriots*, 1930, which gives an interesting survey of the press which is supplemented by three Appendices (C, D, and E) containing carefully annotated lists of periodicals and dailies; besides this chapter, Robert de Jouvenel's spicy comments in *La République des Camarades*, first published in 1914, under the heading "Le Quatrième Pouvoir," pp. 201 ff., are worthwhile. For the Fourth Republic, Philip M. Williams, *Crisis and Compromise — Politics of the Fourth Republic*, 1964, does not, surprisingly, contain a discussion of the press, though random references abound in it.

18. *The Ross Report*, cmd. 7700, 1947–1949, has been superseded by more recent ones which alarmed public opinion by its pessimistic assessment of the future of the press in England. For background, cf. Morison, op. cit.

19. Cf. the *Report* as cited in the previous note.

20. Douglass Cater, *The Fourth Branch of Government*, 1959; J. Westerstahl and C. A. Janson, *The Political Press*, 1958. For historical background, besides Walter Lippmann's two classics, *Public Opinion*, 1922 and *The Phantom Public*, 1925; cf. A. M. Lee, *The Daily Newspaper in America*, 1937, and the special histories: Allan Nevins, *The Evening Post; a Century of Journalism*, 1922; John LaPorte Given, *Making a Newspaper*, 1907; O. G. Villard, *Some Newspapers and Newspapermen*, 1923, and *The Press To-day*, 1930.

21. Zachariah Chafee, Jr., *Government and Mass Communications*, 2 vols., 1947, Vol. II, p. 717.

22. The figure for *Time*'s circulation is from its Market Research Bureau, as of April 4, 1967.

23. For France see John Waline, "L'Agence France-Presse" 80 *Revue du Droit Public* 612, 1964, for a history of the Agence. Martin Harrison, in "Government and Press in France during the Algerian War," 58 APSR 280, 1964, reports that in 1960 M. Debré tried to acquire for the government a majority on the administrative council of the Agence, on the grounds that 60% of its income came from official sources.

24. For pertinent material see Oliver Gramling, *AP: The Story of News*, 1940. For the competition between radio and news services, see Paul Lazarsfeld, *Radio and the Printed Page*, 1940, Chs. V and VI; also the *Hearings* (Summary) of the FCC under order no. 79, 1941.

25. Cf. Bernard Rubin, *Political Television*, Belmont, California, 1967, where these figures, as well as additional ones from Elmo Roper and Associates, *The Public's View of Television and Other Media, 1959–64*, Television Information Office, 1965, are found.

26. See Thomas Grandin, *The Political Use of Radio*, 1939; Arno Huth, ed., *Radio Today*, 1942.

27. Lincoln Gordon, *The Public Corporation in Great Britain*, 1938, p. 166. See also William A. Robson's study of the BBC in the volume he edited, *Public Enterprise*, 1937; and H. of C. Debates, April 29, 1936, 311; 955 ff.; July 6, 1936, 314: 865 ff.; Dec. 17, 1936, 318: 372 ff.; 1946: 414–432.

28. H. R. G. Greaves, *Constitution*, 6th ed., 1950, p. 234.

29. Greaves, ibid. See for this issue James R. Angell, *War Propaganda and the Radio*, 1940; Harwood L. Childs and John B. Whitton, eds., *Propaganda by Short Wave*, 1942, and the author's "Controlling Radiobroadcasting in Wartime" in *Studies in the Control of Radio*, reprinted from *Public Policy*, II, 1941. The cold war and peace-time perspectives are ably developed in *Peoples Speaking to Peoples*, 1946, by Robert D. Leigh and Llewellyn White.

30. For the details of the 1964 reform, see Michel Bouisson, "Le statut de l'O.R.T.F."

80. *Revue du Droit Public* 1109, 1964, and for statistics on television and radio listening, Guy Michelat, "Television, moyens d'information et comportement electoral," 14 *Revue francaise de science politique* 877, 1964.

31. Donald R. Reich, "Court, Comity and Federalism in West Germany," *Midwest Journal of Political Science*, VII, 1963; Gerard Braunthal, "Federalism in Germany; The Broadcasting Controversy," *Journal of Politics*, XXIV, 1962.

32. Cf. the Annual Reports of the SSR for the earlier situation; cf. my *Radiobroadcasting and Higher Education*, 1944.

33. For the statute see 47 *U.S.C.* 606 (c). See also the references given in the GENERAL NOTES. The basic psychological study is Cantril and Allport, *The Psychology of Radio* (1935). Lazarfeld, op. cit., also is very important. Much valuable insight can be gained by reading the FCC's "Report of the Committee appointed by the Commission to Supervise the Investigation of Chain Broadcasting (Commission Order No. 37 — Docket No. 5060)" (June 12, 1940), and "Digest and Analysis of Evidence Presented in the Hearing on Commission Order No. 37 (Docket 5060) and of the Files of the Commission." But they are, of course, presenting a particular view. See the author's article, "The FCC 'Monopoly' Report: a Critical Appraisal," in *Public Opinion Quarterly*, September, 1940 (Vol. IV, No. 3, pp. 526–532).

34. The Commission's Report is entitled "Public Service Responsibility of Broadcast Licensees" and was published on March 7, 1946. Cf. also Charles Siepmann, *Radio's Second Chance*, 1946; and the analysis in C. J. F., "Radiobroadcasting and Higher Education" in *Studies in the Control of Radio*, No. 4, 1942; and Llewellyn White, *The American Radio*, 1947.

35. See the FCC *Report and Digest* cited previously, as well as J. H. Rose, *National Policy for Radiobroadcasting*, 1940, and Thomas P. Robinson, *Radio Networks and the Federal Government*, 1943.

36. David Walker, "The Future of ETV," *The New Republic*, February 11, 1967, p. 35.

37. Report of the Carnegie Commission on Educational Television, *Public Tele-

vision — *A Program for Action,* 1967. Cf. for an earlier assessment W. Y. Elliott, ed., *Television's Impact on American Culture,* 1956.

38. See for the U.S. Bernard Rubin, *Political Television,* 1967, p. 193, who developed some of the key materials and viewpoints offered in the Report to which note 40 refers. See also C. A. H. Thomson, *Television and Presidential Politics,* 1952.

39. See Theodore White, *The Making of a President,* 1960, p. 293. A similar view was taken by Charles A. Siepmann, "Were They Great?" in *The Great Debates —* *Background, Perspective, Effects,* ed. Sidney Kraus, 1962, which contains a number of significant contributions. The texts of the debates were published in Senate, 87th Congress, *Freedom of Communications,* Final Report, Part III, Dec. 11, 1961. Cf. also Sidney Kraus in op. cit.

40. APSA, *Report of the Commission on Presidential Debates,* 1964. The Commission was chaired by the author, while the staff work was done by Bernard Rubin and associates, assisted by the APSA staff.

41. For the general problems see: Harold Levine and James Wechsler, *War Propaganda and the United States,* 1940; James R. Mock and Cedric Larson, *Words that Won the War,* 1939; and Harold D. Lasswell's pathfinding study, *Propaganda Technique in the World War,* 1927. For the second world war, see Lerner, ed. op. cit.; Thompson, op. cit.; and Linebarger, op. cit. A new and perplexing chapter has been opened by government propaganda and the various pressure groups during the Vietnam war, but it is too early for a scientific assessment.

42. See Martin Harrison, "Government and Press in France during the Algerian War," 58 APSR 273, 1964; and Jacques Robert, "Propos sur la liberté de la presse," *Recueil Dalloz* (Chroniques) 189, 1964.

43. Cf. Riesman, loc. cit. above, note 13. Shils, op. cit., especially Ch. 1, and the works by Chafee, as well as the Commission report cited in the GENERAL NOTES. The constitutional issues are treated in J. Edward Gerald, *The Press and the Constitution, 1931–1947,* 1948. For France, cf. Roger Pinto, *La Liberté d'Opinion et d'information — contrôle juridictionel et contrôle administratif,* 1955; for Germany Peter Fliess, *Freedom of the Press in the German Republic, 1918–1933,* 1935; and P. Dagtoglou, *Wesen und Grenzen der Pressefreiheit,* 1963.

44. Lucian W. Pye, ed., *Communications and Political Development,* 1963. Cf. also Pye's paper at Brookings Conference, September, 1966 on "The Theory and Practice of Political Development."

45. It has not been possible to deal here with the interesting problems of the motion picture industry. Two studies are especially valuable in this connection: Leo C. Rosten, *Hollywood — The Movie Colony,* 1941, and Ruth A. Inglis, *Freedom of the Movies,* 1947. See also John E. Harley's *World-Wide Influences of the Cinema: A Study of Official Censorship,* 1941.

46. These facts were confirmed in a research study, carried forward under the author's supervision by A. A. Ulin in *Studies in the Control of Radio,* and entitled "Small Station Management and the Control of Radiobroadcasting." Compare also the interesting study by H. Brucker, Freedom of Information, 1949.

XXIV. Direct Popular Action

GENERAL NOTES

Direct popular action, that is to say participation of individuals in the shaping of public policy, has lost the glamour it possessed at the turn of the century for democratic thought. Its abuse by the totalitarian regimes, combined with its equivocal results elsewhere, as well as its manipulation in the settling of international boundary conflicts have made it seem questionable as an alternative to representative procedures. The extensive development of public opinion polls, controversial at best, has at the same time meant the rapid spread of an extraconstitutional and unofficial plebiscitary procedure. Searching inquiries, like V. O. Key, Jr., *Public Opinion and American Democracy*, 1961; and Robert Lane, *Political Life*, 1959, have served to provide empirical evidence for propositions developed earlier by various writers. The small local community apart — we have dealt with its problems in a previous chapter — the doubts and hesitations, though not the alarmist apprehensions concerning the referendum and initiative, as well as plebiscites, have been confirmed. A. L. Lowell, to be sure, went into the general phases of the problem both in his *Public Opinion and Popular Government* (1913) and in *Public Opinion in War and Peace* (1923). English writers such as Bagehot usually gave it just passing notice, to discard it in favor of the English representative system. The debates preceding the adoption of the German and Swiss programs are rather interesting sources for an elaborate argument both pro and con direct popular action within the context of a constitutional order. The expression "direct democracy" has often been used in continental Europe; it is rather misleading in view of the implied contention that the introduction of the initiative and referendum changes the whole tenor of the constitutional order. In France, where direct popular action had been widely favored during the revolution (following Rousseau), it has always found a place in general treatises, although its application has been discredited. It is here that the relationship to dictatorial plebiscites has most readily suggested itself, and both topics were treated, for example, in A. Esmein's *Eléments de Droit Constitutionnel Français et Comparé*, particularly Vol. I, pp. 435 ff. From the present writer's standpoint this is the most comprehensive treatment in contemporary literature, although his approach was different. An important treatise appeared in a remote place and has therefore not received the recognition it deserves, Professor Axel Brusewitz' *Folkomröstningsinstitutet i den Schweiziska Demokratien — Dess Förutsättningar, Former och Functioner*, which was published by the Department of Justice of Sweden in 1923, the official reference being *Statens Offentliga Utredningar*, 1923:10. In spite of its specialized title (*The Institution of Popular Votes in the Swiss Democracies — Their Conditions, Forms and Functioning*), the general discussion is carried to an advanced point, the ideological background carefully examined, and a general conclusion reached which is comprehensive and accurate, as far as direct popular action within a constitutional framework is concerned. Karl Loewenstein made several important studies which are now systematized in Ch. IX *of Political Power and the Government Process,* 1957, especially pp. 263 ff. He distinguishes, rightly I believe, between the constituent, the legislative and the plebiscitary function; he gives reference to his earlier writings there. Cf. also his *Political Reconstruction,* 1946, pp. 200 ff. and 280 ff. An interesting special aspect was explored by Leicester Webb, *Communism and Democracy in Australia: A Survey of the 1951 referendum,* 1954. The abuse of the referendal procedures under the Weimar Republic by the Communists and Nationalists, while not to my knowledge explored in detail, points a similar lesson; it has been clearly stated by Karl J. Newmann, *Zerstörung und Selbstzerstörung der Demokratie,* 1965, especially pp. 158 ff., with statistics.

REFERENCES

1. V. O. Key, *The Responsible Electorate,* 1966.
2. TD, Ch. 13.
3. Ernst Fraenkel, *Die repräsentative und die plebiszitäre Komponente im demokratischen Verfassungsstaat,* 1958, especially pp. 48 ff.
4. Rousseau's argument against representation is found in *Contrat Social,* Book II, Ch. XV. Cf. also R. Polin, ed., *Rousseau et la Philosophie Politique, Annales de la Philosophie Politique* V, 1965, especially the papers by Barth, Fetscher, Friedrich and Plamenatz.
5. Cf. my paper in op. cit., note 4.
6. For Napoleon I, see F. M. Kircheisen, *Napoleon I, sein Leben und seine Zeit,* 1911–1932, particularly Vols. V and VII. The figures are found in Vol. V, p. 270, and Vol. VII, pp. 10–12, respectively. A special study is: Karl Loewenstein, "Opposition and Public Opinion under the Dictatorship of Napoleon the First," in *Social Research,* Vol. IV, 1937. The need for continuous victories is brought out in H. C. Deutsch, *The Genesis of Napoleonic Imperialism,* 1938. For the data concerning Napoleon III, see P. de la Gorce, *Histoire du Second Empire,* Vols. I and VI. The particular data are found in the former on pp .12–13 and 105, and in the latter in *livre* XXXVIII, particularly pp. 115 ff. More recently, G. Grother has analyzed these problems in *Herzog von Morny,* 1966, Ch. VI. What is true of the plebiscites of the first Napoleon is equally true of those of the third. In fact, there seems to exist an unprinted study of these which is cited by Charles Seignobos, "La Révolution de 1848, le second Empire," in *Histoire de France contemporaine,* ed., Ernest Lavisse, Vol. VI. See also Réné Arnaud, *Le Coup d'État du 2 Décembre,* 1926.
7. For this paragraph see Theodore Curti, *Die Resultate des Schweizerischen Referendums,* 2d ed., 1911; Robert C. Brooks, *Civic Training in Switzerland,* 1930, pp. 107 ff. The most comprehensive study of the Swiss initiative and referendum, however, has appeared in Sweden: Axel Brusewitz, op. cit. A rather general analysis is given in W. E. Rappard; *La Constitution Fédérale de la Suisse — 1848–1948,* 1948, pp. 328 ff.

8. Marcel Bridel, *Droit Constitutionel et Public Suisse*, 1965, Vol. 1, pp. 75 and 85 ff.

9. Robert C. Brooks, *Government and Politics of Switzerland*, p. 164.

10. The discussion of this paragraph was originally based on A. L. Lowell, *Public Opinion and Popular Government*, new ed., 1926, Chs. XI, XIII, and XIV; and A. N. Holcombe, *State Government in the United States*, 3d ed., 1931, Ch. XVI. The quotations at the end of the paragraph are found in Holcombe, op. cit. pp. 551 and 569. See also V. O. Key, Jr., and W. W. Crouch, *The Initiative and Referendum in California*, 1939; and Key, op. cit., 1961, especially Ch. 16.

11. Cf. the study cited above, note 3; cf. also the valuable discussion in A. H. Birch, *Representative and Responsible Government*, 1964, Part. V.

12. For a discussion of the constitutionality of the referenda, see Henry W. Ehrmann, "Direct Democracy in France," 57 APSR 883, 1963; Constantin Zilemenos, *Problèmes Politiques et Constitutionnels en France et en Italie*, 1964; Maurice Duverger, *Institutions Politiques et Droit Constitutionnel*, 1965; and articles by Philip Williams and Martin Harrison on the January 1961 and April 1962 referenda in Vols. 14 and 15 of *Parliamentary Affairs*, 1961 and 1962; cf. also F. Goguel, ed., *Le Referendum du 8 Janvier, 1961*, 1962, and *Le Referendum du 8 Avril, 1962*, 1963.

13. For this paragraph, see Sarah Wambaugh, *A Monograph on Plebiscites, with a Collection of Official Documents* (1920), and Johannes Mattern, *The Employment of the Plebiscite in the Determination of Sovereignty* (1921).

14. See Sarah Wambaugh, *Plebiscites since the World War* (1933), and the literature cited there. Two maps in rather elaborate form are found there, Vol. I, pp. 87 and 266. The map showing the results of the Schleswig plebiscite is based on "Kort over Afstemmings–Resultaterne i Sønderjylland." That for the plebiscite in Upper Silesia is based on a map published by the British Section, Interallied Administrative and Plebiscite Commission. The Saar plebiscite has been described with detachement, though with sympathy toward the technique, by Sarah Wambaugh, *The Saar Plebiscite* (1940).

15. Konarad Adenauer, *Lebenserinnerungen*, Vol. I, 1962, provides the background.

16. For a good summary cf. Alfred Grosser, *La Democratie de Bonn*, 1958, pp. 236 ff.

17. Cf. Philip M. Williams, *Crisis and Compromise*, 1964, Ch. 2.

18. On the 1946 French referenda, see Gordon Wright, *The Reshaping of French Democracy*, 1948, especially pp. 79 ff., 176 ff., 224 ff., and 260. For statistics on all past referenda see Maurice Duverger, *Constitutions et Documents Politiques*, 1964, p. 285; see also Williams, op. cit.

19. Cf. studies cited in note 11 above.

20. See Piero Calamandrei, "Cenni introduttivi sulla Costituente e suoi lavori," in Calamandrei & Levi, *Commentario sistematico all costituzione italiana*, 2 vols., 1950, Vol. I, pp. LXXXIX ff.

21. See Edward H. Litchfield, ed., *Governing Germany*, Chs. 2 (Litchfield), and 4 (Wells); cf. also Peter H. Merkl, *The Origin of the West German Republic*, 1963.

22. *Considerations on Representative Government*, 1873, p. 3.

XXV. Constitutional Dictatorship and Emergency Powers

GENERAL NOTES

Emergencies have become the order of the day in the twentieth century. Hence emergency power arrangements have acquired crucial importance. Even so, the literature on the subject remains quite limited. Basic are some older writings, to wit Frederick M. Watkins, *The Failure of the Constitutional Emergency Powers under the German Republic,* 1939, and his more general study in PP I, 1940. Charles Fairman, *The Law of Martial Rule,* 1930, Clinton Rossiter, *Constitutional Dictatorship,* 1948, and Michel Dendias, *Le Renforcement des Pouvoirs du Chef de l'Etat dans la democratie parlementaire,* 1932. For Britain, cf. John Eaves, *Emergency Powers and the Parliamentary Watchdog: Parliament and the Executive in Great Britain, 1939–1951.* The problems posed by survival in general are treated in my *Constitutional Reason of State: The Survival of the Constitutional Order,* 1957. The problem has been treated from a different viewpoint by Benjamin E. Lippincott, *Democracy's Dilemma — The Totalitarian Party in a Free Society,* 1965.

For military government we note Ernst Fraenkel, *Miliary Occupation and the Rule of Law,* 1944; Hajo Holborn, *American Military Government — Its Organization and Policies,* 1947; Carl J. Friedrich and associates, *American Experience in Military Government in World War II,* 1948; W. Friedmann, *Allied Military Government in Germany,* 1947; and Lucius D. Clay, *Decision in Germany,* 1950; for a more recent assessment, cf. John D. Montgomery, *Forced to be Free — The Artificial Revolution in Germany and Japan,* 1957. The Committee on Comparative Politics of the SSRC held a conference in 1967 to evaluate the impact of military occupation in Germany and Japan upon political change; these papers will be published in PP.

These writings need to be seen within the context of the broader problem of dictatorship. Totalitarian dictatorship as analyzed in *Totalitarian Dictatorship and Autocracy,* by CJF and Z. Brzezinski, 2d ed., 1965, apart, the basic study in English is Alfred Cobban's *Dictatorship: its History and Theory,* 1939; cf. also Hans Kohn, *Revolutions and Dictatorships,* 1939, for broad historical perspective. Franz Neumann dealt with the issue in terms of what he chose to call the "authoritarian" state in *The Democratic and the Authoritarian State,* 1957. For a general review of the most recent scholarship and its literature, cf. my article "Dictatorship" in the encyclopedia *Sowjetsystem und Demokratische Gesellschaft;* it includes a brief review of the Communist position on dictatorship. Cf. also Maurice Duverger, *De la dictature,* 1961.

The problem of emergency powers and military goverment is closely related to that of the role of the military in constitutional regimes. In view of the numerous military take-overs, especially in developing countries, cf. John J. Johnson, ed., *The Role of the Military in Underdeveloped Countries*, 1962, and discussions about militarism in Germany and Japan, cf. e.g. Gordon A. Craig, *The Politics of the Prussian Army, 1640–1945*, 1955, and John M. Maki, *Japanese Militarism*, 1945, have made this problem paramount; see above, Ch. III and literature. Very good also S. E. Finer, *The Man on Horseback — The Role of the Military in Politics*, 1962.

REFERENCES

1. The most significant older general discussion of constitutional dictatorship is given by J. J. Rousseau, *Contrat Social*, Book IV, Ch. VI.
2. Bodin's discussion is to be found in Ch. II of Book III of his *De Republica*, Frankfurt ed., 1609, pp. 424 ff.
3. For the Roman problem, see Theodor Mommson, *Römisches Staatsrecht*, ed. 1874, Vol. II, 1, pp. 125 ff.
4. The ruling of the Supreme Court is found in *Ex parte Milligan*, 4 *Wall* 2, 1866. Regarding the statement of Judge Mackintosh, see Charles M. Clode, *The Administration of Justice under Military and Martial Law*, 1872, p. 166. For a recent reassessment cf. Robert Rankin and W. Dallmayr, *Freedom and Emergency Powers in the Cold War*, 1964.
5. Jürgen Seifert, *Gefahr im Verzuge — Zur Problematik der Notstandsgesetzgebung*, 1963.
6. See the study by Ulrich Scheuner in the *Festschrift* for Heinrich Bruening, 1967.
7. Concerning the Defense of the Realm Act, cf. Charles Fairman, *The Law of Martial Rule*, 1930. See also *The Federalist*, Vol. LXXIV, and James Bryce, *The American Commonwealth*, rev. ed., 1924, Vol. 1, pp. 55 ff.
8. See Martin Harrison, "The French Experience of Exceptional Powers: 1961," 25 *The Journal of Politics* 139, 1963, as well as relevant sections in Duverger, *Institutions Politiques*, 1965, D. Pickles, *The Fifth French Repbulic*, 1962, and R. Macridis, *Supplement to The De Gaulle Republic*, 1963.
9. For the Conseil d'Etat, see Ch. VI, pp. 121 ff.
10. F. M. Watkins, "The Problem of Constitutional Dictatorship" in PP I, 1940, p. 353.
11. *Ex parte Merryman* is found in 17 Fed. Cas. 144, the quotation in Jackson, op. cit., at p. 153.
12. Concerning Machiavelli, see, for example, *Discourses*, Book III, and Friedrich Meinecke's classic, now in English under the title *Machiavellism — The Doctrine of Raison d'Etat and its Place in Modern History*, 1957.
13. Besides the works cited in the GENERAL NOTES, cf. John Gimbel, *A German Community under American Occupation*, 1961, Eugene Davidson, *The Death and Life of Germany — An Account of the American Occupation*, 1959, and the works cited below, note 21.

14. Re Lieber see art. 22 of General Order no. 100, U. S. War Department, 1863. The Hague Conventions are found in Carnegie Endowment for International Peace, Division of International Law, *Hague Conventions*, pamphlet Nos. 3-20, 1914–1915.

15. For the Rhineland occupation, consult I. L. Hunt, *American Military Government of Occupied Germany 1918–1920* (mim. 1920, printed 1943), and the evaluation by Ernst Fraenkel, *Military Occupation and the Rule of Law* (1944), with a thorough critical bibliography. See also (General) Henry T. Allen, *The Rhineland Occupation* (1927). The most dramatic critical evaluation from a political standpoint is B. T. Reynolds, *Prelude to Hitler* (1933). Fraenkel was sharply critized by William F. Sollmann, *APSR*, Vol. XXXVIII, pp. 976 ff., regarding his estimate of the German political situation.

16. The quotation is from Merle Fainsod, "The Development of American Military Government Policy during World War II," in Friedrich and associates, *American Experiences in Military Government in World War II*, p. 51.

17. This document is given as Appendix C in Friedrich and associates, op. cit., pp. 415–416. JCS 1067 and JCS 1067 revised are found ibid., pp. 381 ff. and 402 ff. They are also included in James K. Pollock and Associates, *Germany under Occupation — Illustrative Materials and Documents*, rev. ed., 1949, pp. 76 ff. and 91 ff. This helpful collection contains General Clay's remarkable self-restraining ordinance of June 4, 1947 instructing American military elements to respect the rights of Germans under constitutionalism.

18. See my "Military Government as a Step toward Self-rule" in *Public Opinion Quarterly*, VII, 1943, pp. 527 ff., and what is said above Ch. VI on the rule of law. For a discussion of different national interpretations of the rule of law, see the symposium on "The Rule of Law as Understood in the West," 9 *Annales de la Faculté de Droit d'Istanbul* 24, 1959.

19. See the Italian constitutional treatises, cited earlier, especially *La Costituzione della Repubblica Italiana* by Falzone, Palermo, and Cosentino, where the constitutional debts are digested. The position of the judiciary is given in commentary on articles 101–113, pp. 185 ff. The Control Council Law is found in Pollock, op. cit., pp. 34–35.

20. On Japanese responses to the military occupation, cf. the work by Montgomery, in the GENERAL NOTES, especially Ch. IV, pp. 150 ff., and Robert E. Ward, "Reflections on the Allied Occupation and Planned Political Change in Japan" a paper read to the Conference mentioned above, GENERAL NOTES, 1967, and containing references to Japanese sources and interviews. See also SCAP, Supreme Commander for the Allied Powers, Government Section, *Political Reorientation of Japan*, 1949, and also Arthur Maass in Friedrich, ed., as cited in GENERAL NOTES.

21. Peter H. Merkl, "Strategies of Directed Political Change: the Occupation of Germany," and Carl J. Friedrich, "The Legacies of the Occupation of Germany," 1967, both read to the Conference cited above, GENERAL NOTES. Cf. also Peter H. Merkl's *Origin of the West German Republic*, 1963, and Edward H. Litchfield, ed., *Governing Postwar Germany*, 1953, especially Chs. 1, 2, and 5. For the

British, besides the study by Friedmann cited above in the GENERAL NOTES, see Raymond Ebsworth, *Restoring Democracy in Germany — The British Contribution*, 1960; for the French, F. Roy Willis, *The French in Germany, 1945–1949*, 1962.

XXVI. Constitutionalism in Emergent Nations

GENERAL NOTES

The political development of the nations emerging from colonial rule has been a subject of systematic study and analysis only in recent years. To be sure, there have been studies, especially by anthropologists and ethnologists, of the political order of many "primitive" peoples, such as the renowned James George Frazer's *The Golden Bough*, 1890, or the work of E. E. Evans–Pritchard and his school, accessible in the work edited by him and M. Fortes, *African Political Systems*, 1940, or more recently in the challenging studies edited by John Middleton and David Tait, *Tribes without Rulers*, 1958, and Marc J. Swartz and Associates, *Political Anthropology*, 1966, and Michael Banton, ed., *Political Systems and the Distribution of Power*, 1965. Much of this work has been conveniently synthesized by Lucy Mair, *Primitive Government*, 1962, and most of it is characterized by much cultural sophistication that is not equalled by its understanding or even acquaintance with political theory. It is to be hoped that such works as *Man and His Government*, 1963, and Gabriel A. Almond and G. Bingham Powell, Jr., *Comparative Politics — A Developmental Approach*, 1966, which seek to utilize the work of anthropologists as much as possible, will bring about a breakdown of these interdisciplinary walls.

Because of the richness and variety of specific cultural background that has to be known to assess elements of the political order adequately, much of the general work in the development field has been presented in the form of collaborative works. Considering our interest in constitutionalism and democracy, the following has been found particularly helpful; but there are a few works by individuals that are of rather general interest, notably Rupert Emerson, *From Empire to Nation*, 1960; Lucien W. Pye, *Politics, Personality and Nation-Building*, 1962; Barbara Ward, *The Rich Nations and the Poor Nations*, 1962; Edward A. Shils, *Political Development in the New States*, 1962; S. M. Lipset, *The First New Nation*, 1963; A. F. K. Organski, *The Stages of Political Development*, 1965; and Richard Behrendt, *Soziale Strategie der Entwicklungsländer*, 1965.

Among the collaborative works, I should like to mention the following as germane to our concerns: Gabriel A. Almond and James S. Coleman, eds., *The Politics of the Developing Areas*, 1960; Ralph Braibanti and Joseph J. Spengler, *Tradition, Values, and Socio-Economic Development*, 1961; Max F. Millikan and Donald L.

M. Blackmer, eds., *The Emerging Nations — Their Growth and U. S. Policy*, 1961; John H. Kautsky, ed., *Political Change in Underdeveloped Countries*, 1962; Karl W. Deutsch and William J. Foltz, *Nation-Building*, 1963; Kurt London, ed., *New Nations in a Divided World*, 1963; John H. Hallowell, *Development for What?*, 1964; Alexander Gerschenkron, *Economic Backwardness in Historical Perspective: A Book of Essays* (all by G.), 1935; Ralph Braibauti, ed., *Asian Bureaucratic Systems Emergent from the British Imperial Tradition*, 1966; Herbert J. Spiro, ed., *Patterns of African Development*, 1967; John D. Montgomery, *Approaches to Development: Politics, Administration and Change*, 1967. There are also significant more specialized studies, such as William Y. Elliott, *Education and Training in the Developing Countries — The Role of U. S. Foreign Aid*, 1966; Ralph Braibanti and Joseph J. Spengler, *Administration and Economic Development in India*, 1963, or Gwendolyn M. Carter, ed., *Five African States — Responses to Diversity*, 1963. Very interesting comparative suggestions are contained in William N. Chambers, *Political Parties in a New Nation: The American Experience, 1776–1809*. Of real importance also is Paul E. Sigmund, Jr.'s, *The Ideologies of Developing Nations*, rev. ed., 1967. All the leading journals are publishing in this field, of course, but special mention should be made of the succession of whole sections of highly significant articles in *Public Policy*, edited by John Montgomery and Arthur Smithies; e.g. Vol. XV, 1966, with articles by Karl W. Deutsch, George F. Gant, Ward Elliott, Stanley S. Reiser, Donald Wilhelm, Jr., Robert Erwin (on feudalism), Scott R. Pearson, and Raymond Vernon.

REFERENCES

1. The following discussions are from my paper "Some Reflections of Constitutionalism for Emergent Political Orders" in Herbert J. Spiro's *Patterns of African Development*, 1967.
2. See Clyde Kluckhohn, *A Mirror for Man*, 1949, for competent and searching professional criticism of this position. Cf. also MG for much of what follows.
3. Max Weber, *Wirtschaft und Gesellschaft*, 1921, Ch. III.
4. Cf. for this MG. The serious objections to the "charismatic" notion are explored ibid., Ch. 10, and in my article in the *Journal of Politics*, Vol. 23, 1961, pp. 3 ff.
5. Guiglielmo Ferrero, *The Principles of Power*, 1942, employs this term. Cf. for legitimacy, MG, Ch. 13.
6. Cf. G. Sartori, "Constitutionalism: a preliminary discussion," in APSR, Dec., 1962, and the critique by W. H. Morris–Jones, "On Constitutionalism," ibid., June, 1965 with rejoinder by Sartori.
7. See Ch. VIII above. It is there shown why the constituent power must neither be confused with the amending power, nor be superseded by it.
8. Edward Shils, "The Fortunes of Constitutional Government in the Political Development of the New State" in *Development for What?*, John Hallowell, ed., 1964, pp. 103–143, at p. 104. Italics added.

9. See J. J. Johnson, ed., *The Role of the Military in Underdeveloped Countries,* 1960.

10. This lack of a clearly defined concept of constitutionalism mars the otherwise very broadly suggestive discussion of Shils, loc. cit. note 8, with which I find myself nonetheless in general agreement.

11. For a fuller exploration of these problems see TD, Ch. 10. The suggestion that such constitutions are mere façade is made with special emphasis by G. Sartori in his "Constitutionalism: a preliminary discussion," APSR, Vol. LVI, 1962, pp. 853 ff; it has been recurrent in recent writings, e.g. Herbert Spiro, *Government by Constitution,* 1959, especially pp. 437 ff.

12. See for a fuller treatment of succession MG, Ch. 28.

13. Shils, op. cit., p. 129. Cf. for the role of the military also the informative volume edited by J. J. Johnson, op. cit., covering Latin America, Indonesia, Burma, Thailand, the Middle East, and Africa, with a broad introductory essay by Shils. For an excellent case study, see Richard D. Robinson, *The First Turkish Republic, A Case Study in National Development,* 1963, especially Ch. IX; and E. Oxbudun, *The Role of the Military in Recent Turkish Politics,* Occasional Papers, No. 14, Harvard University Center for International Affairs, 1966.

14. See above, Ch. VIII. Within the context of a suggestive application of the Hegelian dialectic of master and servant, Clement Henry Moore, in a study on "Mass Party Regimes in Africa" in Herbert Spiro, ed., *Africa — The Primacy of Politics,* 1966, pp. 85 ff. at pp. 99–104, delineates the emergence of a "pays réel," an organized political system before independence is actually achieved. Significantly, the nationalist rather than the constitutionalist thrust is in the foreground of attention.

15. See my *Transcendent Justice — The Religious Foundations of Constitutionalism,* 1964. Cf. also such classical studies as J. G. A. Pocock, *The Ancient Constitution and the Feudal Law — English Historical Thought in the Seventeenth Century;* and Charles H. McIlwain, *The High Court of Parliament and Its Supremacy,* 1910. Pocock rightly stresses that the common law tradition retained the medieval "almost universally respected doctrine that the law should be above will," op. cit. p. 51.

16. Cf. my *Puerto Rico — Middle Road to Freedom: Fuero Fundamental,* 1959, and the literature cited there. Since that publication several important studies have greatly deepened our understanding of the underlying belief structure. Cf. especially Robert W. Anderson, *Party Politics in Puerto Rico,* 1965; Gordon K. Lewis, *Puerto Rico,* 1963; and the several studies put out by the United States — Puerto Rico Commission listed in GENERAL NOTES, Ch. XI, especially Robert H. Hunter, *Historical Survey of the Puerto Rico Status Question, 1898–1965;* Sidney W. Mintz, *Puerto Rico — An Essay in the Definition of a National Culture.*

17. Rexford Tugwell, *The Stricken Land,* 1947, and the skillful appraisal of Tugwell's role in Charles T. Goodsell, *Administration of a Revolution — Executive Reform in Puerto Rico under Governor Rexford Tugwell, 1941–1946,* 1965.

18. Robert W. Anderson, op. cit., p. 222.

19. Ismael R. Bou, *Esbozo de un tema — La Nuevas Generacions en Puerto Rico,* 1963.

20. Joseph J. Spengler, "Theory, Ideology, Non-Economic Values, and Politico-Economic Development," in Ralph Braibanti and Joseph J. Spengler, eds., *Tradition, Values, and Socio-Economic Development,* 1961, p. 8.

21. Daniel Lerner, ed., *The Passing of Traditional Society,* 1958, p. 43.

22. Intrinsically careful studies are W. D. Reeve, *Public Administration in Siam,* 1951; Sir Charles Collins, *Public Administration in Ceylon,* 1951; or Ralph Braibanti and Joseph J. Spengler, eds., *Administration and Economic Development in India,* 1963. There the quoted sentence on p. V.

23. Cf. for a recent striking illustration the report *Development Administration in Malaysia,* by John D. Montgomery and Milton J. Ehman, Kuala Lumpur, 1966. There on p. VI the acute observation is made that "development administration" means at once "development of administration" and "administration of development."

24. Charles Drekmayer, *Kingship and Community in Ancient India,* 1962, has gone much further back, but his discussion of the *Arthashastra* in Chs. 11 and 12 illustrates our point well.

25. This point is developed at greater length in TD, Chs. 2 and 28. Cf. also Kurt London, ed., *New Nations in a Divided World,* 1963, especially Part III, papers by David T. Cattell, "The Soviet Union Seeks a Policy for Afro-Asia (pp. 163–179), Sergius Jakobson, "The U.S.S.R. and Ethiopia: a Case of Traditional Behavior" (pp. 180–192), and William E. Griffith "Communist Polycentrism and the Underdeveloped Areas" (pp. 274–286). These problems also constitute a major theme in MG.

26. These ideas appear in expanded form in an essay entitled "Power, Authority, and Legitimacy: Political Theory and the Problems of Developing Countries" which will appear in a forthcoming book on aspects of political development to be published by the Brookings Institution.

27. What follows is more fully developed in MG, Ch. 35.

28. For a full justification of the argument, the theoretical analysis of all the issues, as attempted in MG, or another general theory is needed. Cf. Charles Merriam, *Systematic Politics,* 1945; George E. G. Catlin, *Systematic Politics,* 1965; Harold Lasswell and A. Kaplan, *Power and Society,* 1950; Georges Burdeau, *Traité de Science Politique,* 7 vols., 1949–57.

29. For an elaboration of this model, see MG, pp. 664 ff.

30. Bertrand de Jouvenel, *L'Art de la Conjuncture,* 1964, offers the statement of the general position which has inspired the work of his center and its publications, notably the publication *Futuribles* (since 1960 and more formally since 1966). Cf. also Zbigniew Brzezinski and Samuel Huntington, *Political Power USA/USSR,* 1964. In the interesting paper by Hadley Cantril, "The World in 1952: Some Predictions" *Clinical Supplement to the Journal of Abnormal and Social Psychology,* Vol. 38, 1943, pp. 6–47, my prediction is reported.

31. The following is from my article "Pan-Humanism, Culturism and the Federal Union of Europe" in *Philosophy, Religion, and the Coming World Civilization — Essays in Honor of William Ernest Hocking,* Leroy S. Rouner, ed., 1966, pp. 330–339.

Industrialization, 29
Inflation, medieval, 97
Initiative, 542–545
Inner six, 499
Inns of Court, 111
Insecurity, personal, 376–377
Institutional background, 173–174
Instrument of Government, 129, 174–175
Integration, political, 183, 187; and political parties, 447; representation as, 308–310
Intelligence function, 366f.
Interest groups, 454–474, 490
Internal Security Committee, 461
International Children's Emergency Fund (U. N.), 83
International Labor Office, 464
International Monetary Fund, 83
International planning, 499–500
International War Crimes Trials, 108
Investigative function, 360–361, 422
Iran, 598
Iraq, constitutional weaknesses, 587
Ireland, 215; national elections, 298; nationalism, 329, 332
Iron curtain, 72
Israel, 583
Italy, 7, 9, 10, 15, 18, 21, 22, 23, 134, 159, 200, 219, 314, 341, 486; administrative system, 47; Christian Democrats, 451; fascism in, 69, 70; judiciary, 261; local government, 221; military government, 579; proportional representation, 301; referendum, 554; Renaissance, 91; revolution, 134; socialism in, 34, 35; socialization in, 482, 490, 491, 494; trade unions, 465; unconstitutional dictatorship, 572; unification, 11

Jackson, Andrew, 32
James I (England), 11, 27, 105, 106, 111, 112, 114, 126, 174, 251
James, William, 72
Japan, 598; atom bomb, 63; military government in, 579
Jefferson, Thomas, 23, 161, 252, 258, 259
Jennings, W. Ivor, 585
Jews, and political parties, 443
Joachim, Friedrich (Elector of Brandenburg), 42
John of Salisbury, 90
Johnson, Dr. Samuel, 202, 327
Judaism, and modern law, 16
Judges, disinterestedness, 259–260; and propertied interests, 258–259
Judicial function, 102–119
Judicial independence, 130
Judicial organization, in Europe, 109–111
Judicial process, 107–108; rule of precedent, 108–109
Judicial restraint, and constitutional government, 114
Judicial review, of constitution, 249–265; and precedents, 251
Judiciary, 179ff.; constitutional, 210–212; and Act of Settlement, 111–112; in England, 139; federal, 211; in Prussia, 112–114; rationality and, 256; representative quality, 263–265
Justice, 102–119; and government, 102–104
Justinian, code of, 16

Kant, Immanuel, 176, 183, 190
Kennedy, John F., 76, 87; administration of, 437; debates with Nixon, 374, 530
Kerenski, 69, 572
Kev, V. O., 459
Kiesinger, Kurt, 207
Ky, Nguyen, 588

Labor unions, 193
Labour party, 3, 34, 312; and civil liberties, 35; federalism and, 197; minority leadership, 312; proportional representation, 296; rise of, 433, 440; socialization and planning, 486
LaFollette, Robert, 209, 258
Laissez-faire, 90
Lancaster, House of, and War of Roses, 432
Laos, 588
Latin America, 72, 85, 87, 588, 592, 597; constitutional democracy, 585; constitutional weaknesses, 587; federalizing process in, 196; nationalism in, 202; revolutions in, 148–149
Laud, Archbishop, 21
Law, 16, 194; artifiicial reason, 106–107; canon, 111; conceptions of, 104–106; conservation of, 251; disinterestedness, 259–260; due process of, 254–256; Hooker on, 107; importance, 107; Locke on, 107; logic in, 256; in Prussia, 112–114; Roman, 15; Rousseau on, 107; rule of, 58
Laws of Ecclesiastical Polity, 107
Lawyers, and Act of Settlement, 111–112
Leadership, 583; administrative, 48; constitutional, 26–27; party, 439; political, 373–376
League of Nations, 36, 209; balance of power, 85; Covenant, 31; Fourteen Points, 85; and nations' foreign affairs, 362, secretariat, 83; technical experts, 80
League of the Three Emperors, 77
Lecanuet, 374